# ASIAN CORPORATE RECOVERY

## Findings from Firm-Level Surveys in Five Countries

*Edited by Dominique Dwor-Frécaut, Francis Colaço, and Mary Hallward-Driemeier*

THE WORLD BANK
WASHINGTON D.C.

Copyright © 2000
The International Bank for Reconstruction
and Development/THE WORLD BANK
1818 H Street, N.W., Washington, D.C. 20433

All rights reserved
Manufactured in the United States of America
First Printing April 2000

The World Bank does not guarantee the accuracy of the data included in this publication and accepts no responsibility whatsoever for any consequence of their use. The boundaries, colors, denominations, and other information shown on any map in this volume do not imply on the part of the World Bank Group any judgment on the legal status of any territory or any endorsement or acceptance of such boundaries.

The material in this publication is copyrighted. Requests for permission to reproduce portions of it should be sent to the Office of the Publisher at the address shown in the copyright notice above. The World Bank encourages dissemination of its work and will normally give permission promptly and, when the reproduction is for noncommercial purposes, without asking a fee. Permission to copy portions for classroom use is granted through the Copyright Clearance Center, Inc., Suite 910, 222 Rosewood Dr., Danvers, Massachusetts 01923, U.S.A.

ISBN 0-8213-4634-2

**Library of Congress Cataloging-in-Publication Data**

Asian corporate recovery : findings from firm-level surveys in five countries / edited by Dominique Dwor-Frécaut, Francis X. Colaço, Mary Hallward-Driemeier.
    p. cm.
  "Regional conference based on firm-level surveys in Indonesia, Korea, Malaysia, the Philippines and Thailand, Bangkok, March 31–April 2, 1999."--CIP gallery.
  ISBN 0-8213-4634-2
  1. Financial crises--Asian, Southeastern--Congresses. 2. Asia, Southeastern--Economic conditions--Congresses. 3. Industrial management--Asia, Southeastern--Congresses.
  I. Dwor-Frécaut, Dominique, 1962- II. Colaço, Francis X. III. Hallward-Driemeier, Mary, 1966- IV. World Bank.

HB3808 .A853 2000
338.095--dc21

00-024442

# Contents

**Abbreviations and Acronyms** vii

**Abstract** ix

**Acknowledgments** xi

**Foreword** xiii

**Editors' Notes** xv

## Chapter 1 Asian Manufacturing Recovery: A Firm-Level Analysis 1
Data   2
Impact of the Crisis   3
Conclusion   17

## Chapter 2 Corporates' Views of the Constraints to Recovery 21
Impact of the crisis on the surveyed firms' performance   22
Reasons for declining performance and constraints to corporate recovery   25
Constraints to recovery and policy recommendations   32
Conclusions   34

## Chapter 3 Macroeconomic Views of the East Asian Crisis: A Comparison 37
Macroeconomic development   38
Monetary and fiscal policies in the adjustment process   44
Assessment of the adjustment process   49
Policy implications and concluding remarks   50

## Chapter 4 The New Miyazawa Initiative and Response to the Corporate Debt Problem 55
Basic perspectives   55
Issues for the promotion of debt restructuring   56

Approaches to the corporate debt problem under the Miyazawa Initiative   57
The Asian Growth and Recovery Initiative (AGRI)   59
Transparency in markets and stockholder-oriented corporate governance   59
Transparency in markets   59
Conclusion   59

## Chapter 5 Asian Corporate Credit Needs and Governance   61
Structure of corporate finance prior to the crisis and in mid-1998   63
Determining whether credit availability is a constraint to corporate recovery in Asia   69
The firms' views on loan repayment prospects   75
Issues in corporate financial governance   77
Concluding comments   80

## Chapter 6 Financial Sector Restructuring: Progress and Issues   83
The genesis of the crisis   83
Restructuring and recapitalization   85
Strengthening prudential standards and the legal frameworks   89
Interest rates and loan growth   90
Conclusions and lessons   91
Annex 6.A  Financial restructuring in East Asia at a glance   93

## Chapter 7 Publicly Listed East Asian Corporates: Growth, Financing, and Risks   97
The data   98
Performance measures   99
Financial structures   103
Summary   108

## Chapter 8 Corporate Foreign Debt in East Asia: Too Much or Too Little?   111
Introduction   111
The survey data   112
Foreign debt financing   114
Short-term versus long-term debt   116
Unhedged short-term foreign debt: too much or too little?   118
Profitable versus less profitable firms   118
Conclusions   119

## Chapter 9 Corporate Employment and Public Policy   123
Background information   124
Employment performance across countries, sectors, and the export status of the firms   126
Causes of employment changes   128
The characteristics of workers leaving the firms   131
The firms' reactions to the loss of human capital   135
Summary and policy implications   137
Annex 9.A The frequency of use of formal training programs during the crisis   139

## Chapter 10 Indonesia: The Impact of the Economic Crisis on Industry Performance 141
The economic crisis 142
Overview of the competitiveness study 143
Impact of the crisis on firm performance 146
The financial position of the firms 150
Financial characteristics and impact of the crisis 153
The government's response to the crisis 154
The firms' expectations for the next six months 155
Summary and conclusion 155

## Chapter 11 A Study on the Crisis, Recovery, and Industrial Upgrading in the Republic of Korea 159
The survey 160
Analysis of the impact of the crisis on the firms 161
Financial position of the firms before and after the crisis and its impact on the firms' responses to the crisis 166
Concluding remarks and recommendations 172
Annex 11.A Government support programs listed in the questionnaire 175

## Chapter 12 The Asian Financial Crisis: Impact at the Firm Level— The Malaysian Case 177
Framework of the survey 179
Impact of the crisis on the firms 180
Impact of the crisis on the financial position of the firms 184
The policy response 188
Conclusion 191

## Chapter 13 The Impact of the Southeast Asian Financial Crisis on the Philippine Manufacturing Sector 195
Description of the survey 196
Analysis of the impact of the crisis on the firms 198
Financial position of the firms before and after the crisis 206
Transparency 212
Short-run prospects 214
Conclusions and recommendations 215

## Chapter 14 Thailand: The Road to Recovery 219
Description of the survey 220
Corporate adjustments to the crisis 221
Constraints on corporate recovery and policy implications 227
Prospects for the first half of 1999 and policy recommendations 232
Annex 14.A Macroeconomic data 235
Annex 14.B Methodology 237

## References 239

# Abbreviations and Acronyms

| | |
|---|---|
| ADB | Asian Development Bank |
| AGRI | Asian Growth and Recovery Initiative |
| AGRP | Asian Growth and Recovery Program |
| AMC | Asset Management Corporation (Thailand) |
| APEC | Asia-Pacific Economic Cooperation |
| ASEAN | Association of South East Asian Nations |
| ASEM | Asia-Europe Meeting |
| BAAC | Bank for Agriculture and Agricultural Cooperatives |
| BIR | Bureau of Internal Revenues |
| BIS | Bank for International Settlements |
| BMA | Bangkok Metropolitan Administration |
| BNM | Bank Negara Malaysia |
| BOI | Board of Industry (Thailand) |
| CIF | Cost, Insurance, and Freight |
| CRPP | Currency Rate Protection Program (The Philippines) |
| CDRC | Corporate Debt Restructuring Committee (Malaysia) |
| CPI | Consumer Price Index |
| DOLE | Department of Labor and Employment (The Philippines) |
| EBIT | Earnings Before Interest and Taxes |
| EBITDA | Earnings Before Interest and Taxes (but adding back depreciation) |
| EFAL II | Economic and Financial Adjustment II program, World Bank |
| EIU | Economist Intelligence Unit |
| ESCL | Exchangeable Subordinated Capital Loans |
| EXIM | Export Import Bank of Thailand |
| FIDF | Financial Institutions Development Fund (Thailand) |
| FDI | Foreign Direct Investment |
| FOB | Free On Board |
| FRA | Financial Restructuring Agency (Indonesia) |
| FSC | Financial Supervisory Commission |
| GAAP | Generally Accepted Accounting Principles |
| GDP | Gross Domestic Product |
| GHB | Government Housing Bank |
| HRDF | Human Resource Development Fund (Malaysia) |
| IBRA | Indonesian Bank Restructuring Agency |
| IFCT | Industrial Finance Corporation of Thailand |

| | |
|---|---|
| ILTD | Linkages and Technology Development Study (Malaysia) |
| IMF | International Monetary Fund |
| ISIC | International Standard Industrial Classification |
| ISIS | Institute of Strategic and International Studies (Malaysia) |
| JEXIM | Export-Import Bank of Japan |
| KAMCO | Korean Asset Management Company |
| KDIC | Korean Deposit Insurance Company |
| LE | List of Establishments (The Philippines) |
| M&As | Mergers and Acquisitions |
| MATRADE | Malaysia External Trade Development Corporation |
| MDB | Multilateral Development Bank |
| NAFTA | North American Free Trade Agreement |
| NCR | National Capital Region (The Philippines) |
| NERP | National Economic Recovery Plan |
| NICs | Newly Industrialized Countries |
| NPLs | Nonperforming Loans |
| NSO | National Statistics Office |
| OECD | Organization for Economic Cooperation and Development |
| OECF | Overseas Economic Cooperation Fund |
| RA | Republic Act (The Philippines) |
| ROA | Return On Assets |
| SAL | Structural Adjustment Loan |
| SBGFC | Small Business Guarantee and Finance Corporation (The Philippines) |
| SBI | Sertifikat Bank Indonesia |
| SCB | Siam Commercial Bank |
| SEC | Securities and Exchange Commission |
| SFIs | Specialized Financial Institutions |
| SITC | Standard Industrial Trade Classification |
| SIFC | Small Industry Finance Corporation |
| SIP | Social Investment Program (Thailand) |
| SMEs | Small and Medium Enterprises |
| SPVs | Special Purpose Vehicles (Thailand) |
| SSN | Social Safety Net |
| SSS | Social Security System (The Philippines) |
| TFB | Thai Farmer's Bank |
| UNDP | United Nations Development Program |

# Abstract

This volume presents the main findings of surveys of 3,700 manufacturing firms in Indonesia, The Republic of Korea, Malaysia, the Philippines, and Thailand, conducted by the governments of these countries from November 1998 to February 1999. The resulting papers were prepared for a conference on Asian corporate recovery, held in Bangkok in March and April of 1999, and are collected in this book. The papers compare the effect of the 1997–99 crisis on various countries, sectors, and types of firms, in terms of output, exports, and employment. They analyze the causes of corporate decline and assess the policy options to foster corporate recovery. The impact of the financial sector crisis on the corporate sector is discussed through an analysis of corporates' financial structure and credit needs. The extent of foreign corporate indebtedness is reviewed, as well as the role debt played in the propagation of the crisis. Each of the five survey countries prepared a report; these reports are also included in this volume.

# Acknowledgments

The World Bank wishes to thank the governments of Indonesia, the Republic of Korea, Malaysia, the Philippines, and Thailand for their undertaking of the survey work. Financial support was provided by Japan's Policy and Human Resource Development Fund and by the Asia-Europe Meeting Trust Fund, as well as by regional private sector organizations.

The surveys were coordinated and the conference organized by a team led by Dominique Dwor-Frécaut and consisting of Francis Colaço, Mary Hallward-Driemeier, and Charu Adesnik. Flavia Fernandes provided secretarial assistance. The team wishes to thank Kyle Peters, without whose support this work could not have been carried out.

# Foreword

Asian corporate recovery from the devastating effects of the financial crisis of 1997 is in its initial stages in some economic sectors and some companies in certain parts of Asia. For sustained recovery, the region needs to adopt a balanced response that combines expansion of domestic demand with accelerated corporate and financial restructuring. This was the key conclusion reached by participants at the *Conference on Asian Corporate Recovery: Corporate Governance, Government Policy,* organized by the World Bank in Bangkok, Thailand, from March 31 to April 2, 1999.

New data emerged at the conference showing that economic revival programs in Indonesia, the Republic of Korea, Malaysia, the Philippines, and Thailand are beginning to pay off in certain sectors. The participants acknowledged, however, that much remains to be done to stimulate a wider and fuller recovery.

The participants were responding to extensive new surveys of nearly 4,000 firms in the five crisis countries mentioned above. Substantial information on how small and medium-sized firms and those listed on stock exchanges are faring is now available for the first time. This important information, in addition to the standard macroeconomic data, is pointing the way to the kind of policy and institutional reforms most likely to engender sustained recovery.

After two days of discussions on the survey results, the participants agreed on the following points:

- Stimulation of domestic demand alone is not enough, since the crisis was caused primarily by structural problems. Stimulation of domestic demand is, however, necessary to facilitate the accelerated restructuring of banks and other financial institutions and corporate restructuring;
- Corporate and financial restructuring must take place simultaneously for both to succeed;
- The institutional framework for corporate finance needs urgent strengthening to improve the efficiency of credit allocation. Laws to regulate bank-

ruptcies, foreclosures, and mergers and acquisitions are needed to facilitate the transfer of resources from less to more viable activities;
- Financial transactions need greater transparency through improved reporting, accounting, and auditing;
- According to business responses to the survey, the demand for credit has declined as sales have fallen. However, many firms reported difficulties in securing adequate credit. As demand grows, credit availability will become a bigger issue;
- Excess capacity has both a cyclical and structural nature, so macroeconomic policies need to be supplemented with measures to improve corporate competitiveness;
- The development of longer-term instruments and bond markets needs urgent attention;
- More discussion is required to design competitiveness strategies;
- The speed of adjustment must be balanced with the social costs and the need for social safety nets.

Asia has been through a dramatic adjustment in a very short period. The task, however, is not complete. Incipient recovery should not deter continuing efforts at corporate and financial restructuring. The key to sustained recovery is to balance accommodative macroeconomic policies and restructuring in the financial and corporate sectors.

The five countries that participated in the collection and analysis of the survey information are to be commended. The World Bank is also to be commended for having organized this unique conference with entirely new firm-level information and for having brought together such an impressive group of individuals from business, government, academia, and research institutes from Asian countries. It is to be hoped that efforts to collect firm-level information will continue, since this a valuable additional element that can give policymakers confidence in making recommendations.

Recent events indicate that Asia constitutes a distinct region in the global context. They have also highlighted the linkages between countries. Asia's successes have spread from one country to the next, and recently so have difficulties. Further effort is thus needed to continue similar regional discussions on key issues of interest, based on good and timely data and systematic analysis.

Dr. Il Sakong
Former Minister of Finance
CEO, Institute for Global Economics
Seoul, Korea

# Editors' Notes

This volume contains papers presented at a regional conference on "Asian Corporate Recovery: Corporate Governance, Government Policy," organized by the World Bank with the financial support of the Policy and Human Resource Development Fund (Japan) and the Asia-Europe Meeting (ASEM) Trust Fund, and cosponsored by regional private sector organizations.

The regional conference—based on firm-level surveys in Indonesia, the Republic of Korea, Malaysia, the Philippines, and Thailand—was held in Bangkok from March 31 to April 2, 1999. The surveys covered some 3,700 firms in seven manufacturing sectors: electronics, textiles, garments, food processing, chemicals, machinery, and auto parts. They were conducted between December 1998 and February 1999 by the respective governments, with technical assistance from the World Bank. Two-thirds of the companies were small and medium-size enterprises with fewer than 150 workers while the rest were large companies. About 20 percent of the firms were publicly listed.

The conference brought together 60 senior government officials, business people, academics, and researchers in a roundtable format to examine the prospects for Asian corporate recovery based on the unique and new data made available by firm-level surveys. The chairperson of each session was a senior Asian policymaker: Dr. Il SaKong, a former Minister of Finance of Korea and currently Chairman and CEO of the Institute for Global Economics Institute; Dr. Zeti Akhtar Aziz, Deputy Governor of Bank Negara Malaysia; M.R. Chatu Mongol Sonakul, Governor of the Bank of Thailand; Secretary Benjamin Diokno, of the Department of Budget and Management of the Philippines; and Dr. Mari Pangestu, Executive Director of the Center for Strategic and International Studies of Indonesia. Each session consisted of paper presentations, followed by designated lead commentators and a general discussion by the participants.

The conference had five sessions:
- Macroeconomic Constraints to Corporate Recovery, and Country Presentations on Thailand and Korea;

- Corporate Domestic Credit and Financial Fragility, and Country Presentations on Indonesia, Malaysia, and the Philippines;
- Corporates and Foreign Financing;
- Corporate Employment and Public Policy; and
- Summing Up.

The principal issues taken up in the lively exchange of views among the participants in this roundtable and closed-door regional conference were (a) corporate recovery's current status and the major constraints it faced, observed from macroeconomic and firm-level perspectives—and (b) a number of interrelated financing questions: Is there a "credit crunch?" Is firm-level indebtedness a major constraint? What is the role of short-term indebtedness? What is the role of foreign financing? Is there "labor hoarding" and what is its impact on corporate restructuring and on the nature of government social policies? What are the policy options for accelerated corporate recovery on a regional basis?

The regional conference took place against the backdrop of an incipient corporate recovery in some sectors and in some, but not all, countries. A general point emphasized in the discussions was that the crisis had neither affected all five countries at the same time, nor had its intensity been of the same magnitude. Accordingly, the constraints to recovery also varied by country, as did the policy options. Caution had to be exercised, therefore, in making generalizations. (See the Foreword for the principal conclusions of the conference.)

The issues of macroeconomic demand stimulation and the so-called "credit crunch" were at the center of discussions during the first two sessions. Ito, commenting on the papers by Atchana Waiqwamdee and Dwor-Frecaut, Hallward-Driemeier and Colaço, drawing on a study that he had undertaken of Thai financial institutions immediately after the onset of the July 1997 crisis in Thailand, indicated that he had found there was indeed evidence of a credit crunch. He also cautioned that there might be a "survival bias" in the firm survey results (since only those firms in existence at the time of the survey could be interviewed). Other discussants noted that it was important to distinguish between the early postcrisis period when there had been a major spike in domestic interest rates following the initiation of stabilization programs, and the period covered by the survey when interest rates had returned to precrisis levels. The definition of "credit crunch" must also be clarified, allowing for the rational behavior of financial institutions in limiting the allocation of credit only to viable firms. Differences across countries (for example, Korea and the Philippines) and between firms (exporters versus nonexporters) must be kept in mind. It was acknowledged that "survival bias" was an unavoidable feature of such surveys. While it called for caution in interpreting the results, the fact was that in two consecutive firm-level surveys undertaken in Thailand following the crisis, only 10 percent of the firms in the sample had not survived. The large size of the sample also reduced the impact of this bias.

The firm-level surveys indicated that the collapse of domestic demand was a critical factor hindering corporate recovery. They stressed the importance of stimulating consumption demand, without further damaging a country's creditworthiness. They also underlined the importance of improving competitiveness to take advantage of buoyant foreign markets. Others indicated that a lesson Asian countries could learn from the crisis was avoiding the kind of rapid contraction that had taken place. It was also pointed out that demand stimulation had to be accompanied by required corporate and financial restructuring for international competitiveness.

The discussion on foreign financing raised the issues of excessive borrowing and the availability of hedging instruments. Grenville noted that the crisis had highlighted the prominent issue of how to open an economy without excessive capital inflows, an overappreciation of the exchange rate, and a vulnerability to changes in investor sentiment. He stressed the difference between perceived and real profits. According to Grenville, the perception of high profits in the region was overblown. As these economies opened, there was a huge inflow of capital. Hedging alone would have provided insufficient protection. Many firms decided not to hedge not because of the insufficient development of such instruments, but because the cost of hedging was high. Other participants of the foreign financing roundtable noted it was not surprising that the more profitable firms were those that had not borrowed in foreign currencies; they also expressed caution regarding the quality of financial data, stressed the importance of further development of corporate legal systems, and indicated the importance of resumed capital inflows for corporate recovery.

The discussion on corporate employment and public policy elicited a wide range of comments. Siamwalla cautioned that official unemployment numbers might be underestimating the number of unemployed, as there had been a substantial move to nonparticipation in the labor force, particularly by women. He made a plea for compulsory severance pay and an employment insurance system. Choi argued that the degree of labor market flexibility was inversely related to firm size and degree of unionization. Others noted that there was significant evidence of labor hoarding in Indonesia, Malaysia, and Thailand; that with wages not having adjusted fully, significant labor restructuring might still be ahead; that the human costs of the crisis and of restructuring needed to be given adequate attention; and that the social cost of the crisis had been unevenly distributed and mitigated since the bulk of the redundancies was among younger and less skilled workers.

This regional conference provided an opportunity for senior Asian policymakers, business representatives, academics, and researchers to exchange views on Asian corporate recovery on the basis of a unique set of systematically collected and analyzed firm-level data. Some lessons on crisis management were drawn. The incipient signs of recovery, even though they were uneven between countries and sectors, have led to increased attention being paid to issues of corporate restructuring for international competitiveness. There are indications that the five countries, and possibly others in the region, will undertake further such surveys as a basis for returning Asian countries to strong international competitiveness in the next few years of the new millennium.

Dominique Dwor-Frécaut
Francis X. Colaço
Mary Hallward-Driemeier

# chapter one

# Asian Manufacturing Recovery: A Firm-Level Analysis

*Mary Hallward-Driemeier*
*Dominique Dwor-Frécaut*
*Francis X. Colaço*

Macroeconomic studies investigating the causes of the crisis in East Asia abound. However, until now, there have been little systematic or comparable data across the crisis-hit countries to provide a microeconomic explanation of the last two years' events. Recognizing the importance of filling this information gap, the governments of Indonesia, the Republic of Korea, Malaysia, the Philippines, and Thailand, with the technical assistance of the World Bank, undertook an extensive survey of 4,000 firms between November 1998 and February 1999.

The surveys have two areas of focus. The first is understanding the extent of the impact of the crisis on firms and identifying their constraints to recovery. The second is looking at the determinants of productivity and longer-run issues of structural impediments to growth. This paper provides the overview to the first of these topics. It is based on the survey results and the conclusions of a regional dialogue attended by senior policymakers and private sector representatives from across Asia.[1]

The paper explores the impact of the crisis by looking at changes in capacity utilization, export performance, and employment practices. The causes for the decline are then examined from the perspective of the surveyed firms. Given the attention paid to issues of credit availability, this issue is discussed at length. One of the contributions of the data set is that it provides information on the financial position of small and medium enterprises (SMEs) and unlisted large companies. It relates the extent of the firms' leverage and their reliance on different sources of capital to their reported access to credit. One of the principal findings of the survey is that the nature of the firms' cash flow position is the key to understanding their response to the crisis. These firms had been relying heavily on internal funds—and as sales fell with the slump in demand, the costs of imported inputs rose and nominal interest rates increased, severely hampering cash flow position. One of the policy messages is that the lack of demand was the main constraint reported by the firms. Stimulating demand is a priority, but the survey also demonstrates other structural problems, and that any stimulation must be complemented by simultaneous restructuring of the financial and corporate sectors.

## Data

Close to 4,000 firms were individually interviewed as the basis of the survey. The firms were selected from the principal manufacturing sectors in each country: electronics, textiles, garments, food processing, chemicals, machinery, and auto parts. The sectoral composition differs somewhat across countries, with each country selecting five of the seven sectors. Each sector was chosen by at least three countries, enabling regional comparison (see table 1.1).

The sample was designed in conjunction with the statistical agency in each country. Rather than focus on the largest firms, a random sample of surveyed firms was drawn so that the results would be significant for the larger population of firms in the economy. Participating firms were drawn from the population of firms with 20 or more employees in the selected sectors. Approximately two-thirds of the resulting sample consists of SMEs (firms with fewer than 150 workers), and one-third is

### TABLE 1.1
### Characteristics of the sample

|  | Size (%) | | Export orientation (%) | | FDI firm (%) | | Sector (%) | | | | | Total |
|---|---|---|---|---|---|---|---|---|---|---|---|---|
|  | Small | Large | Nonexporters | Exporters | No | Yes | Food | Text. and garm. | Elec. mach. | Chem. | Auto. |  |
| *Country* |  |  |  |  |  |  |  |  |  |  |  |  |
| Indonesia | 56 | 44 | 64 | 36 | 82 | 18 | 32 | 26 | 12 | 30 | — | 816 |
| Korea, Rep. of | 65 | 35 | 25 | 75 | 83 | 17 | — | 23 | 35 | 28 | 14 | 857 |
| Malaysia | 74 | 26 | 53 | 47 | 74 | 26 | 26 | 31 | 20 | 20 | 4 | 693 |
| Philippines | 48 | 52 | 48 | 52 | 64 | 36 | 26 | 37 | 21 | 16 | — | 564 |
| Thailand | 63 | 37 | 43 | 57 | 70 | 30 | 10 | 54 | 16 | — | 20 | 659 |
| *Sector* |  |  |  |  |  |  |  |  |  |  |  |  |
| Food | 66 | 34 | 64 | 36 | 84 | 16 | — | — | — | — | — | 649 |
| Textiles and garments | 63 | 37 | 48 | 52 | 82 | 18 | — | — | — | — | — | 1194 |
| Electronics, electr. mach. | 58 | 42 | 29 | 71 | 61 | 39 | — | — | — | — | — | 752 |
| Chemicals | 61 | 39 | 44 | 56 | 73 | 27 | — | — | — | — | — | 717 |
| Auto parts | 63 | 37 | 44 | 56 | 75 | 25 | — | — | — | — | — | 277 |
| *Size* |  |  |  |  |  |  |  |  |  |  |  |  |
| Small | — | — | 60 | 40 | 85 | 15 | 19 | 34 | 20 | 20 | 8 | 2077 |
| Large | — | — | 24 | 76 | 62 | 38 | 16 | 33 | 23 | 21 | 8 | 1257 |
| *Export orientation* |  |  |  |  |  |  |  |  |  |  |  |  |
| Nonexporters | 80 | 20 | — | — | 90 | 10 | 25 | 35 | 14 | 19 | 8 | 1629 |
| Exporters | 46 | 54 | — | — | 64 | 36 | 12 | 33 | 28 | 20 | 8 | 1923 |
| *FDI firms* |  |  |  |  |  |  |  |  |  |  |  |  |
| No | 69 | 31 | 54 | 46 | — | — | 20 | 36 | 17 | 20 | 8 | 2792 |
| Yes | 38 | 62 | 19 | 81 | — | — | 12 | 25 | 33 | 22 | 8 | 889 |
| *Indebtedness* |  |  |  |  |  |  |  |  |  |  |  |  |
| Low | 63 | 37 | 49 | 51 | 73 | 27 | 17 | 33 | 22 | 20 | 8 | 1204 |
| High | 55 | 45 | 36 | 64 | 76 | 24 | 12 | 35 | 24 | 19 | 9 | 772 |
| *Foreign borrowing* |  |  |  |  |  |  |  |  |  |  |  |  |
| No | 67 | 33 | 49 | 51 | 80 | 20 | 16 | 36 | 21 | 20 | 8 | 1911 |
| Yes | 37 | 63 | 13 | 87 | 58 | 42 | 6 | 29 | 30 | 21 | 13 | 700 |
| Total | 2000 | 1221 | 1570 | 1861 | 2688 | 872 | 649 | 1194 | 752 | 717 | 277 | 3589 |

*Note:* Percentages represent the share of the row variable that has the corresponding column characteristic.
*Source:* World Bank, Firm-Level Survey.

made up of large companies. The ownership structure of these firms varies across countries, but on average 20 percent are publicly listed companies, 55 percent are private corporations, and the remainder are partnerships, single proprietorships, cooperatives, or other forms of business.

While the chosen sectors represent tradable goods industries, just over one-half of the firms export some of their output. The extent to which the firms export also varies, with less than 20 percent exporting the majority of their products. A significant number have a relationship with a foreign partner; about a quarter are classified as foreign direct investment, with a foreign partner holding at least a 10 percent ownership stake.

The firms were asked two kinds of questions. The first are quantitative questions regarding production, employment, and balance sheet information. The questions cover the period from 1996 through the first half of 1998. The second part of the questionnaire asked qualitative questions that were answered by the owner or senior manager during an interview. These questions referred to the time of the interview—between November 1998 and February 1999.

Some important caveats need to be kept in mind in interpreting the data. First, while the survey was endorsed by the governments, the firms' compliance was voluntary. Verification of responses can be scrutinized using internal consistency checks, but it was not possible to obtain external confirmation of responses. This caveat is particularly relevant with regard to the financial data. Second, this survey, as with any other, suffers from a survival bias. Only firms that were still in existence were available for interviewing. To gain some measure of the extent of the problem, the statistical agencies kept track of the nonresponse rate owing to bankruptcies or closures. On average, 10 percent of the firms selected for the sample were no longer in operation at the time of the interview.[2]

## Impact of the crisis

### Capacity utilization

The firms were asked to report their capacity utilization in 1996, the first half of 1997, the second half of 1997, and the first half of 1998 as a measure of the impact of the crisis (see figure 1.1).[3] Since the onset of the crisis in July 1997, 71 percent of the firms have reported declining levels of capacity utilization. With investment plans virtually halted, this decline corresponds very closely to decreases in output. The proportion was highest in Indonesia, followed by Thailand, Malaysia, the Philippines, and Korea. Indonesia also experienced the largest magnitude in the decline, with declines averaging about 20 percent. The lowest average decline was in the Philippines, at 9 percent. This is consistent with other evidence that the Philippines was less affected and felt the impact at a later date. Korea saw its largest drop in the first half of 1998, again corresponding to the later date of the onset of its financial crisis.

Comparing exporting and nonexporting firms, the capacity utilization of the former remained less affected than nonexporters. While levels were comparable in 1996, by 1998 the exporters' capacity utilization was nine percentage points higher than the nonexporters'. The hardest hit sector was auto parts, with 90 percent of the firms experiencing a decline. The average decline for auto parts was almost 22 percent, followed by declines for electronics (13 percent), chemicals (10.7 percent), garments and textiles (9.3 percent), and finally food processing (8.4 percent).

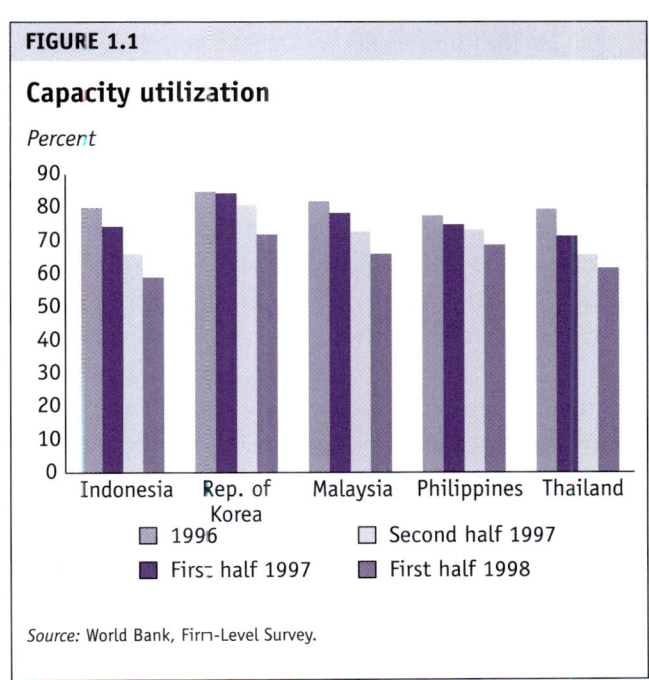

**FIGURE 1.1**

**Capacity utilization**

*Source:* World Bank, Firm-Level Survey.

The exporting firms in Korea, Malaysia, and Thailand were also asked to report on changes in their export performance. Just over half of the firms in these countries export some of their output, with the highest proportion found in Korea. The surveyed firms were more likely to report an improvement from 1996 to 1997 than from 1997 to 1998—despite the continued devaluation. However, one-third of the firms reported that their export performance had declined, on average 10–25 percent. As discussed below, with a significant share of exports sold to neighboring countries, the regional recession has created an impact on the demand for exports. Coupled with falling dollar prices in many sectors, it is not surprising that the export performance of firms after the devaluation was mixed.

It is clear from the data that the fall in capacity is not just a cyclical story associated with the financial crisis. Particularly noticeable in Thailand is that capacity utilization was already falling prior to the devaluation in July 1997. Data are available on inputs and outputs from 1996 to 1998 that will allow this to be investigated further in a separate paper. In certain sectors, part of the explanation is the worldwide overcapacity, such as in electronics and auto parts.

### Prospects for capacity utilization

Firms in Korea are the most optimistic that recovery is likely in the first half of 1999 (see figure 1.2). Approximately 70 percent of the sample firms in Korea and the Philippines believe that they will maintain or increase their capacity utilization. In contrast, more than 35 percent of the firms in Indonesia, Malaysia, and Thailand believe that their capacity utilization will decrease in the next six months. The financial position of the firms gives insights into these differences that will be addressed further below. Among the sectors, auto parts firms are the most optimistic. Having suffered the greatest declines in capacity utilization, many believe that their position will improve as demand picks up again.

Table 1.2 provides information on which firms have in fact experienced some recovery, with either capacity utilization or export performance having improved in 1998 relative to the end of 1997. It is clear in this information too that Korean firms, particularly exporting firms, have been able to increase their output in recent months. However, it should be noted that there is only a loose correlation between the firms' expectations and their actual performance in the prior year.

### Employment

The survey data provides information on the extent to which the crisis has affected employment and the causes for employment reductions.[4] These data have implications for the social costs associated with the crisis and for the likely extent of human capital loss for firms, and they provide an indication of the extent to which firms are undertaking restructuring. One of the principal findings is that employment changes are only loosely correlated with changes in capacity utilization; there is evidence of labor hoarding in Indonesia, Thailand, and Malaysia. Thus, while the data indicate that Korea has made the most progress in adjusting its labor force to the new market conditions, significant labor reductions could still be on the horizon.[5]

Almost half the firms in the survey currently employ fewer workers than they had prior to the crisis (see figure 1.3). The rate is highest in Korea, where 60 percent have fewer workers. Korea and Thailand are also the countries where the proportion of redundancies are greatest, with over a quarter of the firms reporting a decline in employment of over 25 percent. In Korea, the reduction in total employment was close to 20 percent. Malaysia is the country where the impact on

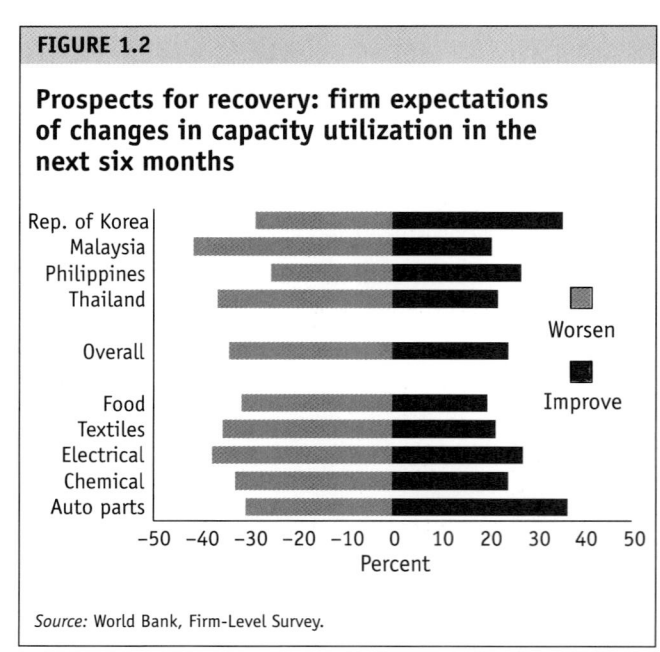

**FIGURE 1.2**

**Prospects for recovery: firm expectations of changes in capacity utilization in the next six months**

*Source:* World Bank, Firm-Level Survey.

### TABLE 1.2
**Who is recovering: characteristics of the firms that expanded in 1998 relative to the end of 1997**
Reported as percent (by country) of firms that have expanded

|  | By size | | By export orientation | | FDI firm | | Sector | | | | | | |
| --- | --- | --- | --- | --- | --- | --- | --- | --- | --- | --- | --- | --- | --- |
|  | Small | Large | Non-exporters | Exporters | No | Yes | Food | Text. and garm. | Elec. mach. | Chem. | Auto | Total | % Sample |
| *Increase in capacity utilization* | | | | | | | | | | | | | |
| Indonesia | 43.1 | 56.9 | 40.1 | 59.6 | 79.4 | 20.6 | 47.6 | 7.9 | 17.5 | 26.9 | — | 51 | 6.3 |
| Korea | 70.1 | 29.1 | 21.9 | 78.1 | 81.9 | 18.1 | — | 31.4 | 25.0 | 32.4 | 1.0 | 103 | 12.0 |
| Malaysia | 65.1 | 34.9 | 39.3 | 60.7 | 68.5 | 31.5 | 31.5 | 19.1 | 20.2 | 27.0 | 2.3 | 86 | 10.6 |
| Philippines | 43.9 | 56.3 | 33.8 | 66.2 | 59.8 | 40.2 | 25.6 | 40.2 | 19.5 | 14.1 | — | 71 | 12.6 |
| Thailand | 56.0 | 44.0 | 25.9 | 74.1 | 67.0 | 33.0 | 12.1 | 66.4 | 12.9 | — | 8.6 | 100 | 15.2 |
| Total | 57.9 | 42.1 | 30.8 | 69.2 | 71.2 | 28.8 | 20.4 | 36.3 | 21.3 | 19.1 | 2.9 | — | — |
| *Increase in exports* | | | | Percentage of exporters | | | | | | | | | |
| Korea | 50.0 | 50.0 | — | 55.1 | 77.6 | 22.4 | — | 21.8 | 38.2 | 27.9 | 12.1 | 348 | 40.6 |
| Malaysia | 39.9 | 60.1 | — | 59.2 | 52.4 | 47.6 | 14.0 | 22.6 | 25.6 | 33.5 | 4.3 | 164 | 29.1 |
| Thailand | 41.3 | 58.7 | — | 40.3 | 56.6 | 43.4 | 10.1 | 61.1 | 16.1 | — | 12.8 | 149 | 22.6 |
| Total | 45.7 | 54.3 | — | — | 66.7 | 33.3 | 12.1 | 30.86 | 30.1 | 29.7 | 10.3 | — | — |
| *Total sample* | | | | | | | | | | | | | |
| Indonesia | 47.9 | 37.1 | 55.1 | 31.4 | 82.5 | 17.5 | 32.1 | 26.2 | 11.8 | 29.9 | — | 816 | — |
| Korea | 62.7 | 33.4 | 24.9 | 73.7 | 83.0 | 17.0 | — | 23.2 | 34.5 | 28.4 | 13.9 | 857 | — |
| Malaysia | 68.1 | 24.8 | 52.3 | 47.7 | 73.8 | 26.2 | 21.9 | 26.0 | 17.0 | 17.0 | 3.3 | 814 | — |
| Philippines | 42.6 | 45.9 | 45.4 | 49.1 | 63.3 | 34.9 | 25.7 | 37.2 | 20.7 | 16.3 | — | 564 | — |
| Thailand | 53.9 | 31.4 | 43.1 | 56.1 | 68.3 | 28.8 | 9.7 | 54.5 | 15.9 | — | 19.9 | 659 | — |
| Total | 62.3 | 37.7 | 45.9 | 54.1 | 75.9 | 24.1 | 17.5 | 32.2 | 20.3 | 22.6 | 7.4 | — | — |

*Source:* World Bank, Firm-Level Survey.

employment has been mildest. Across sectors, auto parts experienced the largest reductions with 73 percent of the firms reducing their work forces, followed by electronics and machinery.

Comparing the declines in employment with capacity utilization changes, there are stark differences across countries (see figure 1.4). In Indonesia and Thailand, the countries with the largest declines in capacity utilization,

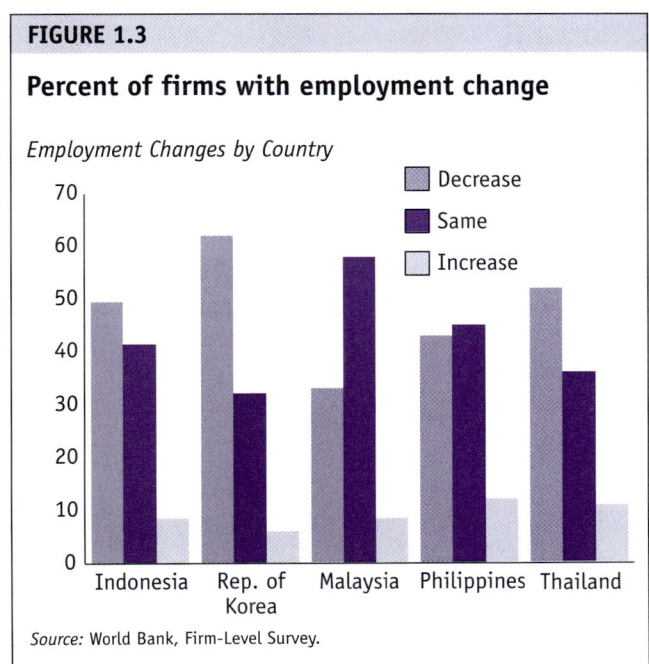

**FIGURE 1.3**
**Percent of firms with employment change**
*Source:* World Bank, Firm-Level Survey.

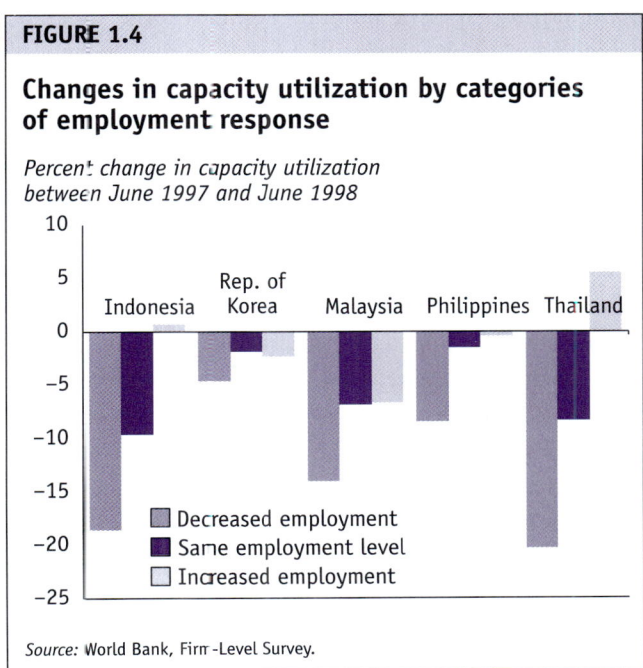

**FIGURE 1.4**
**Changes in capacity utilization by categories of employment response**
*Source:* World Bank, Firm-Level Survey.

there are also large declines in employment. However, there are also a significant number of firms that have maintained their employment levels despite declines in capacity utilization averaging 5–10 percent. A similar phenomenon is discernible in Malaysia. This is consistent with labor hoarding.[6]

Labor hoarding could be the result of inflexible labor markets. A high cost of firing workers can lead firms to maintain higher than optimal levels of employment. Further investigation is needed to examine the specific labor market institutions in each country and to ascribe to them the cross-country differences in the data. What is particularly striking, however, is that Korea, the country with the strongest union movement is also the country with the highest redundancies and the least labor hoarding. One explanation is that with the crisis there has been an introduction of measures that have loosened the restrictions on firing workers. Furthermore, union activism seems to have been curbed by workers' worries about job security in the face of rising unemployment. Many firms may have taken advantage of this to undertake desired restructuring. Such a line of reasoning is most consistent with the *chaebols,* the conglomerates with large labor forces. This explanation is also consistent with further evidence on the types of workers that were made redundant.

From another perspective, labor hoarding can be optimal if real wages have fallen or if the firms wish to maintain firm-specific human capital and the shock is perceived to be short-term. Research on the changes in real wages continues, with preliminary indications that real wages have fallen—in some cases, substantially. The age, tenure, and position of workers who have been made redundant do indicate that the firms are trying to minimize the loss of human capital.

Younger workers were disproportionately made redundant in all countries but Korea (see figure 1.5). Most of the lost jobs had formerly been held by 21–30 year-old workers. Likewise the job losses were concentrated in the production jobs rather than managerial or technical staff. Production jobs represent close to two-thirds of the jobs, but represent three-quarters of the lost jobs. This is most striking in Malaysia and Thailand. The average tenure of those made redundant was one to three years. The implication of these patterns is that younger workers with less firm-specific human capital have been those that are let go.

Minimizing the loss of human capital is consistent with rational behavior on the part of the firms. Looking at it from the social perspective, younger people are less likely to have family responsibilities and likely to be easier to train, thus lessening the social cost dimension of the lost employment.

The one exception to this pattern is Korea. In Korea, almost half of the lost jobs had been held by workers in their 30s. Korean firms also had a lower share of production job losses, consistent with the lower overall share of production jobs in Korea, but this category still bore a disproportionate share of the lost jobs. Like firms in the Philippines, those in Korea lost a higher share of workers with six to ten years tenure. This could represent a significant loss of human capital. However, bearing in mind the loosening of inflexible labor markets, this is consistent with Korean firms' using the opportunity to substantially restructure their workforces. This explanation is consistent with the fact that Korean firms are also the most likely to be filling vacancies; a sign that they are reacting to meet changes in labor demand.

That only firms in Korea show substantial signs of restructuring their work force does not bode well for the extent of labor adjustment that could be on the horizon. If demand does pick up soon, the labor hoarding

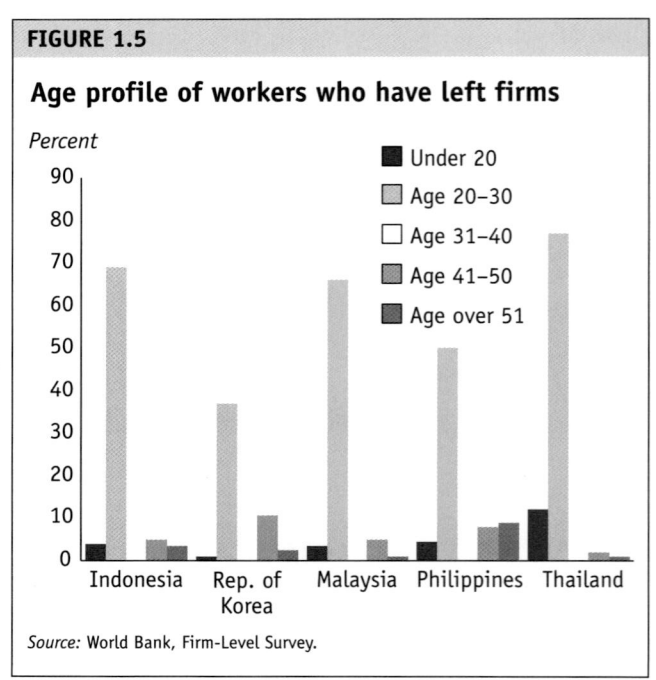

**FIGURE 1.5**

**Age profile of workers who have left firms**

*Source:* World Bank, Firm-Level Survey.

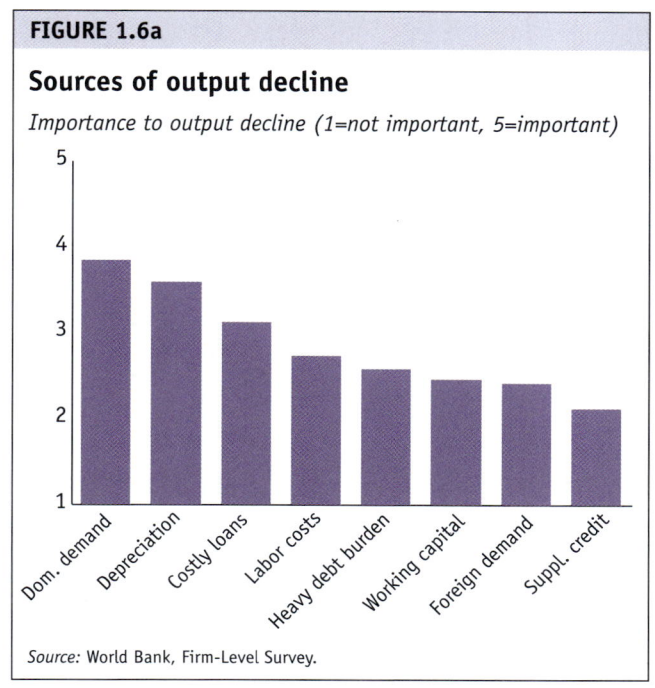

**FIGURE 1.6a**

**Sources of output decline**

*Importance to output decline (1=not important, 5=important)*

Categories: Dom. demand, Depreciation, Costly loans, Labor costs, Heavy debt burden, Working capital, Foreign demand, Suppl. credit

*Source:* World Bank, Firm-Level Survey.

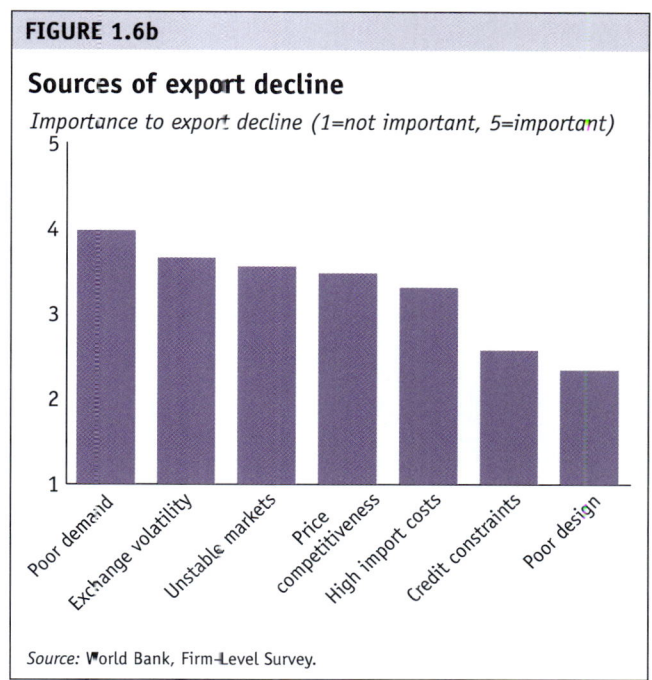

**FIGURE 1.6b**

**Sources of export decline**

*Importance to export decline (1=not important, 5=important)*

Categories: Poor demand, Exchange volatility, Unstable markets, Price competitiveness, High import costs, Credit constraints, Poor design

*Source:* World Bank, Firm-Level Survey.

may have been justified, but only if there is little substantial shift in the skills needed by the firms in the post-crisis period. If significant labor shedding develops in the upcoming months, the need will grow for continued improvements in the expansion of social safety nets and a further balancing of the speed of adjustment with social costs. Clearly this is an area that justifies careful monitoring in the months ahead.

## Corporate views of the causes of the output decline

The firms were asked to list and rank the causes of output decline.[7] The responses are shown in figure 1.6a and table 1.3.[8] The first four causes were, in order of decreasing importance, domestic demand, the rise in imported input costs caused by the depreciation, high interest rates, and labor cost. It should be kept in mind that the answers to this qualitative question were based on the firms' position and the economic environment prevailing in the time period from the end of 1998 to early 1999.[9]

*The main complaint of the firms in all countries, with the exception of the Philippines, was the collapse of domestic demand for their products.* This complaint is mirrored by the macroeconomic data showing a sharp decline in investment and consumption. As emphasized by Cho and Rhee,[10] the withdrawal in capital flows that took place in 1997 translated more into a sharp rise in interest rates than into a contraction of money supply as governments continued to extend liquidity support to their fledgling financial sectors (see figure 1.7). Nominal and real interest rates jumped to historical highs. Because East Asian firms were highly leveraged, the rise in interest rates translated to a sharp decline in the firms' investment demand. The collapse of this demand had a large impact on aggregate demand because before the crisis, investment in these countries accounted for 40 percent of gross domestic product (GDP), with the exception of the Philippines where investment represents only about 20 percent of GDP. The restrictive fiscal policies initially adopted in response to the withdrawal of capital flows further contributed to the collapse of domestic demand.

*The second cause of the output collapse reported by the firms was the rise in the cost of imported inputs caused by the devaluation.* (Filipino firms reported this as the most important cause of output decline.) This complaint can be expected in countries that have devalued their currency. The rise in input costs caused by the devaluation reduces the profit margins of nonexporting firms and provides them with the incentive to redirect

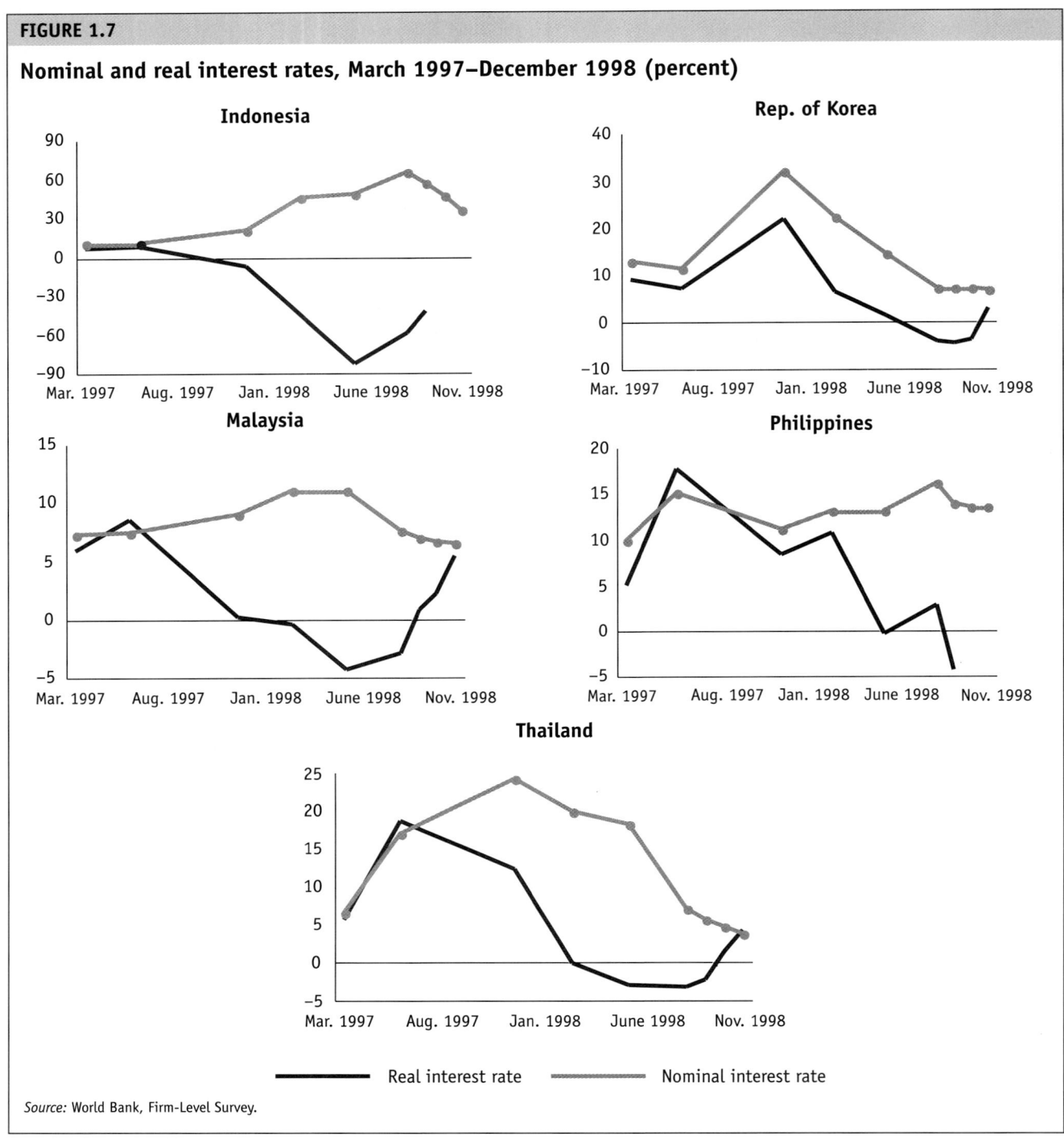

**FIGURE 1.7**

**Nominal and real interest rates, March 1997–December 1998 (percent)**

*Source:* World Bank, Firm-Level Survey.

their production to the tradable sector, which eventually results in an increase in the volume of exports and in the restoration of the firms' profits. Indeed, in 1997 the expectation was for a rapid recovery led by exports.

However, the export-led recovery did not materialize. The survey results shed some light on the reasons. Exporters in Korea, Malaysia, and Thailand were asked for the causes for the decline in export performance (see figure 1.6b and table 1.4). The most important one given was the lack of foreign demand and the lack of stability in foreign markets. The collapse of domestic demand in the five countries and the recession in Japan also hurt exporters, because of the importance of intraregional trade. Including Japan, about half of the exports of the five countries go to the region (the exception is the Philippines, which sells a greater share of its exports to the United States). The firms have reported fewer complaints about the impact of the decline in foreign demand on overall output, not so much because the decline in foreign demand has been less pronounced, but rather because the firms sell a smaller share of their output abroad.

The second main reason given by exporters as the cause of their decline was exchange volatility and the lack of price competitiveness. Export prices in the five countries had started to decline before the crisis hit.[11] And after the crisis, they declined sharply: in the year following the devaluation of the Thai baht, export volumes in the five countries rose by about 20 percent, but nominal export values in U.S. dollars remained flat, with the exception of the Philippines where nominal export values continued to grow at a 20 percent clip. Thus, exporters and domestic producers trying to reorient their production to the export markets were hit simultaneously by shrinking markets and declining prices.

*The third cause of output decline reported by the firms was the high level of interest rates.* At the time when the question was asked (late 1998 to early 1999), nominal interest rates were back to their precrisis levels.

**TABLE 1.3.**

**Change in level of output after the crisis and source of output decline**

|  | By change in level of output (%) | | By source of output decline (%) | | | | | | | | | | |
|---|---|---|---|---|---|---|---|---|---|---|---|---|---|
|  | Increase or same | Decrease | Dom. demand | Depreciation | Costly loans | Labor costs | Heavy debt burden | Wk. capital | Fgn. demand | Raw materials | Expans. credit | Suppl. credit | Not deliver goods |
| Country |  |  |  |  |  |  |  |  |  |  |  |  |  |
| Indonesia | 24 | 76 | 3.5 | 3.6 | 3.1 | 2.6 |  | 2.1 | 1.8 | 2.5 | 2.1 | 1.8 | 2.1 |
| Korea | 33 | 67 | 4.3 | 2.9 | 3.1 | 2.0 | 2.3 | 2.6 | 2.8 | 2.3 | 2.2 | 2.1 | 2.1 |
| Malaysia | 33 | 67 | 4.0 | 3.6 | 2.8 | 2.5 | 2.5 | 2.3 | 2.4 | 2.1 | 2.2 | 2.1 | 2.0 |
| Philippines | 31 | 69 | 3.2 | 3.9 | 3.4 | 3.3 |  | 2.7 | 2.4 | 2.6 | 2.4 | 2.3 | 2.3 |
| Thailand | 27 | 73 | 4.0 | 4.0 | 3.3 | 3.4 | 2.9 | 2.7 | 2.8 | 2.3 | 2.2 | 2.4 | 2.1 |
| Sector |  |  |  |  |  |  |  |  |  |  |  |  |  |
| Food | 34 | 66 | 3.4 | 3.6 | 3.0 | 2.7 | 2.3 | 2.2 | 1.8 | 2.7 | 2.0 | 1.9 | 2.1 |
| Textiles and Garments | 32 | 68 | 3.7 | 3.7 | 3.2 | 3.0 | 2.7 | 2.6 | 2.5 | 2.3 | 2.3 | 2.3 | 2.2 |
| Electronics and elect. mach. | 26 | 74 | 3.9 | 3.3 | 2.9 | 2.5 | 2.4 | 2.3 | 2.9 | 2.1 | 2.1 | 2.0 | 1.9 |
| Chemicals | 33 | 67 | 3.9 | 3.6 | 3.2 | 2.6 | 2.5 | 2.5 | 2.2 | 2.4 | 2.3 | 2.2 | 2.0 |
| Auto parts | 7 | 93 | 4.6 | 3.6 | 3.3 | 2.7 | 2.8 | 2.7 | 2.6 | 2.3 | 2.2 | 2.2 | 2.1 |
| Size |  |  |  |  |  |  |  |  |  |  |  |  |  |
| Small | 26 | 74 | 4.0 | 3.5 | 3.0 | 2.7 | 2.5 | 2.4 | 2.2 | 2.3 | 2.1 | 2.1 | 2.1 |
| Large | 34 | 66 | 3.6 | 3.6 | 3.2 | 2.7 | 2.6 | 2.5 | 2.8 | 2.3 | 2.3 | 2.1 | 2.0 |
| Export orientation |  |  |  |  |  |  |  |  |  |  |  |  |  |
| Nonexporters | 21 | 79 | 4.1 | 3.6 | 3.0 | 2.7 | 2.5 | 2.3 | 1.7 | 2.3 | 2.0 | 2.1 | 2.1 |
| Exporters | 37 | 63 | 3.6 | 3.6 | 3.3 | 2.7 | 2.6 | 2.6 | 3.2 | 2.4 | 2.4 | 2.2 | 2.1 |
| FDI firms |  |  |  |  |  |  |  |  |  |  |  |  |  |
| No | 28 | 72 | 3.9 | 3.6 | 3.2 | 2.7 | 2.6 | 2.5 | 2.2 | 2.4 | 2.2 | 2.1 | 2.1 |
| Yes | 34 | 66 | 3.5 | 3.6 | 2.9 | 2.8 | 2.4 | 2.3 | 3.0 | 2.1 | 2.1 | 2.0 | 1.9 |
| Indebtedness |  |  |  |  |  |  |  |  |  |  |  |  |  |
| Low | 28 | 72 | 3.9 | 3.6 | 3.0 | 2.8 | 2.4 | 2.2 | 2.4 | 2.3 | 2.1 | 2.0 | 2.0 |
| High | 27 | 73 | 3.9 | 3.6 | 3.4 | 2.8 | 2.8 | 2.6 | 2.6 | 2.4 | 2.3 | 2.3 | 2.1 |
| Foreign borrowing |  |  |  |  |  |  |  |  |  |  |  |  |  |
| No | 26 | 74 | 3.9 | 3.6 | 3.2 | 2.8 | 2.7 | 2.5 | 2.4 | 2.4 | 2.3 | 2.2 | 2.1 |
| Yes | 35 | 65 | 4.0 | 3.3 | 3.2 | 2.4 | 2.5 | 2.6 | 3.0 | 2.2 | 2.2 | 2.1 | 1.9 |
| Capacity utilization |  |  |  |  |  |  |  |  |  |  |  |  |  |
| Increase |  |  | 3.4 | 3.7 | 3.3 | 3.1 | 3.3 | 2.7 | 2.6 | 2.7 | 2.5 | 2.4 | 2.4 |
| Same |  |  | 3.5 | 3.5 | 2.9 | 2.8 | 2.5 | 2.3 | 2.4 | 2.3 | 2.1 | 2.0 | 2.0 |
| Decrease |  |  | 4.0 | 3.6 | 3.2 | 2.7 | 2.6 | 2.5 | 2.4 | 2.3 | 2.2 | 2.1 | 2.1 |
| Total | 29 | 71 | 3.8 | 3.6 | 3.1 | 2.7 | 2.6 | 2.5 | 2.4 | 2.3 | 2.2 | 2.1 | 2.1 |

*Source:* World Bank, Firm-Level Survey.

## TABLE 1.4
### Source of export decline by firm characteristics

|  | By change in export (%) | | | By source of export decline (%) | | | | | | |
|---|---|---|---|---|---|---|---|---|---|---|
|  | Decrease | Same | Increase | Poor demand | Exchange rate volatility | Unstable markets | Price competitiveness | High import cost | Credit constraints | Design |
| **Country** | | | | | | | | | | |
| Indonesia | — | — | — | — | — | — | — | — | — | — |
| Korea | 29 | 11 | 60 | 3.68 | 2.94 | 3.55 | 3.28 | 2.71 | 2.30 | 1.97 |
| Malaysia | 38 | 15 | 46 | 4.24 | 3.64 | 3.22 | 3.48 | 3.76 | — | 2.82 |
| Philippines | — | — | — | — | — | — | — | — | — | — |
| Thailand | 36 | 20 | 44 | 3.93 | 3.96 | 3.96 | 3.76 | 3.84 | 3.12 | — |
| **Sector** | | | | | | | | | | |
| Food | 40 | 21 | 39 | 3.79 | 3.85 | 3.26 | 3.55 | 3.57 | 3.17 | 2.63 |
| Textiles and garments | 31 | 15 | 54 | 3.85 | 3.89 | 3.70 | 3.60 | 3.43 | 2.81 | 2.36 |
| Electronics and elect. mach. | 34 | 14 | 52 | 3.97 | 3.45 | 3.49 | 3.36 | 3.30 | 2.19 | 2.32 |
| Chemicals | 32 | 14 | 55 | 3.99 | 3.45 | 3.45 | 3.52 | 3.12 | 2.44 | 2.40 |
| Auto parts | 38 | 10 | 52 | 4.02 | 3.79 | 3.73 | 3.20 | 3.48 | 2.82 | 2.14 |
| **Size** | | | | | | | | | | |
| Small | 38 | 17 | 45 | 3.98 | 3.66 | 3.67 | 3.49 | 3.31 | 2.48 | 2.35 |
| Large | 27 | 11 | 62 | 3.85 | 3.71 | 3.35 | 3.46 | 3.32 | 2.68 | 2.36 |
| **Export orientation** | | | | | | | | | | |
| Nonexporters | — | — | — | — | — | — | — | — | — | — |
| Exporters | 33 | 14 | 52 | 3.93 | 3.68 | 3.55 | 3.47 | 3.34 | 2.58 | 2.36 |
| **FDI firms** | | | | | | | | | | |
| No | 33 | 13 | 53 | 3.79 | 3.59 | 3.53 | 3.42 | 3.18 | 2.48 | 2.26 |
| Yes | 34 | 16 | 50 | 4.18 | 3.79 | 3.56 | 3.54 | 3.62 | 2.82 | 2.56 |
| **Indebtedness** | | | | | | | | | | |
| Low | 35 | 15 | 50 | 4.03 | 3.66 | 3.84 | 3.43 | 3.34 | 2.31 | 2.39 |
| High | 33 | 15 | 52 | 3.94 | 3.63 | 3.76 | 3.44 | 3.34 | 3.01 | 2.31 |
| **Foreign Borrowing** | | | | | | | | | | |
| No | 35 | 15 | 50 | 3.84 | 3.67 | 3.65 | 3.43 | 3.28 | 2.49 | 2.20 |
| Yes | 31 | 12 | 58 | 3.96 | 3.67 | 6.47 | 3.47 | 3.20 | 2.55 | 2.40 |
| *Total* | 33 | 14 | 52 | 3.93 | 3.68 | 3.55 | 3.47 | 3.34 | 2.58 | 2.36 |

*Source:* World Bank, Firm-Level Survey.

Real interest rates, measured by the consumer price index (CPI) were also below their precrisis level. However, because of producer price deflation, real interest rates measured by the producer price index (PPI) were above their precrisis level.[12] Furthermore, with the decline in output prices, precrisis real interest rates were likely to be perceived by firms as "too high."

*The fourth cause of output decline reported by the firms was the high level of labor costs.* This is a surprising finding in view of the nominal depreciation of about 40 percent in nominal terms between mid-1997 and the end of 1998. This particular complaint has to be put in the context of declining output prices. Moreover, the currencies in the five countries were devalued within months of each other. As the countries, particularly Indonesia, Malaysia, the Philippines, and Thailand have fairly similar exports, their overall competitiveness has not increased by much. Finally some of the countries, particularly Korea and Thailand had experienced several years of real wage growth that was higher than productivity growth in the manufacturing sectors. As mentioned previously, the decline in the rate of capacity utilization prior to the crisis suggests that structural problems were at play before the crisis hit.

To sum up, the firms in Indonesia, Korea, Malaysia, and Thailand, were hit by a collapse in domestic demand and a decline in profitability caused by sharply higher imported costs but could not successfully switch their production to exports because of shrinking export markets, declining export prices, and competitiveness problems that predated the crisis.

*The firms in the Philippines seem to have had a somewhat different experience.* First, as mentioned above, of the five countries, Filipino firms had the lowest rate of capacity utilization in 1996 but the smallest decline in capacity utilization as a result of the crisis. Second, Filipino firms ranked costs—imported inputs, high interest rates, and labor costs—as more important causes of output decline than a lack of domestic or foreign demand.

This is likely to reflect a different macroeconomic and international environment. The international environment for Filipino firms seems to have been more favorable, with firmer export prices and a greater reliance on the U.S. market, in which import demand has been sustained throughout the crisis. Furthermore, the contraction of GDP in 1998 was much smaller than in the other countries. The Philippines has not been hit by a collapse in investment demand comparable to that of other countries. The rise in real interest rates was much less pronounced than in Korea and Thailand,[13] and as mentioned above, the ratio of investment to GDP in the Philippines is smaller than in other countries. Rather, the Philippines has been hit by a supply shock: the 1998 drought led to a contraction of output in the agricultural sector, as well as to higher costs of foodstuffs that fed into higher inflation.

The low level of capacity utilization in 1996, the decline in capacity utilization prior to the crisis, and Filipino firms' complaints about costs despite a more favorable international environment suggest that the decline of output of Filipino firms and the recent slowdown in export growth have been caused more by structural competitiveness problems than by the collapse in domestic and foreign demand.

## Credit availability, corporate credit needs, and governance

By the end of 1998, the firms did not report credit availability as a major source of output decline, despite the systemic problems experienced by the financial sectors of many countries. The surveys shed some light on this surprising finding by providing information on the relationship between the banking sector and the firms.

The crisis has greatly curtailed the availability of credit. Bank liquidity and capital have been severely affected by mounting stocks of nonperforming loans. Estimates of peak nonperforming loans vary from 30 percent of the total loan portfolio of banks in Korea to 75 percent in Indonesia,[14] while the Filipino banking sector has not so far suffered from systemic difficulties (see table 1.5). Second, many countries had initially adopted policies that tightened capital adequacy and loan classification rules. These policies have further reduced the availability of credit because banks have found it more difficult than expected to mobilize capital from private sources, especially foreign ones. In view of the lack of interest on the part of foreign investors, governments have had to intervene and provide distressed banks with liquidity and capital. However, with perhaps the exception of Korea, governments have generally been slow in restructuring and recapitalizing the banking sector. Eventually, the tightening of capital adequacy ratios had to be reversed or phased in over a longer period of time. A third reason for the decline in credit availability has been an increased degree of risk aversion on the part of banks, a phenomenon that has been observed in most banking crises. Figure 1.8 shows that, on aggregate, real credit to the private sector has declined since mid-1997 in Indonesia, the Philippines, and Thailand. In the case of Thailand, the decline in the supply of credit is also well documented in a paper by Professor Takatoshi Ito and Luis Pereira da Silva.[15]

Compared with the sharp output declines that occurred, and reduced demand for credit, these aggregate numbers do not indicate that there were large aggregate shortfalls in credit availability. Despite the decline in banks' capability to extend credit, the surveyed

### TABLE 1.5
### Peak nonperforming loans and losses

|  | NPLs (percentage of loan portfolio) | Net loss as percentage of GDP | Losses/capital percent |
|---|---|---|---|
| Indonesia | 75 | 30 | 474 |
| Malaysia | 35 | 20 | 120 |
| Korea | 30 | 16 | 126 |
| Thailand | 50 | 34 | 248 |

*Note:* Assumptions on recovery rates: Indonesia 25 percent; Thailand 30 percent; Malaysia and Korea, 50 percent. Net loss is defined as the deterioration in bank capital resulting from the implied write-down of loans. June 1997 balance sheet data on loans and capital are used as a base.
*Source:* Deutsche Bank Research.

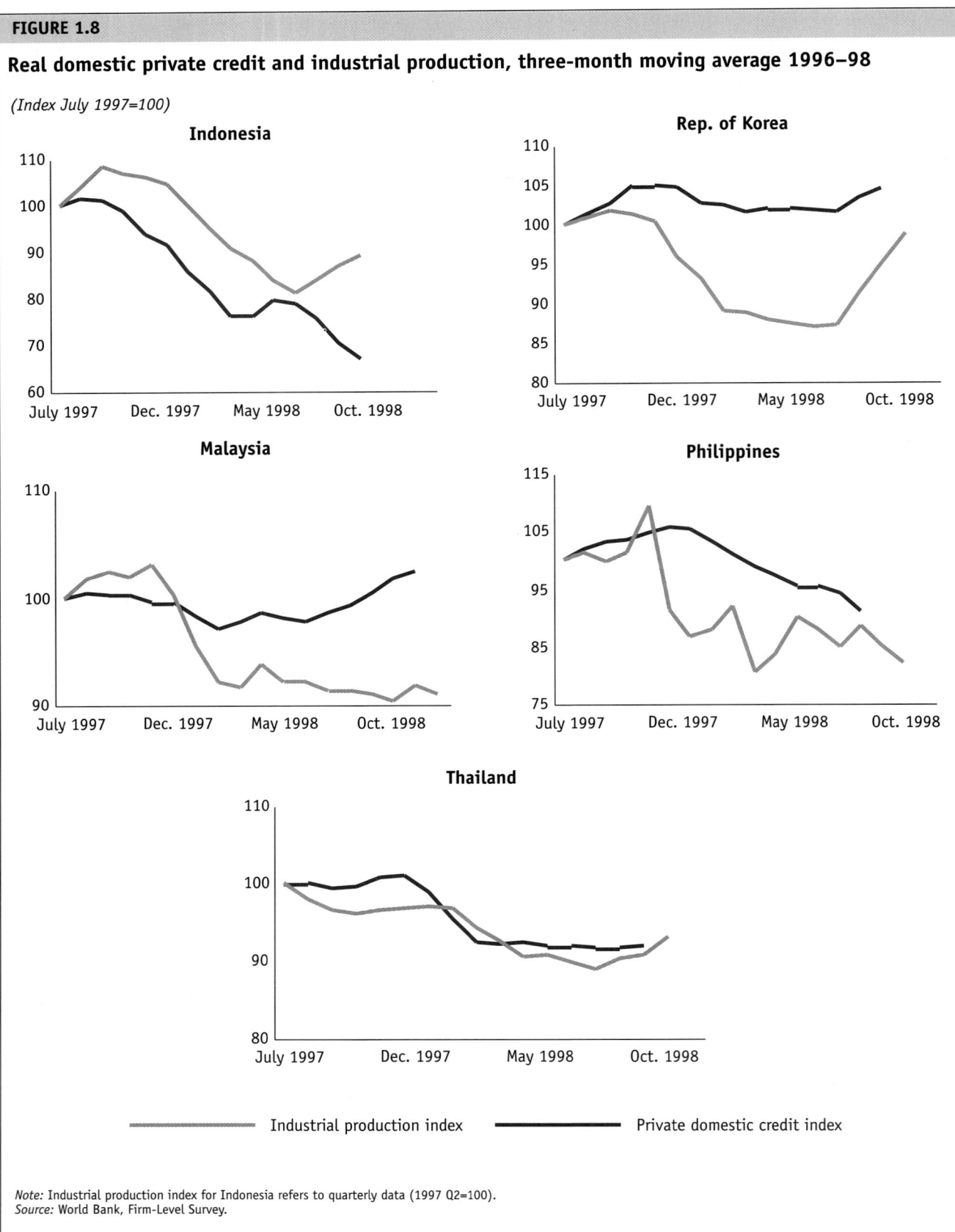

**FIGURE 1.8**

**Real domestic private credit and industrial production, three-month moving average 1996–98**

*Note:* Industrial production index for Indonesia refers to quarterly data (1997 Q2=100).
*Source:* World Bank, Firm-Level Survey.

firms did not report credit availability as a major source of output decline—and exporters reported that the top causes of decline were a fall in demand and a lack of price competitiveness. With the decline in the demand for their products, the firms' credit demand is likely to have declined as well so that credit availability is not an immediate constraint to corporate recovery. However, as countries implement expansionary fiscal policies, the demand for the firms' product and the firms' demand for credit are likely to increase. Financial sector restructuring and recapitalization have to proceed in step with fiscal expansion.

Furthermore, credit aggregates do not indicate whether there were deficiencies in the way credit was allocated. The survey data indicate that despite overall credit availability, many firms felt severely constrained in undertaking viable projects. In part this is due to the distinction between credit and liquidity. Liquidity is a broader concept, including the important financing provided by internal funds. About 40 percent of the firms overall reported experiencing inadequate liquidity to finance production (see figure 1.9). Thailand and Korea were the two countries in which liquidity problems were the most acute, and, in general, exporters found it easier than nonexporters to secure adequate liquidity. When the firms were asked about the causes of inadequate liquidity, they listed as the main causes lower revenues and higher input costs caused by the devaluation. The burden of servicing their debts and insufficient working capital ranked much lower (see figure 1.10). In other words, factors affecting cash flow received more attention than credit.

The importance of cash flow over credit reflects the structure of working capital of firms in the sample, two-thirds of which are small and medium. Only about 20 percent (in Indonesia and Malaysia) to 35 percent (in Thailand) of working capital requirements of surveyed firms comes from loans; the bulk (between 50 and 65 percent) comes from retained earnings (see figure 1.11). Also, Thai and Indonesian firms get about one-third and Korean, Malaysian, and Filipino firms about one-tenth of their working capital from informal sources of financing—family, partners, and informal money lenders. Thus Thailand, the country with the highest reliance on loans to finance working capital, is also the country where surveyed firms complained the most about the lack of loans for working capital.

The firm-level data shows that caution needs to be exercised against drawing broad generalizations regarding the issue of credit availability. Clearly the supply of credit has been reduced, but so too has the demand for credit. First, distinctions between the time periods after the onset of the crisis need to be taken into account. During the stabilization phase when interest rates were raised significantly, the demand for credit was obviously lower. With output down, the demand

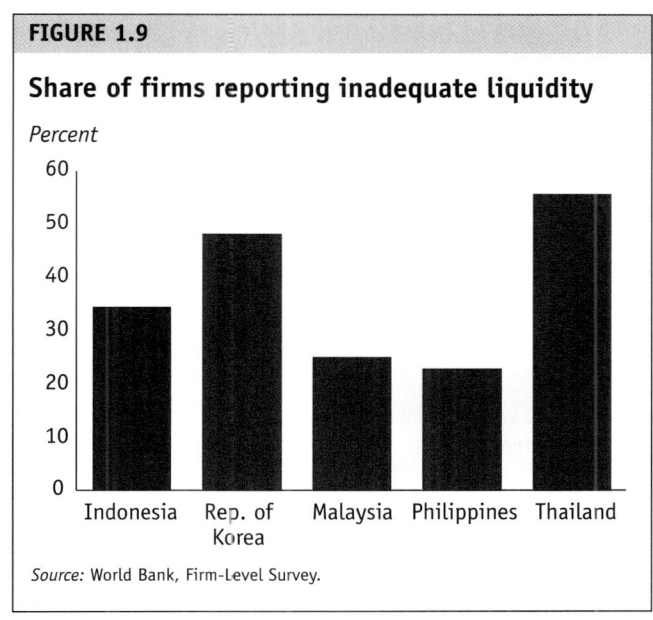

**FIGURE 1.9**

**Share of firms reporting inadequate liquidity**

*Source:* World Bank, Firm-Level Survey.

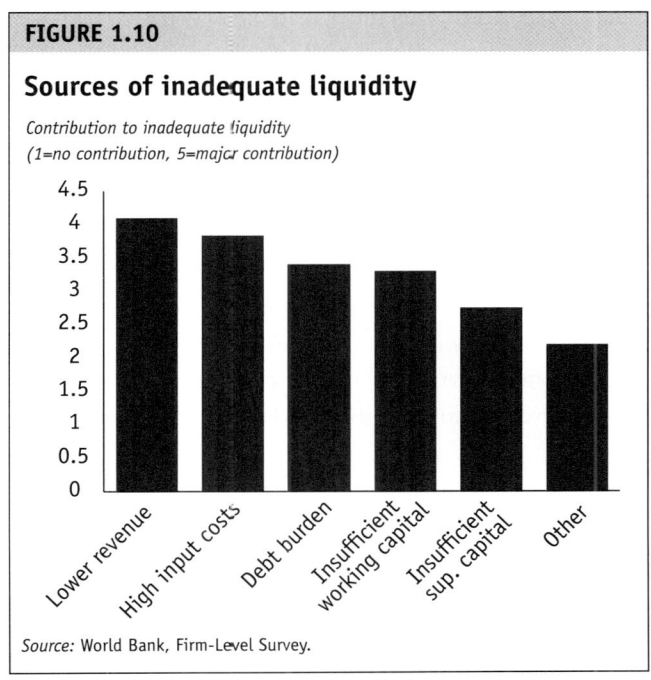

**FIGURE 1.10**

**Sources of inadequate liquidity**

*Source:* World Bank, Firm-Level Survey.

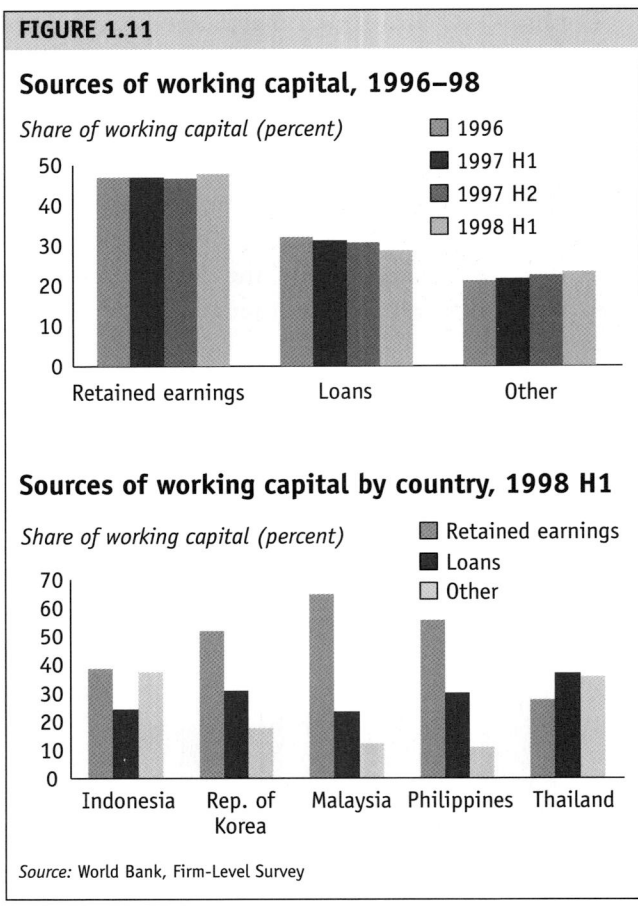

**FIGURE 1.11**

**Sources of working capital, 1996–98**

*Source:* World Bank, Firm-Level Survey

for credit has remained lower. However, since interest rates have been lowered, as recovery picks up, the demand for credit could well rise, increasing the difficulty of obtaining adequate financing if banks remain cautious about extending new loans. Second, there are important differences between the firms depending on their initial level of credit in their total financing, their recourse to bank lending for working capital and for longer-term investments, and the sectors in which they operate. Another factor is whether the firms export or are oriented toward the domestic market. The new microeconomic data available here complements the more aggregate analysis that has so far been undertaken.

## Foreign indebtedness

Short-term borrowing in foreign currency and the sudden reversal of capital flows are often cited as important causes of the financial crisis. However, these data illustrate that for the manufacturing firms, foreign borrowing was concentrated in a small number of firms.[16] Based on the survey results, the manufacturing sector does not seem to have been a major player, particularly relative to the real estate and financial services sectors. With the exception of Korea, less than 10 percent of financing was in foreign currency (see figure 1.12). Korea is notable for its greater reliance on foreign borrowing, with a quarter of the surveyed firms engaging in this practice. That there are more listed companies in the Korean sample is one explanation for this. Of the share of financing that is in foreign currency, only in Korea and Malaysia is the majority of it not short-term. However, it remains true that most of the effect of the depreciation would have been transmitted through alternative channels (for example, the impact on banks) than through the balance sheets of manufacturing firms.

However, one finding does indicate a more worrisome pattern. The firms that qualified for foreign currency loans were more likely to be the unprofitable firms (see figure 1.13). Conversely, more profitable firms had a lower share of their financing denominated in foreign exchange. It is certainly possible that the more profitable firms had less need to borrow, but this provides further evidence that the financial sector needs to scrutinize its clients carefully in deciding whether or not to extend loans.

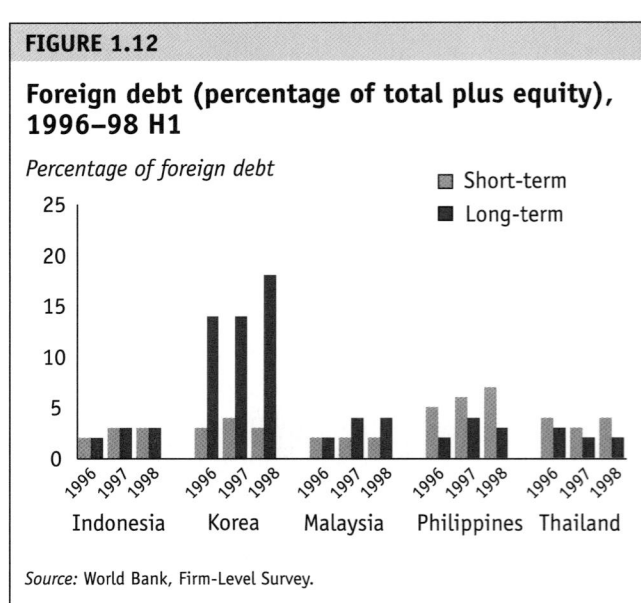

**FIGURE 1.12**

**Foreign debt (percentage of total plus equity), 1996–98 H1**

*Source:* World Bank, Firm-Level Survey.

A policy implication of the surveys is that even though there is no evidence of an overall shortfall of credit availability, credit allocation from domestic and foreign sources is not always efficient. Some firms have seen their working capital needs increase as their source of liquidity decreased; they could benefit from additional credit. At the same time, exporters attribute their decline to a lack of competitiveness, which suggests that additional credit would have to be extended in the context of improvements in competitiveness. These latter improvements require a combination of government competition policies and corporate restructuring to increase productivity.

## The firms' views on loan repayment prospects

The questionnaire, as noted earlier, in addition to seeking quantitative information from the firms, sought their qualitative views on their ability to meet required loan payments, if interest rates remained at current—in other words, end-of-1998 through early 1999—levels. The firms were asked to indicate their perceived ability to meet required loan payments, by three-month intervals, over the next twelve months and beyond. About 2,000 firms in the five countries responded to this question.

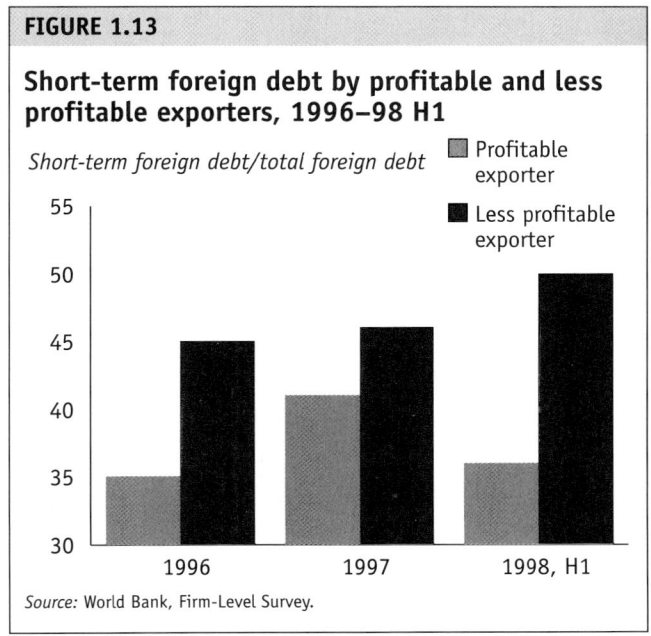

**FIGURE 1.13**

**Short-term foreign debt by profitable and less profitable exporters, 1996–98 H1**

Source: World Bank, Firm-Level Survey.

The firms' responses to this question are shown in figure 1.14. In the five countries, a first category of firms that indicate that they do not expect to have problems in servicing their loan repayments range from over two-thirds in Korea, Malaysia, and Thailand, to one-half in Indonesia and the Philippines. A second category of firms indicating that they expect to be able to meet loan payments for the following twelve months but not beyond that period is populated by 10–15 percent of the firms in Thailand and Malaysia, and 20–25 percent in Indonesia, Korea, and the Philippines. A third category of firms indicated that they are currently having difficulties in meeting loan repayments, or expect to be able to meet loan repayments only for the next three months and not beyond: about 20 percent in Indonesia, Thailand, the Philippines, and Malaysia, and 10 percent in Korea.

Table 1.6 shows the characteristics of firms in the three categories. A comparison of the firms in the first and third categories indicates that those not reporting loan repayment difficulties, on average:
- Have experienced smaller declines in capacity utilization (a significant exception is Korean firms);
- Are exporting more (exceptions are Korean and Thai firms);
- Are financing a greater portion of their working capital with retained earnings (Filipino firms are an exception); and
- Have experienced much less difficulty in securing adequate amounts of liquidity for production.

The above information indicates that surveyed firms in the five countries see themselves at various stages in the recovery process, as well as in their access to liquidity required for production. The bulk of the firms in Korea, Malaysia, and Thailand consider themselves to be in good financial condition. This is less the case in Indonesia and the Philippines. There remain, however, a significant number of firms in all five countries that were either experiencing loan repayment difficulties at the time of the survey, or thought that they would find themselves in that situation in the near future, if economic conditions (in particular, demand and interest rate levels) were to persist. This financial fragility of a significant proportion of the firms is linked both to macroeconomic conditions and the pace of bank and corporate restructuring.

### FIGURE 1.14

**Ability to meet loan payments, by country**

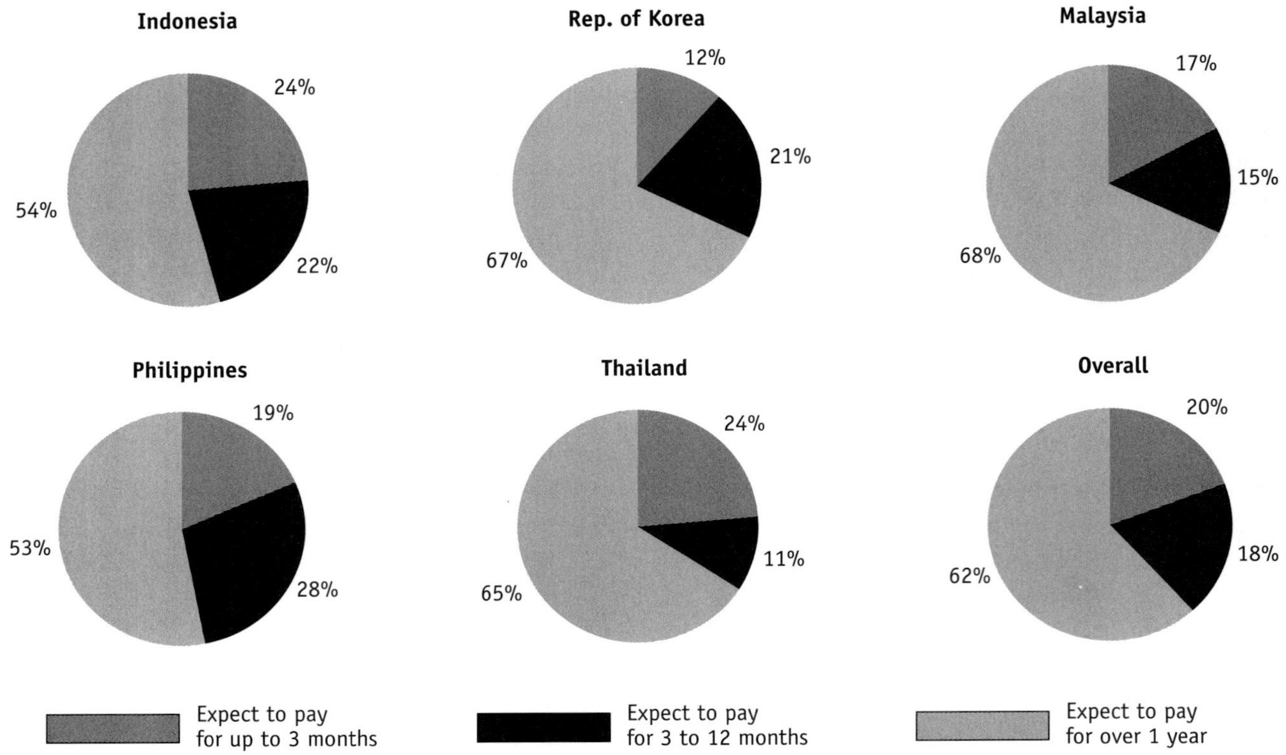

Indonesia: 24%, 22%, 54%
Rep. of Korea: 12%, 21%, 67%
Malaysia: 17%, 15%, 68%
Philippines: 19%, 28%, 53%
Thailand: 24%, 11%, 65%
Overall: 20%, 18%, 62%

- Expect to pay for up to 3 months
- Expect to pay for 3 to 12 months
- Expect to pay for over 1 year

*Source:* World Bank, Firm-Level Survey.

## Governance

A central issue of corporate governance is the relationship between the firm and its financial institution(s). The disclosure and transparency of information is of particular interest. The firms were asked whether they were required to provide audited statements to receive a loan. Of those with 20 percent or more of their financing provided by bank or financial company loans, the share that are so required ranged from 40 percent in Indonesia and Thailand to 70 percent in Korea, Malaysia, and the Philippines (see figure 1.15). If the firms are only interested in securing a letter of credit for trade finance, the issue of transparency is not so important. But to the extent that many of the firms' only source of finance is short-term trade credit—which they in fact use to finance investment or other long-term activities—the issue is still pressing.

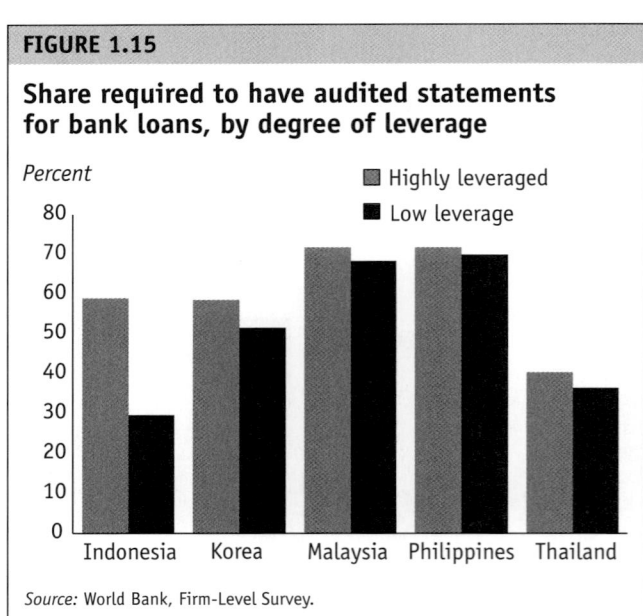

### FIGURE 1.15

**Share required to have audited statements for bank loans, by degree of leverage**

*Source:* World Bank, Firm-Level Survey.

16  Asian Corporate Recovery: Findings fron Firm-Level Surveys in Five Countries

While the survey provides evidence in favor of accelerating standard accounting methods and disclosure requirements, there is another side to the story. It is true that more highly leveraged firms are more likely to be required to provide audited statements. The ones least likely to be required to present them are small firms, which tend to have long-standing relationships with their financial institutions. On average, these firms have done business with the same primary financial institution for over half of the life of the firm. Informal relationships can be an efficient way of learning about a firm and having needed credit extended. In credit markets that discriminate against SMEs, such relationships-based financing may indeed be efficient. However, the development of more transparent financial institutions and improved allocation of credit should see the replacement of relationship-based loans with more market-based criteria. This is a long-term endeavor. In the short term, what is needed is a clear set of prudential regulations and disclosure requirements that should be imposed on banks and financial institutions with regard to their loans—including those extended to SMEs.

## Conclusion

The main conclusions of the survey results and the conference discussions, as outlined by the five senior Asian policymakers who chaired the sessions, are summarized below:[17]

### TABLE 1.6
**Profile of firms with different expectations on remaining current on debt payments**
(Percentage of firms in each category)

*Firms that expected to remain current for more than a year*

|  | Indonesia | Korea | Malaysia | Philippines | Thailand | Average |
|---|---|---|---|---|---|---|
| Experienced output decline | 80 | 70 | 71 | 77 | 73 | 74 |
| Capacity utilization[a] | 59 | 71 | 69 | 70 | 64 | 66 |
| Small size | 51 | 67 | 63 | 54 | 64 | 57 |
| Exporter | 45 | 63 | 51 | 55 | 42 | 49 |
| Low indebtedness | 67 | 37 | 75 | 47 | 63 | 60 |
| Foreign debt | 17 | 44 | 20 | 14 | 28 | 27 |
| Liquidity is a problem | 36 | 60 | 23 | 28 | 55 | 42 |

*Firms that expected to remain current for more than 3 months and less than 1 year*

|  | Indonesia | Korea | Malaysia | Philippines | Thailand | Average |
|---|---|---|---|---|---|---|
| Experienced output decline | 76 | 72 | 86 | 81 | 73 | 77 |
| Capacity utilization[a] | 63 | 67 | 64 | 61 | 60 | 63 |
| Small size | 55 | 77 | 76 | 53 | 68 | 64 |
| Exporter | 38 | 65 | 48 | 41 | 69 | 51 |
| Low indebtedness | 71 | 54 | 91 | 40 | 66 | 62 |
| Foreign debt | 10 | 40 | 20 | 11 | 28 | 22 |
| Liquidity is a problem | 30 | 58 | 46 | 36 | 69 | 44 |

*Firms that were not current or did not expect to remain current for more than 3 months*

|  | Indonesia | Korea | Malaysia | Philippines | Thailand | Average |
|---|---|---|---|---|---|---|
| Experienced output decline | 80 | 73 | 73 | 81 | 88 | 81 |
| Capacity utilization[a] | 56 | 69 | 58 | 62 | 52 | 57 |
| Small size | 62 | 42 | 71 | 49 | 62 | 57 |
| Exporter | 38 | 85 | 52 | 50 | 52 | 51 |
| Low indebtedness | 62 | 42 | 72 | 57 | 45 | 55 |
| Foreign debt | 21 | 54 | 12 | 23 | 28 | 26 |
| Liquidity is a problem | 45 | 70 | 62 | 43 | 85 | 61 |

a. Average capacity utilization.
*Source:* World Bank, Firm-Level Survey.

- The stimulation of demand alone is not enough. It needs to be combined with accelerated restructuring of banks and other financial institutions if corporate recovery is to be robust.
- Corporate and financial restructuring must take place simultaneously for both to succeed.
- The institutional framework for corporate finance needs urgent strengthening to improve the efficiency of credit allocation. Laws to regulate bankruptcies, foreclosures, and mergers and acquisitions, are needed to facilitate the transfer of assets of failed companies to viable ones.
- Financial transactions need greater transparency through improved reporting, accounting, and auditing.
- According to business responses to the survey, the demand for credit has declined as sales have fallen. However, many firms reported difficulties in securing adequate credit. As demand grows, availability will become a bigger issue.
- Excess capacity has both a cyclical and a structural nature; therefore, macroeconomic policies need to be supplemented with measures to improve corporate competitiveness.
- The development of a bond market needs to be started now because it is a long-term endeavor.
- More discussion is required to design competitiveness strategies.
- The speed of adjustment must be balanced with the social costs and the need for social safety nets.

## Notes

Mary Hallward-Driemeier and Dominique Dwor-Frécaut are with the World Bank. Francis Colaço is with Asia-Pacific Management Consultants, Inc. The authors would like to thank Giuseppe Iarossi, Stacy Nemeroff, Dennis Tao, Hairong Yu, and Hosook Hwang for invaluable help in assembling the data set and for excellent research assistance. They have also benefited from the comments of the participants of the Asian Corporate Recovery Conference held in Bangkok, March 31–April 2, 1999 and from the seminars held at the World Bank and in Kuala Lumpur, Jakarta, Singapore, Manila, Hong Kong, Tokyo, Seoul, and at the meeting of the Association of Southeast Asian Nations (ASEAN) Chambers of Commerce and Industry. The findings, interpretations, and conclusions expressed in this paper are those of the authors and do not necessarily represent the views of the World Bank, its Executive Directors, or the countries they represent.

1. The surveys provide the basis for regional conferences on these issues of corporate recovery and the determinants of productivity. The first was held in Bangkok from March 31 to April 2 and was attended by 150 senior policymakers and private sector representatives from around the region. The second conference is planned for November 1999. A research conference is also under discussion for the spring of 2000.

2. Thailand provides a special case as this was the second such survey it had carried out. Twelve hundred firms had been interviewed by the end of 1997. These same firms were then contacted a year later, and again, close to 10 percent had gone out of business. A follow-up paper will examine the characteristics of the firms that closed during 1998 to gain insights into the most vulnerable firms and as a predictor for the likely extent of future bankruptcies.

3. See Waiquamdee, Krairiksh, and Phongsanarakul, 1999, "Corporates' Views of the Constraints to Recovery," paper prepared for the conference on Asian Corporate Recovery, Bangkok March 31–April 2.

4. Care has been taken not to classify all the redundancies as layoffs or fired workers. Many of the countries have restrictions on firing, including large severance packages. Thus, many firms have found alternative ways to reduce the number of workers, and the number of layoffs is significantly lower than the overall reductions in employment.

5. See Xin Meng and Ronald Duncan, 1999, "Corporate Employment and Public Policy," paper prepared for the conference on Asian Corporate Recovery, Bangkok March 31–April 2.

6. In Thailand, and to a lesser extent Indonesia, firms with increased employment also increased capacity utilization, implying that their markets were expanding. In contrast, in Malaysia, firms with greater employment were still experiencing lower levels of capacity utilization. Further investigation, particularly regarding movements in wages, is underway to explain this pattern.

7. See Waiquamdee, Krairiksh, and Phongsanarakul, 1999, "Corporates' Views of the Constraints to Recovery," paper prepared for the conference on Asian Corporate Recovery, Bangkok March 31–April 2, and presented in this volume.

8. There is considerable variation in the responses of individual firms to this question, indicating that managers did differentiate between the severity of different sources of problems. The reported results are the mean responses, but if percentile ranks are used, the ordering is the same.

9. Care must also be taken in interpreting these qualitative results, as the firms report their partial equilibrium view of the world. Thus is it possible that the decline in domestic demand is "overreported"

as a problem, since many suppliers to a large credit-constrained firm will report that a decline in demand is the main constraint, when the root cause is the large buyer's access to credit. However, one piece of evidence that mitigates this concern is that there is no statistically significant difference between the responses of firms that produce intermediate goods and those that produce final goods.

10. Cho and Rhee, 1999, "Macroeconomic Views of the East Asian Crisis: A Comparison," paper prepared for the conference on Asian Corporate Recovery, Bangkok March 31–April 2, and presented in this volume.

11. See Dasgupta and Imai (1998).

12. There is some controversy about how best to calculate real interest rates in a period of rapidly changing expectations as the ex ante expected inflation and ex post inflation can differ substantially.

13. See Dwor-Frecaut, Hallward-Driemeier, and Colaço, 1999, "Asian Corporates' Credit Needs and Governance," paper prepared for the conference on Asian Corporate Recovery, Bangkok March 31–April 2, and presented in this volume.

14. See Javad K. Shirazi, 1999, "The East Asian Crisis: Financial Sector Restructuring—Progress and Issues," paper prepared for the conference on Asian Corporate Recovery, Bangkok March 31–April 2, and presented in this volume.

15. Ito and Pereira da Silva (1998). The paper analyzes aggregate data on the Thai financial sector and the responses from 17 banks (7 Thai and 10 foreign) that returned questionnaires in April and May of 1998.

16. See Masahiro Kawai, Hongjoo Hahm, and Giuseppe Iarossi, 1999, "Corporate Foreign Debt in East Asia: Too Much or Too Little?" paper prepared for the conference on Asian Corporate Recovery, Bangkok March 31–April 2, and presented in this volume.

17. These conclusions are taken from the press conference written by the five chairs of the Asian Corporate Recovery conference, Bangkok, March 31–April 2: Dr. Il Sakong (former Finance Minister of Korea and President of the Institute for Global Economics), Dr Zeti Akthar Aziz (Deputy Governor of Bank Negara Malaysia), M.R. Chatu Mongol Sonakul (Governor of the Bank of Thailand), Secretary Benjamin Diokno (Secretary of Budget and Management, the Philippines), and Dr. Mari Pangestu (Executive Director, Center for Strategic and International Studies, Indonesia).

## chapter two

# Corporates' Views of the Constraints to Recovery

*Economic Research Department, Bank of Thailand*

The economic and financial crisis that has swiftly and devastatingly swept through Asia is undoubtedly the steepest and most prolonged downturn witnessed in recent decades. It has wiped out the economic gains that have been laboriously accumulated over the years—inevitably resulting in widespread social suffering.

More than one year after it first struck Thailand and its contagion effect was felt throughout Asia, the crisis has now brought to the fore a number of widely debated issues, especially with regard to the suitability of competing prescriptions for crisis management. Thus far, policy response by most countries has been characterized by austerity measures commonly in the form of fiscal discipline, interest rate hikes, and strengthening financial supervision (although there have also been alternative approaches, most notably the imposition of capital controls combined with the easing of positions regarding fiscal and monetary policy). What is often overlooked in these discussions, however, is that policy implementation, regardless of methods, has only been based on the top-down macroeconomic approach. Indeed, while conventional macroeconomic indicators have shown the relative extent to which the crisis has affected the different countries, a common comparison among the countries in terms of the microeconomic impacts is yet to be done. Therefore, the surveys conducted by the national authorities in collaboration with the World Bank are timely and appropriate, in that they have enabled us for the first time to step back and gauge the extent of the crisis and its impact on the real sector of the economy. More important, this bottom-up approach allows us to formulate or fine-tune policies—though not necessarily implying a preference of one macroeconomic approach over the other—that could support an early economic recovery.

In this paper, the aim is to identify the impact of the crisis on surveyed firms in Indonesia, the Republic of Korea, Malaysia, the Philippines, and Thailand and assess the relative contributions of the different factors to economic contraction. In so doing, it will be possible to identify the major constraints that these firms perceive to be hampering their recovery, and draw policy recommendations accordingly.

As the details collected from the surveys are quite extensive and voluminous, and have many combinations of dimensions and breakdowns, this paper will attempt to highlight only the salient points and features of the firms in the five countries. It is structured to answer three basic questions: what happened, why it happened, and how it can be solved. Specifically, the paper is structured as follows: The next section looks at the impact of the crisis on the firms' performance, particularly in terms of capacity utilization, export performance, and expansion plans. This is followed by a section that will identify the reasons for the worsened performance, and another section that outlines the factors perceived to be the major constraints to the firms' recovery, and collates and synthesizes the entire paper with the relevant policy recommendations. The final section provides concluding remarks.

## Impact of the crisis on the surveyed firms' performance

Prior to identifying the relative importance of the various causes of the economic downturn, it is necessary to illustrate the impact of the crisis on the firms' performance. In this regard, issues relating to capacity utilization, export performance, and expansion plans will be assessed.

### Capacity utilization

It was observed that about 71 percent of all the firms surveyed in the five countries had experienced output declines since the onset of the regional crisis in 1997. The proportion was highest in Indonesia (76.3 percent), followed by Thailand (73.1 percent), Malaysia (69.6 percent), the Philippines (68.7 percent), and Korea (67.3 percent) (see table 2.1).

In terms of the magnitude of the decline in capacity utilization, it was observed that the decline during 1996–1998 was most severe in Indonesia (reduction of capacity utilization by 20.8 percentage points), followed by Thailand (17.6 percentage points), Malaysia (15.6 percentage points), Korea (12.7 percentage points), and the Philippines (9 percentage points). The lowest level of capacity utilization in the first half of 1998 was found in Indonesia (at 59.2 percent) and highest in Korea (at 72.1 percent). Corresponding to the fact that Thailand was the first country to experience the crisis, Thai firms experienced a sharp decline during the first and second half of 1997. Interestingly, Indonesia suffered a marginally greater fall in 1997. For the first half of 1998, Korea saw the highest drop in capacity utilization rate, followed by Indonesia, Malaysia, the Philippines, and Thailand (see table 2.2).

The largest drop appeared most common in the auto parts and electronics industries (see table 2.3).

As for the capacity utilization levels of exporters, it is not surprising to note that they were generally higher than those of nonexporters (see table 2.4). Sectors in which exporters experienced the smallest decline in capacity utilization were found in the garment and textiles, and food industries. Alternatively, output decline of exporters—a concept that is different from but related to capacity utilization—appeared most common in the auto parts sector, with over 90 percent of both exporters and nonexporters of auto parts in

### TABLE 2.1
**The firms: a profile**
(percent)

| Country | Output since July 1997 | | Export status | | Liquidity | | Partnership | | |
|---|---|---|---|---|---|---|---|---|---|
| | Decline | Not decline | Exporter | Nonexporter | Problems | No problem | Foreign | Domestic | None |
| Indonesia | 76.3 | 23.7 | 36.0 | 64.0 | 34.8 | 65.2 | 11.9 | 25.6 | 62.5 |
| Korea | 67.3 | 32.7 | 74.8 | 25.2 | 48.2 | 51.8 | 13.2 | 4.5 | 82.3 |
| Malaysia | 69.6 | 30.4 | 47.6 | 52.4 | 25.3 | 74.7 | 1.5 | 3.4 | 95.2 |
| Philippines | 68.7 | 31.3 | 52.0 | 48.0 | 23.3 | 76.7 | 5.5 | 2.8 | 91.7 |
| Thailand | 73.1 | 27.0 | 56.8 | 43.3 | 55.8 | 44.2 | 7.6 | 5.4 | 87.0 |
| Total | 71.0 | 29.0 | 54.0 | 46.0 | 37.9 | 62.1 | 8.2 | 8.9 | 82.9 |

*Source:* World Bank, Firm-Level Survey.

### TABLE 2.2
#### Capacity utilization levels of the five countries
(percent)

| | | Capacity utilization | | | |
|---|---|---|---|---|---|
| | 1996 | 1997 | | 1998 | 1996–1998 H1 |
| Country | | First half | Second half | First half | |
| Indonesia | 80.0 | 74.5 | 66.2 | 59.2 | 20.8 |
| Korea | 84.8 | 84.3 | 80.9 | 72.2 | 12.7 |
| Malaysia | 81.9 | 78.5 | 72.9 | 66.3 | 15.6 |
| Philippines | 77.7 | 75.1 | 73.3 | 68.8 | 8.9 |
| Thailand | 79.4 | 71.4 | 66.0 | 61.8 | 17.6 |
| Average | 81.1 | 77.2 | 72.1 | 65.7 | 15.4 |

*Source:* World Bank, Firm-Level Survey.

### TABLE 2.3
#### Sectoral breakdown of capacity utilization: 1997–1998 H1
(percentage points)

| Sectors | Capacity utilization decline during 1997–98 H1 |
|---|---|
| Auto parts | −21.7 |
| Electronics | −13.0 |
| Chemical | −10.7 |
| Garment and textiles | −9.3 |
| Food | −8.4 |

*Source:* World Bank, Firm-Level Survey.

Korea, Malaysia, and Thailand experiencing output declines. The smallest proportion of exporters facing output declines were again exporters of garments, textiles, and food.

As regards prospects for capacity utilization over the next six months, one-quarter of the firms expected an increasing rate of utilization (see table 2.5). Exporters particularly seemed to have a more positive view than domestic producers. The most pessimistic seemed to be the Malaysian corporates, with as high as 41.4 percent expecting a decline, followed by Indonesia, Thailand, and the Philippines. In terms of sectoral breakdown, electronics and electrical machinery, particularly in Indonesia and Malaysia, were exceptionally pessimistic, with 45 percent and 50 percent, respectively, predicting that their capacity utilization would fall. This contrasts with Korea, where more electronics firms were optimistic than pessimistic. The auto parts industry, having suffered the most dramatic decline, is now the sector that is most optimistic about reversing its position and increasing capacity utilization. Overall, firms in Korea and the Philippines seemed to be the most optimistic, with over 70 percent of all firms expecting stable or increasing capacity utilization rates over the next six months.

### TABLE 2.4
#### Capacity utilization levels of exporters and nonexporters
(percent)

| | 1996 | | 1997: First half | | 1997: Second half | | 1998: First half | |
|---|---|---|---|---|---|---|---|---|
| Country | Nonexporter | Exporter | Nonexporter | Exporter | Nonexporter | Exporter | Nonexporter | Exporter |
| Indonesia | 80.8 | 79.3 | 75.2 | 74.9 | 65.0 | 68.5 | 56.6 | 65.1 |
| Korea | 85.1 | 84.8 | 84.2 | 84.5 | 79.6 | 81.3 | 68.5 | 73.7 |
| Malaysia | 81.8 | 82.0 | 77.7 | 79.4 | 70.6 | 75.5 | 63.9 | 68.9 |
| Philippines | 76.6 | 78.8 | 73.3 | 76.8 | 70.0 | 76.2 | 64.8 | 72.4 |
| Thailand | 79.3 | 79.7 | 68.5 | 73.8 | 60.7 | 70.0 | 54.9 | 66.7 |
| Average | 80.7 | 81.6 | 75.6 | 79.0 | 68.4 | 75.5 | 61.0 | 70.0 |

*Source:* World Bank, Firm-Level Survey.

### TABLE 2.5
**Expectations of capacity utilization over the next six months**
(percent of firms)

| Country | Expectations of capacity utilization over the next 6 months | | |
|---|---|---|---|
| | Worsened | Same | Improved |
| Indonesia | 36.9 | 47.3 | 15.9 |
| Korea | 28.7 | 35.5 | 35.9 |
| Malaysia | 41.4 | 37.6 | 20.9 |
| Philippines | 25.1 | 47.9 | 27.0 |
| Thailand | 36.2 | 41.5 | 22.3 |
| Average | 34.1 | 41.5 | 24.4 |

*Source:* World Bank, Firm-Level Survey.

## Export performance

Approximately 54 percent of the firms surveyed were exporters but questions on export performance were only provided to firms in Korea, Malaysia, and Thailand. For these countries, about half of the exporters claimed that their exports had increased during 1996–97 and 1997–98, although slightly larger proportions claimed improved performance during 1996–97 than 1997–98 (54.8 percent against 50.7 percent of exporters for the two respective periods). Improved performance was most common for Korean exporters. Interestingly, a significant proportion of exporters remained (28.9 percent and 34.7 percent for the two periods) who noted that their performance had declined during 1996–97 and 1997–98, respectively, with Thai exporters having the most common instances of worsened performance for 1996–97 (32.2 percent) and Malaysia for 1997–98 (41.7 percent) (see table 2.6). In terms of the magnitude of export performance, the most commonly cited magnitude for both the improved and worsened performance was in the range of 10–25 percent.

As for sectoral breakdown, a number of respondents in the Thai auto parts industry noted that their exports had dropped from 47 percent in 1997 to only 37 percent in 1998. The garment and textiles sector in Thailand reported improved export performance (47 percent claimed an increase during 1996–97 and 49 percent claimed an increase during 1997–98), while those in Malaysia experienced quite a sharp drop (66 percent claimed an increase during 1996–97 but only 56 percent claimed an increase during 1997–98).

In terms of prospects for export performance this year, proportionately more exporters expected their exports to increase (43 percent of exporters) than decrease (24 percent) or remain the same in 1999 (33 percent). The average for Korean exporters was somewhat higher at about 50 percent for those with high expectations, but lower at only 39 percent and 37 percent for Malaysian and Thai exporters. Overall, auto parts exporters were most optimistic about their future prospects.

In the questionnaires, all exporters were also asked to report the reasons for both their improved *and* declined export performance in volume terms in 1998 as compared with 1997. The exporters in Korea, Malaysia, and Thailand thus cited the different reasons both for their improved and worsened performance, not necessarily claiming that their overall performance had fallen into one or the other category.

For those with worsened export performance, the most relevant contributing factor to the decline was poor demand. Unstable conditions in the export market,

### TABLE 2.6
**Export performance**
(percent of exporters)

| Country | Performance in 1997 | | | Performance in the first half of 1998 | | | Expected performance in 1999 | | |
|---|---|---|---|---|---|---|---|---|---|
| | Improved | Worsened | Same | Improved | Worsened | Same | Improved | Worsened | Same |
| Korea | 64.0 | 25.9 | 10.1 | 59.9 | 29.4 | 10.7 | 49.7 | 21.6 | 28.8 |
| Malaysia | 47.4 | 30.4 | 22.2 | 42.5 | 41.7 | 15.8 | 38.6 | 25.4 | 36.0 |
| Thailand | 47.9 | 32.2 | 19.9 | 44.3 | 35.6 | 20.1 | 37.4 | 26.4 | 36.2 |
| Average | 54.8 | 28.9 | 16.3 | 50.7 | 34.7 | 14.7 | 43.0 | 24.0 | 33.0 |

*Source:* World Bank, Firm-Level Survey.

lack of price competitiveness, and exchange rate volatility were also cited as significant contributing factors. Meanwhile, inferior product design, and to a lesser extent, credit constraints, were regarded as the least relevant (details also shown later in table 2.13).

As regards improved export performance, the exchange rate effect and price competitiveness were universally cited as the most important factors contributing to the improvement, while low dependence on imported inputs was the least relevant. It should be noted that the average rating (on a scale from 1 to 5, with 5 being an extremely important factor) was highest for Malaysia (3.91) and lowest for Thailand (2.98). This implied that the mentioned factors were most relevant for Malaysian firms and least relevant for Thai firms.

It should also be noted that with questions on capacity utilization and export performance being separately asked in the questionnaires, firms with lower capacity utilization could still give reasons for improved export performance if the volume of their exports, not output, had increased, thus reflecting their increasing reliance on the export market.

## Expansion plans

The last impact of the crisis to be addressed concerns expansion plans: How have plans for expansion changed with the onset of the crisis and what are the expectations over the next six months?

As expected, plans for expansion have been continuously scaled back since the crisis, but the outlook for 1999 is generally better than 1998. In 1997, 44 percent of surveyed firms had said that they considered expansion, but by 1998 this figure had dropped to 15.4 percent. It rebounded to 22.2 percent for 1999. Also, most of the firms without expansion plans before the crisis did not have plans to expand in 1998 or 1999 either. Conversely, only half of those firms that planned to expand before the crisis actually did expand. Interestingly, despite the many uncertainties, Indonesian firms seemed to be the most optimistic compared with other countries, with 27.2 percent of Indonesian corporates expecting to expand in 1999, compared with 18.9 percent in Korea, 23.6 percent in Malaysia, 25.9 percent in the Philippines, and 15.5 percent in Thailand.

By analyzing the impact of the crisis on the firms' performance in terms of capacity utilization, export performance, and expansion plans, two important findings have been illustrated. First, in line with the general expectations, there is consistent evidence throughout all five countries that the crisis has severely affected capacity utilization levels. The most depressed sectors seemed to be auto parts and electronics. The former particularly seemed to be a serious concern for exporters in Korea, Malaysia, and Thailand, as it probably reflected the limited capacity of the export markets to absorb the excess domestic supply, as well as the regional slump in demand for automobiles. Secondly, a notable number of firms have indeed reported improved export performance. Even in the auto parts industry in which capacity utilization declined most, a third of the exporters in Thailand reported having improved export performance. Nevertheless, there are two important features questioning the widespread perception that exporters represent the major stimulus to economic recovery. The first is that only half of all exporters noted improved export performance despite large currency depreciations in 1997. In addition, poor demand (the reason cited as the most relevant for the worsened performance) is likely to persist given the regional turmoil—while the exchange rate effect and price competitiveness (the factors previously driving export performance) are likely to be less supportive as currencies stabilize and strengthen. Therefore, the outlook for export performance does not necessarily support optimistic expectations regarding an export-led economic recovery. A slight counter-argument to this view is that several firms, in fact, thought that they had already turned the corner. This is not to say that some firms had already recovered from the crisis, but rather that they had improved expectations of the future direction of the economy—a somewhat positive sign.

## Reasons for declining performance and constraints to corporate recovery

The previous section illustrated that apart from some exporters, the performance of the surveyed firms across countries and sectors has deteriorated since the onset of the crisis, while prospects for an export-led recovery remains somewhat questionable. Among the many factors, the major reasons cited for the declined performance were reduced demand, credit constraints, and other cost- and supply-related factors. Each of these will be carefully analyzed in this section to determine which elements are seen by the firms as constraints to their recovery.

## Reduced demand and revenue

The firms' responses confirmed that contraction in demand had played a very important role in lowering capacity utilization and export performance.

For domestic demand, the data show that its decline significantly contributed to a reduction in output for the majority of surveyed firms—but to a much lesser extent in the Philippines than in the other four countries. When the firms are further divided into exporters and nonexporters, the data indicate that proportionately more nonexporters than exporters considered the reduction in domestic demand to be an important reason for output decline.

In contrast, changes in foreign demand were largely perceived to have less influence on the firms' output level, particularly in Indonesia (see table 2.7). As expected, however, a notable proportion of exporters—24.3 percent in Korea, 33.8 percent in Malaysia, 37.5 percent in the Philippines, and 39.9 percent in Thailand—regarded the decline in foreign demand to have significantly contributed to lowering their capacity utilization.

In terms of export performance, responses from Korea, Malaysia, and Thailand elaborated on the extent to which this had been affected by poor external demand. In this regard, the majority of those exporters whose exports suffered (79.5 percent in Malaysia, 68.3 percent in Thailand, and 61.8 percent in Korea) believed that poor demand had significantly affected their export performance.

In addition to looking directly at the role of reduced demand on capacity utilization and export performance, it would also be useful to see whether the firms were seeking foreign partners as a means of expanding market access to compensate for the reduced demand. On the whole, however, it appeared that the majority (62.8 percent in Indonesia, 79.3 percent in Korea, 94.8 percent in Malaysia, 92.1 percent in the Philippines, and 90.0 percent in Thailand) did not seek foreign partners. This finding, therefore, rejects the notion that the firms were compelled to seek foreign partners as a means to expand overseas market access. Nevertheless, for those actually seeking foreign partnership, securing access to a foreign market was deemed as the most important consideration (as expressed by 61.3 percent of Indonesian firms, 52.0 percent of Korean firms, 85.7 percent of Malaysian firms, 83.3 percent of Philippine firms, and 77.3 percent of Thai firms).

Apart from having direct and adverse impacts on capacity utilization and export performance, the problem of reduced demand also affected revenue. This would inevitably have important implications on liquidity and a host of other factors. To confirm this point, of those firms experiencing inadequate liquidity—which surprisingly amounted to only 37.9 percent of all firms—about three-quarters (74.5 percent) cited lower

### TABLE 2.7
**Impact of reduced demand on output**
(percent of firms with reduction in output)

| Country | Reduction in domestic demand | | | Reduction in foreign demand | | |
| --- | --- | --- | --- | --- | --- | --- |
| | None | Limited | Significant | None | Limited | Significant |
| Indonesia | 12.3 | 27.8 | 60.0 | 66.4 | 18.8 | 14.8 |
| Korea | 5.0 | 11.4 | 83.7 | 28.2 | 37.1 | 34.7 |
| Malaysia | 9.9 | 19.5 | 70.6 | 48.4 | 21.2 | 30.4 |
| Philippines | 27.6 | 23.4 | 49.0 | 52.9 | 16.1 | 31.0 |
| Thailand | 11.5 | 17.9 | 70.5 | 35.4 | 27.0 | 37.6 |
| Average | 12.1 | 19.9 | 67.9 | 46.4 | 24.4 | 29.2 |

*Note:* The surveyed firms were asked in the questionnaires to give ratings on a scale from 1 to 5. "None" refers to a rating of 1, meaning that the factor had no relevance to the question being asked. "Limited" refers to the ratings of 2 and 3, meaning that the factor had some, but limited, relevance. "Significant" refers to the ratings of 4 and 5, at which point the factor's degree of relevancy was highest.
*Source:* World Bank, Firm-Level Survey.

**TABLE 2.8**
**Impact of lower revenue on liquidity**
(percent of firms with liquidity problems)

| | Impact of lower revenue | | |
|---|---|---|---|
| Country | None | Limited | Significant |
| Indonesia | 12.5 | 25.0 | 62.5 |
| Korea | 5.0 | 17.6 | 77.4 |
| Malaysia | 10.2 | 12.6 | 77.2 |
| Philippines | 15.4 | 17.1 | 67.5 |
| Thailand | 5.8 | 13.2 | 81.0 |
| Average | 8.4 | 17.2 | 74.5 |

Source: World Bank, Firm-Level Survey.

revenue as a significant contributing factor. The average was even higher for respondents in Thailand (81.0 percent) and surprisingly lowest in Indonesia (62.5 percent) (see table 2.8). Meanwhile, lower sales were more likely to cause a liquidity shortage among nonexporters than exporters, apart from the Philippines.

In all, therefore, it appeared that demand, and thus revenue considerations, were the overriding factors in driving down capacity utilization and export performance, as well as contributing to liquidity problems.

## Liquidity and the credit crunch

The second major reason for the decline in capacity utilization is associated with liquidity and credit considerations. Liquidity and credit are two different notions—the former generally refers to a firm's cash flow, which is partially but not completely influenced by credit. In this section we will first determine, based on exporting status, the extent of the liquidity problems in different countries and in different sectors of industries. Then we will discuss the degree to which the lack of credit contributed to liquidity problems and other related issues.

Although there is certain evidence of inadequate liquidity among firms in the five countries, the extent of the problem may not be as severe or widespread as some might have expected. As commented above, a little over one-third (37.9 percent) of the surveyed firms reported experiencing inadequate liquidity. Thailand was the country with the largest proportion of firms facing the problem (56.8 percent), followed by Korea (48.2 percent), Indonesia (34.8 percent), Malaysia (25.3 percent), and the Philippines (23.2 percent). In addition, this was more common among nonexporters than exporters throughout, and most exporters (over 70 percent, except in Korea and Thailand) on average had adequate liquidity to finance production. The major departure from this trend was observed in Korea and Thailand, where a much smaller proportion of exporters had adequate liquidity (54.6 percent and 47.2 percent, respectively). If exporters are taken to be the engine of economic recovery, then this finding highlights the urgent need to address their liquidity problems. This does not necessarily mean that nonexporters were better off than exporters in absolute terms, however. Instead, the lack of liquidity for exporters can be interpreted such that they had demand but not enough cash flow to produce, while nonexporters faced much more pressing concerns, for example, from the reduced demand than inadequate liquidity (see table 2.9).

Alternatively, in terms of country and sector breakdowns, the most common instances of liquidity-constrained firms in Indonesia were domestic producers of garments and textiles. In Korea and Malaysia, domestic producers of auto parts consistently reported the problem, while the most common instances in the Philippines were reported by domestic producers of textiles, and in Thailand by producers of garments, textiles, and auto parts.

Having determined that liquidity problems existed, the remaining issue to be evaluated is the conventional perception that liquidity and credit shortages are both reasons for the decline in performance and a constraint to recovery. Specifically, there are four questions to be addressed—to what extent credit shortage has affected capacity utilization, how the liquidity shortage was driven by a credit crunch, why the problem with credit access has prompted the search for partners, and how credit constraints have affected export performance.

**TABLE 2.9**
**Problems of inadequate liquidity**
(percent of exporting firms, or of nonexporting firms)

| | Exporters | | Nonexporters | |
|---|---|---|---|---|
| Country | Problem | No problem | Problem | No problem |
| Indonesia | 27.2 | 72.8 | 40.4 | 59.7 |
| Korea | 45.4 | 54.6 | 56.8 | 43.2 |
| Malaysia | 20.4 | 79.6 | 29.7 | 70.3 |
| Philippines | 19.7 | 80.3 | 27.2 | 72.8 |
| Thailand | 52.9 | 47.2 | 59.9 | 40.1 |

Source: World Bank, Firm-Level Survey.

*Cost and availability of credit as causes of the decline in capacity utilization.* The surveyed firms were asked to give ratings to the various factors that they perceived to have contributed to the decline in their capacity utilization. Among the factors relating to the cost and availability of credit are supplier credit, credit for working capital, credit for expansion, high interest rates, and heavy debt burden.

First of all, based on the empirical evidence, the notion that insufficient credit extension by suppliers had any contribution to the decline in capacity utilization was rejected.

Likewise, insufficient credit for working capital at prevailing interest rates was largely rejected as the reason. However, there remained a notable proportion of firms in the Philippines (35.8 percent) and Thailand (36.0 percent), suggesting that this factor had significantly contributed to the decline of capacity utilization. A more worrying feature is the breakdown in exports—as there was a higher proportion of exporters than nonexporters in Malaysia, Indonesia, and Thailand that regarded the lack of working credit as a significant cause of the drop. This meant that those few firms in Malaysia, Indonesia, and Thailand facing significant problems associated with access to working credit were largely exporters.

There was also little evidence that the insufficiency of credit for expansion had contributed to the decline in capacity utilization or output. (It should be noted that technically an increase in credit for expansion would initially raise capacity, thus lowering capacity utilization—defined as output per capacity. Therefore, had there been insufficient credit for expansion, we would have been able to explain the decline in capacity utilization entirely by the reduction in output.) Only 13.1 percent of the firms said that credit for expansion was a severe constraint. This observation implies that the supply of credit at prevailing interest rates was not really a concern. The relevancy of this factor in determining capacity utilization was highest in the Philippines and lowest in Korea. Interestingly, however, in all countries proportionately more exporters than nonexporters regarded availability of expansion credit as a significant contributing factor. This finding supports the previous view that the lack of expansion credit was unfortunately a more relevant contributing factor for exporters than nonexporters, thus confining the economic recovery prospects.

High interest rates per se were not unanimously perceived to be a significant cause of the decline: about 30 percent of all respondents rejected it as a factor. The finding here, though not rejecting the general wisdom, is far less conclusive about the problem of high interest rates. The country-wide differences also bring out some quite interesting features. A large proportion of Malaysian (39.1 percent) and Indonesian (34.2 percent) firms reported that high interest rates had no adverse consequences on their capacity utilization, while conversely, almost half (48.9 percent) of all respondents suggested that high interest rates had significantly contributed to it. This proportion was over one-half for the Philippines (55.5 percent), Thailand (53.7 percent), and Indonesia (51.3 percent)—but merely 40.5 percent in Malaysia. Unfortunately, there was again a consistent, disturbing pattern among exporters: a higher proportion of exporters than nonexporters observed that high interest rates had caused their capacity utilization to fall, and the reverse proportion was observed for those noting that high interest rates had no contribution. A comfort that could be derived from this finding is that interest rate levels have come down significantly from their previous levels, thus the recovery prospects, especially for exporters, should be somewhat more favorable.

Finally, with regard to debt burden, there is again no conclusive evidence that this is an influence in the decline by way of leaving insufficient internal funds. Responses to this question were only available in Korea, Malaysia, and Thailand. Over one-third (36.9 percent) of the firms whose output had declined rejected the notion that heavy debt burden had left insufficient internal funds and thus caused capacity utilization to fall, while almost another third (32.1 percent) regarded it as having some relevance. Definite affirmation was highest from Thai firms at 40.5 percent and lowest from Indonesian firms at 21.4 percent. Again, relatively more exporters were affected by the debt burden than nonexporters.

In summary, only certain aspects of cost and availability of credit were regarded as important factors in determining the level of capacity utilization, and the most relevant was deemed to be high interest rates. Throughout these breakdowns, Indonesian firms consistently regarded the various credit considerations as unimportant, while those affected by credit considerations in all countries were proportionately more often exporters than nonexporters. However, it should be emphasized that these observations only illustrate the link between credit and capacity utilization. Therefore, firms having lower capacity utilization may not necessarily be driven by credit considerations and, vice versa, firms with insufficient credit may not have lower capacity utilization. In other words, problems associated with credit—whether high interest rates or availability of credit—extend far beyond the realms of capacity utilization; for example, there are also profitability and liquidity dimensions, which this section alone cannot cover.

*Insufficient credit as a cause of inadequate liquidity.* The next issue to be discussed is whether inadequate liquidity was caused by insufficient credit and whether or not there existed a credit crunch; that is, at current interest rates, whether credit is being rationed and viable projects go unfunded. A reduction in the supply of credit alone is not sufficient evidence of a credit crunch. In the questionnaires, credit considerations included loans for working capital, supplier credit, and the burden of servicing outstanding debt as it is affected by interest rate levels.

Although a decline in internal revenue that is attributable to depressed demand was the primary source of inadequate liquidity reported by the firms, there is sufficient evidence that the shortage of loans for working capital was also a contributing factor, as about half (50.9 percent) of them considered it important. When surveyed firms regarded insufficient loans for working capital as an important factor for their inadequate liquidity, Indonesian firms ranked lowest (39.0 percent), implying that Indonesia was least affected, and Thailand highest at 61.7 percent. Meanwhile, proportionately more exporters than nonexporters in all countries except Thailand attributed insufficient loans for working capital as a cause of their liquidity problems, thus reinforcing the views expressed in the previous findings.

In terms of supplier credit, there is no conclusive evidence that this had significantly contributed to the firms' liquidity problems. Although about one-third (33.2 percent) of the firms confirmed that it had had a notable or major impact on liquidity, over a quarter (29.9 percent) conversely said that there was no correlation of any kind, while another 36.9 percent said that it had had only a limited or moderate impact. As with the previous findings, it appeared that Indonesia was only partially affected by supplier credit, while Thailand and the Philippines were most affected. Moreover, there is a consistent pattern emerging in Indonesia, Malaysia, and the Philippines that exporters were proportionately more affected in terms of being liquidity-constrained by insufficient supplier credit than nonexporters. This is indeed a worrying finding although it does not necessarily mean that the absolute magnitude of the problem is greater for exporters.

Finally, there is significant evidence that the burden of debt servicing had left the firms with insufficient internal funds and was deemed as a major cause of liquidity constraint. On average, only 17.0 percent of firms with inadequate liquidity said that the burden of debt servicing had no meaningful significance, while over one-half (52.1 percent) confirmed that it had had a notable or major impact on liquidity. Surveyed firms from Indonesia and the Philippines did not provide responses for this question. The problem was most severe among Thai firms as over half of those with inadequate liquidity (56.3 percent) regarded the burden of debt servicing as an extremely important factor in contributing to their liquidity problems. The breakdown of exporting status once again reveals that those affected by the burden of debt servicing in Malaysia, Korea, and Thailand were more likely to be exporters. One point to note here is that the high burden of debt servicing is either caused by the high level of indebtedness or interest rates. It would have, therefore, been interesting to see the responses from the firms on their ability to service loan payments at current interest rates, as this would have determined the extent to which the high burden of debt servicing was driven by high interest rates.

Overall, there is supportive evidence of inadequate liquidity and insufficient supply of credit. In particular, there is evidently a close association between inadequate liquidity, and the burden of debt servicing and loans for working capital. Thus, the first criterion for a credit crunch has been met, that there is insufficient supply of credit. Concerning the second and most important criterion, however, it is not possible to deduce from the survey results that credit is being rationed at the prevailing interest rates.

*Problems with credit access as a cause of the firms' seeking partners.* In this subsection, the question of why firms wanted to seek partnership will be addressed. If evidence suggests that firms were compelled to follow this path in order to secure alternative access to credit, then it further supports the view that there is inadequate supply of domestic credit.

Overall, firms seeking partners were most common among Indonesian firms (38.1 percent) and least common in Malaysia (6.1 percent), and were proportionately more common among exporters than nonexporters. When analyzed by sector, the most common instances of the search for partners were reported by the exporters of food (57.1 percent) and garments and textiles (42.3 percent) in Indonesia. Meanwhile, the least common instances varied among sectors of different countries. In terms of the perceived contributing factors, foreign market, technology, supplier relationship, and access to working and expansion credit, were regarded as the most important considerations for the firms in their search for partners, while equity participation was the least relevant.

More specifically, for those firms seeking foreign partners, it appeared that access to credit for working capital was an important consideration. On average, about 60 percent of those looking for foreign partners confirmed that this had had a notable or major influence on their search. Interestingly, a large proportion of the firms in Indonesia (26.1 percent) said that their search was not driven by this consideration, while the issue was most important for the firms in Malaysia (83.3 percent), followed by the Philippines (72.0 percent), Thailand (68.9 percent), Korea (62.4 percent), and Indonesia (45.5 percent).

Meanwhile, there was also supportive evidence to suggest that access to credit for expansion was a significant cause for the firms' search for foreign partners. On average, 57.2 percent of the firms confirmed that it had had a notable or major influence on their search. Again, Indonesia alone was the home country for half (21 out of 42) of those firms saying that their search was not driven by expansion credit considerations.

The evidence is far less conclusive for equity participation, since 25.9 percent said that it had had no contribution, and the remaining was equally divided between those saying that it had had either a moderate influence, or significant influence.

Although there is little accuracy in these numbers—since relatively few firms were seeking foreign partners—it should be noted that Indonesia, despite being the country with the largest proportion of firms seeking partners, consistently did not consider access to credit an important reason. In general, however, it appeared that credit considerations played a significant role in inducing firms to seek partnership, thus supporting further the view that there was insufficient domestic credit—though the evidence is still not strong enough to conclude that there was a credit crunch.

*The role of credit constraints in hampering export performance.* The last issue to be addressed concerning credit constraints is how these have affected export performance. This is a different issue from inadequate liquidity that was discussed earlier; this question specifically addresses the issue of credit constraints. In this regard, there appears to be *no* conclusive evidence to suggest that credit constraint was the reason for any decline in export performance in Korea and Thailand during 1997–98 (only Korean and Thai firms provided answers to this question). While about a quarter (23.7 percent) of the firms confirmed that it had had a notable or major influence on their export performance, almost one-third (29.7 percent) said that it had had no contribution and the rest (46.6 percent) said that it had had only a limited or moderate influence. Nevertheless, quite a large number of Thai firms (40 percent) with worsened export performance suggested that the problem was significantly driven by the problem of credit constraint.

By looking at the various aspects of credit, it has been demonstrated that there was indeed an insufficient supply of credit, which contributed to liquidity problems and subsequently compelled the firms to seek partners—though evidently the issue was not regarded as a major cause of the decline in capacity utilization. The widely perceived problem of a credit crunch, which can neither be confirmed nor rejected by the survey, may in fact have been just a problem caused by the firms' being unable or unqualified to secure financing in the first place; this is different from the concept of a credit crunch in which viable firms go unfunded. Had a direct question been asked about the nature of credit availability at current interest rates and not merely about its impact, the notion of a credit crunch could then have been clearly identified. Alternatively, given that the firms' viability concept cannot be readily identified from the survey results—as responses were only provided by firms whose output had declined—it would have also been interesting to see the same responses of firms whose output had increased, since this would have represented a proxy for the firms' viability. If the firms complained that they had been constrained from obtaining credit despite their increased output, the story of a credit crunch would then have been confirmed.

## Costs and supply considerations

It is generally perceived that among many factors, high costs associated with currency depreciation and interest rates have lowered the firms' performance. This section, therefore, attempts to evaluate this supposition by looking at the various aspects of costs.

*The contribution of increased costs to the decline in output.* In addition to the many factors mentioned earlier, this subsection attempts to evaluate the extent to which the decline in capacity utilization was caused by the different aspects of costs—namely, currency depreciation, labor costs, raw material shortage, and disruption in supplies.

First, increased costs of imported inputs arising from currency depreciation seems to have played a major role in curtailing capacity utilization. On average, almost two-thirds (60.4 percent) of the firms confirmed that the issue had had a notable or major impact and another 23.5 percent said that it had had a limited or moderate impact. In fact, over two-thirds of the surveyed firms in Indonesia (67.6 percent), Philippines (70.8 percent), and Thailand (71.5 percent) named the problem as a contributing factor. A breakdown in exporting status also reveals that exporters in Malaysia experienced proportionately greater difficulties from currency depreciation than nonexporters. This may be attributable to the fact that exporters in Malaysia are relatively more dependent on imported inputs than exporters elsewhere.

Second, with regard to increased labor costs, although the firms did not unanimously perceive this issue to be a cause of the decline in their capacity utilization, a notable 35.4 percent of Thai firms responded that it had had very significant implications on their capacity utilization. In addition, a slightly higher proportion of exporters than nonexporters in Korea and Malaysia said that the problem of increased labor costs was a cause of the decline, implying that these exporters were affected more than a proportional distribution between them and nonexporters would have dictated. The problem may not merely be a new factor, but one that has in fact persisted unidentified long before the crisis, and that was only seriously felt by the firms when economic activities contracted.

Third, there was significant evidence to suggest that shortages of raw materials were not a cause of the decline in the firms' capacity utilization. The majority of the firms (40.7 percent) confirmed that the issue had no relevance to the decline and only 12.0 percent said that it was a severe constraint.

As with shortage of raw materials, disruption of supplies was not generally perceived to be a cause, as almost half (47.9 percent) of the represented firms revealed that it had no relevance and only 7.8 percent said that it was a severe constraint.

On the whole, therefore, it appeared that only currency depreciation and, to a somewhat lesser extent, labor costs, were contributing factors in the decline of capacity utilization.

*Input costs as a cause of inadequate liquidity.* For those firms that experienced liquidity problems, increased input costs seem to have played a significant contributing role (firms in the Philippines did not provide answers to this question). While very few firms (7.2 percent) said that the issue had no relevance, about two-thirds (66.4 percent) believed that increased input costs had notably affected their liquidity. Thailand appeared to be hardest-hit by the problem as two-thirds of the surveyed firms (66.2 percent) complained that increased input costs had severely hampered their liquidity, while only 16.2 percent in Korea, 24.7 percent in Indonesia, and 52.9 percent in Malaysia agreed.

*Access to foreign inputs as a cause of the search for foreign partners.* In an uncertain economic environment, forming a foreign partnership can help a great deal in securing the much-needed foreign inputs. This supply consideration is one way of reducing uncertainty and costs.

Indeed, there was some supporting evidence that the reason for seeking foreign partners was attributable to supplier relationship. Over half (57.0 percent) of the respondents commented that the supplier relationship was a notable or serious reason driving their search for a foreign partner.

There was much more evidence in support of new technology as the reason behind the search for foreign partners—only 6.5 percent (18 of the 278 firms) that were seeking foreign partners said that it had no relevance. Large percentages of the firms seeking foreign partners in the Philippines (84.6 percent), Malaysia (83.3 percent), and Thailand (82.2 percent) cited access to new technology as the overriding motivation.

Management expertise appears to have been another important consideration in the search for foreign partners—only 13.4 percent of the firms seeking foreign partners rejected that it had any relevance. Again, a great majority of the firms seeking foreign partners in Malaysia (75.0 percent) and Thailand (73.3 percent) cited access to management expertise as the overriding reason, while, as expected, Korean firms ranked lowest at 33.7 percent.

Overall, therefore, access to foreign inputs seems to have played an important role among Thai and Malaysian firms in establishing foreign partnership.

*Input costs as possible factors hampering export performance.* In addition to demand and credit considerations, which we looked at earlier, cost and supply considerations may have also contributed to the worsened export performance in 1998.

Price competitiveness seems to have been a factor, although only firms in Korea, Malaysia, and Thailand provided responses to this question. A large proportion of Thai exporters that experienced poor export performance (61 out of 96 firms, or 63.5 percent) cited price competitiveness as a notable or significant reason.

Likewise, there is evidence in support of high costs of imported inputs and unstable conditions in export market as reasons for poor export performance. Interestingly, almost three-quarters of those exporters experiencing poor export performance in Thailand (70.1 percent) cited unstable conditions as a notable or significant reason.

The only area in which there appears to be no connection with poor export performance was **inferior** product design, although only firms in Korea and Malaysia provided responses to this question.

Suffice it to say that in line with general expectations, the various elements of costs have evidently contributed to output decline, worsened export performance, inadequate liquidity, and the search for foreign partners.

## Constraints to recovery and policy recommendations

This paper has been structured so as to identify the reasons for the decline in capacity utilization and export performance, which are inevitably related to three considerations—(a) the reduction in demand and revenue; (b) problems associated with liquidity and credit constraints; and (c) other cost and supply factors. In so doing, bottom-up policy formulations can be devised to address specific areas that the firms regard as the major constraints to corporate recovery.

This section will first attempt to identify these major constraints by reexamining the previous findings looking from a slightly different perspective. Specifically, we will *rank* the reasons cited for the firms' output decline, problems with liquidity, search for partnership, and worsened export performance, and based on the outcome give policy recommendations.

### Constraints to recovery

The firms were asked in the questionnaires to give ratings to the eleven factors that might have contributed to their decline in capacity utilization. The most important constraints can, therefore, be interpreted as those pressing factors with average ratings of above 3 (on a scale from 1 to 5), which were domestic demand (3.9), increased input costs arising from currency depreciation (3.6), and high interest rates (3.1). (See table 2.10.)

Regarding problems with liquidity, lower revenue (4.1), high input costs (3.8), burden of servicing debt (3.4), and insufficient loans for working capital (3.3) were regarded as the most significant contributing factors (see table 2.11).

As regards the search for a new partner, the most important factors (those exceeding 3.5) driving firms to seek a new partner appeared to be foreign market (3.6), technology (3.5), supplier relationship (3.5), and working credit (3.5) considerations (see table 2.12).

Finally, the most important factors (those exceeding 3.0) that contributed to the worsened export performance were poor demand (4.0), unstable markets (3.6),

### TABLE 2.10
**Ratings of factors perceived by the firms as causes of output decline**

| | Domestic demand | Depreciation & input costs | High interest rates | Labor costs | Debt burden | Working credit | Foreign demand | Raw material costs | Expansion credit | Supplier credit | Disruption of delivery |
|---|---|---|---|---|---|---|---|---|---|---|---|
| Indonesia | 3.5 | 3.6 | 3.1 | 2.6 | — | 2.1 | 1.8 | 2.5 | 2.2 | 1.8 | 2.1 |
| Korea | 4.4 | 2.9 | 3.1 | 2.1 | 2.3 | 2.6 | 2.8 | 2.3 | 2.1 | 2.1 | 2.1 |
| Malaysia | 4.0 | 3.5 | 2.8 | 2.5 | 2.6 | 2.4 | 2.5 | 2.2 | 2.2 | 2.2 | 2.0 |
| Philippines | 3.2 | 3.9 | 3.4 | 3.3 | — | 2.7 | 2.4 | 2.6 | 2.4 | 2.3 | 2.3 |
| Thailand | 4.0 | 4.0 | 3.4 | 3.4 | 2.9 | 2.7 | 2.8 | 2.3 | 2.2 | 2.4 | 2.1 |
| Average | 3.9 | 3.6 | 3.1 | 2.7 | 2.6 | 2.5 | 2.4 | 2.3 | 2.2 | 2.1 | 2.1 |

—. Not available.
*Source:* World Bank, Firm-Level Survey.

### TABLE 2.11
**Ratings of factors perceived by the firms as causes of inadequate liquidity**

| Country | Lower revenue | Input costs | Burden of servicing debt | Insufficient working credit | Insufficient supplier credit |
|---|---|---|---|---|---|
| Indonesia | 3.5 | 3.7 | — | 2.9 | 2.5 |
| Korea | 4.2 | 3.4 | 3.1 | 3.3 | 2.5 |
| Malaysia | 4.2 | 4.1 | 3.3 | 3.4 | 3.0 |
| Philippines | 3.8 | - | — | 3.3 | 2.8 |
| Thailand | 4.4 | 4.3 | 3.9 | 3.7 | 3.2 |
| Average | 4.1 | 3.8 | 3.4 | 3.3 | 2.8 |

—. Not available.
*Source:* World Bank, Firm-Level Survey.

### TABLE 2.12
**Ratings of factors for the search of a new partner**

| Country | Foreign market | Technology | Supplier relationship | Working credit | Local market | Expansion credit | Management | Equity participation |
|---|---|---|---|---|---|---|---|---|
| Indonesia | 3.2 | 3.1 | 3.3 | 3.0 | 3.5 | 3.0 | 3.1 | 2.8 |
| Korea | 4.0 | 3.9 | 3.9 | 3.7 | — | 3.3 | 2.9 | 2.5 |
| Malaysia | 4.0 | 3.9 | 3.5 | 4.3 | — | 4.3 | 3.3 | 3.8 |
| Philippines | 3.9 | 4.0 | 3.3 | 4.1 | 3.0 | 4.1 | — | 3.7 |
| Thailand | 4.0 | 4.0 | 3.8 | 4.0 | — | 3.3 | 3.7 | 3.3 |
| Average | 3.6 | 3.5 | 3.5 | 3.5 | 3.4 | 3.3 | 3.1 | 3.0 |

—. Not available.
*Source:* World Bank, Firm-Level Survey.

lack of price competitiveness (3.5) and high cost of imported inputs (3.3) (see table 2.13).

These simple illustrations show that the perceived major constraints to recovery, in order of importance, were invariably associated with (a) the lower demand for their products; (b) higher costs; (c) insufficient credit; and (d) other supply considerations.

## Policy Recommendations

Based on the above findings, general policy recommendations can be deduced as follows. First and foremost, it is most crucial to boost domestic demand in order to help kick-start the revival process. The austerity measures that have severely depressed demand and squeezed

### TABLE 2.13
### Ratings of factors for the worsened export performance

| Country | Poor demand | Unstable markets | Price competitiveness | Imported inputs | Credit constraints | Design |
|---|---|---|---|---|---|---|
| Korea | 3.7 | 3.6 | 3.3 | 2.7 | 2.3 | 2.0 |
| Malaysia | 4.3 | 3.3 | 3.5 | 3.6 | 0.0 | 2.7 |
| Thailand | 3.9 | 4.0 | 3.8 | 3.8 | 3.1 | 0.0 |
| Average | 4.0 | 3.6 | 3.5 | 3.3 | 2.6 | 2.3 |

*Source:* World Bank, Firm-Level Survey.

credit should be adjusted. Lower interest rates, though necessary, may be futile on their own, as consumer demand is also influenced by other factors such as employment and income uncertainties, while new bank lending is likely to be limited by the weak capital bases and low asset quality. A combination of increased monetary and fiscal stimuli, and a relaxation of certain rules and regulations relating to consumer expenditure should significantly help raise domestic demand.

In terms of credit and liquidity dimensions, additional credit facilities should be urgently provided to exporters to help relieve their liquidity positions. This could be done through government-owned financial institutions such as export-import banks and development banks. The authorities should also actively support the small and medium enterprises as they represent a large part of the industrial sector. In relation to this, the process of corporate debt restructuring should be promoted and supported by the necessary legal infrastructure, as there appeared to be some evidence that high interest rates and burden of debt servicing had affected capacity utilization.

Finally, in response to the complaints on cost and supply factors, the authorities should strive to maintain currency stability, since this would provide confidence and predictability in the computation of cost and revenue—a vital consideration for businesspeople and entrepreneurs. As for longer-term considerations, the authorities should undertake to facilitate the firms' access to management expertise and technology by increasing investment in education, training, and research and development in order to enhance competitiveness and truly reflect labor costs.

These general recommendations are broadly in line with the current policy directions, but each should be further fine-tuned and tailored according to the circumstances in each country.

## Conclusions

This paper has both confirmed and rejected the many perceptions surrounding the "whys" and "wherefores" of the economic crisis. On the one hand, there is clear evidence that capacity utilization declined across all countries and sectors of industries, driven largely by the contraction of domestic demand. In addition, the firms' export performance was generally in line with the subdued macroeconomic export numbers, with only about half of the exporters claiming that their performance in volume terms had improved. On the other hand, however, inadequate liquidity was not generally perceived to be a major problem, and its cause was heavily weighted on the side of the demand for goods rather than the supply of credit—which indicates an urgent need to boost domestic demand. Indeed, there was an insufficient supply of credit, but it cannot be confirmed that there was technically a credit crunch. Finally, while several of the surveyed firms held the view that the worst of the crisis is over, there is also an implied notion that exporters may not be able to provide an immediate engine for economic recovery, unless certain constraints are removed.

It must be made clear, though, that views expressed in the surveys and the conclusions reached cannot in any way be interpreted as a judgment of the authorities' policy response to the crisis. One must be particularly careful not to merely draw conclusions from a subjective perspective. In other words, it cannot simply be concluded that the stabilization policy of high interest rates, for example, has failed or even that it has inflicted more harm than good on the economy by depressing domestic demand, making loans more costly, and increasing debt servicing costs. In principle, the time dimension must also be considered and, in doing so, will alter this conclusion considerably. Specifically, as the currencies have now stabilized and confidence somewhat resumed, the authorities should take a proactive role in relieving the painful pressure faced by corporates, brought on by the abrupt adjustment process. Demand stimulus and continued restructuring of the economy are necessary measures to promote a recovery.

## Note

This paper was the result of a joint collaboration effort undertaken by Dr. Atchana Waiquamdee, Mr. Soravis Krairiksh, and Dr. Wasana Phongsanarakul of the Economic Research Department, Bank of Thailand.

## chapter three

# Macroeconomic Views of the East Asian Crisis: A Comparison

Yoon Je Cho
Changyong Rhee

The financial crisis has brought unprecedented economic and social distress to the Asian economies. The average growth rates in Indonesia, the Republic of Korea, and Thailand had been well above 7 percent during the early 1990s but they dropped dramatically to –13.7, –5.7 and –6.5 percent, respectively in 1998. No one had expected such a severe contraction of the Asian economies. Only in the second half of 1998 did the East Asian countries start to move from the free fall to stabilization. But the recovery has been quite moderate and uneven across countries.

The purpose of this paper is to examine the role of the macroeconomic environment in the adjustment processes of the East Asian crisis. We first document the macroeconomic adjustment in the five East Asian countries (Indonesia, Korea, Malaysia, Thailand, and the Philippines) and contrast the degree to which each country has been affected by macroeconomic constraints. Based on the observation of what has occurred so far, we attempt to identify which factors contributed most to such a severe contraction and uneven recovery.

Our findings can be summarized as follows. The severe downturn was caused mainly by the precipitous drop in investment and, to a lesser degree, consumption. Many factors contributed to the sharp fall. The magnitude of capital flow reversal was remarkable and the concurrent huge depreciation of the currencies worsened the balance sheets of financial institutions and corporations that had large unhedged foreign-currency liabilities. To prevent depreciation-inflation spirals, some period of tight monetary policy was inevitable but the resulting high interest rates had a profound effect on the credit crunch and corporate bankruptcies. The negative effect was exacerbated because the stabilization policy was imposed in conjunction with rapid financial restructuring.

Ironically, it was the sharp economic downturn that contributed to the stabilization of the exchange rates and interest rates in the second half of 1998, and thereby laid the ground for recovery. The sharp fall in demand and the resulting decline in imports brought about a drastic reversal of current account positions and in turn helped to build up a substantial increase in foreign reserves. This speedy adjustment to stabilization was possible since the East Asian countries were more open and private sector–oriented. This was taken into account in the design of the International Monetary Fund (IMF) adjustment program. The essence of the IMF adjustment program is to stabilize the exchange market in the short run through belt-tightening—and the private sector's belt is easier to tighten than the government's. Also the recession in the domestic market could generate a larger improvement in current account balances since these economies were more open and export-oriented.[1]

Despite the common characteristic of a sharp initial downturn, the adjustment process varied widely across the countries. The example of Indonesia shows that a policy for stabilization cannot be effective if structural problems remain unsolved. Uncontrolled monetary expansion in bailing out troubled financial institutions not only delayed recovery but also brought Indonesia to the verge of hyperinflation. The Malaysian case also shows that the belt-tightening policy alone is not sufficient in stabilizing the exchange rate market and that the resumption of foreign capital inflows is essential for recovery. Until mid-1998, Malaysia adopted a "virtual IMF" policy package of austerity but, unlike Korea and Thailand, it failed to stabilize the foreign exchange market. This may be a reflection of the difference in the availability of external financing opportunities through official program loans or private capital inflows.

The paper is organized as follows. In the following section we briefly review the macroeconomic development after the crisis and the recovery prospects for the region. Next comes a section in which we discuss the role of monetary and fiscal policy in the adjustment process. Based on the developments so far, the subsequent section attempts to make preliminary assessments on what caused such a severe economic contraction and recent recovery in this region. The final section concludes and draws some policy implications.

## Macroeconomic development

### Initial conditions

The East Asian crisis has many common features—weak financial systems, excessive unhedged short-term foreign borrowing, lack of transparency in business practices, and so on. Nonetheless, there exist significant differences between the countries regarding the origins and the preconditions.[2] Among these countries, the signs of deteriorating economic conditions and overheating pressures were most visible in Thailand. Key macroeconomic indicators were stronger in Korea, but the country could not sidestep the crisis because of its serious liquidity problem: the ratio of short-term external debt to official foreign reserves in Korea exceeded 100 percent from the mid-1990s onward. Recently, the Philippines has been recovering from its decade-long economic crisis after gaining political stability in 1992.

Indonesia's macroeconomic performance was also strong until mid-1997. But it had its own structural weakness, which exposed Indonesia to the contagion from the Thai and Korean crises in the latter half of 1997. Short-term external debt had been rising rapidly and the country's weak financial system cast doubts on the government's ability to defend the currency peg. In addition, political uncertainty arising from the elections in late 1997 and the presidential election in March 1998 compounded economic problems. El Nino's effects included forest fires and caused a long-lasting drought, inflicting serious damage on the forestry and agricultural sector, reducing exports, and raising food prices.

Prior to the crisis, the Malaysian economy had showed the strongest macroeconomic performance among the five East Asian countries. It had enjoyed the highest growth rates of 8–9 percent with the lowest inflation of around 3 percent, and virtually full employment. Only the widening current account deficits in the mid-1990s showed signs of imbalance, but these were regarded as inevitable and sustainable considering the country's high levels of growth and investment. Also, unlike Korea and Thailand, the current account deficit was covered mostly by long-term capital (primarily foreign direct investment) rather than short-term capital. Moreover, the financial system in Malaysia was known to be in better shape than those of other Southeast Asian countries, even though the belief must be questionable in hindsight.[3]

## Sharp economic contraction and the reversal of the current account position

Reflecting these differences in preconditions, the adjustment processes also were uneven in these East Asian countries. Nevertheless, there were substantial common trends in the adjustment processes. First, they all experienced severe economic contraction and a drastic reversal of current account balances. Second, they all geared their macroeconomic policy stance toward expansion starting in the middle of 1998, cutting interest rates and expanding fiscal deficits. Third, the signs of recovery have been evident (starting late in 1998), but it is still premature to judge whether they will become a trend.

*Economic contraction.* As can be seen in table 3.1, the economic slowdown in these countries was historically unprecedented. The average growth rates in these countries had been well above 7 percent prior to the crisis. But in 1998, the real gross domestic product (GDP) declined by 15, 6, 6, and 7 percent in Indonesia, Korea, Malaysia, and Thailand, respectively. These drops constitute the countries' worst postwar economic records. The growth rate dropped from 5 percent in 1997 to –0.4 percent in 1998 in the Philippines. The fall of industrial production was even more dramatic. In the first quarter of 1998, industrial production indexes in Thailand and Korea declined by 18 and 8 percent, respectively, compared with those of the same period in 1997.

The financial meltdown in these countries resulted in more people losing their jobs and being forced into poverty. The unemployment rates in Indonesia, Korea, and Thailand reached 8–10, 8, and 4.4 percent, respectively, at the end of 1998. Prior to the crisis, these countries, except for the Philippines, enjoyed virtually full employment.

*Capital flows, exchange rates, and stock markets.* In the 1990s, almost two-thirds of all private capital flows to developing countries flowed into East Asia. Table 3.2 summarizes capital flows as a percentage of each country's GDP during the 1990s.[4] The reversal of the foreign capital flows in 1997 was remarkable. The most extreme cases were seen in Thailand and Malaysia. Annual capital inflows into these two countries averaged over 10 percent of GDP during the 1990s, and at one point they reached 13 percent and 17 percent of GDP. However, capital inflows abruptly changed direction in 1997. For example, in Thailand, capital outflows reached 11 percent of GDP in 1997 alone. Therefore, between 1996 and 1997, Thailand experienced a sudden reversal of private capital inflows amounting to about 20 percent of GDP. The other countries faced a similar fate.

The large capital outflows depreciated the currencies precipitously and the stock markets in the region plummeted. Between January and December 1997, the Korean won was depreciated by 121 percent and its composite stock price index declined by 50 percent. The value of Thailand's baht and composite stock price index declined by 139 and 52 percent respectively during a similar period. In Indonesia, Malaysia, and the Philippines, the exchange rate depreciated by 85, 40, and 44 percent, respectively, against the dollar between mid-1997 and 1998. Their stock markets fell by more than 53, 50, and 40 percent, respectively, during a similar period.

*Inflation and interest rates.* The sharp depreciation provided inflationary pressure. Together with the increase of import prices, expected inflation soared, since the market participants anticipated that the central banks of these countries would inject massive liquidity support to save the banking system. The inflation rates in Thailand, Korea, and the Philippines increased swiftly almost twofold by the first half of 1998, reaching 10, 9, and 10 percent, respectively. The inflation rate in Indonesia soared to 58 percent in 1998 from 6 percent in 1997. In Malaysia, the inflation rates soared to 5.3 percent from 2.7 percent during the same period, even though expansionary monetary policies now being pursued could accelerate inflation to a much higher level (see table 3.3).

Owing to higher inflation and tight monetary policies, nominal interest rates drastically increased. At its

## TABLE 3.1
### Growth and unemployment

**I Real GDP growth rates**
(percent change over the same period of the previous year)

|  | 1996 | | | | | 1997 | | | | | 1998 | | | | |
| --- | --- | --- | --- | --- | --- | --- | --- | --- | --- | --- | --- | --- | --- | --- | --- |
|  | 1Q | 2Q | 3Q | 4Q | AVG | 1Q | 2Q | 3Q | 4Q | AVG | 1Q | 2Q | 3Q | 4Q | AVG |
| Indonesia | 5.7 | 6.7 | 8.4 | 10.3 | 7.8 | 7.7 | 6.6 | 3.3 | 2.4 | 5.0 | −6.4 | −16.8 | −17.4 | −19.5 | −15.0 |
| Korea | 7.6 | 6.7 | 6.6 | 7.4 | 7.1 | 5.7 | 6.6 | 6.1 | 3.9 | 5.6 | −3.9 | −6.8 | −6.8 | — | −5.8 |
| Malaysia | 8.3 | 8.4 | 8.1 | 8.2 | 8.3 | 8.5 | 8.4 | 7.4 | 6.9 | 7.8 | −2.8 | −6.8 | −8.6 | — | −6.1 |
| Philippines | 5.3 | 6.1 | 6.9 | 4.9 | 5.8 | 5.5 | 5.6 | 4.9 | 4.8 | 5.2 | 1.6 | −0.8 | −0.7 | −1.9 | −0.4 |
| Thailand | — | — | — | — | 5.5 | — | — | — | — | −0.4 | — | — | — | — | — |

**II Industrial production index growth rates**
(percent change over the same period of the previous year)

|  | 1996 | | | | | 1997 | | | | | 1998 | | | | |
| --- | --- | --- | --- | --- | --- | --- | --- | --- | --- | --- | --- | --- | --- | --- | --- |
|  | 1Q | 2Q | 3Q | 4Q | AVG | 1Q | 2Q | 3Q | 4Q | AVG | 1Q | 2Q | 3Q | 4Q | AVG |
| Indonesia | — | — | — | — | — | — | — | — | — | — | — | — | — | — | — |
| Korea | 9.2 | 9.6 | 8.0 | 8.3 | 8.8 | 4.4 | 6.2 | 7.2 | 3.4 | 5.3 | −6.1 | −12.1 | −10.9 | −0.1 | −7.3 |
| Malaysia | 11.6 | 9.8 | 10.7 | 12.0 | 11.0 | 11.5 | 11.6 | 9.7 | 10.1 | 10.7 | −0.8 | −6.0 | −10.5 | −5.6 | −5.7 |
| Philippines | 11.5 | 2.5 | 4.9 | −1.9 | 4.2 | −3.2 | 3.6 | 6.5 | 13.9 | 5.2 | −3.0 | −9.3 | −13.0 | — | −8.4 |
| Thailand | 8.0 | 6.0 | 9.7 | 9.3 | 8.3 | 7.0 | 7.6 | −4.1 | −11.3 | −0.2 | −17.0 | −15.4 | −9.9 | — | −14.1 |

*Note:* Indexes of Thailand and Philippines are manufacturing production indexes.

**III Unemployment rate**
(percent)

|  | 1996 | | | | | 1997 | | | | | 1998 | | | | |
| --- | --- | --- | --- | --- | --- | --- | --- | --- | --- | --- | --- | --- | --- | --- | --- |
|  | 1Q | 2Q | 3Q | 4Q | AVG | 1Q | 2Q | 3Q | 4Q | AVG | 1Q | 2Q | 3Q | 4Q | AVG |
| Indonesia | — | — | — | — | — | — | — | — | — | — | — | — | — | — | — |
| Korea | 1.8 | 2.0 | 2.0 | 2.2 | 2.0 | 2.5 | 2.6 | 2.4 | 2.6 | 2.5 | 4.7 | 6.9 | 8.4 | — | 6.7 |
| Malaysia | — | — | — | — | 2.9 | — | — | — | — | 3.0 | — | — | — | — | — |
| Philippines | 8.3 | 10.9 | 7.7 | — | 9.0 | 7.7 | 10.4 | — | 7.9 | 8.7 | — | 7.3 | 8.9 | 9.6 | 8.6 |
| Thailand | — | — | — | — | 1.5 | — | — | — | — | 1.9 | — | — | — | — | 4.4 |

*Note:* Existing monthly value is used as the data for that quarter.
*Sources:* International Financial Statistics, IMF
JP Morgan 1999.
Bank Indonesia, Indonesian Central Bureau of Statistics.
Bank Negara Malaysia (Central Bank of Malaysia).
Bank of Korea, Korea National Statistical Office.
Bank of Thailand.
Banko Sentral ng Pilipinas (Central Bank of Philippines).

highest, the benchmark corporate bond yield rates in Korea rose to above 30 percent from their precrisis average of 12 percent. In Thailand, Malaysia, and the Philippines, the interbank lending rates increased to 24, 11, and 19 percent from their precrisis level of 10, 7, and 11 percent, respectively. Indonesia's interest rates rose to above 70 percent from their precrisis level of 12 percent. The punitive level of interest rates strangled businesses, including those that would have been viable and robust otherwise. Bankruptcy and unemployment rates skyrocketed.

*Current account.* The magnitude of the economic slowdown during the crisis was most visible in the dramatic responses of current account adjustment. In Malaysia, the current account surplus is expected to be about 7 percent of GDP in 1998, increasing from its 1997 value of −5 percent. The surplus is likely to reach 14 and 9 percent of GDP in Korea and Thailand, respectively (see table 3.4).[5] The sharp improvement of the current account was forced by harsh recessions. It was mainly due to the decrease in imports rather than the increase in exports. In Korea, imports declined by more than 23 percent in the first half of 1998 while export growth remained stagnant.[6] The decline of imports was mainly attributable to the precipitous fall of investment demand. Compared with the same period in 1997, the private investment demand declined by 28 percent, whereas consumption declined by 12 percent in the first half of 1998 in Korea.

In Indonesia, despite the sharp recession, export performance did not significantly improve, and the current account surplus in 1998 is expected to be only 5 percent of GDP, which is significantly lower than those in Thailand and Korea. The poor performance shows that

### TABLE 3.2
### Capital flows, exchange rates, and stock prices

**I Capital flows**
(percent of GDP)

|  |  |  |  |  |  |  | 1997 | | | | 1998 | |
|---|---|---|---|---|---|---|---|---|---|---|---|---|
|  |  | 1993 | 1994 | 1995 | 1996 | 1997 | Q1 | Q2 | Q3 | Q4 | Q1 | Q2 |
| Indonesia | Capital flows | 3.6 | 2.2 | 5.1 | 5.1 | −0.3 | 7.2 | 4.1 | 3.3 | −15.8 | −29.5 | 1.0 |
|  | Use of fund credit | — | — | — | — | 1.4 | — | — | — | 5.6 | — | 4.7 |
|  | Change in reserves | −0.4 | −0.4 | −0.8 | −2.0 | 2.3 | −1.4 | −4.2 | 2.4 | 12.2 | 23.2 | −9.7 |
| Korea | Capital flows | 1.0 | 2.8 | 8.5 | 5.0 | −2.1 | 3.8 | 6.1 | 0.7 | −18.9 | −6.5 | −0.3 |
|  | Use of fund credit | — | — | — | — | 2.5 | — | — | — | 10.0 | 5.3 | 2.5 |
|  | Change in reserves | −0.9 | −1.2 | −1.5 | −0.3 | 2.7 | 3.0 | −3.6 | 2.3 | 9.0 | −12.2 | −14.7 |
| Malaysia | Capital flows | 16.8 | 1.8 | 8.5 | 9.5 | 2.8 | — | — | — | — | — | — |
|  | Use of fund credit | — | — | — | — | — | — | — | — | — | — | — |
|  | Change in reserves | −17.7 | 4.4 | 2.0 | −2.5 | 3.9 | — | — | — | — | — | — |
| Philippines | Capital flows | 6.0 | 8.0 | 7.2 | 11.5 | 6.1 | 9.4 | 14.6 | 7.5 | −6.9 | 5.0 | — |
|  | Use of fund credit | 0.2 | −0.3 | −0.5 | −0.4 | 0.6 | −0.2 | −0.3 | 3.2 | −0.3 | −0.1 | — |
|  | Change in reserves | −0.8 | −3.3 | −1.2 | −4.8 | 3.1 | −2.0 | 3.4 | 1.3 | 9.8 | −3.6 | — |
| Thailand | Capital flows | 8.4 | 8.4 | 13.0 | 10.7 | −10.3 | 6.5 | −10.3 | −15.1 | −22.1 | −17.5 | −12.0 |
|  | Use of fund credit | — | — | — | — | 5.4 | — | — | 12.4 | 9.3 | 8.1 | 1.8 |
|  | Change in reserves | −3.1 | −2.9 | −4.3 | −1.2 | 6.4 | 0.3 | −5.3 | 5.1 | 5.1 | −1.7 | 3.0 |

Note:
1. Quarterly figures are the ratios of capital flows to one-fourth of annual GDP.
2. Use of Fund Credit includes exceptional financing.
3. Minus sign in change in reserves signifies the increase of foreign reserves.

**II Exchange rate**
(period average, national currency unit per dollar)

|  | 1996 | | | | | 1997 | | | | | 1998 | | | | |
|---|---|---|---|---|---|---|---|---|---|---|---|---|---|---|---|
|  | 1Q | 2Q | 3Q | 4Q | AVG | 1Q | 2Q | 3Q | 4Q | AVG | 1Q | 2Q | 3Q | 4Q | AVG |
| Indonesia | 2318.2 | 2344.0 | 2350.0 | 2357.0 | 2342.0 | 2403.0 | 2437.2 | 2791.3 | 4005.7 | 2909.0 | 9433 | 10460 | 12252 | — | 10715 |
| Korea | 782.9 | 786.2 | 817.1 | 831.6 | 804.5 | 865.4 | 891.7 | 898.6 | 1143.8 | 949.9 | 1612.0 | 1395.0 | 1324.9 | 1281.5 | 1403.2 |
| Malaysia | 2.5480 | 2.5012 | 2.4952 | 2.5193 | 2.5159 | 2.4858 | 2.5081 | 2.7771 | 3.4818 | 2.8132 | 3.9960 | 3.8451 | 4.0570 | — | 3.9660 |
| Philippines | 26.190 | 26.187 | 26.212 | 26.276 | 26.216 | 26.330 | 26.371 | 29.798 | 35.384 | 29.471 | 40.693 | 39.379 | 42.865 | — | 40.979 |
| Thailand | 25.25 | 25.31 | 25.33 | 25.54 | 25.36 | 25.91 | 25.90 | 34.31 | 42.37 | 32.12 | 45.56 | 40.31 | 40.63 | 36.48 | 40.75 |

**III Stock market index**

|  | 1996 | | | | | 1997 | | | | | 1998 | | | | |
|---|---|---|---|---|---|---|---|---|---|---|---|---|---|---|---|
|  | 1Q | 2Q | 3Q | 4Q | AVG | 1Q | 2Q | 3Q | 4Q | AVG | 1Q | 2Q | 3Q | 4Q | AVG |
| Indonesia | — | — | — | — | — | 686.2 | 690.9 | 587.3 | 434.6 | 599.8 | 503.2 | 442.2 | 366.8 | 361.7 | 418.5 |
| Korea | 868.6 | 900.5 | 797.6 | 711.8 | 819.6 | 679.9 | 735.1 | 689.5 | 418.3 | 630.7 | 535.8 | 350.4 | 321.3 | 472.6 | 420.0 |
| Malaysia | 1096.3 | 1155.6 | 1107.4 | 1210.9 | 1142.6 | 1230.2 | 1087.4 | 877 | 601.5 | 949.1 | 687.1 | 540.0 | 359.7 | 497.6 | 521.1 |
| Philippines | — | — | — | — | — | 3320.1 | 2755.6 | 2231.8 | 1819.8 | 2531.8 | 2150.9 | 1984.3 | 1353.2 | 1899.7 | 1847.0 |
| Thailand | — | — | — | — | — | 740.3 | 585.0 | 570.8 | 405.1 | 575.3 | 494.3 | 335.0 | 245.0 | 350.0 | 356.1 |

Sources: International Financial Statistics, IMF; JP Morgan 1999.

## TABLE 3.3
### Inflation and interest rates

**I Nominal interest rate**
(percent per year)

|  | 1996 | | | | | 1997 | | | | | 1998 | | | | |
| --- | --- | --- | --- | --- | --- | --- | --- | --- | --- | --- | --- | --- | --- | --- | --- |
|  | 1Q | 2Q | 3Q | 4Q | AVG | 1Q | 2Q | 3Q | 4Q | AVG | 1Q | 2Q | 3Q | 4Q | AVG |
| Indonesia | 16.24 | 15.41 | 14.76 | 13.31 | 14.93 | 13.25 | 13.69 | 23.48 | 28.50 | 19.74 | 47.00 | 59.80 | 69.65 | 37.50 | 53.48 |
| Korea | 11.8 | 11.6 | 12.2 | 12.6 | 12.1 | 12.7 | 11.7 | 12.4 | 24.3 | 15.3 | 19.0 | 16.6 | 12.5 | 8.3 | 14.1 |
| Malaysia | 7.11 | 7.33 | 7.36 | 7.33 | 7.28 | 7.28 | 7.53 | 8.03 | 9.08 | 7.98 | 10.85 | 11.10 | 7.15 | 6.25 | 8.83 |
| Philippines | 12.88 | 13.07 | 11.59 | 11.68 | 12.31 | 9.72 | 10.97 | 14.96 | 18.10 | 13.43 | 15.78 | 15.00 | 13.80 | 13.50 | 14.52 |
| Thailand | 6.58 | 8.78 | 12.93 | 12.12 | 10.10 | 8.34 | 15.10 | 23.87 | 21.70 | 17.26 | 20.57 | 18.60 | 7.17 | 2.63 | 12.24 |

Note:
1. Indonesia—1-month interbank deposit rate
2. Korea—yield rate on corporate bond with 3-year maturity
3. Malaysia—3-month interbank rate
4. Philippines—91-day treasury bill rate
5. Thailand—weighted average interbank lending rate

**II Inflation**
(CPI, percent change over the same period of the previous year)

|  | 1996 | | | | | 1997 | | | | | 1998 | | | | |
| --- | --- | --- | --- | --- | --- | --- | --- | --- | --- | --- | --- | --- | --- | --- | --- |
|  | 1Q | 2Q | 3Q | 4Q | AVG | 1Q | 2Q | 3Q | 4Q | AVG | 1Q | 2Q | 3Q | 4Q | AVG |
| Indonesia | 12.5 | 9.9 | 8.9 | 8.2 | 9.9 | 4.5 | 4.9 | 6.4 | 9.2 | 6.2 | 27.7 | 49.7 | 76.3 | 78.4 | 58.0 |
| Korea | 4.7 | 4.9 | 5.1 | 5.1 | 4.9 | 4.7 | 4.0 | 4.0 | 5.0 | 4.4 | 8.9 | 8.2 | 7.0 | 6.0 | 7.5 |
| Malaysia | 3.4 | 3.7 | 3.6 | 3.3 | 3.5 | 3.2 | 2.5 | 2.3 | 2.7 | 2.7 | 4.3 | 5.7 | 5.7 | 5.4 | 5.3 |
| Philippines | 11.0 | 10.4 | 8.1 | 6.7 | 9.1 | 5.3 | 5.3 | 5.9 | 7.2 | 5.9 | 7.9 | 9.9 | 10.4 | 10.6 | 9.7 |
| Thailand | 7.4 | 6.2 | 5.2 | 4.6 | 5.9 | 4.4 | 4.3 | 6.2 | 7.5 | 5.6 | 9.0 | 10.3 | 8.2 | 5.0 | 8.1 |

*Source:* JP Morgan 1999.

## TABLE 3.4
### Current account balances
(percent of GDP)

|  | 1996 | | | | | 1997 | | | | | 1998 | | | | |
| --- | --- | --- | --- | --- | --- | --- | --- | --- | --- | --- | --- | --- | --- | --- | --- |
|  | 1Q | 2Q | 3Q | 4Q | AVG | 1Q | 2Q | 3Q | 4Q | AVG | 1Q | 2Q | 3Q | 4Q | AVG |
| Indonesia | -3.6 | -4.6 | -3.7 | -1.9 | -3.4 | -4.3 | -2.1 | -2.6 | -0.4 | -2.3 | 4.8 | 3.2 | — | — | 4.0 |
| Korea | -3.6 | -4.2 | -6.0 | -5.2 | -4.7 | -6.6 | -2.5 | -1.9 | 3.6 | -1.8 | 14.2 | 14.3 | 12.4 | — | 13.6 |
| Malaysia | — | — | — | — | -4.6 | — | — | — | -4.9 | — | — | — | — | — | 7.5 |
| Philippines | -3.7 | -9.3 | -0.2 | -5.7 | -4.7 | -2.5 | -8.0 | -7.0 | -3.3 | -5.2 | -0.4 | — | — | — | -0.4 |
| Thailand | -7.3 | -10.6 | -7.8 | -5.9 | -7.9 | -5.5 | -8.1 | -1.9 | 7.5 | -2.0 | 14.2 | 9.4 | 11.5 | — | 11.7 |

Sources: JP Morgan 1999.
Bank Indonesia, Indonesian Central Bureau of Statistics.
Bank Negara Malaysia (Central Bank of Malaysia).
Bank of Korea, Korea National Statistical Office.
Bank of Thailand.
Banko Sentral ng Pilipinas (Central Bank of Philippines).

Indonesia is suffering from the worst crisis among the five East Asian countries and its economy has not been stabilized yet.

## Stabilization and the prospects for recovery

*Korea and Thailand.* After the free fall in the first half, macroeconomic indicators started to stabilize in the second half of 1998 in Korea and Thailand. Real GDP and industrial production figures improved, notably in Korea. By the end of 1998, over half of the sharp initial exchange rate depreciation had been reversed in Korea and Thailand. Compared with the level in December 1997, the stock price index in Korea increased by 49 percent. And most important, foreign investors' confidence improved and foreign private capital inflows resumed. The yield spread between a dollar-denominated Korean government bond and the U.S. Treasury bond was reduced significantly in the second half of 1998, reflecting the decline of sovereign risk. The inflation rates were also well contained and became lower than the precrisis level. High nominal interest rates, which strangled these highly leveraged countries, have since dropped drastically owing to the relaxed monetary policy. In Thailand and Korea, the interest rates in the last quarter of 1998 were significantly lower than their precrisis values. Only the performance of unemployment rates had yet to show signs of improvement, but it is understandable that employment would require a more sluggish adjustment process on the road to recovery.[7]

Despite the recent signs of stabilization in Korea and Thailand, it is still premature to conclude that recovery has developed into a trend. There is reason for concern. The improvement in the growth rates of real GDP and industrial production in the last quarter of 1998 might be only a statistical phenomenon that is attributable to a sharp recession at the beginning of the crisis. Also, the recent GDP growth was mainly due to the changes in inventory investment. Figure 3.1 shows the movement of the ratio of inventory investment to GDP during the crisis in Korea. After the crisis erupted, inventory investment fell sharply to −15 percent of GDP. The sharp decline in inventory investment was historically unprecedented in Korea and quite different from the stylized cyclical pattern observed in the literature.[8] It clearly indicates how panicky the businessmen felt because of the crisis; the decline was largely associated with fire sales and exports of existing stocks, especially raw materials. High interest rate expenses, exchange rate depreciation, and the lack of cash flows must have forced the disposal of existing stocks.

After the free fall, the inventory investment reached almost zero in the last quarter of 1998. The concurrent increase in inventory investment from −15 percent of GDP to zero (not the increase in inventory stock) was the main factor behind the sharp increase in the recent GDP growth rate. It is not certain at this stage whether inventory restocking and thereby production increase will follow in the near future. If the prospect for economic recovery is not bright, sellers might not want to rebuild inventory stocks, and production would stagnate. Even if recovery is a reality, there is a possibility that inventory restocking can be done through the increase of imports. This negative scenario is likely—considering the nature of previous fire sales and the export of raw materials. If so, the inventory stocking would have a larger negative impact on current account balances instead of having a positive effect on production.

*Indonesia.* Unlike Thailand and Korea, Indonesia showed no sign of recovery even as of the second half of 1998.[9] Political uncertainties seem to play an important role in undermining reform progress and delaying recovery in Indonesia. For example, the implementation of the IMF program was derailed by severe civil unrest, which led to the resignation of President Suharto in May 1998. However, it was the mismanagement of monetary policy that prevented recovery and brought the danger of hyperinflation in Indonesia. Facing the financial sector strain and the danger of bank runs, the Bank of Indonesia injected massive liquidity support to troubled financial institutions and made a limited effort to sterilize it. Between November 1997 and March 1998, the increase in net domestic assets of the central bank amounted to more than twice the entire stock of base money in the beginning of that period.[10] The growth rate of M2 rose to 80 percent in the second quarter of 1998, well above its growth rate in 1997, which was 25 percent. Uncontrolled monetary expansion with no progress in structural reform pushed the economy to the verge of a vicious circle of hyperinflation and currency depreciation. Indonesia's experience highlights the fact that relaxed macroeconomic

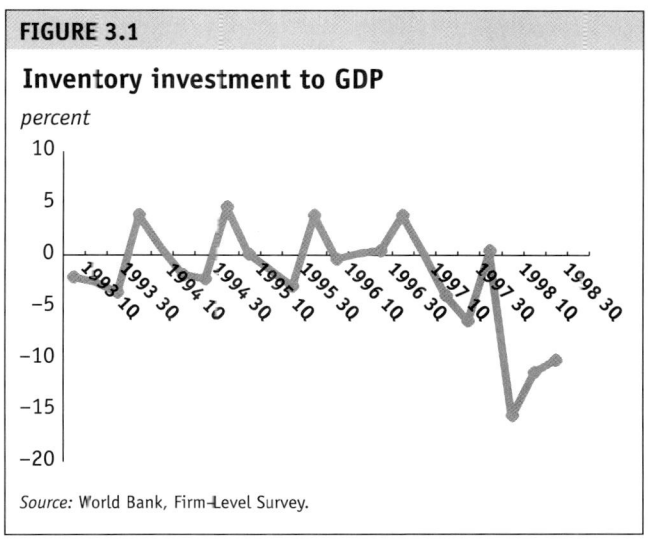

**FIGURE 3.1**

**Inventory investment to GDP**

*Source:* World Bank, Firm-Level Survey.

policies can aggravate the crisis if structural problems remain unresolved.

*Malaysia.* Until mid-1998, Malaysia's response to the crisis can be described as the "virtual IMF" policy package of austerity measures—except that the country tried to cut imports by increasing import duties and imposing other regulations.[11] In December 1997, Malaysia announced a program to slow down the economy and to raise foreign investors' confidence to cope with the regional crisis. The growth outlook was adjusted downward and the current account deficit was targeted to decrease to 3 percent of GDP. Public expenditures including mass development projects were reduced and reprioritized with significant budget cuts of 18–20 percent. Monetary policy was tightened, credit expansion was placed under control and the benchmark interest rate was raised. In sum, the same prescription of the standard IMF package was implemented in Malaysia until mid-1998 without being officially bound by IMF conditionalities.

However, the tight monetary and fiscal policies failed to stabilize the Malaysian economy in the first half of 1998. The resulting credit crunch slowed economic growth and aggravated the recession. Despite the higher adjustment of interest rates, the exchange rates were steadily depreciated and remained volatile. Frustrated with the worsening economic performance, Malaysia decided to reverse the policy direction toward expansion. In July 1998, it announced the National Economic Recovery Plan (NERP), which focused on easing monetary and fiscal policy to provide a stimulus to economic activities. In order to alleviate the credit crunch, prudential standards were relaxed even though they remained tighter than precrisis levels. In September, the government introduced capital controls on outflows of capital and fixed the exchange rates at 3.805 rupiah to the dollar. It intended to gain flexibility for easing monetary policy. Following the adoption of these measures, the interest rates were reduced to the precrisis level.

There are some recent signs that after the introduction of this expansionary policy, the economy started to stabilize in Malaysia. However, reaching judgment on this would still be premature, given the short span of time in which the new policies were introduced. The consensus on capital control seems to be that it could bring benefits in the short run, but not in the long run.

Changing the policy focus from stabilization to expansion could provide short-term relief to Malaysia. However, it should not be forgotten that resumption of foreign capital inflows is critical for bolstering the economy in the long run. Whether foreign capital will return despite the experience of capital controls is a key risk facing the country. Also, completing corporate and financial sector reforms while providing liquidity supports is a major challenge. The outcome of the capital control policy in Malaysia will be an interesting touchstone for evaluating the standard IMF policy in the future.

*The Philippines.* The Philippines were also severely damaged by the spillover effects of the Thai crisis, but it was able to at least sidestep the free fall of economic activity. Even though the real GDP growth rate dropped from 5 percent in 1997 to –0.4 percent in 1998, this reflected more the impact of the disastrous weather than of the regional crisis. Excluding the agricultural sector, the Philippine real GDP would have grown 1.1 percent, instead of –0.4 percent. The structural reform, particularly the financial sector reform, which had been steadily pursued from the early 1990s protected the Philippines from the full brunt of the regional crisis, even though its external debt–to-GDP ratio was the highest among these five countries. However, despite relatively less severe economic contractions, the prospect of recovery for the Philippines is not necessarily brighter. While the external situation has showed some improvement in the second half of 1998, it is still beset with ongoing problems such as a high budget deficit, rising inflation, and increasing poverty. The currency depreciation also increased debt-servicing costs significantly and could delay its recovery.

## Monetary and fiscal policies in the adjustment process

The severe contraction of the East Asian countries raised serious questions as to whether the initial response of the IMF packages was unnecessarily tight for these countries. The critics argue that instead of having favorable impacts on foreign investors' confidence, the stringent macroeconomic policies and the consequent high interest rates have had a negative effect on these highly leveraged countries. This section reviews the magnitude and the impact of the tightened monetary and fiscal policies in the evolution of the crisis.

## Monetary policy

Figure 3.2 shows the movement of monetary aggregates in Indonesia, Korea, Malaysia, Thailand, and the Philippines. They are the monthly stock of reserve money, M2 and domestic credit deflated by the consumer price index (CPI).[12] Several features are apparent. In Indonesia, they increased significantly in the first half of 1998, showing that the Indonesian government was losing control of the money supply in bailing

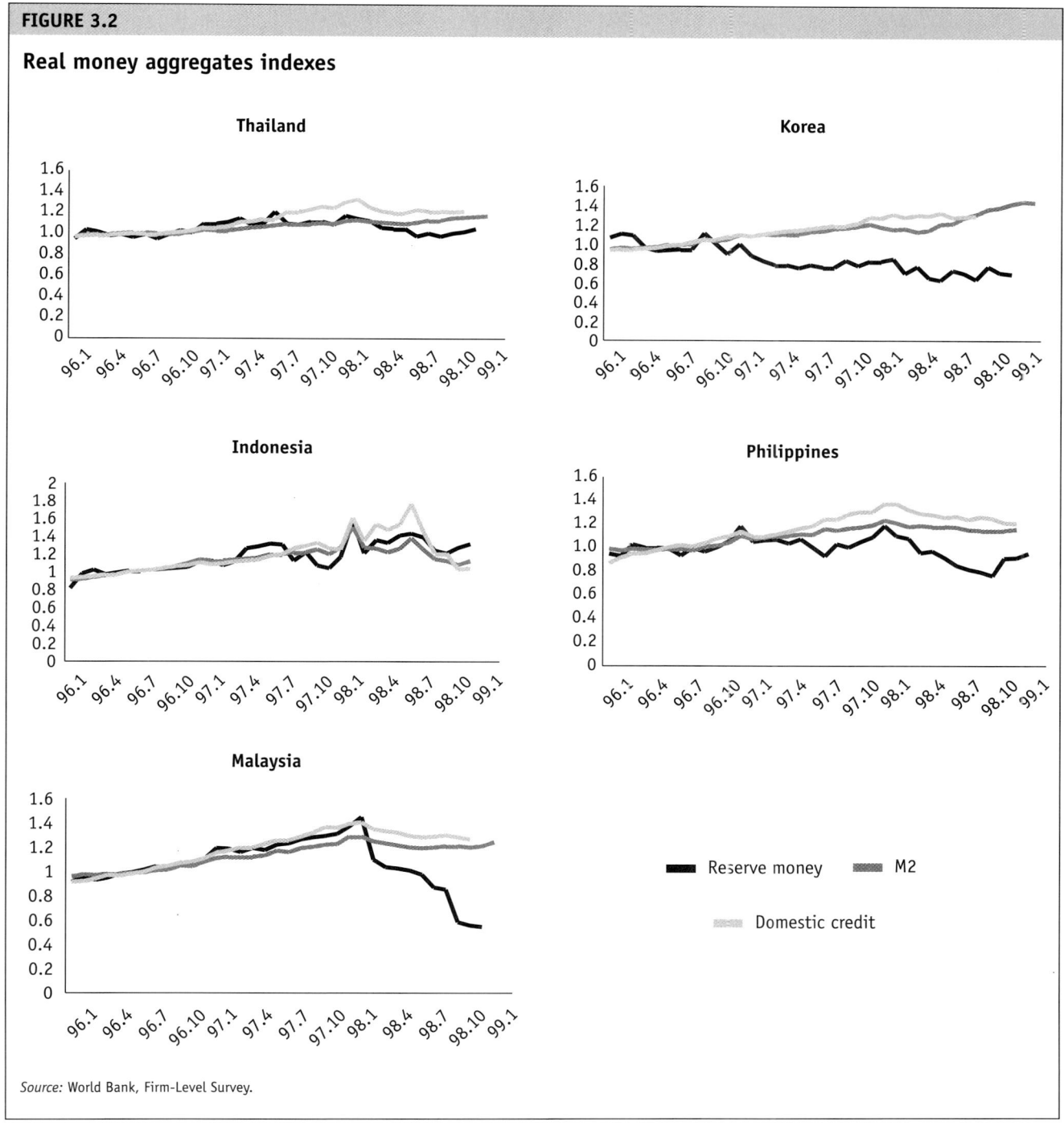

FIGURE 3.2

**Real money aggregates indexes**

*Source:* World Bank, Firm-Level Survey.

out troubled financial institutions and preventing bank runs. In contrast, real M2 and credit in Malaysia steadily decreased in 1998. Even after abandoning the "virtual IMF" policy in July 1998, there was no sign of significant monetary expansion in Malaysia until the very end of the year. It is harder to judge how tight the monetary policies in Korea, Thailand, and the Philippines are by looking at the figures. Reserve money and M2 decreased little or grew at slightly slower rates than previously in the first half of 1998. But from the second half of 1998, there was no sign of monetary contraction, particularly in Korea. In sum, real monetary aggregates and credit in Korea, Thailand, and the Philippines did not seem to be severely contracted except for the brief period at the beginning of 1998.

*Initial monetary policies were tight and caused a credit crunch.* Based on the fact that the slower growth rates of real money and credit were not dramatic, some raised doubts about the view that the tight monetary policy was the main cause of the sharp economic downturn in the East Asian countries.[13] However, quantity changes in monetary aggregates may not be fully adequate in reflecting the severity of credit tightening. Despite the decrease in supply, the equilibrium quantity of monetary aggregates may not change much if the demand for credit does not change and becomes interest-inelastic. Needless to say, the firms' investment demand fell drastically after the crisis erupted, but it was only a part of the demand. Facing increasing uncertainties, precautionary demand for credit increased to prepare for the anticipated loan recall, loss of trade credit, expected increase in interest rates and operating costs, and so on. Servicing existing debt to avoid bankruptcies also made the demand for credit highly inelastic to the changes in interest rates. As a consequence, when the monetary policy tightened, interest rates soared even though the equilibrium growth rate of credit was not drastically slowed down. Therefore, the changes in interest rate, not the quantity of monetary aggregates or credit, may be a better measure of a credit crunch for the duration of the crisis.[14]

Figure 3.3 shows the behavior of nominal and real interest rates in these five countries.[15] In Indonesia, even though nominal interest rates were increased significantly, real interest rates were consistently negative from late 1997 to mid-1998 owing to high inflation. In Korea, Malaysia, and Thailand, a high but brief surge of inflation made real interest rates low immediately after the crisis erupted. But soon after the onset of the crisis, real interest rates soared to a historical high. The increase was highest in Korea where real interest rate rose from 7.2 percent prior to the crisis to 20 percent at its peak. In Malaysia, Thailand, and the Philippines, the increase was relatively mild, from 5 to 10 percent in Malaysia, from 5 to 14 percent in Thailand, and from 5 to 10 percent in the Philippines.

Lane and others (1999) argue that these initial increases in real interest rates were not atypical compared with those seen in other crisis-hit countries. However, even though it is true that the magnitude of the increase was not exceptional, high interest rates imposed a crushing burden on real economic activity. Highly leveraged corporate structures made these economies extremely vulnerable to the increase of interest rates. Especially, business investment demand collapsed. Moreover, the interest rates in figure 3.3 underestimate the severity of the credit crunch. To truly evaluate the severity of the credit crunch, we have to measure the increase of interest rates that marginal firms are facing. Given the lack of adequate data that measure the interest rates prevailing at the secondary market, it is hard to evaluate rigorously the degree of the credit crunch in these East Asian countries. But there is ample anecdotal evidence that it was widespread. For example, as shown in figure 3.4, only the very large conglomerates with low bankruptcy probabilities were able to issue corporate bonds after the crisis erupted in Korea. The share of corporate bonds issued by the five largest conglomerates increased from 47 percent prior to the crisis to 87 percent in the first quarter of 1998.[16] There were many anecdotes showing that small and medium-size firms did not even dare to sell their bonds in the market in the first half of 1998. The interest rate differentials between the corporate bonds issued by the five largest conglomerates and by the others widened from 0.12 percent prior to the crisis to 3.5 percent in March 1998. This gap still underestimates the risk premium because of the sample selection bias, which dictated that only a few qualified medium-size corporations could sell their bonds in the market. Ding, Domac, and Ferri (1999) also document that the "flight to quality" phenomenon was widespread and had negative impacts, particularly on small banks and enterprises in the other East Asian countries.

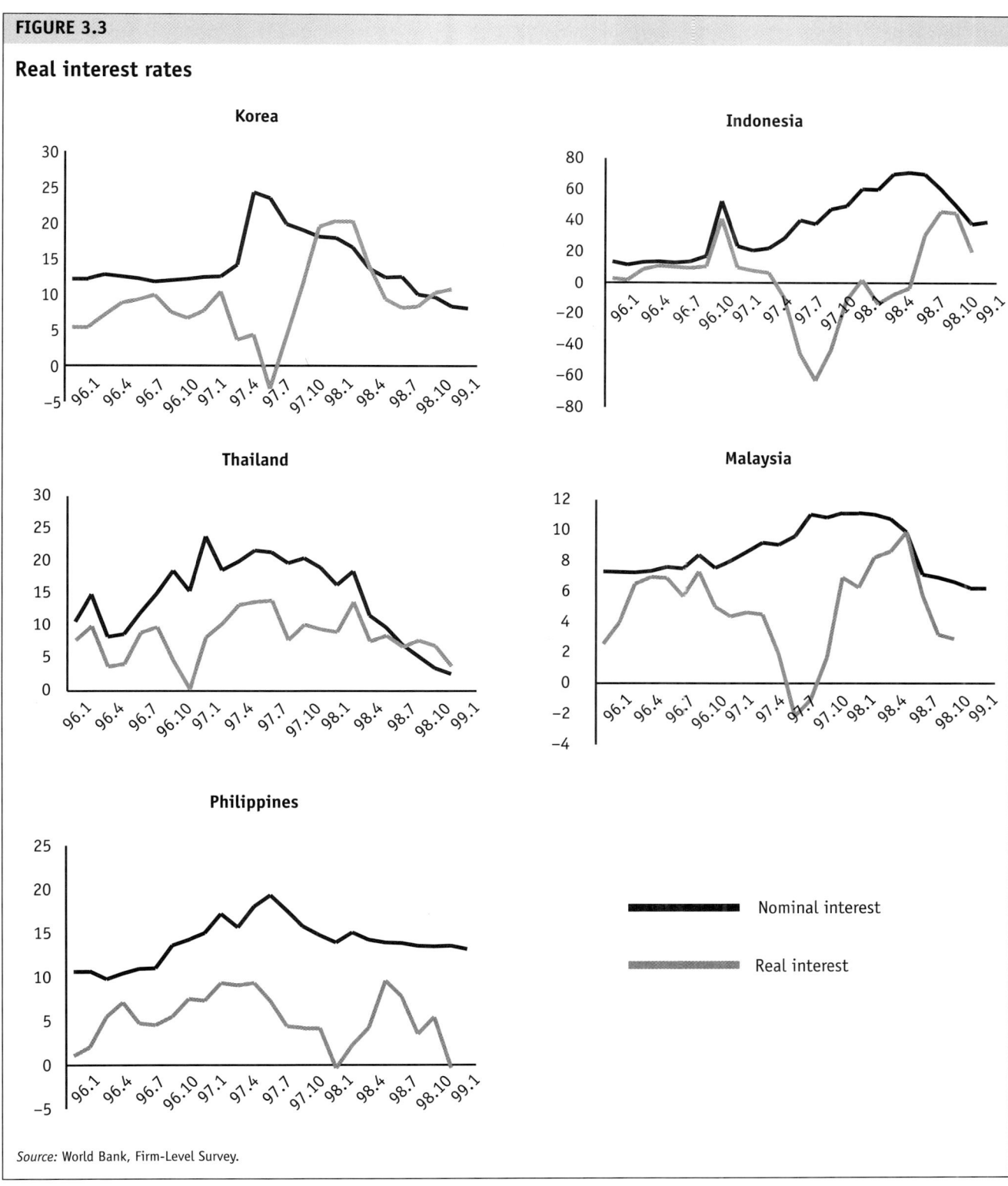

**FIGURE 3.3**

**Real interest rates**

*Source:* World Bank, Firm-Level Survey.

*Tight monetary policy alone was not able to achieve exchange rate stability.* The initial tight monetary policy ordered by the IMF was aimed at preventing the large currency depreciation from initiating depreciation-inflation spirals. In hindsight, the IMF clearly underestimated the negative effects of interest rate hikes in these highly leveraged economies. However, it is hard to deny that some period of high interest rates must

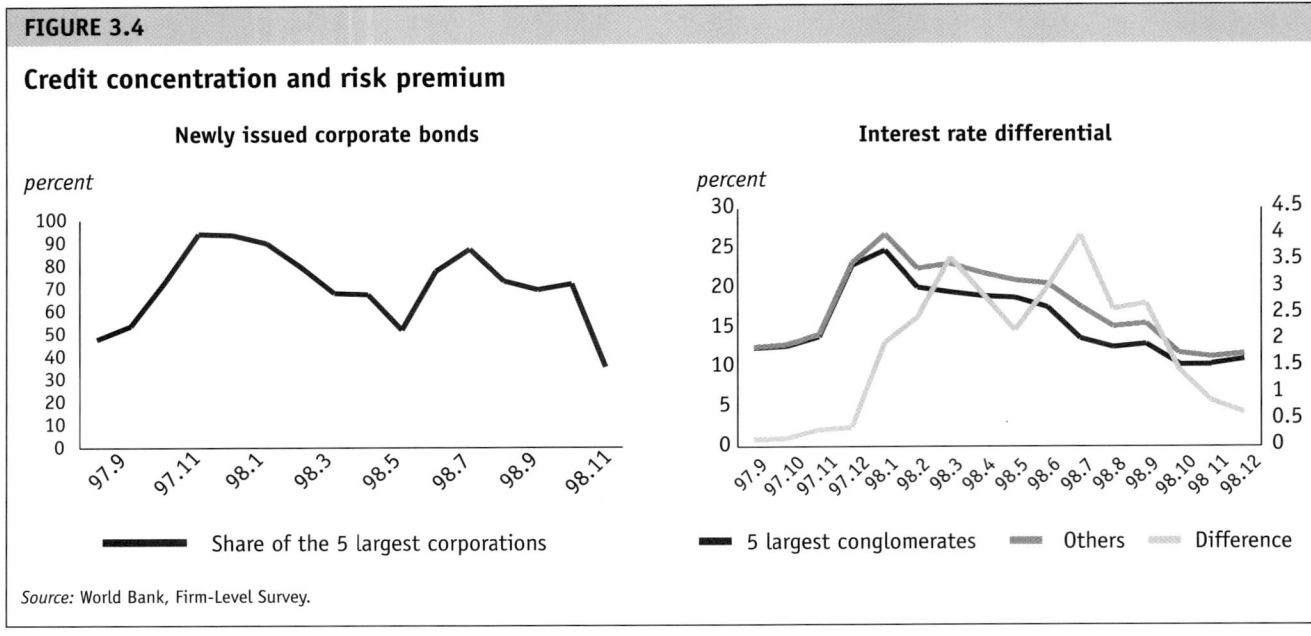

FIGURE 3.4

**Credit concentration and risk premium**

Source: World Bank, Firm-Level Survey.

have been unavoidable in order to stabilize the exchange rates. Two channels had been important in achieving this goal. First, the increase in interest rates was called for mainly to stem the outflow of capital. The high interest rate failed to restore foreign investors' confidence and bring back capital inflows in the midst of the crisis, but it was effective in preventing a sharp increase in demand for foreign currency by domestic firms and individuals. Second, the severe recession induced by the tight monetary policy was a main factor in reducing imports and rapidly improving current account balances in Korea, Malaysia, and Thailand. Without a significant current account surplus, restocking foreign reserves and restoring foreign investors' confidence would not have been possible.

The tight monetary policy, however, did not succeed in stabilizing the exchange rate market in all of the countries. In Korea and Thailand, the exchange rate market started to stabilize steadily in the second quarter of 1998, allowing room for the government to relax the monetary policy. Consequently, these countries' interest rates in the last quarter of 1998 became even lower than their precrisis levels, leading the recovery of real activities. However, the "virtual IMF" policy in Malaysia failed to stabilize the exchange rate market. After showing a brief sign of stabilization at the beginning of 1998, the riggit started to depreciate again and remained volatile until Malaysia introduced its own initiated policy in July 1998. As figure 3.3 shows, the real interest rate started to fall only after the government started to regulate interest rates and introduced capital controls.

The Malaysian case shows that tight policy alone is not sufficient to restore exchange rate market stability. Stemming capital outflows and building foreign reserves by belt-tightening is not enough to reduce the panic. Resumption of capital inflows, especially private capital inflows, seems to be the key factor. Korea and Thailand benefited from official program loans by the IMF and other international financial institutions immediately after the crisis erupted. The Korean government also succeeded in rolling over the short-term external debt of the banking sector in March 1998. Thanks to the private debt rescheduling, the proportion of short-term debt in Korea decreased from 60 percent to 21 percent and significantly alleviated liquidity problems. In contrast, a "virtual IMF" package implemented by Malaysia did not benefit from official program loans. The country's political instability and the restrictive government policy in capital flow probably deterred the resumption of private capital inflows. The lack of capital inflows implies that

Malaysia had to achieve a more drastic current account adjustment and face a deeper contraction even though its precrisis economic environment was better than that of Korea and Thailand.

*Relaxed monetary policy proved effective only when accompanied by structural reforms.* The relaxed monetary and fiscal stance since the second half of 1998 contributed to the rapid decline of interest rates and the recovery in Korea and Thailand, where corporate and financial reforms have been progressing significantly. However, it should be emphasized that expansionary macroeconomic policy alone cannot have a large impact if structural problems remain unsolved. In Indonesia, uncontrolled monetary expansion not only delayed recovery but also brought the country to the verge of hyperinflation. By contrast, the rapid decline of interest rates and fast recovery in Korea was the result of the progress in the country's structural reform as well as the expansionary monetary policy. The reform progress reduced sovereign risk premium and inflation expectation by offsetting the initial worries that the government would monetize bailing-out costs for troubled financial institutions. As little as the origin of the East Asian crisis has to do with macroeconomic imbalances, it is understandable that macroeconomic policy alone cannot solve its problems. Eventually the recovery must depend on the structural reform that addresses the roots of the problems that caused the crisis in the first place.

## Fiscal policy

In the same fashion as monetary policy, tight fiscal policy was initially tried in the East Asian countries after the crisis erupted. The initial tight fiscal policy was introduced to improve current account balance by increasing government savings, and to alleviate the need to squeeze private savings excessively. It also aimed at securing noninflationary funds for financial restructuring. But starting in early 1998, the severity of the economic downturn made it necessary to expand the fiscal stance. As the effectiveness of the monetary policy was constrained by the credit crunch, the fiscal policy had to play a greater role. As a result, budget deficits increased in these East Asian countries in 1998. Prior to the crisis, government budgets were in balance or in surplus in these countries. But in 1998, budget deficits in Indonesia, Korea, Malaysia and Thailand amounted to about –7, –5, –1, and –4.5 percent of GDP.

However, so far the fiscal expansion has not been as effective as the increased budget deficit figures suggest. Instead of being a discretionary change, they were mostly induced by the fall of tax revenues owing to the severe economic downturn and sharp exchange rate depreciation. In fact, even though budget deficits were widened, instead of increasing, the government consumption expenditures decreased by 9 percent in Korea in 1998. Also, among government expenditures, the proportion of transfer payments increased owing to the increase in demand for social expenditures. As long as transfer payments have a smaller multiplier effect than government purchases of goods and services, the expansionary effect of the increased budget deficits must be limited.

Irrespective of their effectiveness in boosting the economy, budget deficits in these Asian countries are likely to grow in the near future. The unemployment problem will not be resolved any time soon and the demand for social expenditures will rise. More important, the governments' support is essential in financial restructuring. Considering the upcoming need for more government expenditures, it is fortunate that the East Asian countries had maintained nearly balanced budgets prior to the crisis. It made it possible for these countries to allow temporal budget deficits in the future without incurring negative side effects.

## Assessment of the adjustment process

Many factors contributed to the sharp fall of economic activities in these countries. Among them, our previous discussion highlighted the three most important factors: (a) drastic reversal of capital flows, (b) tight monetary policy, and (c) uncertainty caused by financial restructuring. It is hard to deny that some period of tight macroeconomic policy was unavoidable to prevent depreciation-inflation spirals and eventually the recovery should depend on the progress of financial reform. However, in the short run, these three factors exacerbated the degree of the credit crunch and their contractional impacts were greater than anyone, including the IMF, had imagined. Only at the end of 1998 did signs of recovery became visible in the region, particularly in

Korea and Thailand. In this section, we review some forces behind the recent recovery.

## High market sensitivity of the open and private sector economies

The quick response to stabilization as well as expansionary policies was possible since the East Asian countries were more open and private sector–oriented. The crisis in East Asia was caused by private sector overinvestment, not by public sector overexpenditure, and the adjustment of the private sector under the changed macroeconomic circumstances tends to be much quicker than that of the public sector. Also, the recession in the domestic market could generate a larger improvement in current account balances since these economies were more open and export-oriented.

Table 3.5 shows the degree of difference in the openness and private sector orientation between East Asian and Latin American economies. Mexico is a good example. In the 1982 crisis, Mexico was less open and more public–sector dominated. After the crisis, its current account balance improved owing to severe recession but the change was not as fast as those of the East Asian cases. The current account balance was –7.9 percent of GDP in 1981, –3.8 percent in 1982, and 4.3 percent in 1983.[17] By contrast, in 1994 Mexico had a smaller budget deficit and became more open after the North American Free Trade Agreement (NAFTA) was passed. In the 1994 crisis, the real GDP growth fell from 4.5 percent in 1994 to –6.2 percent in 1995 and the current account deficit improved sharply within a year from –11 percent to –0.6 percent of GDP. This fast response happened because the economy became more open and private–sector oriented. Unless the economy is led by the private sector and export-oriented, we believe that such a dramatic improvement in the current account positions as experienced in Korea and Thailand in 1998 would be virtually impossible.

## Favorable development of the external environment

The favorable turn in the external environment also helped bring about a quick recovery of these economies. The appreciation of the Japanese yen with three consecutive cuts in U.S. interest rates starting in mid-1998 allowed Korea and Thailand to cut domestic interest rates substantially without destabilizing their exchange rates. The Japanese yen appreciation also reduced the possibility of the Chinese yuan's devaluation and indirectly contributed to the stabilization of the exchange market in Korea and Thailand.

## Policy implications and concluding remarks

In our review of the adjustment processes of the five East Asian countries since the currency crisis erupted in Thailand in 1997 we observe that after covering enormous economic and social costs, the real wages have been substantially reduced, interest rates have dropped below the precrisis level, currency overvaluation has been corrected—perhaps somewhat excessively—and

### TABLE 3.5
**Openness and private sector orientation in selected countries**
(percent)

| Indonesia | Korea | Malaysia | Philippines | Thailand | Mexico | | Brazil | | Argentina | | Chile | |
|---|---|---|---|---|---|---|---|---|---|---|---|---|
| 1996 | 1996 | 1996 | 1996 | 1996 | 1982 | 1995 | 1982 | 1995 | 1982 | 1995 | 1982 | 1995 |
| 40.8 | 57.8 | 158.0 | 65.8 | 69.1 | 21.3 | 32.7 | 13.8 | 14.2 | 16.9 | 14.7 | 30.0 | 49.0 |

*Note:* (Export + Import)/GDP

| Indonesia | Korea | Malaysia | Philippines | Thailand | Mexico | | Brazil | | Argentina | | Chile | |
|---|---|---|---|---|---|---|---|---|---|---|---|---|
| 1996 | 1996 | 1996 | 1996 | 1996 | 1982 | 1995 | 1982 | 1995 | 1982 | 1995 | 1982 | 1995 |
| 14.6 | 18.3 | 22.6 | 18.5 | 16.1 | 30.0 | 16.1 | 9.1 | 14.0 | 20.3 | 14.5 | 36.0 | 19.9 |

*Note:* Government Expenditure/GDP
*Source:* IMF, International Financial Statistics.

rental costs have plummeted in these countries. This development now provides a much more favorable business environment in these economies that had been suffering for a while from the weakening competitiveness of their exports and structural inefficiencies owing to the rigidity in the labor and financial markets.

Nevertheless, there still remain formidable constraints to recovery. Among other things, the list includes continuing low aggregate demand in both domestic and foreign markets; a persistent credit crunch that is attributable to the unresolved financial instability; weakness in the corporate financial structure and overcapacity; and lack of foreign capital inflow. In connection with these constraints, the following policy implications may follow from the review and the comparison of the adjustment experiences of these economies so far.

First, accommodative macroeconomic policies will be needed for a while to prevent further contraction in domestic demand and weakening of the corporate financial structure. This is also important in preventing asset deflation, which would have a significant adverse impact on the corporate and financial restructuring process. Since the corporate sector of these economies, particularly in Korea and Thailand, is highly leveraged, a tight monetary policy would accelerate corporate bankruptcies and asset deflation. This would then impose a heavier burden in resolving financial instability.

However, striking the right balance between the accommodative macroeconomic policies and driving timely financial and corporate sector reforms will be an important challenge to these economies. In practice, the accommodative macroeconomic policies can give signals to corporate firms to be complacent and hang on to their overcapacity. The experience of Indonesia has made it clear that the expansionary monetary policy without necessary financial and corporate sector reforms is ineffective in bringing recovery—and it causes hyperinflation. Through the experience of the Philippines, we can glimpse the importance of the quality and sustainability of recovery. What shielded the Philippines from the full brunt of the regional crisis was its structural reform, particularly the financial sector reform, which had been steadily pursued starting in the early 1990s. Because the root cause for the financial instability in this region was the structural weaknesses of the corporate and financial sector, full recovery of these economies will be realized only after these problems have been properly resolved.

Second, resumption of capital inflow will be a key factor for the fast recovery of these economies. Malaysia adopted a less tight monetary policy than Korea did in the first half of 1998, but its economic contraction was at least as severe as Korea's and its exchange market remained more unstable. If Malaysia had been able to receive external financial assistance organized by the IMF or another institution, it could have avoided such a severe economic contraction. Judging from this experience, the right mix for the economies in this region may have been a less strict stabilization policy package and a larger amount of financial assistance that was heavily front-loaded. Since it would be hard to expect a quick resumption of the private capital inflow to a crisis-hit country, there is an urgent need to expand the available financial resources through multilateral and regional financial institutions.

In this regard, it is encouraging to see recent discussions on the expansion and establishment of emergency financing facilities such as the contingent financing facility under the IMF and the enhancement of its role as an effective lender of last resort in the international capital market (see Fischer (1999), and McKinnon (1998)). Discussions on the establishment of regional financing facilities are also an encouraging step toward this end. However, it is equally important in these discussions to include schemes for involving greater participation of the private sector so as to facilitate the orderly workout of debt rescheduling, a fairer sharing of losses, and quicker resumption of private capital inflows.

Third, more serious and comprehensive efforts are necessary to encourage the development of the capital markets in these economies. One of the key factors in achieving successful corporate restructuring—which will facilitate full economic recovery, particularly in Korea and Thailand—is to reduce the corporate leverage ratio. Substantial inflow of foreign capital, particularly foreign direct investment, will be necessary to this end, especially when the prospect of the new domestic funding is poor as it is now.

However, given the huge size of the overall debt of the corporate firms in these economies, this ultimately will have to be achieved by a substantial conversion of debt to equity, and the change of domestic financial market structure to support this conversion. Corporate financial structure mirrors the structure of the financial market and patterns of financial savings of households in an economy. Improvement in corporate financial structure could hardly be expected unless there is concomitant change in the domestic financial market structure. Therefore, serious efforts have to be made to expand the equity market in these economies by encouraging collective investment vehicles, including mutual funds and investment and trust businesses. Further stabilization of domestic interest rates will play a crucial role for this purpose.

Finally, we may draw some lessons for reference in future currency crises. The experience of the East Asian economic adjustment suggests that policy packages to be imposed on the crisis-hit countries will need to be better tuned to individual market circumstances. In economies such as Korea and Thailand, which are quite open, private–sector oriented, and have a very high leverage ratio in the corporate sector, the sensitivity to a stabilization package could be higher than in other economies.

The main purpose of the stabilization policy in the economies facing currency crisis is belt-tightening and strengthening the foreign debt service capacity. But in these economies, the stabilization policies may far overshoot their original goals. Sharply increased interest rates and depreciated exchange rates in the initial stage have enormous balance sheet effects on highly leveraged economies and lead to drastic declines in domestic investment and employment. Furthermore, the stabilization policy package that is implemented in conjunction with the tight schedule of bank restructuring can accelerate the credit crunch and systemic corporate bankruptcies. This tight monetary policy is inevitable in order to be able to prevent further deterioration of foreign exchange market stability in the earlier stage of the currency crisis. But here again, the maintenance of a careful balance between the conflicting goals of stabilizing the exchange rates and preventing massive bankruptcies and rapid aggravation of financial instability is essential to avoid severe economic contraction and resulting social problems.

## Notes

Yoon Je Cho is with the Graduate School of International Studies at Sogang University in Seoul, Korea, and Changyong Rhee with the faculty of Economics at Seoul National University, Korea. The authors are grateful to Dominique Dwor-Frécaut, Mary Hallward-Driemeier, the participants of the conference for their valuable comments, and Chung-Chul Chung, Han Kyu Lee, Sam Ho Lee, and Sun Hyeong Lee for excellent research assistance. Any errors in the text, however, remain the responsibility of the authors.

1. Mexico is a good example. In the 1980s, when Mexico had a large government budget deficit, the stabilization policy was not very effective in curtailing current account deficits. In 1994, when Mexico had a smaller budget deficit and became more open after the North American Free Trade Agreement (NAFTA) was passed, the stabilization policy brought sharp swings in the current account balance.

2. The structural weaknesses were of a different nature as well. In Korea, the poor governance of corporate and financial sectors was the main cause of the country's structural weakness. In Thailand, the liberalization of the financial system and the external capital accounts without an adequate regulatory and supervisory system played a more significant role.

3. The Bank for International Settlements (BIS) (1997) official estimates for actual nonperforming loans in Malaysia in 1996 was 3.9 percent of total loans, which was significantly lower than those of Thailand (7.7 percent) and Indonesia (8.8 percent). But it was higher than those of Korea (0.8 percent). The other estimates show that the ratios were not significantly lower in Malaysia than in the other crisis-hit countries in 1997 and 1998. See table 5 in Goldstein (1998).

4. The financial capital flows in table 2 are not totally private. They include portfolio investment and direct investment by the governments.

5. The Thailand figure is the most recent estimate of the IMF, and is different from the number in table 4, which does not cover the last quarter of 1998.

6. It is true that the export volume increased significantly after the initial depreciation of the Korean won. But its growth slowed down quickly thereafter. Moreover, there was no improvement of exports in dollar-denominated terms.

7. See Lee and Rhee (1998) for the stylized pattern of employment growth in previous IMF program countries and its policy implications.

8. When an unanticipated demand shock occurs, production usually follows final demand with a lag, implying that inventory stocks rise in the short run. See Bernanke and Gertler (1995), Christiano, Eichenbaum, and Evans (1994), and Sims (1992).

9. Only very recently did the Indonesian crisis start to show signs of abating.

10. In December 1997, the Bank of Korea also injected massive liquidity support (more than one-third of reserve money) in preventing the collapse of the banking system. However, in contrast to Indonesia, the Bank of Korea sterilized the injection.

11. See Yusof (1998) for a detailed explanation of the shift in Malaysian economic policy from mid-1997 to the end of 1998.

12. For comparison, the graph shows the indexes whose average value in 1996 is equal to 100.

13. Lane and others (1999) pointed out that the degree of monetary tightening in the East Asian countries was not as draconian as in the cases of other countries facing an exchange rate crisis. For example, the growth rate of real money in Mexico declined by almost 26 percent in 1995. Dollar and Hallward-Driemeier (1998) also provide microeconomic evidence that shows only weak support of a credit

crunch story. Using the survey results of 1200 manufacturing firms in Thailand, they concluded that the fall in demand, not the restricted access to credit, was the main constraining factor in slowing down the Thailand economy.

14. The fact that the issuing of corporate bonds increased while domestic credit by the banking sector decreased in Korea can be indirect evidence that the supply of credit, not the demand for credit, is a constraining factor. Also, monetary and credit aggregates do not indicate how credit is allocated within the economy, which is a main theme of this conference.

15. Real interest rates are constructed by subtracting a three-month moving average of monthly CPI inflation rates (previous month, current month, and one month ahead) from nominal interest rates.

16. To prevent the concentration of the funds in the five largest conglomerates, the government started to regulate the maximum amount of corporate bonds issued by the five largest conglomerates that financial institutions could hold, starting with October 1998. Therefore, the figures after October should be interpreted with care.

17. The country's real GDP growth rate was 8.5 percent in 1981 but it dropped to −0.6 percent in 1982 and −3.5 percent in 1983.

## chapter four

# The New Miyazawa Initiative and Response to the Corporate Debt Problem

*Kiyoto Ido*

The currency and financial crisis that started in Thailand in July 1997 had a major impact not only there and in neighboring Asian countries, but on the global economy as a whole. Various causes for this crisis have been identified, such as a rigid exchange rate system, short-term capital flows as typified by hedge funds, and fragility in the private financial sector—and included with them is also the lack of corporate governance. Soon it will be two years since the currency crisis erupted, and we are now seeing some hopeful signs in the economies involved in the crisis. However, it would be difficult to claim that adequate progress has necessarily taken place with regard to the corporate debt problem.

Given this situation, it is very good timing, indeed, that the present conference sponsored by the World Bank offers us an opportunity to discuss issues of corporate governance.

In what follows, I would like to address how the problem of corporate debt should be dealt with and what the New Miyazawa Initiative currently being implemented by the Japanese government can do to assist with this problem.

## Basic perspectives

As indicated in table 4.1 and figure 4.1, even among countries that experienced the same currency crisis, corporate debt problems differ by country in, among other things, their scale (relative to GDP and total external debt) and in the composition of indebted corporations (domestic financial institutions, foreign financial institutions, nonfinancial institutions, and so on). Therefore, specific

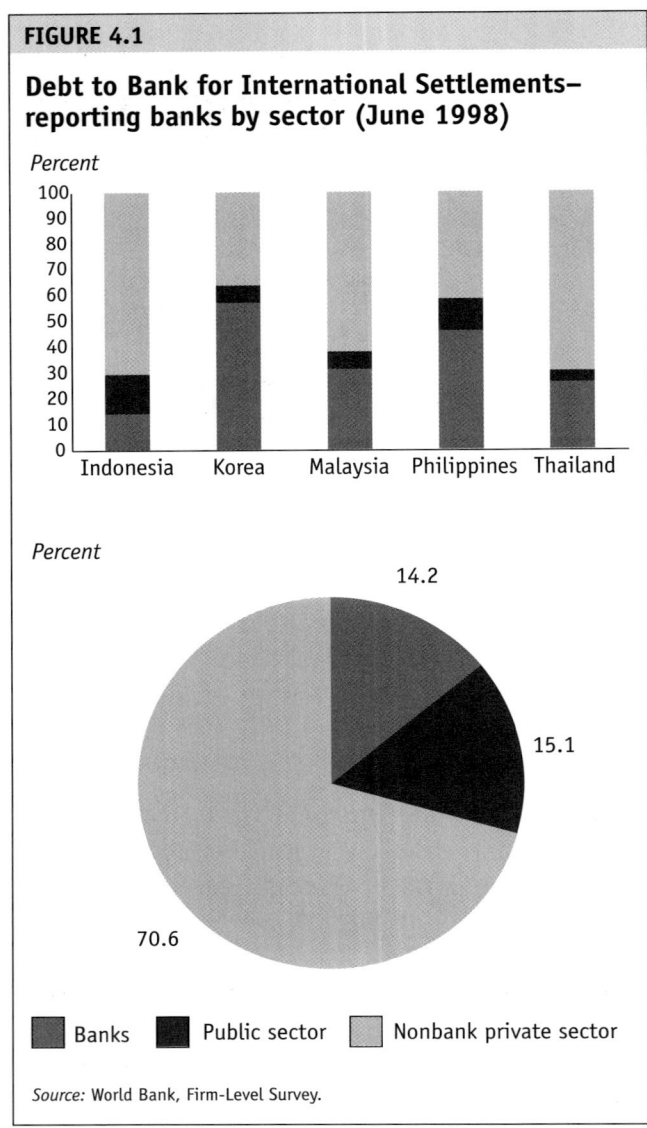

**FIGURE 4.1**

**Debt to Bank for International Settlements–reporting banks by sector (June 1998)**

Banks ■ Public sector ■ Nonbank private sector ▨

Source: World Bank, Firm-Level Survey.

measures applicable to actual situations must be taken in each country.

Most cases have one thing in common, however: the handling of corporate indebtedness is closely tied to the problem of bad debt among domestic financial institutions. Early resolution of corporate indebtedness is essential for the recovery of function in the financial system, and it is necessary to tackle the corporate debt problem at the same time as the problem of nonperforming loans in the financial sector.

At the same time, ensuring that the debtor corporations themselves engage in proper activity is also of the greatest importance for macroeconomic recovery. To that end, it is not enough to just reduce their burden of debt. The underlying premise of the solution is corporate restructuring and the question we must bear in mind is how to ensure an appropriate capital flow to these corporations. In this sense, we must not only work to restore sound management in the financial institutions I mentioned, but we must grapple with the development of capital markets in the medium and long run.

## Issues for the promotion of debt restructuring

To achieve a resolution of corporate indebtedness along these lines, we will be required to tackle the problem from a number of different angles. With respect to the restructuring of corporate debt currently underway in each country, a variety of bottlenecks have been identified. Here, I would like to point out some items that must be considered in connection with the promotion of debt restructuring.

### Establishing relationships of mutual trust between debtors and creditors

In order to move negotiations toward a successful conclusion, it is vital for the parties involved to establish relationships of mutual trust. To that end, it is necessary that they share information, and it is essential that there be a greater degree of transparency and disclosure on the part of the indebted corporations as a group, including the activities, assets, and liabilities of overseas corporations. I would also like to add that when people responsible for decision-making at indebted corporations take part in discussions, it is important for them to respond to their creditors with responsibility and good faith.

### Improvement of the legal environment

Inadequacies in the basic legal framework relating to the execution of obligations, such as bankruptcy laws and accounting systems, have delayed resolution of the problem of corporate indebtedness. The provision of a legal environment and the creation of an atmosphere that will facilitate the progress of negotiations on restructuring are important tasks.

On this point, we welcome Thailand's efforts to amend its bankruptcy laws (which have passed its upper house) and other progress in developing a legal system. It is important for the future not only to enact and amend laws and ordinances, but also to reinforce capacity building as necessary among those who are in charge of conducting business, and in such ways that would establish effective operation of the system.

## Clear setting of the framework for negotiation

For solving the debt problem, initiation of bankruptcy proceedings should be the last recourse. Prior to that, negotiation should be sought between creditors and debtors on the basic premise that indebted corporations should be preserved. From this perspective, the kind of comprehensive framework for promoting negotiations on indebtedness that we find in the Bangkok Initiative and Jakarta Initiative are of great importance. It is essential on these occasions to make clear to the parties involved the procedures for implementation and authority of reform, and to make it possible for both creditors and debtors to participate in the scheme without apprehension. Negotiation is a matter that principally involves the creditors and debtors, but the government of the countries concerned must also provide the leadership needed to bring both sides together on a level playing field.

Moreover, the substance of restructuring should not rely on such methods as uniform debt reduction to enlist the support of debtors. Rather it should present a flexible menu of voluntary options that reflect the specific needs of different situations. It is important in these cases that the schemes make it easier for debtor corporations to continue obtaining domestic and international capital for their continuing survival.

## Provision of working capital

When corporations are making proper efforts to revive themselves and are carrying on a restructuring of debt as described above, it is important to serve an environment in which appropriate working capital can be extended to corporations. In this respect, multilateral agency assistance and bilateral support can be effective as well. As I will explain next, Japan is also implementing assistance through the New Miyazawa Initiative to provide capital to manufacturing industries.

## Approaches to the corporate debt problem under the Miyazawa Initiative

As corporate indebtedness is a problem that occurs in private enterprise relationships, it should basically be settled within the private sector. However, it should also be noted that when the governments of Asian countries affected by the currency crisis are making comprehensive efforts to deal with the problems of corporate debt

TABLE 4.1
**External debt of four Asian countries**
(billions of U.S. dollars)

|  | Thailand | | Indonesia | | Malaysia[b] | | Korea, Rep. of | |
| --- | --- | --- | --- | --- | --- | --- | --- | --- |
|  | Dec. 1997 | Dec. 1998 | Dec. 1997 | Mar. 1998 | Dec. 1997 | Sept. 1998 | Dec. 1997 | Dec. 1998 |
| External debt | 93.4 | 86.2 | 137.4 | 138.0 | 43.6 | 39.6 | 158.1 | 149.4 |
| Short-term debt | 34.8 | 23.5 | n.a. | n.a. | 11.2 | 7.0 | 63.2 | 30.8 |
| Private sector debt | 69.1 | 54.7 | 74.0 | 72.5 | 26.8 | 22.9 | 135.8 | 112.9 |
| Corporate debt | 29.5 | 25.7 | 58.8 | 64.5 | 18.4 | 18.3 | 46.2 | 41.0 |
| *External debt per GDP (percent)[a]* | | | | | | | | |
| External debt | 60.7 | 56.0 | 63.9 | 64.2 | 44.5 | 40.4 | 35.7 | 33.8 |
| Short-term debt | 37.3 | 27.2 | n.a. | n.a. | 25.7 | 17.7 | 40.0 | 20.6 |
| Private sector debt | 74.0 | 63.4 | 53.8 | 52.5 | 61.4 | 57.8 | 85.9 | 75.6 |
| Corporate debt | 31.6 | 29.8 | 42.8 | 46.7 | 42.2 | 46.2 | 29.2 | 27.4 |

a. Per nominal GDP in 1997.
b. Corporate debt for Malaysia is figured by subtracting short-term banking sector debt from private sector debt.
*Sources:* Official data by each individual country.

and the financial sector, considerable amounts of resources will be required.

As you are aware, in October 1998, Japan announced a New Initiative to Overcome the Asian Currency Crisis ("the New Miyazawa Initiative"), to solve the economic difficulties of Asian countries affected by the recent crisis and to stabilize international financial markets. Specific support measures have been decided for the five countries, and we are working steadily to implement those measures.

The object of this scheme is to help fulfil the financial needs of the following measures for recovery of the crisis-hit countries' real economies:
- Providing support for corporate debt restructuring in the private sector and measures to make financial systems sound and stable;
- Strengthening the social safety net;
- Stimulating the economy (promoting public works to increase employment); and
- Taking measures to address the credit crunch (facilitating trade finance and assisting small and medium-sized enterprises).

To deal with the problem of corporate debt and credit crunch that are linked with each other, the following support measures have been declared under the New Miyazawa Initiative.
- *Thailand*. To sustain the reform of the financial and industrial sectors and strengthen the competitive fundamentals of the economy, Japan is providing the yen equivalent to US$600 million for economic and financial adjustment in cofinancing with the World Bank's Economic and Financial Adjustment II (EFAL II) program. In addition, the Export-Import Bank of Japan (JEXIM) is providing the yen equivalent of US$50 million in untied two-step loans to the Industrial Finance Corporation of Thailand and the Krung Thai Bank to make capital available in the manufacturing sector for investment in plant and working capital.
- *Malaysia*. A yen loan in the amount of approximately Y16.3 billion is being provided to the Fund for Small and Medium Scale Industries to make capital available to small and medium-sized enterprises for investment in plant and working capital.
- *The Philippines*. A loan cofinanced with the World Bank will provide the yen equivalent of US$300 million for a banking system reform project intended to take a further step in structural reinforcement of the banking sector and avert worsening of the domestic credit shortage. In addition, JEXIM is providing the equivalent of US$500 million in untied two-step loans to the Development Bank of the Philippines to make capital available for investment in plant and working capital in the private sector.
- *Republic of Korea*. JEXIM is providing the yen equivalent of US$1.3 billion in untied two-step loans to the Industrial Bank of Korea to make capital available to small and medium-sized enterprises for investment in plant and working capital.

Japan has been supporting these countries' efforts to overcome the problem of nonperforming assets by continuing to give careful scrutiny of their capital needs. Moreover, as we work for close cooperation among the countries and multilateral agencies involved, we are studying such policies as the following.

First, in order to facilitate fundraising by the Asian countries in international financial markets, JEXIM will guarantee sovereign bonds issued by these countries. Guarantees from JEXIM will make it possible for them to issue bonds at higher ratings and lower cost, and so promote the smoother acquisition of capital. It will be necessary to amend the law before JEXIM can guarantee bond issues, and such a revised law is now being presented to the legislature. It is hoped that in the long run this scheme will lead to the establishment of a new international guarantee institution focused on the Asian countries.

Second, in order to provide guarantees and interest subsidies, Japan will establish and fund an Asian Currency Crisis Support Facility. This facility will guarantee loans to Indonesia, Malaysia, the Philippines, Thailand, and other countries affected by the currency crisis provided through cofinancing by the Asian Development Bank (ADB) and private financial institutions, as well as bonds issued by countries receiving ADB support. The facility will also provide capital for bond guarantees and interest subsidies to reduce the burden of repayment for countries that receive loans cofinanced by ADB and JEXIM or private financial institutions. It is our intention in Japan to make this Support Facility into an open framework that is also accessible to other Asian countries not affected by the recent currency crisis, and we hope to see more countries participate.

## The Asian Growth and Recovery Initiative (AGRI)

The Asian Currency Crisis Support Facility is to be utilized in part for the Asian Growth and Recovery Initiative (AGRI). Japan, the United States, the World Bank, and the ADB are the core members of the initiative, and the AGRI aims to help facilitate Asian countries' efforts to finance restructuring of financial institutions and the corporate sector. This was announced jointly by Prime Minister Obuchi and President Clinton on the occasion of the Asia-Pacific Economic Cooperation (APEC) Summit on November 16, 1998.

This initiative has four major components: the Asian Growth and Recovery Program (AGRP) that assists the financing of Asian countries to promote restructuring of financial institutions and private sector corporations; expansion of trade finance; mobilization of private sector capital; and enhancement of technical assistance.

The AGRP component aims to mobilize $5 billion through guarantees, loans, and bond purchases. A part of the Asian Currency Crisis Support Facility will be utilized for this program.

To promote implementation of this initiative, Japan, the United States, the World Bank, and ADB, as well as potential donor and beneficiary countries, and Germany, which is chairing the Asia-Europe Meeting, have been invited to participate in a meeting in Singapore on April 12, 1999. At this meeting, the current status of restructuring efforts will be presented by Thailand, Korea, and Indonesia; and the overview of AGRP and multilateral development banks' (MDBs') policies concerning guarantees and related matters will be explained by the World Bank and ADB.

## Transparency in markets and stockholder-oriented corporate governance

Up to this point, I have spoken about issues of corporate debt restructuring in Asian countries, and Japan's support in that regard. In providing this support, however, we also seek efforts on the part of recipient countries to establish transparency in their markets and shareholder-oriented corporate governance.

## Transparency in markets

In several crisis-hit Asian countries, collusive relationships between corporations and financial institutions have produced a fundamental lack of transparency. Consequently, the financial institutions failed to conduct adequate reviews, and this resulted in loans and unplanned capital investment by corporations, which in turn brought about the accumulation of nonperforming loans and excessive debt. When accurate information on a corporation's activities and financial situation are made available in a timely fashion within an environment that provides sufficient transparency, internal and external checking mechanisms can function properly and this enables firms to avoid problems such as experienced currently.

## Establishing stockholder-oriented corporate governance

As another matter related to the question of transparency, the clarification of stockholders' rights and the protection of those rights will enable stockholders to function as a restraining influence on top management. This is also important in terms of fostering sound corporate management.

## Conclusion

The corporate debt problem, which was brought to light by the Asian crisis, is in some respects rooted in business practices that could be characterized as "Asian," and reform and improvement of this deep-rooted issue will require considerable time and cost. However, the goal is to have the Asian countries achieve sustainable growth for the coming twenty-first century, and not to fall behind other emerging economies. In order to accomplish this goal, we must take this opportunity to work out methods for dealing with corporate debt and establishing proper corporate governance. Corporate governance, in particular, is an issue that Japan also must address. In this regard, too, the Japanese government recognizes that the Asian countries must reinforce their cooperative framework further.

## Note

Kyoto Ido is a Deputy Director General with the International Bureau, Ministry of Finance, Japan.

## chapter five

# Asian Corporate Credit Needs and Governance

*Dominique Dwor-Frécaut*
*Mary Hallward-Driemeier*
*Francis X. Colaço*

The nature of corporate finance and its governance has been considered to be at the core of the major economic downturns in all five East Asian "crisis" countries—Indonesia, the Republic of Korea, Malaysia, the Philippines, and Thailand. It has been argued by some that the structure of corporate finance, in particular high exposure to short-term debt (principally loans from banks) and high debt-equity ratios (or leveraging), has made it extremely difficult for East Asian corporates to manage the turbulence in financial and currency markets of recent years.[1] Also, the slow pace of corporate recovery in these countries has been attributed primarily to a continuing lack of credit for financially and economically viable projects and firms, at prevailing interest rates. These hypotheses can now be examined directly with firm-level data that have recently become available.

The five "crisis" countries surveyed a total of 3,700 manufacturing firms between November 1998 and February 1999. The quantitative indicators in the surveys include information for 1996, the first and second halves of 1997, and the first half of 1998, while the qualitative information refers to the firms' views in the period from November 1998 to February 1999. The quantitative information deals with production, employment, and balance sheet indicators. The qualitative questions that were answered by the owner or senior manager of the firm in a personal interview dealt with views regarding the prospects for recovery and the impediments to it. This information provides for the first time a basis for examining the structure of domestic finance prior to the crisis at the firm level—not just for firms listed on the stock exchange, but also for unlisted companies and small and medium enterprises. It also provides a valuable source for the qualitative views of the sample firms on what problems they confront and on what needs to be done to accelerate corporate recovery.

The sample was designed in conjunction with the statistical agency in each country. The firms were selected from the principal manufacturing sectors in each country. The sectors selected were auto parts, chemicals, electronics, food processing, garments, machinery, and textiles. The sectoral composition differs across countries, but each sector was chosen by at least three countries, thus providing a basis for regional comparisons. A random sampling technique was used to select firms, in order for the survey to be representative of the population of firms in each sector of each country. Approximately two-thirds of the resulting sample, drawn from firms with more than 20 employees, comprises small and medium enterprises (firms with fewer than 150 employees), and one-third is made up of large firms (see table 5.1). Just over one-half of the firms in these tradable goods sectors export some of their output. Less than 20 percent export the majority of their production. A quarter of the firms have a foreign partner holding at least a 10 percent ownership stake. The ownership structure varies across countries: on average 20 percent of the firms are publicly listed, 55 percent are private corporations, and the remainder are partnerships, single proprietorships, cooperatives, and other forms of business.

This paper, drawing on the surveys, presents in the next section the structure of corporate finance prior to the crisis and in mid-1998 in the five crisis countries, including leveraging (or debt-equity ratios) of the firms included in the surveys. It considers issues relating to the allocation of credit, and the financing of the firms' requirements for working capital, investment, and exports. In particular, it examines the role of short-term debt and of financing by domestic and foreign banks.

### TABLE 5.1
### Characteristics of the sample
(percent)

| | Size | | Export orientation | | FDI firm | | Sector | | | | | Total |
|---|---|---|---|---|---|---|---|---|---|---|---|---|
| | Small | Large | Nonexporters | Exporters | No | Yes | Food | Text. and garments | Electr. Mach. | Chem. | Auto. | |
| *Country* | | | | | | | | | | | | |
| Indonesia | 56 | 44 | 64 | 36 | 82 | 18 | 32 | 26 | 12 | 30 | — | 816 |
| Korea, Rep. of | 65 | 35 | 25 | 75 | 83 | 17 | — | 23 | 35 | 28 | 14 | 857 |
| Malaysia | 74 | 26 | 53 | 47 | 74 | 26 | 26 | 31 | 20 | 20 | 4 | 693 |
| Philippines | 48 | 52 | 48 | 52 | 64 | 36 | 26 | 37 | 21 | 16 | — | 564 |
| Thailand | 63 | 37 | 43 | 57 | 70 | 30 | 10 | 54 | 16 | — | 20 | 659 |
| *Sector* | | | | | | | | | | | | |
| Food | 66 | 34 | 64 | 36 | 84 | 16 | — | — | — | — | — | 649 |
| Textiles and garments | 63 | 37 | 48 | 52 | 82 | 18 | — | — | — | — | — | 1194 |
| Electronics and electrical machinery | 58 | 42 | 29 | 71 | 61 | 39 | — | — | — | — | — | 752 |
| Chemicals | 61 | 39 | 44 | 56 | 73 | 27 | — | — | — | — | — | 717 |
| Auto parts | 63 | 37 | 44 | 56 | 75 | 25 | — | — | — | — | — | 277 |
| *Size* | | | | | | | | | | | | |
| Small | — | — | 60 | 40 | 85 | 15 | 19 | 34 | 20 | 20 | 8 | 2077 |
| Large | — | — | 24 | 76 | 62 | 38 | 16 | 33 | 23 | 21 | 8 | 1257 |
| *Export orientation* | | | | | | | | | | | | |
| Nonexporters | 80 | 20 | — | — | 90 | 10 | 25 | 35 | 14 | 19 | 8 | 1629 |
| Exporters | 46 | 54 | — | — | 64 | 36 | 12 | 33 | 28 | 20 | 8 | 1923 |
| *FDI firms* | | | | | | | | | | | | |
| No | 69 | 31 | 54 | 46 | — | — | 20 | 36 | 17 | 20 | 8 | 2792 |
| Yes | 38 | 62 | 19 | 81 | — | — | 12 | 25 | 33 | 22 | 8 | 889 |
| *Indebtedness* | | | | | | | | | | | | |
| Low | 63 | 37 | 49 | 51 | 73 | 27 | 17 | 33 | 22 | 20 | 8 | 1204 |
| High | 55 | 45 | 36 | 64 | 76 | 24 | 12 | 35 | 24 | 19 | 9 | 772 |
| *Foreign borrowing* | | | | | | | | | | | | |
| No | 67 | 33 | 49 | 51 | 80 | 20 | 16 | 36 | 21 | 20 | 8 | 1911 |
| Yes | 37 | 63 | 13 | 87 | 58 | 42 | 6 | 29 | 30 | 21 | 13 | 700 |
| Total | 2000 | 1221 | 1570 | 1861 | 2688 | 872 | 649 | 1194 | 752 | 717 | 277 | 3589 |

*Note:* Percentages represent the share of the row variable that has the corresponding column characteristic.
*Source:* World Bank, Firm-Level Survey.

With this factual basis, the paper next explores a central issue that is important for policy: is corporate recovery constrained by the availability of credit? The following section takes up a selected number of issues regarding corporate financial distress, including the profitability of the firms, and more important, the firms' views as reflected in the surveys on their ability to service loan repayments in the twelve months beyond the time of the surveys. Then the paper examines some issues that are important to evaluating corporate financial governance and the institutional framework in which it occurs. The final section presents the conclusions of the analysis and their implications for policy.

## Structure of corporate finance prior to the crisis and in mid-1998

Approximately two-thirds of the firms, as noted above, are categorized as small and medium, and one-third are large (more than 150 workers). The survey sample includes a preponderance of unlisted firms (in other words, firms that are not listed on stock exchanges), from which financial information has been collected for the first time. These firms do not generally have carefully audited financial statements, and they are not accustomed to answering detailed questions on financial matters. The survey results on corporate finance, therefore, have to be interpreted with caution.

It should also be noted that this survey, as is also true of other similar surveys, suffers from a survival bias, in that only the firms that had survived until the end of 1998 could be included in the sample. Statistical agencies, in order to get some measure of this bias, noted the nonresponse rate of firms that no longer existed because of bankruptcies or closures. On average, 10 percent of the firms in the sample were no longer in operation at the time of the interviews.[2] Thus, the results are likely to represent a more optimistic view of the reaction to the crisis relative to the entire population of the firms in mid-1997. The focus of this paper is on the prospects for recovery of the firms that existed at the time of the survey. The analysis should not be affected by this form of bias. Nevertheless, the results are presented as reflecting a broad tendency rather than point-specific quantitative estimates. The qualitative answers represent a brand new source of information for how the firms see their problems and prospects.

## Corporate finance: liquidity, credit, domestic and foreign debt

Before examining issues of credit availability, it is important to be familiar with the financial characteristics of the firms. As the database represents a set of firms for which little prior information was available, the description of the financial position of firms, especially of the small and medium enterprises (SMEs) and unlisted firms, is of particular interest in itself.

## Financing of working capital and investment

In analyzing corporate finances, it is important to distinguish between "liquidity" (or cash flow) and credit (in other words, the firms' debt). The former is a broader concept that includes internal earnings, owners' equity, and credit from domestic and foreign banks, financial institutions, and suppliers. Credit refers to only the latter items. The distinction will be important in the discussion below of liquidity problems and the role of credit constraints.

Almost 40 percent of the total financial resources available to the firms in the survey, both for short-term financing and investment, came from internal earnings in both early 1997 and in 1998 (see figure 5.1). In fact, these ratios showed a slight increase after July 1997 as the tendency to resort to borrowing decreased. Borrowing from domestic banks and other financial institutions, which covered about 38 percent of short-term liquidity needs and 43 percent of long-term needs in the first half of 1997, had declined to 34 percent and 38 percent respectively in the first half of 1998. The share of financing coming from internal sources is particularly high in Malaysia and lowest in Thailand. The extent of the reliance on internal earnings as a source of funding helps explain why many firms do not regard credit constraints as the chief obstacle to recovery in 1999.

Looking specifically at the sources of working capital, the bulk (between 50 and 65 percent) of working capital requirements of the firms in Korea, Malaysia, and the Philippines were met out of retained earnings. By contrast, this ratio was 39 percent for Indonesian and only 27 percent for Thai firms (see figure 5.2). Around 30–40 percent of working capital requirements came from loans in all five countries, with the remainder

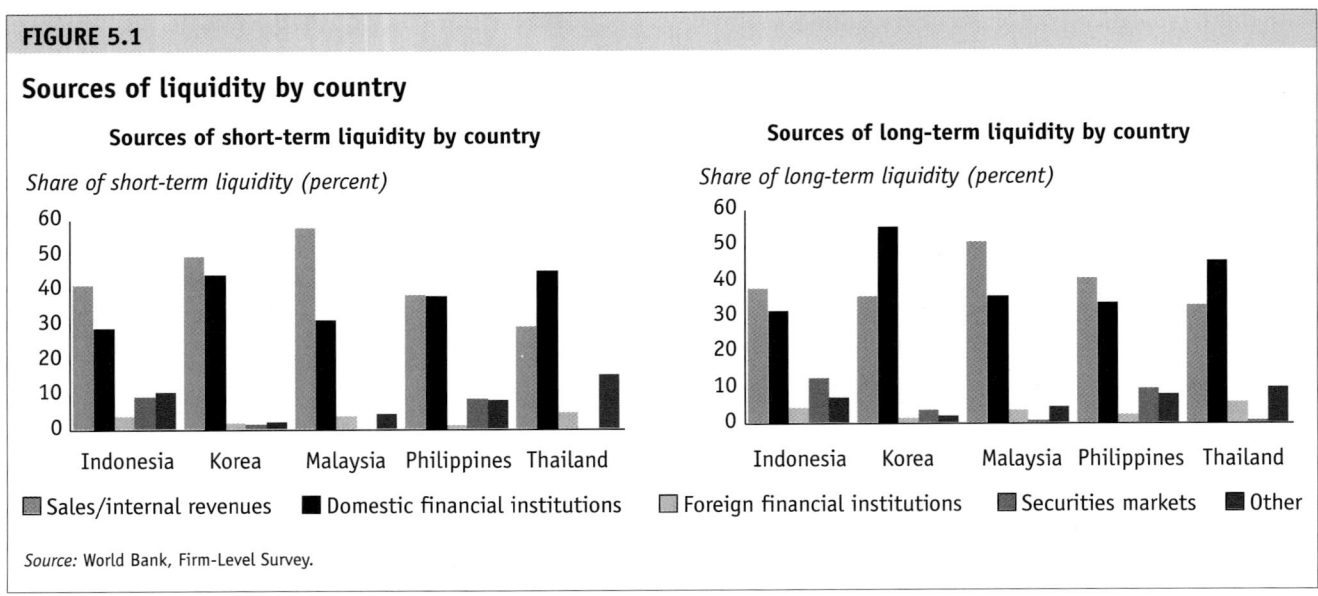

FIGURE 5.1

Sources of liquidity by country

Source: World Bank, Firm-Level Survey.

coming from informal sources of financing—family, partners, and informal moneylenders. In the case of Indonesian and Thai firms, these latter sources provided about one-third of total working capital requirements; in the case of Korean, Malaysian, and Filipino firms, only about 15 percent came from these sources. There does not seem to be much variation across sectors in the tendency to seek informal sources of finance for working capital. Curiously, large firms seem to rely more on informal sources to meet their working capital needs than do small firms.

Turning to credit, figure 5.3 illustrates the differences between SMEs and large firms in the source of credit they rely on. The chart indicates both the reliance on credit and the shares of credit represented by domestic financial institutions, foreign banks, securities markets, and other, more informal, channels of lending. Korea is the only country where large firms rely less on credit than SMEs. Although SMEs generally have a smaller share of credit in their overall financing, domestic financial institutions represent roughly equal shares of the credit borrowed by SMEs and large firms. Much more striking is the large firms' share of credit from foreign banks, at four times the rate of SMEs. SMEs relied to a greater extent on more informal sources of borrowing for their credit needs in every country but Korea. The average was 21 percent of credit versus 14 percent for larger firms.

## Financing in foreign currency

While foreign banks appear to play a small role as a source of credit, a distinction must be made between using foreign banks and borrowing in foreign currency. While few firms borrowed from foreign banks, the share of foreign currency debt was higher—17 percent on average. For large firms and exporters, the share of foreign debt is approximately one-quarter of their total borrowing. The predominance of large firms and of exporters helps explain why foreign credit was higher in Korea (29 percent) than in Indonesia, Malaysia, the Philippines, and Thailand (between 6 and 14 percent). (See table 5.2).

While foreign debt as a proportion of total debt declined in Indonesia and Korea from 1996 to the first half of 1998 and remained relatively steady in the Philippines, it increased in Malaysia and Thailand. Reflecting the export-oriented nature of activities, as well as the existence of foreign joint-venture partners, firms in the auto parts and electronics sectors had the largest exposure to foreign debt, which nevertheless represented only 21–26 percent of total debt.

The relatively low exposure of the firms in this sample—two-thirds of which are SMEs—to foreign financing implies that the fluctuations in international finance (supply, exchange rates, and interest rates) were primarily transmitted to the largest number of

## FIGURE 5.2

**Sources of working capital, first half of 1998**

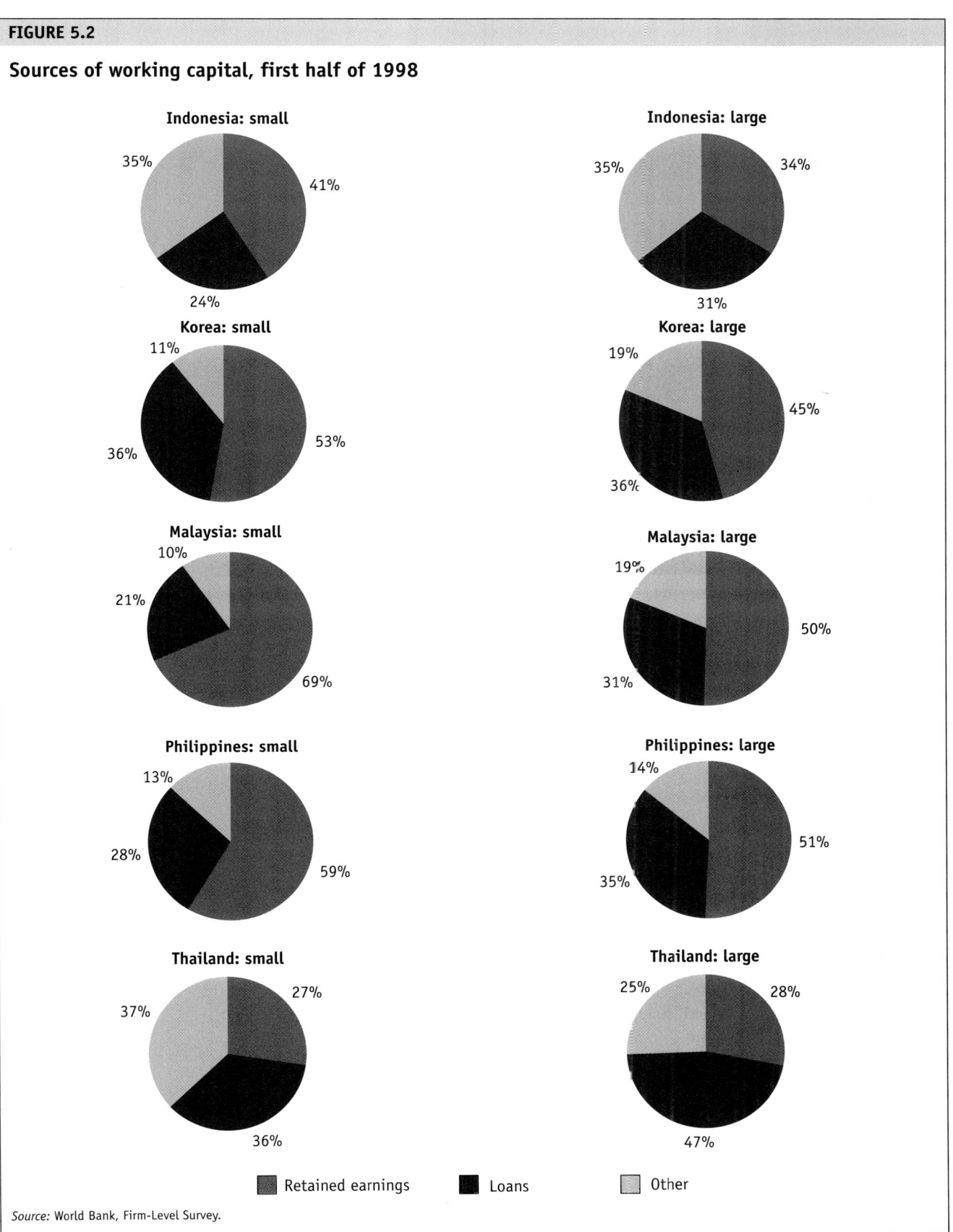

Source: World Bank, Firm-Level Survey.

### FIGURE 5.3
**Sources of short-term credit, first half of 1998**

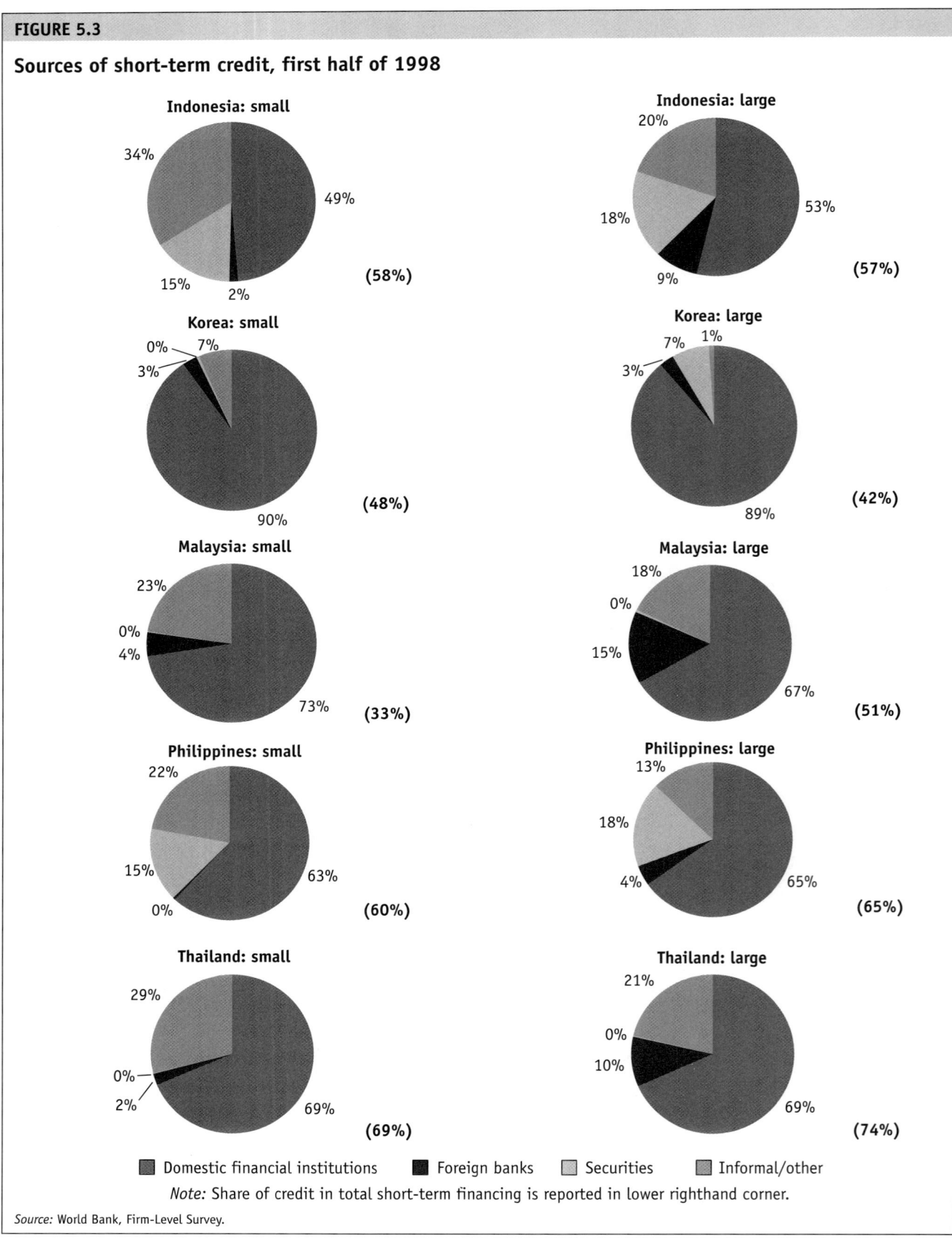

*Note:* Share of credit in total short-term financing is reported in lower righthand corner.

*Source:* World Bank, Firm-Level Survey.

## TABLE 5.2
### Financial structure by firm characteristics
(percent)

| | Total equity/ total financing | | | Short-term debt/ total debt | | | Foreign debt/ total debt | | | Share of working capital financed with internal funds | | |
|---|---|---|---|---|---|---|---|---|---|---|---|---|
| | 1996 | 1997 | 1998 first half | 1996 | 1997 | 1998 first half | 1996 | 1997 | 1998 first half | 1996 | 1997 | 1998 first half |
| *Country* | | | | | | | | | | | | |
| Indonesia | 52.7 | 53.7 | 56.3 | 55.4 | 55.1 | 56.2 | 6.9 | 6.0 | 6.1 | 38.1 | 38.3 | 38.5 |
| Korea | 35.3 | 34.7 | 41.9 | 50.9 | 51.9 | 50.0 | 36.9 | 29.7 | 29.2 | 49.7 | 50.1 | 51.9 |
| Malaysia | 44.6 | 46.2 | 45.5 | 52.5 | 53.1 | 52.8 | 8.5 | 9.8 | 10.0 | 64.9 | 64.4 | 64.8 |
| Philippines | 37.6 | 43.9 | 44.3 | 51.3 | 55.8 | 55.5 | 8.7 | 8.9 | 8.8 | 55.9 | 55.5 | 55.6 |
| Thailand | 47.1 | 46.8 | 51.1 | 55.3 | 57.6 | 56.8 | 10.7 | 12.4 | 13.2 | 27.7 | 27.5 | 27.4 |
| *Sector* | | | | | | | | | | | | |
| Food | 48.7 | 50.5 | 51.3 | 53.6 | 54.2 | 53.9 | 5.7 | 5.6 | 5.0 | 51.5 | 51.7 | 52.4 |
| Textiles and garments | 43.1 | 44.9 | 48.9 | 53.3 | 55.6 | 55.9 | 14.2 | 12.7 | 13.2 | 43.2 | 43.4 | 44.5 |
| Electronics and electrical machinery | 40.4 | 41.7 | 44.5 | 53.8 | 55.5 | 54.9 | 23.1 | 21.9 | 21.3 | 50.4 | 50.9 | 52.2 |
| Chemicals | 44.4 | 45.9 | 49.6 | 51.4 | 52.3 | 49.9 | 19.5 | 17.7 | 17.6 | 47.3 | 46.8 | 48.4 |
| Auto parts | 42.0 | 43.2 | 46.6 | 52.4 | 53.3 | 52.5 | 26.4 | 22.1 | 23.5 | 42.0 | 40.4 | 37.0 |
| *Size* | | | | | | | | | | | | |
| Small | 46.6 | 48.2 | 51.6 | 50.2 | 51.4 | 50.9 | 11.6 | 10.6 | 10.7 | 50.8 | 50.5 | 50.2 |
| Large | 39.1 | 40.4 | 43.0 | 56.3 | 58.3 | 57.9 | 25.0 | 22.5 | 22.7 | 40.1 | 40.8 | 43.3 |
| *Export orientation* | | | | | | | | | | | | |
| Nonexporters | 49.4 | 51.1 | 53.7 | 50.2 | 51.9 | 51.8 | 5.1 | 5.6 | 5.3 | 51.5 | 51.0 | 49.9 |
| Exporters | 39.1 | 40.3 | 44.0 | 54.7 | 56.1 | 55.1 | 25.4 | 22.4 | 22.6 | 43.2 | 43.6 | 46.0 |
| *FDI firms* | | | | | | | | | | | | |
| No | 43.8 | 45.3 | 48.5 | 50.9 | 52.4 | 51.6 | 14.1 | 11.9 | 12.0 | 47.3 | 47.4 | 47.9 |
| Yes | 42.8 | 44.4 | 47.3 | 59.0 | 60.7 | 60.4 | 27.4 | 27.8 | 27.8 | 45.7 | 45.4 | 47.1 |
| Total | 43.6 | 45.1 | 48.3 | 53.0 | 54.5 | 53.8 | 17.4 | 15.8 | 15.9 | 46.9 | 46.9 | 47.6 |

*Source:* World Bank, Firm-Level Survey.

firms indirectly through the domestic banks and financial institutions that were the major borrowers from foreign sources.[3] The domestic financial system has thus played a critical role in the downturn in corporate activity and must be a central factor in its recovery. For the large firms, and those that are exporters, there was also a direct impact, since their foreign debt exposure was higher.

The major role of banks, in particular domestic banks, in financing the firms' both working capital and investment, reflects the state of development of domestic financial markets.[4] It is not a reflection necessarily on the quality of corporate governance by the firms included in this survey. The paucity of financial instruments and limited variety of financial institutions, as well as the lack in many cases of bankruptcy and foreclosure laws and institutional limitations (the predominant use of real property) on collateral, constrains the ability of the firms to manage risks and returns through the use of financial instruments. The essence of good corporate financial governance is the ability to manage risk through financial instruments.

## Short-term debt and leveraging

The high recourse to short-term debt and the high level of leveraging (debt-equity ratios) have been advanced as characteristics of East Asian firms that reflect inadequacies in corporate governance and make them vulnerable to financial crises. The results of the surveys illustrate the extent of the accuracy of this portrayal, allowing for some important distinctions based on firm characteristics.

As can be seen in table 5.2, the proportion of short-term debt in total debt was reasonably high in these five countries—just over 50 percent for all five countries. Domestic banks and suppliers provided the bulk of this. Foreign currency debt accounts for 6 to 13 percent of the total, with the exception of Korea where foreign debt was almost one-third of the total debt.[5] There is

### TABLE 5.3
### Median debt-equity ratios by sector and size, 1997

|  | Food processing | Textiles and garments | Electronics and electrical machinery | Chemicals | Auto parts | Country average |
|---|---|---|---|---|---|---|
| **Small firms** | | | | | | |
| Indonesia | 0.6 | 0.3 | 1.2 | 0.7 | — | 0.57 |
| Korea | — | 3.2 | 2.1 | 2.1 | 2.3 | 2.15 |
| Malaysia | 0.7 | 0.6 | 0.6 | 0.7 | 0.6 | 0.67 |
| Philippines | 1.0 | 1.5 | 2.9 | 1.3 | — | 1.47 |
| Thailand | 1.2 | 1.1 | 1.4 | — | 0.8 | 1.10 |
| **Large firms** | | | | | | |
| Indonesia | 1.0 | 1.5 | 2.1 | 1.4 | — | 1.53 |
| Korea | — | 4.1 | 1.9 | 1.5 | 2.7 | 2.40 |
| Malaysia | 0.7 | 1.0 | 0.9 | 0.9 | 3.3 | 0.96 |
| Philippines | 1.4 | 2.4 | 1.0 | 1.3 | — | 1.77 |
| Thailand | 1.7 | 1.9 | 0.8 | — | 1.7 | 1.56 |

### Mean debt-equity ratios by sector and size, 1997

|  | Food processing | Textiles and garments | Electronics and electrical machinery | Chemicals | Auto parts | Country average |
|---|---|---|---|---|---|---|
| **Small firms** | | | | | | |
| Indonesia | 1.4 | 0.9 | 1.3 | 1.5 | — | 1.29 |
| Korea | — | 4.1 | 2.7 | 2.7 | 2.8 | 2.98 |
| Malaysia | 1.4 | 1.4 | 1.3 | 1.9 | 2.5 | 1.53 |
| Philippines | 1.7 | 2.4 | 3.3 | 3.7 | — | 2.75 |
| Thailand | 2.4 | 2.1 | 2.7 | — | 2.3 | 2.28 |
| **Large firms** | | | | | | |
| Indonesia | 1.9 | 2.5 | 2.8 | 2.3 | — | 2.37 |
| Korea | — | 4.6 | 3.3 | 2.3 | 4.2 | 3.47 |
| Malaysia | 2.5 | 3.1 | 2.3 | 3.0 | 3.6 | 2.80 |
| Philippines | 2.6 | 4.0 | 1.6 | 3.2 | — | 2.95 |
| Thailand | 2.5 | 2.6 | 2.2 | — | 2.9 | 2.58 |

*Source:* World Bank, Firm-Level Survey.

not much variation in the reliance on short-term debt across sectors. However, exporters and large firms do have somewhat higher ratios. The average short-term debt in this sample is just over 50 percent of the total, compared with about 25 percent for firms in the United States and 45 percent for firms in Germany. Country variation was greater in the use of suppliers' credits, a form of self-liquidating short-term debt. It represented 30 to 40 percent in Thailand and Indonesia, and over 50 percent in the other three countries, reaching 65 percent in the Philippines. One consequence of the crisis is that the share of both inputs and outputs financed with suppliers' credits declined (11 percent and 4 percent, respectively) between the first half of 1997 and the end of 1998, as firms that found themselves in tight liquidity positions restricted their provision of credit. This was true across all sectors.

On average for all firms included in the surveys, debt represented 55 percent, and equity 45 percent, of total financing. However, there is considerable variation across countries, sectors and firm size (see table 5.3). Overall, the median ratios are lower than the means, indicating a skewed distribution with some firms having quite high debt-equity ratios.[6] Korean firms stand out as having higher debt-equity ratios, with significantly higher median ratios than the other countries. The median ratio is 2.19 and the mean is 3.13 in Korea compared with a median of 0.88 and mean of 1.78 in Indonesia, or of 0.67 and 1.99, respectively, in Malaysia. In almost every category, large firms have much higher debt-equity ratios than small firms. The overall mean for small firms is 2.19 versus 2.77 for large firms. This reflects the greater access large firms have to external financing, particularly to foreign banks and to equity and bond markets. Across sectors, electronics, auto parts, and textiles have higher debt-equity ratios, reflecting the greater capital intensity of these industries. While not reported in table 5.3, there is a shift in the ratios over time. The pattern appears to be an initial increase in 1997 relative to 1996, followed by a decline in 1998. This can be explained by the initial rise in debt owing to both exchange rate effects on foreign currency liabilities and the firms' borrowing more to finance the higher cost of imported inputs. However, with the rise in interest rates and the decline in domestic demand, the demand for loans declined. This was coupled with a decreased willingness to lend on the part of the financial sector. From 1997 to 1998, the amount of debt did decline on average across all countries.

The above debt-equity ratios compare with 1.03 for listed firms in the United States and 1.51 for those in Germany. The leverage ratios of firms included in this East Asian sample are higher than those of firms in more industrialized countries and even of those of large firms in Latin American countries.[7] These high leveraging ratios indicate the riskiness of the financial structures of the East Asian firms included in the surveys, and their vulnerability to financial fluctuations and movements in interest rates and exchange rates. For example, the rapid increase in interest rates following the adoption of stabilization programs by these countries, as discussed below, put severe strains on the capacity of the firms to maintain required debt-service payments and simultaneously to generate the funds to cover working capital needs.

## Corporate profitability

In a recent paper using data only for listed companies in 1996 (that is, prior to the onset of the crisis), Claessens, Djankov, and Lang (1999) conclude that in terms of return on assets, Indonesia, the Philippines, and Thailand had the most profitable firms in their Worldscope sample of 46 countries, with Malaysia following close behind. With the onset of the crisis this performance changed dramatically. The survey data indicate that profit margins declined between 1996 and the first half of 1998 in all five countries. The declines were smaller in Indonesia and Korea, and up to 5 percent in Thailand. The sample firms in the auto parts sector suffered the largest declines in profitability, reflecting the fact that the sector experienced the sharpest fall in domestic demand. The firms in food, and textiles and garments experienced smaller declines, while the firms in electronics and electrical machinery, and chemicals actually saw their average profitability rise. The most important predictor for whether a firm's profit margin fell was its level of indebtedness. Highly leveraged firms were significantly more likely to have lower profits, consistent with the need to cover larger interest payments as interest rates rose sharply following the implementation of stabilization programs.

## Determining whether credit availability is a constraint to corporate recovery in Asia

Firms in the crisis countries have been hit by a combination of collapse in domestic demand, currency depreciations, and increases in interest rates following the implementation of stabilization programs. The declines in domestic demand, except for the firms that have been able to shift sales to foreign markets, have resulted in reductions in sales revenues, the principal source of liquidity. Currency depreciations have substantially increased input costs and reduced profit margins and available retained earnings. Higher interest rates have increased debt-service payments, especially for firms that borrowed heavily from domestic banks for working capital and investment needs. These factors have strained the liquidity positions of the firms, particularly as banks and other financial institutions have become more selective in credit provision.

A much-debated issue of significant policy importance is whether at the time of the survey (from November 1998 to February 1999) the sample firms' recovery was being constrained by the availability of credit. The five country papers on Indonesia, Korea, Malaysia, the Philippines, and Thailand, prepared for the Conference on Corporate Recovery, all come to the same conclusion. Firms included in the surveys see the collapse in demand and the high cost of inputs, resulting from the increases in interest rates and the major currency devaluations, as significantly more important factors accounting for their present predicament than aggregate credit availability. Broader studies by the Economic Research Department of the Bank of Thailand[8] and Swati R. Ghosh[9] come to a similar conclusion.

However, policymakers have in some cases been persuaded that increases in aggregate credit availability are necessary, and may even be critical, for corporate recovery. In this section we examine the evidence from the survey data on this important issue.

In the earlier discussion, a distinction was made between "liquidity" or cash flow and credit—it was noted that the former is a broader concept that subsumes the latter. Here the concern is with credit, or the availability of financing from sources external to the firm, be they domestic or foreign. The issue, at one level, is whether in the aggregate the demand for credit for viable projects exceeds its aggregate supply at prevailing interest rates.[10] At another level, and one to which the survey data are specifically relevant, the issue has to do with the allocation of credit and the availability of credit to specific firms and projects at prevailing interest rates.

In formulating policies it is important to understand the nature of an aggregate credit availability constraint, if it exists. The very fact that the aggregate supply of credit has decreased does not, in and of itself, imply that there are viable firms and projects that are not securing credit at prevailing interest rates. It is important to examine both the supply and demand for credit for viable projects at prevailing interest rates. The firms' demand for credit depends on their production and sales prospects. There could simultaneously have been an even larger decrease in demand in response to the decrease in demand for the firms' output—such that there would be, at prevailing interest rates, an excess supply, rather than a shortage of credit. If, however, there is an excess demand for credit, then measures to increase liquidity are required. Increases in liquidity would also have the impact of lowering interest rates.

The trajectory of nominal interest rates could thus be an indicator of the tightness of credit conditions. Rising nominal interest rates would be an indicator of excess aggregate demand for credit, while falling interest rates would indicate excess aggregate supply of credit.

Credit aggregates, however, do not indicate whether there is rationing of credit, or inefficiencies in the allocation of credit. Credit rationing is a normal function of financial institutions. Credit rationing involves the selection of viable firms and projects for financing at prevailing interest rates. It is thus a desirable role for financial institutions. If this principle is systematically violated—that is, if credit is systematically provided to firms and projects that are not viable at prevailing interest rates—it leads to financial crises. There is evidence that it was this kind of behavior by financial institutions that contributed to the recent financial crises in East Asia and elsewhere. In this case, increases in the aggregate supply of credit are not the recommended policy because they might lead to further expansions in loan portfolios, worsen problems of capital inadequacy, and delay financial and corporate restructuring. Rather, increases in the pool of viable projects are to be fostered by stimulation of aggregate demand accompanied by financial and corporate restructuring.

It could be, however, that when interest rates are high, there is adverse selection and an exaggerated perception of risk by lending institutions. This could arise because of imperfections in information about the true quality of firms and projects, or owing to lending institutions' exaggerated aversion to risk. In such a case, improvements in transparency and information availability, through improved accounting and auditing, could reduce perceived risks. Also, institutional improvements, such as required legal changes for bankruptcy and foreclosures, and mergers and acquisitions would facilitate required corporate and bank restructuring.

Nevertheless, to the extent that there is a group of firms and projects, within the total set of firms and projects that are economically and financially viable at prevailing interest rates, that are not receiving required credits, special measures may be required. Such measures, however, should be carefully designed to meet the specified needs of the adversely affected groups of firms and projects, while maintaining lending standards, and not retarding bank and corporate restructuring. Information of the kind collected in the present surveys could be useful in coming to judgments about required measures.

The next two sections of this paper will examine the evidence on the role of credit availability as a constraint to corporate recovery in 1999 for firms in the sectors and countries included in the surveys. We will start by examining the evolution of aggregate supply of credit to the private sector, as well as the evolution of nominal and real interest rates, both of which have important implications for the viability of firms and projects. We will then present the firms' views on the impact of liquidity availability on their ability to expand output and exports.

## Aggregate supply of credit to the private sector and interest rates

Despite a reversal in capital flows, which represented on average 10 percent of the gross domestic product (GDP) in the five countries, there was no commensurate decline in credit to the private sector.[11] The evolution of domestic credit to the private sector is shown in figure 5.4; credit to the private sector declined between mid-1997 and mid-1998 in Indonesia, the Philippines, and Thailand.[12] This decline is mirrored by the decline in industrial production.

The crisis and the stabilization programs that were adopted in the immediate aftermath greatly curtailed

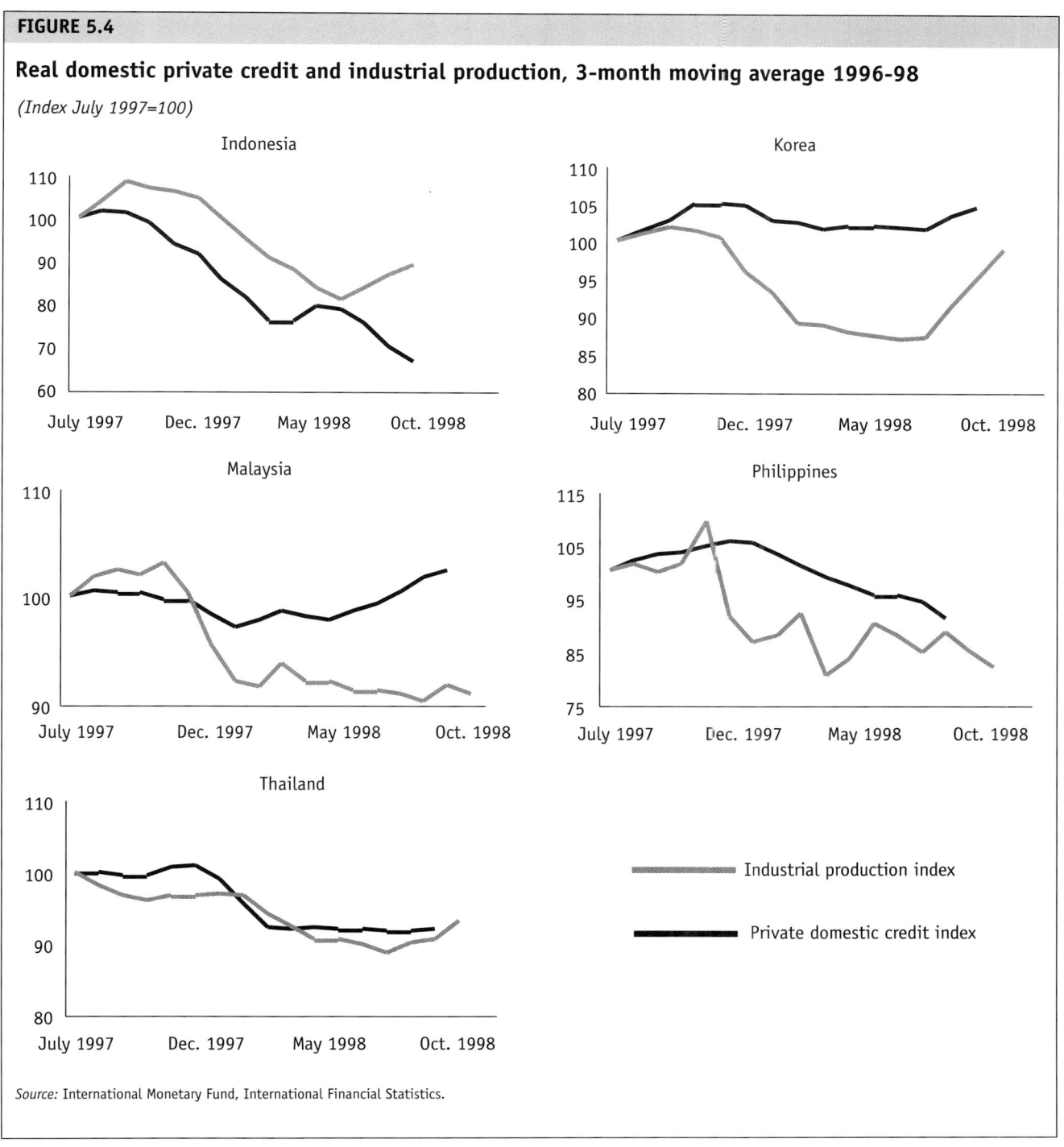

FIGURE 5.4

**Real domestic private credit and industrial production, 3-month moving average 1996-98**

(Index July 1997=100)

Source: International Monetary Fund, International Financial Statistics.

the availability of credit. Bank liquidity and capital were severely affected by mounting stocks of nonperforming loans. Estimates of peak nonperforming loans ranged from 30 percent of the total loan portfolio of banks in Korea to 75 percent in Indonesia, while the banking sector in the Philippines did not experience systemic difficulties.[13] The credit constraint was exacerbated in the immediate postcrisis period by the tightening of capital adequacy and loan classification rules that were implemented. Obviously, and consistent with historical experience in financial crises, risk aversion by banks increased. This issue of credit allocation, however, cannot be examined with aggregate data. The survey data indicate (as discussed below) that some firms felt severely credit-constrained in undertaking viable projects.

The evolution of nominal interest rates is an indicator of the balance between the supply and demand for credit over time. The main impact of the reversal of capital flows has been on domestic interest rates. The evolution of nominal and real interest rates over the period 1997–98 is shown in figure 5.5. Nominal interest rates rose sharply soon after the crisis hit, in mid-1997 in Indonesia, the Philippines, and Thailand, and at the end of 1997 in Korea, indicating an excess demand for credit at prevailing interest rates. In Malaysia, which had lower short-term foreign indebtedness, nominal interest rates rose progressively starting in mid-1997, but by much less than in the other countries. In the five countries, nominal interest rates declined in the second half of 1998; in Korea, Malaysia, and Thailand they are now below their precrisis levels. This supports the view that in the period after the second half of 1998, a period when the current survey was undertaken, excess credit demand had been met.

The behavior of real interest rates—that is, nominal interest rates adjusted with the producer price index—however, was somewhat different. Real interest rates rose sharply immediately after the crisis hit and then began a rapid decline, particularly in Indonesia, owing to the surge of inflation, which occurred following the currency devaluations. Inflation then slowed markedly in the second half of 1998, and real interest rates rose in the five countries, except for the Philippines. While nominal interest rates were at historical high levels but declining in 1998, real interest rates remained negative through most of 1998 in these countries. In all five countries, real interest rates by the end of 1998 were below their precrisis levels.

## Liquidity constraints and output and exports

The surveys included qualitative questions. These asked firms to rank on a scale from 1 (least important) to 5 (most important), the factors that accounted for the decline in output and exports. These qualitative questions were asked in the period between December 1998 and January 1999, 18 months after the onset of the crisis. The results are summarized in figure 5.6. Surveyed firms in all countries expressed the view that the collapse of domestic demand was the most important factor leading to declines in output; this was followed by the increased costs of inputs and by the high cost of credit. The lack of working capital, of credit for expansion, and the debt burden seem to have played a lesser role.[14]

In the case of exports, their decline was attributed to a combination of loss of competitive advantage, credit constraints, and to higher import costs associated with currency devaluations.[15] The survey asked whether the firms encountered problems in having adequate liquidity to finance production. On average 40 percent of the firms in the five countries reported experiencing liquidity constraints.

Figure 5.7 and table 5.4 show the breakdown of the sample firms by various categories. About one-half of Korean and Thai firms claimed to be experiencing liquidity problems. Such problems were most acute in the auto parts sector and least acute in the food products sector. Small firms, nonexporters, and firms selling mainly to the domestic market were more affected by liquidity difficulties, than were large firms, exporters, or those that had foreign direct investment. Firms that were highly indebted were more liquidity-constrained, while there was little difference in the firms' exposure to foreign debt. This latter finding, while puzzling given the extent of the depreciation, is consistent with the fact that larger, exporting firms with foreign partners were predominantly those that borrowed in significant amounts in foreign currency. However, even if they were not severely liquidity-constrained, there are still a number of large firms, exporters, and more dynamic firms complaining that credit constrained their ability to export.

## FIGURE 5.5

**Nominal and real interest rates, March 1997–December 1998**

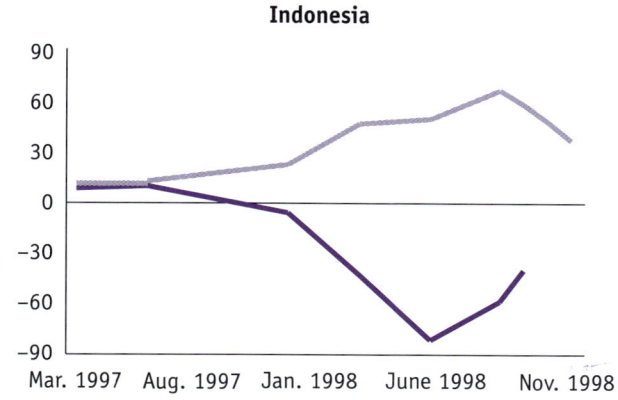
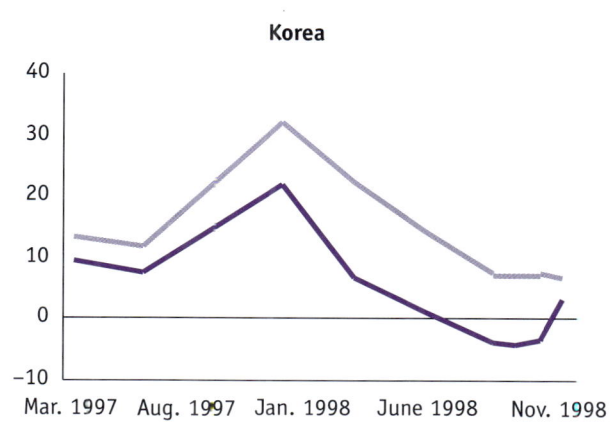
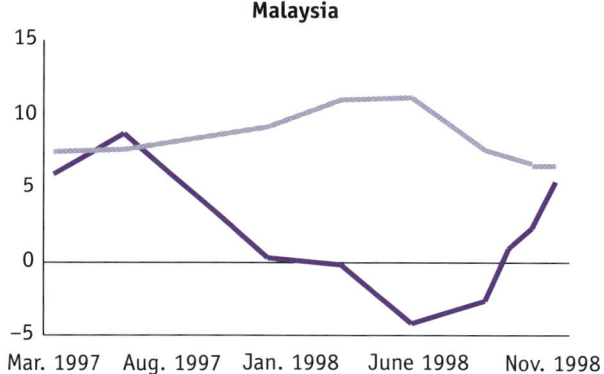
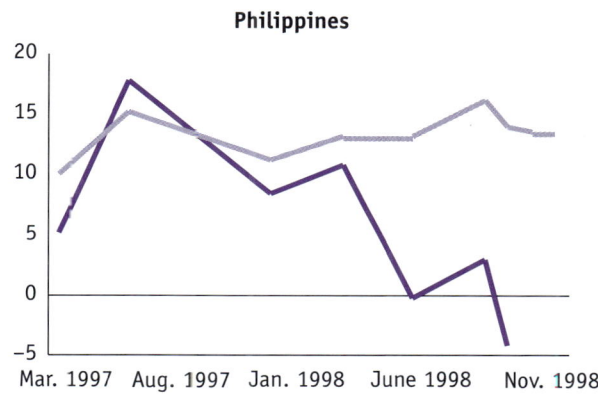

a. Producer price index is used as deflator.

*Source:* International Monetary Fund, International Financial Statistics.

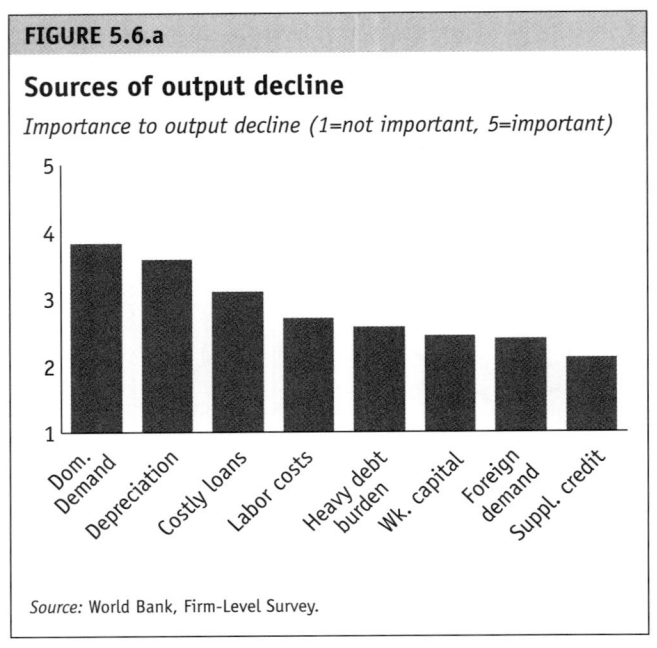

**FIGURE 5.6.a**

**Sources of output decline**

*Importance to output decline (1=not important, 5=important)*

Source: World Bank, Firm-Level Survey.

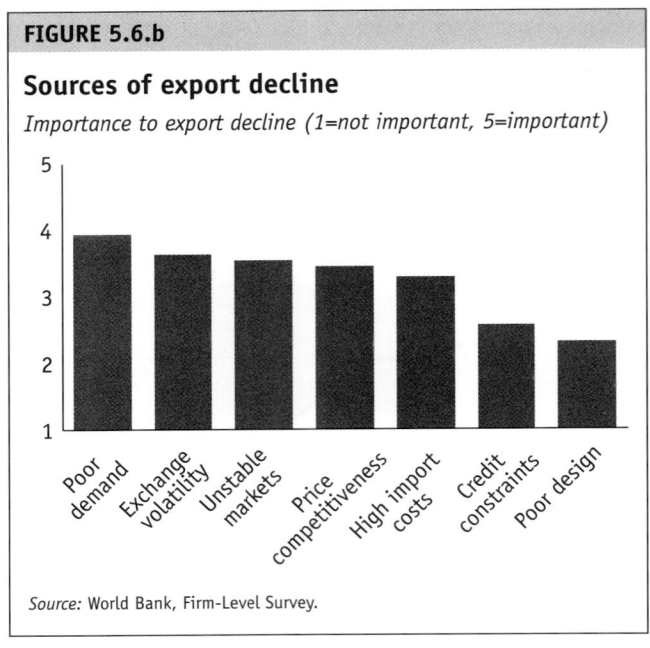

**FIGURE 5.6.b**

**Sources of export decline**

*Importance to export decline (1=not important, 5=important)*

Source: World Bank, Firm-Level Survey.

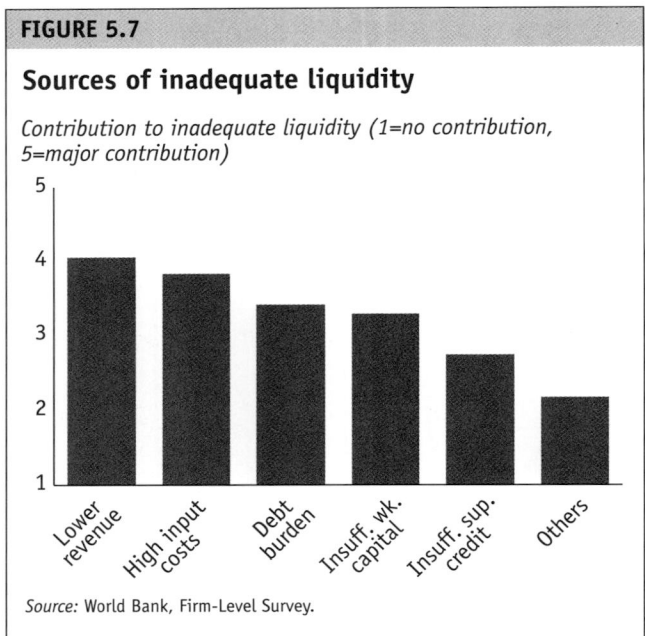

**FIGURE 5.7**

**Sources of inadequate liquidity**

*Contribution to inadequate liquidity (1=no contribution, 5=major contribution)*

Source: World Bank, Firm-Level Survey.

When asked about the causes of their liquidity problems, the firms listed in declining order of importance the following: the decline in revenues, higher input costs that had raised the need for working capital and the burden of servicing outstanding debt, and the lack of loans for working capital. These answers reflect the sample firms' structure of working capital, which as noted earlier, relied on retained earnings to finance almost one-half of the total. Thus, factors that affected cash flow rather than credit received the most attention by these firms. Firms in Thailand, the country that has seen the largest decline in capacity utilization, gave the highest score to lower revenue. Thailand is also the country where loans finance the largest share of working capital—and Thai firms complained the most about the lack of loans for working capital. Similarly, firms in the auto parts sector, which also saw the largest sectoral decline in capacity utilization, also gave the highest score to revenue factors.

A policy implication of these survey results is that, even though there is no evidence that at the time of the surveys (from November 1998 to February 1999) there was in the aggregate a shortfall of credit availability, credit allocation from domestic and foreign sources is inefficient. Small and medium firms, which constitute two-thirds of the sample, have traditionally had difficulties in getting credit from the banking system. The surveys indicate that this problem has been exacerbated by the crisis. Also, many viable firms complain that they are squeezed out of credit while their working capital needs have increased and other sources of liquidity have decreased. Policy and institutional changes to address these problems, some of which are long-standing, are required along with selective credit measures.

### TABLE 5.4
### Source of liquidity problem

| | Share claiming inadequate liquidity (percent) | By source of problem | | | | | |
|---|---|---|---|---|---|---|---|
| | Yes | Lower revenue | High input costs | Debt burden | Insuff. wk. cap. | Insuff. sup. crd. | Others |
| *Country* | | | | | | | |
| Indonesia | 35 | 3.5 | 3.7 | — | 2.9 | 2.5 | 1.8 |
| Korea | 48 | 4.1 | 3.4 | 3.1 | 3.2 | 2.5 | 2.5 |
| Malaysia | 25 | 4.1 | 4.0 | 3.3 | 3.3 | 2.9 | 1.8 |
| Philippines | 23 | 3.8 | — | — | 3.3 | 2.8 | 2.3 |
| Thailand | 56 | 4.4 | 4.3 | 3.9 | 3.7 | 3.2 | 4.2 |
| *Sector* | | | | | | | |
| Food | 28 | 3.7 | 3.7 | 3.3 | 3.0 | 2.5 | 2.0 |
| Textiles and garments | 42 | 4.0 | 4.0 | 3.5 | 3.4 | 2.9 | 2.4 |
| Electronic and electrical mach. | 37 | 4.3 | 3.7 | 3.2 | 3.3 | 2.7 | 2.0 |
| Chemicals | 33 | 3.8 | 3.7 | 3.3 | 3.1 | 2.6 | 2.0 |
| Auto parts | 61 | 4.6 | 3.9 | 3.6 | 3.5 | 2.8 | 3.0 |
| *Size* | | | | | | | |
| Small | 42 | 4.2 | 3.8 | 3.3 | 3.2 | 2.7 | 2.1 |
| Large | 32 | 3.8 | 3.8 | 3.7 | 3.4 | 2.8 | 2.3 |
| *Export orientation* | | | | | | | |
| Nonexporters | 41 | 4.1 | 3.9 | 3.4 | 3.2 | 2.6 | 1.9 |
| Exporters | 36 | 4.0 | 3.8 | 3.5 | 3.4 | 2.9 | 2.5 |
| *FDI firms* | | | | | | | |
| No | 41 | 4.1 | 3.8 | 3.4 | 3.3 | 2.7 | 2.1 |
| Yes | 30 | 4.0 | 4.0 | 3.6 | 3.2 | 2.7 | 2.4 |
| *Indebtedness* | | | | | | | |
| Low | 34 | 4.1 | 4.0 | 3.4 | 3.3 | 2.7 | 1.9 |
| High | 44 | 4.2 | 3.9 | 3.5 | 3.5 | 3.0 | 2.5 |
| *Foreign borrowing* | | | | | | | |
| No | 40 | 4.2 | 3.9 | 3.4 | 3.4 | 2.9 | 3.1 |
| Yes | 40 | 4.0 | 3.7 | 3.6 | 3.4 | 2.6 | 2.7 |
| Total | 38 | 4.1 | 3.8 | 3.4 | 3.3 | 2.7 | 2.2 |

*Source:* World Bank, Firm-Level Survey.

## The firms' views on loan repayment prospects

The questionnaires, as noted earlier, in addition to seeking quantitative information from the firms, sought their qualitative views on their ability to meet required loan payments, if interest rates remained at current—that is, end-of-1998 to early 1999—levels. The questions asked the firms to indicate their perceived ability to meet required loan payments, by three-month intervals, over the next twelve months and beyond. About 2,000 firms in the five countries responded to this question.

The firms' responses are shown in figure 5.8. In the five countries, a first category of firms that indicate that they do not expect to have problems in servicing their loan repayments range from over two-thirds in Korea, Malaysia, and Thailand, to one-half in Indonesia and the Philippines. A second category indicates that the firms expect to be able to meet loan payments for the following twelve months but not beyond that period. In this category are 10–15 percent of the firms in Thailand and Malaysia, 20 percent in Indonesia and Korea, and one-third in the Philippines. A third category is of firms

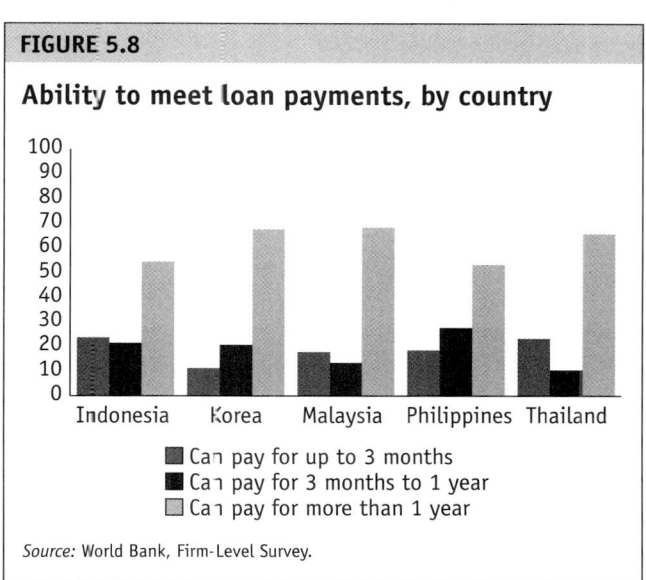

**FIGURE 5.8**

**Ability to meet loan payments, by country**

*Source:* World Bank, Firm-Level Survey.

that have indicated that they are currently having difficulties in meeting loan repayments, or expect to be able to meet loan repayments only for the next three months and not beyond. About 25 percent of the firms in Indonesia and Thailand, 20 percent in Malaysia, and 10 percent in Korea fit this category.

Firms in the first category—in other words, those that do not expect to have loan repayment difficulties—are mainly small (see table 5.5) especially in Korea, Malaysia, and Thailand, and less so in Indonesia and the Philippines. The majority of these firms in Korea, Malaysia, and the Philippines are exporters; Thai firms are evenly distributed between exporters and nonexporters, and Indonesian are mainly oriented to the domestic market. On average, capacity utilization for this group had declined by 15 percentage points since 1996 and 11 percentage points since the first half of 1997. About three-quarters of Malaysian firms and two-thirds of Thai and Indonesian firms in this category reported low levels of overall indebtedness. By contrast, two-thirds of Korean firms and one-half of Filipino firms report high overall indebtedness. The majority of firms in this category, except for those in Korea and Thailand, indicate that securing adequate liquidity is not an issue. Despite high levels of indebtedness, Korean firms in this category indicate fewer difficulties in securing external financing. Thai firms, however, despite having lower indebtedness levels than those in Korea, indicate difficulties in securing bank financing and required liquidity for production. This could be an indication of the different pace of corporate and bank restructuring.

Firms in the second category—those that do not expect to be able to meet loan payments beyond 12

### TABLE 5.5
**Profile of firms with different expectations on remaining current on debt payments**
(Percentage of firms in each category)

*Firms that expected to remain current for more than 1 year*

|  | Indonesia | Korea | Malaysia | Philippines | Thailand | Average |
|---|---|---|---|---|---|---|
| Experienced output decline | 80 | 70 | 71 | 77 | 73 | 74 |
| Capacity utilization[a] | 59 | 71 | 69 | 70 | 64 | 66 |
| Small size | 51 | 67 | 63 | 54 | 64 | 57 |
| Exporter | 45 | 63 | 51 | 55 | 42 | 49 |
| Low indebtedness | 67 | 37 | 75 | 47 | 63 | 60 |
| Foreign debt | 17 | 44 | 20 | 14 | 28 | 27 |
| Liquidity is a problem | 36 | 60 | 23 | 28 | 55 | 42 |

*Firms that expected to remain current for more than 3 months and less than 1 year*

|  | Indonesia | Korea | Malaysia | Philippines | Thailand | Average |
|---|---|---|---|---|---|---|
| Experienced output decline | 76 | 72 | 86 | 81 | 73 | 77 |
| Capacity utilization[a] | 63 | 67 | 64 | 61 | 60 | 63 |
| Small size | 55 | 77 | 76 | 53 | 68 | 64 |
| Exporter | 38 | 65 | 48 | 41 | 69 | 51 |
| Low indebtedness | 71 | 54 | 91 | 40 | 66 | 62 |
| Foreign debt | 10 | 40 | 20 | 11 | 28 | 22 |
| Liquidity is a problem | 30 | 58 | 46 | 36 | 69 | 44 |

*Firms that were not current or did not expect to remain current for more than 3 months*

|  | Indonesia | Korea | Malaysia | Philippines | Thailand | Average |
|---|---|---|---|---|---|---|
| Experienced output decline | 80 | 73 | 73 | 81 | 88 | 81 |
| Capacity utilization[a] | 56 | 69 | 58 | 62 | 52 | 57 |
| Small size | 62 | 42 | 71 | 49 | 62 | 57 |
| Exporter | 38 | 85 | 52 | 50 | 52 | 51 |
| Low indebtedness | 62 | 42 | 72 | 57 | 45 | 55 |
| Foreign debt | 21 | 54 | 12 | 23 | 28 | 26 |
| Liquidity is a problem | 45 | 70 | 62 | 43 | 85 | 61 |

a. Average capacity utilization.
*Source:* World Bank, Firm-Level Survey.

months following the surveys—are relatively few, particularly in Korea, Malaysia, and Thailand, and even less so in the Philippines and Indonesia. On average, they are evenly distributed between exporters and nonexporters, with country differences: about two-thirds are exporters in Korea and Thailand, but only about 40 percent in Indonesia and the Philippines. On average, capacity utilization has declined by 18 percentage points since 1996 and 13 percent since the outset of the crisis. About two-thirds of Thai and Indonesian firms, over half of Korean firms, and 90 percent of Malaysian firms in this category reported low levels of indebtedness. However, 60 percent of Filipino firms in this category reported high indebtedness. The majority of the firms in this category reported that securing adequate liquidity was not an issue, except for those in Korea and Thailand.

Firms in the third category—those currently having or expecting in the near future to have loan repayment difficulties—are mainly nonexporters in Indonesia, predominantly (85 percent) exporters in Korea, and divided equally between exporters and nonexporters in the other three countries. In Malaysia, Thailand, and Indonesia the great majority are small firms, while in Korea they are mainly large firms. On average, capacity utilization for the firms in this group has decreased by 20 percentage points since 1996, and 15 percentage points since the first half of 1997. About 60 percent of the firms in this group also reported difficulties in securing adequate liquidity for production—70 percent in Korea, 85 percent in Malaysia and Thailand. In Indonesia and the Philippines, the majority of the firms in this category did not report liquidity access problems, perhaps because the demand for their production had declined substantially and they were not seeking access to liquidity. Finally the majority also report low levels of indebtedness. A high debt stock, with the exception of the firms in Korea, does not seem to have been a major factor in loan repayment difficulties.

A comparison of the firms in the first and third categories indicates that, on average, the firms that are not reporting loan repayment difficulties:
- Have experienced smaller declines in capacity utilization (Korean firms are a significant exception);
- Are exporting more (Korean and Thai firms are exceptions );
- Are financing a greater portion of their working capital with retained earnings (Filipino firms are an exception); and
- Have experienced far fewer difficulties in securing adequate amounts of liquidity for production.

The above information indicates that the sample firms in the five countries see themselves at various stages in the recovery process, as well as in their access to liquidity required for production. The bulk of the firms in Korea, Malaysia, and Thailand consider themselves to be in good financial condition. This is less the case in Indonesia and the Philippines. There remain, however, a significant number of firms in all five countries that were either experiencing loan repayment difficulties at the time of the survey, or thought that they would find themselves in that situation in the not too distant future. This financial fragility of a significant proportion of firms in the five countries is linked both to macroeconomic conditions and the pace of bank and corporate restructuring.

## Issues in corporate financial governance

The surveys included a number of questions on corporate financial governance, use of audited financial statements, and the nature and use of collateral. This information has to be interpreted with caution, taking into account the nature of the firms included in the sample and the institutional context in which they operate. The samples contain a predominant number of small and medium-size firms that find it costly and difficult to produce good-quality financial information. Instead they and their credit sources tend to rely on well-established and long-standing relationships that have proved reliable for credit decisions. As firms grow, however, the more formal instruments and organizational arrangements become mechanisms for ensuring greater transparency.

### Audited statements

The surveys asked whether the firms were required to produce audited statements when they applied for loans. There is considerable variation across countries in the responses. The audit rate is highest in the

Philippines (65 percent), Korea (63 percent), and Malaysia (61 percent)—and below 40 percent in Thailand and Indonesia (see figure 5.9). These audit rates, however, give no indication of the quality of auditing standards across countries.

It is not the case, however, that firms without audited statements do not have access to bank credit. For firms that receive at least 20 percent of their credit from banks or finance companies, over one-third do not use audited statements. The numbers are the same for both short-term working capital and longer-term investment financing. Within this group, Malaysian firms are most likely to have audits, with over 80 percent reporting that they provide audited statements, while the proportion is two-thirds for Korean and Filipino firms, and less than one-half for the Indonesian and Thai firms.

Audited firms are, in principle, better informed of their financial positions, and disclosing this information to potential creditors should reduce the risk assessed with the loan, making access to credit somewhat easier. However, the surveys do not reveal this pattern across all countries (see figure 5.10). While this pattern does hold in Indonesia and Korea, in Malaysia, the Philippines, and Thailand, firms that are not required to provide audited statements are less likely to report having adequate liquidity. A similar pattern

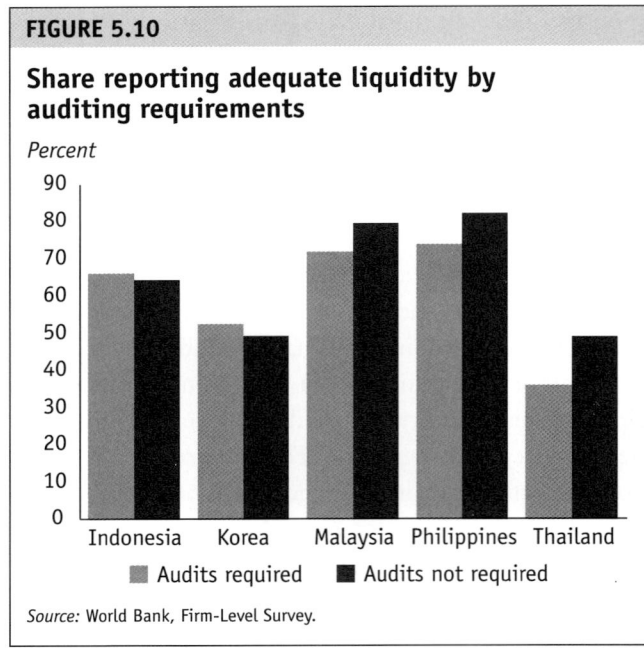

**FIGURE 5.10**

**Share reporting adequate liquidity by auditing requirements**

*Source:* World Bank, Firm-Level Survey.

emerges from the related issue of auditing practices in firms with inadequate liquidity. In Indonesia and Korea, those with liquidity problems are less likely to audit their statements, while in the other three countries, those with liquidity problems are more likely to be required to submit audited statements.

In all countries, highly leveraged firms with substantial access to bank credit are more likely to have audits than is the average firm (see figure 5.11). However, only in Indonesia is the difference between highly leveraged firms and low-leveraged firms very striking. Within this group of highly leveraged firms, however, there are still significant proportions—40 percent in Indonesia and Korea, and 60 percent in Thailand—that do not provide audits.

While highly leveraged firms are more likely to provide audited statements, there is surprisingly no clear relationship between the maturity of the credit obtained and whether audited statements are required. Thus, the firms that have a substantial share of long-term credit are not more likely to have been required to have audited statements than the firms without long-term debt. Likewise, the firms that are required to have audited statements do not have significant differences in the share of long-term debt to total debt than the firms that are not so required. This may also reflect the fact that long-term investments are often financed by rolling over short-term credits.

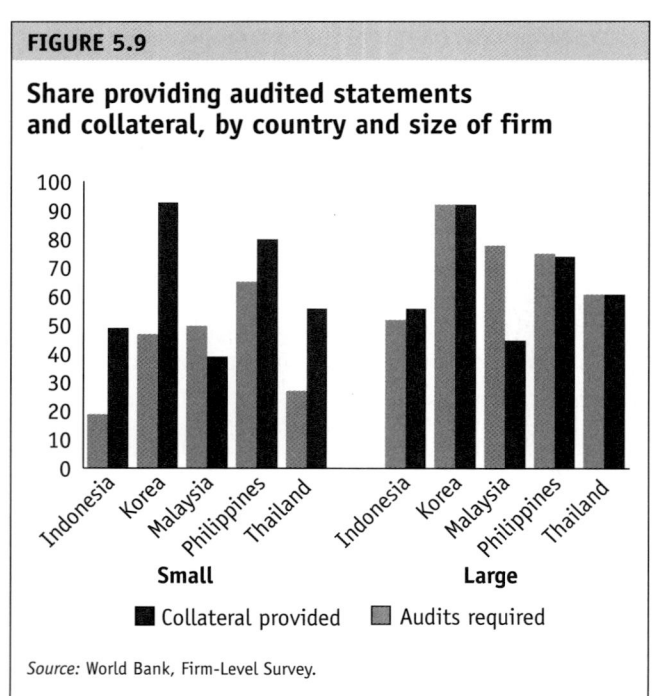

**FIGURE 5.9**

**Share providing audited statements and collateral, by country and size of firm**

*Source:* World Bank, Firm-Level Survey.

The more striking difference is for firms that borrow in foreign currency. Here the pattern is more similar across countries. Such firms are significantly more likely (85 percent) to have audited statements. The same is true for large firms and exporters.

The legal organization of the surveyed firms is also correlated with whether or not they audit their financial statements. Partnerships and single proprietorships (20 percent of the sample) are much less likely to do so; two-thirds of incorporated companies, however, have external audits. In Korea, almost all private corporations do provide the required external audits, while in Malaysia and Indonesia only 50 percent of the corporations have external audits, and less than 10 percent of unincorporated firms have them.

The correlation between legal organization and size is also reflected in the survey data. Three-quarters of the large firms provided audited statements versus 40 percent of the small firms. For the smaller firms, developing a relationship with the creditor is often seen as more reliable than the system of accounts used in such firms. Small firms have dealt with their primary creditor for 70 percent of the life of the firm. (The high is 88 percent in Thailand and the low is 60 percent in Indonesia). Thus small firms that do not provide audited statements are often characterized as having a long-standing relationship with their primary creditor.

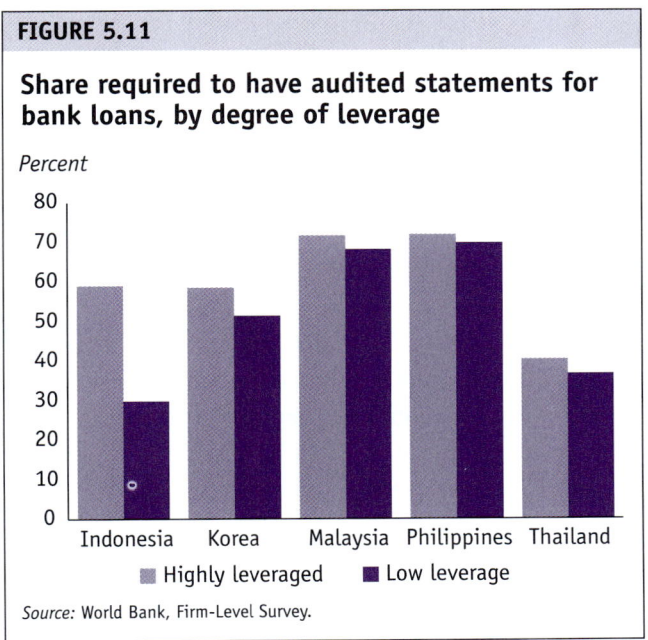

**FIGURE 5.11**

**Share required to have audited statements for bank loans, by degree of leverage**

Source: World Bank, Firm-Level Survey.

## Collateral

Land and physical assets are the principal form of collateral in these countries, representing at least part of the collateral in 90 percent of the cases in which collateral is provided. Machinery and equipment is the second most common form, and in Korea the use of financial instruments is starting to increase. The use of collateral in securing loans is by far the most common in Korea where 90 percent of firms have collateralized loans. In Malaysia, 40 percent of firms provide collateral, and between 50 and 60 percent of firms in the other countries do so.

Firms that provide collateral are slightly less likely to have liquidity problems, although this is not uniformly the case. In fact, two-thirds of the firms with collateral in Thailand are facing liquidity problems. In Indonesia, Malaysia, and the Philippines, two-thirds of the firms with collateral are not liquidity-constrained. In Korea the ratios are even.

Other than in Malaysia, highly indebted firms are significantly more likely to have to provide collateral for loans. But as with the auditing results, there are still over 30 percent of highly indebted firms in each country, except Korea, that qualify for loans without collateral. In Indonesia and Malaysia, firms that rely to a major extent on short-term debt are less likely to provide collateral, although little difference is discernible in Korea and Thailand.

The information on collateral usage needs to be supplemented with other information available to lenders. Other questions in the survey indicate that financial institutions do have information about their clients that they might be using instead of relying on collateral. On average, sample firms have worked for over nine years with their primary financial institution. These traditional relationships may be efficient substitutes for some of the more common financial reporting requirements, in view of the high cost of reducing information asymmetries for small and medium-size firms.

## Governance

Only one-third of the firms in Korea have independent directors on their boards. In Indonesia the corresponding figure is 10 percent, in Thailand 14 percent, in the Philippines 20 percent, and in Malaysia 25 percent.

Employee representation on boards is highest in the Philippines at 18 percent, almost triple the rate in the other four countries. Only in Malaysia and the Philippines, however, is the board likely to have a dominant say in decisions. In Korea, management has the dominant role. In Indonesia and Thailand, the original owners control the firms.

In a sample of listed companies analyzed by Claessens, Djankov, Fan, and Lang,[16] there are significant cross-ownership links between firms and financial institutions, which could lead to preferential access to credit. In this sample, on first evidence and without detailed examination, it seems that only 3 percent of the firms have reported financial institutions with an ownership stake in them.

However, there is a heavy concentration of ownership, as also evidenced in the sample provided by Claessens and others (1999). Approximately 20 percent of the firms have 10 or more shareholders. Among these firms, the top 10 shareholders own three-quarters of the firm. This concentration raises issues about minority shareholder rights.

## Concluding comments

This paper has analyzed the evidence regarding corporate credit needs and governance from the surveys of some 3,700 firms in five countries—Indonesia, Korea, Malaysia, the Philippines, and Thailand, covering major manufacturing and export sectors. The surveys were completed in February 1999. The quantitative information relates to the period between 1996 and the first half of 1998; the qualitative information covers the survey period from November 1998 to February 1999. The survey sample includes firms that are listed on stock exchanges, as well as those that are not; the latter represent 80 percent of the sample. For this latter group of firms in particular, financial information has been collected for the first time, and therefore may not be of the same quality as for the listed firms. Accordingly, the survey results are presented as general indications of tendencies rather than as point estimates.

The principal findings of this paper are as follows:
- The international financial fluctuations of recent years were transmitted to the firms primarily through their impact on domestic banks. Only for a small subset of large firms is short-term foreign currency debt a significant share of total debt. The surveyed firms, with the exception of those in Korea, had relatively low exposures to foreign financing, and relied primarily on domestic banks and financial institutions for their credit needs. The higher exposure to foreign finance by banks, combined with their less than careful approach to loan evaluation, has resulted in overexposed positions, and consequent reluctance to lend.
- The firms do not think that there is an aggregate shortage of credit relative to their needs for financing viable projects. In other words, at prevailing interest rates, credit availability in the aggregate is not seen by the surveyed firms as being a major impediment to corporate recovery. Their principal concern is with the low level of domestic demand. The surveys, however, offer evidence that there are inefficiencies in the allocation of credit, and that some firms, including small and medium-size firms, feel credit constrained.
- The great majority of the sample firms in Korea, Malaysia, and Thailand believe they will be able to meet loan repayments as required. This is less the case in Indonesia and the Philippines. However, there remain significant numbers of firms in all five countries that were either experiencing loan repayment difficulties at the time of the survey, or thought that they would find themselves in that situation in the near future if prevailing macroeconomic conditions persisted. This weak financial condition of a significant proportion of the firms is linked to both macroeconomic conditions and the pace of bank and corporate restructuring. Traditional relationships are important between small and medium-size firms and their lenders, and have compensated for weaknesses in commonly accepted aspects of corporate governance, including availability and utilization of audited financial statements, collateral requirements, and corporate management structures. Improvements in financial transparency are required for more efficient allocation of credit and reduction in its cost.
- The corporate recovery is taking place at an uneven pace between countries, sectors, and firms, with significant weaknesses remaining.

## Notes

Dominique Dwor-Frécaut and Mary Hallwood-Driemeier are with the World Bank. Francis Colaço is with Asia-Pacific Management Consultants, Inc. The authors gratefully acknowledge comments received from participants at the Conference on Corporate Recovery held in Bangkok from March 31 to April 2, 1999, and seminars at the World Bank in Washington and in Kuala Lumpur, Manila, Jakarta, Singapore, Hong Kong, Tokyo and Seoul, and the meeting of the Association of South East Asian Nations (ASEAN) Chambers of Commerce and Industry. The views expressed in the paper are strictly those of the authors and should not be attributed to the World Bank or its affiliated institutions. The authors would also like to thank Stacy Nemeroff, Giuseppe Iarossi, Dennis Tao, and Hairong Yu for research assistance.

1. Claessens, Djankov, and Lang (1999). This paper is based on information for 5,500 firms listed on stock exchanges in nine countries including Japan, Hong Kong, Singapore, Taiwan (China), Indonesia, the Republic of Korea, Malaysia, the Phillipines, and Thailand. The results of that paper and the current one are, therefore, not strictly comparable, and should rather be seen as complementary.

2. Thailand represents a special case as another survey, in late 1997, was carried out in addition to the present one. Both use the same sample of firms. In Thailand, 10 percent of the firms had gone out of business between the two surveys. In order to get clearer indications of the characteristics of the firms that closed during 1998, a follow-up study of the Thai data is underway using these two sets of data. A further follow-up survey in the five countries, planned for early 2000, will also give an indication of normal attrition rates.

3. The listed companies in the sample show higher reliance on foreign borrowing, so certainly some of the exchange rate shocks were transmitted directly to the corporate sector.

4. Demirguc-Kunt and Maksimovic (1995).

5. For a more in-depth discussion of the patterns of foreign currency borrowing, please see Kawai, Hahm, and Iarossi (1999), prepared for the Asian Corporate Recovery Conference.

6. Care was taken to remove obvious outliers or firms with inconsistencies in their reported financial data, so the higher means are not due to a few very high observations.

7. Claessens, Djankov, and Lang (1999).

8. Waiquamdee, Kraiiksh, and Phongsanarakul (1999).

9. Ghosh (1998).

10. See Stiglitz and Weiss (1981).

11. Cho and Rhee (1999).

12. In the case of Thailand, the decline in the supply of credit is well documented in the paper by Takatoshi Ito and Luis Pereira da Silva (1999). The paper analyzes aggregate data on the financial sector of Thailand, and the responses from 10 foreign and 7 Thai banks that returned questionnaires in April and May 1998.

13. See Shirazi (1999).

14. Unfortunately the option of the impact of the debt burden was not included in the Phlippines and Indonesia.

15. Again, this option was not included in the Philippines and Indonesia.

16. Claessens and others (1999).

# chapter six

# Financial Sector Restructuring: Progress and Issues

*Javad K. Shirazi*

This paper provides a review of the progress and the key issues in restructuring the financial systems of the countries at the center of the 1997–98 East Asian crisis—Indonesia, the Republic of Korea, Malaysia, and Thailand.[1] The first section contains an overview of the genesis of the crisis. The paper then examines the restructuring and recapitalization of these countries' financial institutions. This is followed by a section summarizing the steps taken to strengthen the prudential standards and the legal frameworks to facilitate debt recovery and restructuring. Then a brief discussion on interest rates, spreads, and loan growth is included. The final part of the paper attempts to draw some conclusions and lessons from the Asian crisis and the steps taken to restore health to the financial sector. The paper is not intended to be an exhaustive survey.

## The genesis of the crisis

In early 1997, despite signs of mounting currency pressures in Thailand, few—if any—observers could have predicted that East Asia would face a financial and economic crisis of the intensity and duration that it has. With a stellar growth performance spanning two decades, and a sustained record of broadly prudent economic management, the region was the envy of the developing world and attracted substantial and growing inflows of international capital from the industrial countries as a sign of confidence. What led to the unprecedented crisis that engulfed the region?

While much has been written on the origins of the crisis,[2] its root causes can be summarized simply as follows:

- Private investment booms in the 1990s and the associated asset bubbles that were fueled by (perceived) cheap foreign credit, mostly in the form of short-term bank lending to both financial institutions and corporates;
- Large (Malaysia and Thailand) and growing (Indonesia and Korea) current account deficits, incurred under fixed or nearly fixed exchange rate regimes with the exchange rate pegged to a rising dollar;
- Declining productivity of investment, as manifested in rapidly rising incremental capital–output ratios, and erosion of export competitiveness, particularly in Thailand, caused by real wage increases significantly outstripping productivity growth;
- Weak and inadequately regulated financial systems, which could not handle the rapid growth of domestic credit and price risks appropriately; and
- Questionable and nontransparent corporate practices and governance.

Once the financial turbulence began in one country, the contagion effects were strong, generating a widespread crisis of confidence and ensuing panic, which on the whole was clearly unwarranted on the basis of the "fundamentals," but perhaps not irrational from the vantage of individual market players, given the rapidly growing realization of actual and perceived systemic vulnerabilities.

It is beyond the scope of this paper to examine in any detail all of the above factors;[3] however, two aspects that are particularly relevant to the subject matter under discussion—the financial sector—need to be highlighted. The first is the scale of external capital inflows, and the second, the pace of expansion of domestic credit (to the private sector). Net private capital inflows into Asia 5 (Indonesia, Korea, Malaysia, Philippines, and Thailand) totaled some $US178 billion in 1995 and 1996, exceeding the combined flows of the preceding five years (see figure 6.1). Productive absorption of these flows proved to be infeasible. The countries also experienced rapid expansion of domestic credit relative to output growth. By 1997, credit-GDP ratios were in the range of 1.4–1.6 in all of these countries except for Indonesia, which had levels substantially higher than at the beginning of the 1990s (see table 6.1). By contrast, in Mexico, at the time of its banking crisis, the credit-GDP ratio was less than 0.5.

The unprecedented capital inflows into the region played a critical role in fueling the rapid growth of banks' and other financial intermediaries' balance sheets. The quality of assets being acquired was often poor and there was inadequate appreciation of, and pricing for, liquidity and credit risks. The massive credits extended to the real estate sector are indicative of this phenomenon. As the exchange rate crises unfolded and the interest rates were raised, the impact on the balance sheets of financial institutions and corporations was severe. The subsequent contraction of economic activity exacerbated the damage. Ironically, the large-scale capital inflows, which were in part attracted by sound macroeconomic policies, led to the buildup of external and domestic financial imbalances that made the systems highly vulnerable to loss of confidence, speculative

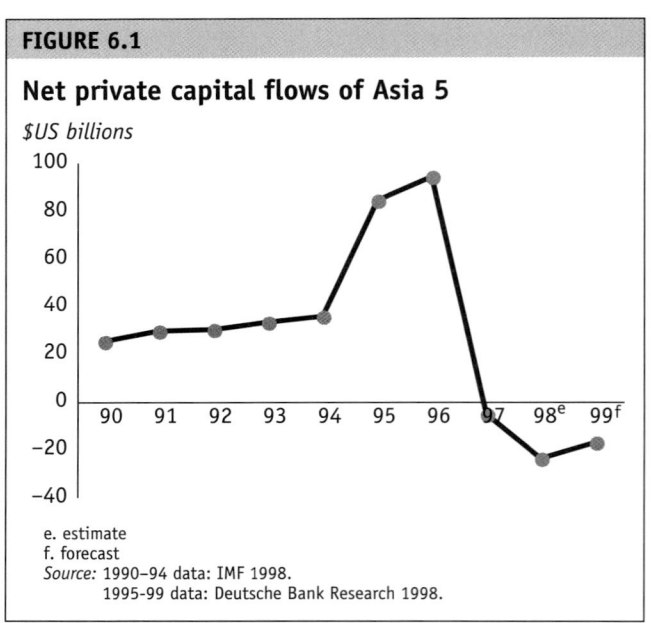

**FIGURE 6.1**

**Net private capital flows of Asia 5**

$US billions

e. estimate
f. forecast
Source: 1990–94 data: IMF 1998.
1995–99 data: Deutsche Bank Research 1998.

**TABLE 6.1**
**Domestic credit and growth rates**

| Country | Credit (percent of GDP) 1991 | Credit (percent of GDP) 1997 | CAGR (percent) 1991–97 |
|---|---|---|---|
| Indonesia | 50.3 | 65.4 | 21.5 |
| Korea | 94.5 | 137.9 | 19.0 |
| Malaysia | 116.7 | 165.4 | 19.9 |
| Thailand | 96.3 | 147.7 | 19.1 |

CAGR: Compound Annual Growth Rate.
Source: Deutsche Bank Research 1998.

attacks, and strong contagion effects. Credit as a percentage of GDP rose particularly rapidly between 1991 and 1997, despite the strong growth of nominal GDP (see table 6.1).

In an earlier paper,[4] the author argued that the reversal of capital flows after the onset of the crisis was particularly punishing and laid the grounds for the subsequent economic dislocations experienced. In 1997, the reversal amounted to more than 10 percent of the combined preshock GDP of Asia 5. The large real exchange rate depreciations, the financial sector and asset price distress, the collapse of investment activity, and the erosion of incomes and consumer confidence must be seen and understood in light of this extraordinary reversal of external flows. In a comparative perspective, what happened in East Asia in 1997 is tantamount to a reversal of $800 billion or about 70 percent of an entire year's private capital formation in the case of the U.S. economy. Paul Krugman, in a recent paper, attempted to shed light on the East Asian crisis by formally modeling the large required adjustments in the current account through real exchange rate depreciation, recession, or both, and the consequent erosion of the firms' balance sheets.[5] It is this dynamic that lies at the heart of the financial sector and corporate distress faced in these countries. The fragility that may have existed in the financial sector and corporate balance sheets received a large shock caused by the very policies put in place to cope with the precipitous fall in the exchange rate and to restore external balance stability. Krugman's tentative conclusion, which merits serious reflection, is that "even a very clean and prudent banking system may not be enough to protect open economies from the risk of self-reinforcing financial collapse."[6]

Accordingly, the conventional wisdom about the Asian crisis that generally apportions much of the blame to weaknesses in the financial sector and corporate governance is at best simplistic. Belatedly, there is a welcome recognition in western policy circles that the root cause was not so much the weaknesses of the financial sectors (a common feature in developing economies), but rather the excessiveness of capital inflows relative to the system into which they must be absorbed.[7] This recognition is particularly important in terms of shifting the emphasis of the current discussions to reforming the international financial architecture and to strengthening the developing countries' economic policymaking and monitoring institutions. This strategy will enable us to reduce the risks of future crises in an increasingly globalized setting in which markets can inflict disproportionate punishment for policy mistakes and reassessed structural weaknesses.

## Restructuring and recapitalization

### The scale of the problem and the fiscal impact

By any standard, the scale of the financial sector distress in East Asian countries is large. Given the dynamic of the crisis in East Asia, the moral hazard problems that arise from weak bankruptcy and foreclosure laws and their enforcement, and uncertainty over the timing and strength of recovery, estimation of the health of bank portfolios in a dynamic sense is fraught with uncertainty and could embody significant margins of error. Nevertheless, many estimates are available from private and official sources and all indicate that the scale of the problem and the fiscal impact are extremely large. As indicated in table 6.2, peak nonperforming loans (NPLs) as a percentage of loan portfolios are estimated to range from 30 percent in Korea to 75 percent in Indonesia. In relation to GDP, the projected net losses range from 16 percent in Korea to 34 percent in Thailand. The sharp currency depreciation and decline in asset values combined with a strong downturn in economic activity led to a mounting deterioration in bank asset quality throughout 1998. For example, estimated NPLs for Thai banks rose from 43 percent at the end of September to 49 percent at the end of the year (see table 6.3). Many observers, however, feel that NPLs will peak during the first half of 1999 in most of the crisis-affected countries.

Converting NPLs into estimates of ultimate losses involves a number of assumptions, including those on peak NPLs and recovery rates from the disposal of collateral. One set of projections, prepared by Deutsche Bank Research, indicates that the total loan net losses could range from 16 percent of GDP in Korea to 34 percent in Thailand, based on the June 1997 portfolio data. In aggregate terms, potential losses on NPLs would exceed by varying margins the total capital of the financial institutions in these countries, with Indonesia

### TABLE 6.2
**Peak nonperforming loans and losses**

| Country | NPLs (percentage of loan portfolio) | Net loss (percentage of GDP) | Losses/capital (percent) |
|---|---|---|---|
| Indonesia | 75 | 30 | 474 |
| Korea | 30 | 16 | 126 |
| Malaysia | 35 | 20 | 120 |
| Thailand | 50 | 34 | 248 |

*Note:* Assumptions on recovery rates are 25 percent for Indonesia, 30 percent for Thailand; and 50 percent for Malaysia and Korea. "Net loss" is defined as the deterioration in bank capital resulting from the implied writedown of loans. June 1997 balance sheet data on loans and capital are used as a base.
*Source:* Deutsche Bank Research 1998.

### TABLE 6.3
**Thai nonperforming loans**

| Financial organization | NPLs/loans (percent) Sept. 1998 | NPLs/loans (percent) Dec. 1998 |
|---|---|---|
| Thai banks | 43 | 49 |
| Private banks (8) | 37 | 42 |
| State-owned banks (8) | 55 | 63 |
| Foreign banks | 8 | 10 |
| Total banking system | 38 | 44 |
| Finance companies (35) | 61 | 70 |
| Total financial system | 40 | 46 |

*Source:* Bank of Thailand.

and Thailand affected particularly heavily. (This does not, of course, imply that all the financial institutions are insolvent.) Estimates of the fiscal and quasi-fiscal costs of restructuring will depend not only on the ultimate levels of NPLs and recovery rates, but also on the loss-sharing arrangements between the government and the private sector. Projections by multilateral institutions and private analysts indicate a range of 10–20 percent of GDP for Malaysia and Korea, and 30–40 percent for Indonesia and Thailand. Assuming that government bonds at market interest rates are used to finance the recapitalization, the annual government interest expense would range from about 1.5 percent to 3 percent of GDP in these countries. The government outlays and obligations for financial sector restructuring, deficit spending for other purposes, and the other crisis-related fiscal costs will sharply raise government indebtedness in the four countries (see table 6.4). While the debt projections are subject to the usual uncertainties, the pace of buildup is alarming, particularly in Indonesia and Thailand. The fact that the precrisis debt-GDP ratios were relatively modest in these countries will help mitigate the future debt-servicing burden.

## Restructuring approaches and country experiences

The financial sector crisis in Indonesia, Korea, Malaysia, and Thailand has clearly proved to be a systemic one that requires major restructuring. Broadly speaking, the approaches adopted in the four countries have been similar and have involved elements of both the "flow" and "stock" solutions, with the emphasis on the latter. The former has entailed injection of central bank liquidity (for example, through the Financial Institutions Development Fund in Thailand) and regulatory forbearance (Indonesia and Malaysia in particular). The "stock" solutions have focused on the closure of deeply insolvent financial institutions, takeovers, carving out and transferring bad assets to a central agency, and capital injection from private and public sources.

Given the scale of the financial management distress, governments have had to inject substantial sums to prevent a complete collapse of the payment systems and to speed up the rehabilitation process. In this respect, Korea has acted expeditiously. By the end of 1998, public funds injected into the banking system since the inception of the crisis amounted to nearly US$31 billion, with an additional US$18 billion programmed for 1999. The Korean Asset Management Company (KAMCO) and the Korean Deposit Insurance Company (KDIC) are the two institutions engineering the removal

### TABLE 6.4
**Government debt as percentage of GDP**

| Country | 1996 | 1999[a] | 2000[a] |
|---|---|---|---|
| Indonesia | 51.1 | 93 | 98.3 |
| Domestic | 25.1 | 57 | 64.3 |
| Foreign | 26 | 36 | 34 |
| Korea | 28.2 | 41.3 | 40.7 |
| Domestic | 19.2 | 25.3 | 24.7 |
| Foreign | 9 | 16 | 16 |
| Malaysia | 47.7 | 59.5 | 63.3 |
| Domestic | 31.7 | 36.5 | 39.3 |
| Foreign | 16 | 23 | 24 |
| Thailand | 11 | 55.4 | 52.7 |
| Domestic | 2 | 26.4 | 24.7 |
| Foreign | 9 | 29 | 28 |

a. Projected.
*Source:* World Bank.

of NPLs from the banks and their disposition. Bonds in exchange for bad assets have been the main instrument for the asset swaps. KAMCO has disposed of the acquired assets in a variety of ways, including auctions and direct sales. KDIC has covered the deposits of the 16 merchant banks that were shut down and has injected new capital to facilitate the acquisition of the nonviable banks by viable institutions and to prepare the sale of Korea First Bank and Seoul Bank, both of which were acquired by the government at the onset of the crisis. Fifty-one percent of the shares of the former has been acquired by a U.S. investment company and 70 percent of the latter is reported to have been acquired by a foreign bank. These sales were effected through international auctions. The Korean strategy, which has involved nationalization, closures, disposition of NPLs, and injection of capital by specialized agencies, mergers and subsequent privatization, has been adequately funded and rapidly implemented as market conditions permitted. In moving forward to establish "clean banks," the authorities have applied stringent safeguards to minimize moral hazard and public losses.

Thailand's approach to financial sector restructuring has entailed two distinct components: the finance companies and the banks. In the case of the former, by December 1997, all but two of the 58 finance companies suspended earlier in the year had been closed down. An independent entity, the Financial Restructuring Agency (FRA), was set up in October 1997 to deal with the 58 suspended finance companies, and an Asset Management Corporation (AMC) was formed to manage and dispose of the bad assets of the banks. The assets of the 56 closed finance companies amounted to 371 billion baht at face value. Financial Institutions Development Fund (FIDF) outlays to these entities exceeded 1 trillion baht or the equivalent of about 18 percent of the 1998 GDP.

On December 15, 1997 the FRA auctioned over US$11 billion of the commercial and real estate loans from the 56 finance companies that had been closed down. The auction, which included both foreign and Thai bidders, generated only 11.66 billion baht (about US$3 billion) for 9 tranches (out of the 45 tranches tendered). Negotiations following the auction raised the total disposed to 41 percent of the portfolio initially offered. The FRA's realization is reported to have been 25 percent of book value of the assets sold. Another auction covering about US$6 billion of the loans of the defunct finance companies was held on March 19, 1998. Reportedly, the bids averaged 18 percent of the face value of the loans and AMC purchased over three-quarters of the value of the assets auctioned.

To deal with the restructuring and recapitalization of the banking sector, the Thai government unveiled a plan in August 1998. This plan offered public funds as capital injection for banks that were prepared to restructure up front, accelerate corporate debt restructuring, and undertake new lending. The support facilities provide both Tier I and Tier II capital, involving funding on a matching basis to that of new private capital. Losses are to be borne fully by existing shareholders up to their equity limits, with additional losses, if any, to be shared by the government and new investors. The plan also includes the purchase of preferred shares by the government to bring Tier I capital up to 2.5 percent. Above that level, the government will match the amount injected by private investors. About 200 billion baht have been earmarked for Tier I. However, financial institutions must fully meet the central bank's loan loss provisioning requirements and submit an acceptable plan for organizational restructuring. For Tier II capital, the plan calls for placing some 100 billion baht of nontradable government bonds in exchange for bank debentures for a maximum of two percent of risk-weighted assets. The amount of funds available would hinge on write-downs of earnings resulting from corporate restructuring and the expansion in new loans to the private sector.

Despite the massive losses suffered by Thai banks in 1998 (see table 6.5) and the rising levels of NPLs, banks have not availed themselves of the facilities set up by the government (particularly the Tier I facility), because they are reluctant to write down their capital in return for public money and accept the dilution of the ownership that comes with the deal. Thus far, only one bank (Siam Commercial Bank) has formally requested Tier I support. Thai Farmers Bank has raised capital through the issuance of linked preferred stocks and subordinated debentures. Two other banks are following a similar approach. These new instruments are perceived as temporary solutions and there is concern about the extent of fresh money actually raised since over one-half of the buyers are depositors of the issuing bank or other

TABLE 6.5
**Net profit (loss) and assets of Thai banks**

| Bank | Net profit (loss) (Baht millions) 1997 | 1998 | Assets (Baht millions) Sept. 1998 | Losses/assets (percent) Sept. 1998 |
|---|---|---|---|---|
| Krung Thai Bank | 210 | (60,079) | 1,143,637 | 5.3 |
| Bangkok Bank | 4,057 | (49,500) | 1,302,192 | 3.8 |
| Thai Farmers Bank | 801 | (39,883) | 733,272 | 5.4 |
| Siam Commercial Bank | 3,194 | (12,861) | 699,658 | 1.8 |
| Bank of Ayudhya | 1,962 | (9,203) | 482,527 | 1.9 |
| Thai Military Bank | 1,368 | (7,700) | 361,596 | 2.1 |

*Source:* Far Eastern Economic Review 1999.

Thai banks.[8] The five state-owned commercial banks are raising capital from the government.

It would be fair to conclude that the Thai experience thus far points to a restructuring process for commercial banks that is moving rather slowly and hence can impede the restoration of normalcy in the financial and corporate sectors. Recent statements by the authorities have indicated that Bank of Thailand may take further steps to accelerate recapitalization if the voluntary actions fall short of the central bank's expectations. This would be justified given broader concerns about economic recovery and the role of the banking system in that process.

Indonesia's banking system, though smaller in terms of assets relative to GDP, is clearly the most distressed in the region because of weaker precrisis conditions, the sharper depreciation of the currency in a setting in which the private sector has very large external liabilities, and the worst contraction in economic activity experienced in 1998 by any country in the region. Several early steps to restructure the banking system were taken in the early phases of the crisis. These included the formation of a bank restructuring agency (the Indonesian Bank Restructuring Agency or IBRA), the closure of 23 private banks, the placement of 61 private banks under the supervision of IBRA, and the formation of a new bank (Bank Mandiri) to absorb four state banks. After the initial progress, however, the pace of restructuring proved to be sluggish, owing largely to the sheer size of the problem coupled with political uncertainty and interference in the decision-making authority of IBRA.

It was only on March 12, 1998 that the government announced a much-awaited comprehensive bank restructuring and recapitalization plan. Thirty-eight banks were closed down, their assets to be managed by IBRA. Seven banks were taken over by the government in order to facilitate the payment system. Seventy-three banks with capital asset ratios equal to or greater than 4 percent will remain open. The government will issue bonds in order to provide up to 80 percent of the financing for the recapitalization of nine banks. The remaining 20 percent will be provided by the owners of these banks. The terms of the government's interest in these nine banks will be restricted to decisions on strategic issues, leaving the day-to-day affairs to the private owners. The original shareholders will have the opportunity to buy back their shares within three years. Otherwise the government will sell its shares in the open market over the next two years. The gross cost of the restructuring package is estimated at 300 trillion rupiah (30 percent of the fiscal 1998 GDP). The recapitalization of the nine private banks amounts to less than 10 percent of the total cost with the liquidation of the 38 banks and the recapitalization of the central bank responsible for the lion's share of the expenses. Some 73 private banks that were not closed down or marked as candidates for recapitalization assistance will be closely supervised.

Compared with Indonesia and Thailand, Malaysia's banking sector difficulties were less pronounced before the crisis began to unfold. The risk-weighted capital adequacy ratio of commercial banks was 10.8 percent at the end of 1996. As the regional crisis unfolded, nonperforming loans rose from 8 percent of total loans at the end of 1997 to 13.6 percent at the end of 1998 (measured on a three-month classification standard), as reported by Bank Negara Malaysia (Central Bank). The overall capital-adequacy ratio at the end of 1998 was reported to have fallen to 8.7 percent. Between October 1997 and March 1998, the authorities announced a series of measures that involved tightened regulations regarding loan classification and higher capital adequacy ratios, but the new norms were subsequently relaxed in September 1998 (see the section on strengthening prudential standards and the legal frameworks below). The government then took the initiative to establish entities similar to those set up in Korea. Danaharta, an asset management company, was set up in May 1998 with a total funding of 15 billion ringgit, and is mandated to acquire NPLs from financial institutions and to maximize their recovery value. By the end of 1998, it had acquired 8.11 billion ringgit of NPLs at an average discount of 61 percent. Additionally, Danaharta managed 11.62 billion ringgit of bad loans in 1998 and expects to complete the acquisition of the remaining bad loans in the system by June 1999.

A second agency, Danamodal, was established in August 1998 with an expected funding of 16 billion ringgit (10.7 billion has been raised so far). Danamodal is expected to recapitalize and consolidate the banking sector. Institutions availing themselves of the assistance of Danamodal are required to sell to Danaharta their NPLs in excess of 10 percent of their loan portfolios. Thus far, Danamodal has injected 4.5 billion ringgit into nine financial institutions in the form of Exchangeable Subordinated Capital Loans. Danaharta's estimated funding was derived based on the basis of the more lenient six-month classification of NPLs. Based on the three-month definition, the funding requirements would have been larger. Malaysia's approach to restructuring centers on balance sheet cleanup—but not liquidity injection, since the payment for NPLs is in the form of long-dated zero coupon bonds.

A major difference in the financial sector restructuring strategy of Malaysia compared with the three other countries has been its reluctance to close or nationalize banks and finance companies. With the exception of MBf Finance Bhd and Kewangan Bersatu Bhd, 2 independent finance companies that were taken over by Bank Negara in January 1999, Malaysia has been unable to complete its plans for the consolidation of 40 finance companies into 8. In all likelihood Danamodal could end up bearing more of the burden of recapitalization than shareholders, unless the government takes a firmer stand in its position regarding closures.

## Strengthening prudential standards and the legal frameworks

As a central feature of financial restructuring in the crisis-affected countries, all the countries have moved toward adopting international standards for loan classification, income recognition, and minimum capital-adequacy ratios. The general approach has understandably introduced the tighter norms in a phased manner. In Korea, the Financial Supervisory Commission (FSC) has spearheaded the introduction of international standards for accounting and reporting.[9] In June 1998, all financial institutions were required to follow a step-by-step schedule to switch over to a mark-to-market basis for accounting for securities. By July 1998, loan classification procedures had been revised to fully reflect capacity to pay. In addition, it became mandatory for banks to disclose connected lending information and manage their foreign exchange exposure in order to avoid maturity mismatches. The calculation of capital asset ratios was modified in order to incorporate a more conservative standard—loan provisions classified as substandard or lower were deducted from Tier II capital. Thailand has set a legal minimum for capital adequacy ratios of 8.5 percent for banks and 8 percent for finance companies, with January 15, 1999 as the deadline. Thai authorities have also shortened the basis period for mandated disclosure of NPLs from 12 to 6 months, though eventually they plan to establish a three-month basis by the year 2000.

In Indonesia, the authorities announced a sharp increase in minimum capital requirements for banks and tightened loan classification and provisioning guidelines in January 1998. However, the increase in capital requirements was later reversed. Current standards are a minimum capital-asset ratio of 4 percent, to be increased to 12 percent by 2001. The three-month definition for overdue loans will be in effect by then as well. In January 1998, Malaysia tightened loan loss provisioning standards by establishing a three-month classification and higher capital adequacy ratios for finance companies in order to strengthen the banking system. However, in September 1998 the government rescinded some of these banking regulations to reduce the severity of the credit crunch, which they believed had been caused by the new regulations. The classification of NPLs is once again based on a six-month rather than a three-month standard (see table 6.6).

In comparison to the other countries facing financial sector distress, Malaysia ranks fairly high in having a viable legal framework for bankruptcy and foreclosure. The Indonesian and Thai legal systems, by contrast, have required major changes to facilitate bank and corporate restructuring. In the former much remains to

### TABLE 6.6
**Prudential standards**

| Country | Definition of NPLs (months overdue) | Capital-asset ratio (percent) |
|---|---|---|
| Indonesia | 3 (by 2001) | 4 (12 by 2001) |
| Korea | 3 | 8 |
| Malaysia | 6 | 8 (10 by 1999) |
| Thailand | 3 (by 2000) | 8.5 |

*Source:* Country authorities.

be done. In Thailand, the signing of a bill in February to establish a Bankruptcy Court paved the way for the reform of the legal system. In mid-March, the Thai Senate approved the pending revisions in the remaining key bankruptcy and foreclosure laws (the Bankruptcy Bill, the Petty Cases Bill, and the Foreclosure Bill), which were subsequently ratified by the Lower House. These new legislations, which are major achievements, provide the impetus for speedier resolution of NPLs. However, their ultimate effectiveness will depend heavily on the efficacy of the judicial system to move the process forward.

In Korea, corporate restructuring has been traditionally handled through workouts rather than the legal process. In February 1998, exit barriers were diminished through a simplification of the legal procedures applicable to corporate restructuring and bankruptcy.

## Interest rates and loan growth

Broadly, the crisis countries have experienced a similar pattern with respect to lending volumes and interest rate movements—that is, there has been a sharp slowdown in credit growth and rising spreads even as nominal interest rates were being lowered in response to the stabilization of the currencies, falling inflation rates and the need to stimulate economic activity (see figure 6.2). Because of mounting NPLs, however, banks have tended to opt for higher spreads to cushion, at least in a modest way, the impact of rising losses. Thai spreads, defined as the difference between the minimum lending rate and a weighted deposit rate, rose from approximately 4.25 percent in July 1997 to 4.75 percent a year later, reaching 7 percent in September 1998, before declining to 5.5 percent (see figure 6.3). An unofficial survey done by the Bank of Thailand in October 1998 estimated that the current spreads, though historically

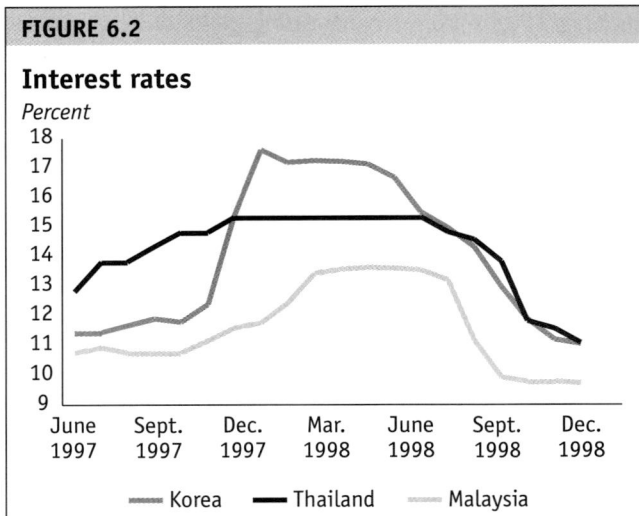

### FIGURE 6.2
**Interest rates**

*Note:* Korean rates are lending rates on general loans for up to one year. Thai rates are minimum lending rates for commercial banks. Malaysian rates are average lending rates for commercial banks.
*Source:* Bank of Korea, Bank of Thailand, and Bank Negara Malaysia.

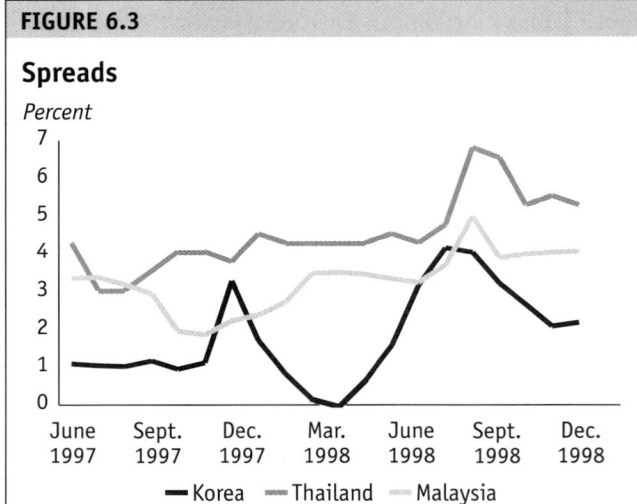

### FIGURE 6.3
**Spreads**

*Note:* Korean spreads are the difference between lending rates on general loans for up to one year and fixed deposit rates for between one and two years. Thai spreads are minimum lending rates for commercial banks minus deposit rates. Malaysian spreads are the difference between average lending rates for commercial banks and one-year fixed deposit rates.
*Source:* Bank of Korea, Bank of Thailand, and Bank Negara Malaysia.

high, are not sufficient given the level of NPLs and the recapitalization requirements. To stay financially viable, banks would need to maintain spreads as high as 12 percent, which would be infeasible.

Loan growth in Thailand in January 1999 relative to a year earlier had slowed to 2.5 percent (see figure 6.4). A similar pattern has emerged in Malaysia, where the loan volume, which grew 26 percent in 1997, barely increased in 1998 (see figure 6.5). The Malaysian credit crunch was very likely exacerbated by tighter banking standards introduced in October 1997, which the government then rescinded in September 1998. Recognizing the fact that high interest rates were contributing to the credit crunch, the government lowered interest rates and directed banks to reduce their maximum spreads over the base lending rate to 2.5 percent. In Korea, though deposit rates have come down, lending rates remain relatively high, reflecting built-in risk. Loan growth (adjusted for NPLs bought by the government) was essentially stagnant in 1998, compared with a growth of 15 percent in 1997. In Indonesia, where the inflation rate and nominal interest rates were very high during much of 1998, the spreads between lending and deposit rates rose sharply between July and December 1998 (from about 9 percent to over 14 percent).

## Conclusions and lessons

The pace of financial sector restructuring, recapitalization, and return to some semblance of "normalcy" has been slower than envisaged in all of the crisis countries, with the possible exception of Korea. This is understandable given the extent of distress in the sector and the deepening economic dislocation during most of 1998. Just as the magnitude of the economic contraction unleashed by the events of 1997 was repeatedly underestimated by international institutions and domestic policymakers, as well as many private analysts, the scale of asset destruction in the financial sector was also inaccurately predicted. These two misjudgments were of course not unrelated.

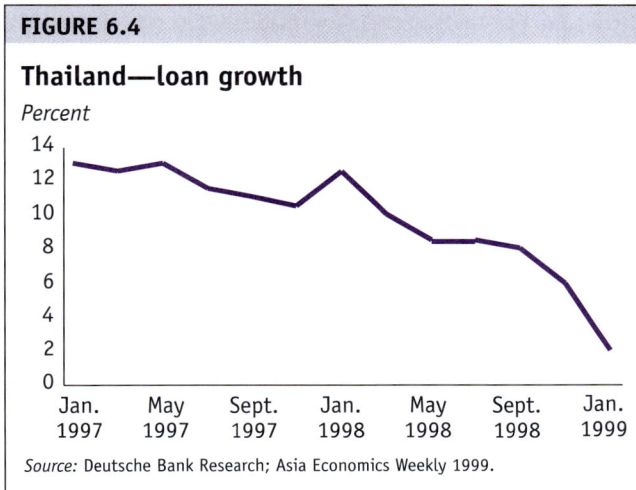

**FIGURE 6.4**

**Thailand—loan growth**

Source: Deutsche Bank Research; Asia Economics Weekly 1999.

The initial optimism about market-based solutions, particularly a recapitalization strategy predicated on private sector funding, has proved unjustified. Despite some early successes in Thailand, it has increasingly become evident that the investor appetite for Asian banks' equity was very limited. Hence, greater public sector involvement in recapitalization has become essential. An earlier appreciation of this reality would have perhaps led to the design and implementation of resolution packages with greater emphasis on closures of deeply insolvent institutions and on government participation in recapitalizing potentially viable ones (as was done in Korea, for example), as well as a more forceful way of inducing bad debt recognition and write-offs on the part of private shareholders.

The extent of domestic debt overhang (essentially the losses in the banking and corporate sectors) has been simply too large to allow for governments to avoid socializing the vast bulk of the costs of asset quality deterioration. An earlier realization of the dynamics set in motion by the pernicious combination of large currency depreciation, high interest rates engineered to defend the currencies, declining terms of international trade, and the sharp decline in domestic demand (particularly investment spending), would have led to more realistic external financing, fiscal stance, and financial

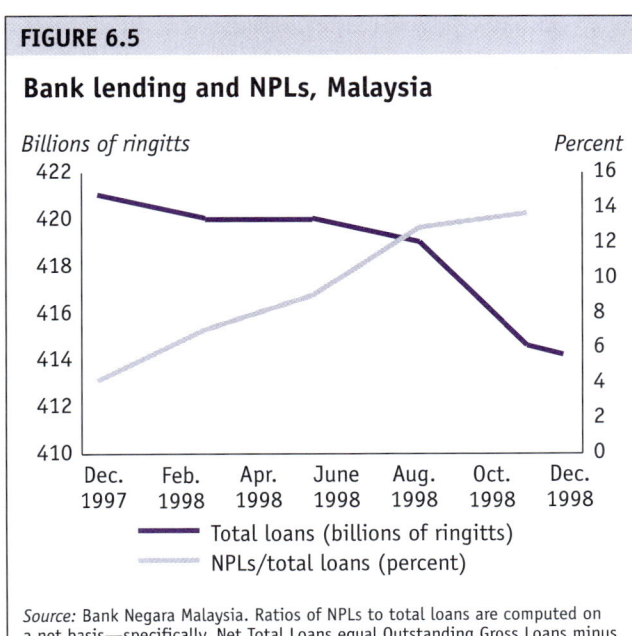

**FIGURE 6.5**

**Bank lending and NPLs, Malaysia**

Source: Bank Negara Malaysia. Ratios of NPLs to total loans are computed on a net basis—specifically, Net Total Loans equal Outstanding Gross Loans minus Interest-in-Suspense and Specific Provisions.

sector restructuring strategies (including judicious use of forbearance). These in turn could have mitigated the extent of the loss of wealth and output.

International experience indicates that countries are far more successful in restoring the solvency of their banking systems than in engineering increases in profitability. Thus far, there is no evidence suggesting that the East Asian experience will prove to be different.

The rapid decline in domestic inflation rates and the deflationary pressures affecting export prices do not bode well for the remaining agenda of cleaning up the banking systems and corporate debt restructuring. Stagnant or falling wholesale prices have offset the decline in nominal interest rates, implying a rise in the firms' debt burden in real terms. Given that the operational restructuring (in other words, measures aimed at increasing efficiency) of the banking system has barely begun, and considering the need to generate margins that facilitate recapitalization, the prospects for easing the debt burden of the borrowers are not bright.

In this context, accelerating the overhaul of bankruptcy and foreclosure laws and, more important, putting in place effective implementation mechanisms, are critical for separating expedient defaulters from others and for facilitating debt-equity swaps. This is an aspect of the financial sector–corporate restructuring nexus that has moved forward at an extremely slow pace.

Dealing with the inevitable large increases in the government debt burden arising from financial sector restructuring and with the other aspects of the crisis can prove to be destabilizing in the medium term. Therefore, privatization of public enterprises and steps designed to broaden the tax base and strengthen tax administration have particular importance for managing the medium-term fiscal consequences of the crisis.

The crisis underscores the need for redoubling efforts to develop domestic debt markets. The underdeveloped debt markets led to excessive reliance on banks and finance companies as the principal vehicles for term financing during the crisis. More developed domestic debt markets would have lowered the risks of maturity mismatch faced by banks and also would have reduced the probability of sharp and sudden reversals of capital flows, as the debt markets would have more effectively intermediated the surge in inflows.

In the early 1990s, it had become an article of faith among most economists that developing countries needed to generate fiscal surpluses in order to accommodate the absorption of private capital inflows. As long as external capital inflows (equity or debt) were being utilized to finance private investment, it was argued, the authorities did not need to be concerned with the volumes and maturities of these inflows. The naiveté of this view—particularly in terms of understanding institutional weaknesses in credit allocation and risk management in developing economies—has been starkly exposed by the experience of the past two years. Policymakers are once again reminded of the close linkages between the management of domestic financial markets, international private capital flows, and overall country debt management.

# Annex 6.A

## Financial restructuring in East Asia at a glance

### Indonesia

- Until recently, the Indonesian Bank Restructuring Authority (IBRA) had not been funded or given proper authority. However, 23 private banks have now been closed, 61 have been placed under the supervision of IBRA and 5 state banks have been merged under a new entity called Bank Mandiri.
- On March 12, 1998 the government announced a restructuring and recapitalization package, the cost of which is estimated to be 300 trillion rupiah (30 percent of the fiscal 1998 GDP).
- The largest part of the cost will be the liquidation and closure of 38 banks and the recapitalization of the central bank to compensate it for large liquidity injections incurred in 1998.
- Nine banks will be recapitalized up to 80 percent of the amount needed to resume a Tier-I capital ratio of 4 percent, with the original shareholders contributing at least 20 percent in cash at a cost of about 10 percent of the recap package.
- 73 banks with capital ratios equal to or greater than 4 percent will remain open.
- Seven large private banks (with 80,000 or more deposit accounts) will be taken over by the government to minimize disruption to the payments system.
- The government has set new capital adequacy targets—banks must achieve a capital-adequacy ratio of 4 percent, 8 percent, and 10 percent by the end of 1998, 1999, and 2000, respectively.

### Korea

- The Korean government has mobilized 64 trillion won in capital for the recapitalization and disposal of nonperforming loans. By the end of December 1998, 41 trillion won had already been spent.
- The Korean asset management corporation, (KAMCO) had disposed of NPLs with a face value of 12.6 trillion won by the end of 1998, with an additional 15.4 trillion won scheduled for 1999.
- A second agency, KDIC, injected 21 trillion won of funds into the financial system, of which one-third covered the deposits of 16 distressed merchant banks closed by the government, another third covered losses for viable financial institutions (mainly 5 banks), and the rest was channeled toward mergers of banks that were not considered viable.
- The government has privatized two of its banks. The sale of 51 percent of Korea First Bank to Newbridge Capital has been finalized and a memorandum of understanding has been signed for the sale of 70 percent of Seoul Bank.
- The FSC has also set a strict timetable for the adherence of commercial banks and non-banks to 8 percent capital ratios by the year 2000, as well as to other international standards.

### Malaysia

- The Malaysian government has set up two agencies to aid in the financial sector restructuring: Danaharta (an asset management company) and Danamodal (to provide liquidity and recapitalization).
- Danaharta has purchased 8.11 billion ringgit of nonperforming loans at a discount of 61 percent, for which it paid 4.26 billion ringgit out of its total funding of 15 billion. Danaharta also managed 11.62 billion ringgits of bad loans in 1998.
- Danamodal has injected 4.5 billion ringgit into nine financial institutions in the form of Exchangeable Subordinated Capital Loans. The government has estimated that Danamodal would require approximately 16 billion ringgit, of which it has raised 10.7 so far.
- Two finance companies, MFf Finance Bhd and Kewangan Bersatu Bhd have been taken over by Bank Negara.
- Prudential standards were tightened in April 1998. Nonperforming loans were defined as those loans that were three months overdue.

- In September 1998, standards were relaxed again and the definition of nonperforming loans changed to six months overdue.

## Thailand

- The government unveiled a financial restructuring plan on August 14, 1998, which pledged a total of 300 billion baht in Tier I and Tier II capital to undercapitalized banks. For both schemes, a capital adequacy standard of 4.25 percent is required.
- In the Tier I scheme, banks are required to first write down their capital by recognizing losses upfront and then change management in return for official money. Siam Commercial Bank (SCB) has applied for Tier I capital, and another application is being considered.
- In Tier II, incremental government capital is provided to individual banks depending on the bank's corporate restructuring performance. Two applications for Tier II capital assistance have also been approved—for TFB (Thai Farmer's Bank) and SCB.
- Thai Farmer's Bank and Bangkok Bank have independently raised Tier I capital through issues of preferred shares, debentures, refinancing and recognizing capital gains.
- Krung Thai Bank has merged with First Bangkok City Bank and taken over Bangkok Bank of Commerce and received 77 billion in assistance from the FIDF, with an additional 108 billion forthcoming after its restructuring plan is approved.
- The FRA auction held in December 1998 resulted in sales of 41 percent of the commercial and real estate loans worth a total of 371 billion baht. FRA's receipts amounted to nearly 25 percent of the book value of the assets. Another auction ($6 billion in loans) was held on March 19, 1999.
- Legislature pertaining to Bankruptcy Court has already been ratified. Three bills—Bankruptcy, Foreclosure, and Petty Cases Bills—were passed in mid-March by the Senate and the Lower House, giving a major boost to progress in the reforms that are critical to Thailand's financial and corporate restructuring.

### TABLE 6.A.1
### The consolidation of banks and finance companies

| Country | Intervened or under supervision | To be closed | Merged | Nationalized | Sold |
|---|---|---|---|---|---|
| Indonesia | 57[a] | 61[b] | 4[c] | 11 | 0 |
| Korea | 17[d] | 16[e] | 11[f] | 2 | 0[g] |
| Malaysia | 0 | 0 | 0 | 2 | 0 |
| Thailand | 0 | 56[h] | 3 | 4 | 2 |

### Notes to table

a. Placed under IBRA. Shareholder rights were suspended and a state-owned bank appointed to manage and control the bank.

b. Depositors' accounts were transferred to the largest state bank.

c. Four state banks are being merged into one entity along with the corporate section of Bank Rakyat Indonesia.

d. Three commercial banks are still under the supervision of FSC; 14 merchant banks have to comply with a timetable to achieve capital adequacy ratios.

e. Sixteen merchant banks were closed.

f. This number refers to 5 commercial banks whose proposals were rejected, 2 that were able to merge and 4 others that did not meet capital adequacy standards.

g. None have been sold yet but a Memorandum of Understanding has been signed between Korea First Bank and Newbridge Capital, and between Seoul Bank and a British bank.

h. Of these 56 finance companies, 12 have been merged under Krungthai Thanakit.

## Notes

The author is a regional head of Deutsche Bank in Asia. The views expressed in this paper are solely those of the author. They should not be attributed to the World Bank, to the financial or other cosponsors of the Conference or to Deutsche Bank, with which the author is currently affiliated. The author wishes to thank Shonar Lala for research assistance in the preparation of this paper.

1. The Philippines are not covered in this paper, as its banking system, which had gone through a restructuring exercise a few years earlier, was not significantly affected by the crisis. The authorities implemented a number of precautionary steps in 1998. The country's small private external debt and low debt-equity ratios also made the system less susceptible to shocks.

2. See, for example, World Bank 1998 and IMF 1998.

3. For an elaboration, see Shirazi 1998.

4. Shirazi (1998).

5. Krugman (1999). A concise summary of Krugman's paper is provided by the Deutsche Bank's Angus Armstrong (see Armstrong 1999).

6. See Krugman (1999), p. 20.

7. See, for example, Larry Summer's remarks in Tokyo on February 26, 1999 as reported in Sunday (Singapore) Times 1999.

8. World Bank (1999).

9. See for details, Republic of Korea 1998.

## chapter seven

# Publicly Listed East Asian Corporates: Growth, Financing, and Risks

*Stijn Claessens*
*Simeon Djankov*

Using a database of 5,550 publicly-listed corporations in nine East Asian economies over the period 1988–1996, we find large differences in performance and financial structures across economies. Profitability, as measured by real return on assets in local currency, was relatively low in Hong Kong, Japan, the Republic of Korea, and Singapore throughout the period, while corporates in Indonesia, the Philippines, and Thailand had high real returns—on average twice as high as those recorded in Germany and the United States. Nominal returns in dollars were high as well in the region, but reflected in part the real appreciation of currencies. During 1994–1996, measured performance declined in several economies, especially in Japan and Korea. This did not show up as much in terms of a decline in sales growth because investment rates were high and they continued to drive output growth rates in many economies. The combination of high investment and relatively low profitability in some economies meant that much external financing was needed. As outside equity was used sparingly, leverage was high in most East Asian economies relative to other economies, and on the rise in Korea, Malaysia, and Thailand. Short-term borrowing became increasingly important, especially in Malaysia, Taiwan (China), and Thailand. Some of the vulnerabilities in corporate financial structures that have now become a highly visible factor in triggering and aggravating the East Asian financial crisis were thus already in existence in the early 1990s. As a result of these vulnerabilities the impact of interest and exchange shocks has been large—43 percent of the corporations in our sample are estimated to face liquidity problems and 17 percent face solvency problems.

The East Asian financial crisis has in part been attributed to the weak performance and risky financial structures of corporates. In retrospect, it has become clear that the operational performance of East Asian corporates was indeed not as stellar as many had thought and in fact involved investments with high risks. Also with hindsight, it has become apparent that the financial structures of many East Asian corporates were not strong enough to withstand the combined shocks of increased interest rates, depreciated currencies, and large drops in domestic demand. This poor performance and these risky financing structures were not, however, notably featured by observers writing on East Asia prior to the financial crisis. Quite to the contrary, East Asian corporates were considered an important contributing part of the region's miracle and were generally viewed as highly competitive and adept at exploiting new market opportunities; they consequently attracted considerable amounts of foreign capital.

Reconciling the differences between these ex post and ex ante views will likely be a topic of much future research.[1] In this short paper, we are less ambitious and start with documenting the basic record in corporate performance and financing structures for a number of large, publicly listed East Asian corporates over the last decade. Specifically, we use a database of balance sheet and income statement data for 5,550 East Asian firms listed on stock exchanges in nine economies over the period 1988–1996 for establishing the stylized facts on corporate performance and financing structures. The main data sources are the annual reports of the companies filed with the major stock exchanges in the region.

We find large differences in performance and financial structures across economies. Profitability, as measured by real return on assets (ROA) in local currency, was relatively low in Hong Kong, Japan, Korea, and Singapore throughout the period, while corporates in Indonesia, the Philippines, and Thailand had high returns, on average twice as high as those recorded in Germany and the United States over the same period. In the years 1994–1996, measured performance declined somewhat in several East Asian economies, especially in Japan and Korea. These differences in performance did not show up as much in sales growth, as investment rates were high and continued to drive output growth rates in all economies. These facts suggest that the East Asian miracle was indeed based on a vibrant corporate sector.

However, the combination of high investment and relatively low profitability in some economies meant that much external financing was needed. Since outside equity was used sparingly, partly because stock markets were depressed (as was the case in Japan) or insiders preferred to retain control, leverage was high in most East Asian economies and on the rise in Korea, Malaysia, and Thailand. This created large risks as short-term foreign exchange borrowing became increasingly important in the last few years, especially in Malaysia, Taiwan (China), and Thailand. Some of the vulnerabilities in corporate financial structures that have now become a highly visible factor in triggering and aggravating East Asia's financial crisis, were thus already in existence in the early 1990s.

As a result of these vulnerabilities, the impact of interest and exchange shocks over the last year has been very large. Using the balance sheet and profit and loss statements for a subset of corporations in our sample, we quantify the impact of the currency and interest rate shocks on individual firms' liquidity and solvency. We find that 43 percent of the firms in the five most affected economies (Indonesia, Korea, Malaysia, the Philippines, and Thailand) are currently illiquid and 17 percent could be technically insolvent. Worst affected is Indonesia with 64 percent of its firms illiquid and 53 percent insolvent, followed by Korea and Thailand. Malaysia has the smallest proportion of insolvent firms, 1.5 percent, but 41 percent of its firms are illiquid, which is about the same percentage as in the Philippines and Thailand. While these amounts are substantially lower than those in the spring of 1998, when interest and exchange shocks were much worse, financial distress in East Asia's corporate sector is still of systemic proportions. Furthermore, about one-third of solvent firms are illiquid, and risk insolvency unless their liquidity constraints are relieved.

## The data

The data come from annual reports of the companies listed on the major stock exchanges in the region and also from Worldscope and Extel databases. The data sets are unbalanced—that is, the number of observations varies from year to year. We excluded companies that reported data less than three times over the period 1988–96. We excluded also financial and banking institutions (Standard Industrial Classification [SIC] 6000–6999). Finally, in any given year, we excluded companies that did not include all of the following variables—net sales, net income after taxes, cost of goods sold, total assets, and the value of common equity. The data set consists of 588 companies in Hong Kong, 317 companies in Indonesia, 2,526 companies in Japan, 392 companies in Korea, 772 companies in Malaysia, 170 companies in the Philippines, 348 companies in Singapore, 265 companies in Taiwan (China), and 564 companies in Thailand.

Several caveats apply to the data. First, the statistics we report do not attempt to correct for cross-economy differences in industrial structure. If an economy data set has many utility firms, for example, average leverage might be higher and profitability lower. The data also cover mainly large firms—the median size of the 5,550 firms is 1,612 employees, with the largest company employing more than 150,000 employees. This selection pattern arises since the firms have to be listed on a stock exchange in order to enter the database, and listed companies tend to be large.

Table 7.1 provides descriptive statistics on the size of the firms in our sample, broken down by country or economy. We use three measures of size: sales revenue, the value of fixed assets, and employment. Japanese and Korean firms have the largest sales revenue and assets. The median firm in these two countries produces half a billion U.S. dollars worth of goods or services, and uses slightly less than half a billion dollars of assets. In contrast, the median Indonesian, Malaysian, and Thai firm has less than 100 million dollars in sales revenue and only about 50 million dollars in assets. The ranking in sales and asset size is not matched by a ranking by employment. Indonesian and Philippine firms have now the largest number of workers, more than 2,000, while the median firm in Taiwan (China) has less than 1,000 employees. This of course reflects the differences in capital- versus labor-intensity across our sample of economies with very different levels of economic development. We can compare our sample with those used by M. Kawai, H. Hahm, and G. Iarossi; D. Dwor-

### TABLE 7.1
**Summary statistics of size, 1996**
(Medians, sales, and assets are in US$1,000)

| Economy | Number of firms | Sales | Assets | Employment |
|---|---|---|---|---|
| Hong Kong | 463 | 202,124 | 121,387 | 2,194 |
| Indonesia | 264 | 91,254 | 54,284 | 2,675 |
| Japan | 2,234 | 488,076 | 457,648 | 1,436 |
| Korea | 258 | 502,486 | 411,116 | 1,631 |
| Malaysia | 636 | 63,853 | 44,563 | 1,872 |
| Philippines | 146 | 108,776 | 52,344 | 2,232 |
| Singapore | 283 | 142,789 | 86,248 | 1,416 |
| Taiwan, China | 222 | 284,717 | 180,624 | 966 |
| Thailand | 427 | 69,712 | 45,582 | 1,587 |

Source: World Bank, Firm-Level Study.

Frecaut, M Hallward-Driemeier, and F. Colaco; and other papers submitted to this conference. Table 7.1 shows that our sample of companies in East Asian economies complements these authors' sampling of smaller and medium-size firms, as the average size is much larger and the number of employees per firm about 10 times as high.

## Performance measures

As our first measure of performance we use the real rate of return on assets in local currency. This is calculated at the firm level as the earnings before interest and taxes (EBIT) in local currency over total assets, minus the annual inflation rate in the economy. The advantage of this measure is that it is not influenced by the liability structure of the corporate, as it excludes interest payments, financial income, and other income or expenses. Table 7.2 shows that across economies, East Asian corporates have had quite different ROAs. Relatively low profitability rates have been recorded by corporates from Hong Kong, Japan, Korea, and Singapore, with real ROAs averaging about 5 percent. High-profitability economies, at least for most of the period we study, have been Indonesia, the Philippines, and Thailand. Corporates in these economies averaged real ROAs of about 9–10 percent for the whole period. ROAs for corporates in Malaysia and Taiwan (China) fall in between these two groups, but their returns of about 7 percent are still closer to the high performers. These ROAs can be compared to ROAs of about 5 percent in Germany and the United States,[2] providing support to the notion that the corporate sector contributed significantly to the so-called "East Asian Miracle" during most of this period.

As a further comparison of the performance of East Asian corporates, we plot the average 1988–96 ROA for corporates in all other economies that report to Worldscope (see figure 7.1). Thailand, the Philippines, and Indonesia have the highest ROAs in this sample of 46 economies, while Taiwan (China) and Malaysia are close behind. At the other end, Korea and Japan have the lowest ROAs in the sample, together with Norway, Sweden, and Austria. Singapore and Hong Kong have also relatively low ROAs in real local currency.

Next we calculate the return on assets in U.S. dollars, adjusted for the effects of currency movements (see table 7.3). This measure of performance presents the point of view of an international investor who can allocate resources across several economies. With the exception of Japan (6.6 percent) and Taiwan, China (8.4 percent), all East Asian economies have ROAs in U.S. dollars that are higher than the U.S. median (8.7 percent). The Philippines (18.7 percent), Thailand (14.7 percent), and Indonesia (13.0 percent) have the highest average returns over the 1988–96 period.

The high returns in table 7.3 are driven to some extent by the real exchange rate appreciation in the respective economies. Correcting for the real exchange rate appreciation in relation to the U.S. dollar, we find

### TABLE 7.2
**Return on assets for nine Asian economies, Germany, and the United States**
(percent, medians, in real local currency)

| Economy | 1988 | 1989 | 1990 | 1991 | 1992 | 1993 | 1994 | 1995 | 1996 | 1988–96 |
|---|---|---|---|---|---|---|---|---|---|---|
| Hong Kong | 5.1 | 5.3 | 4.9 | 4.8 | 4.5 | 3.8 | 3.9 | 3.9 | 4.1 | 4.6 |
| Indonesia | — | — | 9.4 | 9.1 | 8.6 | 7.9 | 7.4 | 6.2 | 6.5 | 7.1 |
| Japan | 5.7 | 5.4 | 4.6 | 4.7 | 4.8 | 4.5 | 4.1 | 3.8 | 3.6 | 4.1 |
| Korea | 4.4 | 3.9 | 4.1 | 4.0 | 3.9 | 3.6 | 3.4 | 3.6 | 3.1 | 3.7 |
| Malaysia | 5.4 | 5.6 | 5.4 | 6.2 | 6.0 | 6.5 | 6.3 | 6.1 | 5.6 | 6.3 |
| Philippines | — | — | — | 7.1 | 6.4 | 8.1 | 8.5 | 6.8 | 8.4 | 7.9 |
| Singapore | 4.9 | 4.5 | 4.2 | 3.9 | 5.2 | 4.6 | 4.5 | 3.9 | 4.0 | 4.4 |
| Taiwan, China | — | — | — | 5.1 | 6.2 | 6.5 | 6.8 | 6.5 | 6.6 | 6.7 |
| Thailand | 10.8 | 11.0 | 11.7 | 11.2 | 10.2 | 9.8 | 9.3 | 7.8 | 7.4 | 9.8 |
| United States | 4.7 | 4.8 | 5.1 | 4.9 | 5.2 | 5.4 | 5.3 | 5.2 | 5.2 | 5.3 |
| Germany | 5.3 | 5.5 | 5.5 | 5.7 | 5.6 | 5.2 | 5.1 | 4.9 | 5.0 | 4.7 |

— : not available
Source: World Bank, Firm-Level Survey.

### TABLE 7.3
**Return on assets for nine Asian economies and the United States**
(percent, medians, in nominal U.S. dollars)

| Economy | 1988 | 1989 | 1990 | 1991 | 1992 | 1993 | 1994 | 1995 | 1996 | 1988–96 |
|---|---|---|---|---|---|---|---|---|---|---|
| Hong Kong | 8.0 | 8.4 | 7.2 | 12.9 | 14.3 | 12.5 | 11.5 | 8.0 | 10.3 | 10.3 |
| Indonesia | — | — | 16.0 | 13.7 | 12.6 | 15.3 | 11.7 | 10.7 | 11.2 | 13.0 |
| Japan | 6.5 | -6.0 | 13.3 | 14.8 | 7.0 | 16.2 | 15.6 | 1.0 | -9.2 | 6.6 |
| Korea | 25.1 | 10.3 | 7.3 | 7.2 | 6.4 | 5.9 | 12.1 | 9.9 | -1.0 | 9.2 |
| Malaysia | -0.8 | 8.8 | 7.2 | 9.9 | 14.8 | 6.1 | 15.5 | 12.2 | 9.5 | 9.2 |
| Philippines | — | — | — | 23.2 | 21.2 | 5.4 | 29.4 | 7.5 | 16.5 | 17.2 |
| Singapore | 8.9 | 9.4 | 15.6 | 13.6 | 6.9 | 9.3 | 16.4 | 9.0 | 6.8 | 10.7 |
| Taiwan, China | — | — | — | 6.2 | 12.0 | 4.6 | 12.4 | 6.3 | 8.9 | 8.4 |
| Thailand | 13.9 | 14.6 | 19.3 | 16.9 | 13.4 | 13.1 | 16.6 | 13.2 | 11.5 | 14.7 |
| United States | 8.7 | 9.6 | 10.5 | 9.1 | 8.3 | 8.4 | 7.9 | 8.0 | 8.1 | 8.7 |

— : not available
Source: World Bank, Firm-Level Survey.

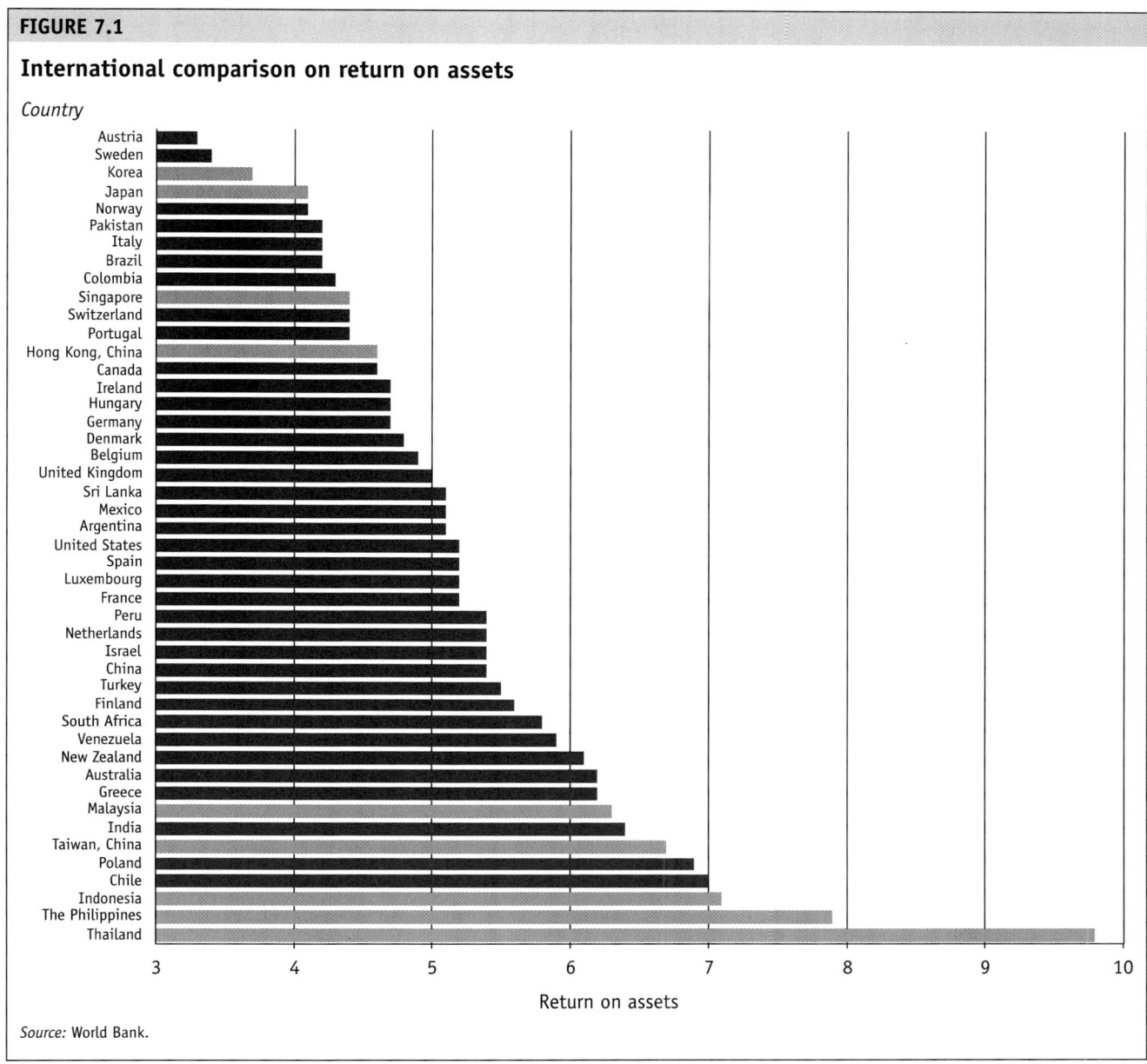

**FIGURE 7.1**

**International comparison on return on assets**

*Source:* World Bank.

significantly lower ROAs. For example, the return in U.S. dollars once a correction is made for real currency appreciation is 8.4 percent in Korea in 1988. Mathematically, this is the sum of the real ROA in Korean won (4.4 percent) and the inflation rate in the United States (4.0 percent)—all other terms cancel out in the calculation. This implies that the relative comparisons of the ROAs corrected for real exchange rate appreciations are the same as those in table 7.2.

Our third measure of profitability is operational margin, calculated as the difference between sales and costs of good sold, as a share of sales (see table 7.4). The liability structure or other income and expenses of the corporate do not influence this measure either, but the capital intensity of the individual corporate does. The operational margin measure shows less cross-economy differences and has been stable for most economies throughout the period. The cross-economy differences may indicate that firms across East Asia were exposed to differing degrees of (international) competition. Relatively lower-margin producers seem to be Singapore, followed by Hong Kong, Malaysia, and

Korea. Surprisingly, Japanese firms have higher margins on goods sold ratios than these developing economies, which may reflect the high capital intensity of Japanese firms and the lower level of competition within Japan, as is often argued. Relatively high-margin producers are the Philippines, Indonesia, and Thailand, which may reflect the degree of domestic competition, lower wages, and the high share of natural resources in their exports (the last factor is especially prominent in the case of Indonesia). No strong trend appears over time; however, there is some decrease in operational margins for Hong Kong, Indonesia, and Singapore. This may be reflective of these economies' higher wage growth coinciding with their facing increased competition.

The cross-economy differences in returns on assets do not reflect themselves directly in differences in sales growth, which are also more variable over time (see table 7.5). Most East Asian corporates recorded on average high, real sales growth over the period. Malaysia, Indonesia, and Thailand stand out, with averages of 11.9, 10.6, and 9.7 percent, respectively, followed by Taiwan (China) with 9.3 percent. Other economies also had high sales growth rates, which are about double those of Germany (2.6 percent) and the United States (3.7 percent). The economy with the lowest corporate sales growth in East Asia is Japan, averaging 7.7 percent. These high sales growth rates mirror the high growth in export and domestic demand that has characterized this region over the last decade. We do observe some slowdown in 1996, however, in sales growth for Indonesia, Japan, Singapore, Taiwan (China), and Thailand, possibly reflecting lower export growth rates.

### TABLE 7.4
**Operational margin for nine Asian economies, Germany, and the United States**
(percent, medians)

| Economy | 1988 | 1989 | 1990 | 1991 | 1992 | 1993 | 1994 | 1995 | 1996 | 1988–96 |
|---|---|---|---|---|---|---|---|---|---|---|
| Hong Kong | 23.5 | 19.5 | 22.2 | 19.6 | 17.4 | 16.6 | 17.3 | 14.6 | 14.2 | 18.7 |
| Indonesia | — | — | — | 35.7 | 33.3 | 34.4 | 32.8 | 31.2 | 30.6 | 32.9 |
| Japan | 22.2 | 22.7 | 22.9 | 22.4 | 21.9 | 21.8 | 21.8 | 23.1 | 23.3 | 22.1 |
| Korea | 13.7 | 16.8 | 17.3 | 16.9 | 19.2 | 18.7 | 19.6 | 21.4 | 22.1 | 19.6 |
| Malaysia | 16.4 | 16.3 | 17.1 | 17.3 | 17.6 | 17.4 | 18.4 | 19.5 | 25.5 | 18.1 |
| Philippines | — | — | — | 36.1 | 26.4 | 26.4 | 27.5 | 30.8 | 33.3 | 27.7 |
| Singapore | 17.3 | 16.7 | 16.8 | 15.5 | 15.5 | 15.2 | 14.1 | 13.6 | 13.1 | 14.9 |
| Taiwan, China | — | — | — | 25.4 | 21.4 | 22.7 | 22.6 | 22.3 | 21.9 | 22.6 |
| Thailand | 21.9 | 24.3 | 25.7 | 27.3 | 25.9 | 25.1 | 24.9 | 24.7 | 22.7 | 25.2 |
| United States | 14.1 | 13.9 | 14.1 | 14.3 | 15.5 | 14.0 | 14.7 | 14.8 | 14.6 | 14.4 |
| Germany | 13.2 | 13.4 | 13.7 | 13.5 | 13.8 | 14.1 | 15.6 | 16.7 | 17.1 | 14.6 |

— : not available
Source: World Bank, Firm-Level Survey.

### TABLE 7.5
**Real sales growth (year-on-year) for nine Asian economies, Germany, and the United States**
(percent, medians)

| Economy | 1989 | 1990 | 1991 | 1992 | 1993 | 1994 | 1995 | 1996 | 1988–96 |
|---|---|---|---|---|---|---|---|---|---|
| Hong Kong | 10.1 | 11.6 | 10.2 | 12.4 | 9.8 | 9.4 | 9.7 | 11.8 | 9.2 |
| Indonesia | — | — | — | 10.7 | 12.1 | 12.4 | 9.4 | 8.3 | 10.6 |
| Japan | 7.4 | 8.2 | 8.4 | 8.3 | 8.8 | 8.5 | 7.2 | 4.3 | 7.7 |
| Korea | 8.4 | 8.7 | 8.2 | 8.3 | 7.6 | 7.3 | 7.2 | 8.6 | 8.2 |
| Malaysia | 9.7 | 12.3 | 11.8 | 12.7 | 13.1 | 12.6 | 11.7 | 11.9 | 11.9 |
| Philippines | — | — | — | 8.4 | 6.7 | 7.6 | 10.6 | 12.2 | 8.2 |
| Singapore | 8.4 | 8.6 | 8.1 | 9.4 | 11.6 | 11.8 | 10.2 | 7.7 | 8.7 |
| Taiwan, China | — | — | — | 7.1 | 11.3 | 10.3 | 9.7 | 8.4 | 9.3 |
| Thailand | 11.6 | 10.3 | 10.8 | 9.6 | 8.3 | 10.1 | 10.7 | 5.7 | 9.7 |
| United States | 4.3 | 3.4 | −1.8 | 4.3 | 2.8 | 6.9 | 4.1 | 4.3 | 3.7 |
| Germany | 5.0 | 4.4 | 5.1 | 1.1 | −4.2 | 2.3 | 1.3 | 4.7 | 2.6 |

— : not available
Source: World Bank, Firm-Level Survey.

### TABLE 7.6
**Capital investment for nine East Asian economies, Germany, and the United States, 1988–1996**
(percent, medians)

| Economy | 1988 | 1989 | 1990 | 1991 | 1992 | 1993 | 1994 | 1995 | 1996 | 1988–96 |
|---|---|---|---|---|---|---|---|---|---|---|
| Hong Kong | 14.3 | 16.6 | 8.3 | 7.6 | 7.2 | 13.8 | 7.6 | 5.8 | 9.3 | 8.3 |
| Indonesia | — | — | — | 12.4 | 13.4 | 3.6 | 15.8 | 13.8 | 11.8 | 12.7 |
| Japan | 11.6 | 14.2 | 8.3 | 4.6 | 7.6 | 5.8 | 7.3 | 7.5 | 7.1 | 8.0 |
| Korea | 15.6 | 13.8 | 13.2 | 19.6 | 11.6 | 11.2 | 12.2 | 12.4 | 13.7 | 13.6 |
| Malaysia | 8.6 | 7.6 | 8.9 | 9.6 | 11.3 | 13.4 | 15.2 | 14.6 | 16.1 | 10.7 |
| Philippines | — | — | — | 9.1 | 8.9 | 7.8 | 13.5 | 14.1 | 14.5 | 10.8 |
| Singapore | 7.8 | 7.6 | 7.4 | 8.8 | 9.6 | 11.3 | 13.4 | 12.5 | 13.5 | 10.4 |
| Taiwan, China | — | — | — | 14.3 | 8.2 | 3.4 | 8.7 | 11.2 | 8.6 | 8.7 |
| Thailand | 10.4 | 12.9 | 12.3 | 15.0 | 14.9 | 15.0 | 14.7 | 14.5 | 5.8 | 13.8 |
| United States | 3.8 | 4.1 | 3.0 | -1.4 | 4.0 | 2.6 | 6.4 | 3.7 | 3.8 | 3.4 |
| Germany | 4.9 | 4.8 | 4.2 | 5.0 | 0.9 | -3.8 | 2.1 | 1.3 | 4.6 | 2.5 |

— : not available
Source: World Bank, Firm-Level Survey.

### TABLE 7.7
**Leverage for nine Asian Economies, Germany, and the United States**
(percent, means)

| Economy | 1988 | 1989 | 1990 | 1991 | 1992 | 1993 | 1994 | 1995 | 1996 | 1988–96 |
|---|---|---|---|---|---|---|---|---|---|---|
| Hong Kong | 1.832 | 2.311 | 1.783 | 2.047 | 1.835 | 1.758 | 2.273 | 1.980 | 1.559 | 1.902 |
| Indonesia | — | — | — | 1.943 | 2.097 | 2.054 | 1.661 | 2.115 | 1.878 | 1.951 |
| Japan | 2.994 | 2.843 | 2.871 | 2.029 | 2.042 | 2.057 | 2.193 | 2.367 | 2.374 | 2.302 |
| Korea | 2.820 | 2.644 | 3.105 | 3.221 | 3.373 | 3.636 | 3.530 | 3.776 | 3.545 | 3.467 |
| Malaysia | 0.727 | 0.810 | 1.010 | 0.610 | 0.627 | 0.704 | 0.991 | 1.103 | 1.176 | 0.908 |
| Philippines | — | — | — | 0.830 | 1.186 | 1.175 | 1.148 | 1.150 | 1.285 | 1.129 |
| Singapore | 0.765 | 0.922 | 0.939 | 0.887 | 0.856 | 1.102 | 0.862 | 1.037 | 1.049 | 0.936 |
| Taiwan, China | — | — | — | 0.679 | 0.883 | 0.866 | 0.894 | 0.796 | 0.802 | 0.820 |
| Thailand | 1.602 | 1.905 | 2.159 | 2.010 | 1.837 | 1.914 | 2.126 | 2.224 | 2.361 | 2.008 |
| United States | 0.798 | 0.848 | 0.904 | 0.972 | 1.059 | 1.051 | 1.066 | 1.099 | 1.125 | 1.034 |
| Germany | 1.535 | 1.552 | 1.582 | 1.594 | 1.507 | 1.534 | 1.512 | 1.485 | 1.472 | 1.514 |

— : not available
Source: World Bank, Firm-Level Survey.

That these sales growth rates were maintained at such a high level—and at rates that are extremely similar across economies—reflects in part the high investment rates in this region (see table 7.6). We measure investment growth in new dollar investments as a share of existing fixed assets. Over this period, Indonesia, Korea, and Thailand stand out, with investment rates of up to 13 percent (and in some years even more), followed by Malaysia, the Philippines, and Singapore, with rates averaging about 10 percent. Hong Kong, Japan, and Taiwan (China) had growth in investment in fixed assets of about 8 percent. Japan has had low investment rates, particularly since 1990. This probably reflects in part its sustained financial and corporate crisis since the early 1990s.

## Financial structures

The degree of riskiness inherent in the liability structures of East Asian corporates is evident from the data. The high investment rates, and relatively low ROAs for some economies, meant that external financing had to be large, as internal sources of capital—in other words, retained earnings—were limited. This high external financing, mostly from the banking systems, has been always a characteristic of the "East Asian Miracle." Leverage, defined as total debt over equity, also has remained high for many East Asian economies, much above that observed in other developing economies and many industrial economies (see table 7.7). The highest leverage over this period was in the case of Korea—

about five times that of the lowest, Taiwan (China). It was also low in Malaysia; but rising in the Philippines, where it was still much below that of Indonesia and Thailand.

Most East Asian economies saw some increase in leverage in the last few years: this was most notable for Japan, Korea, Malaysia, and Thailand. Japan had seen some de-leveraging earlier in the decade—possibly owing to some financial retrenchment in the early 1990s—but lack of equity and corporate sector difficulties may have meant that no new equity was raised and loans were rolled over in the later part of the period. Leverage consequently rose. The rise in leverage in the Philippines is probably the result of its reforms in the mid-1980s, which led to revived corporate and financial sectors and better financing possibilities.

To study the riskiness of the financial structures of East Asian corporates, we next compare their average 1988–96 leverage ratios with the leverage ratios in the other Worldscope economies (see figure 7.2). Korean and Japanese firms have the highest leverage among all corporates in this group of economies, while companies

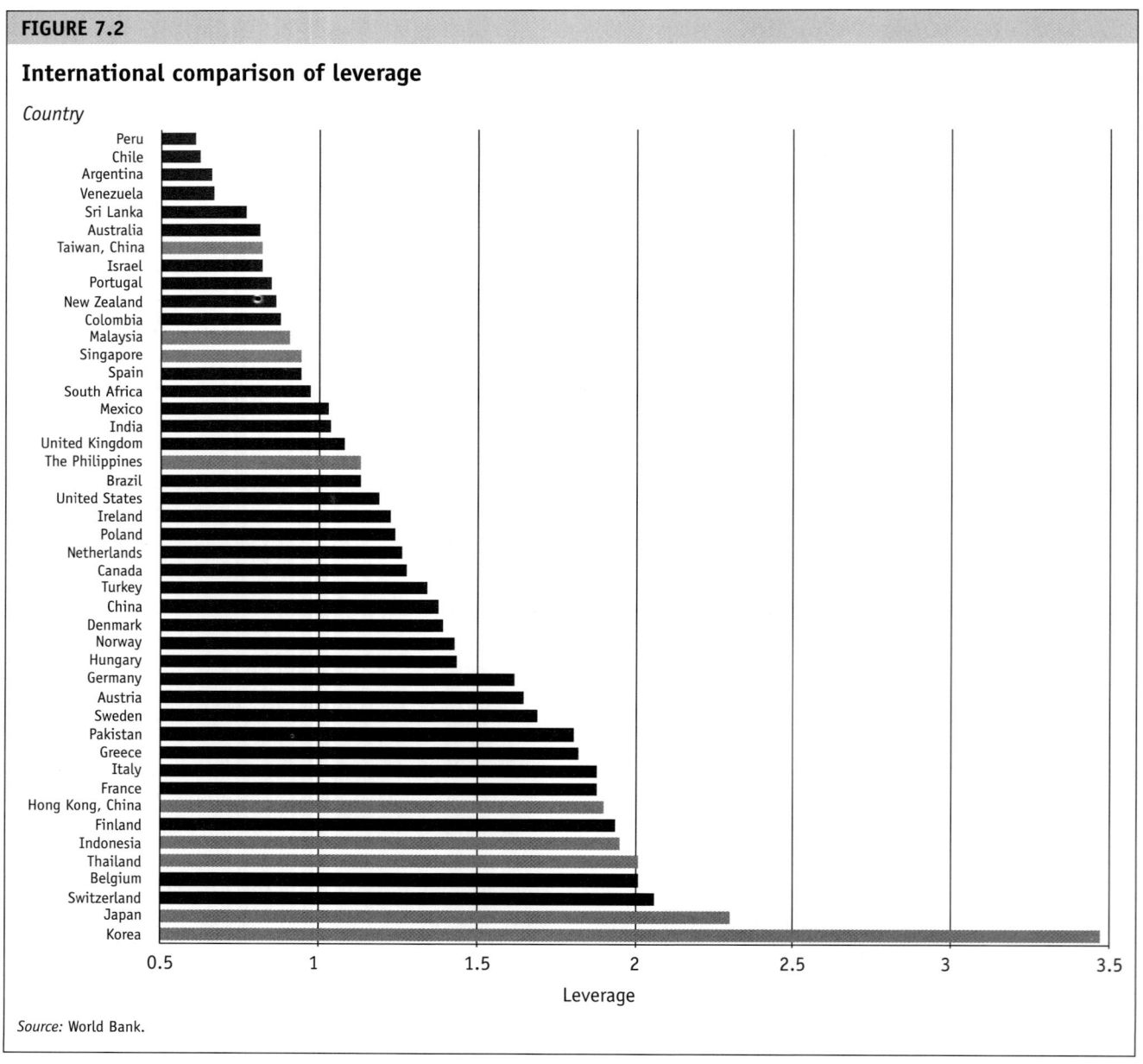

**FIGURE 7.2**

**International comparison of leverage**

*Source:* World Bank.

in Thailand, Indonesia, and Hong Kong also have among the ten highest leverage ratios. At the opposite extreme, firms in Taiwan (China) show relatively low leverage ratios. Firms in the Philippines, Singapore, and Malaysia also have below-average ratios. The pattern across other regions is also interesting. Western European economies typically display high leverage ratios, with Swiss firms having leverage almost as high as Japanese firms. In contrast, corporates in South American economies (Peru, Chile, Argentina, Venezuela, and Colombia) have low leverage, reflecting the less deep banking systems of these economies.

Long-term debt (as a share of total debt) has been low throughout the 1988–96 period in all East Asian economies (see table 7.8). Malaysia, Taiwan (China), and Thailand stand out with less than a one-third share. Japan and the Philippines have the highest share at one-half, while the others have their proportion at about 0.43. In contrast, about three-fourths of U.S. corporate debt is long-term, while in Germany the ratio is 0.55. In spite of the considerable attention given to the role of short-term debt in the East Asian financial crisis, these data do not suggest a massive buildup in short-term debt for the East Asian economies, at least up to the end of 1996, but rather a consistently low share of long-term debt. In fact, only Japan saw some decrease in the share of long-term debt. As these data do not distinguish foreign exchange from domestic debt, it can of course be that the composition may have shifted away from short-term domestic debt toward short-term foreign exchange debt.

The international comparison of the maturity of debt structure (see figure 7.3) reveals that most East Asian economies rank below European and Latin American economies in their share of long-term debt.[3] Among East Asian economies, only corporations from the Philippines have an average share of long-term debt that is greater than 50 percent. There is a general tendency for corporates in richer economies to have larger long-term debt. Some other, low-income Asian economies (Sri Lanka, Pakistan, China, for example) have indeed low shares of long-term debt. But many of the higher-income East Asian economies are outliers to this pattern, as they rely less on long-term debt than what would be expected on the basis of their per capita income level. Japan, for example, ranks below many other developed economies. Among developing economies, Chile stands out as one with an extremely high share of long-term debt.

The structure of debt (domestic vs. foreign; and short- vs. long-term) was different across economies, however. Figure 7.4 reports the distribution of debt across these four categories in 1996 for the six economies most affected by the crisis. Korea has the highest share of foreign short-term debt share, followed by Malaysia and Thailand. In contrast, the Philippines and Taiwan (China) have the largest share of domestic long-term debt.[4]

The data also suggest large differences across economies in interest payment coverage. This is calculated as the ratio of earnings before interest and taxes (but adding back depreciation)—that is, EBITDA or

### TABLE 7.8
**Long-term debt share for nine Asian economies, Germany, and the United States**
(percent, medians)

| Economy | 1988 | 1989 | 1990 | 1991 | 1992 | 1993 | 1994 | 1995 | 1996 | 1988–96 |
|---|---|---|---|---|---|---|---|---|---|---|
| Hong Kong | 59.7 | 59.5 | 53.8 | 56.5 | 44.7 | 44.7 | 43.7 | 37.3 | 36.4 | 44.9 |
| Indonesia | — | — | — | 52.4 | 40.8 | 39.6 | 41.6 | 41.8 | 43.3 | 43.1 |
| Japan | 49.9 | 54.1 | 53.8 | 49.9 | 49.4 | 51.7 | 47.7 | 44.4 | 40.8 | 48.4 |
| Korea | 55.7 | 47.2 | 49.8 | 49.8 | 44.2 | 43.7 | 41.4 | 40.4 | 41.5 | 43.7 |
| Malaysia | 35.8 | 35.5 | 32.5 | 27.1 | 26.9 | 26.6 | 27.2 | 27.8 | 29.9 | 29.2 |
| Philippines | — | — | — | 57.2 | 53.1 | 50.3 | 50.2 | 49.8 | 51.4 | 52.2 |
| Singapore | 57.2 | 55.4 | 54.1 | 33.8 | 33.8 | 33.9 | 40.2 | 38.6 | 41.1 | 43.3 |
| Taiwan, China | — | — | — | 53.9 | 44.4 | 32.8 | 34.6 | 34.3 | 38.9 | 35.9 |
| Thailand | 58.1 | 49.8 | 38.8 | 34.3 | 25.2 | 26.4 | 27.6 | 32.9 | 32.8 | 30.9 |
| United States | 77.7 | 77.2 | 76.3 | 76.7 | 75.8 | 76.2 | 75.2 | 74.6 | 74.1 | 75.9 |
| Germany | 56.8 | 55.4 | 54.5 | 53.9 | 55.2 | 55.4 | 55.4 | 55.3 | 54.7 | 55.3 |

— : not available
Source: World Bank.

operational cash flow—to interest expenses (see figure 7.5). With the low interest rates in Japan, Japanese corporates needed to devote only a small fraction of EBITDA on interest payments, so the interest coverage ratio is about 8 in 1996, followed by Taiwan (China) with 6.1. Thai and Korean corporates had the lowest interest coverage ratios—about 2.7 and 2.1, respectively. Corporates in Hong Kong, Malaysia, Indonesia, and the Philippines averaged between 3 and 4 while Singaporean firms averaged 4.5.

## Effect of exchange rate and interest rate shocks

We next assess the impact of the currency and interest rate shocks these economies have experienced since the second half of 1997 on firm liquidity and solvency.[5] We start by describing the exchange rate and interest rate shocks we use. For each economy, we calculate the average exchange rate over the period February 15–March 1, 1999, and compare that with the average exchange

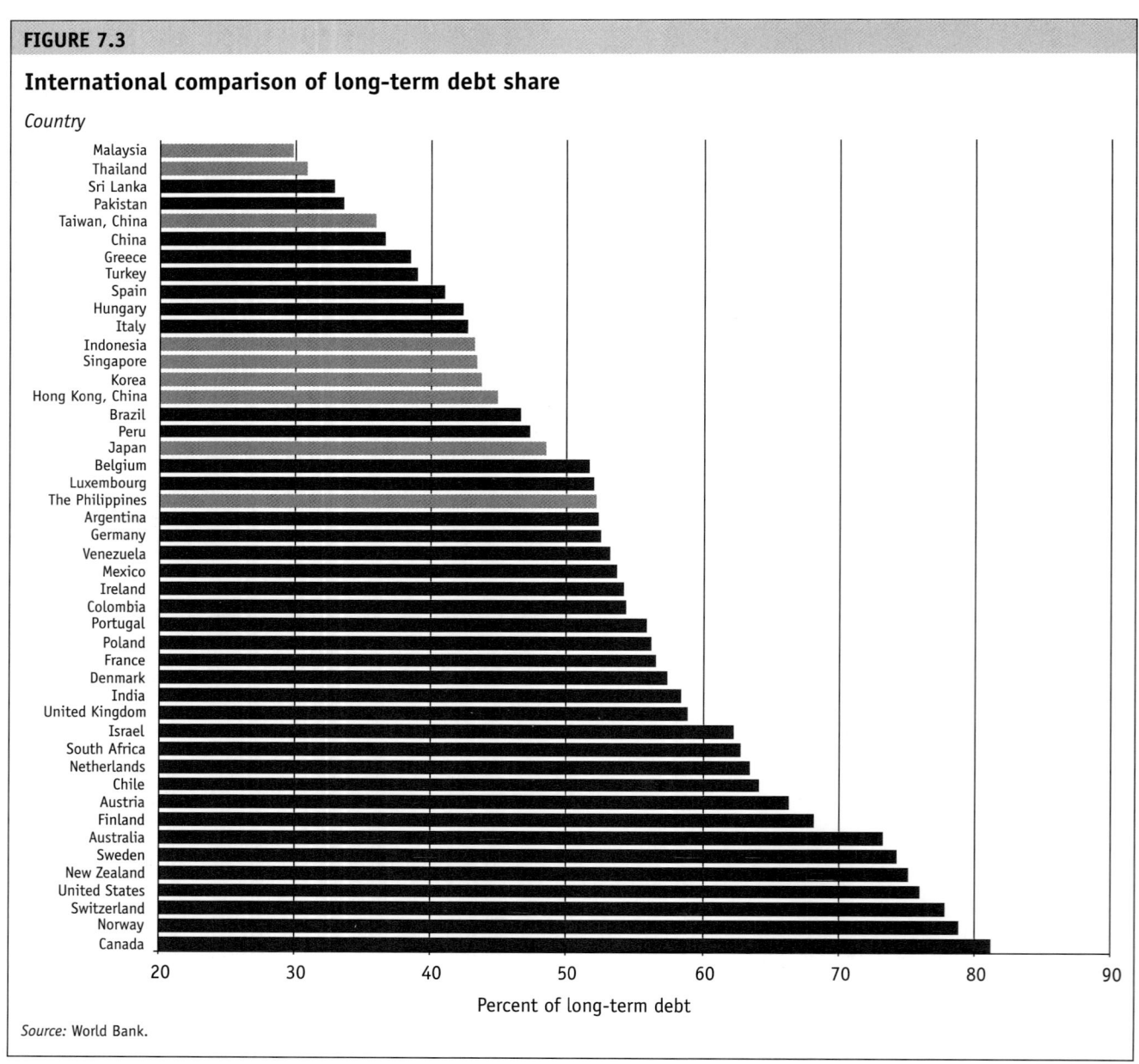

**FIGURE 7.3**

**International comparison of long-term debt share**

*Source:* World Bank.

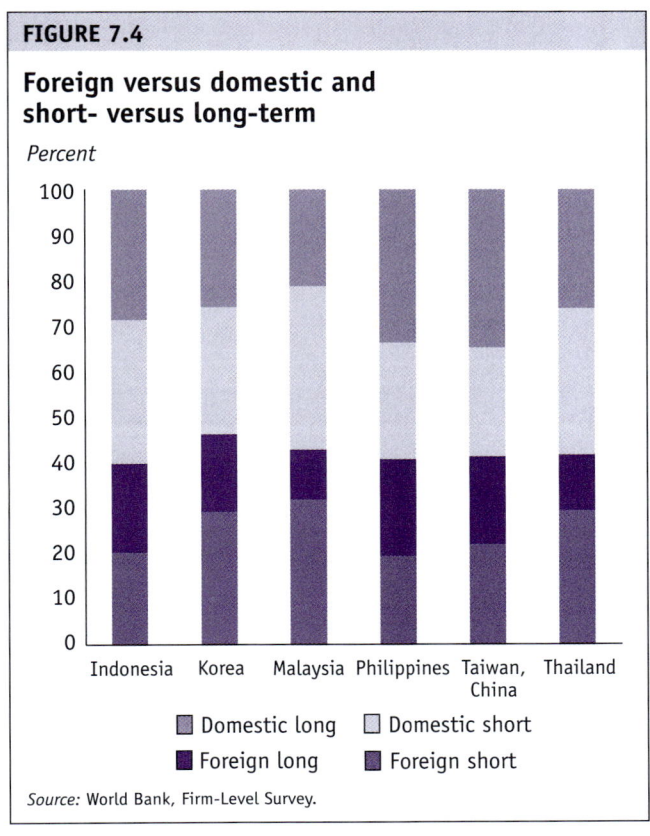

**FIGURE 7.4**

**Foreign versus domestic and short- versus long-term**

*Percent*

Domestic long | Domestic short
Foreign long | Foreign short

*Source:* World Bank, Firm-Level Survey.

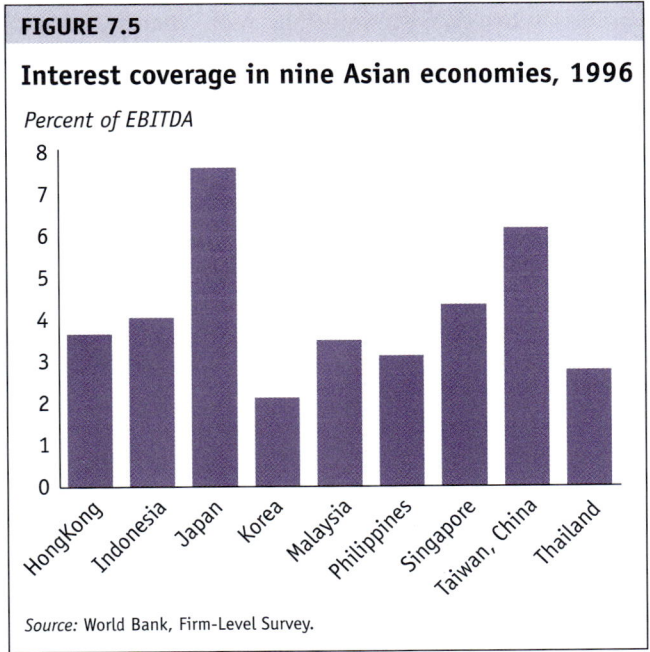

**FIGURE 7.5**

**Interest coverage in nine Asian economies, 1996**

*Percent of EBITDA*

*Source:* World Bank, Firm-Level Survey.

rate in March 1997, taken as the precrisis value. For the interest rate shocks, we compare the average of the domestic currency bank lending rate over the first two months of 1999 with the average lending rates in the first half of 1997, again taking it as the precrisis value. We also revise upward the interest rate paid on foreign currency debt by a factor proportional to the increase in the spread between the economy's rate on U.S. dollar–denominated sovereign bonds and the rate on U.S. Treasury bonds of analogous maturity.[6]

Next, we compute the impact of these shocks in terms of corporate financial obligations using the end-of-1996 balance sheet figures and 1996 profit and loss statements. We define firms as technically insolvent when the increase in financial obligations calculated at new exchange and interest rates exceeds the corporation's end-of-1996 equity. We define firms as illiquid when 1996 EBIT falls short of debt-service obligations projected at new exchange and interest rates. We use both exchange rate and interest rate shocks at the same time.

The increase in financial obligations attributable to the two shocks is computed as follows. The exchange rate shock is calculated as the increase in the value of end-of-1996 foreign currency debt—assumed to be entirely denominated in U.S. dollars—that is attributable to the domestic currency devaluation.[7] The interest rate shock is computed by (a) applying the estimated increase in domestic corporate borrowing rates to the end-of-1996 debt denominated in domestic currency;[8] and (b) applying the estimated (as described above) increase in corporate foreign currency borrowing rates to the end-of-1996 debt denominated in foreign currency.[9]

Table 7.9 reports the share of firms that are technically insolvent, illiquid, or both after the two shocks. On average for the five affected East Asian economies, the share of insolvent firms is 17.3 percent. Indonesia is by far the hardest-hit economy—more than half of its firms are estimated to be insolvent, with the damage to the corporate sector mainly stemming from the large depreciation of the currency. In Korea, about 14 percent of the corporates are technically insolvent at current interest and exchange rates. In the Philippines and Thailand, about 6 and 8 percent, respectively, of the firms are insolvent. Finally, it is worth noting that very few firms in our sample would be technically insolvent in Malaysia and none in Taiwan (China).

Table 7.9 shows also the share of corporates that have become illiquid after the shock. Illiquidity is much more pervasive than insolvency. In the postcrisis scenario, 64 percent of Indonesian firms, 28 percent of Korean

### TABLE 7.9
**Firms facing illiquidity or insolvency**
(percent of all firms in the sample)

| Economy | Illiquid and insolvent | Illiquid and solvent | Liquid and solvent | Liquid and insolvent | Total Illiquid | Total Insolvent |
|---|---|---|---|---|---|---|
| Indonesia | 51.2 | 12.4 | 34.6 | 1.8 | 63.6 | 53.0 |
| Rep. of Korea | 10.5 | 17.1 | 68.4 | 3.9 | 27.6 | 14.4 |
| Malaysia | 1.5 | 39.3 | 59.2 | 0.0 | 40.8 | 1.5 |
| Philippines | 4.1 | 35.0 | 58.9 | 2.0 | 39.1 | 6.1 |
| Thailand | 6.4 | 35.1 | 57.2 | 1.2 | 41.5 | 7.6 |
| Five Countries | 14.7 | 27.8 | 54.9 | 2.6 | 42.5 | 17.3 |
| Taiwan, China | 0.0 | 16.7 | 83.3 | 0.0 | 16.7 | 0.0 |

*Source:* World Bank, Firm-Level Survey.

firms, 41 percent of Malaysian firms, 39 percent of Philippine firms, and 42 percent of Thai firms are illiquid—that is, their earnings do not cover interest payments. Even in Taiwan (China), approximately 17 percent of the firms face illiquidity problems. Across the five economies most affected by the crisis, 43 percent of the firms are illiquid on average, and approximately 17 percent are insolvent.

It is useful to focus on the differences between illiquidity and insolvency problems. Table 7.9 shows that the share of firms that are illiquid but technically solvent is rather large: it averages more than one-third of all firms in the three most affected East Asian economies (Malaysia, the Philippines, and Thailand), and is between 12 and 17 percent in the other three economies. This implies that many solvent firms are at risk of insolvency as their liquidity positions are weak, in the sense that they cannot even cover current debt-service payments from earnings. These firms may have difficulty obtaining outside financing for working capital that would enable them to maintain ongoing operations, and they may be running at (too) low operating levels. Restoring credit flows to these solvent firms would be important for restarting growth in these economies.

## Summary

There were large differences in performance across economies as measured by return on assets. These differences did not show up as much in sales growth, as investment rates were high and those rates drove output rates in many economies. The high investment and relatively low profitability meant that external financing had to remain high in most economies with high leverage, as outside equity was used sparingly. While there were no strong trends in the early 1990s, leverage did increase in Korea and Thailand in the later years—signaling the vulnerability in corporate financial structures, which now has become a highly visible factor in triggering and aggravating the financial crisis. Across economies, the share of foreign short-term debt varied considerably in 1996, as did the ability of the sample firms to cover interest payments through earnings. The underlying causes of decreased profitability and increased leverage are multiple, with financial liberalization, macroeconomic policies, poor corporate governance, and weak financial discipline by domestic and foreign lenders playing a role—but the exact contribution of each of these, and other factors, are currently unknown. But, owing to these vulnerabilities the impact of interest and exchange shocks since mid-1997 has been large on corporations' solvency and liquidity positions.

## Notes

The authors are with the World Bank. Opinions expressed do not necessarily reflect those of the World Bank. We would like to thank Jerry Caprio, Stanley Fischer, Jack Glen, Ejaz Ghani, Guy Pfeffermann, S. Ramachandran, Charles Woodruff, Masahiro Kawai, Dominique Dwor-Frecaut, and Hongjoo Hahm for helpful suggestions on this and related work.

1. Five companion papers use the same data to study specific aspects of the behavior of corporations in East Asia. The paper by Claessens, Djankov, and Lang (1999) studies the ownership and control structures of East Asian corporations. The paper by Claessens, Djankov, Fan, and Lang (1999a) investigates the pattern of diversifi-

cation into vertically related, complementarily related, and unrelated businesses. The paper by Claessens, Djankov, Fan, and Lang (1999b) looks at the relation between ownership structure and diversification decisions and performance. The paper by Claessens, Djankov, Fan, and Lang (1999c) examines the link between ownership structure and the expropriation of minority shareholders. Finally, Claessens, Djankov, and Ferri (1998) had looked at the impact of exchange and interest shocks of the firms' solvency and liquidity positions as of the fall 1998.

2. For all companies listed on the DAX in Frankfurt, and for all NYSE companies in the United States.

3. We present the share of long-term debt rather than the share of short-term debt—the latter can underestimate the amount of liabilities with a short maturity, as it excludes, for example, trade credits.

4. Most of the data in this section refer to a more limited sample that we also use for our simulation exercise on the effects of interest and exchange rate shocks.

5. Claessens, Djankov, and Ferri (1998) undertook a similar exercise in mid-1998 on the basis of the average exchange rate over the period September 1–13, 1998 compared with the average exchange rate in March 1997, and the average domestic currency bank lending rate over the first half of 1998 compared with the average lending rates in the first half of 1997. As exchange rate and interest rates shocks were much larger in the fall of 1998, the percentage of firms found to be in financial distress was consequently much larger (about 63 percent of the firms in the five most affected economies were estimated to be illiquid and 30 percent technically insolvent).

6. Again, the precrisis sovereign spread was that observed at the end of March 1997 and the postcrisis sovereign spread was that observed at the end of February 1999.

7. Notice that, owing to data availability, we could not compute the positive effect of the devaluation in terms of increased value of assets denominated in foreign currency. Neglecting this effect may lead one to overestimate insolvency. We should, however, stress that our analysis neglects also the negative demand shock triggered by the crisis, a shock that likely outweighs any positive effect stemming from the revaluation of foreign currency assets.

8. To account for the repricing of loans, we apply the increase entirely to short-term domestic currency debt, but we apply only one-third of the increase to long-term domestic currency debt. This amounts to assuming that long-term domestic currency debt pays fixed rates and has a three-year maturity.

9. Again, to account for the repricing of loans, we apply the increase entirely to short-term foreign currency debt. We apply only one-third of the increase to long-term foreign currency debt—that is, we assume that long-term foreign currency debt also pays fixed rates and has a three-year maturity.

## chapter eight

# Corporate Foreign Debt in East Asia: Too Much or Too Little?

*Masahiro Kawai*
*Hongjoo J. Hahm*
*Giuseppe Iarossi*

This paper examines a sample of corporate financial data obtained from five East Asian countries—Indonesia, the Republic of Korea, Malaysia, the Philippines, and Thailand—during the period 1996–98. We find that the levels of foreign debt owed by manufacturing and mostly unlisted, small and medium-size enterprises in these countries were, in general, quite low. We find the patterns of foreign debt to be different across countries and sectors. Korea stands out—Korean corporations borrowed more from abroad across almost all sectors compared with their Southeast Asian counterparts. In Southeast Asia, larger firms, export firms, and firms with foreign direct investment (FDI) partners borrowed more from abroad. As a rule, larger firms in Southeast Asia were better able to access foreign funds during the crisis; exporters were better hedged against foreign exchange shocks; and firms with FDI partners were better able to use foreign debt financing. Overall, the size of short-term foreign debt was not large, by international comparisons. But the level of short-term foreign debt as a percentage of total foreign debt was high, and almost all of the debt was unhedged. Profitable export firms proved to be the most resilient sample group throughout the crisis. They were best able to weather the devaluation and interest rate shocks. An interesting result is that the less profitable firms in our sample borrowed more from abroad compared with their more profitable counterparts.

## Introduction

Since most crisis-affected countries maintained strong macroeconomic policy fundamentals before the crisis—low inflation, disciplined fiscal positions (surpluses or minimal deficits), and low public debt to gross domestic product (GDP) ratios—academics and policymakers alike have increasingly pointed to the private sector as the chief culprit in the crisis. Private banks and corporations are seen to have borrowed excessively, especially from short-term external sources, and to have misallocated those resources in the real estate sector and in inefficient manufacturing firms—with adverse impacts on productivity and competitiveness. No doubt, structural problems in the banking sector—such as interest rate ceilings, government-directed lending, relationship-based activities, weak accounting and disclosure practices, and the lack of effective supervisory and regulatory framework—contributed to the misallocation of resources. However, the real force behind the crisis emanated from structural weaknesses in the corporate sector. Restructuring financially distressed private corporations and putting good governance in place are viewed as the way out of the East Asian crisis and the way forward to sustained growth.

It is important to examine the extent of structural weaknesses in the corporate sector. Claessens, Djankov, and Lang (1999), using a comprehensive database of listed, large East Asian firms in nine countries over the period 1988–96, showed that there were large differences in corporate performance across countries, as measured by returns on assets. They demonstrated that East Asian corporate performance began to deteriorate even before the outbreak of the crisis, that corporate debt-equity ratios were already high compared with international norms, and that reliance on external debt financing was significant. Steep exchange rate depreciation and significant interest rate hikes suddenly inflated external debt, measured in local currencies, and increased both domestic and foreign debt servicing obligations of corporations. The domestic demand contraction that followed the currency crisis drove the corporate sector into further financial difficulties.[1] However, information and reliable data on how East Asian corporations have reacted to and fared in the midst of the financial crisis have been scarce.

The objective of this paper is to examine the extent of and changes in patterns of external financing by private corporations during the period 1996–98. Using microlevel survey data, this paper provides a descriptive account of the patterns of foreign debt by types of manufacturing firms in five East Asian countries—Indonesia, Korea, Malaysia, the Philippines, and Thailand. Furthermore, the paper examines the links between foreign debt financing and the profitability of corporations as well as the links between foreign exchange risk management and corporate external trade and financing activities.

The paper is organized as follows. In the next section, we describe the survey technique and data source, including caveats to the data. This is followed by a section in which we present a summary description of the data that points out the main characteristics of the firms engaged in foreign financing. First, we present data on foreign financing broken down by types of corporate borrowers: exporting versus nonexporting firms, firms with or without FDI partners, and medium-size to large versus small firms. Second, we present data on the financing mode (debt versus equity), the maturity composition (short versus long), and the currency composition (domestic versus foreign) of the firms' total liabilities, and offer some analytical interpretations of the results. In three subsequent sections, we examine the extent of short-term versus long-term debt financing, in both domestic and foreign currencies; we examine the extent of hedging undertaken by corporate borrowers; and we investigate the relationship between foreign debt financing and corporate profitability, as measured by returns on equity. In the final section, we conclude by providing policy prescriptions and recommendations that result from our analysis of the survey data.

## The survey data

The collection of firm-level data in Indonesia, Korea, Malaysia, the Philippines, and Thailand was motivated by the desire to improve the availability of corporate financial information in these countries. In the last quarter of 1998, survey interviews of about 800 to 1,000 manufacturing firms were conducted in each of the five countries. The sample of firms was put together randomly from the registry of enterprises maintained in each country. The firms drawn, therefore, included a few large but many small and medium-size enterprises; the majority of the sample was made up of unlisted corporations. The sample was confined to the most important geographic regions that are major centers of manufacturing or industrial activity. The manufacturing subsectors covered in the survey include: Autos and auto parts, Chemicals, Construction materials, Electronics, Food, Garments, Machinery, Textiles, and Wood.

We categorize these firms with respect to their size, their export orientation, and their foreign control. Specifically, a firm is defined as an "exporter" if it exports any amount of its sales; a firm is defined as "medium to large" if it has 150 or more employees; and a firm has "FDI partners" if it receives 10 percent or more in foreign direct investment. Overall, about two-thirds of the sample is comprised of small firms (with the exception of the Philippines); a little over half of the sample is comprised of exporters (with the exception of Korea where 75 percent of the sample is made up of exporters) and 25 percent of firms with FDI partners.

Our analysis is based on data made available as of February 16, 1999 (table 8.1). The survey data draw on approximately 850 Indonesian firms; 860 Korean firms; 820 Malaysian firms; 570 Filipino firms; and 660 Thai firms in manufacturing. The questionnaire was developed in close cooperation with the authorities of each country. Over 80 percent of the questions are the same for all five participating countries, allowing the possibility of cross-country comparison.[2] The major areas covered by the questionnaire are (1) bottlenecks to corporate recovery; (2) the firms' response to the crisis, financial structure, employment practices, prospects for increased exports; and (3) determinants of the upgrading of industry. In this paper, we focus our attention on the firms' financial structure, particularly foreign corporate financing. With regard to the issue of foreign financing, the sample firms were asked questions about the amount and maturity composition of foreign debt and hedging practices over the period from 1996 to 1998.[3] The paper provides a descriptive analysis and interpretation of these data.

We note ex ante some caveats to the data. First, although much time has been spent cleaning up the data and eliminating major outliers and inconsistent data entries, the survey data have all the usual *survey biases* of under- or overreporting a firm's true financial position. We have also found changes in the data over the three-year period, 1996–98, to be minimal, with many firms reporting the same or very similar data for successive years. Second, the survey was conducted only for manufacturing firms, excluding the service sector and other nonmanufacturing activities. This presents a *sample bias*, and examining external liability positions of surveyed firms may mask the true state of corporate external financing undertaken collectively by all corporations in the country as a whole. Finally, the most important caveat is a *winner bias*; that is, the survey only covers firms that are still in existence today. It is thus biased toward firms that have managed to survive until February 1999, and does not include others that have gone bankrupt as a result of the crisis. For all these reasons the results stemming from these data should be examined with a certain degree of caution.

### TABLE 8.1
### Sample characteristics

|  | Size | | Export orientation | | Foreign control | | |
|---|---|---|---|---|---|---|---|
|  | Small | Medium to large | Nonexporter | Exporter | Non-FDI | FDI | Total |
| Indonesia | 410 | 315 | 474 | 266 | 684 | 144 | 853 |
| Korea | 537 | 286 | 213 | 632 | 711 | 146 | 857 |
| Malaysia | 555 | 202 | 427 | 388 | 602 | 213 | 815 |
| Philippines | 241 | 259 | 257 | 278 | 358 | 198 | 566 |
| Thailand | 357 | 210 | 285 | 374 | 455 | 190 | 664 |
| Total | 2100 | 1272 | 1656 | 1938 | 2810 | 891 | 3755 |

Note: Breakdown numbers do not always add up to "total" because of incomplete or no responses.
Source: World Bank, Firm-level Survey Data (see the data description in the text for a more detailed documentation).

## Foreign debt financing

East Asian corporations in our sample, on aggregate, did not rely heavily on foreign debt financing, with the exception of Korea. Domestic debt financing and equity financing, including retained earnings, were predominant (table 8.2). This is because most firms in our sample are unlisted, small and medium-size enterprises, with limited access to foreign financing. Over 80 percent of the firms in our sample did not employ the services of foreign banks. Though equity financing was dominant in a few countries and in certain subsectors (table 8.3), we believe that outside equity was used sparingly because insiders preferred to retain control of their own corporations.[4]

The share of foreign debt, as a percentage of total liabilities, is uniformly low for most countries over the three-year period from 1996 through 1998 (table 8.2 and figure 8.1). In Thailand, Malaysia, and Indonesia, the average firm-level share of foreign debt did not exceed 5 percent as a percentage of total liabilities in 1996 and increased by only 1 percentage point in 1998. In the Philippines, the share of foreign debt as a percentage of total liabilities was moderately higher at about 7 percent in 1996, increasing to 10 percent in 1998.

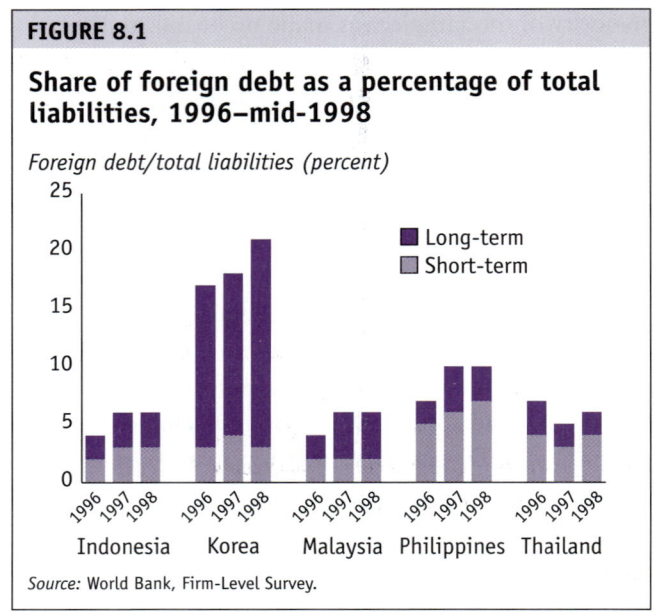

FIGURE 8.1

**Share of foreign debt as a percentage of total liabilities, 1996–mid-1998**

Source: World Bank, Firm-Level Survey.

### TABLE 8.2
**Estimated shares of domestic debt, foreign debt and equity as percentage of total liabilities**

|  | Domestic currency debt | | | Foreign currency debt | | | Equity | | |
|---|---|---|---|---|---|---|---|---|---|
|  | Short-term debt | Long-term debt | Total | Short-term debt | Long-term debt | Total | Foreign owned | Domestically owned | Total |
| **1996** | | | | | | | | | |
| Indonesia | 25 | 18 | 43 | 2 | 2 | 4 | 9 | 44 | 53 |
| Korea | 33 | 16 | 49 | 4 | 13 | 17 | 9 | 25 | 34 |
| Malaysia | 25 | 26 | 51 | 1 | 3 | 4 | 14 | 31 | 45 |
| Philippines | 24 | 29 | 53 | 5 | 2 | 7 | 19 | 21 | 40 |
| Thailand | 28 | 20 | 48 | 3 | 2 | 5 | 10 | 37 | 47 |
| **1997** | | | | | | | | | |
| Indonesia | 25 | 18 | 43 | 3 | 3 | 6 | 8 | 43 | 51 |
| Korea | 34 | 16 | 50 | 5 | 13 | 18 | 8 | 24 | 32 |
| Malaysia | 24 | 24 | 48 | 2 | 4 | 6 | 15 | 31 | 46 |
| Philippines | 29 | 27 | 56 | 7 | 3 | 10 | 19 | 15 | 34 |
| Thailand | 28 | 18 | 46 | 4 | 3 | 7 | 10 | 37 | 47 |
| **Mid-1998** | | | | | | | | | |
| Indonesia | 24 | 18 | 42 | 3 | 3 | 6 | 8 | 44 | 52 |
| Korea | 32 | 6 | 38 | 5 | 16 | 21 | 8 | 32 | 41 |
| Malaysia | 25 | 23 | 48 | 2 | 4 | 6 | 16 | 30 | 46 |
| Philippines | 28 | 22 | 50 | 7 | 3 | 10 | 22 | 19 | 40 |
| Thailand | 26 | 16 | 42 | 3 | 3 | 6 | 11 | 41 | 52 |

*Note:* 1. The foreign and domestic components of equity have been calculated from the FDI share, on the assumption that equity is domestic currency–denominated, whether domestically or foreign-held. 2. Equity includes retained earnings.
*Source:* World Bank, Firm-level Survey Data (see the data description in the text for a more detailed documentation).

## TABLE 8.3
### Domestic and foreign equity ownership by sector, percentage of total liabilities

| | Domestic owned equity | | | | | Foreign owned equity | | | | |
|---|---|---|---|---|---|---|---|---|---|---|
| | Chemicals | Machinery | Auto | Garm. & textiles | Electronics | Chemicals | Machinery | Auto | Garm. & textiles | Electronics |
| *1996* | | | | | | | | | | |
| Indonesia | 43 | — | — | 45 | 26 | 9 | — | — | 9 | 20 |
| Korea | 36 | 46 | 35 | 44 | 36 | 12 | 5 | 9 | 2 | 11 |
| Malaysia | 25 | 0 | 42 | 40 | — | 18 | 39 | 6 | 8 | — |
| Philippines | 24 | — | — | — | 7 | 18 | — | — | — | 30 |
| Thailand | — | — | 37 | — | 22 | — | — | 11 | — | 26 |
| *1997* | | | | | | | | | | |
| Indonesia | 45 | — | — | 42 | 26 | 7 | — | — | 8 | 18 |
| Korea | 35 | 44 | 41 | 39 | 36 | 13 | 6 | 6 | 2 | 11 |
| Malaysia | 25 | –2 | 45 | 43 | — | 19 | 41 | 6 | 8 | — |
| Philippines | 30 | — | — | — | 0 | 17 | — | — | — | 35 |
| Thailand | — | — | 38 | — | 22 | — | — | 11 | — | 26 |
| *Mid-1998* | | | | | | | | | | |
| Indonesia | 48 | — | — | 44 | 29 | 8 | — | — | 9 | 17 |
| Korea | 47 | 50 | 51 | 50 | 42 | 9 | 10 | 5 | 3 | 17 |
| Malaysia | 25 | –3 | 46 | 41 | — | 19 | 42 | 7 | 8 | — |
| Philippines | 35 | — | — | — | 7 | 19 | — | — | — | 34 |
| Thailand | — | — | 39 | — | 20 | — | — | 13 | — | 31 |

— : not available
*Note:* 1. The foreign and domestic components of equity have been calculated from the FDI share, on the assumption that equity is domestic currency–denominated, whether domestically or foreign-held. 2. Equity includes retained earnings.
*Source:* World Bank, Firm-level Survey Data (see the data description in the text for a more detailed documentation).

It was higher in Korea at about 17 percent in 1996, rising to 18 percent in 1997 and to 21 percent in 1998. The firms generally relied on domestic debt as well as equity financing rather than foreign debt financing throughout the three-year time period covered by our survey data.

The sectoral characteristics of the firms that engaged in foreign debt financing appear to reflect each country's specific conditions (table 8.4). The predominant industries in this financing category in Korea, for example, were the machinery and tools sector (in which some 30 percent of financing was in the form of foreign debt), the garments and textiles sector (24 percent), the automobile sector (20 percent), the electronics sector (19 percent), and the chemicals sector (about 16 percent) in 1998. In Indonesia, foreign debt financing was predominant in the electronics sector (13 percent) and the garments and textiles sector (9 percent). In Malaysia, the machinery and tools sector (14 percent) was the major borrower in the foreign debt market. In the Philippines, the electronics sector (16 percent) and the garments and textiles sector (12 percent) engaged in substantial foreign debt financing. In Thailand, mainly the electronics sector (12 percent) borrowed from abroad.

In the four Southeast Asian countries, there were significant differences in the size of foreign debt between exporters and nonexporters, between medium-to-large and small firms, and between foreign joint venture firms and fully locally owned firms. Many exporting firms were larger and tended to have FDI partners. Not surprisingly, foreign debt financing was more predominant among export-oriented firms than among nonexporters in all five countries.[5] Exporters borrowed externally on average 10–15 percentage points more than nonexporters in Indonesia, Malaysia, and the Philippines, and 7 percentage points more in Thailand and Korea. Firm size also mattered. In all countries, larger firms exhibited more foreign debt financing than smaller ones. Medium-size and large firms financed at least 10 percentage points more than small firms from overseas sources in Southeast Asia, and 2 percentage points more in Korea. The difference is starker for firms that had FDI partners, as they universally engaged in

### TABLE 8.4
### Share of foreign debt as a percentage of total liabilities by sector

| | Chemicals | Machinery | Auto | Garments and textiles | Electronics |
|---|---|---|---|---|---|
| *1996* | | | | | |
| Indonesia | 3 | — | — | 7 | 10 |
| Korea | 12 | 29 | 15 | 20 | 13 |
| Malaysia | 5 | 14 | 1 | 5 | — |
| Philippines | 8 | — | — | 9 | 11 |
| Thailand | — | — | 7 | 4 | 10 |
| *1997* | | | | | |
| Indonesia | 5 | — | — | 8 | 13 |
| Korea | 13 | 29 | 15 | 22 | 14 |
| Malaysia | 7 | 13 | 1 | 6 | — |
| Philippines | 7 | — | — | 9 | 15 |
| Thailand | — | — | 7 | 5 | 12 |
| *Mid-1998* | | | | | |
| Indonesia | 5 | — | — | 9 | 13 |
| Korea | 16 | 30 | 20 | 24 | 19 |
| Malaysia | 6 | 14 | 2 | 7 | — |
| Philippines | 7 | — | — | 12 | 16 |
| Thailand | — | — | 8 | 5 | 12 |

— : not available
*Source:* World Bank, Firm-level Survey Data (see the data description in the text for a more detailed documentation).

more foreign debt financing. In Indonesia, Malaysia, and the Philippines, the difference in foreign debt financing by FDI firms in comparison to non-FDI firms was about 15–20 percentage points; and in Thailand, about 12 percentage points. Only Korea had almost no difference, at about 1 percentage point (table 8.5).

To summarize, the patterns of foreign debt financing were quite different across countries and sectors. Korea stands out as an exception, distinguishing itself from the other Southeast Asian countries. First, Korean corporations financed more from abroad in the form of debt across almost all sectors than their Southeast Asian counterparts. Second, in Korea the machinery and tools and the garments and textiles sectors financed their debt externally more heavily, while in Southeast Asia, the electronics sector followed this route more than any of the other sectors. Third, exporters, larger firms, and firms with FDI partners financed their debt more from abroad in Southeast Asia, while only exporters fit this trend in Korea—without exhibiting any difference based on firm size or the presence of FDI partners. As a rule, larger firms were better able to access foreign debt financing during the crisis; exporters were naturally hedged against foreign exchange risks; and firms with FDI partners were better able to utilize foreign debt financing.

## Short-term versus long-term debt

Given the notorious role attributed to short-term external debt in the East Asian financial crisis, we now examine the term structure of total liabilities by East Asian corporations. First, we take up the level of short-term debt (both domestic and foreign) of East Asian corporations.

Our data suggest that the overall size of short-term debt was not large, when compared with international norms. In fact, the ratio of short-term debt to total liabilities (including net worth) is estimated to be 32 percent for U.S. manufacturing firms,[6] which is approximately the same as in our sample. The short-term debt to total liabilities ratio remained relatively constant in East Asia throughout the period 1996–98. In Indonesia, Malaysia, the Philippines, and Thailand this ratio was about 25–30 percent, while in Korea it was higher at close to 40 percent (figure 8.2). The use of

### TABLE 8.5
### Share of foreign debt as a percentage of total liabilities by firm characteristics

|  | Size | | Export orientation | | Foreign control | |
|---|---|---|---|---|---|---|
|  | Medium to large | Small | Exporter | Nonexporter | FDI | Non-FDI |
| **1996** | | | | | | |
| Indonesia | 9 | 1 | 10 | 0 | 14 | 3 |
| Korea | 18 | 16 | 18 | 11 | 17 | 17 |
| Malaysia | 11 | 2 | 9 | 0 | 14 | 1 |
| Philippines | 11 | 3 | 14 | 0 | 17 | 3 |
| Thailand | 12 | 2 | 10 | 1 | 14 | 3 |
| **1997** | | | | | | |
| Indonesia | 12 | 2 | 16 | 1 | 23 | 3 |
| Korea | 20 | 17 | 19 | 12 | 18 | 18 |
| Malaysia | 12 | 2 | 9 | 1 | 15 | 2 |
| Philippines | 13 | 5 | 15 | 3 | 20 | 4 |
| Thailand | 14 | 2 | 10 | 2 | 16 | 3 |
| **1998** | | | | | | |
| Indonesia | 12 | 2 | 15 | 1 | 21 | 4 |
| Korea | 21 | 21 | 22 | 16 | 20 | 21 |
| Malaysia | 13 | 2 | 10 | 0 | 16 | 2 |
| Philippines | 13 | 4 | 17 | 1 | 20 | 4 |
| Thailand | 12 | 2 | 9 | 3 | 15 | 3 |

Source: World Bank, Firm-level Survey Data (see the data description in the text for a more detailed documentation).

short-term debt financing appears to be above the U.S. norm for large firms, export firms, and firms with FDI partners, all of which show an average ratio of almost 40 percent.

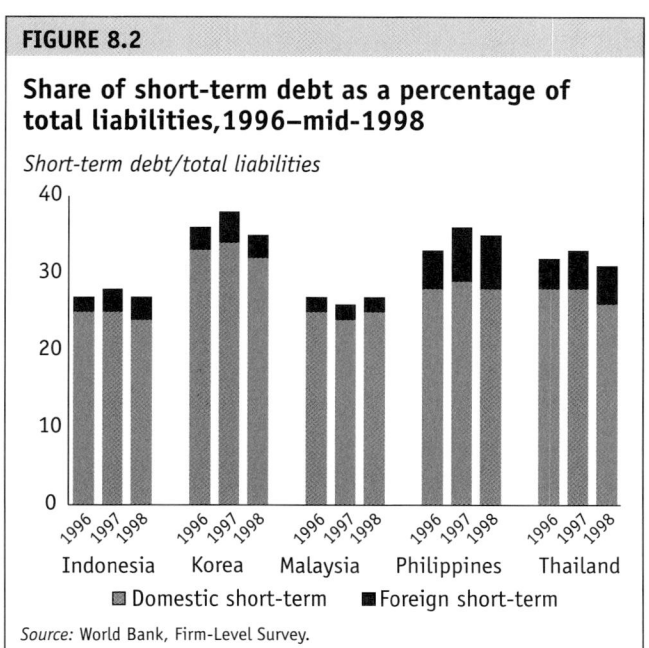

**FIGURE 8.2**

**Share of short-term debt as a percentage of total liabilities, 1996–mid-1998**

Source: World Bank, Firm-Level Survey.

Focusing on the relative size of short-term compared with long-term debt, Indonesia, Korea, and Thailand had larger shares of the former, while Malaysia had a larger share of long-term debt. The Philippines experienced an increase in the share of short-term debt over the period 1996–98. In terms of short-term versus long-term debt as a percentage of total liabilities for each country, Korea's short-term borrowing was about 37 percent and long-term 22 percent (the relative ratio being 1.7); respectively, these figures were 29 percent and 19 percent (1.5) for Thailand; 35 percent and 27 percent (1.3) for the Philippines; 27 percent and 21 percent (1.3) for Indonesia; and 27 percent and 27 percent (1.0) for Malaysia in 1998.

The higher dependence on short-term debt is often explained by the high credit risk that creditors are unwilling to take. Creditors, as a result, would prefer to extend short-term loans, frequently (and sometimes systematically) rolling over these loans. The inability of the sample firms to access long-term funding is also due in part to limited market infrastructure, such as the lack of long-term financial instruments, accounting standards, and portfolio risk management. However, the fact that large firms, export firms, and firms with FDI partners tend to borrow more short-term debt than firms in other categories may suggest that the former types of firms have easier access to domestic suppliers' credit, export-import credit, and FDI partner credit. In this sense, their reliance on short-term debt financing at a time of crisis may have increased their ability to withstand a crisis.

Next, for all countries, short-term debt financing was by and large from domestic sources. Distinguishing short-term domestic versus foreign debt, the relative ratios were about eight to one. In terms of percentage ratios of total liabilities, Thailand borrowed short-term about 26 percent from domestic sources and 3 percent from foreign sources; respectively, Korea borrowed 32 percent and 5 percent; Malaysia 25 percent and 2 percent; the Philippines 28 percent and 7 percent; and Indonesia about 24 percent and 3 percent in 1998.

## Unhedged short-term foreign debt: too much or too little?

In our sample, over 80 percent of the firms do not employ foreign bank services, and only a very small proportion borrows in foreign currency. We therefore examine the ratio of short-term *foreign* debt over total *foreign* debt to take into account only those firms that finance in foreign currency. The overall average ratio of short-term foreign debt to total foreign debt is 48 percent, with the Philippines' ratio the highest at about 70 percent and Korea's ratio the lowest at about 25 percent (figure 8.3).

A striking though not surprising finding is that very few borrowers hedged foreign exchange risk. Clearly, de facto pegged exchange rate regimes and a quarter century of uninterrupted economic growth encouraged short-term foreign debt financing without hedging. In Korea, the country with relatively large foreign debt financing, less than 7 percent of the firms that engaged in foreign debt financing hedged their loans. The ratios were only marginally higher for three of the other countries and much higher for the Philippines. In Malaysia, 11 percent of the firms hedged; in Indonesia, 14 percent; and in Thailand, 19 percent, all in 1997. In the Philippines, almost 30 percent hedged their foreign exchange exposure, which was high among East Asian countries, but still low by international standards.

Interestingly, the degree of hedging did not change in any substantive way from 1997 to 1998, and it did not change significantly across countries except in the case of the Philippines. This was probably because of the higher cost of buying hedging contracts in the aftermath of the crisis. While the degree of short-term foreign debt financing was low in general for our sample firms, the more a firm borrowed short-term from abroad, the more it also tended to hedge (figure 8.4).

## Profitable versus less profitable firms

Using returns on equity as a measure of profitability, we have divided our sample into profitable firms and less profitable firms using the Box-Cox transformation technique.[7] Only 25 percent of our cross-country sample falls under the profitable category using this technique, and the remaining 75 percent is categorized as less profitable.[8] This skewed distribution shows that the majority of the sample firms were already in financial distress before the crisis, and that the distress situation was aggravated by the crisis itself. In fact, while over 25 percent of the firms overall reported profits "above" average before the crisis, this ratio went down to 20 percent after the crisis.[9]

Examination of the distribution of profitable and less profitable firms across export orientation, not surprisingly, reveals that export firms proved to be more profitable than nonexport firms. Export firms are more

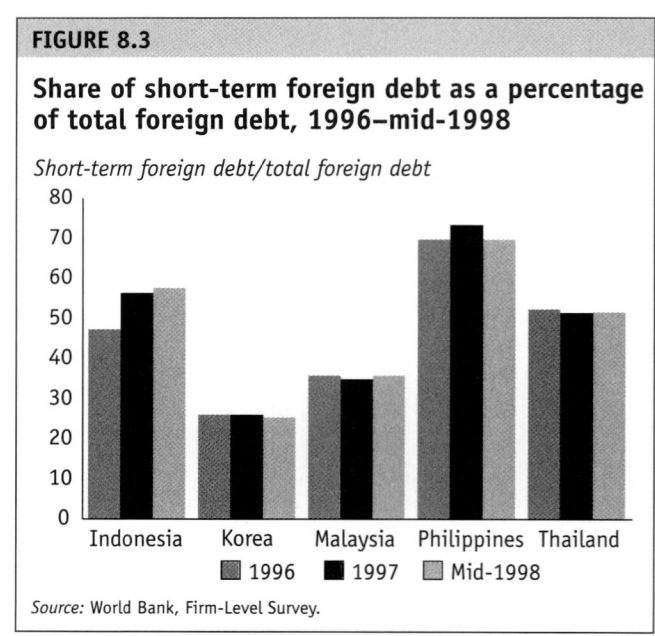

**FIGURE 8.3**

**Share of short-term foreign debt as a percentage of total foreign debt, 1996–mid-1998**

*Source:* World Bank, Firm-Level Survey.

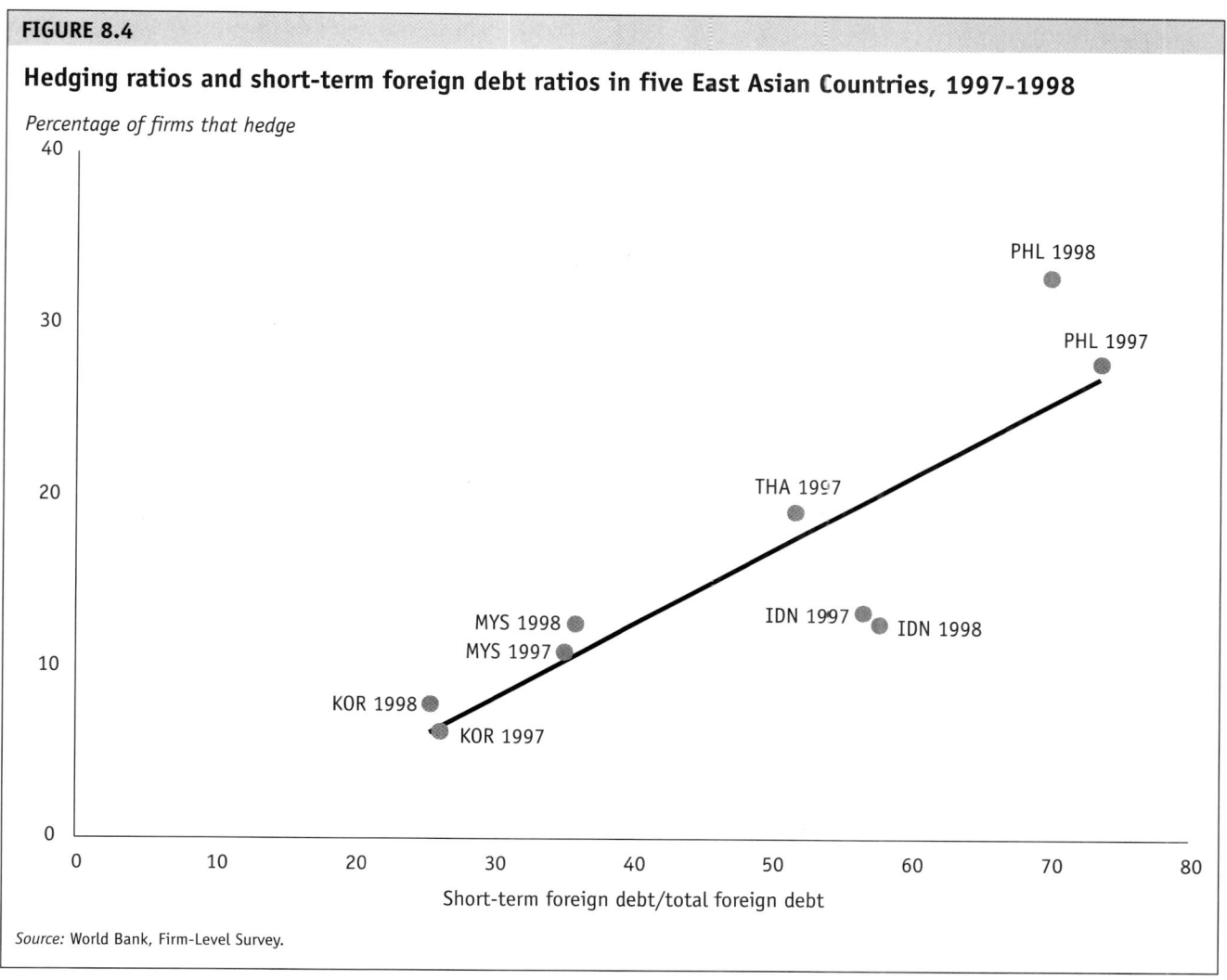

**FIGURE 8.4**

**Hedging ratios and short-term foreign debt ratios in five East Asian Countries, 1997-1998**

*Source:* World Bank, Firm-Level Survey.

resilient and have managed to weather the crisis better. While the percentage of profitable exporters remained unchanged before and after the crises, the percentage of profitable nonexporters fell from 35 percent to 21 percent. This is an indication of the role played by the drop in domestic demand caused by the crisis, which severely affected nonexporting firms.

An interesting result is the difference in the level of foreign debt between profitable and less profitable firms. Firms that were nonprofitable financed more in the form of short-term debt from abroad compared with their more profitable counterparts. On average, the ratio of short-term foreign debt to total foreign debt for less profitable firms was about 44 percent, compared with 37 percent for profitable firms. Foreign creditors were more willing to lend to riskier firms with short-term rather than long-term maturity, expecting higher returns. Throughout the 1996–98 period, these ratios did not change much. Most less profitable firms continued to borrow relatively heavily in the short term in foreign currency. Reliance on short-term foreign debt was accompanied by low levels of hedging across the board. When we examine the level of short-term foreign debt by export orientation, the data show that less profitable exporters, on average, financed their debt from abroad 10 percent more than profitable exporters throughout the 1996–98 period (figure 8.5).

## Conclusions

This paper examined a sample of corporate financial data obtained from five East Asian countries during the period 1996–98. We find that the levels of foreign debt by manufacturing and mostly unlisted, small and

**FIGURE 8.5**

**Short-term foreign debt ratios by profitable and less profitable exporters, 1996–mid-1998**

*Short-term foreign debt/total foreign debt*

■ Profitable exporters  ■ Less profitable exporters

*Source:* World Bank, Firm-Level Survey.

medium-size enterprises in these countries were, in general, quite low. Furthermore, the patterns of foreign liabilities were quite different across countries. Korea stands out: Korean corporations financed more in the form of foreign debt across almost all sectors compared with their Southeast Asian counterparts. In Southeast Asia, larger firms, export firms, and firms with FDI partners relied more on foreign debt for their financing than other categories of firms, while in Korea only export firms tended to finance from abroad. In Southeast Asia, as a rule, larger firms were better able to access foreign debt financing during the crisis; exporters were better hedged against foreign exchange shocks; and firms with FDI partners were better able to use foreign debt financing.

Overall the size of short-term debt was not large, by international comparisons, but the level of short-term foreign debt as a percentage of total foreign debt was higher, especially for exporters, large firms, and firms with FDI partners. The degree of currency hedging was quite limited. Export firms that were profitable proved to be more resilient through the crisis, because they were better able to weather the devaluation and interest rate shocks early in the crisis period. Although firm size helped, it was not a significant factor in affecting firm profitability during the crisis. An interesting result is that firms that were less profitable financed *more* in the form of foreign debt than their more profitable counterparts.

In the light of the analysis of survey results, we can provide three simple policy prescriptions. First, in order to secure credit lines and liquidity and to continue operations at times of crisis, corporations may wish to shift at least part of their products to foreign markets or find FDI partners. Second, corporations that depend on foreign debt financing must find better ways to hedge against exchange risk. Third, corporations that borrow short-term from abroad should make every effort to increase efficiency and rates of return on equity because these firms tend to be less profitable.

We also provide three broader policy recommendations. First, it is important to develop financial markets further to mobilize long-term savings for investment in productive corporate activity. Financial market deepening that would facilitate the growth of long-term capital markets is corollary to this prescription. Second, it is important to deepen the foreign exchange market to enable firms to access foreign currency hedging facilities. Third, it is important to strengthen corporate governance so that corporations can prudently manage their own financial risks and conditions. The three general recommendations are common to all five economies, and are important prerequisite institutional requirements for sustained growth.

## Notes

The authors are with the World Bank. They are thankful to Arvind Gupta, Mary Hallward-Driemeier, Margaret Miller, and other conference participants for valuable suggestions and comments on the earlier drafts, and to David Bisbee for editorial assistance. The findings, interpretations, and conclusions expressed in this paper are those of the authors and do not necessarily represent the views of the World Bank, its Executive Directors, or the countries they represent.

1. See World Bank (1998) and Furman and Stiglitz (1999).

2. Though data for construction materials were collected for Malaysia, this report does not examine this subsector owing to insufficient data in other countries.

3. Note that the data for 1998 refer to the first half of the year.

4. The survey data contain information on the amounts of equity and debt and amounts of short-term and long-term liabilities. The data do not indicate these amounts' respective breakdowns into domestic and foreign components. It is believed, however, that equity falls largely into the category of long-term domestic liabilities on the assumption that equity is domestic currency–denominated.

5. This conclusion is similar to the findings of Dollar, Hallward-

Driemer, Iarossi, and Chakraborty (1998) who studied industrial firms in Thailand.

6. Dun & Bradstreet Credit Services (1999).

7. Our initial attempt to divide the sample of firms using a *sample mean* was hampered by the presence of large outliers. To mitigate the effects of outliers, we used the Box-Cox transformation technique. This technique basically assumes that the true distribution of profitability is normally distributed and transforms the skewed actual distribution into a normal one. The sample mean of the normalized distribution is then used to separate the profitable firms from the less profitable ones.

8. The only exception to this pattern is found in Malaysia. This could be because in Malaysia no negative profit values were reported. All firms in Malaysia reported positive profits for the three-year period 1996–98. This phenomenon, although not completely impossible, seems implausible. As a consequence, the analysis of this section did not include Malaysian data.

9. We define 1996 for Thailand and 1997 for Indonesia, Korea, Malaysia, and the Philippines as "before the crisis"; and 1997 for Thailand and 1998 for Indonesia, Korea, Malaysia, and the Philippines as "after the crisis."

# chapter nine

# Corporate Employment and Public Policy

Xin Meng

Ron Duncan

One of the outstanding features of Asian economic growth has been its rapid development of labor-intensive exports. This has affected Asian economies in several important ways. During the process of economic growth, hundreds of thousands of once-unskilled laborers were trained to handle recently introduced modern technology. Thus, human capital accumulation has been fast in these economies. Since the driving force for the rapid growth was labor-intensive exports, growth brought about faster increases in labor income relative to capital income. This, in turn, brought about a relatively equal income distribution.

The crisis suddenly slowed down markedly these countries' economic growth—and had a substantial impact on employment. While the adverse impact on employment is obvious, the details are not known. For example, who are the most severely affected workers? Which categories of workers were laid off? To answer these questions and to design necessary policy responses, one needs to understand the response of economic agents, especially firms, to the shock. Using the surveys carried out in the crisis countries as a basis, this paper throws some light on how corporate firms reacted to the Asian crisis from the viewpoint of their employment practices. In particular, the following questions are addressed:

- Which particular groups of employees have been most severely affected by the changes in production?
- How have the sample firms reacted to minimize human capital losses?
- How are reductions in the work force associated with demand or labor cost constraints? To what extent have labor costs changed and in what direction? and
- How have labor market institutional factors affected the behavior of surveyed corporate firms in dealing with the crisis?

The next section discusses the background of the five crisis countries, in particular their economic achievements before the crisis, how badly the countries have been affected by the crisis, and the differences in labor market institutions. The next three sections are devoted to the questions of employment change and its contributing factors, the particular groups of employees that have been affected, and the firms' behavior with respect to minimizing human capital losses. The final section discusses the relationship between firm behavior and labor market institutional settings, and provides some policy implications.

## Background information

Four of the five economies had consistently fast economic growth for a long period before the Asian crisis. Table 9.1 shows the real GDP growth of the five countries since the beginning of the decade. The average real GDP growth in the first half of the 1990s for four of the countries (Indonesia, the Republic of Korea, Malaysia, and Thailand) was above 7.5 percent. Even the Philippines, which previously had relatively poor growth, began to register reasonably strong growth from 1994 on, and by 1996 its real GDP growth had reached 5.5 percent. The GDP growth for all five countries, however, declined in 1997 and fell further in 1998. Indonesia, Korea, and Thailand experienced negative growth in 1998.

As a result of the declining economic growth, unemployment in all five countries has increased sharply (see figure 9.1). The reported changes in Indonesia, Korea, and Thailand are dramatic.

In Indonesia, the pressure on employment is not only attributable to the shrinking domestic labor demand, but also to the repatriation of Indonesians working in other parts of East Asia (Economist Intelligence Unit [EIU] 1998a).

The lack of reliable information makes any estimates of the unemployment rate in Thailand suspect. The figure of 6 percent used in figure 9.1 is based on an estimate by the International Labor Organization (ILO). The National Statistics Office and the Ministry of Labor in Thailand have made other estimates that range up to 10 percent. What can be concluded with certainty is that the number of Thailand's unemployed has increased sharply (EIU 1998d).

In Korea, many workers have dropped out of the labor force, a fact which has affected the official unemployment figures. The Confederation of Trade Unions has estimated that the "true" level of unemployment is double the official rate. This "true" rate is a reflection of the large number of people who have dropped out of the labor force, or who are working without pay in family businesses, and casual workers who have not been paid for over a month.

While Malaysia saw almost a doubling of its unemployment rate from 1997 to 1998, its rate is low when compared with much of the rest of East Asia. This is partly attributable to the fact that before the crisis Malaysia was experiencing an extremely tight job market. Urban unemployment rates were believed to be much lower than the official rate. The government noted at the time that skilled and semi-skilled workers were becoming scarce (EIU 1998b).

In percentage terms, unemployment in the Philippines has risen the least of the countries in the study. This is partly because the Philippines is one of the last countries in East Asia seemingly affected by the current financial crisis. It was only in the second quarter of 1998 that the country recorded negative growth. This decline, however, was seen by many as the result of the drought conditions brought on by El Nino and not the result of the crisis. Confirmation of this analysis can be seen in the employment figures for the second half of 1998 when employment rebounded strongly in the agricultural sector, bringing the national unemployment level down to around 10 percent from 13 percent (EIU 1998c).

Employment at firm level is heavily influenced by labor market institutions. Hence, understanding the degree of flexibility of the labor markets in each of the five countries helps one identify the differences in the firms' employment behavior during the crisis.

**TABLE 9.1**
### Change in real GDP: 1991–1998

| Real GDP growth | Indonesia | Korea | Malaysia | Philippines | Thailand |
|---|---|---|---|---|---|
| 1990 | 9.0 | 9.7 | 9.7 | 2.7 | 11.7 |
| 1991 | 8.9 | 9.2 | 8.8 | −0.2 | 8.0 |
| 1992 | 7.2 | 5.0 | 7.8 | 0.3 | 8.1 |
| 1993 | 7.3 | 5.8 | 8.4 | 2.1 | 8.3 |
| 1994 | 7.5 | 8.4 | 9.4 | 4.4 | 8.8 |
| 1995 | 8.2 | 9.0 | 9.4 | 4.8 | 8.7 |
| 1990–95 avg. | 8.0 | 7.5 | 8.7 | 2.3 | 8.4 |
| 1996 | 8.0 | 7.1 | 8.6 | 5.5 | 5.5 |
| 1997 | 5.0 | 5.5 | 8.0 | 5.1 | −0.4 |
| 1998 | −10.0 | −2.5 | 3.0 | 3.3 | −1.5 |

*Source:* Garnaut (1998).

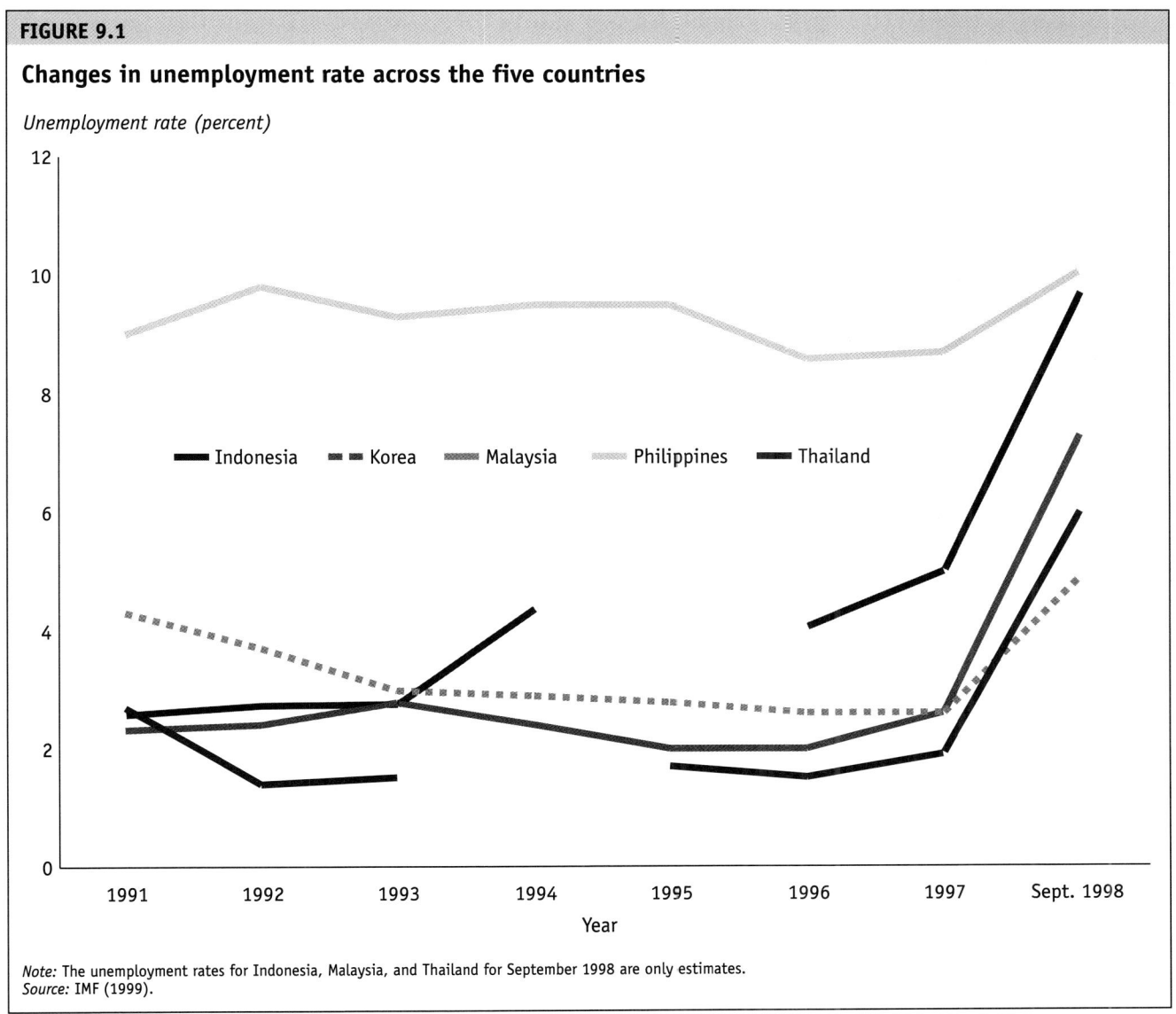

**FIGURE 9.1**

**Changes in unemployment rate across the five countries**

*Note:* The unemployment rates for Indonesia, Malaysia, and Thailand for September 1998 are only estimates.
*Source:* IMF (1999).

Of the five countries, Korea has the strongest union movement. Even though on average only 10 percent of its labor force is unionized, a much higher unionization rate is found in the manufacturing industry. In addition, the unionization rate is highly correlated to firm size. The average firm size in this study is 314 employees, and all the firms are from the manufacturing industry. According to Lee and Kim (1997), the unionization rate is 26 percent in firms with 100–299 employees and 36 percent in firms with 300–499 employees. This implies a 30 percent unionization rate for the firms covered in this study; which may be the highest unionization rate among the five countries. But because smaller firms are less unionized they are likely to be more flexible in responding to economic changes.

During the crisis, unions in Korea once again demonstrated their power. For example, when the Hyundai automobile factory in Ulsan decided to implement a redundancy plan, the workers orchestrated a takeover of the factory, causing US$650 million in lost production costs and driving several suppliers to the edge of collapse. The end result was an agreement allowing the company to lay off 1,300 workers, mostly female cafeteria staff, and permitting another 1,200 workers to go on voluntary unpaid leave (EIU 1998d). Recently, new legislation that allows employers to lay off workers *en masse* was implemented. In the negotiations that led up to this change, labor won a promise from employers that workers would not be "recklessly" laid off. In return, the unions agreed that they would work with management to adjust wages and working hours (Lee 1998:17).

Unions are virtually nonexistent in Malaysia. They were banned until 1988, after which only in-house unions were allowed at plant level, rather than at industry level. Industrial relations legislation provides for compulsory arbitration of disputes and prohibition of the right to strike in sectors providing "essential services" (Athukorala 1998). Indonesia has only one, government-run, union. According to Agarwal (1995), it is more of a government organ than a representative body for workers.

Although unions are prevalent in the Philippines and Thailand, they have lacked bargaining power in both places. In Thailand, the legal requirement for any strike action is support from a majority of workers, which makes such actions extremely difficult (EIU 1998e). In the Philippines, the lack of bargaining power of unions can be seen in their inability to hold employers to legislated minimum wages (EIU 1998c).

On the minimum wage front, Thailand, Indonesia, and the Philippines all have legislation. In some cases, however, the minimum wage level is set rather low so that it is not effective, and in others, governments have no adequate method to reinforce the legislation (EIU 1998a, c, e). Malaysia does not have minimum wage legislation (Athukorala 1998). Korea introduced a minimum wage law in 1987; it was initially applied to manufacturing enterprises employing over 10 workers. In 1990, it was extended to include all industries with over 10 workers. About 2.1 percent of total workers were estimated to be covered by minimum wages (Kim, Rhee, and Lee 1992), a rather low coverage rate.

Although minimum wages may have little application in Korea, the Labor Standard Law introduced in 1953 and reinforced in 1987 has played an important role in the Korean employment system. Employers were prevented from laying off or dismissing workers except for the "right causes." A thirty-day advance notice was legally required. A mandatory employer-financed severance pay scheme was also required (Lee and Kim 1997). In early 1998, the government legalized layoffs to help employers cope with the pressure imposed by the crisis (Veale 1999). However, it is reported that the two major union groups see this as giving in to the demands of employers instead of having firms adopt job-sharing programs and shorter working days.

## Employment performance across countries, sectors, and the export status of the firms

Across the five countries, 50 percent of the surveyed firms reduced employment. The most widespread reductions were in Korea—over 60 percent. Employment reductions appear to have been largest in Korea and Thailand, judging by the reports that upwards of 27 percent of the firms in these countries reduced employment by more than 25 percent. Malaysia had the smallest proportion of firms reducing employment by more than 25 percent.

Figure 9.2 summarizes the employment changes in the five crisis countries in broad magnitudes (increased, unchanged, and decreased). On average, employment fell in about 48 percent of the surveyed firms. Of the five countries, Korea was the most severely affected with about 62 percent of the firms experiencing employment reductions. Thailand and Indonesia were next in this ranking. Although employment was not as seriously affected in the Philippines and Malaysia, more than 30 percent of the sampled firms in these countries reduced their employment levels.

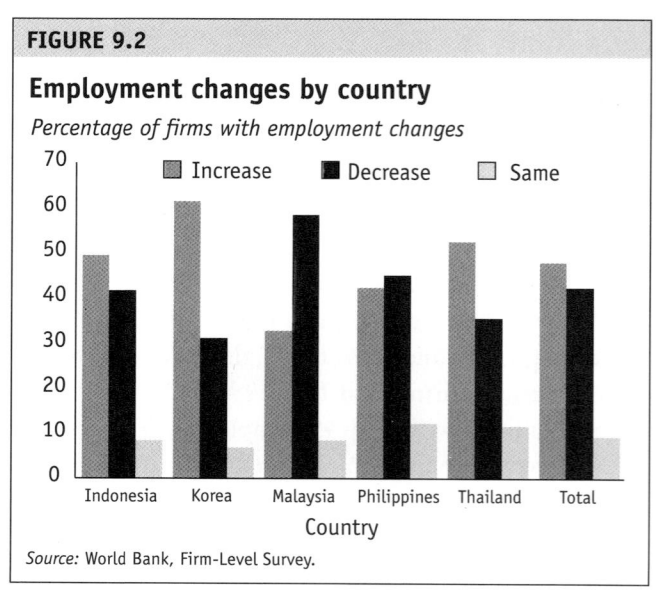

**FIGURE 9.2**

**Employment changes by country**

*Percentage of firms with employment changes*

*Source:* World Bank, Firm-Level Survey.

At the industry level, auto parts, electronics, and machinery are the sectors that have had the largest employment loss (see figure 9.3). In the auto parts industry 73 percent of the firms have reduced employment, while the equivalent figures for the electronics and machinery industries are 56 and 55 percent, respectively. The auto parts and electronic industries also have the highest percentage of firms that have reduced employment by 25 percent or more. While the garments and textiles and chemicals industries have a smaller percentage of firms with large reductions in employment, the absolute number of firms adversely affected is much higher than in other industries. Garments and textiles are also likely to have a high percentage of female employees.

Given that foreign direct investment fell dramatically during the crisis, one might expect that export-oriented firms would have been most adversely affected. From another perspective, as the crisis resulted in huge currency depreciations, the export sector may well have expanded. Thus, whether the crisis has adversely affected the export or domestic sector the most is largely an empirical question. It can be observed from figure 9.4 that an equal percentage of firms from the domestic and export-oriented sectors reduced employment. However, a significantly greater number of firms

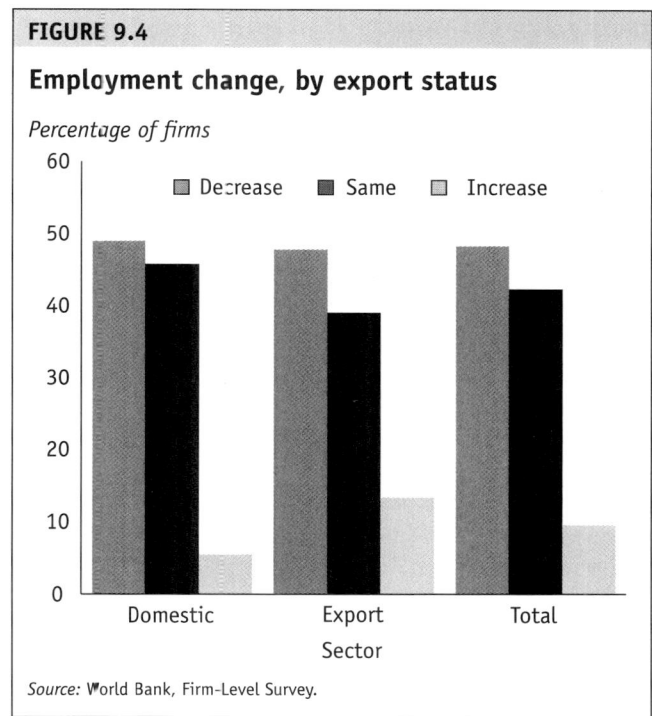

**FIGURE 9.4**

**Employment change, by export status**

*Percentage of firms*

*Source:* World Bank, Firm-Level Survey.

in the export sector increased employment than in domestic firms.

Even though many firms have reduced employment, they may still have job vacancies that cannot be filled by redundant workers for various reasons, such as mismatches in skills. It should be expected that the more capital- and skill-intensive firms, owing to their being involved in more dynamic technologies, would be more likely to fill vacancies while letting workers go. In the survey, the firms were asked whether they were filling vacancies as people left their jobs. The summary of the responses to this question by country and export status is reported in table 9.2. Of the four countries responding, Korea has the highest proportion of firms that answered positively—at 46 percent. If we take into account that 62 percent of Korean firms have reduced employment since the Asian crisis began in mid-1997, the high proportion of firms filling vacancies may also indicate that there may be a shift in demand from one kind of labor to another.

When it comes to laying off workers, firms adopt different practices. Some enforce layoffs, while others encourage workers to quit voluntarily. Some pay redundant workers severance pay; others do not. This variance in firm behavior also reflects labor legislation and has implications for the social impact of the crisis.

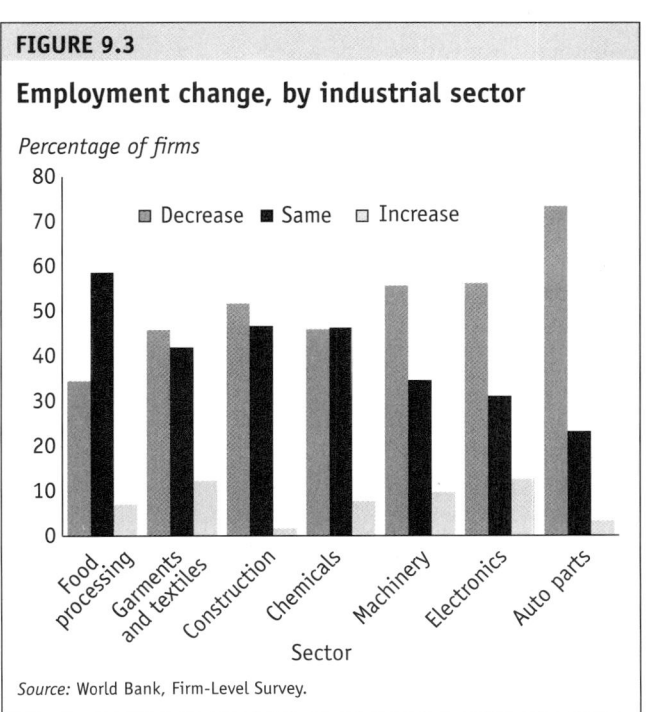

**FIGURE 9.3**

**Employment change, by industrial sector**

*Percentage of firms*

*Source:* World Bank, Firm-Level Survey.

### TABLE 9.2
**Filling vacancies during retrenchment, by country**

| Response | Indonesia | Korea | Malaysia | Philippines | Thailand | Total |
|---|---|---|---|---|---|---|
| Yes (number of responses) | — | 392 | 79 | 214 | 96 | 781 |
| Yes (percent) | — | 46.34 | 29.81 | 39.34 | 28.66 | 39.25 |
| No (number of responses) | — | 454 | 186 | 330 | 239 | 1,209 |
| No (percent) | — | 53.66 | 70.19 | 60.66 | 71.34 | 60.75 |
| Total (number of responses) | — | 846 | 265 | 544 | 335 | 1,990 |

—: not available
*Source:* World Bank, Firm-Level Survey.

### TABLE 9.3
**Employment practices, by country**

| Laid off workers | Indonesia | Korea | Malaysia | Philippines | Thailand | Total |
|---|---|---|---|---|---|---|
| Yes (percent) | 38.89 | 43.65 | 20.38 | 29.23 | 15.98 | 33.05 |
| No (percent) | 61.11 | 56.35 | 79.62 | 70.77 | 84.02 | 66.95 |
| Total (number of responses) | 378 | 850 | 265 | 544 | 338 | 2,375 |

| Severance pay paid | Indonesia | Korea | Malaysia | Philippines | Thailand | Total |
|---|---|---|---|---|---|---|
| Yes (percent) | 67.02 | — | 24.15 | 60.55 | 49.04 | 52.92 |
| No (percent) | 32.98 | — | 75.85 | 39.23 | 50.96 | 47.01 |
| Total (number of responses) | 373 | — | 265 | 469 | 314 | 1,421 |

—: not available
*Source:* World Bank, Firm-Level Surveys.

In the survey questionnaire, the firms were asked the following questions:

(a) Are you laying off or retrenching your workers?
(b) Does your firm pay severance compensation?

The answers to these questions are summarized in table 9.3. Korea has the highest proportion (43 percent) of firms that laid off or retrenched workers. This is rather interesting considering that the enforcement of the Labor Standard Law in Korea has been rather strong. However, it is not clear whether the impact has been mostly felt since layoffs were legalized. In Indonesia and the Philippines the percentage of firms laying off workers is 39 and 29 percent, respectively. Surprisingly, Thailand, with the second highest proportion of firms with reduced employment, has a very low percentage (16 percent) of firms laying off workers.

Once employees are laid off, do firms compensate them? In Indonesia 67 percent do so, while in the Philippines and Thailand 60 and 49 percent of the sample firms, respectively, provide compensation. Only 24 percent in Malaysia receive severance pay.

In cases in which the firms' export status is concerned, there is some difference in employment practices (see table 9.4). A higher percentage of exporting firms lay off workers, have workers leaving voluntarily, and compensate on retrenchment. These features may indicate that the export sector is more dynamic and has a higher labor turnover rate.

## Causes of employment changes

Changes in employment may result from both demand- and supply-side factors. However, in the current context, labor demand should be the main factor. In this section, the main causes of employment change over the crisis period are studied. In particular, the data are analyzed to determine whether the reduction in employment was caused by the reduction in production or by an increase in labor costs.

To investigate the impact of output and wage changes on employment, data on changes in production capacity utilization (measured as the amount of output actually produced relative to the maximum amount that can be produced), changes in the percentage of wage and nonwage labor costs in total production costs, and the variable "the proportional change in employment as

### TABLE 9.4
### Employment practices, by export status
(percent)

| Firm retrenched workers | Nonexport | Export | Total |
|---|---|---|---|
| Yes (number of responses) | 308 | 454 | 762 |
| Yes (percent) | (30.68) | (35.17) | (33.2) |
| No (number of responses) | 696 | 837 | 1533 |
| No (percent) | (69.32) | (64.83) | (66.8) |
| Total (number of responses) | 1,004 | 1,291 | 2,295 |

| Employee left voluntarily | | | |
|---|---|---|---|
| Yes (number of responses) | 608 | 863 | 1471 |
| Yes (percent) | (80.64) | (85.45) | (83.39) |
| No (number of responses) | 146 | 147 | 293 |
| No (percent) | (19.36) | (14.55) | (16.61) |
| Total (number of responses) | 754 | 1,010 | 1,764 |

| Firm paid severance pay | | | |
|---|---|---|---|
| Yes (number of responses) | 378 | 333 | 711 |
| Yes (percent) | (50.27) | (54.77) | (52.28) |
| No (number of responses) | 374 | 275 | 649 |
| No (percent) | (49.73) | (45.23) | (47.72) |
| Total (number of responses) | 752 | 608 | 1,360 |

Source: World Bank, Firm-Level Surveys.

compared with the employment level before the crisis" are used.

Figure 9.5 shows the changes in the capacity utilization rate across the five countries. Over the 1996–98 period, Indonesia, Thailand, and Malaysia experienced the largest reductions in capacity utilization. Korea and the Philippines did relatively better. However, the countries experienced different degrees of reduction during different periods. Four of the five experienced progressively larger reductions. Thailand was the exception, experiencing the greatest reduction at the beginning of the crisis. Korea, by contrast, experienced its largest capacity reduction in 1998. This pattern may simply indicate that the crisis hit the five countries at different times.

Figure 9.6 presents the correlations between the changes in employment and in capacity utilization. The decline in capacity utilization (and presumably, therefore, in output) has had its greatest impact on employment in Indonesia and Thailand. The low level of correlation in Korea suggests that reductions in capacity utilization cannot have played a large part in the comparatively large reduction in employment in that country. In general, there is a positive correlation between changes in the two variables. Nevertheless,

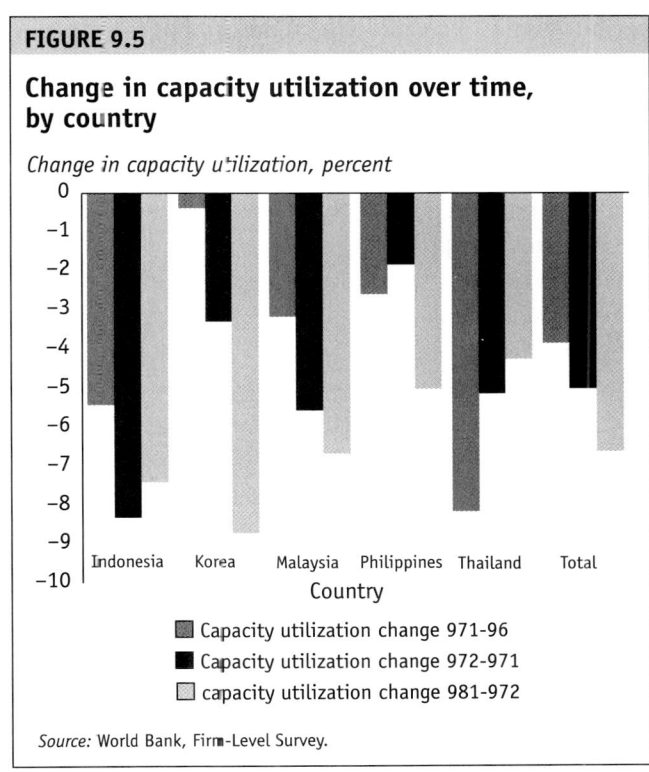

### FIGURE 9.5
### Change in capacity utilization over time, by country

Source: World Bank, Firm-Level Survey.

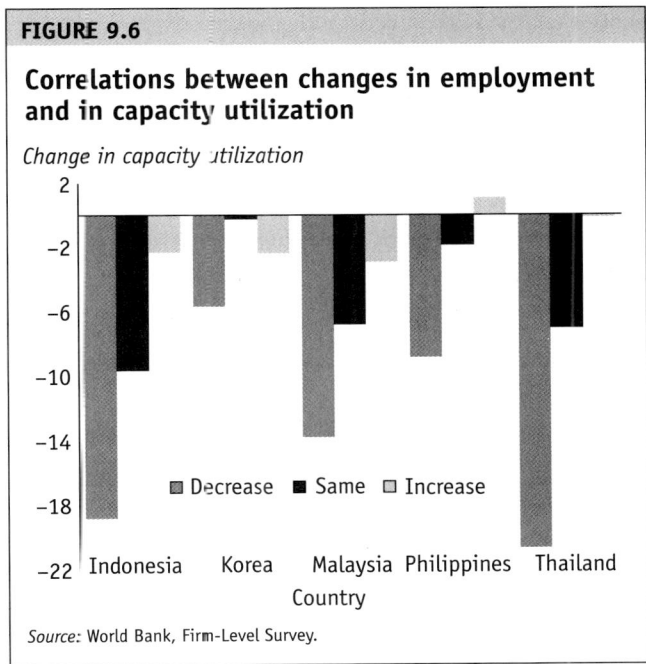

### FIGURE 9.6
### Correlations between changes in employment and in capacity utilization

Source: World Bank, Firm-Level Survey.

labor hoarding is evident, particularly in Indonesia, Thailand, and Malaysia. Labor hoarding is indicated by firms with decreased capacity utilization maintaining levels of employment. For example, in Indonesia, among the 310 firms that did not experience a change in employment, average capacity utilization reduction was around 10 percent. The figure is about 7 percent for Thailand and Malaysia. A surprising observation is that in Indonesia, Korea, and Malaysia, some firms increased their employment level when their capacity utilization declined.

Labor hoarding is more obvious in the nonexport sector than in the export sector. For example, in 657 nonexporting firms with no employment change and 77 firms with an increased employment level, the capacity utilization fell by 8 and 6 percent, respectively.

Labor hoarding can be caused by different factors. First, it may result from inflexible labor market institutions. If there are labor laws preventing employers from laying off workers or high redundancy costs such as severance pay, one may observe at least short-run labor hoarding. Second, the practice may be a rational strategy, in response to what is expected to be a short-run shock, for profit-maximizing employers who want to avoid human capital loss.

As regards the impact of changes in labor costs on changes in employment, one needs a proper measurement of labor costs. At this stage, however, the labor costs variable is replaced by the share of labor costs in total production costs, acting as a proxy. In general, from the limited information available, there has not been much change in the five countries in the share of labor costs in total costs. Table 9.5 presents the changes in this share during the periods 1996–1997 and 1997–1998. In all cases, the change is less than one percentage point. Nevertheless, the standard deviations reported are rather high, indicating considerable diversity across firms.

Correlations between the change in employment and the change in the share of labor costs in total costs are presented in figure 9.7. Korea stands out as having a

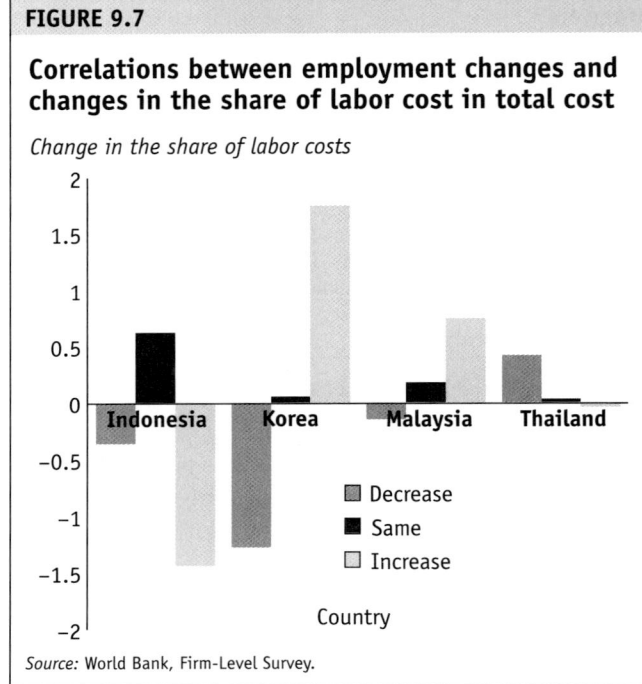

FIGURE 9.7

**Correlations between employment changes and changes in the share of labor cost in total cost**

*Source:* World Bank, Firm-Level Survey.

strong positive correlation, particularly with regard to firms that increased employment. Assuming that Korea has the least labor-intensive industrial sector among the five countries,[1] its firms' labor costs account for a smaller share of total costs. If we assume that in the short run the firms' total costs are fixed, the strong positive correlation between the two variables in Korea may imply that the wage level is relatively inflexible and that the employment effect dominates any adjustments in labor costs. This could explain why the reduction in capacity utilization appears to be less important in Korea in terms of explaining the employment reductions.

Interestingly, although there has been little change in the share of labor costs in total costs, some firms have complained that the increase in labor costs was one of

TABLE 9.5
**Change in the Share of Labor Costs in Total Costs**

| | 1996–97 | | | 1997–Mid-98 | | |
|---|---|---|---|---|---|---|
| Country | Mean | S.D | Number | Mean | S.D | Number |
| Indonesia | — | — | — | −0.05 | 8.76 | 613 |
| Korea | −0.29 | 5.25 | 751 | −0.67 | 6.43 | 751 |
| Malaysia | 0.68 | 4.02 | 697 | 0.08 | 4.97 | 691 |
| Philippines | — | — | — | — | — | — |
| Thailand | — | — | — | 0.15 | 6.20 | 563 |
| Total | 0.18 | 4.72 | n.a. | −0.15 | 6.68 | n.a. |

—: not available
*Note:* S.D. stands for Standard Deviation.
*Source:* World Bank, Firm-Level Survey.

the main reasons for their reduction in capacity utilization. In response to the question "What are the main causes for the reduction in capacity utilization?" the firms were asked to rank seven factors on a scale of 1 to 5, with 1 indicating "not important" and 5 indicating "very important." Here, the five values are grouped into three categories: 1–2 (not important), 3 (average), and 4–5 (very important). Table 9.6 reports the firms' ranking of the importance of an increase in labor costs in contributing to their reduction in capacity utilization. About 50 percent of the firms in the Philippines and Thailand thought the increase in labor costs was an extremely important factor in their reduction of capacity utilization. The figures for Indonesia, Korea, and Malaysia are 27, 8, and 26 percent, respectively.

Assuming that the firms identifying high labor costs as one of the main contributors to the reduction in capacity utilization actually did have increased labor costs during the crisis period, the question is why, with such large currency depreciations, labor costs in these firms still increased. One explanation may be that nominal wages are indexed to the Consumer Price Index (CPI). With a currency depreciation, the prices of imports and import-competing goods increase, and hence the CPI increases. This was apparently true in the case of the Philippines (See Country Report for the Philippines). However, to understand the real reason for the complaints, one needs to ascertain whether the firms that complained about increases in labor costs actually did have these increases.

## The characteristics of workers leaving the firms

Because employment reductions are costly both to the firms and society from the viewpoint of losing firm-specific and general human capital and in creating social hardship, it is important to understand which groups of people were most affected. In this section we study the profiles of workers who left the surveyed firms.

## The age profile of workers who left the sample firms

The firms were asked to state the average age of people who had left the firm. Answers were given in terms of five age groups: under 20, 21–30, 31–40, 41–50, and above 50. To make full use of the answers, one also needs to know the average age of all employees in the firm. For example, if the average age of all employees is 31 to 40 years, whereas the average age of people leaving the firm is 21–30 years, we may conclude that young people are being retrenched disproportionately. However, data on the average age of all employees are not available. Below, we present summaries of the answers to the question broken down by country and by industry (see figures 9.8 and 9.9). While it is hard to judge whether a particular age group was disproportionately retrenched, some cross-country and industry-related differences are identified and some conjectures provided.

Figure 9.8 indicates that apart from Korea, the other four countries mainly retrenched 21–30 year-old workers. Workers who were made redundant in Korea were mainly 31–40 years old. It may be observed that the four countries that mostly fired workers in the 21–30 age group have the more labor-intensive industries and the proportion of production labor is relatively high (see table 9.7). If we assume that production workers are younger than managerial and technical workers, the fact that the 21–30 age group was more likely to be retrenched suggests that production workers are the

### TABLE 9.6
**Contribution of increase in labor cost to reduction in capacity utilization**
(percentage of firms, totals)

| Survey response | Indonesia | Korea | Malaysia | Philippines | Thailand |
|---|---|---|---|---|---|
| Not important | 44.13 | 66.06 | 50.63 | 29.28 | 33.18 |
| Average | 28.52 | 25.45 | 23.52 | 24.64 | 15.14 |
| Very important | 27.35 | 8.48 | 25.85 | 46.09 | 51.67 |
| Total number. of firms | 596 | 495 | 557 | 345 | 449 |

Source: World Bank, Firm-Level Survey.

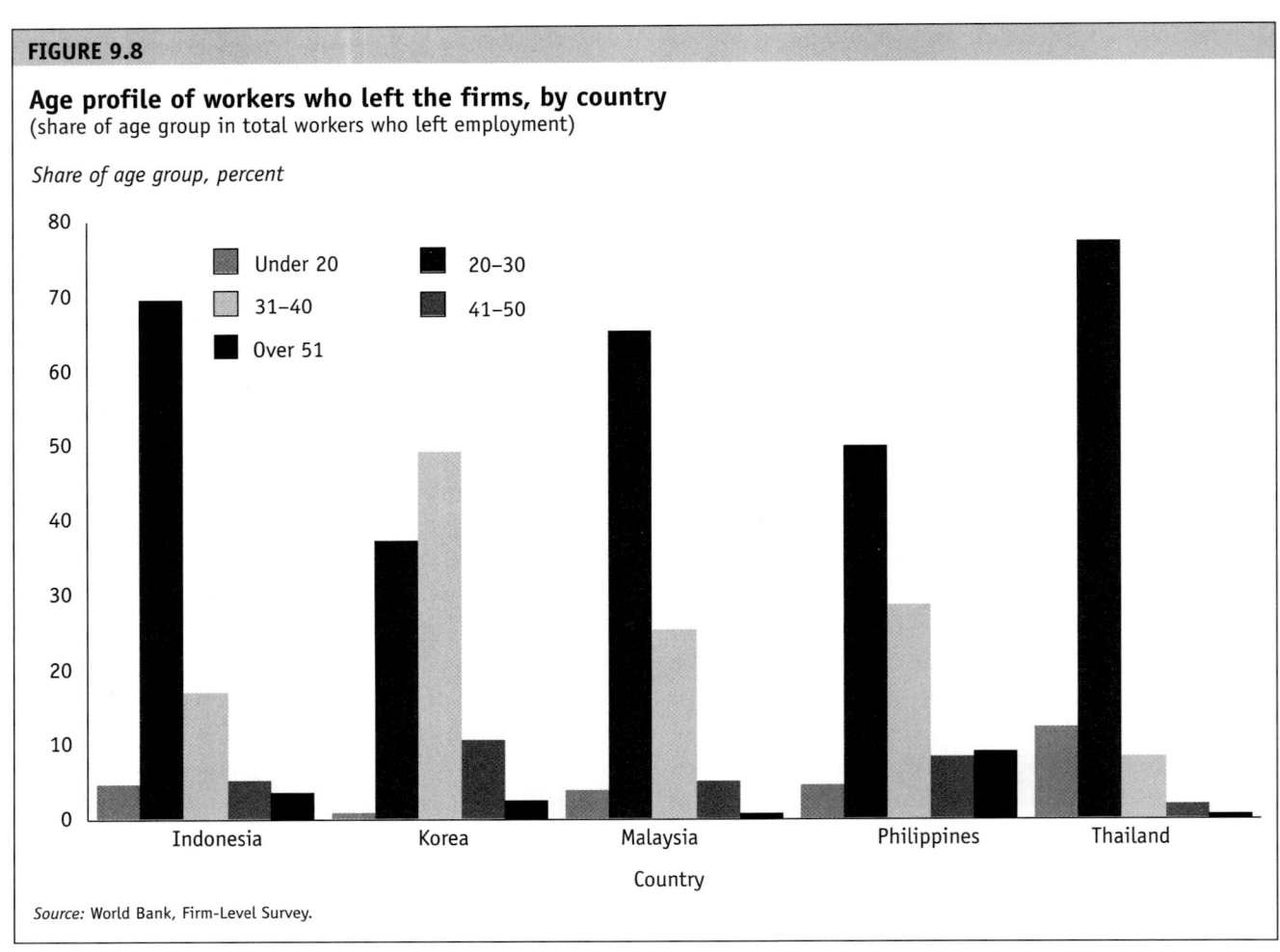

**FIGURE 9.8**

**Age profile of workers who left the firms, by country**
(share of age group in total workers who left employment)

*Source:* World Bank, Firm-Level Survey.

**TABLE 9.7**
**Occupational distribution, by country**

| Country | Average number of employees per firm | | Percent of managerial and technical staff | | Percent of production workers | | Percent of nonproduction workers | |
|---|---|---|---|---|---|---|---|---|
| | 1997 | Mid-1998 | 1997 | Mid-1998 | 1997 | Mid-1998 | 1997 | Mid-1998 |
| Indonesia | 350 | 319 | 6.77 | 7.40 | 74.83 | 75.57 | 18.40 | 17.02 |
| Korea | 354 | 328 | 16.65 | 16.59 | 55.26 | 54.86 | 28.10 | 28.55 |
| Malaysia | 166 | 155 | 18.60 | 19.34 | 70.23 | 68.00 | 11.18 | 12.66 |
| Philippines | 421 | 386 | 8.69 | 8.56 | 81.84 | 82.40 | 9.47 | 9.05 |
| Thailand | 249 | 236 | 10.73 | 11.00 | 76.17 | 75.35 | 13.10 | 13.65 |
| Total | 301 | 278 | 11.90 | 12.18 | 70.48 | 70.18 | 17.62 | 17.64 |

*Source:* World Bank, Firm-Level Survey.

ones who suffered the most from the crisis. This can be verified when the occupational profile of retrenched workers is studied.[2]

Korea, however, has a somewhat different industrial structure. Relative to the other four countries, production labor in Korean firms accounted for a lower proportion of total labor. If the assumption made above also applies in Korea's case—that is, that production workers are relatively younger—we may observe that in Korea it is the relatively older and more skilled age group that has suffered most from the employment reduction.

We also examined the age profile of leaving workers by their industry classification (see figure 9.9). It can be seen that apart from the machinery and chemicals industries, all other industries mainly lost workers whose age was 21–30 years. The machinery and chemicals industries were the most prominent in terms of reducing their workers aged 31–50 years. It is possible that these industries are mainly located in Korea, but it is hard to confirm whether this is a country-specific phenomenon based on the available data.

## The tenure of workers who left the sample firms

In the previous subsection we implied, perhaps optimistically, that young employees who had been laid off would most likely have been those with lower levels of firm-specific skills. In this subsection, we look more closely into the firm-specific skills, measured by length of tenure, of retrenched workers.

Table 9.8 shows the percentage of firms that reduced employment, broken down by worker tenure. More than 70 percent of the firms in Indonesia, Malaysia, and Thailand retrenched workers whose average length of tenure was less than three years. For the Philippines this figure was 45 percent, and for Korea, 57 percent. In the Philippines and Korea more than 20 percent of the firms retrenched workers whose average tenure was more than six years; in the case of the Philippines the figure was 38 percent. Another 20 percent of the firms in these two countries fired workers whose average tenure was four to five years.

These findings indicate that firm-specific human capital losses may have been more serious in the Philippines

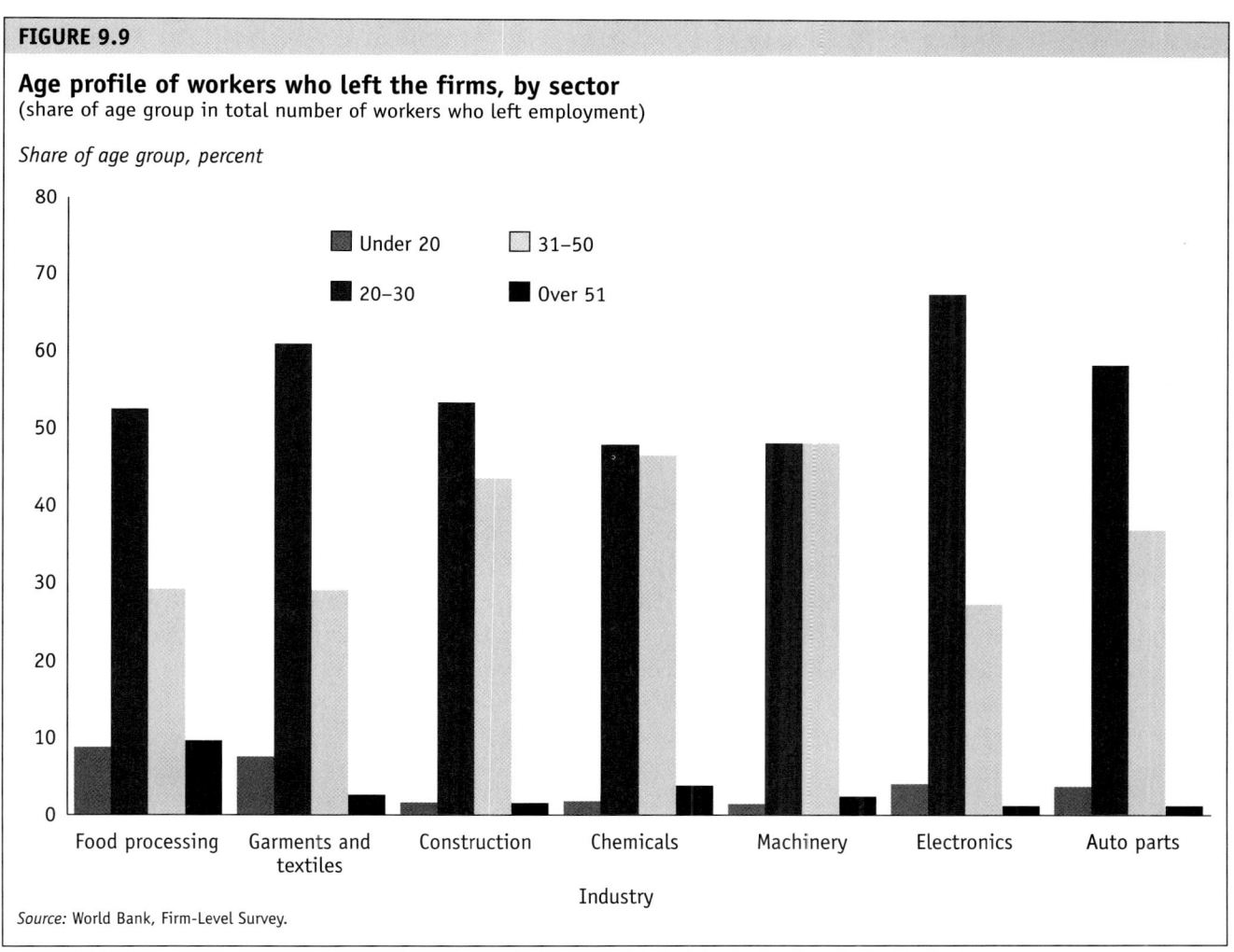

**FIGURE 9.9**

**Age profile of workers who left the firms, by sector**
(share of age group in total number of workers who left employment)

*Source:* World Bank, Firm-Level Survey.

### TABLE 9.8
### Tenure of workers who left firms, by country
(percent, totals)

| Tenure | Indonesia | Korea | Malaysia | Philippines | Thailand | Total number of firms |
|---|---|---|---|---|---|---|
| Less than 1 year | 18.36 | 15.83 | 33.33 | 20.12 | 55.85 | 735 |
| 1–3 years | 50.62 | 41.69 | 42.8 | 25.15 | 35.76 | 984 |
| 4–5 years | 17.62 | 22.03 | 14.02 | 16.7 | 4.59 | 387 |
| 6–10 years | 6.95 | 15.17 | 6.82 | 15.29 | 2.53 | 253 |
| More than 10 years | 6.45 | 5.28 | 3.03 | 22.74 | 1.27 | 195 |
| Total number of firms | 403 | 758 | 264 | 497 | 632 | 2,554 |

*Source:* World Bank, Firm-Level Survey.

### TABLE 9.9
### Tenure of workers who left firms, by sector
(percent, totals)

| Sector | Less than 1 year | 1–3 years | 4–5 years | 6–10 years | More than 10 years | Total number of firms |
|---|---|---|---|---|---|---|
| Food processing | 28.09 | 31.17 | 13.89 | 10.49 | 16.36 | 324 |
| Garments and textiles | 37.58 | 36.24 | 12.19 | 7.16 | 6.82 | 894 |
| Construction | 33.87 | 38.71 | 14.52 | 9.68 | 3.23 | 62 |
| Chemicals | 18.79 | 37.35 | 19.26 | 13.69 | 10.90 | 431 |
| Machinery | 21.89 | 40.80 | 20.40 | 13.93 | 2.99 | 201 |
| Electronics | 23.20 | 46.39 | 15.46 | 9.54 | 5.41 | 388 |
| Auto parts | 27.50 | 44.17 | 16.25 | 10.00 | 2.08 | 240 |
| Total number of firms | 730 | 982 | 386 | 252 | 195 | 2,545 |

*Source:* World Bank, Firm-Level Survey.

and Korea. But why did more firms in these two countries prefer to retrench workers with longer tenure? One possible explanation may be related to labor market institutional settings. If a country has more rigid labor market institutions, the labor turnover rate will be lower on average than in a country where labor market institutions are more flexible. Thus, the average firm tenure of workers should be longer in a more flexible labor market. If this is the case, one may conclude that a higher percentage of firms in countries with less flexible labor market institutions fire workers with longer firm tenure than firms in countries with more flexible labor market institutions.

We also looked to see whether there were any firm-related differences across industries (see table 9.9). It can be seen that the chemicals industry has the highest percentage of firms that have fired workers with a high average length of tenure. About 44 percent of the surveyed firms in this industry laid off workers whose average tenure was four years or more. The food processing and machinery industries were also more likely to fire workers with longer average tenure.

### The occupational status of retrenched workers

It was assumed above that retrenchment was mostly concentrated on production workers, as they normally account for the largest proportion of occupations. In this subsection the question of whether workers in some occupations were made redundant disproportionately is examined. Below, the average percentages of retrenchment across occupations are reported in table 9.10.[3] From the figures presented, it can be seen that production workers were the major group of workers made redundant. However, in Korea and the Philippines, the proportion of production workers made redundant was smaller than the proportion of production workers in the total work force. Indonesia and Thailand, however, lost disproportionately more production workers than workers in other occupations, but only slightly. Nonproduction workers suffered disproportionately in Korea and the Philippines. Managers and technical staff only suffered losses disproportionately in the Philippines.

### TABLE 9.10
**Occupational distribution of workers who left the firms, by country**
(percent)

| Occupation | Indonesia | | Korea | | Philippines | | Thailand | |
|---|---|---|---|---|---|---|---|---|
| | Total | Left the firm | Total | Left the firm | Total | Left the firm | Total | Left the firm |
| Managerial and technical staff | 7.4 | 4.48 | 16.6 | 11.43 | 8.6 | 9.55 | 11.0 | 4.10 |
| Production workers | 75.6 | 77.09 | 54.9 | 43.71 | 82.4 | 76.62 | 75.4 | 77.86 |
| Nonproduction workers | 17.0 | 15.13 | 28.6 | 32.50 | 9.1 | 12.92 | 13.7 | 8.27 |

Source: World Bank, Firm-Level Survey.

### TABLE 9.11
**Occupational distribution of total employees and of those who left the firms, by industry**
(percent)

| Industry | Managerial and technical staff | | Production workers | | Nonproduction workers | |
|---|---|---|---|---|---|---|
| | Total | Left the firm | Total | Left the firm | Total | Left the firm |
| Food processing | 9.03 | 5.19 | 69.42 | 71.02 | 21.55 | 14.56 |
| Textiles | 8.56 | 3.47 | 81.35 | 83.04 | 10.08 | 8.93 |
| Garments and textiles | 6.20 | 2.34 | 84.96 | 83.85 | 8.84 | 6.84 |
| Garments | 6.42 | 5.03 | 77.70 | 65.49 | 15.88 | 22.99 |
| Chemicals | 13.49 | 10.59 | 62.52 | 45.25 | 23.99 | 37.99 |
| Machinery | 22.48 | 12.47 | 61.84 | 59.92 | 15.68 | 26.34 |
| Electronics | 15.43 | 10.45 | 69.97 | 57.57 | 14.60 | 14.64 |
| Auto parts | 15.33 | 9.37 | 57.78 | 70.22 | 26.88 | 12.47 |

Source: World Bank, Firm-Level Survey.

In cases in which the sector of production is concerned, it is seen that for auto parts, a domestic market–oriented industry, retrenchment was most severe on production workers (see table 9.11). The garments, chemicals, and machinery industries disproportionately retrenched nonproduction workers.

Table 9.12 lists the occupational distribution of total employees and those who left the firms, broken down by export and nonexport sectors. It shows that the export sector disproportionately cut nonproduction workers, whereas this is the case for production workers in the nonexport sector. These details appear to line up with the sectoral impact, as chemicals and machinery are likely to be export-oriented, while auto parts is primarily oriented to the domestic market.

## The firms' reactions to the loss of human capital

Layoffs can be extremely costly for firms. In the previous section we observed that our sample firms in general had behaved rationally in favoring workers who possessed more human capital, especially firm-specific human capital. Nevertheless, loss of human capital is inevitable when firms have to retrench workers. In this section we examine how firms have tried to rebuild their human capital stock in the face of employment decline. In particular, how have their training programs functioned during the crisis?

Tables 9.A1, 9.A2, and 9.A3 in the appendix present data describing the average firms' involvement with formal training programs, by country,[4] industry, and export status. The Philippines appear to have the highest

### TABLE 9.12
**Occupational distribution of total employees and those who left the firms, by export status**
(percent)

| Occupation | Export | | Nonexport | |
|---|---|---|---|---|
| | Total | Left the firm | Total | Left the firm |
| Managerial and technical staff | 12.37 | 7.75 | 11.67 | 5.72 |
| Production workers | 70.82 | 64.42 | 65.17 | 74.02 |
| Nonproduction workers | 16.81 | 19.40 | 23.16 | 14.67 |

Source: World Bank, Firm-Level Survey.

proportion of firms that have a formal training program. Of the nine industry categories, the more capital- or technology-intensive ones, such as chemicals, machinery, electronics, and auto parts, have a higher percentage of firms with formal training programs. In addition, export-oriented firms are more likely to have these programs than nonexport firms.

The survey also sought information on the number of employees trained in 1997 and 1998. Unfortunately, there is information on only two of the five countries. Table 9.13 presents the percentage of employees trained in 1997 and 1998 broken down by occupational categories for Malaysia and Thailand. The surveyed firms in these countries put the greatest emphasis on managerial level training, with the firms in Thailand training more than half of their managerial staff in both 1997 and 1998. The emphasis on the training of managerial staff may have been induced by the crisis, since the sharp reduction in domestic and foreign demand required managers to adopt new strategies.

When examining the firms' training behavior across industries, it is found that training managerial staff was the priority task in all industries for both years (see table 9.14). The electronics, garments and textiles, and auto parts industries trained more than 50 percent of their managerial staff in one of the two years. Apart from textiles and electronics, almost all industries increased their efforts in training managerial staff in 1998. In particular, the auto parts industry trained 10 percent more managerial staff in 1998 than in 1997.

Surprisingly, the export sector trained a lower percentage of managerial staff, but a higher percentage of production and nonproduction workers than the nonexport sector (see table 9.15). This may be because the

### TABLE 9.13
**Percentage of employees trained in 1997 and first half of 1998, by occupation**

| | Malaysia | | | Thailand | | |
|---|---|---|---|---|---|---|
| Occupation | Trained in 1997 | Trained in 1998 | 1998–1997 change | Trained in 1997 | Trained in 1998 | 1998–1997 change |
| Managerial staff | 35.92 | 39.20 | 3.29 | 56.07 | 56.19 | 0.11 |
| Technical staff | 34.64 | 30.31 | −4.32 | 14.96 | 14.85 | −0.11 |
| Production workers | 6.60 | 6.11 | −0.48 | 8.12 | 6.87 | −1.25 |
| Nonproduction workers | 7.11 | 6.97 | −0.14 | 28.53 | 29.18 | 0.65 |

*Source:* World Bank, Firm-Level Survey.

### TABLE 9.14
**Employees trained, by occupation and industry, 1997 and first half of 1998**
(percent)

| | Food | Textiles | Garments and textiles | Construct. | Chem. | Machry. | Electron. | Auto parts | Garments |
|---|---|---|---|---|---|---|---|---|---|
| *1997* | | | | | | | | | |
| Managerial | 41.86 | 46.59 | 48.70 | 37.23 | 40.84 | 38.71 | 58.51 | 51.55 | 39.14 |
| Technical | 31.01 | 14.34 | 8.63 | 19.08 | 35.33 | 40.68 | 25.26 | 15.57 | 27.19 |
| Production | 7.04 | 5.71 | 3.02 | 2.82 | 11.78 | 14.53 | 17.11 | 8.58 | 3.15 |
| Nonproduction | 8.87 | 14.75 | 24.54 | 1.11 | 12.93 | 12.19 | 35.84 | 24.52 | 2.66 |
| *1998* | | | | | | | | | |
| Managerial | 47.47 | 44.23 | 51.43 | 45.16 | 41.80 | 40.30 | 56.91 | 61.74 | 32.97 |
| Technical | 27.93 | 10.47 | 10.45 | 33.14 | 32.28 | 32.48 | 20.95 | 13.88 | 21.81 |
| Production | 5.18 | 4.07 | 2.98 | 1.99 | 9.12 | 17.48 | 14.18 | 8.78 | 2.43 |
| Nonproduction | 8.09 | 10.67 | 28.98 | 1.87 | 11.06 | 13.87 | 38.80 | 23.89 | 3.49 |
| *1998–1997 (change)* | | | | | | | | | |
| Managerial | 5.60 | −2.36 | 2.73 | 7.93 | 0.96 | 1.59 | −1.60 | 10.19 | −6.16 |
| Technical | −3.09 | −3.87 | 1.82 | 14.06 | −3.04 | −8.20 | −4.31 | −1.69 | −5.38 |
| Production | −1.86 | −1.64 | −0.05 | −0.82 | −2.66 | 2.94 | −2.93 | 0.20 | −0.72 |
| Nonproduction | −0.78 | −4.07 | 4.44 | 0.76 | −1.87 | 1.68 | 2.97 | −0.63 | 0.83 |

*Note:* Malaysia and Thailand only.
*Source:* World Bank, Firm-Level Survey.

**TABLE 9.15**
**Employees trained, by occupation and by export status, mid-1988**
(percent)

| Occupation | Nonexport 1998 | Export 1998 |
|---|---|---|
| Managerial | 54.70 | 45.27 |
| Technical | 16.25 | 19.85 |
| Production | 3.53 | 9.25 |
| Nonproduction | 6.82 | 14.38 |

*Note:* Malaysia and Thailand only.
*Source:* World Bank, Firm-Level Survey.

export sector has more expatriates working in managerial positions who receive training overseas. In addition, in 1998 the training effort in the export sector did not change as much as it did in the nonexport sector. The domestic sector may have been under greater pressure to shift its market focus because of the relatively larger downturn in domestic demand than in export markets.

The relationship between the firms' employment change and their training behavior was also examined. Table 9.16 presents the percentage of each occupational group trained broken down by decreased, unchanged, and increased employment levels for both countries in both years. Firms with an increased employment level increased their level of training in 1998 relative to 1997, as might be expected. This is especially true for managerial and technical staff. Firms with increased employment levels in Thailand, for example, increased their managerial training by 5 percent. Firms whose employment has been adversely affected by the crisis have not yet begun to put increased effort into reducing their human capital losses, although firms with a reduced employment level in Thailand did train about 60 percent of their managerial staff in both years.

## Summary and policy implications

In this paper, the degree to which the crisis has affected employment and human capital accumulation, the causes of the employment reduction, and the possible social impact of the employment reduction have been studied. Below, the main findings are summarized and policy implications discussed.

Across the five countries, 50 percent of the sample firms reduced employment, while the rate of employment reduction averaged around 15 percent. The most widespread reductions were in Korea where around 60 percent of the firms reduced employment and the total employment reduction was around 19 percent. Thailand and Indonesia also had highly significant declines in employment.

It is found that the decline in capacity utilization and presumably in output has had its greatest impact on employment in Indonesia and Thailand. However, the reduction in capacity utilization does not seem to be

**TABLE 9.16**
**Correlation between employment change and training**
(percent)

| | Malaysia | | | Thailand | | |
|---|---|---|---|---|---|---|
| Employment change | 1997 | Mid-1998 | Mid-1998–1997(change) | 1997 | Mid-1998 | Mid-1998–1997(change) |
| *Decreased employment* | | | | | | |
| Managerial | 36.53 | 38.40 | 1.87 | 59.06 | 58.87 | −0.19 |
| Technical | 34.24 | 30.39 | −3.85 | 16.77 | 16.57 | −0.20 |
| Production | 9.87 | 8.99 | −0.88 | 8.72 | 7.82 | −0.90 |
| Nonproduction | 8.28 | 9.03 | 0.75 | 33.49 | 33.80 | 0.31 |
| *Unchanged employment* | | | | | | |
| Managerial | 33.12 | 38.01 | 4.89 | 55.46 | 53.97 | −1.49 |
| Technical | 33.51 | 30.45 | −3.06 | 12.31 | 10.75 | −1.56 |
| Production | 3.78 | 3.52 | −0.26 | 7.71 | 5.53 | −2.18 |
| Nonproduction | 5.29 | 4.85 | −0.43 | 24.62 | 26.87 | 2.25 |
| *Increased employment* | | | | | | |
| Managerial | 40.70 | 44.76 | 4.06 | 48.89 | 54.29 | 5.40 |
| Technical | 40.98 | 31.33 | −9.64 | 16.79 | 20.57 | 3.79 |
| Production | 12.56 | 11.99 | −0.57 | 9.40 | 9.05 | −0.35 |
| Nonproduction | 12.61 | 11.04 | −1.57 | 25.92 | 23.99 | −1.93 |

*Source:* World Bank, Firm-Level Survey.

able to explain the dramatic decline of employment in Korea. One suggestion yet to be tested is that the greater inflexibility of wages in Korea may have been the cause for the greater-than-average reduction in employment. More rigid labor markets in Korea and the Philippines may also be responsible for the fact that these countries retrenched workers with longer firm tenure than the other countries.

An alternative explanation of the relatively greater redundancies among older, more highly skilled workers in Korea is that there is a restructuring of firm activities underway, perhaps triggered by the financial shock. This restructuring may involve changes in the labor-capital relativity in producing the same products or a shift to new products. Another hint of restructuring in Korea is the disproportionate loss in the share of nonproduction workers, who may be thought of as overhead. Further support for this hypothesis can be found in the relatively higher proportion of firms in Korea filling vacancies when people leave.

Somewhat surprisingly, the firms in Thailand show less evidence of restructuring than in the other countries. This is surprising because rising labor costs in Thailand have been held to be partly responsible for triggering the crisis through the erosion of competitiveness (see Thailand Country Report). If there is a need for firms in Thailand to shift to higher-valued products requiring higher labor skills, the shift has not yet begun.

Interestingly, while 50 percent of the surveyed firms have reduced their employment level, it is found that labor hoarding is a common phenomenon in all of the five countries studied. This is indicated by the fact that firms with reduced capacity utilization kept the same level of employment or even increased employment. Labor hoarding may be the result of two different factors. First, it may be caused by the inflexibility of labor market institutions. Labor laws may restrict employers from laying off workers. Second, it may also be a rational course of action on the part of employers who want to minimize human capital losses. To understand the reasons for labor hoarding in each country, more thorough analysis is needed.

The relationship between the change in employment and the change in the share of labor costs in total costs is also studied. While there is a positive relationship between these variables in Korea and Malaysia, there is a negative relationship in Thailand and Indonesia. Although it is impossible to disentangle the impact of the change in total cost from the change in labor cost, we think that in the short run, given fixed capital costs, the positive relationship may imply relatively inflexible wage settings.

The analyses of the characteristics of workers who left the sample firms revealed interesting patterns. In all countries except Korea, younger workers with short firm tenure—and production and nonproduction workers rather than managerial and technical workers—were more likely to be retrenched. The implication of this behavior is twofold. First, if we assume that firm-specific human capital accumulation is associated with firm-specific work experience, the loss of younger workers with fewer years of firm tenure implies a loss of less skilled workers. In addition, production and nonproduction workers are less skilled when compared with managerial and technical workers. Thus, the profiles of retrenched workers indicate that firms reacted to the crisis in a rational way—by attempting to minimize their loss of human capital.

Second, if we assume that younger people have fewer family responsibilities, the profile of the retrenched workers implies that the social pressure that was attributable to the crisis was minimized. Moreover, younger people will find it easier to learn new skills. Therefore, it will be less costly for industry or government to retrain them so that they can fit in with new trends in labor demand.

However, things are gloomier in Korea, where workers aged 30–50 years, with tenure of between 4 and 10 years were more likely to be laid off. In addition, about 11 percent (the highest among the five countries) of the laid-off workers were managerial and technical staff. This profile indicates that Korea suffered serious human capital losses owing to the crisis, and that the social consequences were also more serious.

# Appendix 9.A

## The frequency of use of formal training programs during the crisis

**TABLE 9.A1**
**Use of formal training, by country**
(percent, total)

| Country | Firms with training program | Firms without training program | Total number of firms |
|---|---|---|---|
| Indonesia | 26.08 | 73.92 | 740 |
| Korea | 31.9 | 68.1 | 840 |
| Malaysia | 22.09 | 77.91 | 815 |
| Philippines | 51.47 | 48.53 | 544 |
| Thailand | 27.19 | 72.81 | 629 |
| Total number of firms | 1,092 | 2,476 | 3,568 |

*Source:* World Bank, Firm-Level Survey.

**TABLE 9.A2**
**Use of formal training, by industry**
(percent, total)

| Industry | Firms with training program | Firms without training program | Total number of firms |
|---|---|---|---|
| Food processing | 31.13 | 68.87 | 604 |
| Textiles | 29.69 | 70.31 | 229 |
| Garments and textiles | 26.79 | 73.21 | 321 |
| Construction | 11.57 | 88.43 | 121 |
| Chemicals | 34.48 | 65.52 | 670 |
| Machinery | 36.81 | 63.19 | 288 |
| Electronics | 46.45 | 53.55 | 422 |
| Auto parts | 37.59 | 62.41 | 266 |
| Garments | 15.37 | 84.63 | 605 |
| Total number of firms | 1,084 | 2,449 | 3,533 |

*Source:* World Bank, Firm-Level Survey.

**TABLE 9.A3**
**Use of formal training, by export status**
(percent, total)

| Training | Nonexport | Export | Total number of firms |
|---|---|---|---|
| Firms with training program | 18.57 | 41.16 | 1,084 |
| Firms without training program | 81.43 | 58.84 | 2,454 |
| Total number of firms | 1,648 | 1,890 | 3,538 |

*Source:* World Bank, Firm-Level Survey.

## Notes

The authors are with the National Center for Development Studies, Australia National University, Canberra, Australia.

1. This should be a reasonable assumption given that Korea is the most developed country and has the highest per capita GDP among the five countries studied. The assumption can be easily tested once the necessary data become available.

2. Another possible explanation might be that many rural migrants are employed in the industrial sectors. Rural migrants are often younger than local workers. Layoffs may have been concentrated on workers from rural areas. However, because there are too many missing values, the location profile of redundant workers is hard to determine.

3. Malaysia did not report on this question.

4. Data for Indonesia are not available.

# *chapter ten*

# *Indonesia: The Impact of the Economic Crisis on Industry Performance*

*National Development Planning Agency (BAPPENAS)*

After two decades marked by remarkable rates of economic growth and structural transformation, fortunes reversed for the Indonesian economy in 1997 with the onset of the financial and banking sector crisis. The crisis quickly spilled over into the real sector, and by early 1998 Indonesia was in its worse economic recession since the 1960s. To better understand the impact of this financial crisis on the real sector and how Indonesian firms are responding to the changed economic conditions, an Indonesian Competitiveness Study is being undertaken by BAPPENAS and the Central Bureau of Statistics with assistance from the World Bank. The project is collecting a unique database of detailed information on about 1,200 firms in five broad sectors: food processing (International Standard Industrial Clasification [ISIC] 31), garments (ISIC 322), textiles (ISIC 321), chemicals and processed rubber (ISIC 35), and electronics (ISIC 383). It includes data on firm behavior during the two years preceding the financial crisis in 1997 as well as the first two years of the crisis. This paper presents the preliminary results of 562 responses.

The analysis provides a number of important findings. First, the impact of the crisis on the firms' economic performance appears to be mixed. While many firms have been adversely affected by the crisis to varying degrees, some are better off because of the depreciation of the rupiah. This depends on the type of industry, whether or not a firm exports part of its production, and differences in the regions' resource endowment. The results of the survey show that domestic-oriented firms had greater reductions in capacity utilization rates and employment levels than medium and large exporting firms and FDI firms. Even within the domestic-oriented group of firms, the impact of the crisis is mixed. The food processing sector had a smaller reduction in capacity utilization rates and employment levels than the other sectors included in the survey. More than one-third of the domestic-oriented firms in the food sector reported no change in production or an increase in production in 1998. Conversely, most domestic-oriented firms in electronics reported reductions in production. Among other factors, this arises because of differences in price and income elasticities of demand for the goods produced by the five sectors. Processed food, for example, is generally more income-inelastic—and thus is relatively less affected by falls in real incomes of domestic consumers. The electronics sector, by contrast, generally has higher income elasticity of demand, and thus is more likely to be adversely affected by falls in real incomes and expenditure switching by consumers. The firms operating in Java had greater reductions in capacity utilization rates and have smaller workforces (as of 1998) compared with those operating outside Java. This provides some support for recent evidence that the regional economies of the outer islands are faring better than Java's.

The second important finding is that it is unclear to what extent the firms' financial position affected their economic activities. The results of the survey actually show that highly leveraged firms or firms with foreign currency liabilities had, on average, smaller reductions in capacity utilization rates and employment levels than did firms with low debt-equity ratios. This arises because a large proportion of the firms in the former group are also relatively efficient medium and large-scale exporters. These firms are less affected by the economic crisis.

Finally, the surveyed firms identified the sharp decline in domestic demand and the effect of the depreciation of the rupiah in raising input costs (and presumably its volatility) as the major causes of the fall in output levels in 1998. The high cost of capital was cited as the third most common cause; access to credit and guarantee of letters of credit were not rated as major causes at the end of 1998.

Indonesian firms have adopted different strategies to cope with the economic crisis. Some have shifted from supplying the domestic market to export markets. Other firms rely more on informal sources of short-term finance such as family, partners, and shareholders rather than banks.

This chapter is organized as follows: the next section briefly reviews the background and context of the Indonesian economic crisis. This is followed by a section describing the competitiveness survey, then another section presenting a descriptive analysis of the immediate impact of the economic crisis on the real sector, as measured by changes in capacity utilization rates and employment. The section analyzes changes in these real sector variables by firm type—ownership, firm size, exporting status—and by region within Indonesia. The two subsequent sections analyze the firms' financial position, and examine the relationship between specific financial indicators and firm performance. The final section summarizes the main findings of the study and provides several policy recommendations for discussion.

## The economic crisis

While the study is primarily concerned with the impact of the crisis on the firms' responses to the crisis and identifying impediments to economic recovery, one would be well-advised to keep in mind the overall macroeconomic context as it affects relative prices, interest rates, aggregate demand, and investment behavior. Without macroeconomic stability, efforts to improve firm performance will face difficulties.

Although a lot more analysis of Indonesia's crisis is still being undertaken, several tentative conclusions have been put forward on the causes. While the Thai crisis was clearly the trigger for the regional financial crisis, there were several macro- and microeconomic factors that combined to exacerbate Indonesia's economic crisis. These included inconsistent monetary and exchange rate policy, weak supervision of the banking and financial sector, accumulation of foreign currency–denominated debts, and the presence of policy distortions in the economy that misdirected resources to less profitable uses.

At the macroeconomic level, Bank Indonesia's commitment to use monetary policy to target an inflation rate, while at the same time maintaining a stable real exchange rate partly contributed to the financial crisis. With relatively high interest rates and a managed exchange rate, it was cheaper for domestic firms to borrow abroad without hedging. Coinciding with the economic boom, particularly in nontradable sectors, there was a rapid buildup of private external debt in recent years. Between 1992 and July 1997, about 85 percent of the increase in external debt was due to private sector borrowing. The average maturity of the credit extended to Indonesia's private sector declined sharply in the last few years; by December 1997, US$20.8 billion had to be paid back in one year or less. While the accumulation of external short-term debt itself is not a direct cause of the crisis, it certainly made corporations vulnerable to changes in outside perceptions. There may have also been a moral hazard problem in that large corporations and banks, mistakenly or not, may have believed that the government would rescue them if there were a financial crisis.

Second, well-recognized flaws in the banking system and weak bank supervision meant that numerous banks were undercapitalized, and some even insolvent, well before the crisis began. Excessive intergroup lending practices often resulted in resources not being put to their most productive use. The depreciation of the rupiah and resulting capital flight exacerbated the problems of these banks and other corporations that were heavily exposed to foreign exchange risk. Another possible cause of the crisis was the prevalence of policy distortions that misallocated resources in the economy. In the past, several sectors were artificially made profitable as a result of protection from imports or other forms of assistance. This diverted resources away from more profitable uses. This structure of protection, while substantially reduced in recent years, hampered the efficiency of the industrial sector.

While further investigation regarding the causes of the crisis is needed, its effects on the economy are much clearer (table 10.1). The dramatic depreciation of the exchange rate and the collapse of confidence in the financial and banking sector triggered capital flight in late 1997 and early 1998. This exacerbated difficulties in the banking sector. The financial crisis quickly spilled over to the real sector. Domestic prices of tradable goods adjusted upwards toward higher world prices (in rupiah terms), as a result of the dramatic depreciation of the exchange rate. This resulted in substantial price inflation in the domestic economy; the consumer price index more than doubled during the first 18 months of the crisis. Bank Indonesia raised commercial interest rates in an effort to arrest the depreciation of the rupiah and to control inflation. Bank Indonesia's SBI* rates reached a peak of around 70 percent in October 1998, but have subsequently declined to 37 percent (as of January 1999). High interest rates coupled with difficulties in the banking system led to a reduction in private-sector borrowing during this period.

Real wages fell in 1998 and investment slowed to a trickle. Coupled with the adverse effect of the El Nino–related weather conditions on farmers' incomes, this led to a fall in real aggregate demand. Real GDP is estimated to have declined by a massive 14 percent in the 12 months prior to December 1998. Construction, manufacturing, and banking and finance sectors were hit hardest in terms of the fall in real value added. Within the manufacturing sector, construction materials, steel production, transportation, and wood products recorded the greatest decline in real value added, between −23 and −55 percent. Indicative of the sharp decline in aggregate demand, imports fell by 36 percent in the 10 months leading up to October 1998 compared with the same period in 1997. While total US$ value exports showed a decline in the eight months prior to August 1998, nonoil exports showed robust growth in US$ terms and certainly more so in rupiah value terms. Agriculture exports grew by 23 percent in US$ values and nonoil manufacturing exports grew by 6.4 percent in the first nine months of 1998 compared with the corresponding period in 1997. The slower growth in nonoil manufacturing exports was due to the fall in plywood exports from US$3.2 billion in the first three quarters of 1997 to US$1.8 billion in 1998, and to falling terms of trade.

However, recent tentative evidence suggests that the impact of the crisis on economic activity and people's real incomes is heterogeneous and differs by income group and region. Not surprisingly, given the origins of the financial and economic crisis in the formal sector, economic activities and real incomes of people in the urban areas have been hit harder than those of people in the rural areas. The recession appears to be more severe for the Javanese economy than those of the outer islands, particularly in comparison with those regions abundant in natural resources and export commodities.

## Overview of the competitiveness study

The Indonesian government conducted the competitiveness study for two purposes. First, to gauge the pattern and magnitude of the impact of the economic crisis

---

*Sertifikat Bank Indonesia, short-term notes issued by the Indonesian Central Bank to manage domestic liquidity

TABLE 10.1
**Macroeconomic indicators**

| Economic growth | 1995 | 1996 | 1997a | 1998b |
|---|---|---|---|---|
| Agriculture, livestock, forestry, and fisheries | 4.38 | 3.14 | 0.72 | 0.43 |
| Mining and quarrying | −11.11 | 27.65 | 1.71 | −11.16 |
| Manufacturing industry | 10.88 | 11.59 | 6.42 | −15.91 |
|   Oil and gas industry | −4.74 | 11.05 | −1.97 | 0.91 |
|   Nonoil and gas manufacturing | 13.09 | 11.66 | 7.42 | −17.73 |
|     1. Food, beverages, and tobacco | 16.52 | 17.16 | 14.91 | −4.90 |
|     2. Textile, leather products, and footwear | 10.45 | 8.71 | −4.44 | −20.17 |
|     3. Wood products | 3.01 | 3.21 | −2.09 | −23.50 |
|     4. Paper and printing | 13.53 | 6.85 | 8.95 | −15.02 |
|     5. Fertilizers, chemicals, and rubber products | 11.93 | 9.05 | 3.36 | −24.20 |
|     6. Cement nonmetallic minerals | 20.14 | 10.98 | 4.46 | 34.17 |
|     7. Iron and basic steel | 18.65 | 8.04 | −1.41 | −32.72 |
|     8. Transport equipment, machinery, and other apparatus | 7.73 | 4.60 | −0.41 | −55.19 |
|     9. Other manufacturing products | 8.86 | 9.73 | 6.02 | −25.41 |
| Electricity, gas, and water supply | 15.91 | 13.63 | 12.75 | 3.28 |
| Construction | 12.92 | 12.76 | 6.43 | −37.49 |
| Trade, hotels, restaurants | 7.94 | 8.16 | 5.80 | −19.28 |
| Transport and communication | 8.49 | 8.68 | 8.31 | −11.84 |
| Financial, ownership, and business services | 11.04 | 6.04 | 6.45 | −18.24 |
| Services | 3.27 | 3.40 | 2.84 | 5.51 |
| Gross domestic product (GDP) | 6.55 | 9.51 | 4.91 | −14.14 |
| GDP nonoil and gas | 9.24 | 8.16 | 5.45 | −14.53 |
| Inflation | 14.7 | 11.8 | 22.0 | 77.6 |
| Growth in nonoil exports | 15.1 | 9.0 | 9.8 | 1.5 |
|   Agriculture | 2.5 | 0.8 | 7.5 | 23.8 |
|   Mining | 49.5 | 12.2 | 2.9 | −21.0 |
|   Industry | 14.1 | 9.5 | 8.9 | 6.4 |
| Total growth in nonoil imports | — | — | — | −36.0 |

— : not available
a. Preliminary estimates.
b. Very preliminary estimates.
Source: Central Bureau of Statistics.

on firms and therefore industry performance, and to better understand how firms are coping with the economic crisis. And second, to identify long-term impediments to resource mobilization. With the assistance of the World Bank, a detailed survey was designed to learn about participating firms' production, labor force, export performance, and financial structure before and during the economic crisis. The surveys gathered information for the period 1996 to October 1998. The survey was conducted during November and December of 1998, and the process of collecting the questionnaires from 1,200 firms is near completion. At the time of writing this report, just under 700 questionnaires had been collected.

This report uses the information from 562 firms to analyze the impact of the crisis on firms operating in Indonesia.[1] The results presented here are preliminary, and should be treated as tentative (see below). However, the results do illustrate clear relationships between performance and firm and industry characteristics and provide insights into both short- and long-term impediments that are pertinent to economic recovery and growth.

Table 10.2 shows the characteristics of the sample. Five sectors were selected based on their importance to the economy in terms of value added, export orientation, and employment, as well as being representative of Indonesian manufacturing. All but one of these industries were included in similar, recent surveys of other Association of South East Asian Nations (ASEAN) countries. These five industries are food processing (ISIC 31), textiles (ISIC 321), garments (ISIC 322), chemicals and processed rubber (ISIC 35), and electronics (ISIC 383). All sectors are well represented. Just under half of all firms export some of their production, although the share of exporters varies across industries. Garments and electronics have the greatest number of exporters: two-thirds of the firms export part of their production, while less than 30 percent of all firms in processed foods and chemicals export a proportion of their production. In this regard, the sample is representative of Indonesian manufacturing—garments and electronics are export-oriented industries, while chemicals and processed foods are more domestic-oriented or import-competing industries. The distinction is important in understanding the varying impacts of the crisis on industry performance and how the firms were able to respond to the crisis.

The size distribution of the sample firms is reasonably representative of Indonesian manufacturing. Small firms (defined here to include firms that employ less than 150 workers) account for about 60 percent of the survey sample. This is similar in all industries except for electronics and textiles, which have a higher proportion of larger firms. Textiles and electronics are typically characterized as large-scale firms. More large firms undertook export activities in 1998 than smaller firms—58.0 percent and 13.6 percent, respectively.

About 12 percent of the surveyed firms are classified as FDI firms (defined here to include all firms with more than 10 percent foreign ownership), accounting for over 20 percent of total employment in the sample. FDI firms are concentrated in electronics, followed by garments and textiles. The tie to a foreign firm is an important factor in providing firms with access to capital and export markets. In the sample, close to 78 percent of the FDI firms exported part of their production, compared with 27 percent of wholly domestic-owned firms.

Care was taken to include firms from outside Java, as these have apparently been less negatively affected by the economic crisis. Twenty-five percent of all firms in the sample operate outside Java. Outer Java provinces covered in the survey are North Sumatra, Riau, South Sumatra Lampung, and South Sulawesi. Slightly less than 50 percent of these firms exported part of their production in 1998.

Before the results of the analysis are presented a few notes of caution need to be made. First, there is the possibility of sample selection bias in the study. Firms surveyed by definition are the ones that have survived the crisis. Unfortunately, the survey was unable to include firms that closed down during 1998. Second, response rates for several important questions included in the survey were disappointing. The survey consisted of two questionnaires. The first consisted of both qualitative and quantitative questions on production, capacity, exports, and employment, and was carried out through interviews. The second questionnaire consisted of a

**TABLE 10.2**
**Characteristics of the sample**

| | By size | | By export orientation | | By volume of exports | | | FDI firm | | Aver. no of employees | Total no. of firms |
|---|---|---|---|---|---|---|---|---|---|---|---|
| | Large | Small | Exporters | Nonexporters | Small | Medium | High | Yes | No | | |
| Sector | | | | | | | | | | | |
| Chemicals and rubber products | 65 | 97 | 76 | 86 | 31 | 32 | 13 | 15 | 147 | 212 | 162 |
| Electronics | 33 | 28 | 45 | 16 | 14 | 7 | 24 | 24 | 37 | 323 | 61 |
| Food | 66 | 117 | 73 | 110 | 35 | 28 | 10 | 14 | 169 | 237 | 183 |
| Garments | 38 | 39 | 45 | 32 | 12 | 6 | 27 | 9 | 68 | 300 | 77 |
| Textiles | 41 | 38 | 35 | 44 | 15 | 16 | 4 | 10 | 69 | 274 | 79 |
| Age | | | | | | | | | | | |
| New | 56 | 81 | 80 | 57 | 25 | 20 | 35 | 38 | 99 | 223 | 137 |
| Old | 187 | 238 | 194 | 231 | 82 | 69 | 43 | 34 | 391 | 262 | 425 |
| Location | | | | | | | | | | | |
| Java or Bali | 183 | 253 | 204 | 232 | 89 | 70 | 45 | 48 | 388 | 254 | 436 |
| Other islands | 60 | 66 | 70 | 56 | 18 | 19 | 33 | 24 | 102 | 259 | 126 |
| Total | 243 | 319 | 274 | 288 | 107 | 89 | 78 | 72 | 490 | 255 | 562 |

*Note:* "Small firm" is defined as a firm with less than 150 workers; "large firm" as a firm with more than 150 workers. "Exporter" is defined as a firm that derives some revenue from export sales. "Large exporter" is defined here to include firms that earn at least 35 percent of revenues from export sales, "medium exporter" is defined as a firm that derives between 5 and 35 percent of revenues from export sales. "Small exporter" is defined here to include firms that derive between 0 and 5 percent of revenue from export sales.
"FDI firm" is defined here to include firms with at least 10 percent foreign ownership.
*Source:* World Bank, Firm-Level Survey.

series of questions on the firms' financial condition, including balance sheet data. This questionnaire was filled out by the firm and collected by or mailed to the Central Bureau of Statistics. While the response rate for the first questionnaire was high, the response rate for the second, financial questionnaire was poor, possibly reflecting the different interview methods used in the study and also the sensitivity involved in disclosing financial data. Less than 50 percent of the firms provided answers to many of the major financial questions. Even fewer firms provided complete information on their financial position. Furthermore, several questions are open to alternative interpretations and this makes it difficult to derive clear conclusions.[2] This limits our scope for detailed analysis of the impact of the crisis on the firms' financial positions and the impact of this on their economic activities.[3] Finally, the survey was only carried out in November 1998 and, while collection and processing of the data have been timely, the process was not completed at the time of writing this paper. As indicated earlier, the results of this paper are based on a smaller sample of 581 firms instead of about 1,200. In this regard, the results are preliminary and should be treated as tentative.

## Impact of the crisis on firm performance

One of the immediate concerns of policymakers is to gauge the impact of the crisis on domestic demand, production, and employment. The sample firms were asked about how capacity utilization has changed, and whether they employ fewer workers now relative to the precrisis 1997 situation. The firms were also asked to attribute current difficulties facing them to different sources including domestic demand, foreign demand, interest rates, and access to capital.

### Capacity utilization

Figure 10.1 shows the average firm capacity utilization rates in the five sectors over the period from 1996 to

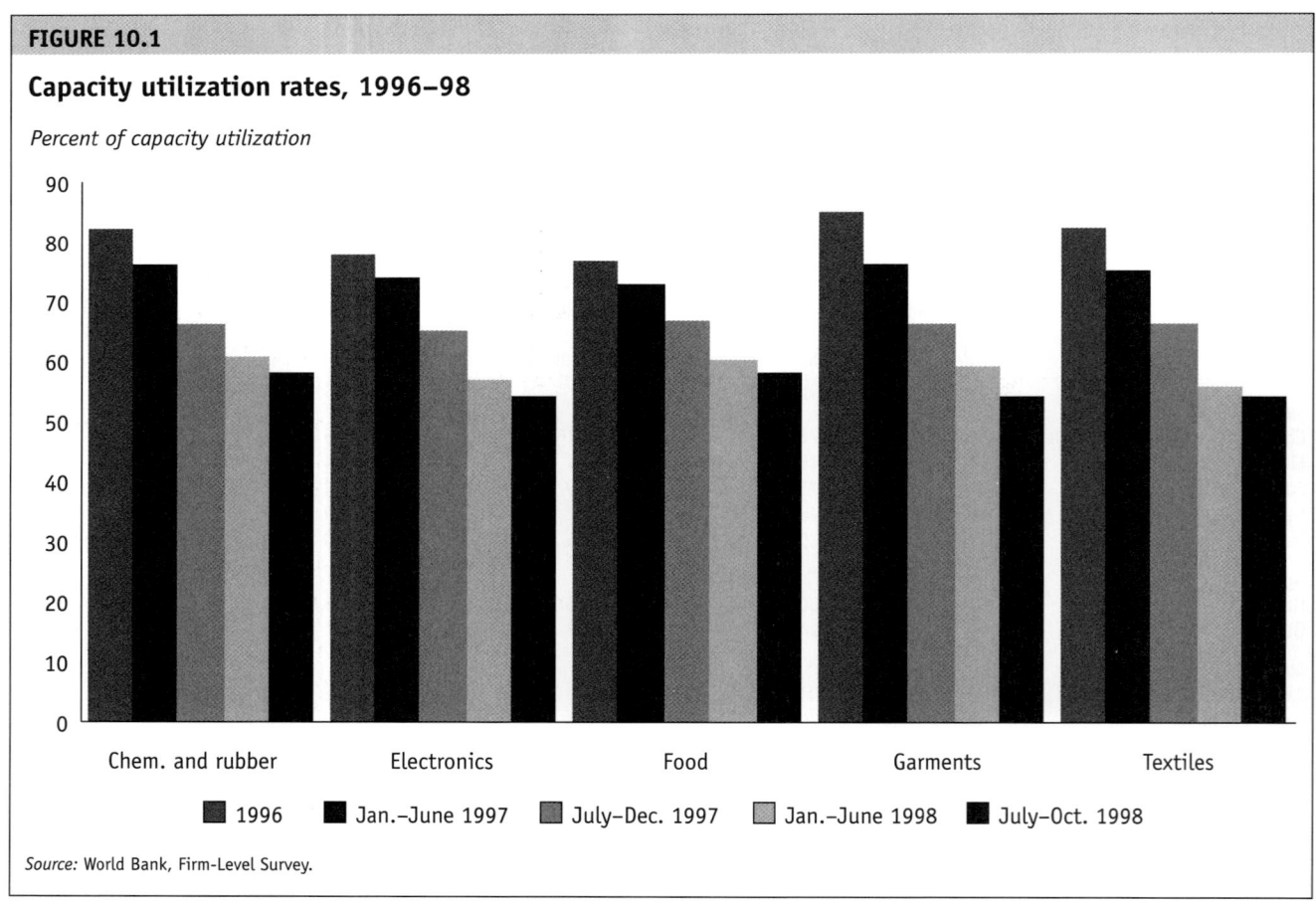

**FIGURE 10.1**

**Capacity utilization rates, 1996–98**

*Percent of capacity utilization*

■ 1996 ■ Jan.–June 1997 ■ July–Dec. 1997 ■ Jan.–June 1998 ■ July–Oct. 1998

*Source:* World Bank, Firm-Level Survey.

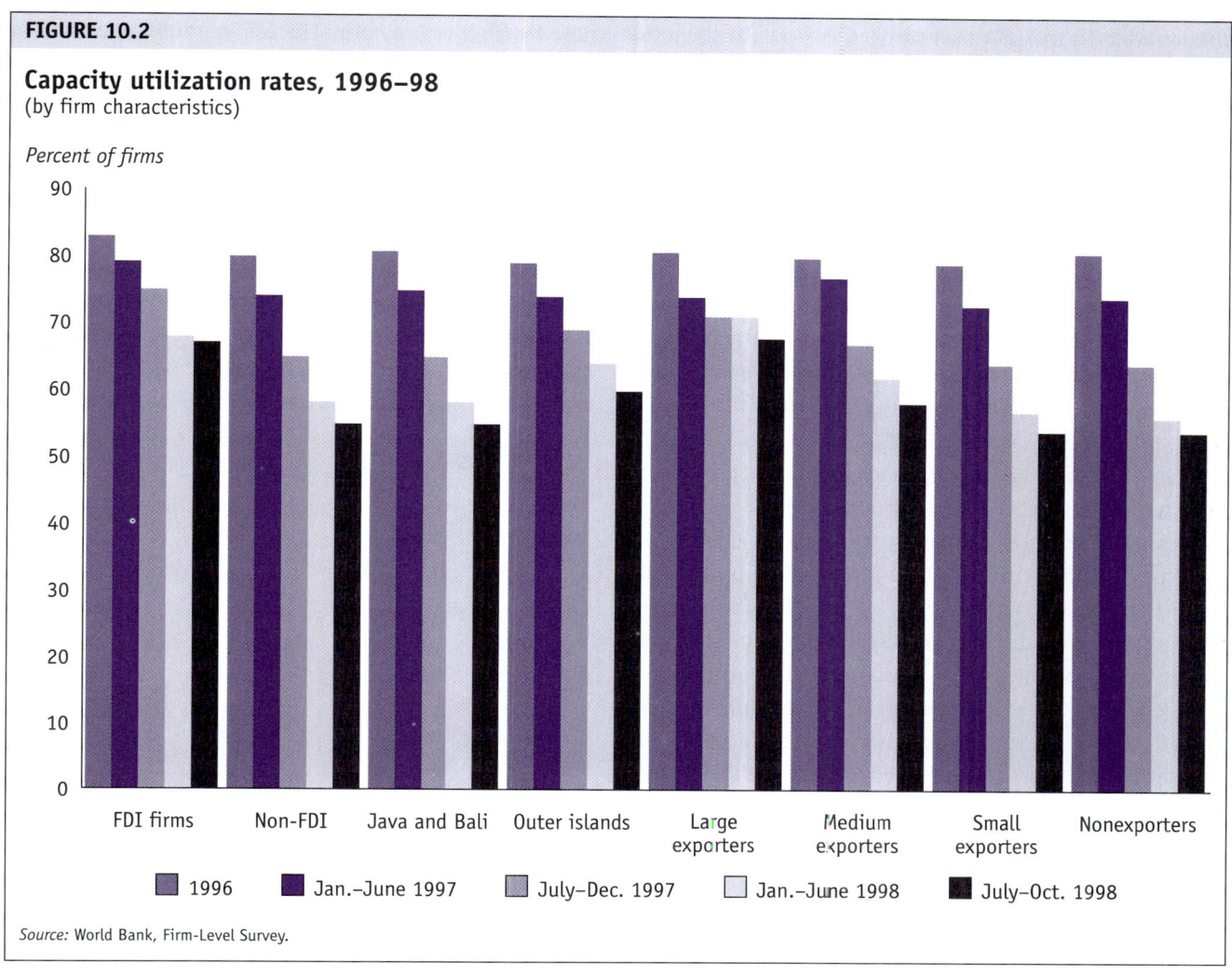

FIGURE 10.2

**Capacity utilization rates, 1996–98**
(by firm characteristics)

Source: World Bank, Firm-Level Survey.

1998. Figure 10.2 shows the average firm capacity utilization rates by firm characteristics. The majority of the firms reported operating at lower capacity in October 1998 than they had been a year before. However, capacity utilization rates also fell in the first half of 1997, indicating a possible slowdown in aggregate demand prior to the financial crisis erupting in July 1997. Dramatic decreases in capacity utilization rates occurred in all industries in the first half of 1998, as the financial crisis accelerated and the economy recorded its third consecutive quarter of negative economic growth. Capacity utilization continued to fall in the second half of 1998, but at a much lower rate than the previous two quarters. It is still too early to know whether capacity utilization has stabilized, although more than 60 percent of the surveyed firms did not anticipate further reductions in output in the first quarter of 1999.

Firm characteristics provide insights into which sectors have been hit hardest by the economic crisis. In general, large and medium-scale exporters are operating at much higher rates of capacity utilization, and have experienced less of a drop in 1998 compared with the other firms. In particular, large-scale exporters (those that export more than 35 percent of their output) reported capacity utilization rates of 15 percentage points higher than nonexporting firms in the third quarter of 1998. Foreign firms also reported higher than average capacity utilization rates, and less of a drop in 1998 compared with non-FDI firms. This is mostly due to the fact that the bulk of the FDI firms in the sample are also large exporters of their production. Compared with smaller firms, large firms are also operating at a higher rate of capacity utilization and have experienced less of a decline. Again, this difference is primarily attributable to the fact that larger firms in the sample are bigger exporters of their products. Controlling for exports, size does not appear to be a determining factor in the impact of the crisis on production. There is a clear regional difference in capacity utilization rates. Firms operating in regions outside Java experienced a lower decline in capacity utilization than did those operating in Java, providing some support for recent evidence that the outer islands are less adversely affected by the economic crisis. This is particularly the case for regions that have abundant resources and produce export commodities. These regions have benefited from the depreciation of the real exchange rate.

Even though average capacity utilization rates declined across sectors, at least a quarter of the firms reported either no change in production levels or increased production in 1998. More than 45 percent of the exporters reported that they were better off in terms of increased production in 1998. Similarly, one-fifth of the domestic-oriented firms reported either no change in production or increased production during this period. There are differences across sectors. Around one-third of all domestic-oriented firms in the food-processing sector were better off in 1998. In electronics, however, less than 15 percent of the domestic-oriented firms were better off in terms of increased output levels in 1998. In contrast, over 40 percent of the electronic firms exporting part of their production reported that they were no worse off or better off than they had been a year earlier. This indicates that the large drop in capacity utilization rates in the electronics industry in 1998 was primarily attributable to the fall in domestic sales for these products. The firms responded in different ways to the fall in domestic sales. From the survey, we identified that about 5 percent of the exporters were newcomers to the category in 1998, indicating that some firms were able to shift sales from the domestic market to export markets in response to the fall in local demand. Unfortunately, the survey did not tell us whether those firms had shifted to new products in response to declining demand for their established products.

## Employment

Figures 10.3 and 10.4 show the percentage of the sample firms that employed fewer workers in 1998 compared with a year earlier. The fall in employment is not as stark as the fall in capacity utilization rates. Less than 50 percent of all sample firms are currently employing fewer workers in the third quarter of 1998 they they did immediately prior to the crisis. The pattern of employing fewer workers differs by type of firm, industry, and region. Consistent with the pattern of change in capacity utilization rates, the firms that export a proportion of their production reported lower rates of worker layoffs; 40 percent of the exporting firms reported employing fewer workers in the third quarter of 1998 relative to the precrisis situation. This compares with around 55

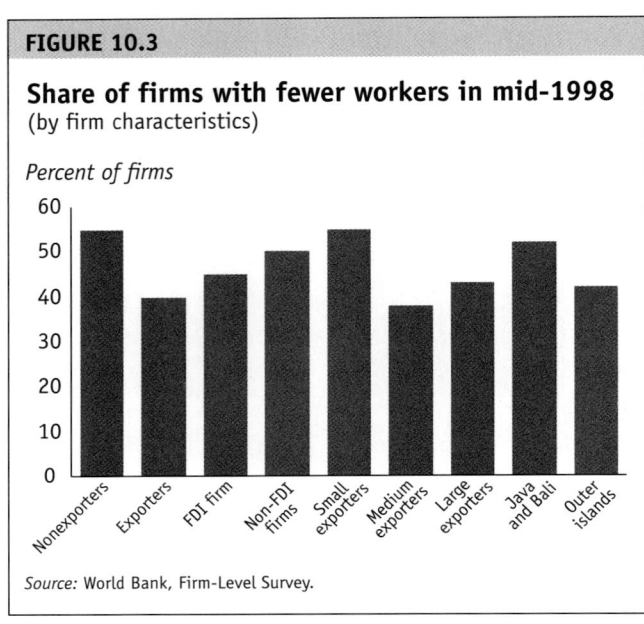

**FIGURE 10.3**

**Share of firms with fewer workers in mid-1998**
(by firm characteristics)

*Source:* World Bank, Firm-Level Survey.

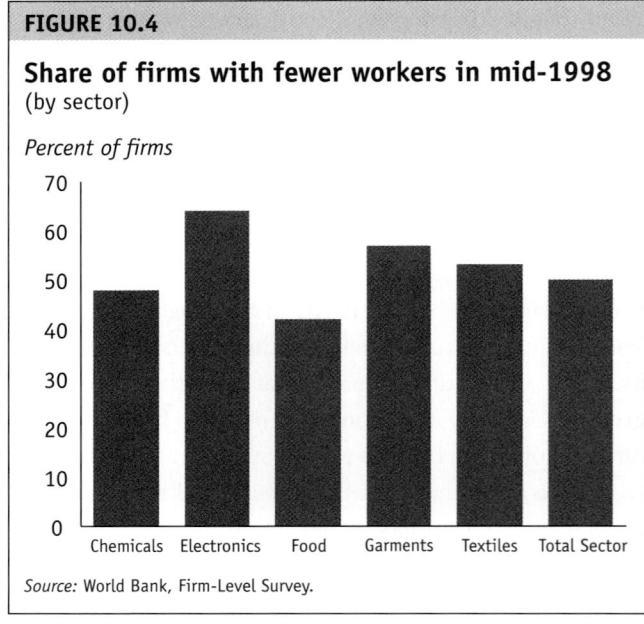

**FIGURE 10.4**

**Share of firms with fewer workers in mid-1998**
(by sector)

*Source:* World Bank, Firm-Level Survey.

percent for nonexporters. Also consistent with the pattern of change in capacity utilization rates, a greater share of the firms operating in Java reported smaller work forces by the end of 1998 than those operating outside Java. Comparing across sectors, more electronic firms reported smaller work forces. Around 65 percent of the electronic firms reportedly downsized their work force in 1998. This is primarily due to the fall in domestic sales of electronics in 1998. Conversely, less than 40 percent of the firms operating in the processed food sector reported smaller work forces at the end of 1998.

The results for capacity utilization and employment suggest that the impact of the crisis on firms and industry performance is mixed. While many firms are adversely affected by the crisis to varying degrees, some are actually better off than they had been before the crisis. Exporting firms are less adversely affected by the economic crisis than domestic-oriented firms. At least 45 percent of the exporters either reported no change or increased capacity utilization in 1998. Even within the domestic-oriented group of firms, the impact of the crisis on economic performance is mixed. Many firms producing in the food processing and chemical-rubber sectors appear to be less negatively affected by the economic crisis than the other three sectors included in the sample. One-third of the firms in the food-processing sector either experienced no change or increased their production in 1998. Among other factors, this arises because of differences in price and income elasticities of demand for the goods produced by the five sectors. Processed food, for example, is generally income-inelastic and, thus, is relatively less affected by falls in real incomes of households. Electronics, by contrast, generally has higher income elasticity and, thus, is more likely to be affected by falls in real incomes of consumers.

The sample firms operating in Java were more adversely affected by the economic crisis than those operating outside Java, providing evidence that the negative effects of the crisis are greatest in Java.

## Perceived causes of the fall in output in 1998

This section examines the respondents' perceived causes of their output decline in 1998. Before discussing the survey results, a few comments on the questionnaire are warranted. The firms were asked to rank the severity of possible causes of their output decline. They were asked to rank a list of 12 factors on a scale of 1 to 5, with 1 representing no problem at all and 5 a severe problem. This question is somewhat problematic, because the firms could list more than one factor as a major cause of their output decline. It would have been preferable if they had been asked to give the major cause of their fall in output. Bearing this in mind, figure 10.5 represents the average scale for the most important perceived causes of output decline. The scale ranges between 1 (minor cause) and 5 (major cause). Table 10.3 presents the percentage of the firms that rated the factors as their most severe problems (for example, those firms that rated factors as number 4 or 5 on the scale).

The sharp decline in demand for the firms' products and the effect of the depreciation of the rupiah in raising input costs (and presumably its volatility) were considered as the major causes of output decline during 1998. The high cost of capital was rated as a distant

### TABLE 10.3
**Perceived causes of the fall in output**
(percentage of firms that rated causes as 4 or 5 on a scale of 1 to 5)

| | Major causes | | | | | |
|---|---|---|---|---|---|---|
| Sector | Domestic demand | Foreign demand | Access to credit | Rupiah depreciation | Interest rates | Labor costs |
| Food | 53 | 8 | 18 | 60 | 46 | 26 |
| Garments | 61 | 18 | 23 | 70 | 57 | 27 |
| Textiles | 68 | 24 | 27 | 73 | 57 | 32 |
| Chemicals and rubber | 64 | 12 | 24 | 75 | 51 | 33 |
| Electronics | 58 | 17 | 25 | 56 | 40 | 29 |
| Exporters | 48 | 33 | 25 | 60 | 47 | 20 |
| Nonexporters | 64 | 6 | 20 | 71 | 50 | 33 |

*Source:* World Bank, Firm-Level Survey.

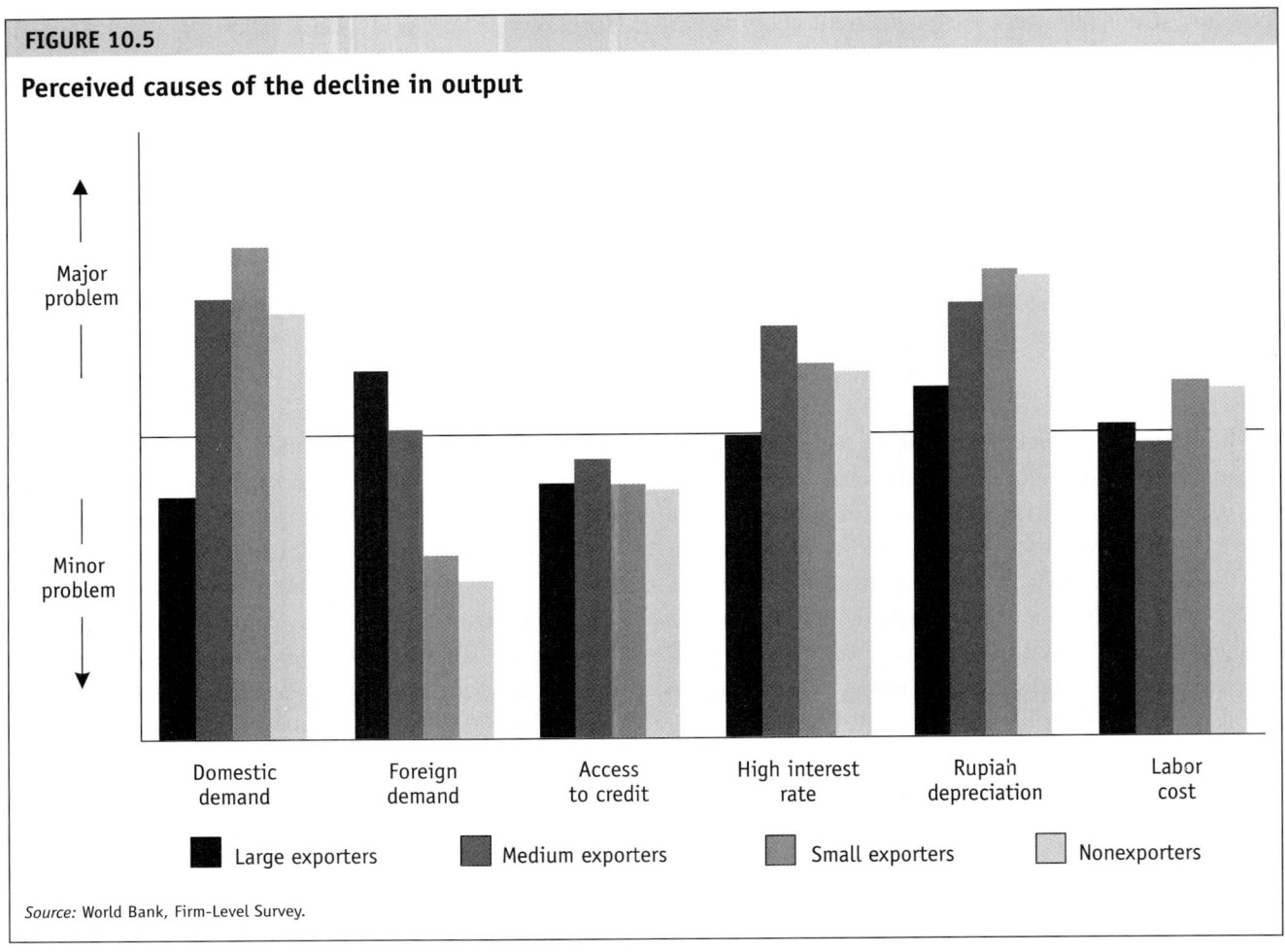

**FIGURE 10.5**

Perceived causes of the decline in output

*Source:* World Bank, Firm-Level Survey.

third major cause of the fall in output, whereas access to credit was not rated as a major cause. This pattern of perceived causes is fairly uniform across different types of firms and sectors. For domestic-oriented firms or nonexporters and small exporters, the fall in domestic demand and the rupiah depreciation were rated as the major causes of their output decline, swamping all other possible causes. Similarly for medium-scale exporters (those firms that export between 5 and 35 percent of their output), the fall in domestic demand and the rupiah depreciation were rated as the major causes of their output decline. For large exporters, the fall in foreign demand was considered the major cause. These results are consistent with the responses detailed above regarding changes in capacity utilization rates and employment changes.

Access to credit was not rated as a major cause of decline in output by the firms in this sample, whether exporting part of their production or not. This is somewhat surprising given the severe problems facing the banking sector and the attention in the media to the notion of a credit crunch that was supposed to be strangling firms. However, this is not to say that access to credit is not a longer-term bottleneck, although this will depend on the speed and success of the government's bank recapitalization program. It appears that among the short-run difficulties, access to credit is swamped by the immediate effect of the fall in domestic demand and the volatility of the rupiah. Similarly, letters of credit guaranteed by domestic banks were not rated as a major problem for exporters, regardless of whether they were small or large firms.

## The financial position of the firms

Given that the crisis began as a financial one in the private sector, it is important to examine in some detail the financial structure of the sample firms and to analyze how this structure has been affected by the financial crisis. This may provide answers to two important questions: (1) to what extent financial distress has affected the firms' economic activities, and (2) how the firms have coped with the their changed financial conditions.

To answer these questions, we investigated two areas: (1) the impact of the crisis on the firms' debt structure, including share of foreign currency liabilities and debt-equity ratios; and (2) sources of funds and their changes during the crisis. The section below on financial characteristics and the impact of the crisis attempts to link the firms' financial positions with their economic performance—capacity utilization, employment, and exports. However, one must repeat the caveat that the survey results on the firms' financial positions are considered weak and, thus, the results presented in this paper are very tentative.

## Impact of the firms' debt structure

*Foreign currency liabilities.* With the dramatic depreciation of the rupiah, firms with foreign currency–denominated debts have experienced substantial increases in their rupiah-equivalent liabilities and debt-servicing costs. However, the results of the survey suggest that firms with substantial foreign currency liabilities were not the most adversely affected ones during the crisis. Firms with foreign currency borrowings actually had lower reductions in capacity utilization rates and work forces compared with those with no foreign currency–denominated debt. This arose because many of the firms with foreign currency–denominated debts are also large and medium-sized exporters, which were less affected by the economic crisis.

Table 10.4 shows foreign currency borrowings broken down by firm categories. Of those firms that provided information on debt, 16 percent reported having debts denominated in foreign currency. The larger borrowers in foreign currency are FDI firms and large and medium-scale exporters. Forty-six percent of the FDI firms had borrowed in foreign currency and 38 percent of large and 27 percent of medium-scale exporters reported having some foreign currency–denominated debts in 1998. In contrast, fewer small firms (4 percent) had some foreign-currency denominated debts.

For medium and large-scale exporters, foreign currency–denominated debts should not be a major problem, as most of their revenues are also in foreign currency. However, foreign currency debts will be a problem for those domestic-oriented firms that have not hedged their positions. Of those with foreign currency debt, only 27 percent said that they had hedged some of this debt. Furthermore, firms with foreign currency debts are more leveraged than the ones that do not have foreign currency debts—an observation that applies both before and after the crisis.

An important question is whether the firms were able to alter their exposure to foreign currency risk by reducing their foreign currency debt levels or, if possible, hedging their positions. Examining changes in the firms' foreign currency liabilities between 1996 and 1998, there is little evidence to indicate that the firms significantly altered their exposure to foreign currency risk. Of those firms that provided information on their liabilities, only a small number had reduced their foreign currency debt obligations. Most of these were FDI firms and exporters, which are less exposed to foreign currency risk anyway. Few domestic-oriented firms had been able reduce their obligations. Furthermore, 76 percent of the firms with foreign currency liabilities still had not hedged their positions by the end of 1998.

*Debt-Equity Ratio.* The substantial depreciation of the rupiah and the relatively high domestic interest rates necessary to stabilize it have important implications for

**TABLE 10.4**
**Profiles of the firms borrowing in foreign currency**

| Firm characteristics | Firms with foreign currency liabilities | |
|---|---|---|
| All firms (percent) | 16 | |
| *By size (percent)* | | |
| Large firms | 28 | |
| Small firms | 4 | |
| *By ownership (percent)* | | |
| FDI | 46 | |
| Non-FDI | 9 | |
| *By exporter status (percent)* | | |
| Exporters | 23 | |
| Large exporters | 38 | |
| Medium exporters | 27 | |
| Small exporters | 6 | |
| Nonexporters(percent) | 4 | |
| Borrowing | Yes | No |
| *Financial indicators* | | |
| Short-term debt/Total debt | 0.61 | 0.55 |
| Debt-equity ratio | 3.17 | 1.72 |
| *Response to the crisis (percent)* | | |
| Capacity utilization rate | 61 | 58 |
| Fewer workers in 1998 | 42 | 54 |

*Source:* World Bank, Firm-Level Survey.

the cost of debt servicing for highly leveraged firms. Debt-equity ratios show that many firms had borrowed heavily prior to the crisis. However, there is some evidence that certain types of firms are acting to reduce their liabilities after the onset of the crisis.

At the end of 1996, debt-equity ratios were high, around 1.8 on average and in some cases above 6. The average ratio increased from 1.8 in 1996 to 2 in 1997, indicating that average leverage of the firms had increased during the crisis (figure 10.6). However, by 1998, debt-equity ratios had fallen to 1.5. The degree of leverage by type of firm shows that medium-size and large exporters have much higher debt-equity ratios than nonexporters. Large firms have higher debt-equity ratios than small firms. FDI firms also have much higher ratios than non-FDI firms. This partly arises because the many large firms and FDI firms are also medium-scale and large exporters of their products.

As indicated earlier, average debt-equity ratios had risen with the onset of the crisis. However, the trend varies by firm type. Not surprisingly, many firms that had foreign currency–denominated debts experienced the greatest increases in leverage between 1996 and 1998 (in rupiah terms). Large firms and exporters experienced increases in their debt-equity ratios during this period, whereas FDI firms, on average, experienced declines—suggesting that these firms were reducing their liabilities during the crisis. Small firms also had slight declines in their debt-equity ratios. This could be evidence consistent with either a fall in the demand for credit or a liquidity crunch story—the firms' debt positions being lower in keeping with the loans not being rolled over.

## Sources of short-term funds

High interest rates and problems in the banking sector mean that the firms have to look for other ways to supplement cash flow or to repay outstanding obligations. There are several possibilities. The firms could rely more on proceeds from sales and increase the rate of turnover of working capital every month. They could inject equity from their own sources, family, or shareholders, or find a new partner. They could also sell nonessential assets to supplement cash flow or to repay loans. Results from the survey suggest that the sample firms are adopting a combination of these strategies.

Figure 10.7 shows fund sources and how these have changed during the crisis. Before the crisis, the firms' two major sources of short-term finance were sales revenue (41 percent of total short-term funds) and the banking sector (32 percent). Other sources included partners', shareholders', and owners' equity (11 percent), and local moneylenders and suppliers (12 percent). Similarly, close to 70 percent of the funds for long-term investment was obtained from sales revenue and banks. The structure of funding sources showed some significant changes during the crisis. First, for both short-term and long-term financing, the proportion of proceeds from sales increased and that of loans from domestic and foreign banks declined. It can be seen in figure 10.7 that the proportion of short-term funds from sales revenue increased from 41 percent in 1996 to 43 percent in 1998, indicating that the firms now rely more on proceeds from sales to finance their business activities than they did before the crisis. Conversely, the proportion of short-term loans from banks fell from 32 percent in 1996 to less than 26 percent in 1998. Sources from other alternative channels also increased during the crisis; the proportion of short-term funds from owners, shareholders, and family increased from 11 percent in 1996 to almost 14 percent in 1998.

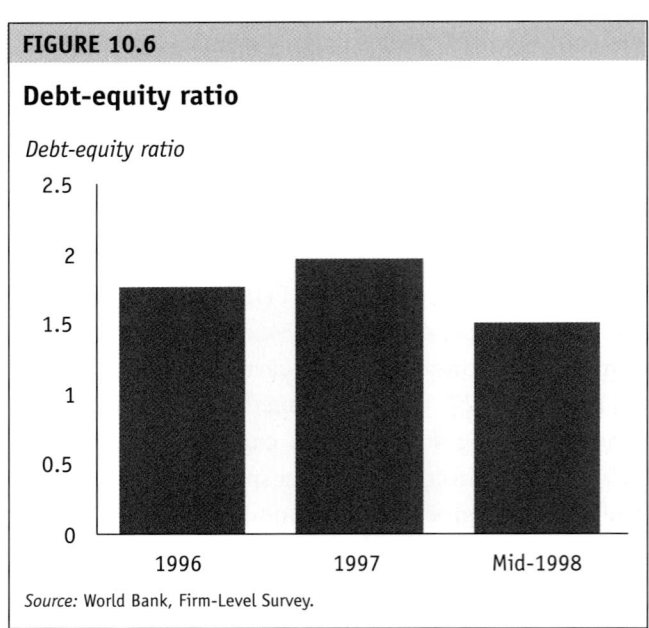

**FIGURE 10.6**

**Debt-equity ratio**

*Source:* World Bank, Firm-Level Survey.

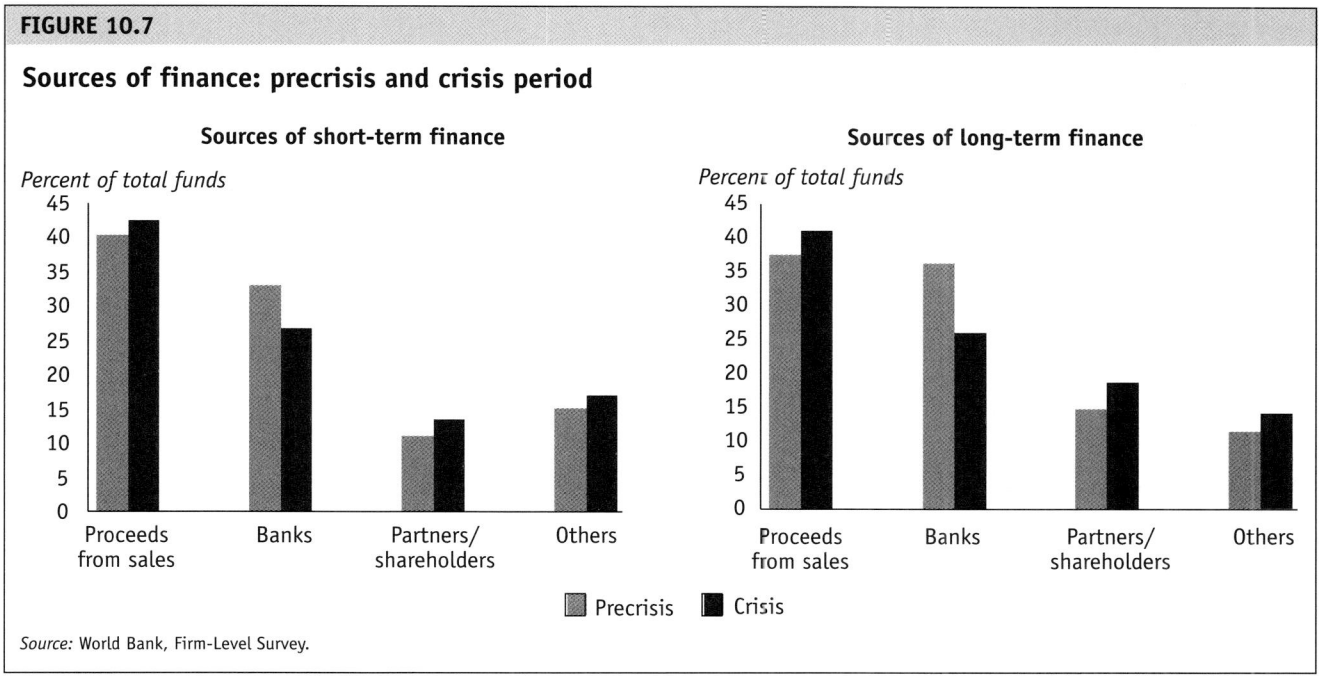

FIGURE 10.7

Sources of finance: precrisis and crisis period

Source: World Bank, Firm-Level Survey.

This change in the structure of financing is consistent with a number of interpretations. First, the fall in the proportion of loans from banks is consistent with the decline in the firms' demand for credit. As demand for a firm's products decline, so does the firm's demand for credit at any given interest rate. Second, the result is also consistent with the high cost of capital and the notion of a credit crunch; if loans are not being rolled over, the proportion of loans from banks obviously declines. While all these factors may partly explain the fall in the proportions of funds from bank loans, we are unable to distinguish the most important factors causing the proportional fall in bank loans. However, the results for the "perceived causes of the fall in output" (discussed above in the section bearing that title) provide some clues to the major causes. As noted earlier there, the firms saw the substantial fall in domestic demand as the major cause of the fall in output, swamping other causes such as the access to credit.[4]

Many firms reported in their balance sheets a reduction in the value of their fixed assets and a corresponding reduction in liabilities. Among other factors, this could indicate that the firms are selling some nonessential assets to keep the business operating. However, we need to be cautious in this interpretation. It might be that the firms have revalued their assets downward as a result of the recession.

## Financial characteristics and impact of the crisis

Table 10.5 shows selected financial indicators and economic performance by different types of firms. Based on the table there appears to be no clear relationship between the firms' financial positions and their responses to the economic crisis. Firms with relatively high debt-equity ratios or foreign currency liabilities are no more affected by the crisis than are those with low debt-equity ratios or no foreign currency liabilities. Indeed, table 10.4 shows that, on average, highly leveraged firms actually had smaller reductions in capacity utilization and work forces. This primarily arises because in our sample a high proportion of highly leveraged firms or firms that have foreign currency liabilities are also efficient medium- and large-scale exporters, of which many are FDI firms. These firms have been less negatively affected by the crisis. Conversely, domestic-oriented firms that are highly leveraged or have significant foreign currency liabilities are most adversely affected by the economic crisis. These firms had greater

### TABLE 10.5
### Firm profiles

|  | Foreign currency loans | | Size | | By volume of exports | | | FDI firm | | Total |
|---|---|---|---|---|---|---|---|---|---|---|
|  | Yes | No | Large | Small | Small | Medium | High | Yes | No |  |
| *Financial indicators* | | | | | | | | | | |
| Short-term debt/Total financing | 0.61 | 0.52 | 0.56 | 0.48 | 0.66 | 0.48 | 0.65 | 0.61 | 0.55 | 0.55 |
| Long-term debt/Total financing | 0.39 | 0.48 | 0.44 | 0.52 | 0.34 | 0.52 | 0.35 | 0.39 | 0.45 | 0.45 |
| Debt-equity ratio | 4.2 | 1.7 | 2.7 | 1.5 | 3.4 | 2.7 | 2.8 | 1.9 | 1.5 | 1.9 |
| *Firm characteristics* | | | | | | | | | | |
| Number of employees | 317 | 249 | 545 | 58 | 279 | 453 | 500 | 434 | 233 | 255 |
| Share of firms that export (percent) | 69.1 | 27.1 | 58.0 | 13.6 | — | — | — | 77.8 | 26.5 | 32.9 |
| Share of firms that are FDI (percent) | 35.1 | 10.2 | 35.1 | 10.2 | 10.2 | 20.2 | 41.8 | — | — | 13.6 |
| *Response to the crisis* | | | | | | | | | | |
| Current capacity utilization (percent) | 63.1 | 55.3 | 62.5 | 51.2 | 53.6 | 58.0 | 67.6 | 66.6 | 55.0 | 56.1 |
| Share with fewer workers (percent) | 36.4 | 51.8 | 44.9 | 54.3 | 54.5 | 38.2 | 42.5 | 45.2 | 50.3 | 49.6 |

—: not available
*Source:* World Bank, Firm-Level Survey.

reductions in capacity utilization rates and work forces during the crisis than other domestic-oriented firms.

## The government's response to the crisis

Under the "government and international donor program," the Indonesian government has introduced a wide range of policy measures in response to the crisis. These policy actions comprise short-term measures aimed at stabilizing the macroeconomy and dampening the adverse effects of the crisis on Indonesia's poor, and long-term structural reforms aimed at improving the competitiveness of the economy.

Short-term measures include a tight monetary policy to stabilize the rupiah and to control inflation. Interest rates on Bank Indonesia's SBIs peaked at 73 percent in October 1998, and declined to 37 percent (as of January 1999). Accompanying tight monetary policy have been improvements in the mechanisms to achieve stable inflation. First, SBIs were auctioned on an open market for the first time in mid-1998. Second, a new central bank law was passed by Parliament, although it had not been enacted when this paper was written. The law ensures that Bank Indonesia's major purpose is to target the rate of inflation. The tight monetary policy has been relatively successful in reducing inflation from a year-on-year peak of 85 percent in September 1998 to 53 percent at the end of February 1999. The decline in the rate of inflation is expected to accelerate over the next six to eight months. A stable price level should then be reflected in a stable foreign currency, assuming there are no new shocks to the economy.

To deal with the severe corporate and bank debt problem, the government has introduced a number of programs. The government has played an important role in facilitating the process between corporate debtors and creditors for debt restructuring. To address bank problems, the government has introduced a bank restructuring program, which includes bank liquidations and recapitalization of banks meeting certain criteria. The government is also in the process of introducing more stringent prudential controls, including raising the required risk-weighted capital-asset ratio of banks above its current level of 4 percent. While progress on bank recapitalization has been slow, it is gaining momentum, and the government is expected to announce further liquidations and the names of banks that have qualified for participation in the bank recapitalization program in mid-March 1999.

To dampen the adverse effects of the economic crisis on Indonesia's poor, the government—with assistance from the World Bank—has implemented a social safety net (SSN) program involving a range of programs such as work schemes and health and poverty alleviation programs. These programs are currently being updated and redesigned to ensure effective targeting and implementation as more information of the mixed impact of the crisis becomes available to the government.

In an effort to improve the competitiveness of industry, the Indonesian government has embarked on a complex policy reform agenda. This includes deregulation of several monopolies and cartels, removal of budget subsidies to industry, acceleration of trade liberalization, a bankruptcy law, and a competition law. Successful implementation of these reforms should lay down the foundation for a competitive, flexible economy.

## The firms' expectations for the next six months

The sample firms were asked about their production expectations for the first half of 1999. Figure 10.8 shows the percentage of firms that expected their production to decrease, experience no change, or increase during 1999. The figure shows that in all five sectors, the majority of the firms expect production levels to remain the same as they were at the end of 1998 or increase in the first quarter of 1999, indicating that most firms feel that the worst of the crisis has passed or the recession has bottomed out. The firms were more optimistic about increases in output in food processing, garments, and chemicals and rubber than they were in electronics and textiles.

## Summary and conclusion

The Indonesian government conducted the Competitiveness Study for two purposes: first, to gauge the pattern and magnitude of the impact of the economic crisis on firm and industry performance, and to better understand how firms are coping with the economic crisis; and second, to identify long-term impediments to resource mobilization. This latter objective will be the focus of a forthcoming conference. This section makes a number of tentative recommendations for discussion and consideration.

### Recovery in aggregate demand

The firms have reported substantial idle productive capacity at the end of 1998, particularly those that supply the domestic market with non-resource-based

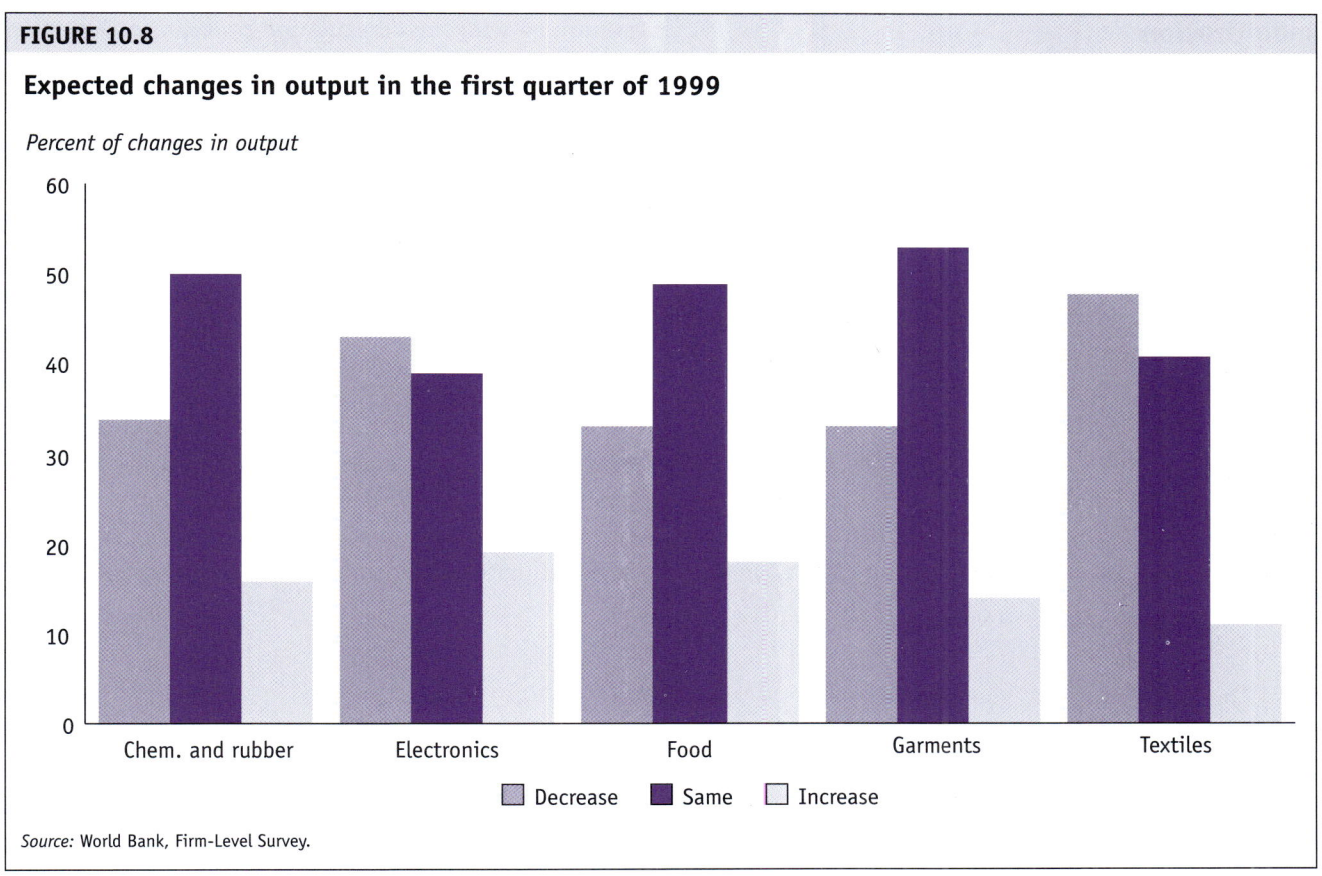

**FIGURE 10.8**

**Expected changes in output in the first quarter of 1999**

*Source:* World Bank, Firm-Level Survey.

products. A major cause of the reported excess capacity is the fall in domestic demand for the firms' products. Economic recovery in the short run, therefore, essentially depends on recovery in aggregate demand, including new investment. Recovery in aggregate demand also depends on consumer expectations about the economy and adjustment in their real incomes. A key issue in restoring the flow of investment is to restore confidence in private sector investors—both domestic and foreign investors—in the economy. This is particularly important given the problems in the banking sector and slow progress in bank recapitalization. Thus, it is important for the government to maintain a stable macroeconomic framework including low inflation. A transparent investment regime that provides equal treatment of foreign and domestic investors as well as removing all impediments to investment goes a long way toward restoring private sector investor confidence in the economy. In the immediate period, the government can stimulate aggregate demand through effective targeting of its social safety net program.

## Removing policy impediments to resource mobilization

The study shows that resources are likely to reallocate to export-oriented sectors and resource-based sectors, as the firms in these sectors have sustained the least damage, and some are better off as a result of the depreciation of the rupiah. It is therefore important to ensure that impediments to resource allocation are removed so that firms can, where possible, shift to new markets quickly. An extensive web of regulations, approvals, and permits is still required to establish and operate businesses at all levels of government (national, provincial, and local) in Indonesia. For example, more than 26 licenses, permits, and approvals are required to establish a fishing business. This raises the cost of doing business and impedes resource mobilization in the economy.

While there has been improvement in this area, more work is needed, in particular removing those nuisance regulations, permits, or approvals that increase the cost of doing business in the country.

## Customs and port facilities

Trade facilitation is also critical to ensuring that resources can shift quickly to profitable sectors such as exports. The sample firms reported problems with customs such as delays in processing imports. Therefore, it is paramount that problems related to customs administration and port facilities are addressed in the medium term.

## Trade and industry policy

As indicated above, the industry and trade sectors have undergone substantial deregulation in the last 12 months. This includes eliminating the statutory basis of several remaining monopolies and cartels, and a commitment to accelerating trade policy reforms, a bankruptcy law, and a competition law. The government has continued with the deregulation process. In December 1998, the government removed all subsidies given to fertilizer producers and removed quantitative restrictions on urea imports. The government is to review other distortions in the economy, including remaining fiscal incentives such as tax holidays, in an effort to improve the competitiveness of the economy.

## Bank restructuring

As indicated earlier, the government has introduced a bank restructuring program, which includes liquidation of some banks and recapitalization of other banks that meet certain criteria. Bank recapitalization is a necessary condition for resuscitating the banking sector and stimulating renewed lending to the corporate sector.

## Notes

The report was prepared by Dr. Ir. Bambang Widianto, MA and Ir. Tb. A. Choesni, MA of the National Development Planning Agency (BAPPENAS), based on surveys conducted by the Bada Pusat Statistik with financial assistance of the World Bank.

1. Around 80 firms were dropped because they provided incomplete information.

2. One example is the question on the sources of short-term and long-term finance. The question was worded to inquire what the sources would be "if the respondent wanted to obtain short-term finance." The potential sources were listed in the questionnaire. The firm was asked to give percentages for each applicable source both before and after the crisis. It is unclear whether those firms that answered the question were referring to actual sources of finance or their preferred source of finance. The fact that the reported patterns of finance before and after the crisis were similar, however, does suggest that the firms interpreted the question as referring to the preferred source of finance in 1998.

3. As a consequence of weaknesses in the financial data, we could not adequately explore the impact of the crisis on the firms' profitability. Thus, the analysis on that is not included in this paper.

4. However, caution must be exercised in interpreting the results presented in figure 10.7. As indicated, the figure shows that about one-quarter of short-term and long-term finance was still sourced from banks in 1998, down from above 30 percent before the crisis. This is somewhat surprising given the severe problems facing the banking sector and the attention in the media to the notion of a credit crunch strangling viable firms. Figure 10.7 indicates that firms were still borrowing from banks in 1998. Interpretation problems with the questionnaire may explain this somewhat confusing result; it is unclear in the survey whether the firms are referring to preferred sources or actual sources of finance in 1998, or whether they are reporting outstanding balances or new borrowings in 1998 (see note 2).

## chapter eleven

# A Study on the Crisis, Recovery, and Industrial Upgrading in the Republic of Korea

*Nakgyooon Choi*
*Du-Yong Kang*

This report presents the results of a comprehensive survey—conducted from November 1998 to February 1999—of 850 firms in key manufacturing sectors in the Republic of Korea. The survey provides microeconomic-level information on the impact of the financial crisis on output, employment, corporate finance, and profitability. It also provides insights into the efficacy of government programs, and the prospects for corporate recovery as seen by these firms. Similar studies undertaken in Indonesia, Malaysia, the Philippines, and Thailand allow for regional comparisons and the possibility to benchmark firm performance.

Since the outbreak of the financial crisis in December 1997, Korea has taken drastic measures to consolidate a base for economic stability. The two national priorities have been to reform the overall economic structure and to build up the depleted foreign exchange reserves. Through successful economic reforms, the Korean economy has regained its vitality—as evidenced by the decreasing exchange rates and interest rates, the increasing stock market indexes, and the improved current account.

This study on Korea's experiences in the recent crisis is one of the World Bank's series on East Asian responses to the current crisis and on long-term competitiveness issues. In particular, the research examines the impacts of the crisis and the resulting policy responses. The causes and impacts of the Korean economic crisis have been heatedly discussed in the international trade and financial forums, thus making it one of the most challenging policy issues. Policymakers' responses to the crisis, however, have been constrained by the paucity and inadequacy of the available economic and financial information. This paper addresses these weaknesses through the development and analysis of a database consisting of information collected through firm-level interviews.

The paper is organized as follows. The first section provides a detailed description of the survey, indicating the industrial sectors covered, sample composition and distribution. This is followed by a section that investigates issues pertaining to the impact of the crisis on the firms surveyed and their views on the causes of the crisis, and another section that deals with the firms' main sources of funding and focuses on investigating the extent of the credit crunch. The final section sums up our discussions and evaluates where Korea's economy is headed as the crisis begins to subside.

## The survey

In order to analyze the impact of and the response to the crisis, we conducted a detailed survey at the firm level. The survey focuses on the change in the firms' production, financial structure, labor force, and technology acquisition from 1996 to 1998. The survey was initiated in November 1998 and was completed in February 1999. Questionnaires were distributed to approximately 2,500 firms, out of which 863 sent responses. The firms were selected from five industrial sectors that adequately reflect the makeup of the Korean manufacturing sector. These sectors are garments and textiles (Standard Industrial Classification [SIC] code 17, 18), chemicals (SIC code 24, 25), machinery (SIC code 29), electronics and electrical machinery (SIC code 2930, 30, 32), and automobiles and automobile parts (34). They are the biggest sectors in Korea's manufacturing industries in terms of both value added and exports.

Within each of the sectors, firms were randomly selected so that the survey would involve a representative mix of firms of different sizes and geographic locations. We selected firms with at least 20 employees. As a combined set, small and medium-size enterprises (SMEs) are defined as those having less than 300 employees. A brief description of the characteristics of the sample is shown in table 11.1. In the sample, the chemicals industry occupies the biggest proportion (244 firms), while the automobile industry has the smallest (118 firms).

Approximately 70 percent of the firms export at least some of their output, which is not surprising if we take into account the outward-oriented nature of the Korean economy. The share of exporters varies across sectors—

### TABLE 11.1
### Characteristics of the sample

| | Size | | Export orientation | | By export volume | | | FDI firm | | Foreign control | | | Average number of employees | Number of firms |
|---|---|---|---|---|---|---|---|---|---|---|---|---|---|---|
| | Small | Large | Export | Nonexport | High | Medium | Small | No | Yes | None | Some | Total | | |
| *Industry* | | | | | | | | | | | | | | |
| Apparel and textiles | 171 | 29 | 131 | 67 | 69 | 35 | 66 | 195 | 5 | 190 | 4 | 2 | 234 | 200 |
| Chemicals | 206 | 38 | 165 | 79 | 44 | 69 | 113 | 200 | 47 | 192 | 20 | 21 | 246 | 244 |
| Machinery | 149 | 7 | 107 | 46 | 29 | 45 | 66 | 143 | 13 | 136 | 10 | 5 | 203 | 156 |
| Electronics | 112 | 33 | 124 | 23 | 65 | 39 | 31 | 122 | 26 | 114 | 24 | 4 | 546 | 145 |
| Automobiles | 96 | 22 | 69 | 51 | 13 | 43 | 61 | 101 | 22 | 99 | 10 | 11 | 453 | 118 |
| *Age* | | | | | | | | | | | | | | |
| Old | 561 | 122 | 493 | 193 | 186 | 195 | 248 | 604 | 89 | 580 | 54 | 36 | 363 | 683 |
| New | 171 | 7 | 103 | 71 | 34 | 36 | 88 | 156 | 23 | 150 | 14 | 7 | 127 | 178 |
| *Location* | | | | | | | | | | | | | | |
| Seoul | 500 | 103 | 425 | 173 | 162 | 152 | 231 | 532 | 77 | 505 | 51 | 29 | 375 | 603 |
| Others | 234 | 26 | 171 | 93 | 58 | 79 | 106 | 229 | 36 | 226 | 17 | 14 | 173 | 260 |
| Total | 734 | 129 | 596 | 266 | 220 | 231 | 337 | 761 | 113 | 731 | 68 | 43 | 314 | 863 |

*Source:* World Bank, Firm-Level Survey.

it is highest in electronics and lowest in automobiles. Among the exporters, the companies whose exports are more than half of their sales were about 28 percent of the group. The firms whose exports are more than 5 percent but less than 50 percent of their sales took up 29 percent, while the firms whose exports are less 5 percent of their sales accounted for 43 percent.

About 13 percent of those surveyed are Foreign Direct Investment (FDI) firms, that is, firms whose foreign ownership is more than 10 percent. These are either part of a joint venture or the subsidiary of a foreign parent. FDI firms are most common in the chemicals industry and are seen least in the textile industry. FDI firms tend to be larger, with an average employee count of 493 versus 289 for non-FDI firms. Foreign ties could be an important factor for firms to access capital or markets overseas.

Concerning the size of the firms in the survey, the sample is representative of the Korean situation since the small and medium-size companies make up a substantial proportion of the sample. Approximately 85 percent of surveyed firms were SMEs, although the share of SMEs also varies across sectors. The share is highest in the machinery industry (96 percent), and lowest in electronics (77 percent).

The sample is also representative of Korea's market situation in terms of firm age as well as location. The surveyed firms are divided into "old" and "new," based on the year of establishment, with the threshold being the year 1990. About 80 percent of the firms are designated old in the sample, and almost 70 percent are located in or near Seoul, the nation's largest city.

## Analysis of the impact of the crisis on the firms

The ultimate goal of the economic reforms imposed on Korea in exchange for the bailout loans from the International Monetary Fund (IMF) was to elevate foreign investors' confidence in the Korean economy and to revive its economic growth momentum. When the Korean economy was hit by the financial crisis, the expected disastrous effects on the domestic as well as external sectors were not easy to figure out. This made the job of policymakers very difficult, and they eagerly sought information about the impact of the crisis on domestic production, trade, and employment. In the survey, the firms were asked about changes that had occurred in capacity utilization, net profitability, and employment numbers since 1997.

### Capacity utilization and exports

In the wake of the crisis, Korean companies suffered from dull domestic demand as well as a credit crunch. Therefore, it is not surprising to find that the capacity utilization on average fell in all five industries from 1997 to the first half of 1998 (figure 11.1). In line with this decrease in capacity utilization, production also dropped. Exactly two-thirds of the firms reported that their production had been reduced since the outbreak of the crisis. The highest mention of production loss was among automobile producers (91.1 percent), followed by the machinery producers (74.4 percent). The chemicals (61.7 percent), electronics (58.8 percent), and apparel and textiles (55.7 percent) sectors reported production losses that were lower than the industry average.

Firm size provides insights into which areas of the economy were hardest hit by the crisis. The large firms were operating at a capacity utilization ratio that was 5.2 percent higher than the small firms in the first half of 1998. These firms experienced a significantly lower drop-off in production than did the small firms. During the same period, firms with links to foreign companies were producing a slight 0.6 percent less than domestic firms, while exporters were 6.0 percent more productive than domestically oriented producers.

In response to questions about expansion plans, 41.7 percent of the firms reported that they had planned to expand their facilities before the crisis occurred. Automobile producers registered the highest proportion of positive answers to the question at 60.2 percent. Only 26.4 percent of apparel and textiles producers reported their plan to expand the capacity before the crisis. The chemicals (43.5 percent), machinery (39.7 percent), and electronics (45.9 percent) sectors turned out to be very close to the mean of the survey results.

However, when the crisis was in full swing in 1998 more than two-thirds of the firms had abandoned their expansion plans. Only 13 percent of the firms reported that they had planned to expand their capacity utilization

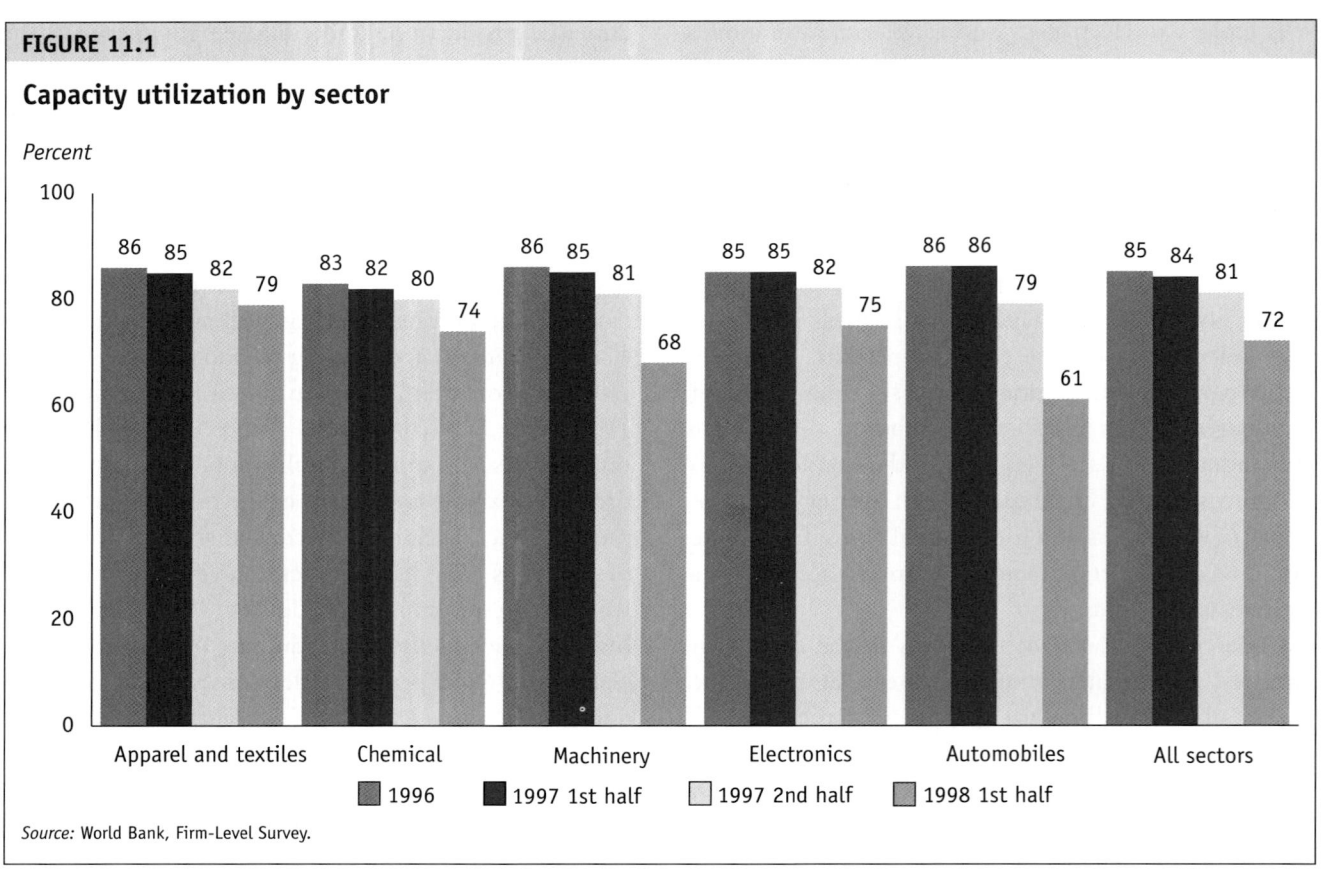

**FIGURE 11.1**

**Capacity utilization by sector**

*Source:* World Bank, Firm-Level Survey.

during the crisis. By sector, electronics producers were most ready to expand their capacity at 20.3 percent, and automobile producers were least likely at 10.6 percent. The apparel and textiles (10.9 percent), chemicals (12.1 percent), and the machinery sectors (14.1 percent) were closest to the mean of the survey results.

The results mentioned above indicate that the domestic demand was frozen in the aftermath of the crisis. They also reveal that automobile and machinery industries were the hardest hit sectors in Korea. The automobile industry had been suffering long before the crisis erupted, owing to the collapse of KIA Motors, one of the big three Korean carmakers along with Hyundai and Daewoo. The machinery industry suffered since it depends on domestic demand rather than exports. The apparel and textiles, chemicals, and electronics industries performed relatively better than the manufacturing average.

The firms were asked whether their exports in 1998 had increased or decreased, compared with 1997. A full 59.2 percent answered that their exports had increased, 29.0 percent answered that their exports had decreased, and 10.6 percent answered that their exports had not changed in 1998. These results indicated that most Korean firms have shown a relatively strong international competitiveness in the world market, despite the reduced production. Rating the factors contributing to their sustained international competitiveness, the firms selected the devalued exchange rates as the most important factor, followed by competitiveness in price, quality, efficient marketing strategies, and expanded market access.

## Net profitability

The fact that the firms had been facing reduced capacity utilization and production, and an increased interest payment burden caused by the higher interest rates, logically led to decreased profitability. The net profit–to-equity ratio was examined after excluding the companies whose capital was reduced to a value below zero. Outliers were eliminated by excluding firms with a ratio that was more or less than the value of the mean by three times the standard deviation. The survey results reveal (figure 11.2) that the net profitability stood at 11.5 percent in 1996, fell to 8.4 percent in 1997, and fell again to 5.7 percent in 1998. The standard deviations of the survey results have increased yearly since 1996 from 0.25 to 0.30 to 0.41. This shows that the uncertainty of profit-making rose sharply after the crisis, with some firms more seriously hurt than others.

By industry, the profitability of the automobile sector suffered the highest drop, with –6.6 percent in 1998. This was a substantial drop from the 11.5 percent enjoyed in 1996 and 10.0 percent in 1997. Next, the machinery sector suffered a drop of 2.7 percent in profitability in 1998; this variable was 4.5 percent in 1997 and 13.6 percent in 1996. On the contrary, the apparel and textiles sector showed a 13.4 percent profitability in 1998, surprisingly better than the 9.4 percent in 1997 and 13.2 percent in 1996. The profitability of the electronics sector (8.6 percent) was worse in 1998 than 1996 (13.1 percent) and 1997 (11.9 percent), but it was still greater than the overall average. The chemicals sector recorded a relatively good result with 8.2 percent in 1998, which exceeds the 7.0 percent of 1997, although it is smaller than the 8.6 percent of 1996.

## Competitors

The firms were asked to identify the categories of firms that were their strongest competitors. The results indicate that the Korean markets were more open in 1998 than 1996 and 1997 (figure 11.3). The share of firms that regard the domestic producers as their strongest competitors decreased to 63.5 percent in 1998 from 71 percent in 1996. The share of firms that perceived the domestic joint ventures as the main competitors rose from 2.7 percent in 1996 to 4.6 percent in 1998.

The survey demonstrates that the share of firms regarding the low-cost producers, newly industrialized countries, or developed countries as the biggest competitors rose every year. The share of firms picking the low-cost producers as the biggest competitors went up from 5.3 percent in 1997 to 6.4 percent in 1998. The share of firms picking the OECD countries as the biggest competitors rose from 12.4 percent in 1997 to 14.4 percent in 1998. Those firms that feel the NICs

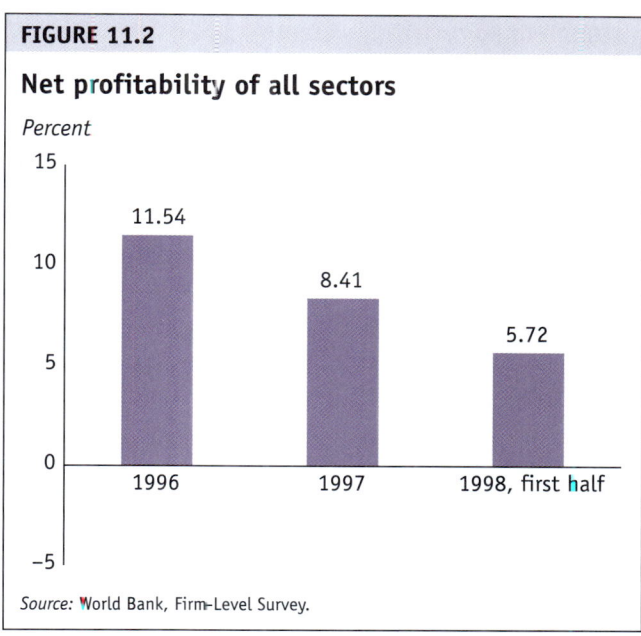

**FIGURE 11.2**

**Net profitability of all sectors**

Source: World Bank, Firm-Level Survey.

are the biggest competitors have remained around 4.9 percent.

Decreasing in all sectors in 1998 from 1996 was the share of firms that regard domestic producers as the strongest competitors. For producers in apparel and textiles, this drop was from 73.1 percent in 1996 to 64.2 percent and 64.2 percent in successive years. For the chemicals sector, the decline went from 71.8 percent to 70.6 percent to 65.7 percent. The share in the case of the machinery sector was 68.6 percent in 1996, and dropped to 62.2 percent in both 1997 and 1998. The drop for the electronics sector was from 63.5 percent to 56.8 percent to 52.7 percent. Finally, the automobile sector responses showed a fall from 78.0 percent to 75.6 percent to 72.4 percent in 1998.

Firm size provides insights into the impacts of the crisis. The larger firms were more likely to choose other domestic firms as the biggest competitors than were the smaller firms. This could be attributable to the larger firms being relatively better off lately in terms of production than the small firms. In 1998 there was a 6.2 percent drop in domestic competitors' profile in the case of large firms, and a 1.9 percent drop for small firms. Regarding the competition in the market, the larger firms have faced tough challenges from the direct competition with strong-performing foreign firms.

Overall, the results revealed that the Korean market is more open to foreign firms than it was in the past.

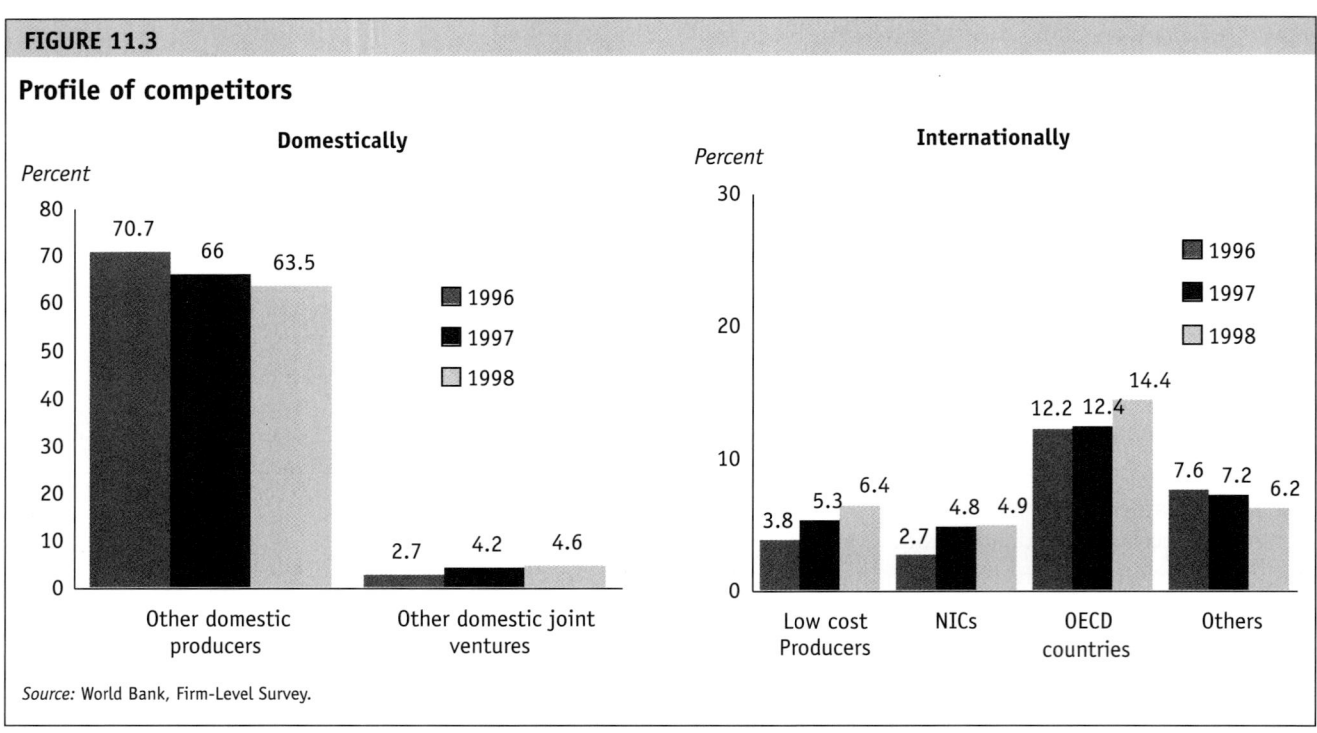

More than one-third of Korean firms now (1998) state that joint ventures and foreign producers are their biggest competitors.

## Employment

A full 63.5 percent of the firms are currently (1998) employing fewer workers relative to December 1997, when the crisis hit the nation full force (figure 11.4). The pattern of firms that are employing fewer workers differs slightly by firm characteristics. Exporters reporting the employment of fewer workers after the crisis accounted for 61.4 percent, while the figure for nonexporters was 66.9 percent. By foreign ownership, 63.5 percent of the firms whose foreign ownership is less than 10 percent are employing fewer workers, while this figure stands at 69.9 percent for the firms whose foreign ownership is less than 50 percent but more than 10 percent, and 60.0 percent for the firms whose foreign ownership is more than 50 percent. These results might indicate that foreign-controlled firms have been operating more efficiently than the domestic ones, and have not been forced to reduce their workforce.

It is interesting that the share of large and small firms employing fewer workers is somewhat different. Of the small firms, 61.2 percent have reduced their workforce, while 79.8 percent of the large firms are employing fewer workers, based on 1998 figures. The small firms have a more difficult time in an economic crisis, but apparently they are also more reluctant to let workers go. Of automobile producers, 80.5 percent have reduced their workforce, while this is 66.0 percent of machinery producers, 62.5 percent of chemicals producers, 57.4 percent of electronics producers and 56.7 percent of apparel and textiles producers.

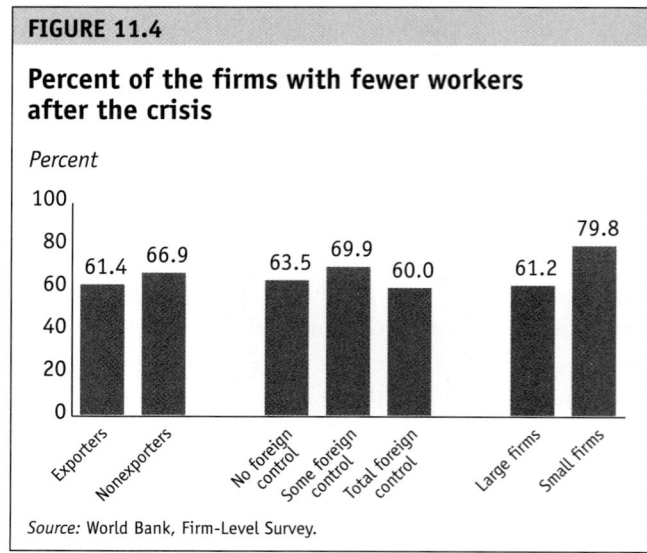

The correlation analysis on the decrease in capacity utilization and employment reveals a different picture. The correlation was –37 percent for the machinery sector, which was the highest, followed by apparel and textiles (–30 percent), electronics (–28 percent), chemicals (–27 percent), and automobiles (–13 percent). This analysis is not surprising since, as usual in a recession of Korean economy, the domestic-demand-dependent sectors (such as the machinery sector) as well as the labor-intensive sectors (such as the apparel and textiles sector) led the decrease in employment in this case.

Asked what percentage of the reduction in employment occurred in various categories, the firms answered that employment dropped in all categories as follows: 31.4 percent of unskilled production workers; 31.1 percent of clerical, sales, and service workers, and 25.3 percent of skilled production workers. The firms also stated that employment figures in administrative and managerial workers, and technical and research workers were reduced by 5.0 percent and 7.3 percent, respectively. This low reduction in knowledge and technical workers implies that the corporate competitiveness in terms of human capital was not diminished.

Regarding the reduction in employment, the firms were also asked to state any alternative to retrenchment they used. More than two-fifths, or 40.4 percent, of the firms reduced the length of working hours and 37.6 percent imposed pay cuts. Only 8.0 percent of the firms carried out rotational work shifts, and 6.1 percent transformed full-time jobs into part-time work. These results reveal that labor unions and management accepted wage cuts rather than retrenchment itself as a compromise to overcome the business crisis.

## Perceived causes of the slowdown

The firms were asked to assess to what extent they attributed the decline in their plant's utilization—with a score of "5" for "major contribution," and "1" for "no contribution." A substantial decline in domestic demand, and the effect of a high interest rate in raising the costs of loan repayments were the most commonly perceived causes of the continuing economic slowdown (figure 11.5). The firms emphasized somewhat the effect of the depreciated won in raising input costs—while increases in labor costs was the least common response.

By type of firm, exporters perceived the decline in domestic and foreign demand and the interest rate as the contributing factors, while nonexporters blamed

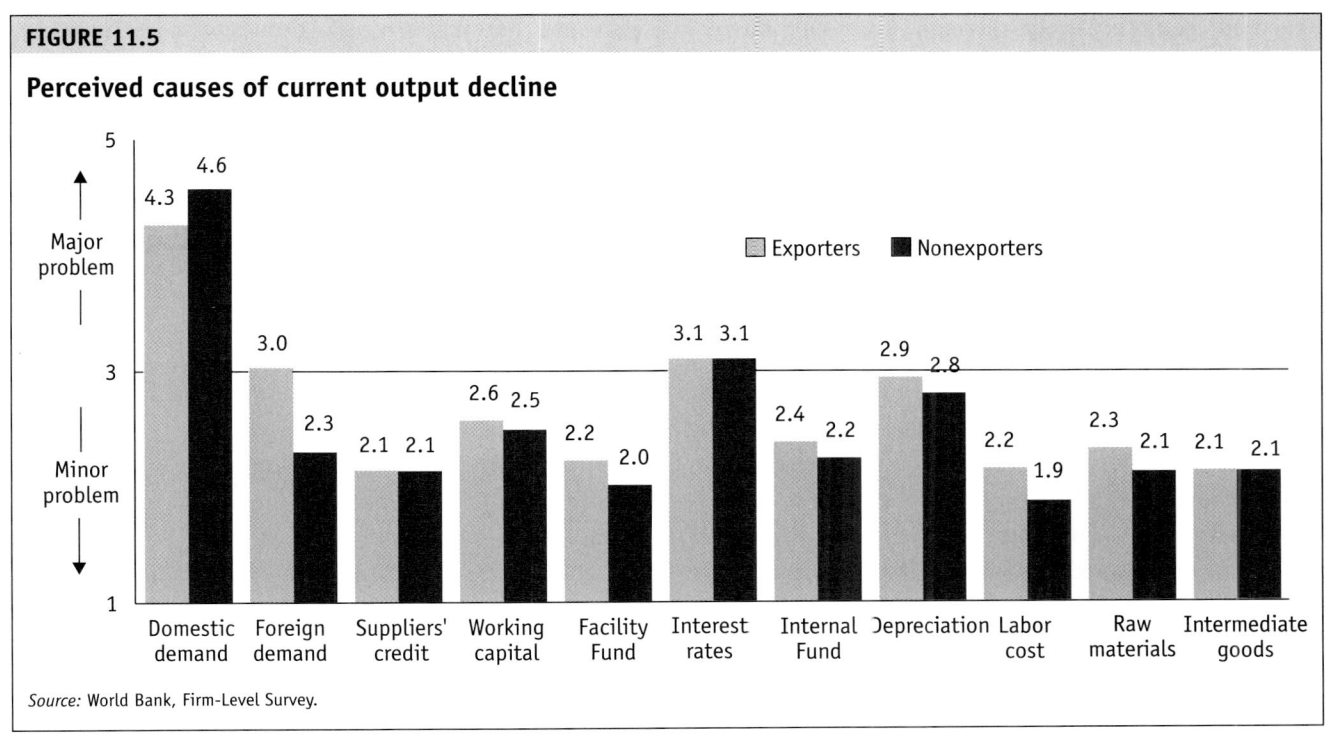

**FIGURE 11.5**

**Perceived causes of current output decline**

Source: World Bank, Firm-Level Survey.

the decline in domestic demand, the high interest rate, and the depreciated Korean won as the causes of their economic troubles. Regardless of the firm type, the survey results reveal that the dull domestic market, high interest rate, and the higher cost of production factors were the primary difficulties. This implies that the crisis can be overcome by the expansion in government spending and the macroeconomic stabilization policy.

## Policy response to the corporate sector

The Korean government provided the export credit facility funds, among others, for the corporate sector. Such policy was very important in helping the firms cope with the crisis. We will discuss the policy environment in the next section.

On the employee side, the government provided the social programs, including the mandated severance pay and the six-month unemployment benefits for laid-off workers. Korean law is an institutional framework set up to protect employees from arbitrary layoffs by management. For example, Korean labor law stipulates that employers are not allowed to lay off employees for reasons other than a business emergency. Korea's minimum wage law stipulates that approximately US$10 per day at the minimum has to be given to the employees. Social programs for unemployment insurance have specified eligibility requirements and methods of financing job training, among other stipulations.

## Financial position of the firms before and after the crisis and its impact on the firms' responses to the crisis

Since Korea's crisis has been largely attributed to the weak financial sector, information on the firms' financial position is of particular importance in assessing the impact of the crisis on the firms and understanding their responses to the crisis. In this section, we investigate the firms' financial positions focusing on five areas. Those are (a) sources of funds and their changes after the crisis; (b) the firms' debt structure (debt-to-equity ratios, share of foreign-currency-denominated debt, and share of short-term debt); (c) the changes in credit availability after the crisis; (d) transparency; and (e) programs offering financial support to the corporate sector and their effects.

## Sources of funds and their changes

The survey investigated the sources of funds and how these changed after the onset of the crisis. Before the crisis (figure 11.6a), the biggest source of short-term liquidity, at about 49 percent, was sales, and the biggest source of long-term funding was loans from domestic banks, also at about 49 percent. The next biggest sources of short-term and long-term funds were loans from domestic banks (38 percent) and sales revenue (35 percent), respectively. More than 80 percent of firms relied mainly on sales for short-term liquidity and on loans from domestic banks for long-term funding. In short, from these two sources, the firms raised most of the funds they needed. Other sources were loans from other domestic financial institutions (6 percent), loans from foreign banks (2 percent), and the bond market (1–2 percent).

This structure of funding sources showed some significant changes with the onset of the crisis (figure 11.6b). First of all, in both short-term and long-term financing, the proportion of sales revenue rose and that of loans from domestic banks fell sharply. The change was so substantial for long-term financing that the first and the second biggest sources were reversed after the crisis. That is, sales revenue became the biggest source (44 percent) followed by loans from domestic banks (41 percent). Before the crisis, domestic loans were the biggest funding source (49 percent) and sales revenue was the second largest (35 percent).

This change can be interpreted in two ways. First, it can be considered as an outcome of the credit crunch. Considering that the sales revenue also dropped substantially, concurrent with the progress of the financial crisis and the subsequent economic recession, the decrease of the relative proportion of loans from domestic banks implies that the amount of loans fell more sharply, serving as evidence of a significant credit crunch after the onset of the crisis.

However, the drop of the proportion of loans from banks can be interpreted as the result of the firms' decreased demand for credit as well. As mentioned above, since the Korean economy fell into a sharp recession after the onset of the crisis (the GDP growth rate fell from 5.5 percent in 1997 to about –6 percent in 1998), we can guess that the firms' financial demand also fell drastically. In this regard, the rise of the proportion of

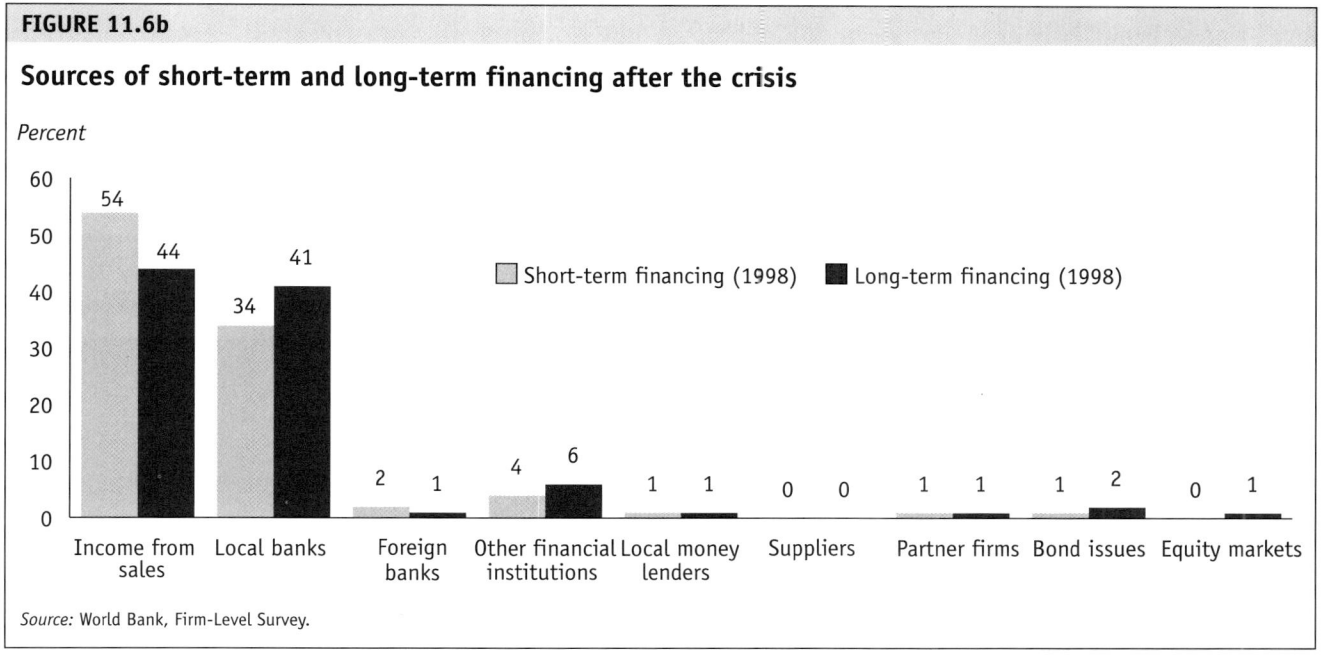

**FIGURE 11.6a**

**Sources of short-term and long-term financing before the crisis**

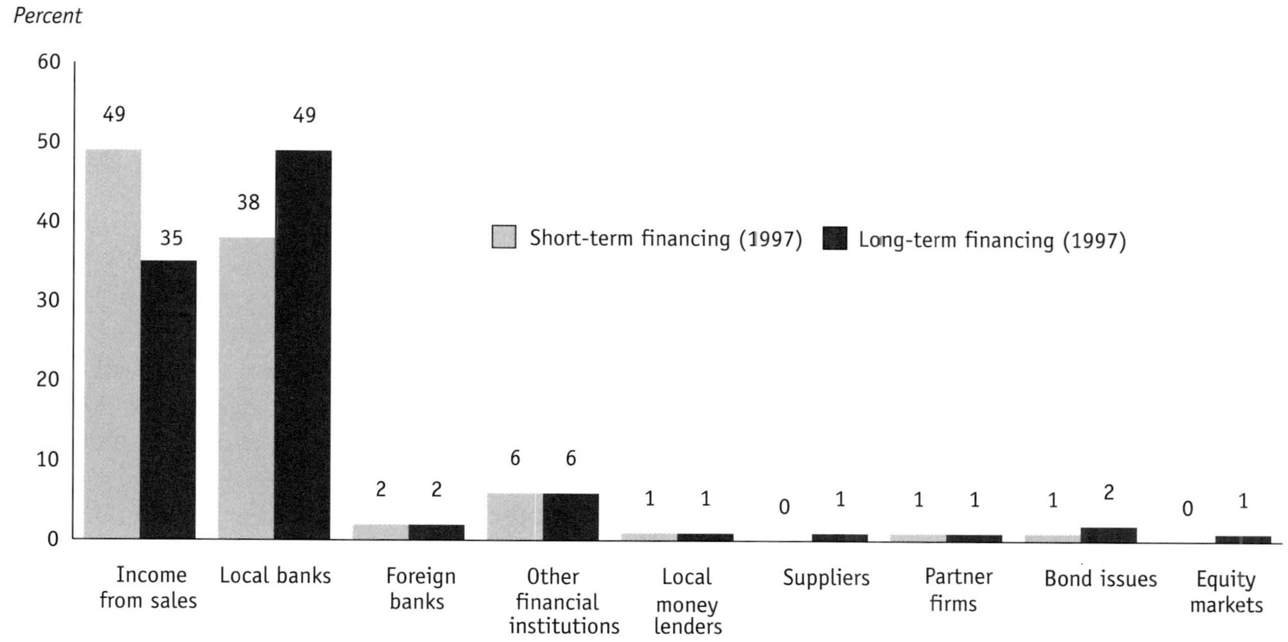

*Percent*

- Income from sales: 49 (short-term 1997), 35 (long-term 1997)
- Local banks: 38, 49
- Foreign banks: 2, 2
- Other financial institutions: 6, 6
- Local money lenders: 1, 1
- Suppliers: 0, 1
- Partner firms: 1, 1
- Bond issues: 1, 2
- Equity markets: 0, 1

*Source:* World Bank, Firm-Level Survey.

**FIGURE 11.6b**

**Sources of short-term and long-term financing after the crisis**

*Percent*

- Income from sales: 54 (short-term 1998), 44 (long-term 1998)
- Local banks: 34, 41
- Foreign banks: 2, 1
- Other financial institutions: 4, 6
- Local money lenders: 1, 1
- Suppliers: 0, 0
- Partner firms: 1, 1
- Bond issues: 1, 2
- Equity markets: 0, 1

*Source:* World Bank, Firm-Level Survey.

sales revenue despite reduced sales and the fall of the proportion of loans from banks may be attributable to the firms' efforts to cut back on their credit demands in the face of falling domestic demand.

On the whole, it seems that these two factors played a role in bringing about the change in the structure of fund sources after the crisis, although the more important contributing factor cannot be distinguished by our survey. Still, we can find some important clues, at least in the case of short-term funds. We asked the firms to assess the contribution of each source to difficulties in financing production, with a score of "5" denoting "major contribution" and "1" denoting "no contribution." The highest rating was lower revenue from sales reduction (4.16), while insufficient loans was the third highest (3.24), following higher costs of inputs (3.42). This seems to imply that difficulties in the relevant sector itself played a bigger role than the credit crunch.

## Debt structure

*Debt-equity ratio.* In the wake of the financial crisis, the IMF advised the Korean government to reduce government expenditures and to implement a very tight monetary policy. As a result, the interest rate soared during the first half of 1998. A high interest rate was considered inevitable in order to avoid capital flight and further depreciation of the Korean won. However, soaring interest rates had an extremely negative impact on Korean firms.

It is widely known that Korean firms had been highly leveraged. This seems to be attributable to their aggressive business behavior in an environment of rapid economic growth on the one hand, and the country's underdeveloped capital market, on the other hand. According to the Bank of Korea, the average debt-equity ratio of Korean manufacturing firms was 3.17 in 1996.

In our sample, the average debt-equity ratio rose from 3.55 in 1996 to 3.96 in 1997 and fell again to 3.70 in 1998. The sharp rise of the ratio over 1996–1997 seems to be deeply related to the onset of the crisis, which began at the end of 1997. The average debt-equity ratio in the official statistics also rose in this period, which seems to be the result of the massive increase of foreign borrowing after Korea joined the OECD in 1996.

Meanwhile, the fall of the debt-equity ratio amidst the crisis can also be interpreted as the result of the two factors mentioned in the previous section: the credit crunch and the decrease of the firms' financial demands (figure 11.7). First, it could be considered that as loans were not rolled over, the ratio fell. At the same time, the ratio might also fall, because the firms' financial demands decreased with the economic recession. While the former is an involuntary reduction in their debt-equity status, the latter can be considered as a voluntary reduction.

Among the five industrial sectors under study, the ratio was lowest in chemicals (2.62 in 1998), and highest in automobiles (5.52 in 1998). In textiles and chemicals, the ratio rose over the 1996–1997 period while falling in 1998. The ratio sustained its growth over 1996–1998 in machinery, automobiles and electronics.

Not surprisingly, the ratio was much higher in large firms than in SMEs. Exporters had higher ratios than nonexporters, and the correlation between export orientation and debt-equity ratio was positive. However, there were a couple of results that contradicted our predictions. First of all, it is notable that firms with foreign-currency debt had lower debt-equity ratios than those that borrowed only in won. More surprisingly, the ratio in firms with foreign-currency debt fell over 1996–1998, although the sharp depreciation of the won over the period was expected to raise the ratio, other things being equal. Second, in spite of the FDI firms' easier access to foreign capital, they showed a lower debt-equity ratio than local firms.

*Issues related to foreign-currency-denominated debt.* Since the crisis came with the dramatic depreciation of the Korean won, it was generally expected that firms with extensive debt denominated in foreign currencies would suffer more severely than those without. However, the survey result suggests that this problem is not as serious as expected. As we mentioned in the above section, debt-equity ratio in firms with foreign-currency-denominated debt was not only lower than those without, but also fell over the 1996–98 period.

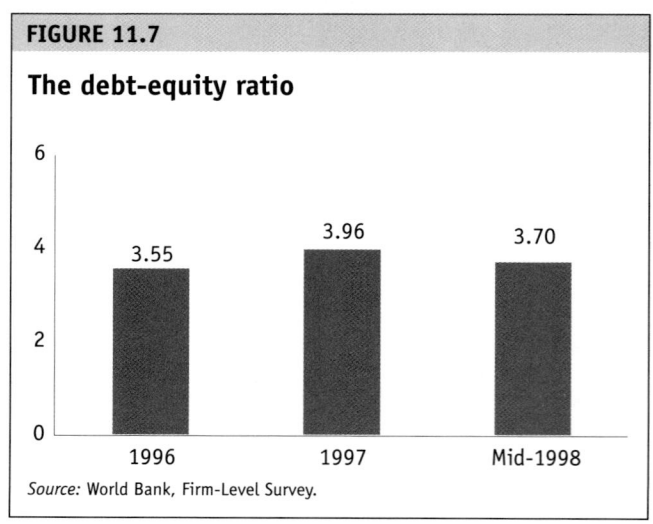

**FIGURE 11.7**

**The debt-equity ratio**

Source: World Bank, Firm-Level Survey.

Of course, as expected, the average amount of foreign-currency debt rose quite rapidly over the period. Particularly, the amount increased sharply over 1996–97 as the won depreciated dramatically at the end of 1997. The average amount of foreign-currency debt doubled from 18,240 million won in 1996 to 36,481 million won in 1997. However, it fell again to 30,501 million won during the first half of 1998, reflecting the appreciation of the won over that period. Moreover, not surprisingly, the average amount of total debt did not increase as much over 1996–98. This is because the share of foreign debt in total debt was not very high. The average share among relevant firms was 19.8 percent in 1998. It rose from 15.2 percent in 1996 to 24.3 percent in 1997 and fell again in 1998.

In addition, for firms with foreign-currency debt, about 42 percent of the survey respondents were larger, more export-oriented, and healthier in financial structure than the firms that borrowed only in won. The average number of employees was 420 in firms with foreign-currency debt, compared with 238 in firms without. And the average ratio of export-to-total sales in firms with foreign-currency debt was 35 percent, while it was 24 percent in firms without. The average share of short-term debt was 49 percent in firms with foreign-currency debt versus 50 percent in firms without. Perhaps reflecting this relative strength, firms with foreign-currency debt showed higher capacity utilization than firms without (see table 11.2).

On the whole, we can suppose, based on these facts, that the existence of foreign-currency debt did not affect the financial structure of firms with debt as seriously as had been feared. This is partly because those firms were relatively stronger than others and also partly because the share of foreign debt was not very high.

*Share of short-term debt.* Although high interest rates after the onset of crisis damaged highly leveraged firms, among them, those with a high proportion of short-term debt suffered more. As the credit crunch emerged, raising money itself became difficult in spite of the high interest rate. Thus, many Korean firms had difficulties in rolling over their short-term debt.

For the sample firms, the average share of short-term debt was 49.9 percent in 1998, which was about 1.5 percentage points lower than before the crisis (figure 11.8). The share rose slightly during 1996–1997, and fell in 1998. The large firms and exporters showed higher shares than SMEs and nonexporters, respectively. The share was positively correlated with export orientation. Firms with foreign debt had a lower share of short-term debt than those without, while local firms had a lower share than FDI firms.

**TABLE 11.2**
**Profile of the firms**

|  | Borrow in foreign currency | | Size | | Export orientation | | Foreign control | | | FDI firm | |
|---|---|---|---|---|---|---|---|---|---|---|---|
|  | Yes | No | Small | Large | Export | Nonexport | None | Some | Total | No | Yes |
| *Financial indicators* | | | | | | | | | | | |
| Short-term liabilities/ total liabilities | 49.5 | 50.2 | 49.0 | 54.1 | 51.3 | 46.2 | 48.4 | 51.5 | 53.4 | 49.0 | 55.6 |
| Long-term liabilities/ total liabilities | 50.5 | 49.8 | 51.0 | 45.9 | 48.7 | 53.8 | 51.6 | 48.5 | 46.6 | 51.0 | 44.4 |
| Debt-equity ratio | 3.53 | 3.86 | 3.59 | 4.18 | 3.87 | 3.25 | 3.82 | 3.37 | 3.81 | 3.75 | 3.37 |
| *First characteristics* | | | | | | | | | | | |
| Number of employees | 420 | 238 | 89 | 1594 | 419 | 96 | 205 | 1638 | 255 | 289 | 493 |
| Share of export | 34.7 | 23.9 | 25.7 | 43.7 | 40.0 | 3.3 | 27.5 | 39.6 | 32.7 | 27.7 | 35.4 |
| Share of FDI firm | 16 | 11 | 12 | 18 | 15 | 9 | n.a. | 69 | 98 | n.a. | 100 |
| *Response to the crisis* | | | | | | | | | | | |
| Current capacity utilization | 74.4 | 70.3 | 71.4 | 76.7 | 74.1 | 67.8 | 72.1 | 70.4 | 73.3 | 72.2 | 72.1 |
| Share with fewer workers | 66.6 | 62.3 | 61.3 | 79.8 | 62.1 | 67.2 | 63.7 | 72.7 | 67.4 | 64.3 | 62.5 |
| Optimistic for future growth | 34.7 | 36.3 | 35.7 | 35.2 | 34.0 | 40.1 | 37.1 | 25.4 | 27.9 | 36.3 | 31.3 |
| Frequency | 363 | 501 | 723 | 128 | 594 | 257 | 722 | 67 | 43 | 750 | 112 |
| Total share | 42.0 | 58.0 | 83.7 | 14.8 | 69.8 | 30.2 | 86.8 | 8.1 | 5.2 | 87.0 | 13.0 |

n.a. not applicable
*Source:* World Bank, Firm-Level Survey.

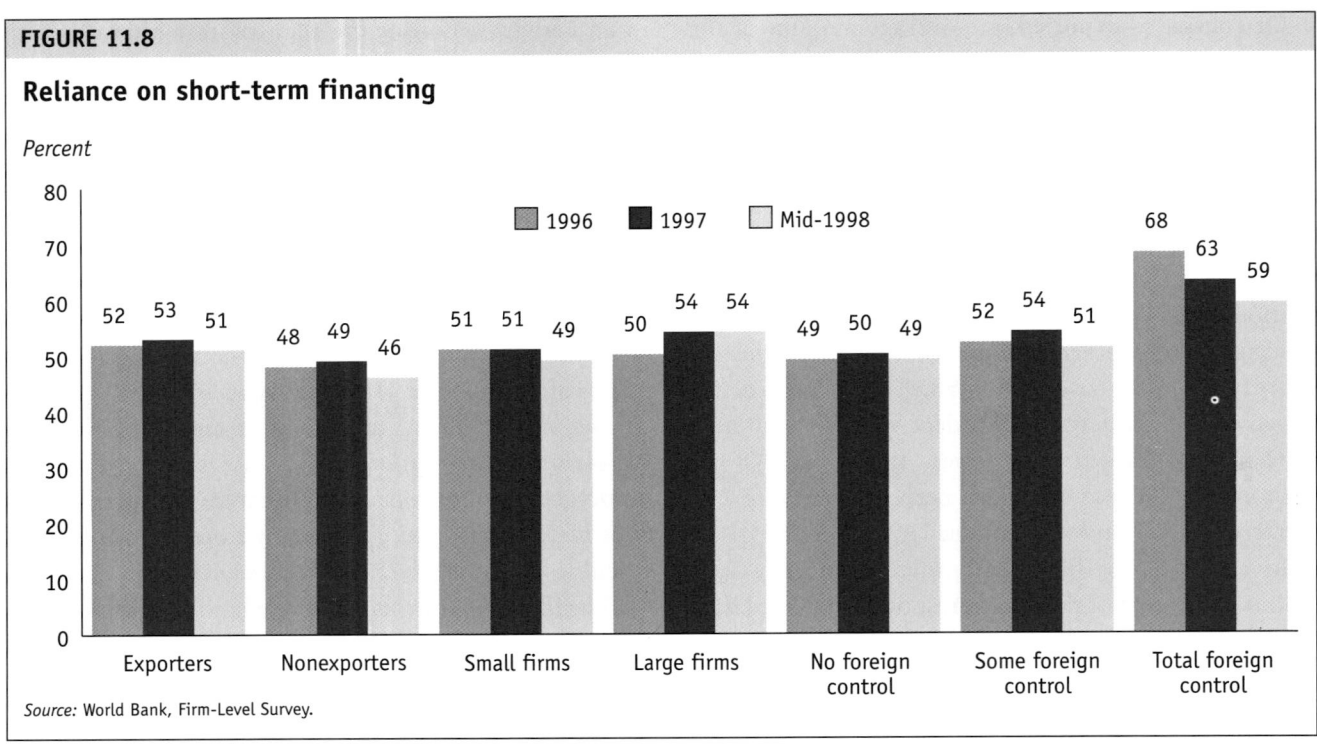

**FIGURE 11.8**

**Reliance on short-term financing**

Source: World Bank, Firm-Level Survey.

Over the investigation period, the share fell more sharply after the crisis began in SMEs than in the large firms, and in nonexporters over exporters. The share in the large firms actually rose slightly after the onset of crisis. Since there is no reason to believe that the large firms and exporters suffered more than SMEs and nonexporters from the economic recession after the outbreak of the crisis, this seems to imply that the former two groups had less difficulty in rolling over short-term debt than did the latter two groups.

## Availability of credit

One of the controversial issues during the crisis was whether the credit crunch existed and how serious it was. Although we already discussed this issue in the above sections, we also directly investigated it with a survey question on the change in the availability of credit. The firms were asked to assess the change in the availability of credit after the onset of crisis—with "5" indicating "much less restrictive," "3" "the same," and "1" "much more restrictive." The survey showed that the availability of credit was substantially restricted in all financial sources (figure 11.9). The answer was less than 2.5 for all financial sources. This implies that a significant credit crunch did, in fact, exist.

The most restrictive sources were local moneylenders (1.9), a source that is generally considered as the most sensitive to the change in the money market. Relatively less restrictive sources were suppliers, partner firms, and domestic banks. Among the financial institutions, domestic banks were the least restrictive credit suppliers.

In another question concerning the availability of credit, we also investigated the proportion of firms that were declined loans by banks or other financial institutions. The survey showed that the proportion rose sharply following the onset of the crisis. The proportion was 14 percent in the first half of 1997, rose to 27 percent in the second half of the year, and rose again to 38 percent in the first half of 1998. Both the proportion and its growth rate were higher in the large firms and local firms than in SMEs and foreign controlled firms, respectively. It is particularly remarkable that the proportion of large firms rejected for loans rose dramatically from 21 percent in the first half of 1997 to 61 percent in the same period of 1998. This does not support the general belief that SMEs suffered more severely from the credit crunch.

## Transparency and disclosure

Even before the financial crisis began unfolding, the East Asian financial system, not excluding Korea's, had often been criticized for its insufficient transparency and disclosure of financial information. Concerning this issue, we asked the firms whether their financial statements were audited by outside accounting firms, whether they needed audited statements to receive a bank loan, and whether they had to secure their loan with collateral.

On the issue of audited statements, about two-thirds of the surveyed firms answered that they were audited by outside accounting firms. Almost all of the large firms and about 60 percent of the SMEs affirmed this. In order to qualify for a bank loan, approximately 62 percent of the firms needed audited statements—specifically, about 95 percent of the large firms and 56 percent of the SMEs. Thus, judging by this response, it can be inferred that there is sufficient transparency and disclosure of financial information in Korea. Therefore, the actual problem in Korea is neither whether firms are audited by outside accounting firms nor whether they provide audited statements to receive a bank loan, but how much credibility the audited statements hold and how much importance banks attach to them in determining loan provisions. Unfortunately, this information cannot be obtained from our survey.

Meanwhile, on the issue of collateral, 86 percent of the firms answered that they had to provide collateral to receive bank loans. This reflects the fact that Korean banks traditionally demand collateral to provide loans, particularly to SMEs. Comparing debt-equity ratios between firms that provide collateral and those that do not, the ratio of the former was much higher: 3.33 compared with 1.88. Perhaps this is because banks are more likely to demand collateral from firms with higher debt-equity ratios. The types of collateral are mostly real estate, such as buildings and land.

## Policy environment

To deal with the crisis, the Korean government has implemented several policies to relieve the credit crunch and to support firms' restructuring efforts. Expanded financial support and taxation relief were provided to SMEs and venture businesses, to spur exporting efforts and corporate restructuring, mergers and acquisitions

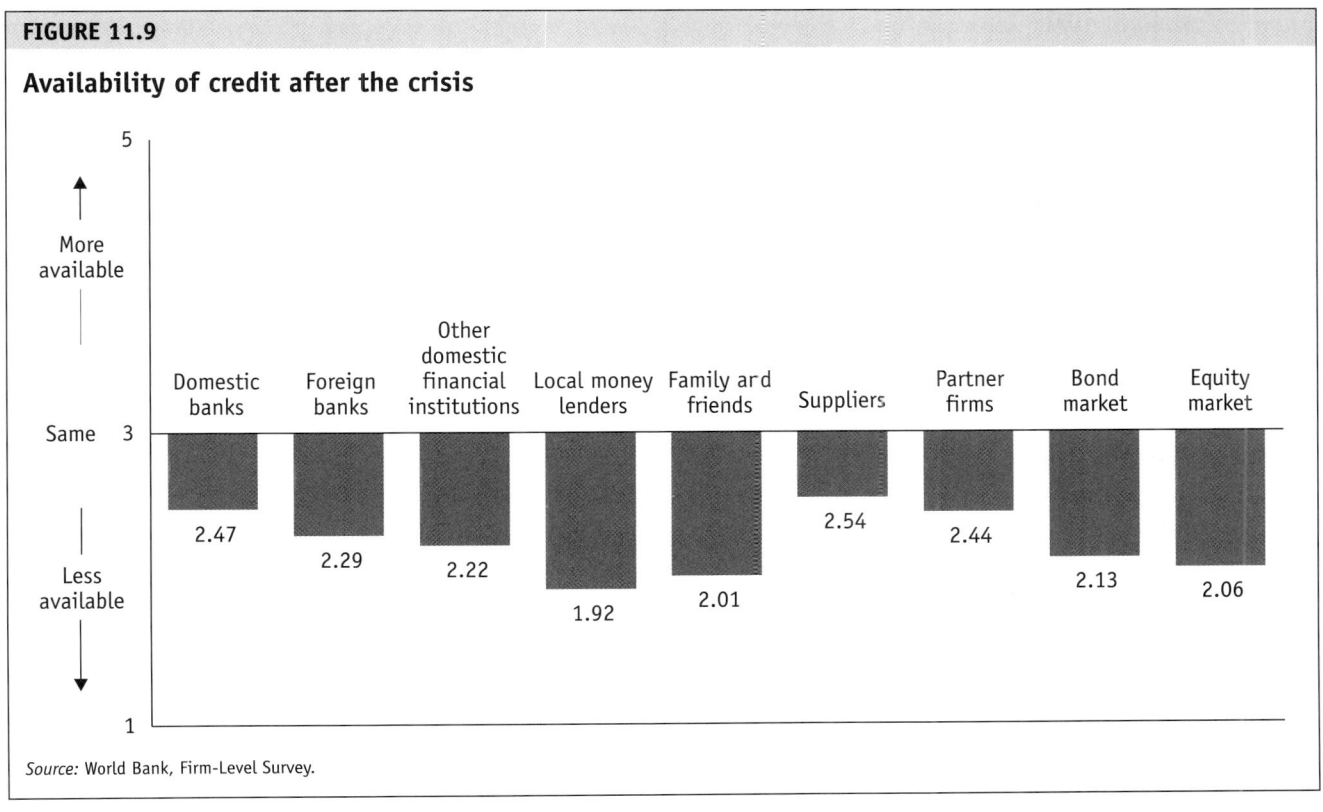

**FIGURE 11.9**

**Availability of credit after the crisis**

*Source:* World Bank, Firm-Level Survey.

(M&As), technology development, and employment. We investigated in the survey whether the firms were aware of these policies and how they assessed their effect.

Most of the firms were well aware of these policies. Approximately 89 percent of the surveyed firms were aware of financial support policy for SMEs. Only 66 percent of firms knew about the M&A promotion policy, which was the least well known policy among firms.

Meanwhile, the proportion of firms that applied for these programs, not surprisingly, varies for each policy program. The proportion was high in credit guarantees for SMEs (46 percent) and technology development funds (38 percent), while it was low in M&A promotion policy (9 percent) and the corporate restructuring fund (15 percent). Low application ratios for the latter two policies can be explained by the fact that they were restricted to only those firms that opted for M&A or corporate restructuring.

Finally, the effect of the supporting policies was regarded as satisfactory. We asked the firms to assess these policies with "5" signifying "major contribution" and "1" "no contribution." The answer was more than 3 for all of the above-mentioned policy programs. Although the variance was small across each policy program, the long-term facility fund from Korea Development Bank scored relatively high (3.91), as did the export and import financing (3.86). The firms gave low ratings to the M&A promotion policy (3.40) and the financial support provided to venture businesses and SMEs (3.47). It is somewhat surprising that the support for venture business and SMEs scored the second lowest rating, considering that this is one of the most important economic policies of the present government. This result suggests that there might be some problems with the efficiency of the policy.

## Concluding remarks and recommendations

Economic growth, the price level, and the balance of payments are among the Korean government's paramount concerns. For the time being, the government agenda will focus on the challenging problem of sustaining the trade surplus. The reason for setting this priority is that the Korean economy, boosted by an outward-looking development strategy, faces dampened economic activities with the current lukewarm growth in exports. In addition, a sufficient trade surplus is needed to upgrade the credit rating of the Korean economy and to repay the borrowed loans from international financial institutions.

The ultimate goal of the IMF program, imposed on Korea in exchange for the bailout loans, was to elevate foreign investors' confidence in the Korean economy. The IMF program is expected to provide the Korean economy with the opportunities to improve its development capacities through structural reforms and a balanced current account. In the short term, however, the IMF program has had the effect of sacrificing the country's economic growth. Specifically, with overly low growth rates prescribed in its action plan, the program curtailed domestic business, including facility investments.

According to the survey results, lower-capacity utilization, declining net profitability, and reduction in employment were bad news for the Korean economy. Specifically, the impact of the crisis on the highly leveraged firms was devastating. Korean export capabilities, however, were shown not to have been damaged by the crisis. This was further evidenced by the export performance of last year, which recorded US$133.2 billion in 1998. Export volume was just 2.2 percent less than that of 1997, which contributed to a huge trade surplus of almost 40 billion U.S. dollars in 1998. Export performance and regained vitality in the manufacturing sectors are signs of Korea's economic recovery in 1999.

The survey results revealed that 36 percent of the firms expected their output to increase in the next six months, while only 28 percent expected their output to decrease in this time period (figure 11.10)—35 percent expected their output not to change at all. Interestingly, 54 percent of automobile producers answered that they expected their output to increase in six months, and only 21 percent expected their output to decrease. As we noted in the previous sections, the automotive sector was the hardest hit by the crisis in terms of production and employment. Of electronics producers, 37 percent expected their output to increase in six months, while 29 percent thought their output would decrease. In the case of the apparel and textiles sector, the proportion of producers who expected their output to increase in six months was smaller than the proportion of producers who expected their output to decline.

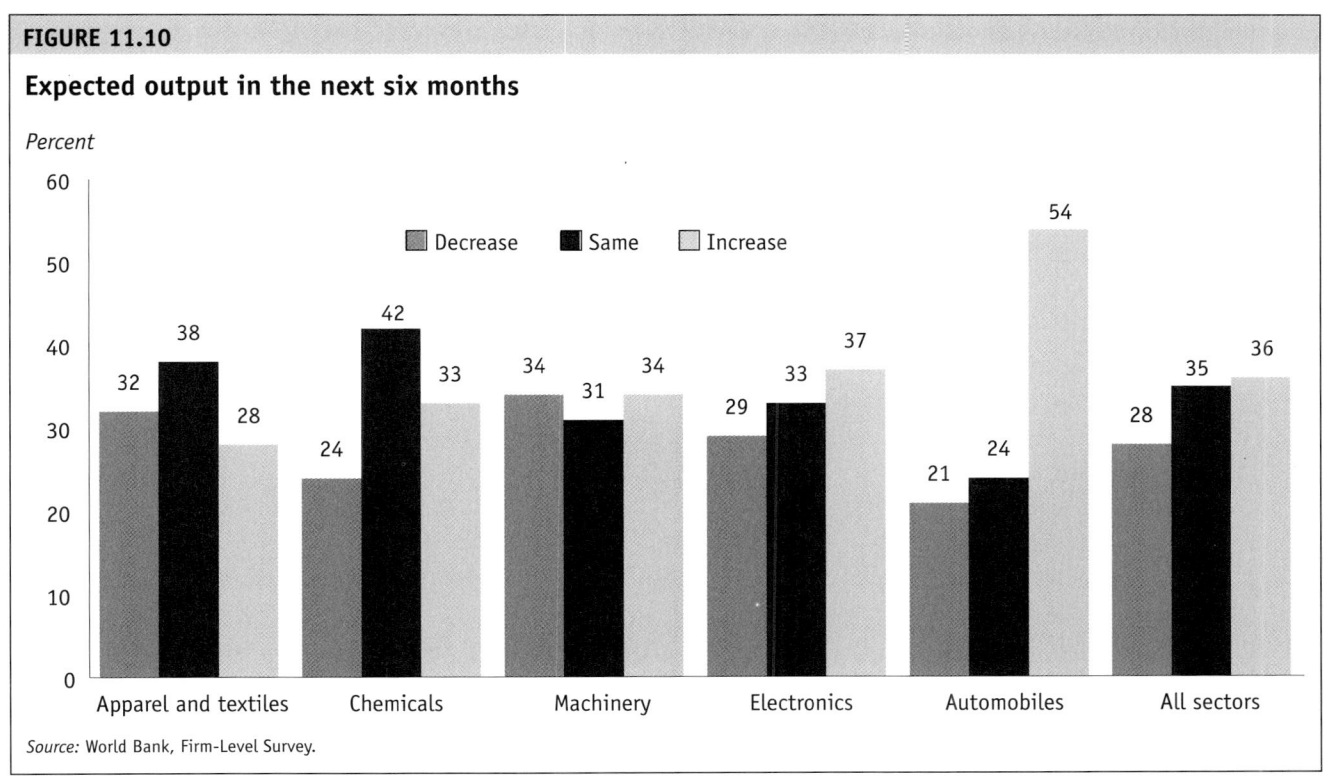

**FIGURE 11.10**

**Expected output in the next six months**

*Source:* World Bank, Firm-Level Survey.

Considering the debt-equity ratios of Korean firms, decreasing exchange rates and interest rates, the increasing stock market indexes, and the improved current account, we can interpret that Korean business will be rejuvenated owing to the economic restructuring. We note that the hard-hit automobile sector shows signs of recovery at this time.

Not surprisingly, Korean firms were alarmed by the skyrocketing interest rates as a result of tightened monetary policy implemented in 1998. This paper will not provide an in-depth analysis on whether higher interest rates contributed to the stabilization of the Korean economy and the activation of foreign direct investment, or whether they were conducive to the aggravated domestic business in the early stages of the financial crisis. However, Korea did agree that the tightened monetary and fiscal policies were necessary to elevate foreign investors' confidence in the Korean economy and to revive its economic growth momentum in the early stages of the crisis management.

In addition, we note that the private-sector austerity program, and public-sector burden sharing programs were effective in tackling the crisis. Korean imports in 1998 were reduced by 35 percent, which demonstrated the people's willingness to optimize their economic activities. The public sector played a leading role in promoting the so-called big four economic restructuring agenda in terms of financial, corporate, labor and management, and public-sector reforms.

The recent macroeconomic indicators—including the economic growth rate, exchange rate, interest rate, and inflation rate—demonstrate the Korean economy's signs of recovery from the financial crisis. At this stage, anti-recession measures such as a relaxed monetary supply and expanded fiscal spending are more desirable than adhering needlessly to the tightened policies. Needless to say, economic restructuring measures will have to be implemented faithfully. Such reforms also conform to the spirit of democracy and market economy, which the President Kim Dae Jung administration has adopted as a framework agenda.

Korea is eager to open its market to foreign producers as well as investors. To this end, it is trying to bring its domestic regulations and institutions up to established international levels. Through its economic restructuring processes, the Korean government has announced drastic market opening measures including the capital market and foreign exchange liberalization, and the abolition of the import diversification policy, among others. Still, the government will have to set up long-term plans to conform to global standards.

Finally, we hope that this project will help strengthen the capabilities of Korean policymakers by allowing them to ascertain what is actually occurring at the firm level. This project will lend support to developing a network of policymakers in East Asian countries through the pooling of information about country experiences.

# Annex 11.A

## Government support programs listed in the questionnaire

### Enlargement of the credit guarantee for SMEs

The fund for credit guarantee was expanded from 600 billion won in 1997 to 1.3 trillion won in 1998 with the fund from IBRD and ADB of about one billion U.S. dollars each. And the ceiling of guarantee for each firm was also raised from won 1.5 billion to won 3 billion.

### Enlargement of the financing to venture businesses and SMEs

Loans to venture businesses and SMEs that became due in 1998 were rolled over for six months. The interest rate for policy loans to SMEs was lowered by 1 percentage point. Thirteen trillion won of special funds was raised by banks for loans to SMEs.

### Activation of M&A

Hostile M&A was allowed by the amendment of the law. The ceiling of treasury stock purchases was raised to 33 percent.

### Financial support for corporate restructuring

Taxation support was given to business activities for restructuring. For example, 50 percent of value added tax credit was given to the sales of real estate for corporate restructuring.

### Technology development fund.

For the development of basic technology, two-thirds of the developing cost is now supported by the government.

### Enlargement of export and import financing

The limit to export-import financing was abolished, and additionally public funds totaling 5.3 billion dollars were raised to support export-import financing.

### Long-term facility fund from the Korea Development Bank

Out of various government funds, loans are currently made to firms' equipment investment with a relatively low interest rate. Although this supporting program had long been implemented even before the financial crisis, the size of the fund was expanded after the onset of the crisis.

## Note

The authors are with the Korea Institute for Industrial Economics and Trade (KIET). This paper discusses the results from an Industrial Survey conducted by KIET with the cooperation of NICE (National Information and Credit Evaluation Inc.). Many thanks are owed to Dr. Mary Hallward-Driemeier of the World Bank for her technical support, Ms. Linda Elmose of KIET for her enthusiastic proofreading, and the World Bank for financial support.

# chapter twelve

# The Asian Financial Crisis: Impact at the Firm Level—The Malaysian Case

*Economic Planning Unit,*
*Prime Minister's Office, Malaysia*

The Asian financial crisis that started in mid-1997 adversely affected the performance of East Asian economies, including Malaysia. The effects of the financial crisis on the real economy became discernible during the last quarter of 1997 when the real GDP growth rate slowed down in comparison with that of the earlier three-quarters. In 1998, the economy contracted for the first time since 1985. Both domestic demand and exports in terms of U.S. dollars declined. All sectors of the economy including manufacturing, which is the leading sector, registered negative growth rates. The performance of selected economic and financial indicators over this period was as shown in table 12.1.

This report evaluates the impact of the financial crisis at the firm level based on the results of the corporate sector survey on the impact of the Asian financial crisis conducted by the Government of Malaysia in collaboration with the World Bank. The survey provides up-to-date information on the effects of the financial crisis on the performance of the firms, particularly with respect to their production, revenue, employment, exports, and investment capability. The results of the survey also illustrate how firm characteristics and the policy environment affect the vulnerability of these firms. The results can serve as a useful input for the formulation of appropriate policies and strategies to initiate the recovery of the corporate sector.

The results of the survey show that in general, most firms have been affected by the crisis in terms of a decline in their output and net profits, with domestic-oriented firms being more severely affected than those specializing in exports. The firms attribute output decline primarily to softening demand and the higher cost of input arising from the depreciation of the ringgit. Export performance

## TABLE 12.1
## Selected economic and financial indicators, 1994–98

|  | 1994 | 1995 | 1996 | 1997 | Estimate 1998 |
|---|---|---|---|---|---|
| *Real sector (percent change)* | | | | | |
| Real GDP | 9.3 | 9.4 | 8.6 | 7.7 | -6.7 |
| Real domestic demand | 12.7 | 13.3 | 7.0 | 6.5 | -25.8 |
| CPI inflation (period average) | 3.7 | 3.4 | 3.5 | 2.7 | 5.3 |
| Unemployment rate (percent) | 2.9 | 2.8 | 2.6 | 2.6 | 3.9 |
| *Savings and investment (percent of GDP)* | | | | | |
| Gross domestic investment | 40.4 | 43.5 | 41.6 | 42.5 | 25.8 |
| Private, including stocks | 27.5 | 30.9 | 30.2 | 30.9 | 14.5 |
| Public | 13.0 | 12.6 | 11.4 | 11.6 | 11.4 |
| Gross national savings | 32.7 | 33.6 | 36.7 | 37.3 | 38.8 |
| Private | 15.1 | 18.6 | 20.8 | 19.1 | 23.6 |
| Public | 17.5 | 15.0 | 15.9 | 18.3 | 15.2 |
| *Fiscal sector (percent of GDP)* | | | | | |
| Federal government balance | 2.3 | 0.9 | 0.7 | 2.4 | -1.8 |
| Revenue | 26.0 | 23.3 | 23.4 | 23.9 | 20.3 |
| Expenditure and net lending | 23.7 | 22.5 | 22.6 | 21.5 | 22.1 |
| Overall public sector balance | 3.5 | 3.2 | 4.0 | 6.3 | -1.7 |
| *Monetary sector (annual percent change)* | | | | | |
| M3 growth | 13.1 | 22.3 | 21.2 | 18.5 | 2.7* |
| Domestic credit growth | 14.7 | 28.6 | 26.7 | 32.0 | -1.6* |
| *Interest rates (percent, end–period)* | | | | | |
| One-month interbank rate | 5.14 | 6.05 | 7.23 | 8.60 | 6.48* |
| Average lending rate | 11.49 | 11.54 | 11.93 | 12.16 | 9.95* |
| *Balance of payments (US$ billion)* | | | | | |
| Trade balance | 1.7 | 0.0 | 4.0 | 4.0 | 17.7 |
| Exports, f.o.b. | 56.6 | 71.6 | 76.8 | 77.7 | 71.9 |
| Imports, f.o.b. | 54.9 | 71.5 | 72.7 | 73.7 | 54.2 |
| Services account balance | -6.5 | -7.7 | -7.7 | -7.7 | -6.0 |
| Current account balance | -5.6 | -8.6 | -4.8 | -5.0 | 9.2 |
| (% of GDP) | -7.8 | -9.9 | -4.9 | -5.1 | 12.9 |
| Capital account balance | 2.5 | 6.9 | 7.3 | 1.2 | 1.1 |
| Medium- and long-term | 4.4 | 6.6 | 5.4 | 6.8 | 2.8 |
| Short-term | -3.2 | 1.0 | 4.1 | -4.0 | -5.5 |
| Portfolio capital | 1.3 | -0.8 | -2.1 | -1.6 | 3.8 |
| Overall balance | -3.1 | -1.8 | 2.5 | -3.9 | 10.3 |
| *International trade (annual percent change)[a]* | | | | | |
| Export volume | 23.5 | 15.2 | 6.9 | 10.6 | 20.8 |
| Import volume | 32.5 | 25.5 | 1.6 | 8.9 | -5.4 |
| Terms of trade | 2.5 | 5.0 | -0.4 | -1.4 | -1.6 |
| *Gross official reserves (US$ billion)* | 26.0 | 25.4 | 27.8 | 21.0 | 25.4 |
| Months of retained imports | 5.5 | 4.1 | 4.4 | 3.4 | 5.7* |
| *External debt* | | | | | |
| Total external debt (US$ billion) | 29.0 | 33.9 | 39.0 | 60.3 | 38.3[b] |
| percent of GDP | 40.0 | 38.9 | 39.3 | 61.6 | 54.0[b] |
| Private external debt[c] (% of total) | 31.8 | 33.0 | 33.3 | 35.7 | 40.2[b] |
| Public external debt[c] (% of total) | 49.5 | 47.9 | 40.5 | 38.6 | 42.2[b] |
| Short-term external debt (US$ billion) | 5.4 | 6.5 | 10.2 | 15.5 | 6.8[b] |
| Debt service ratio | 5.5 | 6.6 | 6.9 | 6.2 | 5.8[b] |
| *Exchange rates* | | | | | |
| RM/US$ (end-period) | 2.6 | 2.5 | 2.5 | 3.9 | 3.8* |
| NEER (1990=100, period average) | 110.3 | 110.3 | 113.7 | 110.6 | 84.9[d] |
| REER (1990=100, period average) | 102.2 | 102.7 | 107 | 104.5 | 82.8[d] |

*Note:* a. EPU estimates.  b. September 1998.  c. Medium- and long-term.  d. January–October 1998, IFS.   * Actual
*Source:* Economic Planning Unit, Prime Minister's Office.

shows mixed results with almost an equal number of firms experiencing an improvement and a deterioration of performance. In terms of employment, all categories of firms employ fewer workers today as a result of the crisis, but exporting, foreign-controlled, and large firms exhibit this trend to a greater degree. In terms of availability of credit since the onset of the crisis, only about a quarter of the firms that rely on local banks found credit less accessible, reflecting that the problem of credit inaccessibility was not widespread. It is also noted that borrowing from local banks continues to be a major source of financing after the crisis, second only to sales revenue.

The first part of the paper sets out the framework of the survey. The paper then follows by evaluating the impact of the crisis on firm output, profitability, export performance, and employment. It then deals specifically with the effect of the crisis on the surveyed firms' financial position. The subsequent section outlines the policy responses by the government, and the paper concludes by alluding to the perception of the firms regarding immediate term prospects.

## Framework of the survey

The survey was limited to firms in the manufacturing sector, that being the leading sector of the economy, contributing 35.7 percent of the GDP in 1997. Thus, the recovery of the economy will largely depend on the revival of growth in the manufacturing sector. The survey covers six major subsectors within manufacturing—namely, electrical and electronics; textiles, garments and footwear; food and beverages; chemicals, rubber and plastic products; construction-related manufacturing; and auto parts—as shown in table 12.2. The six subsectors were identified on the basis of their importance in terms of their value added and exports. They constitute 83 percent of the manufacturing value added and 87 percent of total manufactured exports. The sampling frame was selected from the list of 2,300 firms used in the Linkages and Technology Development (ILTD) Study conducted in 1997. This was done so as to complement the ILTD study and reduce the survey time while meeting the requirements of the current survey. A total of 1,500 firms were selected and to ensure that the sample was representative, a cross-section of large, medium-size and small firms; and domestic- and export-oriented firms were included. The ownership and location factors were also taken into account in constructing the sample. A total of 850 firms (57 percent) responded.

In terms of sectoral distribution, 26 percent of the firms within the sample were from textiles and garments; 22 percent from the food and beverages subsector; 17 percent from electrical and electronics; 17 percent from chemicals; and the remaining from the construction-related and auto parts subsectors (see table 12.3).

In terms of size based on the number of workers employed, 24 percent of the firms were large[1] and the rest medium and small. The electrical and electronics subsector followed by the chemical subsector had the biggest number of large firms, while textile and apparel followed by the food subsector had the biggest number of small firms. As much as 19 percent of the large and 17 percent of the medium and small firms were new firms.[2]

Of the total number of firms selected, 47 percent were export-oriented,[3] with the largest number in electrical and electronics, followed by the chemical subsector. In the category of highly export-oriented industries[4] were largely electrical and electronics, and chemicals sectors; whereas in the category of moderately export-oriented were mostly auto parts and chemicals.[5] As much as 47 percent of both the old and new firms were export-oriented, suggesting that there is no direct relationship between the age of the firm and its export orientation. It was also noted that both export-oriented and domes-

### TABLE 12.2
**Manufacturing sectoral weights, 1997**

| Subsector | Legend | Percent to GDP | Percent to Exports |
|---|---|---|---|
| 1 | Food & beverages | 3.2 | 1.8 |
| 2 | Textiles, garments & footwear | 1.9 | 3.4 |
| 3 | Construction-related | 4.3 | 3.7 |
| 4 | Industrial chemicals, rubber & plastic products | 8.1 | 5.5 |
| 5 | Electrical machinery & electronics | 10.5 | 53.8 |
| 6 | Auto parts | 1.7 | 2.2 |
| | Total | 29.7 | 70.4 |
| Manufacturing sector | | 35.7 | 81.0 |

Source: World Bank, Firm-Level Survey.

### TABLE 12.3
### Characteristics of the sample

| | By employment size[a] | | By export orientation | | By value of exports[b] | | | By foreign control[c] | | | FDI firm | | Average no. of employees | Total no. of firms |
|---|---|---|---|---|---|---|---|---|---|---|---|---|---|---|
| | Jan–Aug 1998 | | | | | | | | | | | | Jan–Aug 1998 | |
| | Large | Small | Nonexporters | Exporters | High | Medium | Small | None | Some | Total | No | Yes | | |
| *Sector* | | | | | | | | | | | | | | |
| 1. Food & beverages | 20 | 158 | 127 | 61 | 17 | 26 | 6 | 166 | 13 | 9 | 164 | 24 | 71 | 188 |
| 2. Textiles, garments & footwear | 41 | 174 | 154 | 70 | 44 | 15 | 2 | 198 | 6 | 20 | 196 | 28 | 158 | 224 |
| 3. Construction-related | 30 | 86 | 60 | 62 | 27 | 22 | 5 | 103 | 10 | 9 | 99 | 23 | 137 | 122 |
| 4. Industrial chemicals, rubber & plastic products | 44 | 84 | 50 | 92 | 39 | 36 | 10 | 77 | 23 | 42 | 74 | 68 | 180 | 142 |
| 5. Electrical machinery & electronics | 63 | 68 | 44 | 99 | 62 | 20 | 3 | 60 | 6 | 77 | 58 | 85 | 411 | 143 |
| 6. Auto parts | 8 | 19 | 14 | 16 | 3 | 8 | 4 | 20 | 9 | 1 | 19 | 11 | 248 | 30 |
| Total | 206 | 589 | 449 | 400 | 192 | 127 | 30 | 624 | 67 | 158 | 610 | 239 | 165 | 849 |
| *Age* | | | | | | | | | | | | | | |
| New[d] | 40 | 96 | 78 | 70 | 39 | 17 | 3 | 101 | 8 | 39 | 100 | 48 | 191 | 148 |
| Old | 167 | 483 | 369 | 330 | 153 | 108 | 28 | 522 | 59 | 118 | 509 | 190 | 182 | 699 |
| *Location* | | | | | | | | | | | | | | |
| Outside capital | 167 | 497 | 391 | 323 | 157 | 99 | 23 | 527 | 52 | 135 | 518 | 196 | 168 | 714 |
| Within capital[e] | 40 | 84 | 56 | 79 | 36 | 27 | 8 | 97 | 15 | 23 | 92 | 43 | 268 | 135 |

*Note:*
a. "Large" if total employment is 150 workers or more; "Small" if less than 150 workers.
b. Exports of most important product.
c. "None" if foreign ownership is less than 10 percent of equity; "Some" if 10 percent or more but less than 50 percent; and "Total" if 50 percent or more.
d. Established in 1990 and thereafter.
e. Includes firms located in the Selangor state.
*Source:* World Bank, Firm-Level Survey.

tic-oriented firms are largely located outside Kuala Lumpur and the neighboring state, Selangor.

In terms of ownership, 19 percent of the firms in the sample were foreign owned,[6] 8 percent had some foreign equity, and the rest were local firms. A total of 66 percent of the firms that were foreign controlled or had some foreign equity were in electrical-electronics and chemical subsectors, while 88 percent of the local firms were in the textiles and food subsectors.

The highest average number of employees was for the firms in the electrical and electronics subsector, followed by the auto parts and chemical subsectors.

## Impact of the crisis on the firms

The survey shows that in general, the firms were adversely affected by the crisis in terms of output, profitability, and export performance, and were compelled to reduce the number of workers as a result.

## Capacity utilization

All firms were operating at a lower capacity in the first half of 1998, reflecting a decline in output when compared with 1996 as well as with the first and second half of 1997 (see figure 12.1). In total, the level of capacity utilization declined to 66 percent in the first half of 1998 from 78 percent in the first half of 1997. It is noted, however, that capacity utilization had in fact begun to decline even before the crisis—as seen in the first half of 1997. The fall in the level of capacity utilization in the first half of 1998 when compared with the first half of 1997 was largest for auto parts (23 percentage points), followed by construction-related manufacturing (20 percentage points), and textiles and electrical (12 percentage points). The fall in capacity utilization in these subsectors correlates with the decline in their output as reflected by the manufacturing production index published by the Department of Statistics, Malaysia.

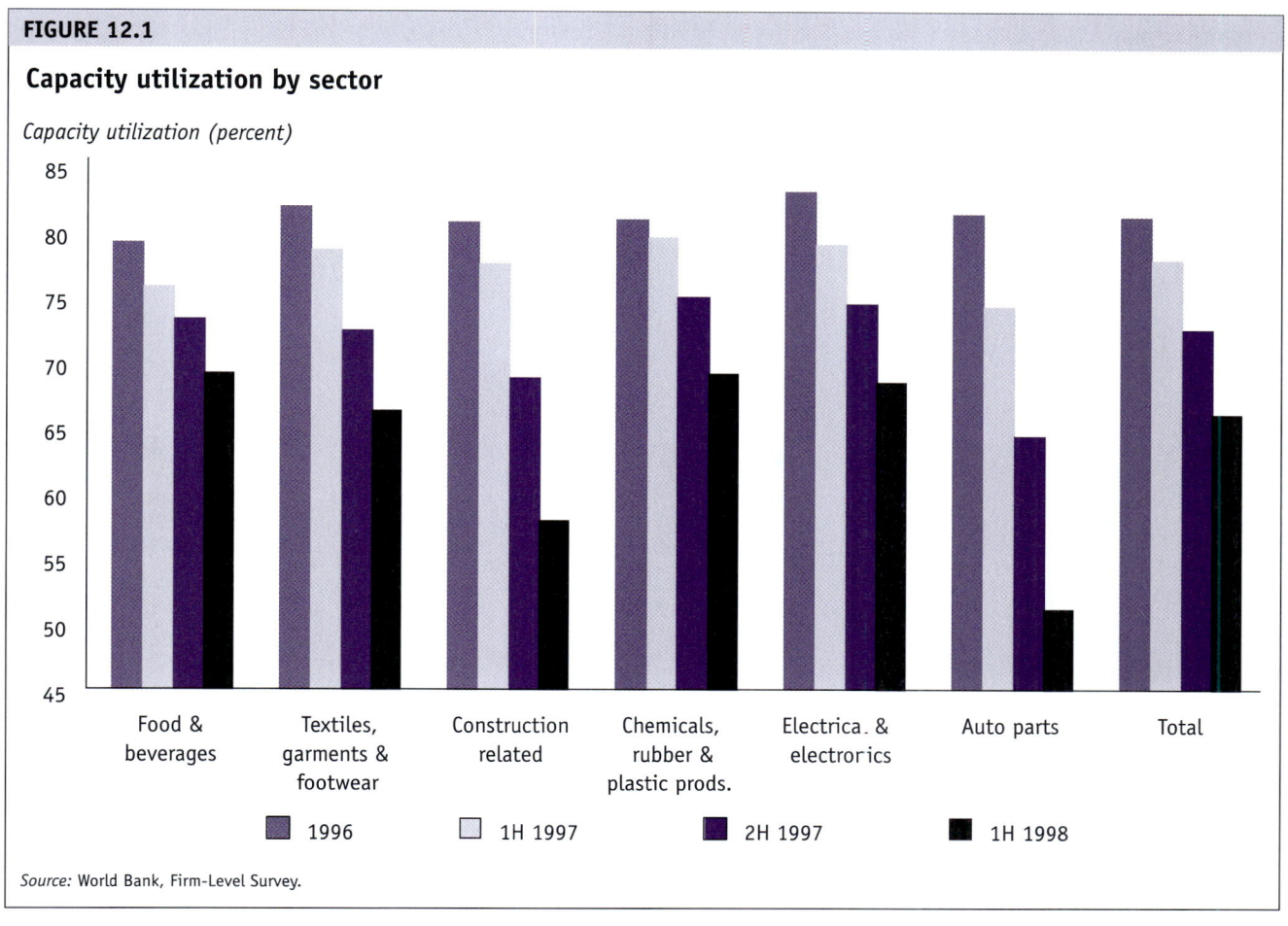

**FIGURE 12.1 Capacity utilization by sector**

Source: World Bank, Firm-Level Survey.

The reduction in the construction-related subsector is also reflective of the negative growth rate registered for the construction sector since the onset of the crisis.

In assessing the major causes for the decline in output, it is noted that exporting firms attributed the fall to higher input prices arising from the depreciation of the ringgit, the drop in both domestic and foreign demand, and the higher interest rate (see figure 12.2). Insufficient credit and shortage of inputs were not perceived as major causes of output decline. Nonexporting firms, by contrast, attributed the cause of output decline largely to a fall in domestic demand and the depreciation of the ringgit, and similar to exporting firms, perceived supply constraints as minor problems.

## Net profitability

In general, the net profitability of firms measured in terms of the average net profit-equity ratio declined from 69 percent in 1997 to 47 percent in the first half of 1998,[7] as shown in figure 12.3. With the exception of food and beverages,[8] all subsectors recorded a decline in net profitability in the first half of 1998 compared with 1997 and 1996. Food and beverages is also the only subsector in which net profitability has increased steadily since 1996. In contrast, firms in the chemicals, rubber and plastic products, and auto parts subsectors, have witnessed on average a constant decline in their net profitability since 1996. When comparing the first half of 1998 with 1997, the most drastic decline in net profitability was for construction-related materials (71 percent) followed by electrical and electronics (54 percent).[9] An analysis in terms of the characteristics of the firms shows that exporting firms were more severely affected than those not exporting.

## Export performance

A total of 44 percent of the firms reported an improvement in export performance in the first half of 1998

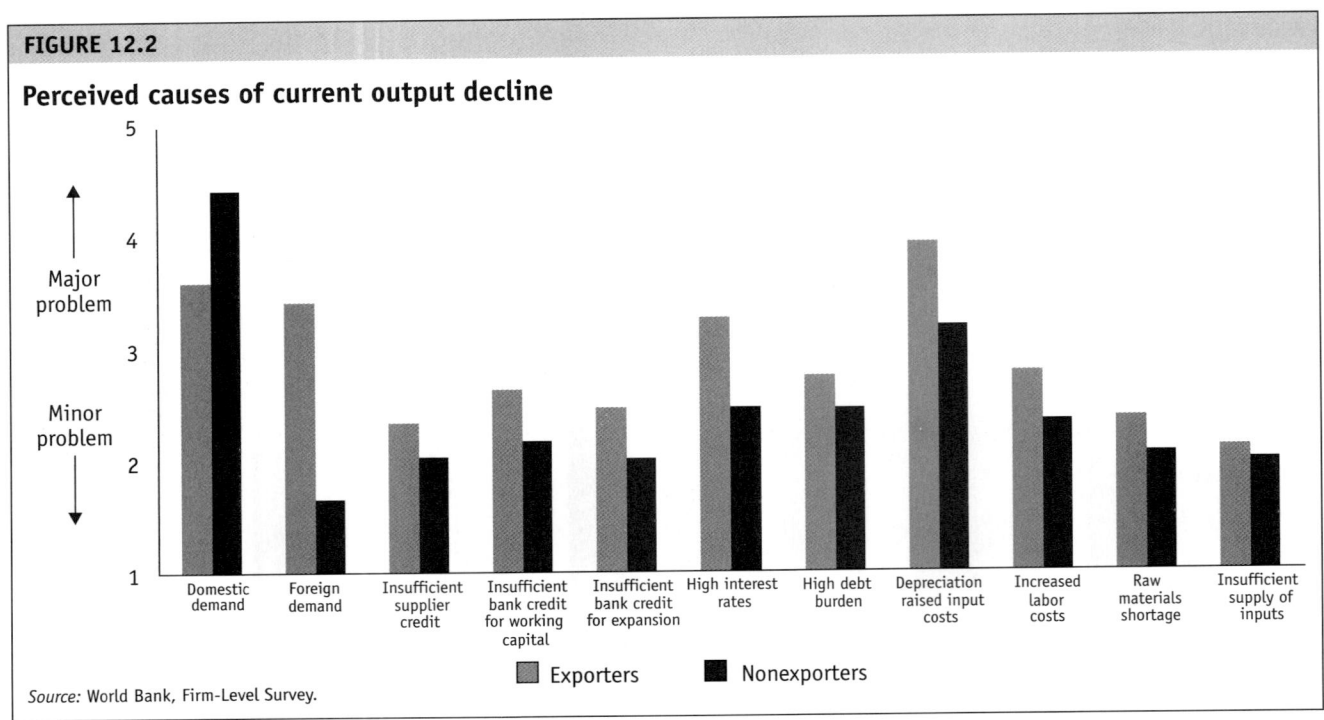

**FIGURE 12.2**

**Perceived causes of current output decline**

Source: World Bank, Firm-Level Survey.

when compared with 1997; 42 percent reported that it had worsened, while the rest declared that there was no change (see figure 12.4). The results of the survey imply that there was no distinct correlation between the type of industry and export performance. Within each type of industry, a significant number of firms witnessed an

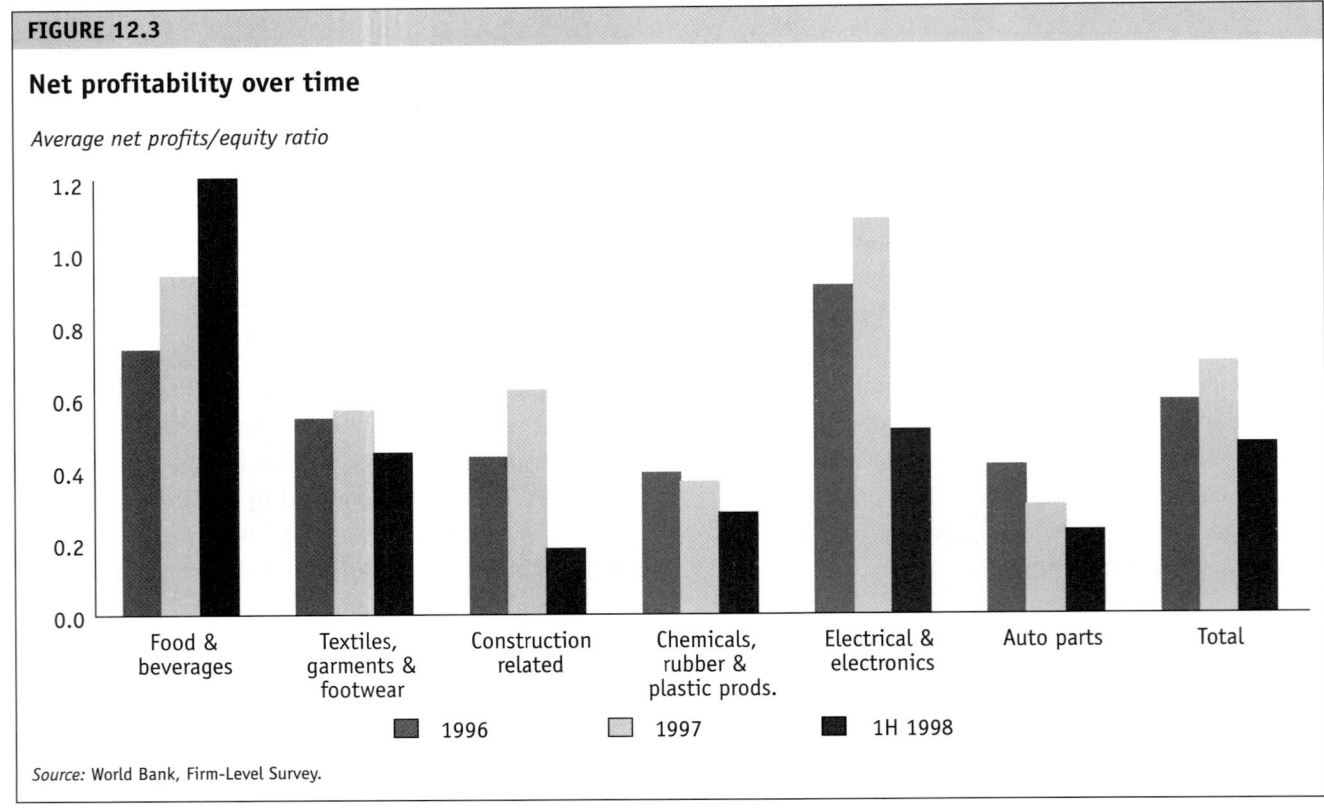

**FIGURE 12.3**

**Net profitability over time**

*Average net profits/equity ratio*

Source: World Bank, Firm-Level Survey.

182   Asian Corporate Recovery: Findings from Firm-Level Surveys in Five Countries

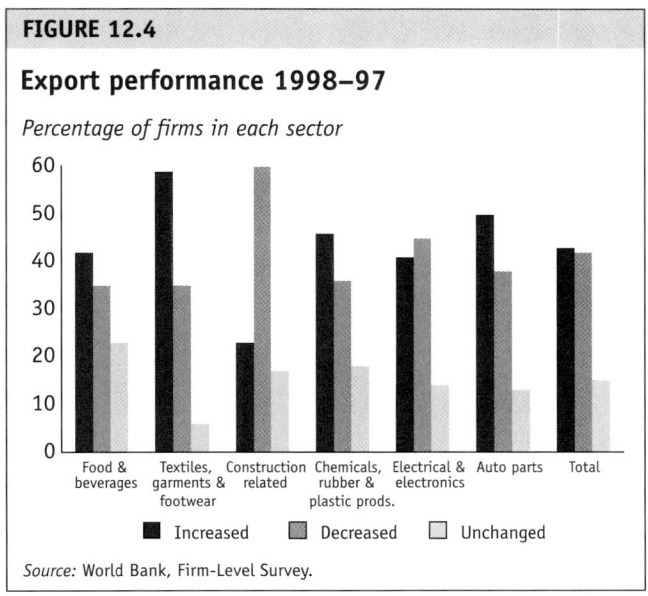

**FIGURE 12.4**

**Export performance 1998–97**

*Percentage of firms in each sector*

Source: World Bank, Firm-Level Survey.

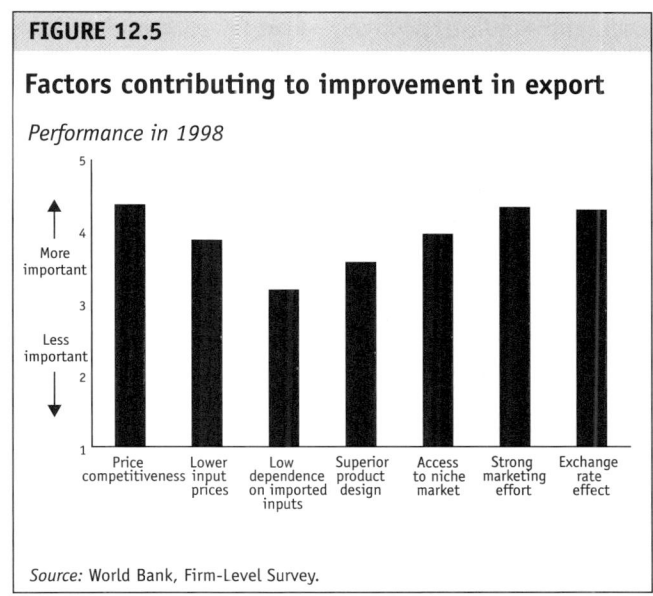

**FIGURE 12.5**

**Factors contributing to improvement in export**

*Performance in 1998*

Source: World Bank, Firm-Level Survey.

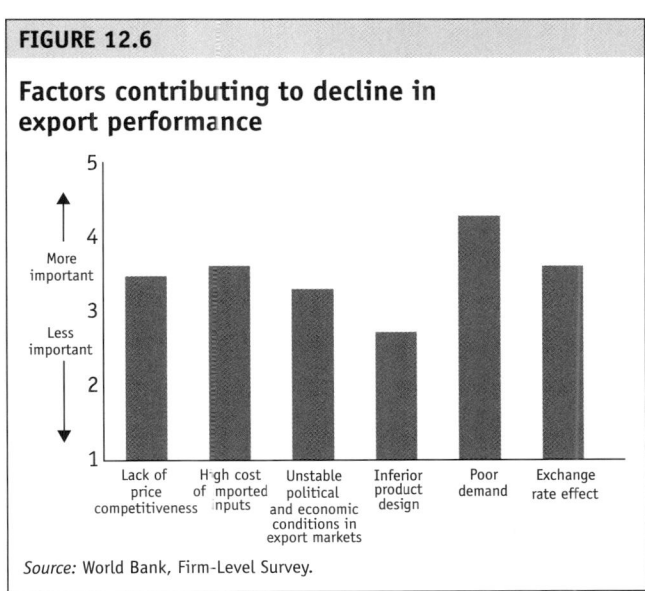

**FIGURE 12.6**

**Factors contributing to decline in export performance**

Source: World Bank, Firm-Level Survey.

improvement in export-performance—as was the case for those that saw a decline. It is noted, however, that the subsector with the highest percentage of firms that experienced an improvement in its export performance was textiles, garments and footwear (59 percent), followed by the auto parts subsector (50 percent). Meanwhile, the subsector with the highest percentage of firms reporting a decline in its export performance was construction-related (60 percent) followed by electrical and electronics (45 percent).[10]

The firms that recorded improvements in export performance attributed the increase in export revenue primarily to price competitiveness, as well as strong marketing efforts and valuation gains arising from the depreciation of the ringgit (see figure 12.5). By contrast, the firms that experienced a decline in their export performance assigned it mainly to poor demand, lack of price competitiveness, and the high cost of imported inputs, as shown in figure 12.6.

## The competitor's profile

The competitor's profile has not changed significantly with the crisis. On average, about 74 percent of the firms continue to perceive other domestic producers as their biggest competitor (see figure 12.7a). While only the remaining 26 percent consider firms outside the country as the biggest competitor for the domestic market, firms from neighboring countries continue to be viewed as the dominant competitor internationally (see figure 12.7b). In addition, an increasing number of firms have come to perceive low-cost producer countries as the biggest competitor, while a smaller number of firms perceive newly industrialized countries (NICs) as the biggest competitor.

## Employment

Overall, 32 percent of the firms at the time of the survey were employing fewer workers relative to before the crisis,[11] as shown in table 12.4. It is observed that a larger percentage of firms that are export-oriented, foreign-controlled and large—as opposed to nonexporting, local, and small, respectively—had fewer workers after the crisis, indicating that a larger number of jobs might have been lost in the former types of firms (see figure 12.8).

In terms of the category of workers, on average, the highest percentage of retrenchments were for production workers, both skilled and unskilled as shown in figure 12.9. Apart from retrenchments, some firms resorted to reducing the length of the work week and imposing pay cuts as shown in figure 12.10.

## Impact of the crisis on the financial position of the firms

### Sources of financing

Prior to the crisis, the sources of short- and long-term financing for the surveyed firms had predominantly been sales revenue loans from local banks. This remains the case to a large extent (see figures 12.11a and 12.11b). The firms continue to depend on their sales turnover (about 56 percent) and on local banks (about 28 percent) to meet both their short-term and long-term financing needs. The reliance on the bond and equity markets to raise long-term financing was less than 1 percent—and it has fallen further after the crisis, reflecting the potential for further development of the capital market in Malaysia.

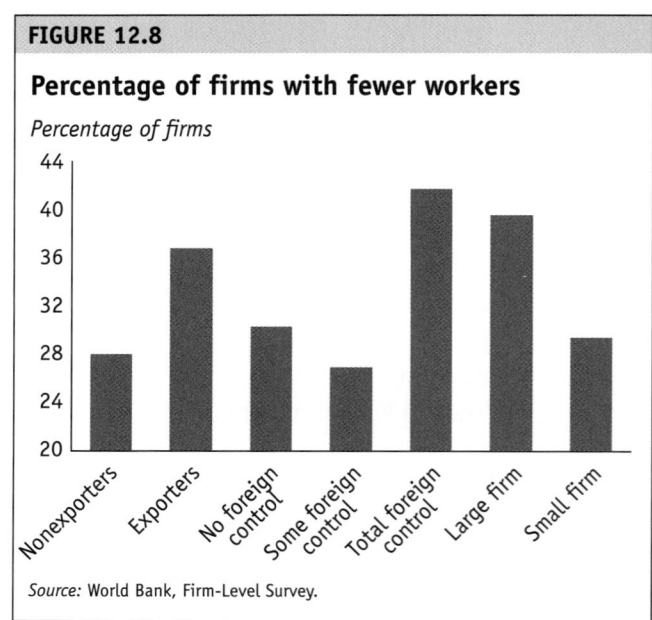

### Reliance on debt

The firms' reliance on debt—measured in terms of average debt–equity ratio—in the first half of 1998 was higher compared with 1997, but lower than it had been in 1996 (see figure 12.12). The higher debt-equity ratio in the first half of 1998 compared with 1997 is attributable to the large increase in liabilities.

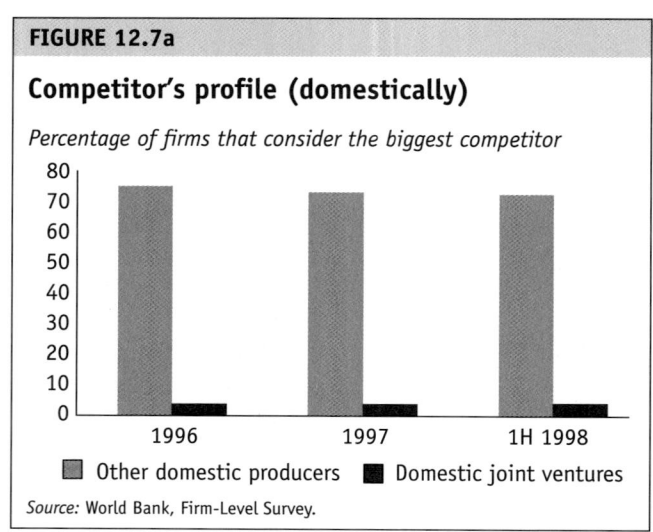

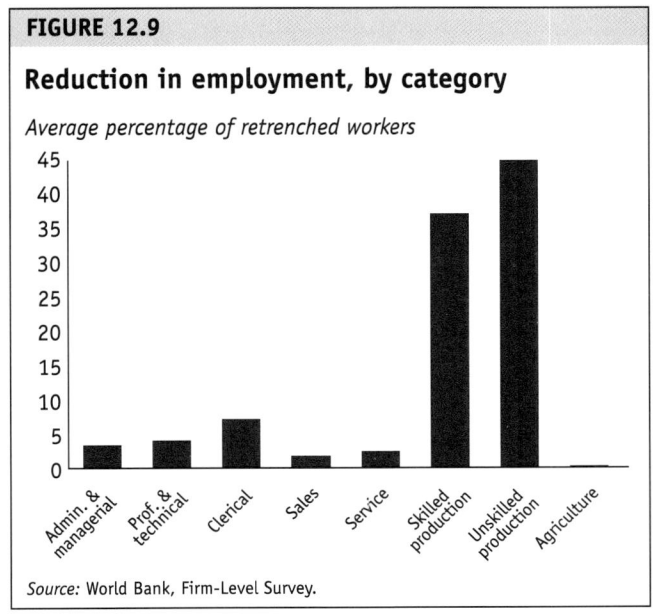

**FIGURE 12.9**

**Reduction in employment, by category**

*Average percentage of retrenched workers*

Source: World Bank, Firm-Level Survey.

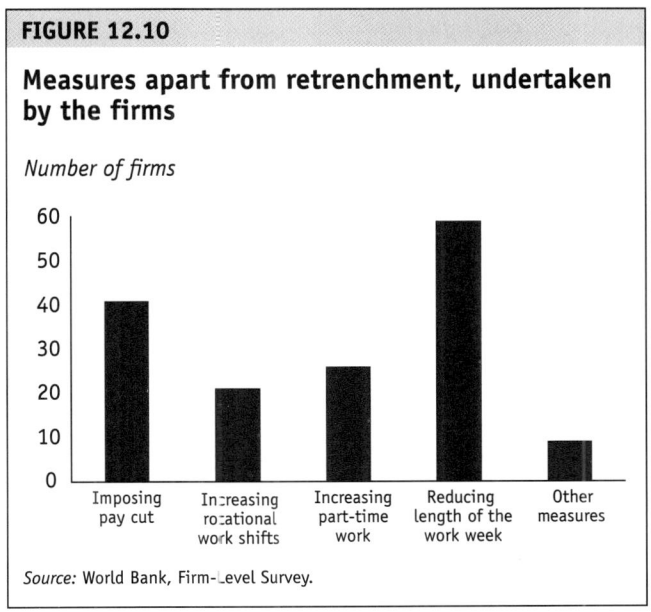

**FIGURE 12.10**

**Measures apart from retrenchment, undertaken by the firms**

*Number of firms*

Source: World Bank, Firm-Level Survey.

**FIGURE 12.11a**

**Sources of short- and long-term financing (before the crisis)**

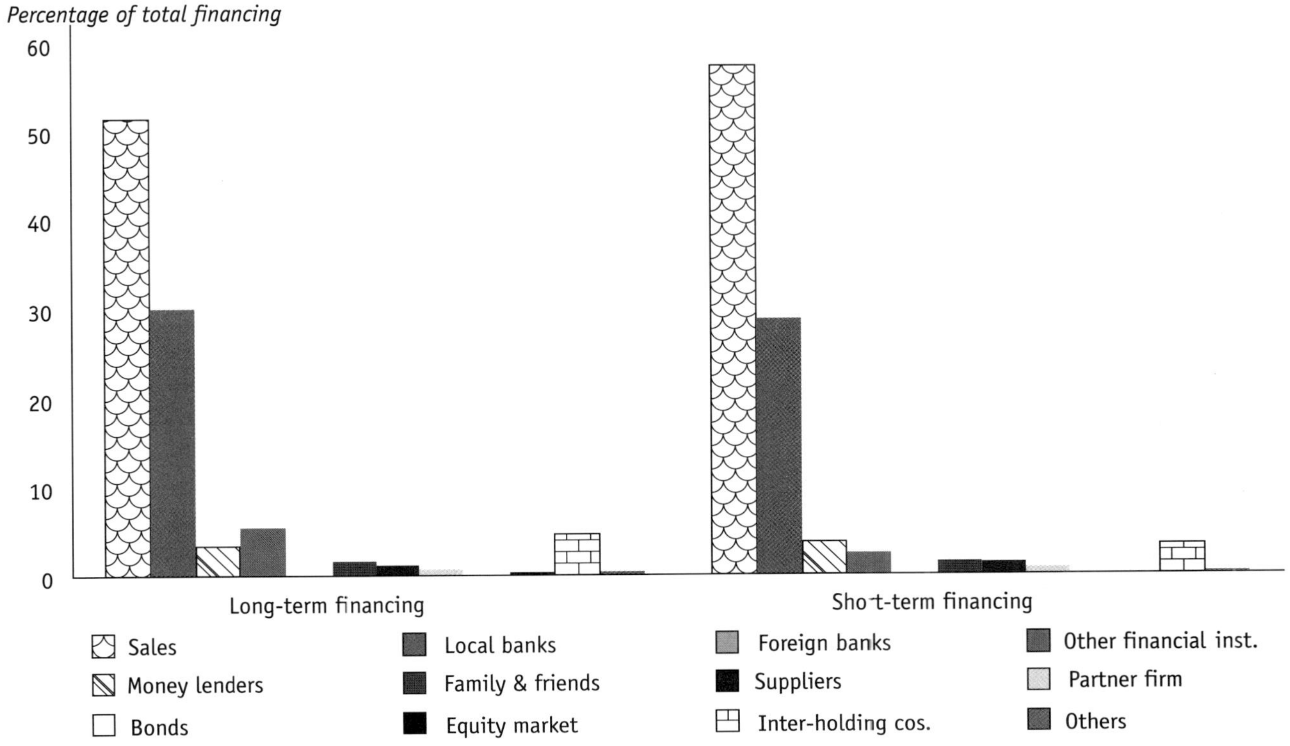

*Percentage of total financing*

- Sales
- Money lenders
- Bonds
- Local banks
- Family & friends
- Equity market
- Foreign banks
- Suppliers
- Inter-holding cos.
- Other financial inst.
- Partner firm
- Others

Source: World Bank, Firm-Level Survey.

### FIGURE 12.11b
**Sources of short- and long-term financing (after the crisis)**

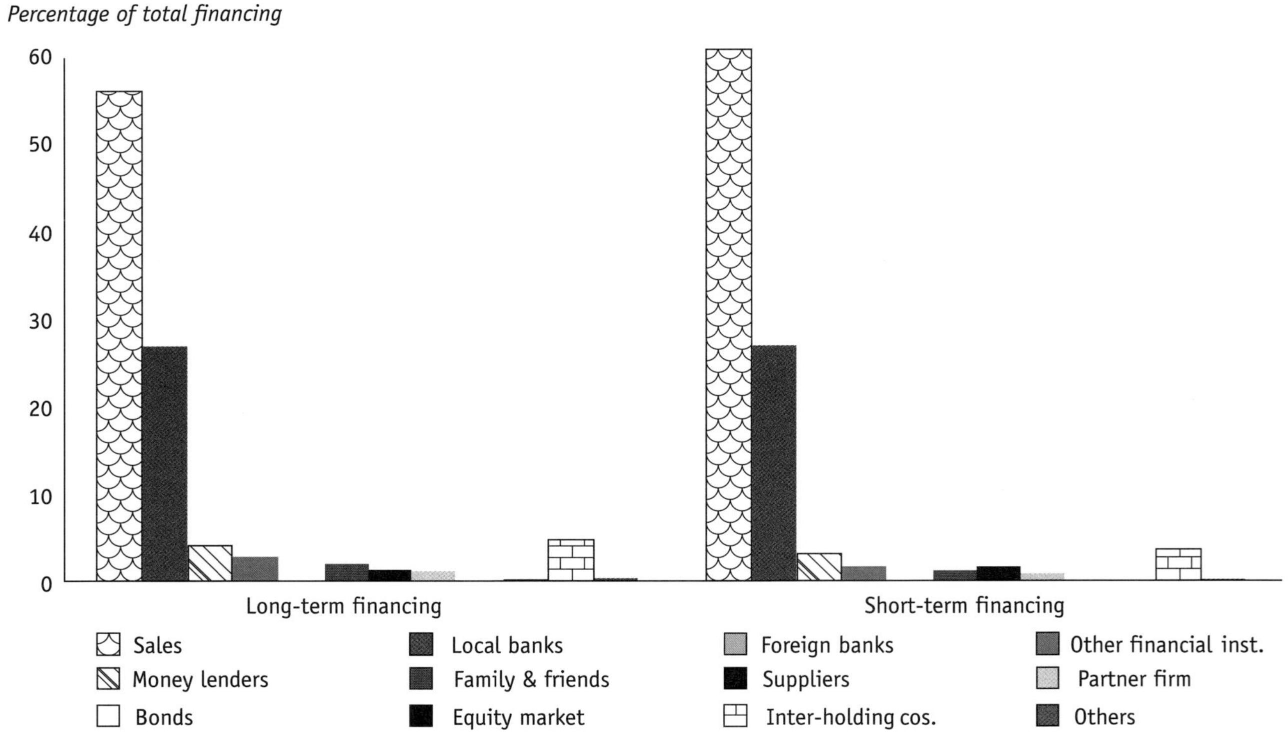

*Percentage of total financing*

Source: World Bank, Firm-Level Survey.

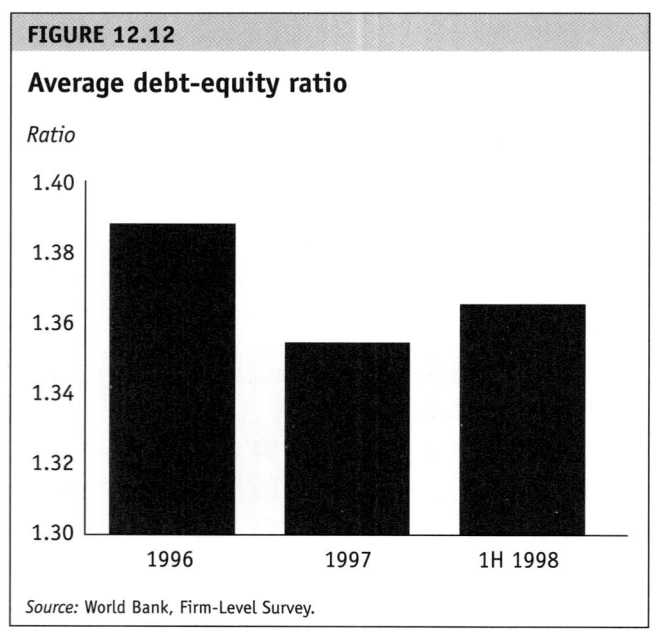

### FIGURE 12.12
**Average debt-equity ratio**

Source: World Bank, Firm-Level Survey.

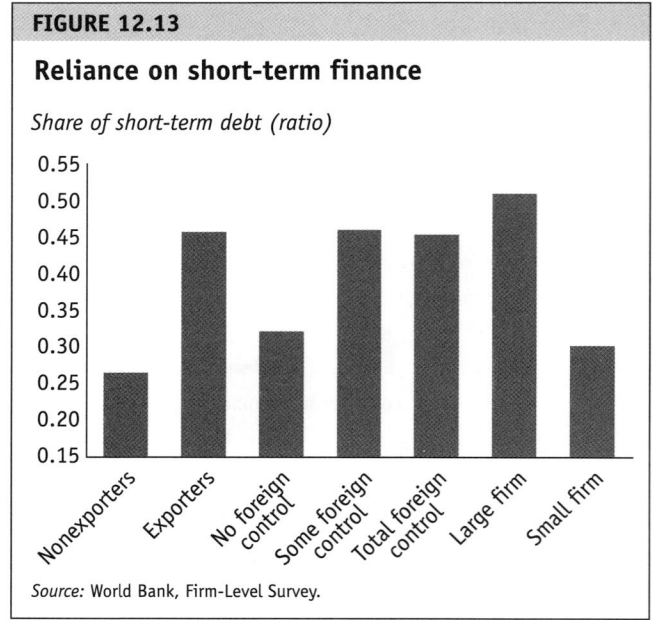

### FIGURE 12.13
**Reliance on short-term finance**

Source: World Bank, Firm-Level Survey.

## TABLE 12.4
### Firm profiles, first half of 1998

| | Borrow in foreign currency | | By employment size[a] | | By export orientation | | By foreign control[b] | | | FDI firm | | Total |
|---|---|---|---|---|---|---|---|---|---|---|---|---|
| | No | Yes | Large | Small | Nonexporters | Exporters | None | Some | Total | No | Yes | |
| **Financial indicators** | | | | | | | | | | | | |
| Short-term debt/ Total financing ratio | 0.31 | 0.61 | 0.51 | 0.30 | 0.27 | 0.46 | 0.32 | 0.46 | 0.45 | 0.32 | 0.46 | 0.36 |
| Long-term debt/ Total financing ratio | 0.69 | 0.39 | 0.49 | 0.70 | 0.73 | 0.54 | 0.68 | 0.54 | 0.55 | 0.68 | 0.54 | 0.64 |
| Debt/Equity ratio | 1.16 | 2.43 | 1.87 | 1.14 | 0.96 | 1.63 | 1.22 | 1.52 | 1.80 | 1.24 | 1.62 | 1.37 |
| **Firm characteristics** | | | | | | | | | | | | |
| No. of employees | 111 | 672 | 584 | 41 | 50 | 338 | 97 | 278 | 501 | 90 | 432 | 184 |
| Share that export (percent to total firms in each category) | 40.1 | 96.7 | 84.5 | 32.7 | — | — | 33.7 | 73.1 | 90.5 | 32.8 | 84.5 | 47.3 |
| Share that are FDI (percent to total firms in each category) | 20.8 | 71.4 | 56.0 | 17.0 | 8.3 | 50.2 | 2.2 | 100.0 | 100.0 | — | — | 28.2 |
| **Response to the crisis** | | | | | | | | | | | | |
| Current capacity utilization (percent) | 64.8 | 71.7 | 72.7 | 64.0 | 63.6 | 68.9 | 64.9 | 64.1 | 71.8 | 65.0 | 69.1 | 66.2 |
| Share with fewer workers (percent to total firms in each category) | 28.8 | 44.0 | 39.6 | 29.4 | 28.0 | 36.8 | 30.3 | 26.9 | 41.8 | 29.8 | 38.1 | 32.2 |
| Optimistic for future growth (% to total firms in each category) | 22.4 | 26.4 | 31.4 | 20.8 | 18.6 | 28.6 | 21.3 | 34.3 | 26.6 | 21.5 | 28.0 | 23.3 |

—: not available.
Note:
a. "Large" if total employment is 150 workers or more; "Small" if less than 150 workers.
b. "None" if foreign ownership is less than 10 percent of equity; "Some" if 10 perccent or more but less than 50 percent; and "Total" if 50 percent or more.
Source: World Bank, Firm-Level Study.

The proportion of short-term to total debt in general was 36 percent, as shown in table 12.4. In terms of the distribution of short-term debt, it is observed that exporting, foreign-controlled, and large firms as opposed to nonexporting, local, and small firms rely to a greater extent on short-term financing, with the former's share of short-term debt to total debt close to 50 percent (see figure 12.13).

## Availability of credit

It is observed in general that after the crisis, the firms found the availability of credit from local banks—and to a lesser extent from suppliers—to be more restrictive relative to other sources as shown in figure 12.14.[12] Only a small percentage of the firms (less than 10 percent) found access to credit from foreign banks less forthcoming. It is noted, however, that even in the case of local banks, the percentage of firms that found it more restrictive was less than 25 percent. This implies that while there was some credit squeeze, the problem may not be as widespread or as severe as has generally been perceived,[13] at least in the manufacturing sector.

## The adequacy of working capital

The structure of working capital did not change after the crisis. The firms, on average, continued to rely predominantly on their retained earnings (64 percent) to finance their working capital as shown in figure 12.15, while bank loans only constituted 25 percent. On average by June 1993, across sectors, almost 75 percent of

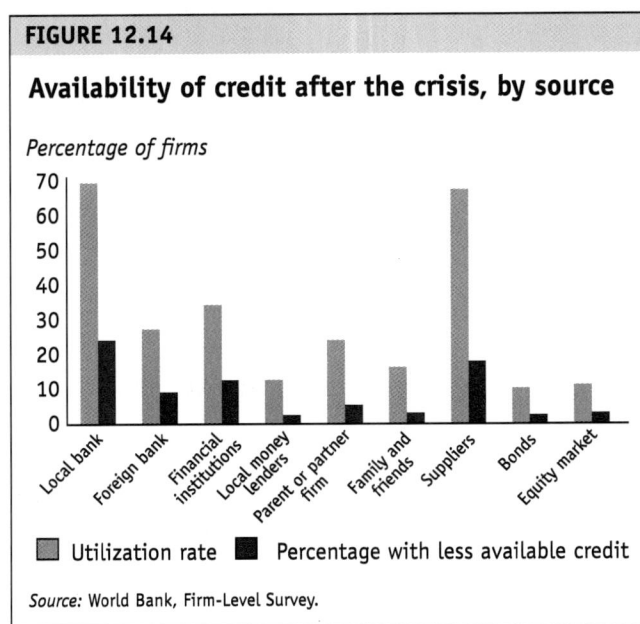

**FIGURE 12.14**

**Availability of credit after the crisis, by source**

*Source:* World Bank, Firm-Level Survey.

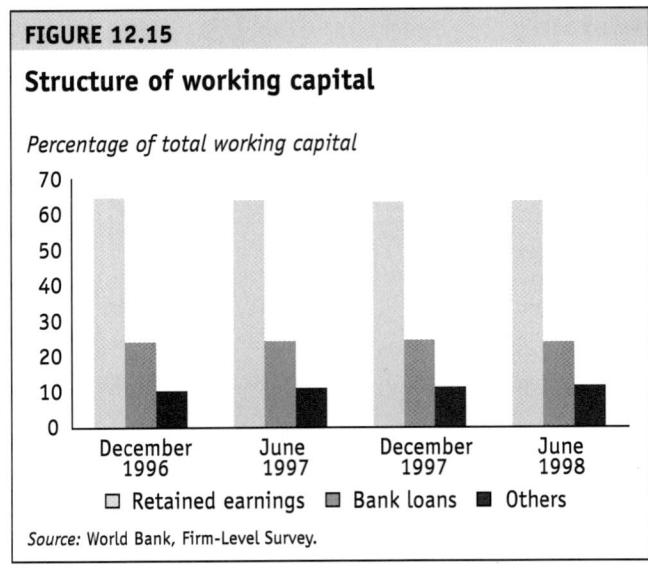

**FIGURE 12.15**

**Structure of working capital**

*Source:* World Bank, Firm-Level Survey.

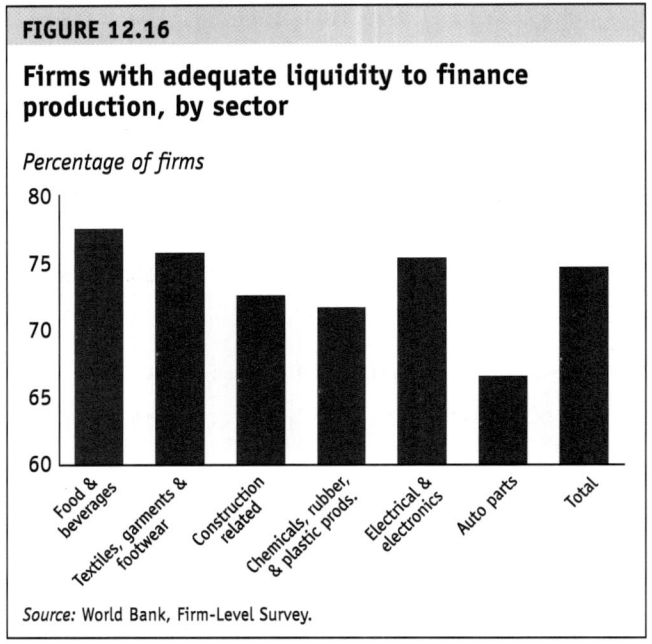

**FIGURE 12.16**

**Firms with adequate liquidity to finance production, by sector**

*Source:* World Bank, Firm-Level Survey.

the firms reported that they had adequate liquidity to finance production, as shown in figure 12.16. Broken down by sector, the highest percentage of firms with adequate liquidity was in food and beverages (78 percent) while the lowest was for auto parts (67 percent).

## The policy response

The government introduced a series of policy packages in line with the changing circumstances during the course of the crisis. Initially, the government tightened both its fiscal and monetary policy in order to address the concerns about inflationary pressure and the persistent current account deficit in the balance of payment. Subsequently, in mid-1998 the government relaxed both its fiscal and monetary policy when economic activities began to slow down, with the objective of reactivating economic growth. At that time, the threat of inflationary pressure had abated and the current account of the balance of payments was beginning to improve. The major policy initiatives, particularly those targeted at reviving the performance of the corporate sector, are summarized below. The measures address the issues of accessibility to credit, stimulating output and exports, and employment.

### Measures to improve accessibility to credit and reduce debt service burden

The following are measures taken to improve credit accessibility and reduce debt service burden:

(a) Reducing the statutory reserve ratio from 13.5 percent of eligible liabilities to 4 percent to address the issue of tight liquidity, thereby making available more funds for bank lending;

(b) Reducing *Bank Negara Malaysia's* (BNM) three-month intervention rate so as to reduce the cost of funds and the debt service commitment of firms and promote investment activities;

(c) Setting up *Pengurusan Danaharta Nasional Bhd.*,[14] an asset management company, to acquire and manage non-performing loans (NPLs) of banking institutions, so that banks can focus on lending to viable corporate ventures;

(d) Setting up Danamodal Nasional Bhd.[15] to recapitalize banking institutions so as to restore their lending capacity and facilitate the process of consolidation. The capital injections are in the form of equity and hybrid instruments, and investment decisions are based on market principles;

(e) Setting up the Corporate Debt Restructuring Committee (CDRC)[16] to facilitate voluntary corporate debt restructuring. The CDRC is intended to minimize losses to creditors, shareholders, and other stakeholders through voluntary coordinated workouts; to preserve viable businesses that have suffered during the current economic slowdown; and implement a comprehensive framework for debt restructuring;

(f) Exempting the construction of residential properties costing less than RM250,000 from the 20 percent limit on lending, which is imposed on the broad property sector;

(g) Requiring banking institutions to achieve a minimum loan growth rate of 8 percent by the end of 1999 to ensure continued funding for viable ventures;

(h) Reclassifying the default period for NPLs by banking institutions from 3 to 6 months so as to give some breathing space to the corporate sector;

(i) Requiring banking institutions to establish Loan Rehabilitation Units to facilitate more intensive management of problem loans; and

(j) Setting up new and increasing budget allocations for existing specialized funds monitored by BNM to ensure accessibility to credit at reasonable cost to the small and medium-size enterprises (SMEs) and selected economic sectors. Among the specialized funds involved are the New Entrepreneur's Fund, Fund for Food (Production) and Fund for SMEs.

## Measures to promote economic activity

The following are measures taken to promote economic activity:

(a) Relaxing the equity guidelines in the manufacturing sector (excluding certain activities), so that all applications received between 31 July 1998 and 31 December 2000 are to be exempted from both equity and export conditions, implying that project owners can hold 100 percent equity and will not need to meet any export requirements;

(b) Providing tax exemption on 70 percent of statutory income arising from the increased value of export sales for companies granted "international trading status" that are at least 70 percent Malaysian-owned or using local facilities such as insurance, shipping and ports, and are registered with the Malaysia External Trade Development Corporation (MATRADE);

(c) Exempting stamp duty for the refinancing of loans for business purposes in order to reduce the cost of doing business;

(d) Abolishing excise duty on refrigerators, televisions, and air conditioners to improve the competitiveness of local firms;

(e) Providing group tax relief for companies engaged in food production, based on certain criteria;

(f) Allocating 200 million Malaysian ringgit (RM) for a new micro-credit scheme to provide assistance to petty traders and hawkers in urban areas. This scheme targets the poor and lower income group, which may have suffered a drop in real income as a result of higher prices and retrenchment. For this purpose, the government has established *Tabung Usahawan Kecil,* which provides funding facilities up to a maximum of RM20,000 and *Tabung Ekonomi Kumpulan Usaha Niaga,* which will be expanded nationwide to provide loans up to a maximum of RM10,000. Both of these funds cater to the financial needs of small entrepreneurs; and

(g) Allowing *Bumiputera* (indigenous) companies facing financial difficulties as a result of the drop in share value to sell their shares to non-*Bumiputera* on a win-win basis.

## Measures related to the labor market

The following are measures taken to deal with issues related to the labor market:

(a) Encouraging the corporate sector to increase investment in export-oriented industries, thereby generating additional employment opportunities;

(b) Amending the Employment Act 1955 to encourage employers to institute part-time employment or flexible working hours and introducing guidelines on retrenchment that include pay cuts and reducing working hours (or days) and shifts instead of retrenchment;

(c) Setting up an electronic labor exchange for the registration, monitoring, and placement of workers to facilitate greater mobility;

(d) Initiating a special fund of RM5.0 million under the Human Resource Development Fund (HRDF) to provide financing for the retraining of retrenched workers;

(e) Recrediting unclaimed training funds by the HRDF to companies to encourage them to undertake training and retraining of their workers;

(f) Exempting companies from contributing to the training levy for a certain period; and

(g) Setting up a graduate entrepreneur scheme to provide basic training in entrepreneurship for the purpose of developing entrepreneurs among unemployed graduates.

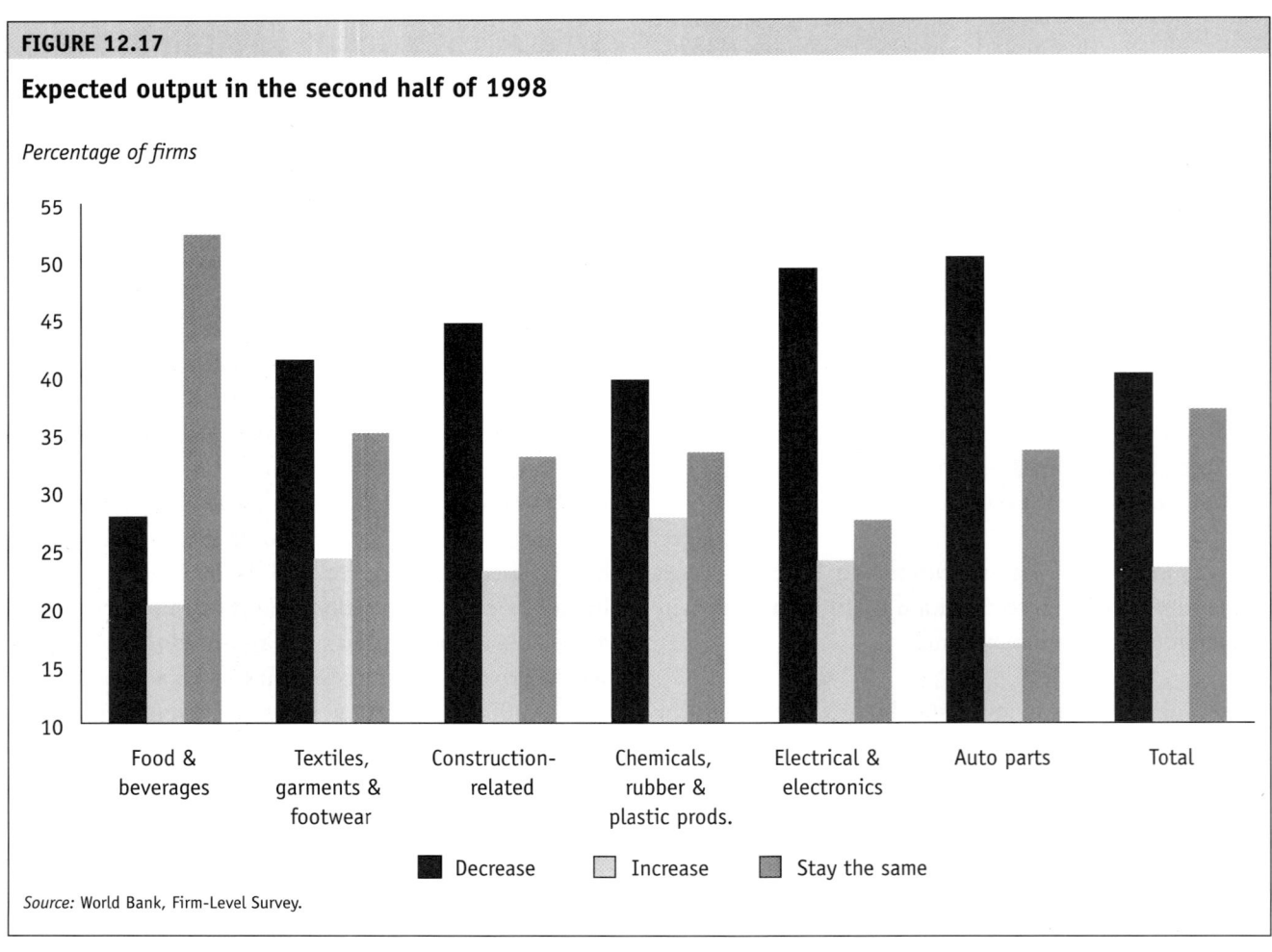

**FIGURE 12.17**

**Expected output in the second half of 1998**

*Source:* World Bank, Firm-Level Survey.

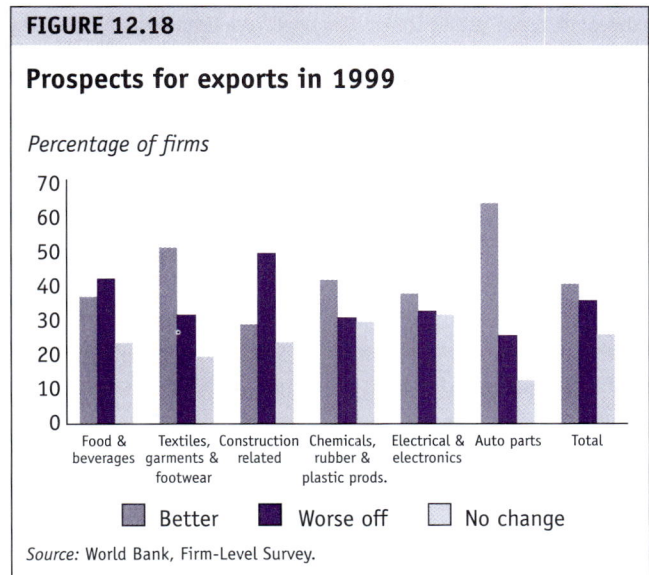

FIGURE 12.18

**Prospects for exports in 1999**

Source: World Bank, Firm-Level Survey.

## Conclusion

The results of the survey show that the Asian financial crisis had a negative impact on all firms. The nature and extent of the impact of the crisis, however, varied (albeit slightly) depending on the characteristics of the firms. In general, all firms experienced a reduction in output, while their export performance was mixed.

At the point of conducting the survey in mid-1998, the perception of the firms regarding their prospects for the next six months was not very encouraging. However, the firms, in general, felt that the prospects for an improvement in export performance in 1999 was better than for a recovery in output (see figures 12.17, 12.18, and 12.19). With respect to their output, 23 percent of the firms expected it to increase over the second half of 1998, 37 percent expected it to remain the same, while the remaining were pessimistic. In terms of subsectors, rubber and plastic products and chemicals

FIGURE 12.19

**Current account (percentage to GDP) and index of exports (1990=100)**

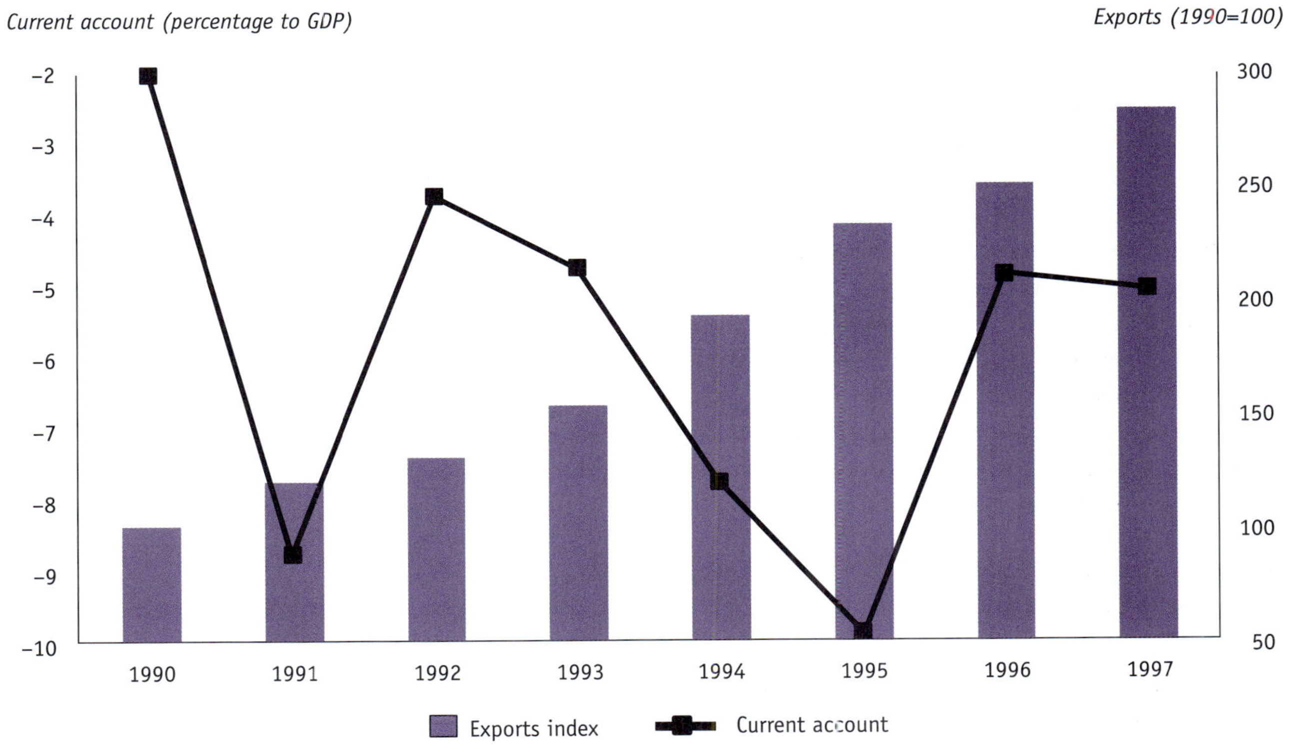

Source: Economic Planning Unit, Prime Minister's Office.

involved the highest percentage of firms that expressed optimism, while auto parts were produced by the largest percentage of firms that expressed pessimism.

In terms of the prospects for exports in 1999, 40 percent of the firms expected an improvement, 25 percent foresaw no change, while the rest believed that exports would decline. Ranked by subsector, auto parts had the highest percentage of firms that envisaged an improvement in export performance, followed by textiles, garments and footwear, while the construction-related subsector had the highest percentage of firms that were pessimistic.

More recent trends in macroeconomic and financial indicators show, however, that signs of recovery are already becoming evident, mainly in response to the measures introduced since mid-1998. Malaysia is projected to achieve a turnaround and register a positive growth in 1999. The growth of the manufacturing sector is also expected to revert to a positive.

## Notes

1. The term "large firms" refers to those employing 150 and more workers; while "medium and small" refers to those employing less than 150.

2. The term "new firms" refers to those established in 1990 and thereafter.

3. "Export-oriented" refers to firms that export some of their output.

4. "Highly export-oriented" refers to firms that derive more than 50 percent of their sales revenue from exports.

5. "Moderately export-oriented" refers to firms that derive 5 or more but less than 50 percent of their sales revenue from exports.

6. The term "foreign-owned firms" refers to those with foreign equity of 50 percent or more, "some foreign equity" refers to those with more than 10 but less than 50 percent foreign equity, and "local" firms are those with less than 10 percent foreign equity.

7. The assessment of net profitability is based on the responses from only 157 firms or 24 percent of the sample size, as the rest did not answer this question. The conclusions derived, therefore, should be viewed with caution.

8. The increase in the net profit–equity ratio for food and beverages is attributed to an increase in net profits. The increase in net profits may be supported by the fact that the value of food exports (including animal and vegetable oils and fats) increased significantly, close to 50 percent in 1998 compared with 1997. The increase in value is attributed mainly to valuation gains from the depreciation of the ringgit. Furthermore, owing to the less elastic nature of demand for this product, its domestic sales may not have been severely affected.

9. The drastic reduction in the net profits–equity ratio for firms in construction-related materials and electrical and electronics is attributable to the combined effect of a decline in net profits and an increase in equity.

10. National Trade Statistics show that the value of exports in terms of the ringgit increased by 41 percent during January–June 1998 compared with the corresponding period in 1997, and the value for 1998 as a whole was about 30 percent higher than that for 1997. The value of exports increased for all the six subsectors covered by the survey. Significant increases in export value were recorded for selected construction-related materials such as iron and steel, nonferrous metal; food and beverages; and textile and apparel.

11. Principal features of the Employment Policy :
- In Malaysia, wages are determined by market forces and are closely linked to worker productivity and company performance. There is no policy defining a minimum wage, except for vulnerable occupations such as shop assistants and stevedores.
- Employment Legislation, among others:
  – Stipulates basic requirements on terms and conditions of service including hours of work, overtime, overtime payments, and benefits including termination benefits, annual leave, public holiday, sick leave, limit on pay deductions, and minimum standard of housing (for those employers providing housing).
  – Provides protection for women and children.
  – Provides avenues for resolving disputes through the referral of cases to the Labour Court, Industrial Relations Department, and the Industrial Court.
  – Provides for the right to organize, which is governed by the Trade Union Act 1959.
  – Provides for social security mainly through the Social Security Act of 1969. It provides protection to workers for contingencies such as employment injuries, occupational diseases, permanent disability, death, and promotes accident prevention and work safety. Among the social security schemes are the Employment Injury Scheme and Invalidity Pension Scheme.

12. A total of 24 percent of the firms that use credit from local banks found it more restrictive, while 18 percent of the firms that use supplier credit found access to supplier credit more restrictive.

13. This finding is supported by the response to a related question that required the firms to answer "yes" or "no" to whether a bank or financial institution declined to grant a loan to them. Only 14 percent of the firms had their loans rejected during the first half of 1998, 10 percent during the second half of 1997, and 6 percent during the first half of 1997. Data at the macroeconomic level, however, appear to indicate the presence of a credit squeeze from the supply side particularly during the first half of 1998, when total outstanding loan

growth from commercial banks (including loans for the manufacturing sector) decelerated rapidly and the interest rate spread widened. Notwithstanding, it must be noted that the decline in loan growth may also have been in response to a decline in demand for credit as the firms were cutting back on output because of falling demand and deferring investments owing to increasing underutilized capacity.

14. As of 31 December 1998, Danaharta had acquired 8.1 billion Malaysian ringgit in gross value of nonperforming loans and managed, on behalf of Bank Negara Malaysia, 11.6 billion ringgit in gross value of nonperforming loans. Excluding what was acquired from offshore banks and development finance institutions, the amount of NPLs that were acquired and managed represents approximately 22 percent of the total NPLs in the banking system based on the six-month classification. This also amounts to 4.8 percent of the total loan portfolio in the banking system.

15. As of 17 March 1999, Danamodal had injected a total of RM6.2 billion into ten banking institutions in the form of exchangeable subordinated capital loans.

16. As of 15 March 1999, the CDRC had received 46 applications involving more than RM24.7 billion.

## chapter thirteen

# The Impact of the Southeast Asian Financial Crisis on the Philippine Manufacturing Sector

Mario B. Lamberte
Caesar B. Cororaton
Margarita F. Guerrero
Aniceto C. Orbeta

There already exists a plethora of studies on the sad performance of the Philippine economy in the wake of the Asian financial crisis.[1] However, most, if not all, of these studies have examined the impact of the crisis from a macroeconomic perspective. Certainly the crisis' impact will vary based on the size of a firm and the economic sector it is in; accordingly, different firms will have different responses to the crisis. Fairly detailed and accurate knowledge of these issues can greatly help in fine-tuning the government policies and programs designed for staging a rapid economic recovery in the short term. This, however, requires good firm-level survey data. Such data had been unavailable prior to this study, which attempts to analyze the impact of the Southeast Asian financial crisis on the Philippine industry and the industry's initial responses to the crisis to stay alive. The data for this study come from a sample of manufacturing firms.

Although the study uses purely descriptive analyses, the results it yields can provide insights that are useful for policy formulation.[2] The survey results clearly show that the capacity utilization rate of Philippine enterprises started to decline even before the crisis struck in July 1997, and it continued to drop as the crisis deepened. This, however, varied across sectors, with the electrical machinery sector being the hardest hit in the most recent period. Nonexporters and small firms were more adversely affected by the crisis compared with exporters and large firms. The firms' net profitability declined along with the capacity utilization rate. Although labor layoffs could not be avoided under this unfavorable circumstance, a large proportion of the firms resorted to other measures, such as cutting down on work hours and days, to preserve some jobs.

The structure of the firms' sources of short- and long-term funds did not significantly change before and after the crisis—reliance to a great extent on income from sales and bank loans to finance operations being the general trend. The overall average debt-equity ratio inched up a little in 1997, but declined in the first half of 1998 as the firms reduced their outstanding debt. At the time of the survey, the share of short-term debt in total financing had not changed substantially in the last two and a half years. On the whole, there seems to be no clear evidence of a supply-side credit crunch, as most firms—regardless of how they are classified, whether by sector, export orientation, or size—claimed to have continued access to credit during the crisis period. Also, most claimed that they had not encountered a liquidity problem during the crisis period. What is worrisome, though, is that an overwhelming majority was pessimistic about business prospects for the next six months.

The following section gives a brief description of the survey of the Philippine industry and a few of the characteristics of the sample firms. The paper then examines issues pertaining to the impact of the crisis on surveyed firms and their views on the causes of the crisis. Another section discusses issues related to the firms' main sources of funding, debt structure, transparency, and policy environment. This is followed by a brief discussion on the firms' assessment of the prospects of their business in the short term. The last section offers concluding remarks and suggests some policies.

## Description of the survey

The *Survey of Philippine Industry and the Asian Financial Crisis* covered establishments engaged in the following manufacturing industries: food products, textiles, apparel and footwear, chemical and rubber products, and electrical machinery.

More detailed descriptions of each sector in terms of the 1994 *Philippine Standard Industrial Classification* are given in annex A. These particular manufacturing sectors are among the top 10 contributors to manufacturing output. In addition, electrical machinery (the sector that includes semiconductors and electronics) and food products sectors rank high among both import-dependent and export-oriented industries.

Standard sampling methodology for Philippine establishment surveys utilize a *List of Establishments* (LE) compiled and updated by the National Statistics Office (NSO). The sampling frame of the survey of Philippine industry was the 1997 updated version of the LE, which included about 3,800 establishments belonging to the five sectors covered by the survey. Food products (32 percent) and apparel and footwear (29 percent) comprised 61 percent of the total number of relevant establishments. In terms of employment size, 68 percent of firms in the sampling frame are listed as having less than 100 workers. Over half of the establishments in the sampling frame are located in the National Capital Region (NCR).

Based on the list, establishments were independently selected from each sector with a goal of spreading the sample across the five sectors roughly equally. The number of engaged workers was used as a stratification variable—a greater number of samples were selected from establishments with more than 100 workers. A simple random sample was drawn within each stratum. Annex B shows the percentage distribution of establishments by sector and classes in the frame and in the resulting sample selected.

The questionnaire consisted of two separate forms. Form 1 was designed to elicit responses from interviews with the sample establishments' chief executive officers. Form 2 was designed as a self-accomplishing schedule for personnel officers, production managers, or financial managers. The questionnaires were fielded from September 1998 to January 1999 by the NSO.

This report is based on the responses of 541 establishments out of a targeted number of 750. Food products, apparel and footwear, and electrical machinery sectors are about equally represented in the set of respondents, with textiles and chemical products having half that number (see table 13.1). This is attributable to the fact that most of the establishments for these two sectors were contacted much later and the retrieval rate was thus lower.

The responding firms had an average number of 388 employees in 1996. Small establishments (defined as those with employment in 1996 of less than 150) dominated the food products and textiles sectors with 57 and 64 percent shares, respectively. Apparel and footwear and electrical machinery sectors are both equally represented in terms of size.

Fifty-six (56) percent of the responding firms were located outside the NCR. More likely than not (65.3 percent of the time) the respondent firms were "old"—in other words, established prior to 1990.

Establishments in the electrical machinery and electronics sector employed more workers than any other sector, averaging about 643 workers. Establishments of "older" firms had more employees than new ones, and establishments located outside the NCR had more employees than those in the NCR.

Exporters comprised 51.9 percent of the sample respondents. For "new" firms and those located outside the NCR, there were more exporters (56 and 58 percent, respectively) than nonexporters but both groups were evenly represented among "older" firms. Among manufacturing sectors, food products and chemicals had more nonexporters; the reverse is true for apparel and footwear and the electrical machinery sectors.

About 53 percent of exporters may be considered as "high" volume exporters—that is, exports comprise more than 50 percent of their sales. Except for the food products and chemicals sectors, in which more firms were small- or medium-volume exporters (meaning, exports comprised less than 50 percent of sales), high-volume exporters dominated all sectors. This is most evident in the electrical machinery sector, which includes the "electronics" sector in which 71 percent were high-volume exporters.

A firm is defined as having "no foreign control" if foreign equity comprises less than 10 percent of the firm's equity. If foreign equity accounts for at least 50 percent of the equity, the firm is said to be under "total foreign control." About 21 percent of the responding firms were under total foreign control. For all sectors, the majority of the firms had "no foreign control." Only 8 percent of the food products sector were under total foreign control, but this figure rose to 39.3 percent in the electrical machinery sector. The proportion of firms with large foreign equity was greater among new firms. Because most industrial estates and technological parks

TABLE 13.1
**Profile of responding firms**

| | By size | | By export orientation | | By volume of exports | | | By foreign control | | | Average number of employees | Total |
|---|---|---|---|---|---|---|---|---|---|---|---|---|
| | Large | Small | Exporters | Nonexporters | Small | Medium | High | None | Some | Total | | |
| Sector | | | | | | | | | | | | |
| Food | 59 | 78 | 51 | 82 | 24 | 8 | 19 | 113 | 13 | 11 | 384 | 137 |
| Textiles | 28 | 49 | 39 | 37 | 14 | 4 | 21 | 58 | 8 | 11 | 242 | 77 |
| Apparel | 61 | 62 | 78 | 42 | 30 | 4 | 44 | 78 | 16 | 29 | 331 | 123 |
| Chemicals | 47 | 40 | 38 | 49 | 19 | 7 | 12 | 62 | 8 | 17 | 250 | 87 |
| Electrical machinery | 59 | 58 | 70 | 46 | 17 | 3 | 50 | 62 | 9 | 46 | 643 | 117 |
| Age | | | | | | | | | | | | |
| New | 71 | 105 | 98 | 77 | 39 | 2 | 57 | 96 | 19 | 61 | 330 | 176 |
| Old | 183 | 182 | 178 | 179 | 65 | 24 | 89 | 277 | 35 | 53 | 413 | 365 |
| Location | | | | | | | | | | | | |
| NCR | 113 | 125 | 105 | 131 | 34 | 19 | 52 | 188 | 22 | 28 | 429 | 238 |
| Others | 141 | 162 | 171 | 125 | 70 | 7 | 94 | 185 | 32 | 86 | 342 | 303 |
| Total | 254 | 287 | 276 | 256 | 104 | 26 | 146 | 373 | 54 | 114 | 388 | — |

—: not available.
*Source:* World Bank, Firm-Level Survey.

are located outside the NCR, it is understandable that more firms outside the NCR had large foreign equity.

Table 13.2 gives a quick look at the profile of the sample firms using 1996 data, except for information referring to the firms' responses to the crisis. The information contained in this table will be the main focus of discussion presented in the subsequent sections of this study.

## Analysis of the impact of the crisis on the firms

### Capacity utilization

The period from 1996 to the first half of 1998 saw a continuous decline in the capacity utilization rate in the manufacturing sectors covered by the survey. From an average high of 78 percent for all sectors in 1996, the rate declined to an average of 69 percent in the first half of 1998 (see figure 13.1).

The performance varied across sectors. Of the five manufacturing sectors, the apparel sector attained the highest capacity utilization rate in 1996 of 82 percent, while the food and textile sectors registered the lowest rate of 75 percent. In the first half of 1998, all sectors experienced a drop. From a high of 82 percent in 1996, the highest rate declined to only 71 percent (the chemical sector) in the first half of 1998. Similarly, the lowest capacity utilization rate dropped from 75 percent in 1996 to 66 percent (the food sector) in the same period.

The percentage changes in the capacity utilization of different sectors that are season-independent can also be computed from figure 13.1. The first half of 1997 had already seen a significant decline in the capacity utilization rate (–3.4 percent relative to the 1996 average for all sectors), with apparel and leather as the worst performer experiencing a –5.5 percent change. Food products also did poorly, reducing the rate by 5.1 percent during the first half of 1997.

Although the decline continued in the second half of 1997, it was not as deep as in the first half. On average, it dropped by only 2.3 percent relative to the first half of the same year.

The results seem to suggest that the recessionary effect took its toll on the Philippine industrial sector during the first half of 1998. The capacity utilization rate declined on average by 6.5 percent relative to the previous period. The worst performer was the electrical machinery sector whose rate shrank by 10.8 percent.

The survey results also show the difference between the capacity utilization rates of exporters and nonexporters—results indicate that the latter were hit harder by the crisis compared to the former. For example, in 1996, exporters and nonexporters had a rate of 78.2 percent and 77.2, respectively. In the first half of 1998, the rate of the latter was down to 65.2 percent, while that of the former decreased to 71.9 percent.

### TABLE 13.2
### Profile of firms

| | Borrow in foreign currency | | Size | | Export orientation | | Foreign control | | | FDI firm | | |
|---|---|---|---|---|---|---|---|---|---|---|---|---|
| | Yes | No | Large | Small | Exporters | Nonexporters | None | Some | Total | Yes | No | Total |
| *Financial indicators* | | | | | | | | | | | | |
| Short-term debt/Total financing | 0.33 | 0.26 | 0.31 | 0.31 | 0.31 | 0.30 | 0.32 | 0.38 | 0.26 | 0.19 | 0.26 | 0.31 |
| Long-term debt/Total financing | 0.27 | 0.15 | 0.23 | 0.24 | 0.22 | 0.25 | 0.25 | 0.24 | 0.17 | 0.30 | 0.31 | 0.23 |
| Debt-equity ratio | 2.95 | 1.57 | 2.19 | 2.32 | 2.14 | 2.66 | 3.00 | 2.79 | 1.41 | 1.65 | 3.00 | 2.27 |
| *Firm characteristics* | | | | | | | | | | | | |
| Number of employees | 485 | 285 | 711 | 58 | 608 | 190 | 283 | 625 | 692 | 668 | 267 | 406 |
| Share that export (percent) | 64 | 36 | 65 | 35 | — | — | 50 | 12 | 38 | 55 | 45 | |
| Share that are FDI (percent) | 34 | 22 | 40 | 15 | 84 | 16 | 5 | 12 | 38 | — | — | |
| *Response to the crisis* | | | | | | | | | | | | |
| Current capacity utilization (percent) | 78 | 77 | 79 | 76 | 78 | 77 | 77 | 84 | 79 | 81 | 76 | 78 |
| Share with few workers (percent) | 69 | 31 | 50 | 50 | 47 | 53 | 72 | 10 | 18 | 29 | 71 | 41 |
| Optimistic of future growth (percent) | 59 | 41 | 28 | 26 | 31 | 23 | 25 | 35 | 30 | 32 | 25 | 27 |
| Total | 61 | 39 | 47 | 53 | 52 | 48 | 69 | 10 | 21 | 34 | 66 | — |

—: not available.
*Source:* World Bank, Firm-Level Survey.

## FIGURE 13.1
## Capacity utilization

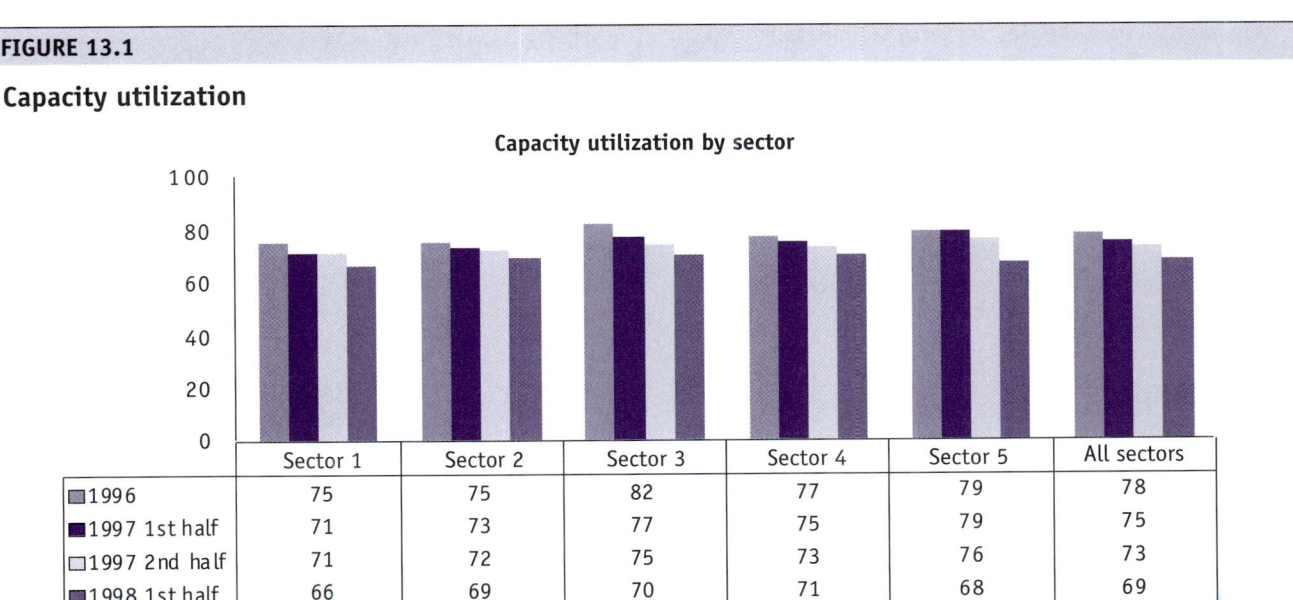

Capacity utilization by sector

|  | Sector 1 | Sector 2 | Sector 3 | Sector 4 | Sector 5 | All sectors |
|---|---|---|---|---|---|---|
| 1996 | 75 | 75 | 82 | 77 | 79 | 78 |
| 1997 1st half | 71 | 73 | 77 | 75 | 79 | 75 |
| 1997 2nd half | 71 | 72 | 75 | 73 | 76 | 73 |
| 1998 1st half | 66 | 69 | 70 | 71 | 68 | 69 |

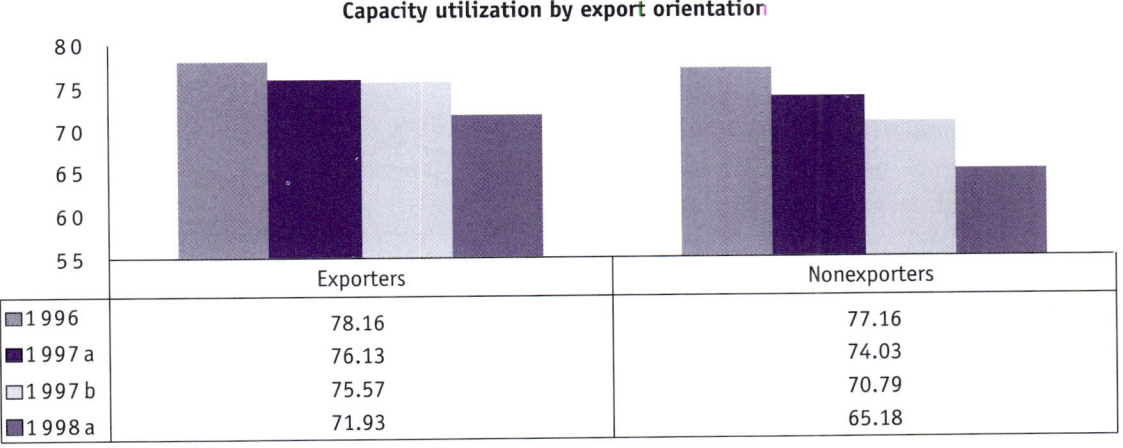

Capacity utilization by export orientation

|  | Exporters | Nonexporters |
|---|---|---|
| 1996 | 78.16 | 77.16 |
| 1997 a | 76.13 | 74.03 |
| 1997 b | 75.57 | 70.79 |
| 1998 a | 71.93 | 65.18 |

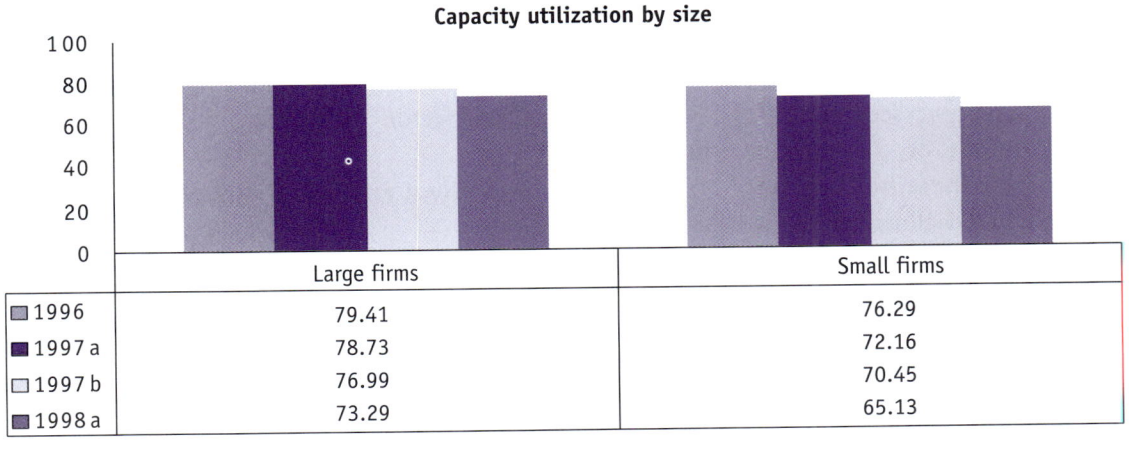

Capacity utilization by size

|  | Large firms | Small firms |
|---|---|---|
| 1996 | 79.41 | 76.29 |
| 1997 a | 78.73 | 72.16 |
| 1997 b | 76.99 | 70.45 |
| 1998 a | 73.29 | 65.13 |

*Source:* World Bank, Firm-Level Survey.

Figure 13.1 also divides the sample firms into two categories: large and small. Based on the trend, it would appear that small firms were hit harder than the large ones. In 1996, small firms had a capacity utilization rate of 76.3 percent. In the first half of 1998, their rate dropped to 65.7 percent (or a decline of 13.9 percent). The drop for large firms was only 9.4 percent over the same period: from 79.4 percent in 1996 to 72 percent in the first half of 1998.

## Profitability

The continuous drop in the firms' capacity utilization rate translated into poor performance in terms of net profitability. From a high of 12.1 percent in 1996, net profitability of the sample firms dropped dramatically to 3.5 percent in 1997 and to 2.1 percent in the first half of 1998 (see figure 13.2).

The average profitability of the firms classified according to export orientation and size shows a consistently declining trend for the last two and a half years. Among the five sectors, the food and electrical machinery sectors exhibited a consistently declining net profitability during this period, while the textile, apparel, and chemical sectors showed a fluctuating profitability.

## Sectoral performance versus broader sector performance

Table 13.3 presents indicators of the general macroeconomic environment in the Philippines during the period of analysis. Real GNP growth reached a peak of 7.8 percent in the third quarter of 1996, subsequently decelerated, and started to contract in the second quarter of 1998. In the fourth quarter of 1998, real GNP contracted by 1.2 percent (see figure 13.3).

The overall output of the manufacturing sector started to contract in the second quarter of 1998. By the fourth quarter, it had declined by 3.4 percent.

In terms of the sectors covered in the study, only apparel registered an improvement in real growth in the gross value added. In particular, this sector registered a peak of 18.2 percent in the second quarter of 1998. The rest of the sectors, however, slowed down considerably—including the electronics sector. The electronics

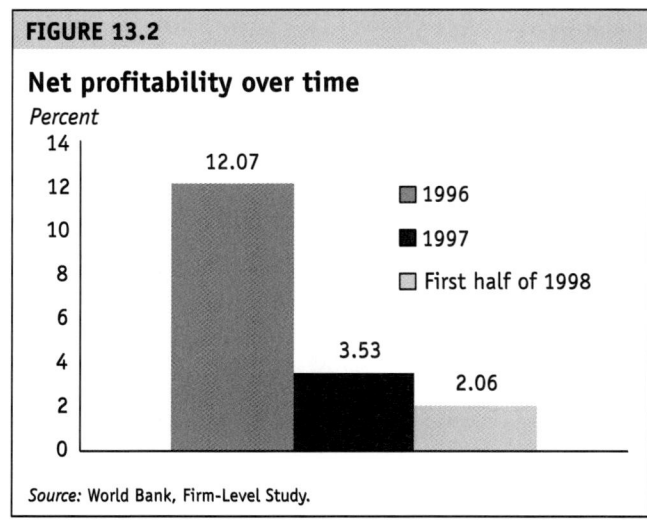

**FIGURE 13.2**

**Net profitability over time**

*Source:* World Bank, Firm-Level Study.

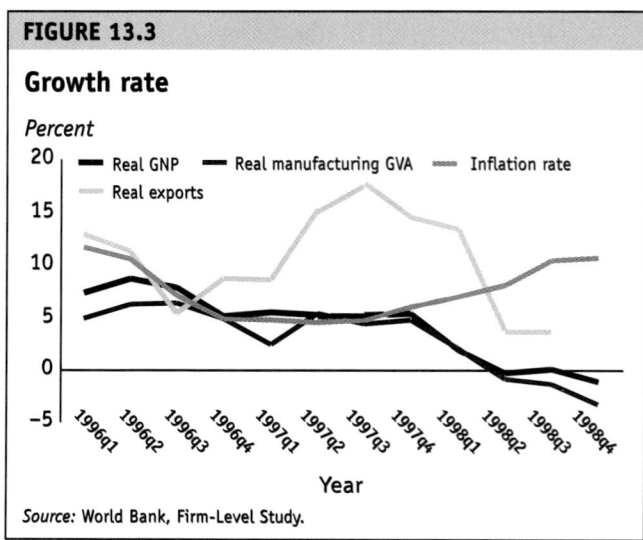

**FIGURE 13.3**

**Growth rate**

*Source:* World Bank, Firm-Level Study.

sector reached a peak of 43.6 percent in the fourth quarter of 1997. Following that period its growth decelerated considerably, although it did not contract.

Based on these indicators, the survey results seem to have confirmed the general slowdown in the manufacturing sector.

## Perceived causes of slowdown

The survey identified ten major causes of output decline. These are (a) decline in domestic demand; (b) decline in foreign demand; (c) insufficient credit being extended by suppliers; (d) insufficient bank credit for working capital; (e) insufficient bank credit for expansion; (f) high interest rates; (g) high cost of raw materials

## TABLE 13.3
**Macroeconomic variables**
(Growth rate)

| | 1996q1 | 1996q2 | 1996q3 | 1996q4 | 1997q1 | 1997q2 | 1997q3 | 1997q4 | 1998q1 | 1998q2 | 1998q3 | 1998q4 |
|---|---|---|---|---|---|---|---|---|---|---|---|---|
| Gross national product | 7.3 | 8.7 | 7.8 | 5.1 | 5.4 | 5.3 | 5.2 | 5.3 | 2.0 | (0.3) | (0.0) | (1.2) |
| Gross domestic product | 5.3 | 6.1 | 6.9 | 4.9 | 5.5 | 5.6 | 4.9 | 4.8 | 1.6 | (0.8) | (0.7) | (1.9) |
| Agriculture, fishery, and forestry | 2.9 | 6.8 | 7.9 | (0.5) | 4.9 | 1.8 | 0.4 | 4.1 | (3.8) | (11.5) | (3.1) | (7.8) |
| Industry sector | 5.8 | 5.5 | 7.0 | 6.5 | 5.1 | 7.6 | 6.4 | 5.6 | 1.6 | (0.2) | (3.5) | (4.4) |
| Mining and quarrying | 4.6 | (19.2) | (3.3) | 3.1 | (13.1) | (1.0) | 1.8 | 23.9 | 17.5 | 5.7 | 0.3 | (16.0) |
| Manufacturing | 4.9 | 6.2 | 6.3 | 4.9 | 2.3 | 5.3 | 4.3 | 4.7 | 2.0 | (0.9) | (1.5) | (3.4) |
| Food | 3.3 | 10.1 | 5.2 | 7.8 | 3.4 | 2.7 | (0.6) | (1.9) | 5.7 | 0.9 | 1.5 | — |
| Textiles | (3.1) | (6.1) | 7.4 | (8.0) | (14.1) | (6.8) | (0.1) | 4.6 | (4.1) | (8.5) | (8.8) | — |
| Apparel, leather | 4.3 | (4.7) | (4.5) | (23.3) | (14.0) | 4.3 | 6.2 | 7.9 | 5.3 | 18.2 | 9.1 | — |
| Chemicals, rubber, plastic[a] | (2.1) | 6.5 | 11.0 | 6.6 | 10.2 | 2.7 | 10.0 | 6.1 | (5.6) | (2.1) | (0.3) | — |
| Electronics | 14.9 | 17.9 | 14.3 | 12.3 | 21.8 | 20.6 | 33.7 | 46.3 | 21.9 | 7.3 | 7.9 | — |
| Construction | 7.6 | 9.3 | 12.8 | 13.8 | 21.3 | 18.5 | 18.1 | 7.6 | (5.0) | (1.8) | (15.6) | (10.0) |
| Service sector | 6.1 | 6.3 | 6.5 | 6.7 | 6.1 | 5.7 | 5.6 | 4.6 | 4.5 | 3.6 | 2.7 | 3.3 |
| Export[b] | 12.9 | 11.3 | 5.3 | 8.7 | 8.6 | 15.2 | 17.6 | 14.5 | 13.4 | 3.7 | 3.7 | — |
| Garments | 11.6 | (7.2) | (12.9) | (6.4) | (13.9) | (5.8) | 9.9 | (9.6) | (0.1) | 8.5 | (8.2) | — |
| Semiconductors | 25.4 | 14.3 | (2.5) | 3.5 | 3.6 | 21.1 | 43.6 | 41.9 | 25.4 | 15.1 | 1.6 | — |
| Inflation rate | 11.6 | 10.5 | 7.0 | 4.8 | 4.8 | 4.5 | 4.8 | 6.0 | 7.0 | 8.0 | 10.4 | 10.6 |
| 1991—Treasury bill rate[c] | 13.0 | 12.8 | 11.5 | 11.5 | 10.1 | 10.5 | 15.3 | 17.7 | 16.6 | 14.0 | 13.8 | 13.4 |

—: not available.
a. Chemicals only.
b. In real peso value.
c. Level of T-bills
*Note:*
Details for Mfg: 1985 constant prices.
1991—T-Bills: End of period was used.
Inflation rate was computed using the average consumer price index.
q1 = first quarter; q2 = second quarter; q3 = third quarter; q4 = fourth quarter.
*Source:* NSO.

owing to the depreciation of the peso; (h) increasing labor costs; (i) shortages in raw materials; and (j) nondelivery of goods by suppliers hurt by the crisis. If one assumes that reduced capacity utilization implies reduced output level, then the above reasons could also be used as causes for the drop in the capacity utilization rate discussed earlier.

Figure 13.4 presents separate sets of results for the exporters and nonexporters with regard to their perception on the possible causes of the decline in output and capacity utilization. In the survey, 1 means that the respondent believes there is no contribution, while 5 identifies the factor as a major contributor. For both exporters and nonexporters, the biggest contributor to the slowdown in output was the increase in input costs owing to the depreciation of the peso. The effect of the currency depreciation was slightly bigger for nonexporters (3.88) than for exporters (3.66). Note that while a peso depreciation would be favorable to all exporters, it would adversely affect some of them because of the relatively high import content of their products.

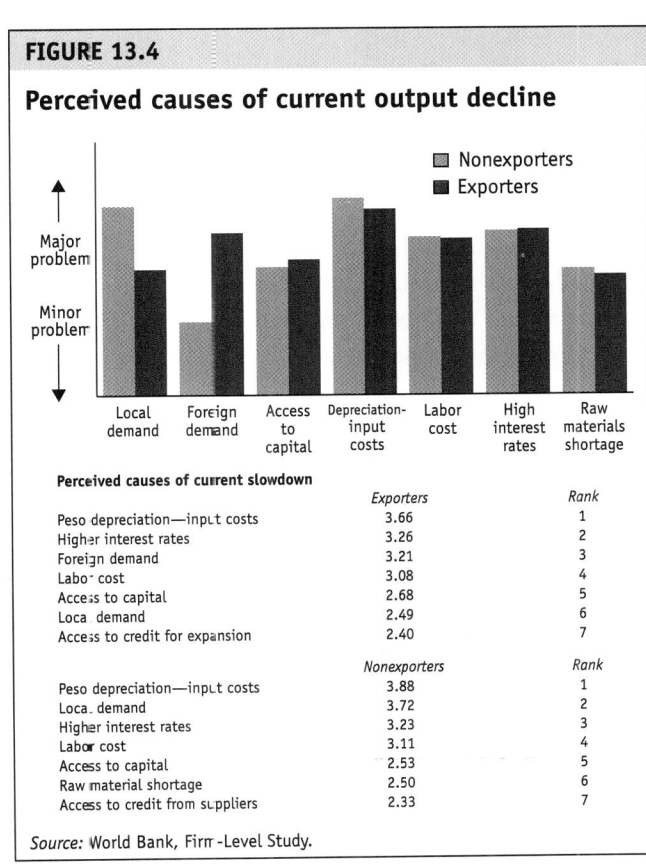

**FIGURE 13.4**
**Perceived causes of current output decline**

*Perceived causes of current slowdown*

| | Exporters | Rank |
|---|---|---|
| Peso depreciation—input costs | 3.66 | 1 |
| Higher interest rates | 3.26 | 2 |
| Foreign demand | 3.21 | 3 |
| Labor cost | 3.08 | 4 |
| Access to capital | 2.68 | 5 |
| Local demand | 2.49 | 6 |
| Access to credit for expansion | 2.40 | 7 |
| | Nonexporters | Rank |
| Peso depreciation—input costs | 3.88 | 1 |
| Local demand | 3.72 | 2 |
| Higher interest rates | 3.23 | 3 |
| Labor cost | 3.11 | 4 |
| Access to capital | 2.53 | 5 |
| Raw material shortage | 2.50 | 6 |
| Access to credit from suppliers | 2.33 | 7 |

*Source:* World Bank, Firm-Level Study.

For the exporters, the second major cause of the slowdown was high interest rates. By contrast, for the nonexporters, the second major factor was the decline in domestic demand.

Changes in foreign demand emerged as the third most important factor causing the slowdown as far as the exporters were concerned, while high interest rates turned out to be the third-ranking factor causing the decline in output for the nonexporters.

For both exporters and nonexporters, the fourth- and fifth-ranking factors were the same—labor cost and access to capital, respectively. For the exporters, the sixth factor and the last factor on the list were local demand and access to credit for expansion. However, for nonexporters, the sixth factor was raw material shortage, while the last on the list was access to credit from suppliers.[3]

From the point of view of a firm facing a competitive market, the results discussed above seem to suggest that the simultaneous drop in demand and increase in the average cost during the crisis period squeezed a firm's profit. The results also seem to suggest that the surveyed firms did not face much difficulty in accessing credit, although they had to pay a higher interest on it.[4]

## Competitor profiles

The results shown in figure 13.5 indicate that for those firms selling to the domestic market, the biggest competitors were other domestic producers owned by local investors or owners. Joint venture companies and multinationals were considered far less of a threat than other domestic producers in terms of competition in the domestic market.

In the international market, the biggest threat to the local exporters in terms of competition were those firms within the neighboring countries (in other words, firms in Malaysia, Indonesia, and Thailand). Not too far behind the first group were firms in low-cost producing countries such as Vietnam, China, Cambodia, Laos, and Myanmar. The third group of firms that posed market competition in the international market were firms in newly industrialized countries (South Korea, Taiwan, Hong Kong, and Singapore). The last group of firms was from developed countries.

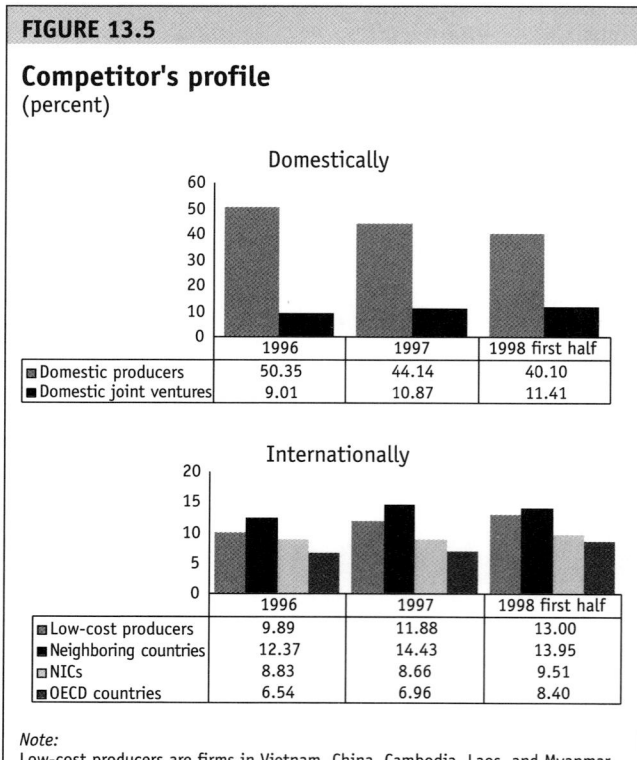

**FIGURE 13.5**

**Competitor's profile**
(percent)

Domestically

|  | 1996 | 1997 | 1998 first half |
|---|---|---|---|
| Domestic producers | 50.35 | 44.14 | 40.10 |
| Domestic joint ventures | 9.01 | 10.87 | 11.41 |

Internationally

|  | 1996 | 1997 | 1998 first half |
|---|---|---|---|
| Low-cost producers | 9.89 | 11.88 | 13.00 |
| Neighboring countries | 12.37 | 14.43 | 13.95 |
| NICs | 8.83 | 8.66 | 9.51 |
| OECD countries | 6.54 | 6.96 | 8.40 |

*Note:*
Low-cost producers are firms in Vietnam, China, Cambodia, Laos, and Myanmar.
Neighboring countries' data are from firms in Malaysia, Indonesia, and Thailand.
NICs' data are from firms in Korea, Taiwan, Hong Kong, and Singapore.
OECD countries' data are from firms in the United States, Japan, and Europe.
*Source:* World Bank, Firm-Level Survey.

## The proportion of firms reducing the number of workers

About two-fifths of the firms surveyed reported that they had been operating with fewer workers since the crisis struck in July 1997 (see figure 13.6). Firms in the apparel and leather sector had the highest proportion (49 percent) that reduced the number of workers in the wake of the crisis, followed by the electrical machinery sector (44 percent). In terms of other criteria, the figure was 46 percent for nonexporters versus 38 percent for exporters; 44 percent for large firms versus 39 percent for small firms; 43 percent for firms with no foreign control versus 41 percent with some foreign control and 35 percent with total foreign control.

## The profile of workers who lost jobs

The survey results show that those leaving the firms were younger workers and newer arrivals (see table 13.4). This is not surprising; the firms had little capital invested in these employees. Also, many of those newly

## TABLE 13.4
### Profile of workers leaving the plan
(percent)

|  | Average age (years) | | | Average tenure (years) | | |
|---|---|---|---|---|---|---|
|  | 30 or less | 31–50 | Above 50 | 3 or less | 4–10 | Above 10 |
| *By sector* | | | | | | |
| Food products | 43 | 42 | 15 | 40 | 31 | 30 |
| Textiles | 51 | 38 | 10 | 41 | 35 | 24 |
| Apparel, leather | 59 | 36 | 5 | 50 | 29 | 21 |
| Chemicals, rubber, plastic | 49 | 42 | 9 | 44 | 31 | 25 |
| Electrical machinery | 71 | 26 | 3 | 53 | 36 | 11 |
| Total | 55 | 37 | 9 | 46 | 32 | 22 |
| *By export orientation* | | | | | | |
| Exporters | 58 | 34 | 8 | 49 | 30 | 21 |
| Nonexporters | 51 | 40 | 8 | 43 | 35 | 22 |
| Total | 55 | 37 | 8 | | 46 | 3221 |
| *By size* | | | | | | |
| Small | 58 | 35 | 7 | 51 | 31 | 18 |
| Large | 52 | 38 | 10 | 41 | 33 | 26 |
| Total | 55 | 37 | 9 | 46 | 32 | 22 |

*Source:* World Bank, Firm-Level Survey.

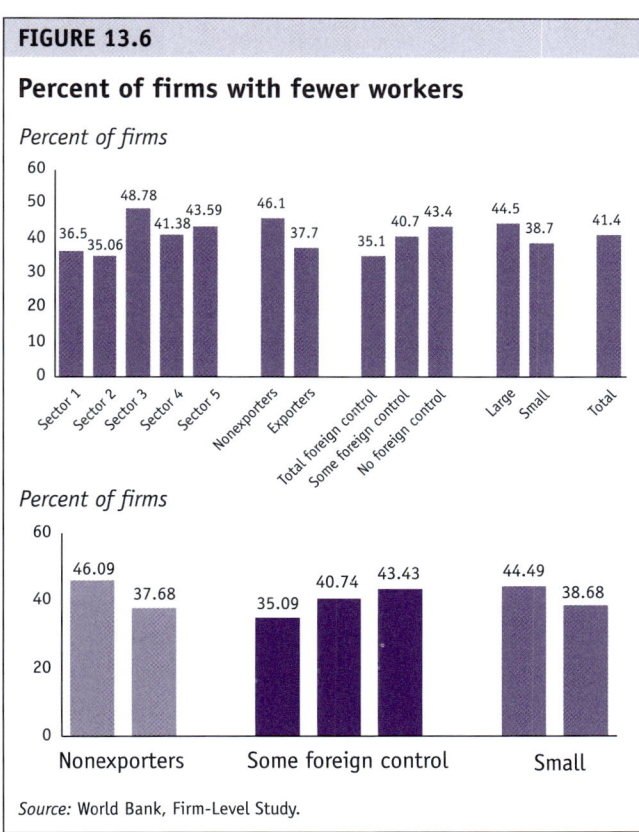

**FIGURE 13.6**

**Percent of firms with fewer workers**

*Source:* World Bank, Firm-Level Study.

hired workers may not have earned their permanent appointment yet.

More than half (55 percent) of the workers leaving the firms were thirty years old or less. Another 37 percent were between 31 and 50. There was a higher proportion of younger and newer workers leaving the firms in the electrical machinery sector than in the other four sectors; in exporting firms than in nonexporting firms; and in small firms than in large firms.

As regards tenure, almost half of the employees had been with the company for 3 years or less while about one-third had been there for 4 to 10 years.

## The proportion of firms retrenching workers or using other methods of reducing labor

Some 39 percent of the surveyed firms were filling up their vacancies as workers left (see table 13.5). However, 29 percent had laid off workers as a result of the crisis. Some 61 percent gave severance pay or benefits to workers who were separated from work.

While the apparel sector (42 percent) and the chemical sector (43 percent) had a higher proportion of firms filling up their vacancies than the other sectors, they also had a higher proportion (34 percent and 37 percent, respectively) laying off workers as a result of the crisis than the other sectors. And the electrical machinery, textiles, and apparel sectors gave severance pay or benefits at a higher rate than other sectors, at 48, 54, and 55 percent, respectively.

A higher proportion of exporting firms than nonexporters filled up their vacancies, but in terms of laying off workers the order was reversed. Nearly equal proportions of firms in each category gave severance benefits to their laid-off workers.

A higher proportion of large firms than small firms filled up their vacancies and laid off their workers. The proportions were about equal in terms of giving severance benefits to laid-off workers.

Aside from laying off workers, firms in general may resort to other measures to respond to an economic crisis that will possibly affect them. These may include (a) cutting down on the work hours or days of workers paid hourly or daily; (b) compressing the work week for workers paid monthly; (c) introducing forced vacation leaves; and (d) freezing salary increases or cutting salaries of rank-and-file workers, management, or both. Almost two-fifths of the sample firms cut down on work hours and days, about one-fifth implemented a compressed work week, about one-fourth used forced vacation, and close to one-third froze the salary increases of rank-and-file employees and management. Only a small proportion of the sample firms implemented salary cuts for rank-and-file (3 percent) and management personnel (5 percent) (see table 13.5).

In terms of sectors, the apparel and leather sector had the highest proportion of firms that cut down on working hours in response to the crisis. The electrical machinery sector had the highest proportion of firms that resorted to compressing the work week for their employees. Forced vacation, by contrast, was used by a higher proportion of firms in the food and electrical machinery sectors than in other sectors. The textile and electrical machinery sectors had a higher proportion of firms that froze salary increases of rank-and-file employees than other sectors. Freezing the salary increases of management personnel was employed by more firms in the food and textile sectors than in other sectors.

In terms of export orientation, the number of firms resorting to compressing the work week and forced vacation was greater for the exporters than for the nonexporters. However, more nonexporters than exporters cut down on work hours or days and froze salary increases of both rank-and-file and management personnel.

In terms of size, a higher proportion of large firms than small firms cut down on work hours or days, compressed the work week, and resorted to forced vacation. In terms of freezing salary increases for rank-and-file workers, however, the ranking was reversed.

Membership of workers in unions was mentioned by 41 percent of the sample firms (see table 13.6). Compared with firms in other sectors, the electrical machinery sector had the lowest proportion (23 percent) of workers who were members of unions. The figures were 43 percent for exporting firms and 53 percent for large firms—surpassing nonexporting and small firms, respectively.

As regards formal training activities, 52 percent of the surveyed firms claimed that they had formal training activities for their workers (see table 13.6). More than half of the firms in the food, chemical, and electrical machinery sectors also made this claim. Exporting firms (61 percent) and large firms (67 percent) had higher proportions in this category than nonexporting and small firms, respectively.

Among those firms that had training activities for their workers, one-fourth reported that they were planning to reduce the amount of training for their workers owing to the crisis. The apparel and leather sector had the highest proportion of firms planning a reduction. Nonexporters had a higher proportion than exporters in this regard. And finally, one-fourth of the large and small firms planned to decrease their training activities.

## Labor policy

*Minimum wage fixing.* The prevailing law governing minimum wage in the country is the Republic Act (RA) 6727 or the Wage Rationalization Act enacted in 1989. It created the National Wage and Productivity Commission,[5] but wage fixing was devolved to the Regional Wages and Productivity Tripartite Boards. In terms of promulgating wage orders, the Tripartite Boards have been proven to be faster than wage legislation despite the required hearing and consultation process to be followed.

## TABLE 13.5
### Responses to crisis: labor
(percent)

| | Filling vacancies | Laying off workers | Paying severance | Reducing hours | Compressing work week | Mandating vacation | Freezing salary: rank & file | Freezing salary: mgt. | Cutting salary: rank & file | Cutting salary: mgt. |
|---|---|---|---|---|---|---|---|---|---|---|
| *By sector* | | | | | | | | | | |
| Food products | 39 | 21 | 68 | 38 | 16 | 26 | 27 | 32 | 2 | 4 |
| Textiles | 31 | 29 | 65 | 36 | 17 | 20 | 29 | 37 | 1 | 9 |
| Apparel, leather | 42 | 34 | 56 | 41 | 20 | 23 | 27 | 29 | 6 | 7 |
| Chemicals, rubber, plastic | 43 | 37 | 70 | 33 | 18 | 23 | 31 | 29 | 4 | 2 |
| Electrical machinery | 38 | 29 | 47 | 40 | 22 | 25 | 28 | 27 | 3 | 4 |
| Total | 39 | 29 | 61 | 38 | 19 | 24 | 28 | 31 | 3 | 5 |
| *By export orientation* | | | | | | | | | | |
| Exporters | 47 | 29 | 59 | 34 | 20 | 26 | 25 | 29 | 3 | 5 |
| Nonexporters | 30 | 31 | 62 | 43 | 18 | 22 | 32 | 33 | 4 | 5 |
| Total | 39 | 30 | 60 | 38 | 19 | 24 | 28 | 31 | 3 | 5 |
| *By size* | | | | | | | | | | |
| Small | 33 | 27 | 59 | 37 | 17 | 16 | 29 | 31 | 4 | 5 |
| Large | 45 | 32 | 62 | 39 | 20 | 32 | 27 | 31 | 2 | 4 |
| Total | 39 | 29 | 61 | 38 | 19 | 24 | 28 | 31 | 3 | 5 |

*Source:* World Bank, Firm-Level Survey.

The minimum wage has been adjusted almost regularly and the past year is not an exception. The inflation rate has been the primary factor contributing to wage hikes. The wage adjustment in 1998 was a response to the increase in the inflation rate brought about by the substantial depreciation of the domestic currency.

*Restrictions on layoffs.* Tenure security is one of the employee rights that is safeguarded by the Constitution. This right prohibits management from terminating the services of a regular employee without just cause and without due process of law.

*Mandated severance pay.* There are authorized causes for termination of employment by employers. These include (a) installation of labor-saving devices; (b) redundancy; (c) retrenchment to prevent losses; or (d) long-term illness or disease. In the case of (a) and (b), the separation pay is one month pay or at least one month pay for every year of service, whichever is higher. In the case of (c) and (d), it is one month pay or one-half month for every year of service, whichever is higher.

## Social programs

In response to the crisis, the Department of Labor and Employment (DOLE) was able to work out on February 6, 1998 a tripartite agreement dubbed the "Social Accord for Industrial Harmony and Stability."

## TABLE 13.6
### Human resource and training
(percent)

| | Workers member of union | With formal training | Decreased amount of training |
|---|---|---|---|
| *By sector* | | | |
| Food products | 45 | 51 | 26 |
| Textiles | 43 | 44 | 21 |
| Apparel, leather | 48 | 44 | 38 |
| Chemicals, rubber, plastic | 49 | 59 | 24 |
| Electrical machinery | 23 | 62 | 18 |
| Total | 41 | 52 | 25 |
| *By export orientation* | | | |
| Exporters | 45 | 61 | 22 |
| Nonexporters | 37 | 42 | 31 |
| Total | 41 | 52 | 25 |
| *By size* | | | |
| Small | 27 | 38 | 25 |
| Large | 55 | 67 | 25 |
| Total | 41 | 52 | 25 |

*Source:* World Bank, Firm-Level Survey.

Under the Accord, employers promised that they would "exercise the utmost restraint in the lay-off, termination or rotation of their employees, which should be availed of only as a last resort." On the part of workers, they pledged that they would "exercise utmost restraint in declaring or going on strikes, slowdown of work and other forms of concerted work stoppages, which should be availed of only as a last resort." Similar accords have been brokered by DOLE in various regions of the country. The statistics on labor strikes seem to suggest that the accord is holding. In particular, the number of recorded strikes has not significantly gone up during the crisis period compared with the period before the crisis.

Moreover, on February 11, 1998, a National Economic Summit was convened by President Ramos to draft a comprehensive response to the crisis. Among the proposals taken up was for DOLE to monitor worker layoffs, provide job placement for displaced workers, disseminate information on job vacancies, and implement programs for retraining, entrepreneurship, and credit and livelihood assistance. It should be noted, however, that these are ongoing activities of the department. The monitoring of worker layoffs is being done by the Bureau of Labor and Employment Statistics, which publishes on its Web site (www.manila-online.net/bless/welcome.htm) the latest update on actual and planned layoffs including the number and firms involved.

While DOLE has prepared the program document for the "Comprehensive Program Package for Displaced Workers," there appears to be no readily available data on actual assistance given to displaced workers. The program includes monitoring, job loss prevention, training, livelihood programs, placement assistance, and educational assistance for the children of displaced workers.

Another recommendation that came out of the Summit was for the Social Security System (SSS) to implement a 200 million peso Emergency Loan Program for displaced workers. According to a published report,[6] P300[7] million had already been disbursed as of December 1998, and the SSS has recently approved the allocation of another P200 million for the program. As reported by the SSS, the program had already approved some 25,815 applications as of February 22, 1999. The program offers a maximum of P12,500 to members at 6 per year payable in 24 equal monthly installments starting after a 12-month grace period. Borrowers are required to be members in good standing and present either termination papers or proof of employment from DOLE and certification from the employer that they have suffered loss in income because of job rotation or reduced work hours. It must be noted that this program violates the government's standing policy of doing away with subsidized credit programs.

Still another program proposed was the setting up of a guarantee facility for loans to small and medium enterprises that are still viable but are under distress owing to the crisis. The program, called the Enterprise Stabilization Guarantee Fund, is being implemented by the Small Business Guarantee and Finance Corporation (SBGFC). The proposed facility will guarantee up to 50 percent of the principal loan balance. While awaiting the proposed financing requirement of P1 billion, the SBGFC has already set aside P200 million from its own funds for the project. As of March 1999, there was still no available record of performance other than the preparation of the guidelines and presentation of the project to government and private institutions that are involved with small and medium enterprises. With the Department of Trade and Industry's endorsement, the project was presented to donor agencies for possible funding support.

## Financial position of the firms before and after the crisis

### The sources of funds

Firms raise short- and long-term funds from internal and external sources. As can be observed from figure 13.7, income from sales and loans from local banks were the two main sources—internal and external, respectively—of short-term and long-term funds for the sample firms before (that is, January to June 1997) and during the crisis period. It should be noted that this source structure has hardly changed at all since the onset of the Southeast Asian financial crisis.

### The firms' reliance on debt

The average debt-equity ratio of the surveyed firms in 1996 stood at 2.27 (see figure 13.8 and table 13.7).[8] It inched up to 2.46 in 1997, but dropped to 2.04 in the first half of 1998, a level that is below that of 1996. This pattern holds true for large and small firms, for exporting and nonexporting firms, and for all sectors but one—namely, electrical machinery, whose debt-equity ratio had already started to decline in 1997. The above results seem to suggest that the surveyed firms

### FIGURE 13.7

**Source of short-term and long-term financing**
(percent of total financing)

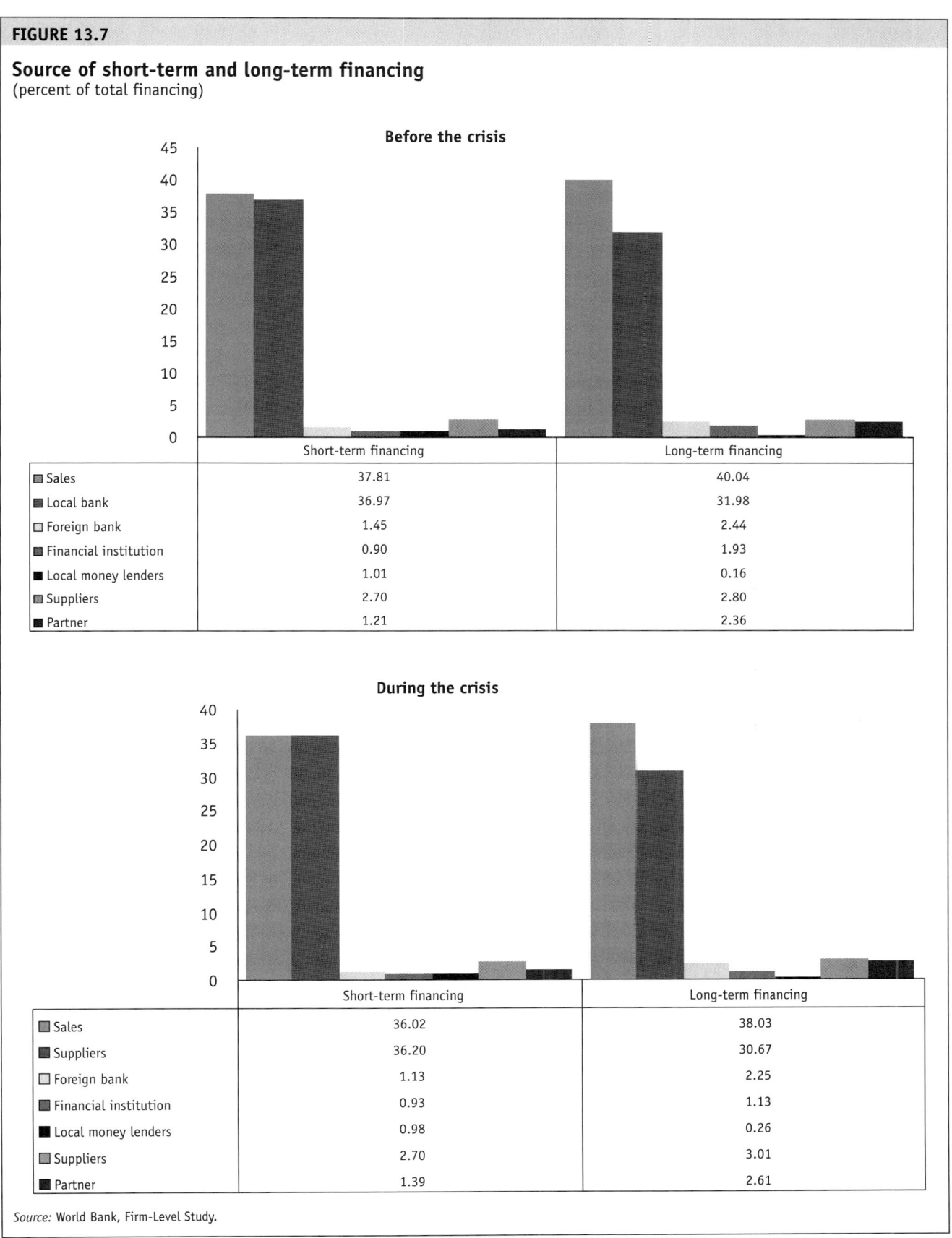

*Source:* World Bank, Firm-Level Study.

The Impact of the Southeast Asian Financial Crisis on the Philippine Manufacturing Sector

### TABLE 13.7
### Financial indicators

| Indicators | Sector | | | | | Size | | Export orientation | | Average |
|---|---|---|---|---|---|---|---|---|---|---|
| | 1 | 2 | 3 | 4 | 5 | Large | Small | Exporter | Nonexporter | |
| *Short-term debt/total financing*[a] | | | | | | | | | | |
| 1996 | 0.29 | 0.30 | 0.34 | 0.27 | 0.33 | 0.31 | 0.31 | 0.31 | 0.30 | 0.31 |
| 1997 | 0.30 | 0.33 | 0.39 | 0.31 | 0.34 | 0.35 | 0.32 | 0.34 | 0.33 | 0.33 |
| First half of 1998 | 0.27 | 0.34 | 0.44 | 0.26 | 0.32 | 0.33 | 0.31 | 0.34 | 0.29 | 0.32 |
| *Long-term debt/total financing*[b] | | | | | | | | | | |
| 1996 | 0.21 | 0.30 | 0.25 | 0.24 | 0.20 | 0.23 | 0.24 | 0.22 | 0.25 | 0.23 |
| 1997 | 0.20 | 0.26 | 0.19 | 0.25 | 0.19 | 0.21 | 0.22 | 0.20 | 0.23 | 0.21 |
| First half of 1998 | 0.19 | 0.26 | 0.17 | 0.25 | 0.20 | 0.21 | 0.21 | 0.19 | 0.23 | 0.21 |
| *Debt-equity ratio* | | | | | | | | | | |
| 1996 | 2.27 | 1.94 | 2.65 | 1.67 | 2.94 | 2.19 | 2.32 | 2.14 | 2.66 | 2.27 |
| 1997 | 2.40 | 2.23 | 2.85 | 2.18 | 2.71 | 2.40 | 2.54 | 2.29 | 2.75 | 2.46 |
| First half of 1998 | 1.80 | 2.18 | 2.40 | 1.56 | 2.19 | 2.12 | 1.92 | 1.98 | 2.16 | 2.04 |

a. Both sectors 2 and 3 include 3 outliers.
b. Sector 2 includes 3 outliers; sector 3 includes 1 outlier.
*Note:*
Sector Codes:
Sector 1—Food products.
Sector 2—Textiles.
Sector 3—Apparel, leather.
Sector 4—Chemicals, rubber, plastic.
Sector 5—Electrical machinery.
*Source:* World Bank, Firm-Level Survey.

attempted to reduce their debt as they began to feel the effects of the financial crisis in 1998.[9] However, the degree of adjustment in the debt-equity ratio seems to vary by firm type. More specifically, the decline in the debt-equity ratio in the first half of 1998 was much larger for nonexporting firms than for exporting firms. Small firms made greater adjustments than large firms during the same period. Among the five sectors, the food and chemical sectors experienced much larger declines compared with the other three sectors. By contrast, the textile sector made the smallest adjustment in the first half of 1998. In 1996, the electrical machinery sector obtained the highest debt-equity ratio, followed by the apparel and leather sector. This ranking was reversed in the first half of 1998.

The shares of short-term and long-term debt in the total amount of financing could serve as a good indicator of the firms' vulnerability to sudden tightness in the credit market. Short-term debt comprised almost one-third of the firms' total financing (see figure 13.9 and table 13.7). The firms' share of or degree of reliance on short-term debt changed little during the period from 1996 to the first half of 1998; this was especially true for large firms regarding the degree of reliance. Regarding changes in share, large firms showed much larger changes than small firms during the indicated period. In the first half of 1998, the large firms' share of short-term debt stood at 33 percent compared with 31 percent for small firms.

Some differences in the behavior pattern of the short-term debt's share among various sectors can also be discerned during this period. The food, chemical and electrical machinery sectors exhibited an inverted U-shape. By contrast, the textile and apparel sectors showed a rising share. It should be noted that the

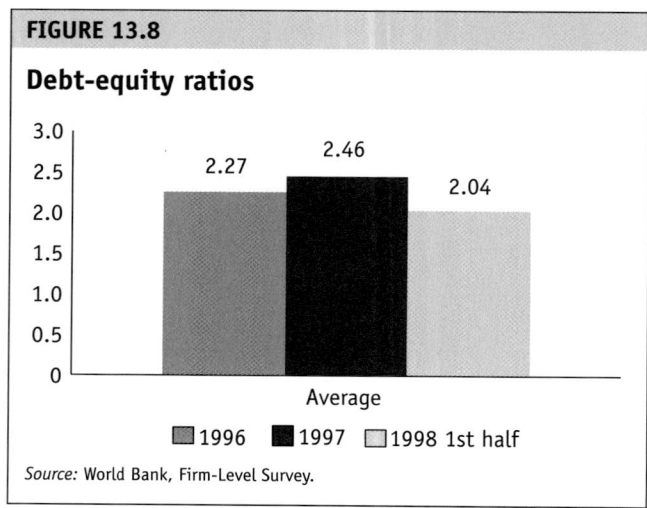

**FIGURE 13.8**
**Debt-equity ratios**
*Source:* World Bank, Firm-Level Survey.

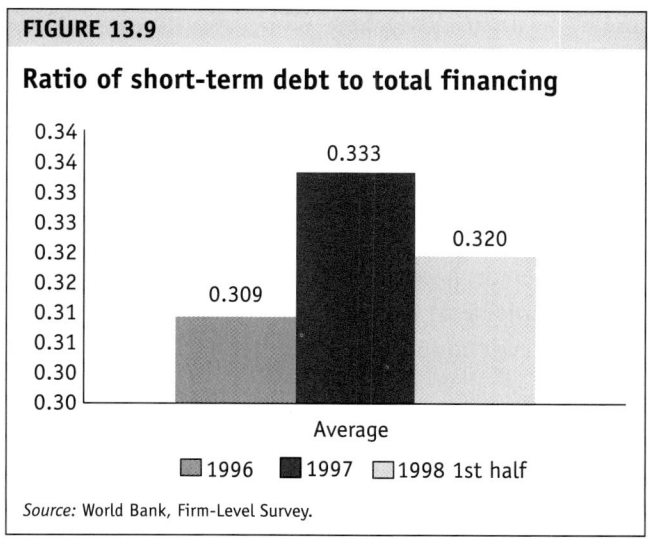

**FIGURE 13.9**

**Ratio of short-term debt to total financing**

1996: 0.309; 1997: 0.333; 1998 1st half: 0.320

*Source:* World Bank, Firm-Level Survey.

apparel sector stood out prominently among the five sectors with its short-term debt accounting for 44 percent of total financing. When the firms are classified according to export orientation, results show that the share of short-term debt of nonexporting firms declined to 29 percent in the first half of 1998 from 33 percent in 1997, whereas that of exporting firms remained the same at 34 percent during the same period.

The surveyed firms' share of long-term debt in total financing declined a little from 23 percent in 1996 to 21 percent in 1997, and stayed at that level during the first half of 1998 (see figure 13.10 and table 13.7). The shares reported by large and small firms had almost the same level and pattern of behavior during the indicated period. Exporters and nonexporters showed a similar pattern, but the former's share of long-term debt was lower than that of the latter. Among the five sectors, the textile and apparel sectors experienced a significant decline, while the other three sectors went through little change. In the first half of 1998, the textile and chemical sectors showed a much higher share of long-term debt than the other three sectors.

The results discussed above suggest that the decline in the debt-equity ratio experienced by the firms in the first half of 1998 can be attributed to the drop in both their short- and long-term debt during the same period.

### The availability of credit

The respondents were asked whether banks or finance companies had declined to grant them a loan before and during the crisis. Only 6 percent answered positively to this question before the Southeast Asian financial crisis—that is, from January to June 1997 (see table 13.8). During the crisis, the proportion of firms being denied bank loans had doubled. It should be noted that this proportion in the first half of 1998 was slightly higher for exporters (14 percent) than for nonexporters (12 percent). Large firms also slightly surpassed small firms, at 15 versus 12 percent. The electrical machinery sector appears to be the least affected by the crisis in terms of

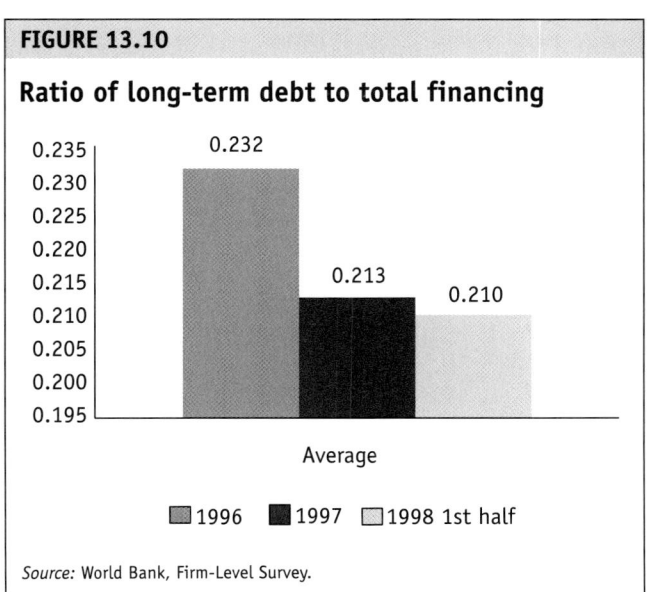

**FIGURE 13.10**

**Ratio of long-term debt to total financing**

1996: 0.232; 1997: 0.213; 1998 1st half: 0.210

*Source:* World Bank, Firm-Level Survey.

**TABLE 13.8**

**Firms that were denied bank loans**
(percent)

| Category | January 1–June 30, 1997 | July 1–December 31, 1997 | January 1–March 30, 1998 |
|---|---|---|---|
| *By sector* | | | |
| Food products | 6.31 | 16.22 | 11.71 |
| Textiles | 6.15 | 9.23 | 15.15 |
| Apparel | 7.48 | 15.89 | 17.59 |
| Chemicals | 6.49 | 10.26 | 15.38 |
| Electrical machinery | 5.61 | 7.55 | 6.54 |
| Total | 6.42 | 12.21 | 12.98 |
| *By export orientation* | | | |
| Exporters | 6.61 | 11.98 | 14.34 |
| Nonexporters | 6.28 | 12.56 | 11.61 |
| Total | 6.45 | 12.26 | 13.03 |
| *By size of firms* | | | |
| Small | 5.24 | 8.66 | 11.16 |
| Large | 7.56 | 15.68 | 14.77 |
| Total | 6.42 | 12.21 | 12.98 |

*Source:* World Bank, Firm-Level Survey.

access to bank credit—only 6 percent of the firms in this sector were turned down for credit in the first half of 1998. By contrast, 18 percent of the apparel sector firms were denied bank loans in the first half of 1998, up from only 7 percent in 1996.

Note that though the percentage of those that admitted having been denied a loan by a bank or finance company had doubled during the crisis period, this is still much smaller than what was generally expected considering the economic uncertainty brought about by the Southeast Asian currency meltdown. In other words, a great majority of the sample firms continued to have access to credit during the crisis period.

Firms typically buy inputs on credit. Seventy-four (74) percent of the surveyed firms confirmed this practice (see table 13.9). This proportion does not significantly differ among different categories. The results seem to suggest that the firms' access to supplier credit during the crisis was not hampered. As table 13.9 shows, 81 percent of the sample respondents said that their input suppliers were still extending credit to them after July 1997. The proportion does not significantly differ among the various categories either.

Firms also typically sell their products to their customers on credit. About three-fourths of the sample firms were doing this before the crisis. During the crisis period, a little over three-fourths of the sample firms claimed to have continued selling their products on credit to their customers. The proportion of firms extending credit to their customers appears to be higher for nonexporters than for exporters, and higher for large firms than small firms. Among the five sectors, the chemical sector had the highest proportion, while the apparel and leather sector had the lowest.

The firms were asked about which usual source of loans or credit had become more restrictive in making credit available to them since the onset of the regional financial crisis in July 1997 (see figure 13.11). Domestic

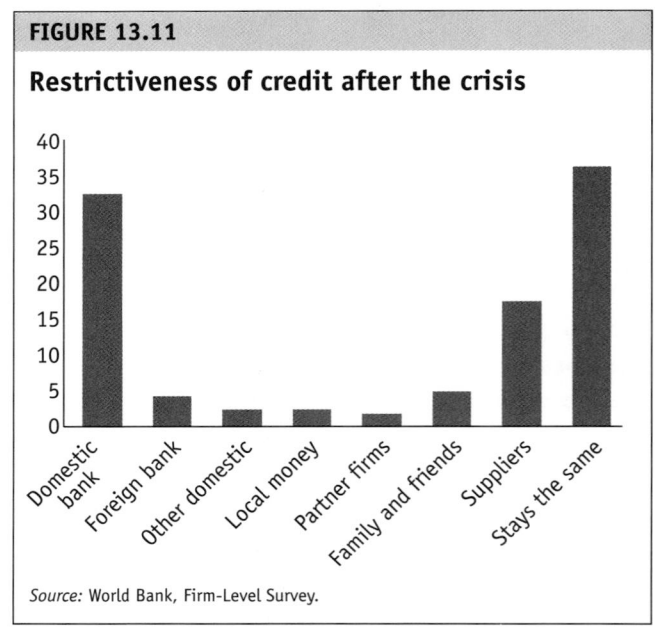

**FIGURE 13.11**

**Restrictiveness of credit after the crisis**

Source: World Bank, Firm-Level Survey.

### TABLE 13.9
**Access to suppliers' credit**
(percent)

| Category | Buying inputs on credit | Suppliers still extending credit (after July 1997) | Selling products on credit | Still extending credit to buyers (after July 1997) |
| --- | --- | --- | --- | --- |
| *By sector* | | | | |
| Food products | 71.43 | 82.30 | 80.45 | 84.96 |
| Textiles | 72.73 | 84.06 | 83.12 | 81.16 |
| Apparel | 69.42 | 75.45 | 55.37 | 59.63 |
| Chemicals | 75.58 | 82.72 | 86.05 | 90.00 |
| Electrical machinery | 80.00 | 83.33 | 80.00 | 79.25 |
| Total | 73.68 | 81.29 | 75.94 | 78.20 |
| *By export orientation* | | | | |
| Exporters | 72.89 | 84.34 | 71.79 | 74.39 |
| Nonexporters | 75.10 | 77.92 | 80.63 | 82.17 |
| Total | 73.95 | 81.25 | 76.05 | 78.15 |
| *By size of firms* | | | | |
| Small | 69.96 | 75.31 | 75.27 | 76.37 |
| Large | 77.91 | 87.19 | 76.71 | 80.00 |
| Total | 73.68 | 81.29 | 75.94 | 78.20 |

Source: World Bank, Firm-Level Survey.

TABLE 13.10
**Adequate liquidity to finance production**
(percent)

| Category | Yes |
|---|---|
| *By sector* | |
| Food products | 75.00 |
| Textiles | 67.57 |
| Apparel | 73.28 |
| Chemicals | 80.95 |
| Electrical machinery | 82.88 |
| Total | 76.22 |
| *By export orientation* | |
| Exporters | 79.77 |
| Nonexporters | 72.18 |
| Total | 76.08 |
| *By size of firms* | |
| Small | 74.36 |
| Large | 78.33 |
| Total | 76.22 |

*Source:* World Bank, Firm-Level Survey.

tation. However, when the sample firms are classified by sector, the electrical machinery sector appears to have a different pattern of responses from the rest. In particular, half of the firms in this sector claimed that their access to credit had not changed at all during the crisis period. Only a little over one-fifth indicated that it had become more restrictive.

## The liquidity problem

The sample firms were also asked whether they, at the time of the survey, had adequate liquidity to finance their production. About three-fourths of the total sample of firms declared having no liquidity problem at that moment (see table 13.10). The claim was made by a roughly equal proportion of small and large firms. The same can be said of exporters and nonexporters. Looking at the responses of the firms broken down by sector, the textiles sector appears to have the lowest percentage.

Among those claiming that they had inadequate liquidity to run their operations, a little over half singled out low revenue as the major reason (see table 13.11). A little over one-third mentioned low collection rates and insufficient loans as the major reason for encountering a liquidity problem during the time of the interview.

banks were the most frequently mentioned source in response, followed by input suppliers. Interestingly, 36 percent of the firms mentioned that the availability of credit from their usual source had remained the same. The same pattern of responses can be observed when respondents are broken down by size and export orientation.

TABLE 13.11
**Causes of inadequate liquidity**
(percent)

| Category | Low revenue | Insufficient loans | Insufficient credit from suppliers | Low collection rate | Others |
|---|---|---|---|---|---|
| *By sector* | | | | | |
| Food products | 44.83 | 32.26 | 24.14 | 37.93 | 13.33 |
| Textiles | 50.00 | 28.57 | 20.00 | 33.33 | 6.67 |
| Apparel | 60.71 | 60.71 | 25.00 | 30.77 | 28.57 |
| Chemicals | 40.00 | 14.29 | 15.38 | 50.00 | 40.00 |
| Electrical machinery | 66.67 | 14.29 | 6.67 | 28.57 | 22.22 |
| Total | 52.63 | 34.26 | 20.00 | 35.58 | 21.43 |
| *By export orientation* | | | | | |
| Exporters | 52.08 | 32.61 | 16.28 | 19.05 | 29.63 |
| Nonexporters | 53.03 | 35.48 | 22.58 | 46.77 | 16.28 |
| Total | 52.63 | 34.26 | 20.00 | 35.58 | 21.43 |
| *By size of firms* | | | | | |
| Small | 59.09 | 35.48 | 25.00 | 38.33 | 22.73 |
| Large | 43.75 | 32.61 | 13.33 | 31.82 | 19.23 |
| Total | 52.63 | 34.26 | 20.00 | 35.58 | 21.43 |

*Source:* World Bank, Firm-Level Survey.

## Transparency

### Financial statements, collateral and guarantees

Accounting information—in other words, balance sheets and income statements—is one of the instruments that can make firms transparent to lenders. The value of this information can be enhanced if it is certified by an independent auditing firm.

Philippine firms and banks are required to maintain appropriate financial records that observe standard and customary accounting and auditing principles and procedures. Out of the total sample of firms in this study, 88 percent claimed to have financial statements audited by an independent auditing firm (see table 13.12). As expected, the proportion of firms having audited financial statements is lower for small firms (82 percent) than for large firms (93 percent). Ninety-three (93) percent of exporting firms maintain audited financial statements, whereas 82 percent of nonexporting firms do so. The rigor involved in competing in the international market is perhaps one of the compelling reasons for exporters to have audited financial statements. Looking at the five sectors, the textile firms appear to have the lowest proportion of firms with financial statements audited (80 percent), followed by food-producing firms (83 percent). The rest have proportions ranging from 89 to 92 percent.

Results show that even though 88 percent of the total sample respondents for this study claimed that their financial statements were audited by independent auditors, only 65 percent said that they typically needed audited financial statements to apply for and receive a bank loan (see table 13.13). As expected, large firms reported a higher proportion (71 percent) than small firms (60 percent) with regard to being required to submit audited financial statements when applying for a loan. The difference is less significant between exporters (68 percent) and nonexporters (63 percent). Among the five sectors, the electrical machinery sector reported the lowest proportion (56 percent) concerning this requirement.

Usually, the longer the maturity of the loan, the greater the chance that a bank will require collateral from a borrower. The results of the survey support this trend. Almost half of the total number of respondents said that they had typically had to provide collateral when they borrowed for 12 months or longer; the percentages were only 27 percent when borrowing for 6 months or longer, and 24 percent for less than 6 months (see table 13.14). There is not much difference in this respect when respondents are grouped by export orientation or size. When classified by sector, the textile sector appears to have the highest proportion of

**TABLE 13.12**
**Financial statements audited by independent auditing firm**
(percent)

| Category | Yes |
| --- | --- |
| *By sector* | |
| Food products | 83.49 |
| Textiles | 80.30 |
| Apparel | 88.89 |
| Chemicals | 91.25 |
| Electrical machinery | 91.74 |
| Total | 87.50 |
| *By export orientation* | |
| Exporters | 92.71 |
| Nonexporters | 81.61 |
| Total | 87.45 |
| *By size of firms* | |
| Small | 81.55 |
| Large | 93.31 |
| Total | 87.50 |

*Source:* World Bank, Firm-Level Survey.

**TABLE 13.13**
**Submission of audited financial statement to apply for a loan**
(percent)

| Category | Required |
| --- | --- |
| *By sector* | |
| Food products | 66.67 |
| Textiles | 63.08 |
| Apparel | 64.81 |
| Chemicals | 78.48 |
| Electrical machinery | 55.96 |
| Total | 65.25 |
| *By export orientation* | |
| Exporters | 67.48 |
| Nonexporters | 62.95 |
| Total | 65.32 |
| *By size of firms* | |
| Small | 59.48 |
| Large | 70.83 |
| Total | 65.25 |

*Source:* World Bank, Firm-Level Survey.

**TABLE 13.14**
**Requirement of a collateral for a loan**
(percent)

| | Loan | | |
|---|---|---|---|
| Category | Less than 6 months | 6 months or longer | 12 months or longer |
| *By sector* | | | |
| Food products | 22.77 | 25.77 | 50.00 |
| Textiles | 37.29 | 41.38 | 55.00 |
| Apparel | 25.25 | 29.90 | 50.49 |
| Chemicals | 18.67 | 19.18 | 56.41 |
| Electrical machinery | 17.65 | 21.00 | 35.64 |
| Total | 23.39 | 26.59 | 48.65 |
| *By export orientation* | | | |
| Exporters | 21.97 | 25.00 | 45.61 |
| Nonexporters | 24.64 | 28.02 | 51.87 |
| Total | 23.27 | 26.48 | 48.64 |
| *By size of firms* | | | |
| Small | 23.56 | 25.49 | 46.98 |
| Large | 23.25 | 27.60 | 50.22 |
| Total | 23.39 | 26.59 | 48.65 |

*Source:* World Bank, Firm-Level Survey.

respondents claiming that they were required to present a collateral for their loans with a maturity period of less than six months. By contrast, the electrical machinery sector had the lowest proportion of firms reporting that they were required to present a collateral for their long-term loans.

Of those who said that they were required by their banks to present collateral, 87 percent mentioned land and buildings they had been using as collateral and 65 percent named machinery and equipment. Only 24 percent mentioned stocks used as collateral.

In some cases, banks have required their borrowers to have guarantors for their loans, especially if the borrowers were unable to present an acceptable collateral or if the collateral was inadequate. Twenty-nine (29) percent of the total number of respondents mentioned having obtained guarantees on their financing. Large firms and exporters had a higher proportion of respondents obtaining guarantees for their loans than small and nonexporting firms. A large proportion of them (60 percent) mentioned their stockholders as their usual guarantors, and one-fourth mentioned other banks.

## The level and depth of accounting practices

Philippine enterprises are duty bound to adopt sound accounting policies and practices, maintain an adequate and effective system of accounts, safeguard the integrity of their assets, and devise a system of internal controls that will help establish the viability of the business.[10] Following the Statements of Financial Accounting Standards, an enterprise must include a description of the accounting policies it has adopted as an integral part of the financial statements. Financial statements are generated by an accounting process that follows the generally accepted accounting principles (GAAP) on three levels: pervasive principles, broad operating principles, and detailed principles.

The enterprise's "accounting principles" are the specific accounting principles and methods that are considered by the enterprise as the most appropriate in presenting its financial position, the changes in said financial position, and the results of operations in accordance with the GAAP. Some examples of disclosure of accounting principles and methods are, among others, depreciation methods, amortization of intangibles, inventory pricing and overall valuation policy, methods of revenue recognition, and gains and losses on disposal of property. The GAAP also require the disclosure of related party transactions including those between a parent company and its subsidiaries, between or among subsidiaries of a common parent, an enterprise and trust for the benefit of employees, and so on. Transactions involving related parties cannot be presumed to be carried out at arm's length because the requisite conditions of competitive, free market transactions may not exist. Finally, the nature of the control relationship among enterprises under common ownership or management control must also be disclosed.

The Philippines has an Auditing and Standards Council, established in 1987, which issues statements on the "Generally Accepted Auditing Standards." These standards are approved by the Board of Accountancy and the Professional Regulation Commission. The standards require the independent auditor to indicate whether the financial statements presented conform to generally accepted accounting principles.

The generally accepted auditing standards are applicable in the audit of the financial statements of banks, related financial institutions, and business enterprises. The primary objective of an audit is the statement of an opinion by the independent auditor on the financial statements of a business enterprise. For this purpose, the auditor studies and evaluates the accounting systems and internal controls, tests the operation of those controls, and assesses the accounting transactions and account balances.

There are more than 200 accounting and auditing firms registered with the Securities and Exchange Commission (SEC). Almost all of them are located in the NCR; however, they also provide auditing services to firms located outside the NCR by sending audit teams.

In conclusion, it can be said that the existing accounting and auditing systems are comparable to those of more developed countries. However, the actual accounting and auditing practices are different from their respective standards. In particular, small- and medium-sized firms seldom keep good accounting systems and this is one of the reasons why banks seldom lend to this group of borrowers. Also, it has been a general practice among firms to keep two books of accounts, one for their creditors (this is called the "in-house financial statement") and one for the Bureau of Internal Revenues (BIR) for tax purposes, and the difference between the two is glaring. This is complicated because auditors certify only the accuracy of the accounting information and methods used, not necessarily the veracity of the information. This is because under the Philippine practice, much depends on the willingness of the firm to disclose pertinent information about itself and the project. Therefore, audited financial statements are as good as the amount and quality of information provided by the firm. Under this environment, the problem of asymmetric information persists.

### Measures to assist Philippine enterprises

Concerned about the rapidly deteriorating condition of the corporate sector as the crisis continued to deepen, the government introduced some measures to alleviate the firms' plight.

The Bangko Sentral ng Pilipinas created in December 1997 the Currency Rate Protection Program, which essentially is a nondeliverable forward facility, to protect corporations with foreign exchange liabilities against currency fluctuation risk. Since this program can spread the demand for dollars between the spot and forward market, it can also ease the demand pressure in both the spot market—caused by corporate borrowers wanting to cover their foreign exchange exposure—and in the domestic interest rate.

The government issued Executive Order (EO) 465 on January 13, 1998, to modify the nomenclature and tariff structure of 22 industries identified as "Philippine winners." These are the industries that have proven to be competitive or shown some potential. EO 465 was the result of the review of the pace of tariff reduction under EO 264 in consideration of the recent Asian financial crisis.

The rates of duty for certain tariff lines were either raised or reduced under EO 465. Other tariff lines had the same rate as set under EO 264. It should, however, be noted that EO 465 was not designed to delay the attainment of a uniform tariff rate of 5 percent by 2004. While it resulted in a small increase in the overall average nominal tariff rate from the pre–EO 465 level, the overall effective protection rate actually went down.

The government secured in December 1998 from the World Bank US$150 million for the Private Enterprise Credit Support Project, which aims to help enterprises restructure and meet their permanent working capital needs, improve productivity, and create jobs. It also secured another US$150 million from the World Bank for its Third Rural Finance Project, which will assist farmers and agribusiness undertake new projects, and finance working capital requirements. A US$7 million microfinance component is included in the project to supplement ongoing microfinance programs and help satisfy demand for credit by small-scale enterprises.

### Short-run prospects

A great majority of the sample firms were not optimistic about the economy in general, and their situation in particular, regarding the six months following the survey. Almost half thought that their capacity utilization rate, which had already significantly dropped since the onset of the crisis, would remain the same, while one-fourth were expecting a further decline (see figure 13.12). Only 27 percent were optimistic—namely, expecting a rebound in their capacity utilization rate in the next six months. In terms of export orientation, results suggest that nonexporters were more pessimistic—they expected the rate to decline further or remain the same in the next six months—than exporters. In terms of size, small firms were more pessimistic than

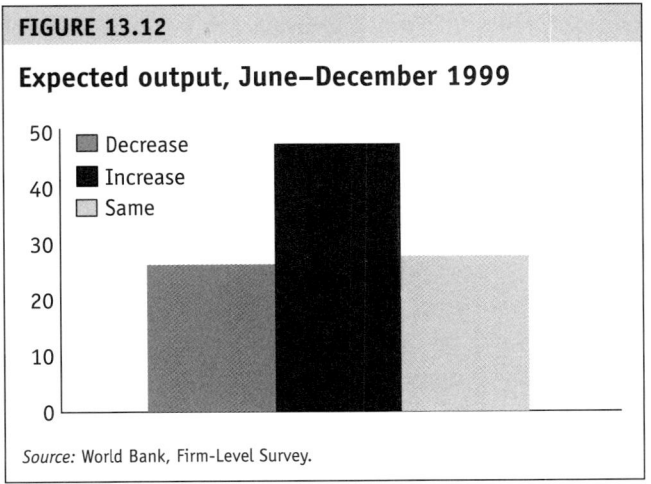

**FIGURE 13.12**

**Expected output, June–December 1999**

*Source:* World Bank, Firm-Level Survey.

large firms. When classified according to sector, it appears that the apparel sector was the least pessimistic and the textile sector the most pessimistic about business prospects in the short-term.

## Conclusions and recommendations

The survey results clearly show that the capacity utilization rate of the Philippine manufacturing firms started to decline even before the crisis struck in July 1997, and that it continued to drop as the crisis deepened. While the recent drop can be attributed to the slowdown in both the domestic and foreign demand for goods and the sudden rise of the interest rate and of the cost of inputs (especially imported inputs), thereby squeezing the firms' profits, the earlier drop could perhaps be attributable to overinvestment made by the firms in building additional capacity given a much more liberal and cheaper access to external sources of funds. Thus, the current capacity underutilization may be attributed to both cyclical and structural factors, which call for demand management as well as industrial restructuring policy measures.

As the crisis deepened, it seems that a consensus emerged: the firms were facing a credit crunch. In other words, institutional lenders had stopped lending to them because of the highly volatile economic situation. The results of this study do not provide clear evidence on the existence of a supply-side credit crunch during the crisis period. It should be noted that a great majority of surveyed firms still had uninterrupted access to institutional loans, albeit at a much higher interest rate.

While banks are now much more discriminating in lending to the business sector, the decline in total loan growth in 1998 could also be attributed to the lower demand for credit, which was brought about by the sharp reduction in demand for goods produced by the firms during the crisis period.

The significant drop in the firms' capacity utilization rate and output during the crisis period would normally have required a drastic cut in the workforce. However, to minimize layoffs, the sample firms resorted to other means, such as reducing the work week or work days, applying forced vacation leave, and freezing salary increases, to save some jobs.

This study has generally confirmed the adverse impacts of the financial crisis on the manufacturing sector; however, it also yields some positive signs that the government can use as a platform for formulating policies and programs to stage a rapid economic recovery. First, most of the firms surveyed were still earning profits, albeit declining in the last two and a half months. If the worst of the crisis has already passed, then these firms can quickly rebound, using partly their profits to finance their growth. Second, most of the firms still have access to credit, although at a relatively higher price. A reduction in the interest rate will surely help them a lot during the recovery period. Third, although the firms resorted to some cost-cutting measures, most of them preferred to preserve jobs, a strategy they think will pay off once the crisis fades away. With most of their core staff intact and excess capacity readily available, a resurgence in demand will certainly be most welcome by them.

All this leads us to conclude that the most appropriate policy that the government could adopt now would be an expansionary one to stimulate aggregate demand. Both monetary and fiscal policies are required to support such an expansionary policy.

There is still some room for relaxing monetary policy. First of all, the inflation rate had already started to come down last February. The agricultural sector—particularly the crop subsector, which suffered a large decline in 1998 as a result of the El Nino weather phenomenon—is expected to rebound in 1999. Second, the reserve money level during the February 1999 test period was found to be P30 billion below the level agreed upon between the government and IMF under the existing standby arrangement program.

The relaxation of the monetary policy, which will push the interest rate down, can accomplish four things. One is that it will lighten the debt-service burden of enterprises, freeing some resources that can be used to meet increased demand for goods. It can also reduce the cost of debt restructuring, whenever resorted to by both enterprises and banks. Still another benefit is that it can stimulate consumer spending and revive the sagging consumer durable goods sector. Finally, it can help arrest the appreciation of the peso in relation to the U.S. dollar and improve the competitiveness of the export sector, which has been stimulating the economy during this crisis period.

There is a limit to how much of the task outlined above can be accomplished by monetary policy. Pushing the interest rate further down and exhorting banks to lend to private enterprises would not be sufficient to stimulate growth unless demand for goods is increased with the help of fiscal policy. Thus, on the fiscal side, the pump-priming measures should continue in 1999, focusing on the critical sectors of the economy, specifically the agriculture sector, which has the most extensive linkages with the rest of the economy, and the social sectors, such as health, education, and housing. However, there are two important programs that the government could launch to help the labor and manufacturing sectors directly. One is to provide skill training programs for those who have been laid off as a result of the retrenchment undertaken by firms in the wake of the crisis. These programs should be offered in various regions of the country so that the benefits can be widely spread. It should be noted that those who were laid off are younger, and therefore most probably less experienced and less skilled—but highly trainable. The government may give incentives to those firms that have resorted to reducing work hours and days to encourage them to offer their unutilized facilities and perhaps the slack time of their senior staff for training.

The other is for the government to stimulate the housing sector, which is a strategy with direct short-term economic and social impact. There is still a huge backlog of housing units, especially for lower middle class and poor households, in the country today. One of the ways of doing this is to strengthen the Home Insurance Guarantee Corporation so that it will have additional resources to provide guarantees to bonds to be issued by local government units for the purpose of financing mass housing projects in their respective localities. Of course, the government housing finance system has to be reformed quickly so that it can efficiently provide the services the public requires of it, without necessarily dissipating its funds.

To support its pump-priming measures in 1998, the government tapped foreign sources of funds to avoid crowding out the private sector and also secure foreign exchange to beef up the country's international reserves. Since private sector demand for funds is still down and the interest rate has already come down to the precrisis level, it would be worthwhile for the government to secure funding for its pump-priming measures for 1999 from the local market, where the cost of financing is now lower than in foreign markets.

Finally, the recent crisis has underscored the importance of keeping a flexible exchange rate policy. However, even if a flexible exchange rate policy is pursued and corporate governance is improved, the level of foreign capital inflows experienced by the country before the Asian financial crisis is unlikely to be attained in the near term unless additional measures are put in place. One way is to liberalize further the entry of foreign banks into the country, preferably allowing foreign banks to wholly own domestic banks—either by establishing new subsidiaries or buying existing ones, especially those that are not well capitalized. The presence of more foreign banks in the country can certainly breathe new life into the banking system and make additional capital available to the Philippine economy.

# Annex 13.A

| Sector | Industry codes | Description |
|---|---|---|
| 1. | **Food products** | |
| | 1512 | Production, processing, and preserving of meat and meat products |
| | 1513 | Production and preserving of fish and fish products and other seafoods |
| | 1514 | Processing and preserving of fruits and vegetables |
| | 1515 | Manufacture of vegetable and animal oils and fats |
| | 152 | Manufacture of dairy products |
| | 154 | Manufacture of starches and starch products |
| | 156 | Manufacture of bakery products |
| | 157 | Manufacture of sugar |
| | 158, 1593, 1594 | Manufacture of coconut-based products |
| | 1591 | Manufacture of cocoa, chocolate and sugar confectionery |
| | 1592 | Manufacture of macaroni, noodles, couscous, and similar farinaceous products |
| | 1595 | Coffee roasting and processing |
| | 1599 | Manufacture of other food products, nec (eg, soup, vinegar, nuts) |
| 2. | **Textiles** | |
| | 171 | Spinning, weaving and finishing of textiles |
| | 172 | Manufacture of other textiles |
| | 173, 174 | Manufacture of knitted and crocheted fabrics and articles; manufacture of embroidered fabrics |
| 3. | **Wearing apparel and footware** | |
| | 181 | Ready-made garments manufacturing |
| | 189 | Manufacture of wearing apparel, nec |
| | 192 | Manufacture of footwear |
| 4. | **Chemical products, rubber** | |
| | 2411 | Manufacture of basic chemicals except fertilizers and nitrogen compounds |
| | 2412 | Manufacture of plastics in primary forms and of synthetic rubber |
| | 2423 | Manufacture of paints, varnishes and similar coatings, printing ink and mastics |
| | 2424 | Manufacture of pharmaceuticals, medicinal chemicals and botanical products |
| | 2425 | Manufacture of soap and detergents, cleaning and polishing preparations, perfumes and toilet preparations |
| | 2429 | Manufacture of other chemical products, nec (e.g. matches, ink, glues and adhesives) |
| | 243 | Manufacture of man-made fibers |
| | 251 | Manufacture of rubber products |
| | 252 | Manufacture of plastic products |
| 5. | **Electrical machinery** | |
| | 311 | Manufacture of electric motors, generators and transformers |
| | 312, 313 | Manufacture of electricity distribution and control apparatus; manufacture of insulated wire and cables |
| | 321, 322 | Manufacture of electronic valves and tubes; manufacture of semiconductor devices and other electronic components |
| | 323, 324 | Manufacture of television and radio transmitters and apparatus for line telephony and line telegraphy; manufacture of television and radio receivers, sound or video recording or reproducing apparatus, and associated goods |

# Annex 13.B

| Industry stratum/sector | | ATE class | | | | % of total |
|---|---|---|---|---|---|---|
| | | 20-49 | 50-99 | 100-199 | >=200 | |
| **Total** | Frame | 46.9 | 21.1 | 15.7 | 16.4 | 100.0 |
| | Sample | 19.3 | 17.2 | 18.0 | 45.5 | 100.0 |
| **Food products** | % frame | 54.1 | 21.0 | 11.5 | 13.3 | 32.0 |
| | % sample | 18.1 | 17.4 | 19.6 | 44.9 | 22.0 |
| **Textiles** | % frame | 40.1 | 24.1 | 11.5 | 13.3 | 32.0 |
| | % sample | 21.3 | 23.2 | 18.5 | 37.0 | 18.0 |
| **Wearing apparel and footware** | % frame | 46.8 | 19.7 | 15.8 | 17.7 | 20.0 |
| | % sample | 15.6 | 12.5 | 13.7 | 58.2 | 22.0 |
| **Chemical products, rubber** | % frame | 46.3 | 22.1 | 19.4 | 12.2 | 23.0 |
| | % sample | 20.3 | 15.2 | 16.9 | 47.6 | 20.0 |
| **Electrical machinery** | % frame | 21.8 | 19.0 | 21.8 | 37.5 | 6.0 |
| | % sample | 21.8 | 19.0 | 21.8 | 37.5 | 18.0 |

## Notes

The authors are with the Philippine Institute for Development Studies (PIDS). The survey of sample firms, which was conducted by the National Statistics Office (NSO), and this report were funded by the World Bank. The authors are grateful to Ms. Ofelia M. Templo, Assistant Director General of the National Economic and Development Authority, for providing direction to the research team. The authors are also grateful to Ms. Ma. Chelo V. Manlagnit and Ms. Hope A. Gerochi for research assistance and to Ms. Juanita E. Tolentino for secretarial assistance. This report is available at the Institute's web site: http://www.pids.gov.ph.

1. For example, see Lamberte (1999) and Virtucio (1998).
2. There is no attempt in this study to do cross-tabulation analysis or regression analysis to test some hypotheses. The authors plan to do this in subsequent studies using the same database.
3. The issue regarding the impact of the crisis on the firms' access to capital is discussed in greater detail below.
4. This issue will be discussed in greater detail below.
5. The NWPC serves as the consultative and advisory body to the President on matters relating to wages, income, and productivity—and also exercises technical and administrative supervision over the RWPTBs.
6. *Business World*.
7. Another P100 million has been added to the initial fund of P200 million.
8. This is based on the median.
9. See below for a discussion on the credit crunch.
10. This section draws on Lamberte and Llanto (1995).

# chapter fourteen

# Thailand: The Road to Recovery

*Fiscal Policy Office and the Office of Industrial Economics, Bangkok, Thailand*

This report presents the results of a comprehensive survey—conducted from October 1998 to February 1999—of 700 firms in key manufacturing sectors in Thailand. The survey provides microeconomic-level information on the impact of the financial crisis on output, employment, corporate finance, and profitability. It also provides insights into the efficacy of government programs, and the prospects for corporate recovery as seen by these firms. Similar studies undertaken in Indonesia, the Republic of Korea, Malaysia, and the Philippines allow for regional comparisons and the possibility to benchmark firm performance.

The macroeconomic story of the crisis has become a familiar one. Until now, however, much less has been known about the microeconomic-level impact of the crisis and how firms have responded over the last 18 months. Based on new information collected from 642 establishments in five principal manufacturing sectors, this paper provides insights into the key difficulties facing the firms and relates them to the policy environment and policy reforms enacted by the government in response to the crisis.[1]

After having enjoyed a real annual growth rate of 9.6 percent between 1986 and 1996, Thailand suffered a sharp economic downturn with the combination of currency and financial crises in 1997 as a result of the unsuccessful defense of the currency and the weak banking system. At the onset of the crisis, Thailand faced four major macroeconomic problems:

- Net international reserves were depleted because of the unsuccessful defense of the Thai baht;
- There were systemic problems in the financial sector;
- The real sector faced a serious liquidity shortage; and
- Regional economic turmoil was a significant constraint in terms of the country's ability to resolve its economic difficulties.

The substantial depreciation of the baht instantly brought soaring costs of foreign debt servicing and foreign exchange losses to those firms that had borrowed heavily abroad or imported their inputs. This compounded the difficulties facing firms whose profits had already been squeezed by rising labor costs throughout the 1990s. Things got even worse after the economic turmoil spread to other Asian tiger countries[1] and became the so-called Asian Financial Crisis. The depreciation of currencies across the region and the growth in excess capacity in many manufacturing sectors meant that firms faced declining export prices in U.S. dollar terms at the same time that many saw their costs increasing.

To restore economic stability swiftly, the government initially pursued tight monetary and fiscal policies by imposing temporary capital controls, raising interest rates and running budget surpluses—which eventually prevented the baht from entering a free fall and brought stability toward the end of the first half of 1998. Unfortunately, economic stability did not come without a price. Domestic demand plunged at both the household and corporate levels. Furthermore, the soaring domestic interest rates raised the firms' costs of debt servicing considerably. The economic slowdown in regional trading partner countries also brought significant falls in foreign demand. Consequently, corporate profits declined sharply, and hence impaired firms' ability to pay back their debts. With accumulating nonperforming loans, the financial sector became risk-averse and was less willing to give credit to the corporate sector. Therefore, many firms were left with insufficient working capital and unable to sell their goods, faced the real prospect of becoming insolvent.

Nevertheless, in recent months financial conditions have continued to improve. The strengthening of market confidence has extended beyond the exchange rate to declining inflation and a leveling-off in indicators of production and demand. Fiscal policy has been assigned the task of supporting domestic demand by expanding fiscal deficits while interest rates have been allowed to decline substantially in line with improved market confidence and falling inflationary pressure. (See figure 14.A.1.)

Using data from the Office of Industrial Economics and the World Bank's 1998–99 Industrial Survey and the already rich findings from Dollar and others (1998), this paper further investigates (a) whether all these issues have become apparent to Thai industries (and in what ways, if they have), and (b) to what extent the recent monetary and fiscal policies have become efficiently implemented from the perspective of key industrial sectors. In line with the previous findings the empirical results indicate that:

- From 1997 to the first half of 1998, macroeconomic stability came at the price of shrinking domestic demand, output decline, and high unemployment.
- There was little evidence of a severe credit crunch after the crisis. However, the survey does show that the availability of credit has been declining.
- Toward the end of 1998, there were some signals of improvement in the firms' financial conditions and growing confidence in the current policy environment. However, substantial corporate restructuring has yet to begin and strengthening long-term competitiveness has become an important issue.

This paper is organized as follows. The next section describes the industrial survey regarding the sectors covered and the sample composition. This is followed by a section discussing the impact of the crisis on the surveyed firms such as changes in demand, level of production, employment, profit margins, and capital structure. The subsequent section presents an in-depth analysis of the constraints to corporate recovery and their implications on government policies. The issues addressed include global demand, credit availability, and industrial competitiveness. Prospects for the first half of 1999 and policy recommendations are discussed in the last main section. Finally, key macroeconomic data and methodology are presented in annexes 14.A and 14.B.

## Description of the survey

The data used in this paper come from the Office of Industrial Economics and the World Bank's 1998–99 survey of Thailand's manufacturing sectors, which is a follow-up to the similar survey conducted between October 1997 and March 1998. (See Dollar and others (1998) for a description of the first survey and its findings.) There were five manufacturing sectors selected for the surveys, based on their contributions to the country's export and GDP. The five sectors are (1) garments, (2) textiles, (3) electronics, (4) food processing, and (5) auto parts. (See tables 14.A.1 and 14.A.2 for sector shares.) In the 1998–99 survey, each establishment was asked over 300 questions on the plant's production, financial structure, and labor force in 1996, 1997, and the current period. Close to 90 percent of the 1,227 establishments surveyed in 1997 (1,107 establishments) survived the year and were still engaged in manufacturing operations in 1998. Out of 1,107 interviewees, 642 establishments were re-interviewed. Thus, a 58 percent response rate was achieved for the second survey during November 1998 and February 1999.

The sectoral coverage of these establishments is distributed unequally, in part as a reflection of the different numbers of establishments in each sector in the broader manufacturing population. Thus, fewer food processing plants are included in the sample, in line with the smaller number of such plants overall. In the sample, about one-third of the firms are relatively new, having been established since 1990; one-third are large, with over 150 employees; 55 percent export at least some of their output, and 29 percent have a partnership or joint venture with a foreign firm. (See figure 14.1 and tables 14.1 and 14.2 for more details regarding the characteristics of the sample.)

While the sample of firms was chosen randomly to minimize possible biases and to allow for statistically significant analysis, it should be noted that as a resuvey, there is a bias in favor of more successful firms. Firms that had to close because of current economic difficulties would have been less likely to participate in the survey, so the results tend to represent upper bounds, or more optimistic projections, of firm performance relative to the entire population of firms in the Thai economy.

## Corporate adjustments to the crisis

This section will use the microeconomic evidence from the survey to analyze the impact of this crisis in five contexts: (1) changes in domestic and foreign demand, (2) changes in the level of production, (3) changes in the level of employment, (4) changes in profit margins, and (5) changes in the capital structure.

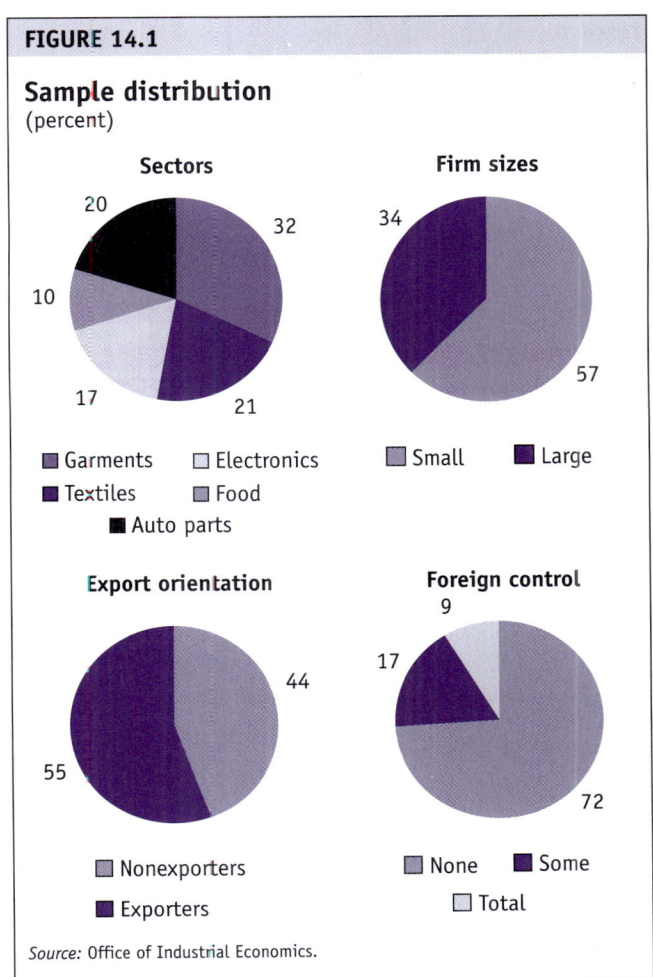

FIGURE 14.1
Sample distribution
(percent)

Source: Office of Industrial Economics.

### Changes in domestic and foreign demand

The downward pressure on the Thai and neighboring economies caused by the currency depreciation brought substantial declines in both domestic and foreign demand. However, from the perspective of the Thai firms that were surveyed, the impact of the contraction of domestic demand was larger than that of foreign demand. Approximately 82 percent of the nonexporters addressed the shrinkage in domestic demand as their major current difficulty, whereas 51 percent of the exporters reported a decline in foreign demand as a significant concern. In part this reflects the fact that not all of these firms export, but also that losses in exports to the crisis countries were partly offset by gains in exports to noncrisis countries such as the ones in the Euro Zone and North America. Firms whose primary export market is within the region (including Japan) were significantly

## TABLE 14.1
### Characteristics of the sample

| | By size | | By export orientation | | By volume of exports | | | By foreign control | | | FDI firm | | Average no. of employees | Total |
|---|---|---|---|---|---|---|---|---|---|---|---|---|---|---|
| | Large | Small | Exporters | Nonexporters | Small | Medium | High | None | Some | Total | Yes | No | | |
| *Sector* | | | | | | | | | | | | | | |
| Garment | 64 | 130 | 133 | 73 | 5 | 23 | 93 | 167 | 31 | 3 | 42 | 159 | 236 | 207 |
| Textiles | 41 | 85 | 53 | 84 | 6 | 19 | 24 | 113 | 15 | 6 | 24 | 110 | 201 | 138 |
| Electronics | 43 | 48 | 68 | 38 | 8 | 18 | 31 | 50 | 20 | 34 | 61 | 43 | 443 | 106 |
| Food | 33 | 22 | 45 | 19 | 7 | 5 | 29 | 42 | 16 | 4 | 22 | 40 | 718 | 64 |
| Auto parts | 40 | 83 | 56 | 68 | 8 | 23 | 16 | 91 | 25 | 9 | 38 | 87 | 268 | 127 |
| *Age* | | | | | | | | | | | | | | |
| New | 86 | 131 | 133 | 94 | 9 | 32 | 74 | 160 | 40 | 22 | 70 | 152 | 342 | 230 |
| Old | 130 | 225 | 214 | 178 | 23 | 23 | 54 | 116 | 288 | 65 | 33 | 113 | 273 | 300 |
| *Location* | | | | | | | | | | | | | | |
| Non-BKK | 47 | 41 | 70 | 30 | 7 | 16 | 36 | 57 | 20 | 23 | 49 | 51 | 502 | 101 |
| Grtr. BKK | 174 | 327 | 285 | 252 | 27 | 72 | 157 | 406 | 87 | 33 | 138 | 388 | 279 | 541 |
| Total | 221 | 368 | 355 | 282 | 34 | 88 | 193 | 463 | 107 | 56 | 187 | 439 | 312 | 642 |

*Source:* Office of Industrial Economics.

## TABLE 14.2
### Profile of the firm

| | Borrow in foreign currency | | Size | | Export orientation | | Foreign control | | | FDI firm | | Total |
|---|---|---|---|---|---|---|---|---|---|---|---|---|
| | Yes | No | Large | Small | Exporters | Nonexporters | None | Some | Total | Yes | No | |
| *Financial indicators* | | | | | | | | | | | | |
| Short-term debt/total financing | 0.43 | 0.29 | 0.42 | 0.27 | 0.39 | 0.25 | 0.32 | 0.29 | 0.52 | 0.36 | 0.31 | 0.32 |
| Long-term debt/total financing | 0.18 | 0.26 | 0.21 | 0.26 | 0.23 | 0.25 | 0.25 | 0.27 | 0.07 | 0.22 | 0.24 | 0.24 |
| Debt-equity ratio | 4.21 | 3.40 | 4.4 | 3.2 | 3.89 | 3.32 | 3.53 | 3.20 | 5.20 | 4.01 | 3.41 | 3.62 |
| *Firm characteristics* | | | | | | | | | | | | |
| Number of employees | 593 | 215 | 736 | 58 | 471 | 130 | 229 | 559 | 653 | 611 | 201 | 312 |
| Share that export (%) | 85 | 44 | 79 | 38 | 100 | 0 | 46 | 77 | 96 | 81 | 45 | 55 |
| Share that are FDI (%) | 59 | 18 | 45 | 17 | 43 | 12 | 5 | 100 | 100 | 100 | 0 | 29 |
| *Response to the crisis* | | | | | | | | | | | | |
| Current capacity utilization (%) | 64 | 60 | 67 | 57 | 67 | 55 | 60 | 64 | 66 | 64 | 60 | 61 |
| Share with few workers | 46 | 53 | 45 | 56 | 41 | 63 | 53 | 52 | 36 | 48 | 53 | 51 |
| Optimistic for future growth | 32 | 19 | 28 | 19 | 30 | 13 | 21 | 20 | 41 | 27 | 21 | 22 |
| Total | 27 | 73 | 34 | 57 | 55 | 44 | 72 | 17 | 9 | 29 | 68 | 100 |

*Source:* Office of Industrial Economics.

more likely to see their exports decline and to cite a fall in foreign demand.

Among the 34 percent of establishments whose export volume declined, 49 percent, 56 percent, and 58 percent identified, respectively, loss of price competitiveness, unstable political and economic conditions in export markets, and a fall in foreign demand as their major concerns. By contrast, 41 percent of the establishments reported an increase in their export volume. Yet, over 60 percent of these establishments identified price competitiveness and exchange rate effects as their major sources of export increases. This opposite effect caused by price competitiveness reflects the currency depreciation of crisis countries and the fact that regional excess capacity helped to drive down dollar-export prices. Increasing export volumes is thus not sufficient to ensure improved firm performance if the values of exports are falling at a higher rate.

## Changes in the level of production

In keeping with changes in demand, 70 percent of the surveyed establishments reported a decline in their level of outputs after the crisis. The average capacity utilization fell down from 71 percent in the first half of 1997 to 61 percent in the first half of 1998, or a 12 percent reduction in utilization rate for each surveyed firm. These establishments cited a contraction in domestic demand and a sharp increase in input costs caused by currency depreciation as their major sources of output decline. Interestingly, these firms perceived access to capital as a less severe problem. Over 70 percent of them identified a fall in domestic demand and higher input costs from currency depreciation as their major problems, while less than 35 percent and 52 percent, respectively, reported access to working capital and costly loans as their main obstacle.

The degrees to which the firms experienced a decline in production varied by firm characteristics. About 84 percent of the nonexporters reported a decline in their output after the crisis, compared with 60 percent of exporters. There was also a significant difference in the reduction in utilization rate between the nonexporters and the exporters; on average, capacity utilization fell by 10 percent more for the former. This reflects the fact that the contraction in domestic demand was larger than that of foreign demand as mentioned in the previous section ("Changes in domestic and foreign demand").

By the same token, 79 percent of the small establishments (compared with 60 percent of the large establishments) reported a decline in output after the crisis. These small establishments experienced a 13 percent decline in utilization rate, compared with 11 percent among the large establishments. This partly reflects the fact that over 60 percent of the small firms were nonexporters, while nearly 80 percent of the large firms were exporters. In addition, being labor-intensive, high labor costs had more impact on the small firms' production costs than on that of the larger firms. Nearly 56 percent of the small establishments identified high labor costs as their major sources of output decline, compared with 38 percent in the large establishments. In addition, suppliers were more willing to give credits and services to larger firms, owing to their higher buying volume. Respectively, 27 percent and 21 percent of the small firms reported supplier credits and goods deliveries as their major difficulties—compared with 16 percent and 5 percent for the large firms.

Likewise, 74 percent of the non-foreign direct investment (FDI) firms reported a decline in output compared with 63 percent of the FDI firms. Firms with no foreign ties were more likely to experience a decline in output than those with foreign ties (that is, those that are under foreign control or are joint venture firms), which is attributable to the smaller share of exporters among the non-FDI firms (45 percent compared with 81 percent in the FDI firms).

The sector that experienced the greatest fall in output is auto parts, with a 25 percent decline in the utilization rate. Of all the sectors, it is the one most influenced by the state of the domestic economy. New cars or motorcycles represent large durable good purchases that many consumers have decided to postpone in this time of crisis. Electronics is the other sector that has been hit particularly hard, with a 22 percent decline in utilization. While geared toward export markets, the firms have suffered from excess capacity within the region and the largest fall in export prices.[2] (See figures 14.2 through 14.4.)

## Changes in the level of employment

The downward trend in the level of production led to a decline in employment during the crisis. However, these changes in employment were smaller than those in output levels. Even though 70 percent of the surveyed establishments reported a decline in their outputs after the crisis, approximately 50 percent reported a decline in employment. This is because these firms, to some extent, were committed to their workers. In addition, labor and welfare regulations (which are costly severance compensation payments) might turn them away from laying off their workers. Therefore, firms preferred other measures (such as reducing the length of the workweek and cutting administrative costs) over laying off workers.

Only 17 percent of the firms that experienced a reduction in employment identified layoffs as the measure they had adopted during the crisis. However, over 70 percent of them reported not filling vacancies and asking for volunteer leave, and about 46 percent reported paying severance compensation as the actions they took. Also, other alternatives were used among establishments whose number of workers either decreased or remained the same. About 41 percent of them used rotational work shifts and 38 percent reduced the length of their work week.

Similar to changes in the level of production, the extent to which surveyed firms experienced a decline in employment—and the employment policies they adopted to cope with the crisis—varied by firm characteristics. Larger shares of the small firms (56 percent) and the nonexporters (63 percent) reported a decline in their level of employment, compared with the large firms (45 percent) and the exporters (41 percent). Close to 80 percent of the small establishments and 60 percent of the large establishments experienced declines in output, whereas, respectively, 56 percent and 45 percent reported decreases in employment. This reflects their difference in work force reduction policies. The management and owners of the small firms tended to have closer ties with their workers. Consequently, aggressive policies such as layoffs and severance compensation payment were more preferable among the large firms, whereas defensive policies such as not filling vacancies and volunteer leave were chosen by the small firms. Of the small establishments, 71 percent and 63 percent,

### FIGURE 14.2
**Capacity utilization by sector**

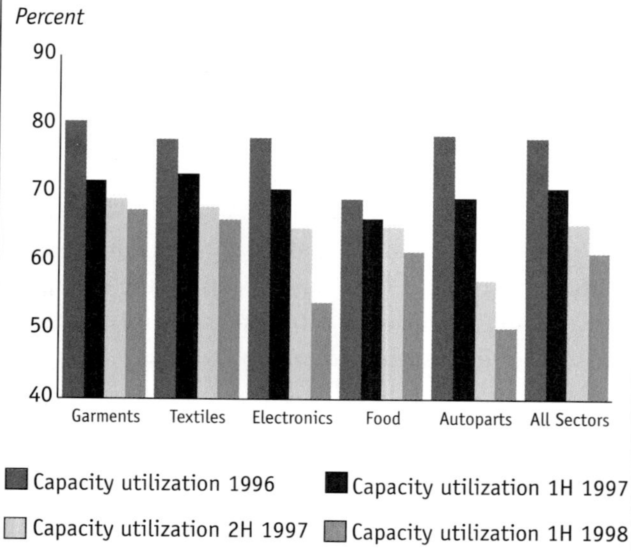

[Bar chart showing capacity utilization percentages across Garments, Textiles, Electronics, Food, Autoparts, and All Sectors for the periods: Capacity utilization 1996, Capacity utilization 1H 1997, Capacity utilization 2H 1997, Capacity utilization 1H 1998.]

Source: Office of Industrial Economics.

### FIGURE 14.3
**Perceived causes of current output decline**

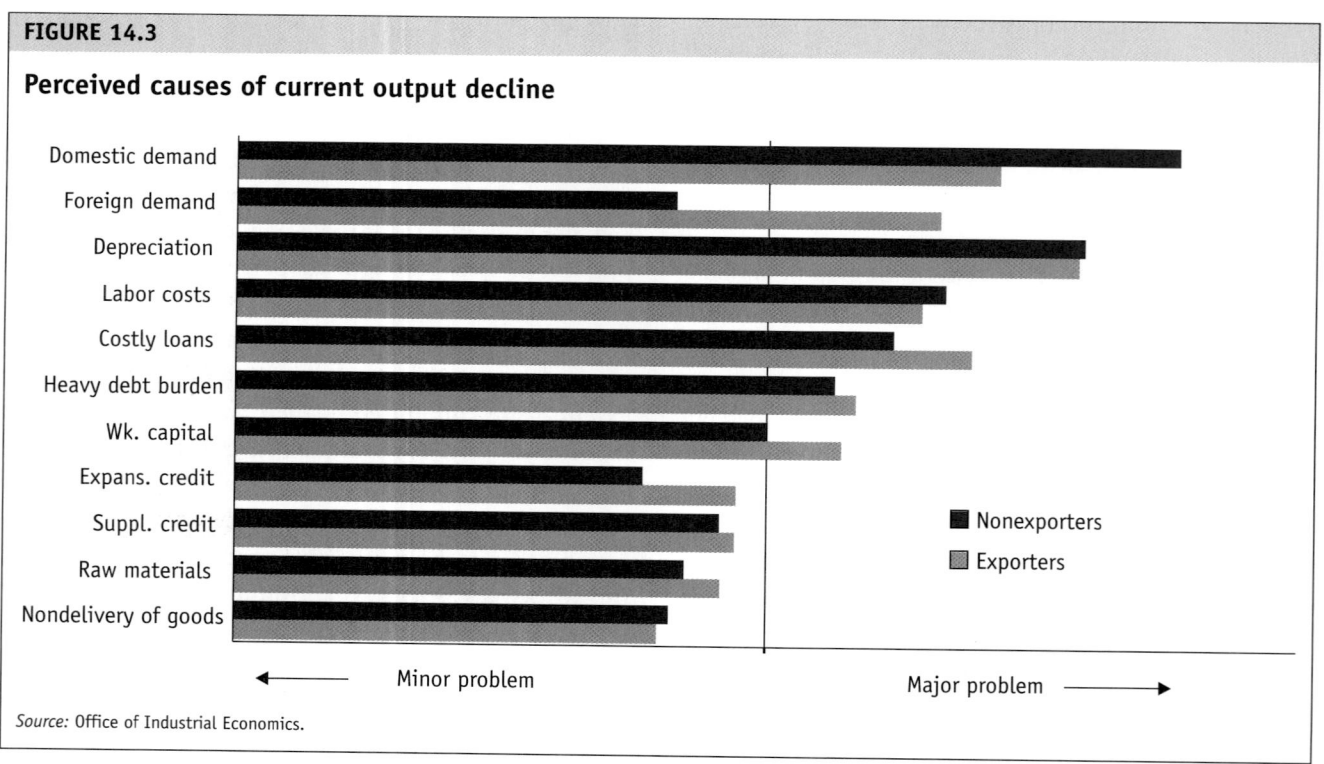

Source: Office of Industrial Economics.

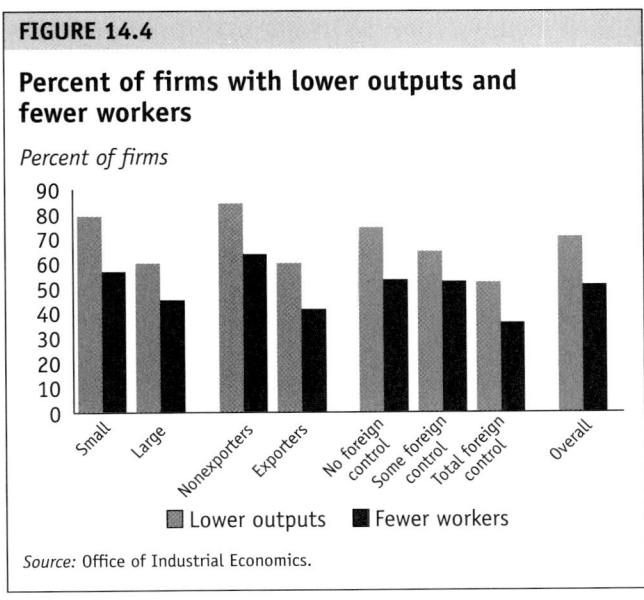

**FIGURE 14.4**

**Percent of firms with lower outputs and fewer workers**

*Source:* Office of Industrial Economics.

respectively, did not fill vacancies and asked for volunteer leave, whereas the figures were close to 72 percent for the large establishments. By contrast, only 13 percent of the small establishments compared with 21 percent of the large establishments laid off their workers. Likewise, 38 percent of the small firms paid severance compensation, while 63 percent of the large establishments did so. (See figures 14.4 and 14.5.)

The profile of jobs being lost also provides an insight to the surveyed firms' employment policies during the crisis. Among establishments that experienced a decline in employment, 77 percent reported the average age of people leaving the plants to be in the range of 20–30 years. Similarly, 88 percent of such establishments reported the average length of tenure of people leaving the plants to be less than three years. Among these plants, the average share of unskilled, skilled, and nonproduction workers leaving the plants were 49 percent, 30 percent, and 8 percent, respectively.[3]

## Changes in profit margins

After the onset of the crisis, approximately 52 percent of the establishments experienced a decline in their profit margins (net income relative to sales).[4] The average profit margins dropped sharply from 3 percent in 1996 to –4 percent in 1997 and experienced a further, albeit slight drop to –5 percent in the first half of 1998. With the exception of the garments sector firms whose majority shares exported more than 50 percent of their outputs and did not have foreign debt (45 percent and 82 percent of garment plants, respectively), the fall in profit margins in 1997 mostly reflects the losses from foreign exchange after the baht devaluation. By contrast, the further decline in profit margins in the first half of 1998 might have resulted from the substantial decline in profit margins of the auto parts firms, which accounted for 20 percent of the surveyed firms. By contrast, the textiles, electronics, and food processing sectors show a possibility for financial stability. However, it is still too soon to judge whether stability has come for the garments sector, since their profit margins were barely at break-even point in the same period.

As shown above, the degree to which surveyed firms experienced a decline in profit margins varied by their financial characteristics. In order to identify the sources of differences in profit margins, this paper will perform analyses on the four major components of net profits: (1) sales revenues, (2) operating expenses (namely, labor, overhead, and input costs), (3) administrative expenses (marketing expenses), and (4) financial expenses (interest expenses and gains or losses from foreign exchange).

First, being exposed to foreign currency losses immediately after the baht depreciation in 1997, the average gains or losses from foreign exchange of those firms that had borrowed abroad dropped sharply from 0 percent in 1996 to –5 percent in 1997 and returned to 0 percent in the first half of 1998. Meanwhile, the firms

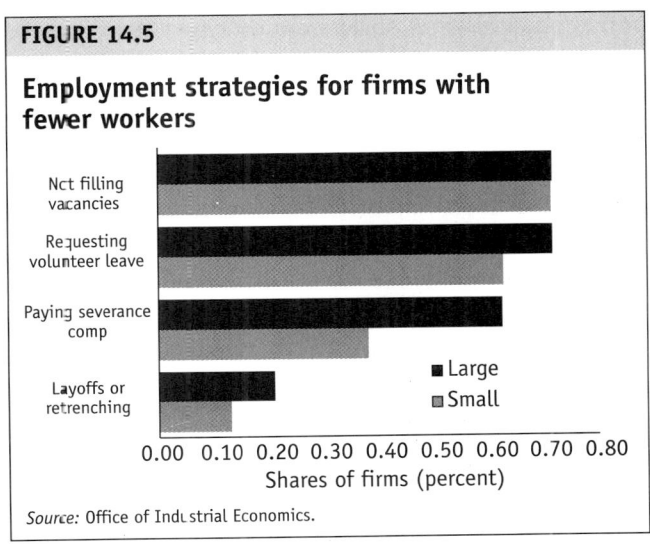

**FIGURE 14.5**

**Employment strategies for firms with fewer workers**

*Source:* Office of Industrial Economics.

that had not borrowed abroad remained at the same −1 percent level in 1996, climbed to 0 percent in 1997, and came back down to −1 percent in the first half of 1998. Therefore, profit margins of firms with foreign debt fell from 3 percent in 1996 to −16 percent in 1997 and rose to −7 percent in the first half of 1998, compared with 3 percent to 1 percent and to −4 percent in the same period for those that had not borrowed abroad.

Likewise, being vulnerable to high interest rates, firms with high leverage tended to experience a fall in profit margins after the Bank of Thailand pursued a high interest rate policy from July 1997 to June 1998 to stabilize the baht. Among establishments with debt-equity ratios greater than 2.0, the average interest expenses relative to sales hovered around 8 percent in 1996 and 1997, then increased to 11 percent in the first half of 1998. However, the figures for firms with lower debt remained at 5 percent in 1996 and 1997 and increased to 7 percent in the first half of 1998. As a result, profit margins of firms with heavy debt burden fell from 1 percent in 1996 to −7 percent in 1997 and rose to −2 percent in the first half of 1998. Meanwhile, margins of firms with less debt burden dropped from 5 percent in 1996 to 4 percent in 1997 and to −1 percent in the first half of 1998.[5]

Similarly, being geared toward domestic economy and paying more on interest expenses, the auto parts sector experienced the greatest fall in profit margins in 1997 and the first half of 1998. This sector's average profit margins decreased from 7 percent in 1996 to −9 percent in 1997, and to −18 percent in the first half of 1998. Interestingly, the average profit margins from the survey shows that exporters did no better than nonexporters in 1997 and the first half of 1998—despite the relatively small difference in their interest expenses and gains or losses from foreign exchange. In other words, we found that interest expenses, gains and losses from foreign exchange, and revenues (which were measured by demand) had no strong relationship with the profit margins function of the surveyed firms. Consequently, we then looked back at production costs of the net profit components as stated in the first paragraph. One might deduce that operating costs and administrative expenses were stronger variables in terms of profit margins than the previous variables. Hence, at this point the issue of eroding industrial competitiveness could arise, resulting in higher operating costs, which will be discussed in the section on "Industrial Competitiveness and Industrial Restructuring" below. (See figures 14.6 and 14.7.)

## Changes in capital structure

The sample firms were reasonably highly leveraged at the onset of the crisis. In 1996, the debt-equity ratio was 3.21 on average. Examining debt financing more closely, we found that the firms relied heavily on short-

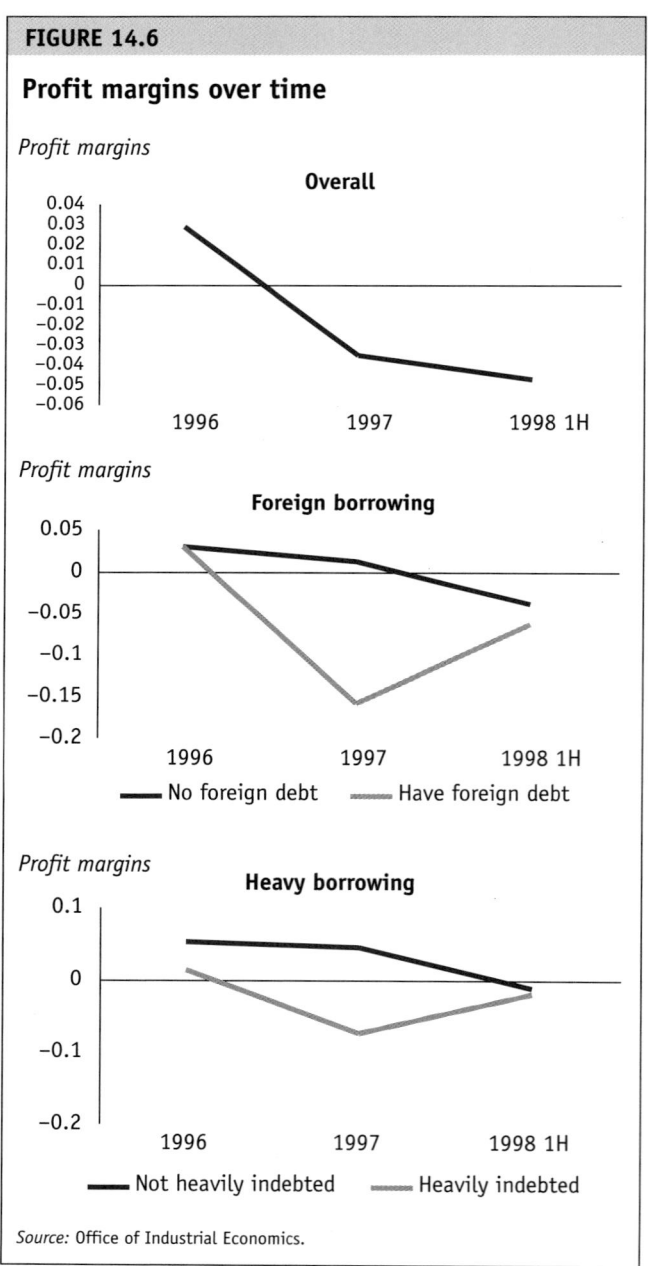

**FIGURE 14.6**

**Profit margins over time**

*Source:* Office of Industrial Economics.

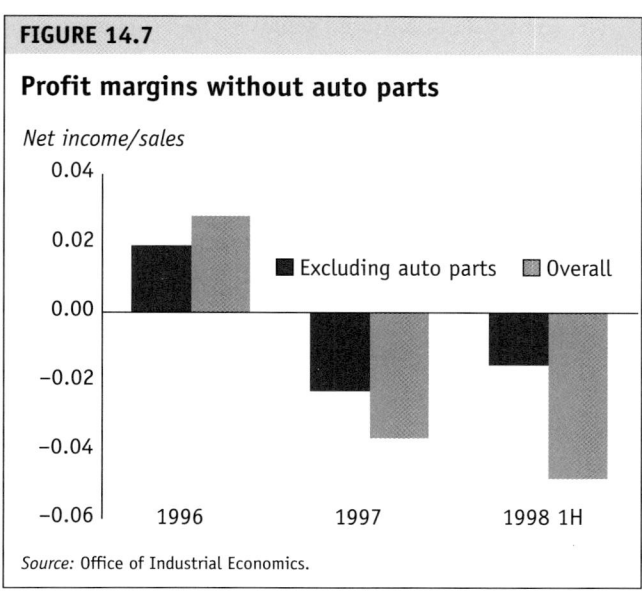

**FIGURE 14.7**

**Profit margins without auto parts**

*Source:* Office of Industrial Economics.

term debt financing. The average short-term debt relative to total financing was about 31 percent in 1996, while that of long-term debt was 24 percent in the same period. As a result, these establishments were extremely vulnerable to changes in the interest and foreign exchange rates, as evidenced by changes in profit margins (see the previous subsection on this topic). After the onset of the crisis, the average debt-equity ratio rose to 3.62 at the end of 1997 and fell back to 2.92 at the end of 1998's first half. Although foreign debt accounted for only 6 percent of the total financing in 1996, the rise in debt-equity ratios in 1997 mostly reflected the substantial increase in foreign debt after the baht depreciation.[6] The debt-equity ratio of surveyed firms with foreign debt increased from 2.84 in 1996 to 4.21 in 1997, while that of firms with only domestic debt increased mildly from 3.35 to 3.40. Foreign debt relative to total financing rose from 19 percent in 1996 to 24 percent in 1997. Meanwhile, overall domestic debt financing decreased mildly from 50 to 49 percent. The small rise in the debt-equity ratio of firms that had not borrowed abroad can be attributed to the increases in short-term debt financing from 28 percent in 1996 to 29 percent in 1997. This is because the decline in profitability left these firms with insufficient working capital, and hence they borrowed to finance their operations.

In contrast, the fall in debt-equity ratios in the first half of 1998 could be attributed to several factors. First, the financial sector was less willing to lend money, owing to the proliferation of nonperforming loans—which meant that loans might not be rolled over. Furthermore, the firms' needs for expansion credit were likely to decrease because of the fall in demand. Long-term debt relative to total financing dropped from 24 to 22 percent, while short-term debt financing only increased from 32 to 33 percent. With the soaring interest rate, the firms might also switch from debt financing to equity financing.[7] Average domestic debt relative to total financing dropped from 49 percent in 1997 to 48 percent in the first half of 1998, while that of foreign debt fell from 24 to 21 percent. Despite these positive changes to the firms' capital structure, there is little evidence that any substantial restructuring has taken place in the corporate sector. Much more strenuous efforts are needed from both the government and the private sector. (See figures 14.8 and 14.9.)

## Constraints on corporate recovery and policy implications

In the previous section, we briefly showed that demand played important roles in the surveyed firms' ability to make a comeback in the first half of 1998. However, this is just one part of the story. Credit availability and the firms' long-term competitiveness are also crucial to the prospect of corporate recovery. In this section, we will examine these issues and their implication on government policies in three dimen-

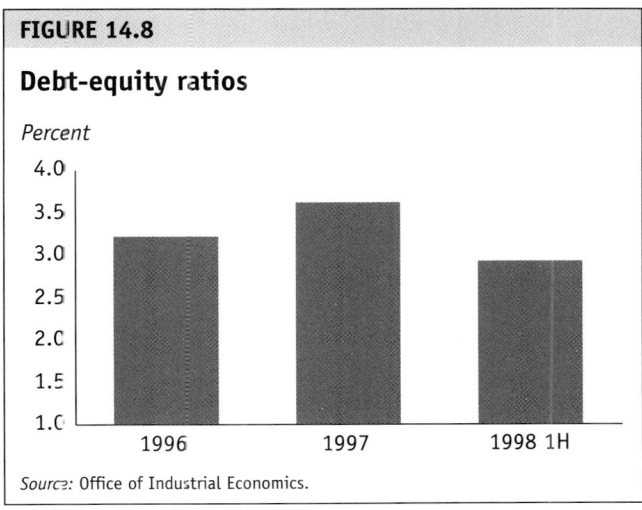

**FIGURE 14.8**

**Debt-equity ratios**

*Source:* Office of Industrial Economics.

Thailand: The Road to Recovery

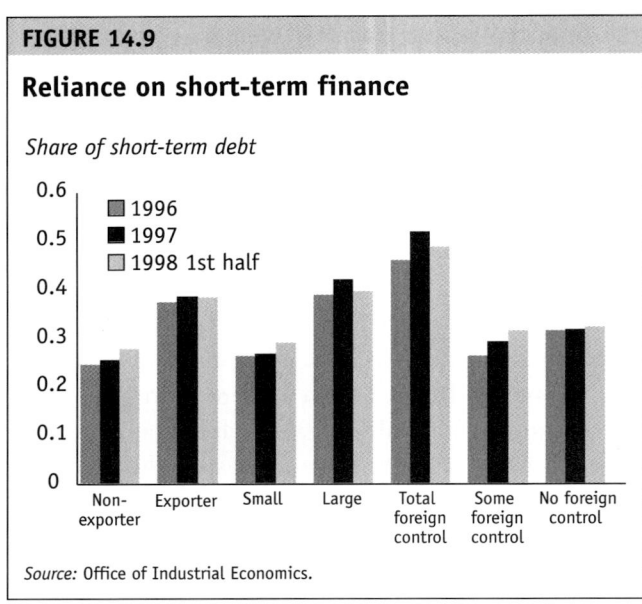

**FIGURE 14.9**

**Reliance on short-term finance**

*Source:* Office of Industrial Economics.

sions: (1) global demand and expansionary policies, (2) availability of credits and financial restructuring, and (3) industrial competitiveness and industrial restructuring.

## Global demand and expansionary policies

Since, as shown previously, Thai firms rely substantially on foreign demand, they are vulnerable to global economic and political conditions. Because foreign competitors' currencies have depreciated and considerable excess capacity exists in regional export sectors, a decreased foreign demand could cause a substantial fall in the firms' profitability. At the moment, there are significant risks of further fall in foreign demand in China, Japan, the United States, and South America. For example, a devaluation of the Chinese renminbi could have dramatic repercussions on the region's currencies, as would a significant correction of the U.S. stock market. The possibility of a contagion from the devaluation of the Brazilian real will also need to be watched. Fiscal expansion in Japan as well as its progress in financial sector reforms will continue to have an important impact on the region. Consequently, Thailand cannot rely only on external demand–led recovery—as the prospect for expansion of global demand seems remote. The government should also focus on generating domestic demand by adopting expansionary monetary and fiscal policies such as interest rate cuts and deficit spending to counteract the crisis.

The survey demonstrated that a lot of firms were cutting off their labor force to stay viable during the crisis; it follows that the rate of unemployment is likely to increase in the coming periods. Thailand's economic growth for 1999 is predicted to be 1 percent while unemployment is predicted to increase from 1.31 million in 1998 to 1.55 million people in 1999.[8] Consequently, the bulk of the additional fiscal stimulus during 1998–1999 will focus on social safety nets, including job training and labor intensive projects.

## Availability of credits and financial restructuring

According to the survey results, there was little evidence of a severe credit crunch.[9] Among 54 percent of establishments with a liquidity problem, 78 percent and 77 percent identified, respectively, revenue decline and high input costs as the sources of their problems, whereas 55 percent, 37 percent, and 59 percent reported, respectively, insufficient working capital, insufficient supplies of credits, and a heavy debt burden. Moreover, only 34 percent of establishments with unchanged or increased output (in other words, the establishments that were more likely to stay viable) reported having a liquidity problem, compared with 62 percent of those with output decline.

However, the survey does show that the availability of credit has been declining. Given the financial sector's growing problem with NPLs, the majority of surveyed establishments had a hard time obtaining credit. With the exception of bond and equity markets whose utilization was not widespread (3–4 percent), the degree of difficulty in getting credits was the highest with domestic financial institutions (83 percent) because many finance companies were closed down after the crisis. Moreover, those remaining were extremely wary of lending and would only do so to the least crisis-affected firms. The decrease in the availability of credits were the lowest in family or friends (57 percent) and partner firms (53 percent) as sources of funds, owing to the close ties between lenders and borrowers. The extent to which surveyed firms experienced a decline in credit availability also varied by the amount of outstanding debts they had on their balance sheet. Approximately 77 percent and 73 percent of heavily indebted establishments reported difficulties in getting credit from domestic and foreign banks, compared with 62 percent and 51 percent of those with lower debts. Firms with lower debt burden were more preferable because the higher their debts, the higher default risks financial institutions faced in lending to these firms. Close to 27 percent of establishments with heavy debts claimed they were unable to meet loan payments at the time of the survey, whereas 15 percent of those with lower debts did so. (See figures 14.10 and 14.11.)

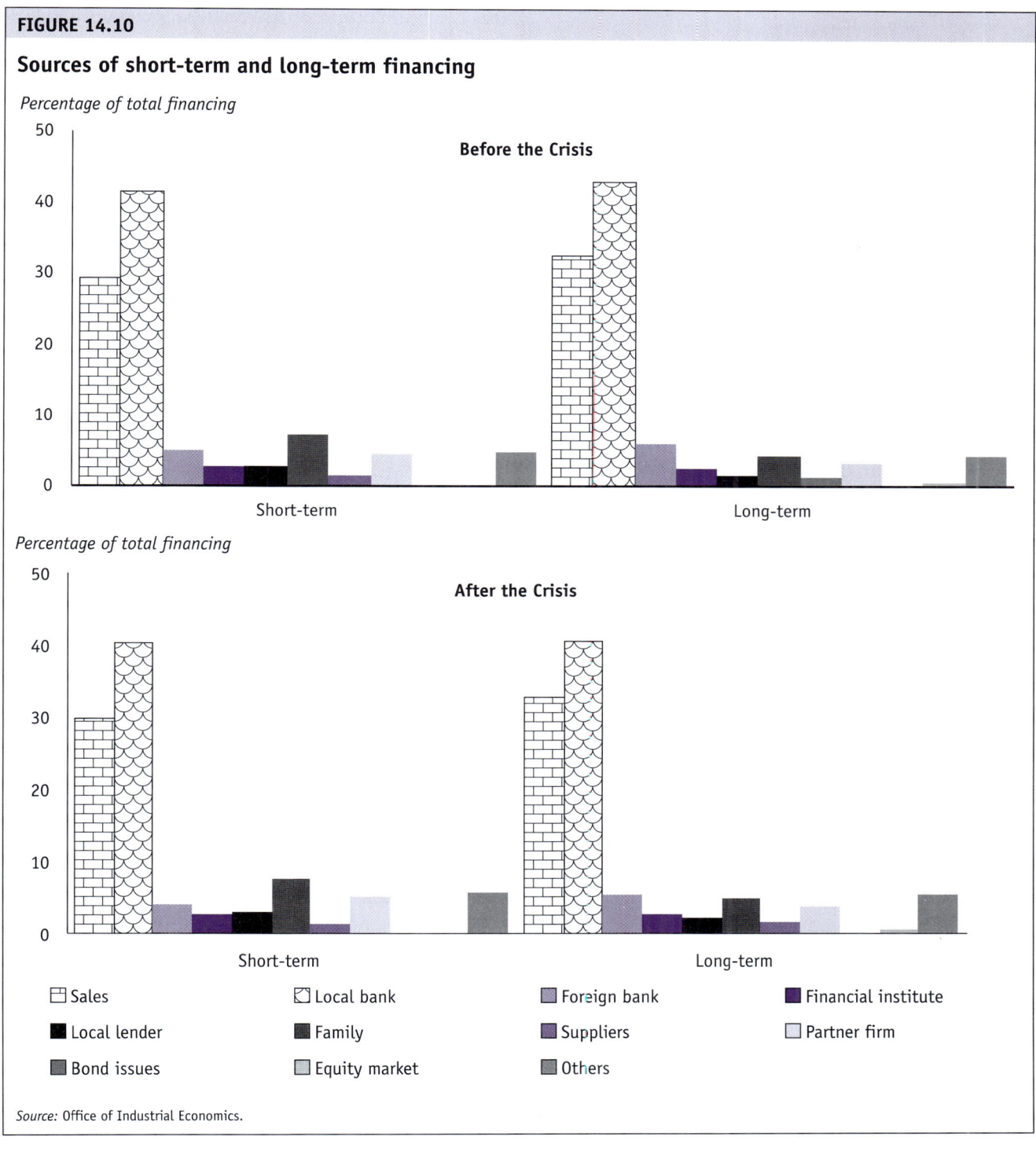

FIGURE 14.10

Sources of short-term and long-term financing

Source: Office of Industrial Economics.

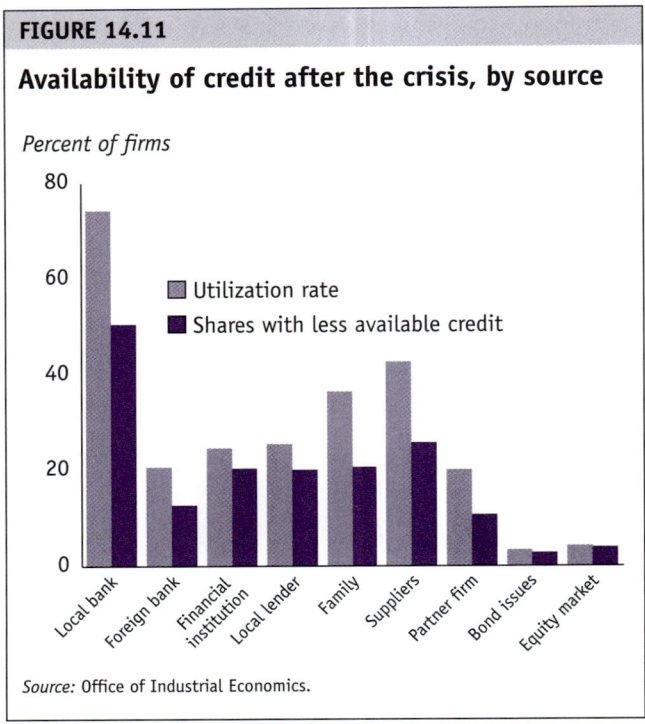

**FIGURE 14.11**

**Availability of credit after the crisis, by source**

*Source:* Office of Industrial Economics.

Given the decline in credit availability and the structural weakness of the financial sector, expansionary monetary policy becomes less effective in directing the domestic economy toward recovery. In this respect, the government is required to take active roles in restructuring both financial and corporate sectors through public incentives and forceful actions. These include (a) recapitalizing the financial sector, (b) restructuring corporate debt, and (c) using credit schemes to increase credit availability.

In addition to financial restructuring to get the financial sector to resume lending, the government might need to review its roles on corporate financial transparency and disclosure of information. Firms and financial institutions are collaboratively required to (a) adopt a joint creditor-debtor review of creditor portfolios and define criteria using clear and sound indicators, and (b) develop a sound and transparent credit rating system of comparison for internal use. According to the survey, collateral was the most common form of lending insurance that the firms provided to their lenders. Close to 59 percent of the surveyed establishments used collateral—especially land—to get loans, while 40 percent and 33 percent used audited statements and guarantees. Among the 59 percent of the establishments that used collateral, 65 percent of the loan value was covered by land, which was the most popular asset the firms used to cover their loans. There is also a point to be made about the transparency problem. Approximately 24 percent of the establishments claimed that they had not been using any form of audited statements, collateral, and guarantees to get financing. This raises the issues of unprofessional financial practices and lack of transparency. As a result, comprehensive financial regulation and supervision is strongly required to improve practices in these areas. In addition, lending requirements (40) need to be augmented with audited statements. During the precrisis period, the lending amount was executed based on the collateral value of the debtor's assets, which reflected the asset-price bubble. However, as the crisis developed, collateral values dropped sharply. Thus, increased financial restraint for private firms and a more transparent approach is required—perhaps with an appropriate mixture of cash flow and collateral lending.

## Industrial competitiveness and industrial restructuring

Will the above expansionary monetary and fiscal policies, financial and debt restructuring, and greater use of credit schemes bring a rebound? Yes. However, these measures cannot guarantee a real recovery. Moving the economy toward that goal also requires corporate sectors to undertake extensive structural reform.

Over the years Thai producers have relied heavily on exploitation of volume and low-cost-based competition with foreign rivals; meanwhile, the value-based competition has not been much utilized. Approximately 62 percent of the surveyed establishments regarded domestic producers, domestic joint venture firms, and multinational corporations in Thailand as their biggest competitors. This indicates that most of the firms are competing among themselves with low degree of foreign competition—as a result, devaluation advantage is nonexistent. Foreign firms that do compete with Thai producers are those in the area of price competition (that is, the low-cost category). Close to 16 percent of the sample establishments regarded low-cost producers (namely, firms from China, Vietnam, Myanmar, and Laos) as their biggest competitors (see figure 14.12). In other words, Thai consumer products in general have little differentiation, low value adding, low degree of production, and little technological enhancement applied to the products. Thai producers can keep such practices and still turn a profit only as long as domestic production costs remain competitively lower than those of foreign firms.

In the globalization age, entities that are more likely to survive are ones that can sell better products at lower prices. Unfortunately, labor costs in Thailand have been rising recently compared with those of the country's low-cost competitors. To make matters worse, there are relatively fewer investments in product and process development and human capital to improve product quality and production efficiency, compared to low-cost competitors. Product and process innovation and investment in human capital was relatively low in the surveyed firms. Only 27 percent and 41 percent of the establishments claimed having, respectively, research and development spending prior to the crisis, and having new product introduction during 1995–1997. Meanwhile, only 54 percent of the establishments reported having formal training of any kind when they were first surveyed.[10] Consequently, Thailand's major and new low-cost competitors have been expanding their market shares successfully, while the country's market shares and profitability have been declining. The present favorable exchange rate cannot fully offset losses from Thailand's eroding long-term competitiveness.

In conjunction with the currently ongoing industrial restructuring initiated by corporate sectors, the National Committee for Industrial Development has developed the "Industrial Restructuring Plan." The action plan for this strategy was approved by the cabinet on June 16, 1998. The plan focuses on upgrading Thailand's competitiveness and increasing positive impact on society through the following six strategies:[11]

- Move toward production of high value added products for the middle-to-higher markets, with higher quality standards, by:
  - Upgrading technology and machinery as well as quality management and
  - Developing product designs in line with market preferences;
- Improve efficiency in terms of production costs, and streamline production process; improve delivery, quick response, and management capability;

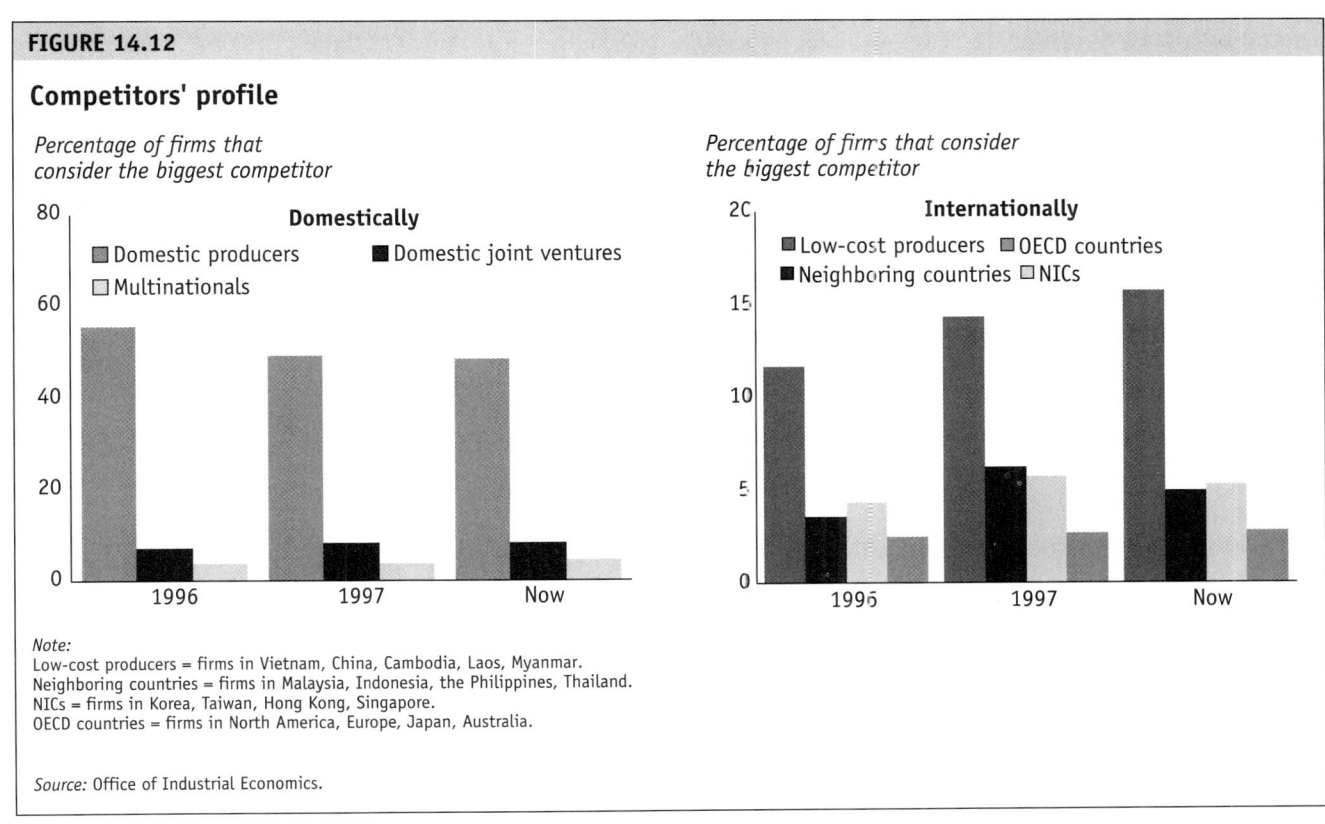

**FIGURE 14.12**

**Competitors' profile**

Note:
Low-cost producers = firms in Vietnam, China, Cambodia, Laos, Myanmar.
Neighboring countries = firms in Malaysia, Indonesia, the Philippines, Thailand.
NICs = firms in Korea, Taiwan, Hong Kong, Singapore.
OECD countries = firms in North America, Europe, Japan, Australia.

Source: Office of Industrial Economics.

- Upgrade knowledge and production skills of industrial personnel;
- Create production and trading alliances with both domestic and overseas companies to penetrate and expand the markets and to enhance technology transfer;
- Decrease industrial pollution through the adoption of clean technology and industrial zoning policies; and
- Disperse industrial employment to regional and rural areas.

## Prospects for the first half of 1999 and policy recommendations

### Prospects for the first half of 1999

The current macroeconomic indicators related to financial stability (namely, the foreign exchange rate, inflation, and the interest rate) all show marked improvement. Moreover, since the third quarter of 1998, there have been indications that various components of domestic demand and production (as measured by the manufacturing production index, value added tax (VAT), the excise tax on motor vehicles, and imported capital goods) have picked up. The problem, however, remains with the expansion of credit given by the financial sector to the real sector.[12]

The survey findings also show improvement in output levels. The surveyed firms are anticipating a better performance in the upcoming year than what they actually experienced in 1998. However, the results do not show a significant progress. This could be attributable to the fact that benefits from the government's expansionary fiscal policies had not been realized at the firm level by the time of the survey.[13] Approximately 62 percent of the surveyed establishments expected their capacity utilization to remain the same or rise, and 35 percent expected a fall in the first half of 1999. In 1998, by contrast, the actual experience yielded 54 percent and 41 percent for the two respective categories.

The extent to which surveyed firms were optimistic regarding output growth in the first half of 1999 also varied by firm characteristics. As the baht stabilized and interest rates fell, 71 percent and 64 percent of the firms that, respectively, had foreign debt and had borrowed heavily expected their capacity utilization to remain the same or rise in the first half of 1999. However, only 49 percent and 52 percent, respectively, actually experienced this trend in the same period of 1998. Likewise, the interest rates for automobile loans were falling. As a result, 36 percent of the auto parts establishments surveyed were expecting a decrease in their capacity utilization in the first half of 1999. However, the actual experience of 1998 was that 50 percent decreased their capacity utilization. The electronics and food processing sectors, and the exporters were also optimistic in their output growth in the first half of 1999. Nevertheless, it is still too early to predict their output growth since they were overly optimistic about their prospects in the first half of 1998. Nearly 44, 33, and 29 percent, in the above respective groups, expected their capacity utilization to decrease in the first half of 1998. In actuality, 53, 53, and 40 percent of them experienced falls in their capacity utilization.[14] (See figure 14.13.)

### Policy recommendations

The firm-level information produced by the survey has given important insights into the impact of the Asian financial crisis on Thai industries, and their responses to the new environment and policy regime. Based on these findings, we propose the following recommendations for further consideration:

*Continuation of fiscal expansion.* As the possibility of export-led recovery seems remote and the domestic

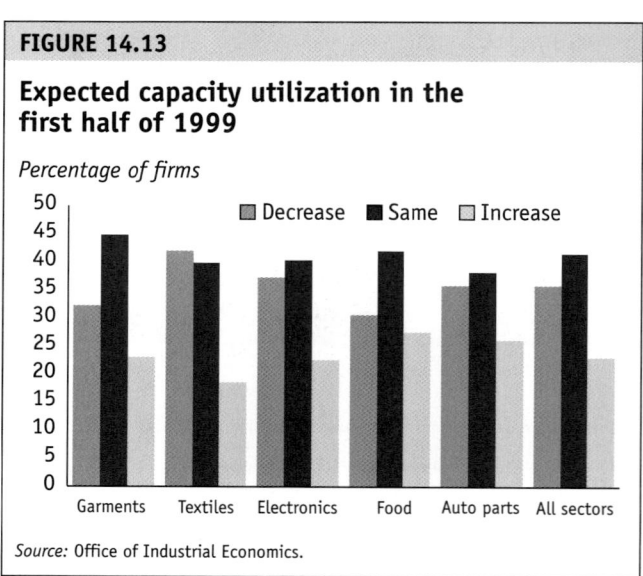

**FIGURE 14.13**

**Expected capacity utilization in the first half of 1999**

*Percentage of firms*

Source: Office of Industrial Economics.

demand contraction is perceived to be the biggest problem by the surveyed firms, the continuation of larger fiscal deficit expansion by external financing is justified to rejuvenate stagnant domestic demand. As already discussed in the paper, Thailand cannot solely rely upon export-led recovery thinking. Therefore, it is important to reinforce the recovery by increasing fiscal stimuli through existing government spending programs. The additional spending should include providing financial resources for the corporate sector and alleviating the social impact resulting from the crisis through (a) public employment, (b) skill-demand based training for the unemployed, and (c) maintaining current social security and public welfare.

*Support for small and medium enterprises (SMEs).* Thai SMEs, which account for 98 percent of the total enterprises in the country, are the ones hardest hit by the crisis—as shown by the amount of output decline, the liquidity problem, and unemployment. Therefore, governmental support for SMEs toward self-sustainability in the long run is recommended. The support for SMEs must be systemically laid down to achieve equilibrium between Thai ownership and access to new technology and product innovation from overseas. This requires a wider range of measures encouraging financial and technical assistance as well as advisory services support that will help integrate SMEs into the market environment. A package of funding through specialized financial institutions totaling 35 billion baht was approved by the government in December 1998. An SMEs Promotion Act and SMEs promotion funds are being set up. A special consultant may be created to assist Thai SMEs with financial advice and management plans for their corporate restructuring and improved cash-flow management, enabling the effective acquisition of additional capital. In addition, with well-developed restructuring plans the government can possibly further strengthen the recapitalization of SMEs by introducing a new equity-financing source that would inject equity capital directly into SMEs.

*Enhancing credit expansion of specialized financial institutions (SFIs).* The SFIs represent an important financing source for the private sector. During a crisis, they have a more important role besides providing credits for their current customers. SFIs must also actively expand their coverage for those who seek liquidity and investments. Consequently, in the short run, SFIs' role would be to affect declining credit expansion of the ailing domestic private financial institutions. However, when economic stability has been restored, the domestic private financial institutions would still be the major vehicle for financing. The progress of loan disbursement is still at an early stage. Moreover, the survey shows that despite the relatively low use of these specialized funds, there has been a clear increase in their availability. Approximately 11, 9, and 11 percent of the surveyed firms claimed using such sources of financing in 1996, 1997, and 1998, respectively. It is expected that specialized credit schemes—particularly export finance, housing finance, rural credit, and SMEs finance—will continue to play an increasingly important role in the recovery of the corporate sector.

*Financial sector reform.* Financial sector reform is unarguably no less important than any earlier points. As already stated, the real recovery cannot be accomplished without financial restructuring. The government should continue its full support for the existing recapitalization measures to further credit expansion. The supervisory and regulatory framework should be strengthened to enhance financial stability and the efficient provision of financial services. Also, disclosure of information has to be incorporated into supervision as well as regulation practices to improve transparency and accountability. In addition, given declining credit availability and low use of debt and equity issues from the survey, capital market development needs to be integrated to increase market liquidity and provide additional sources of funding for Thai corporates. This would create alternatives to borrowing from foreign and domestic financial institutions.

*Facilitating corporate debt restructuring progress.* In our findings, the extent of corporate debt restructuring was relatively small; this can be seen through the debt-equity ratio, profit margins, and debt repayment abilities of the surveyed firm. The likelihood of moral hazards in debt servicing tends to increase given the surge in the amounts tied up in nonperforming loans. The firms might be reluctant to service their debts in the short run, preferring to do so in the longer run. Interestingly, there was a relatively small number of firms (13 percent) claiming that they had been able to meet their loan payments between three months and one year. By contrast, the majority of the surveyed firms (65 percent) reported that they had been able to do so for more than one year, and 22 percent were not able to meet their loan payments. Based on these results it is evident that the government should provide additional measures to stimulate corporate debt restructuring. It should strengthen the legal framework for debt restructuring by adopting such measures as amendments to the bankruptcy and foreclosure laws. Several other initiatives toward a more enabling environment should be accelerated, including steps to promote secure lending, a credit bureau, and liberalization of foreign ownership of business activities and foreign ownership of real property. Operation improvement is also required in accordance with debt restructuring. This is because Thai firms have made many nonstrategic and noncore investments that added fixed cost without increasing operating efficiency and productivity for a long period before the crisis. Finally, the government should call for a more in-depth analysis of the progress of financial and corporate restructuring in relation to NPLs in domestic financial institutions and the extent to which the program has been implemented by the SMEs.

*Additional support for long-term competitiveness enhancement.* Despite improving financial conditions, the survey indicates that corporate structural reform still lags behind and long-term competitiveness needs to be enhanced. Specifically, long-term competitiveness development measures should be set up with respect to the four following criteria: (a) technological development, (b) human resource development, (c) infrastructure investments, and (d) tariff reform. The government should review its roles in supporting technological and human resource development. Given the poor survey results, both the government and Thai firms must collaboratively design their ideal training, and research and development programs in order to maximize the utilization of such programs. These programs were unsuccessful in reaching the firms, especially the small ones and the nonexporters. The findings on the effectiveness of government programs for research and development (R&D) and technology development (for example, those of the National Science and Technology Development Agency, the Ministry of Industry (MOI), Board of Industry (BOI) incentives for R&D, and BOI unit for Industrial Linkage Development) were astounding. Relatively small numbers of firms were informed about such programs. Among these programs, the ones administered by the MOI were the best known at 31 percent. However, only 42 percent of the surveyed establishments claimed having used them. (See figure 14.14.) Moreover, the necessity of infrastructure investments must not be undermined by the crisis—these fundamentally attract foreign direct investment and improve income and wealth distribution to the population. And finally, tariff reform needs to be undertaken to rationalize the tariff structure and to strengthen the competitive edge of Thai industries in the long run.

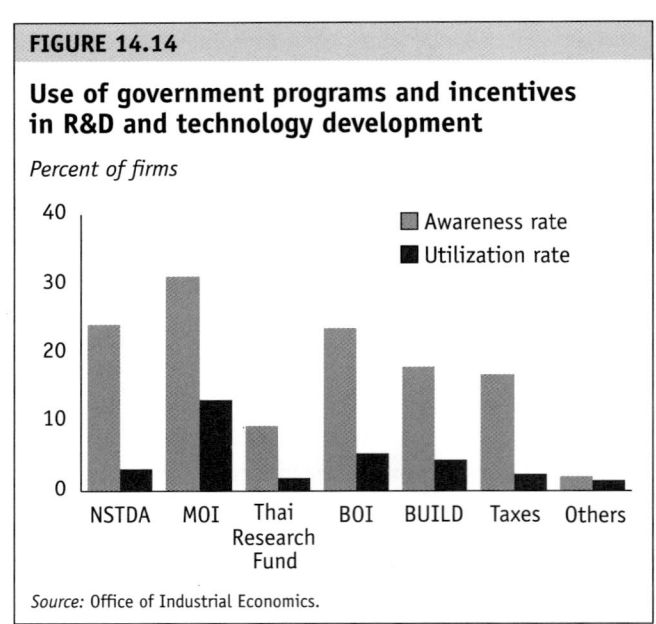

**FIGURE 14.14**

**Use of government programs and incentives in R&D and technology development**

*Source:* Office of Industrial Economics.

# Annex 14.A

## Macroeconomic data

### List of tables and figures

**Figure 14.A.1** Changes in Thailand's key economic indicators.

**Table 14.A.1** GDP shares of manufacturing commodities.

**Table 14.A.2** Exports shares by commodity group.

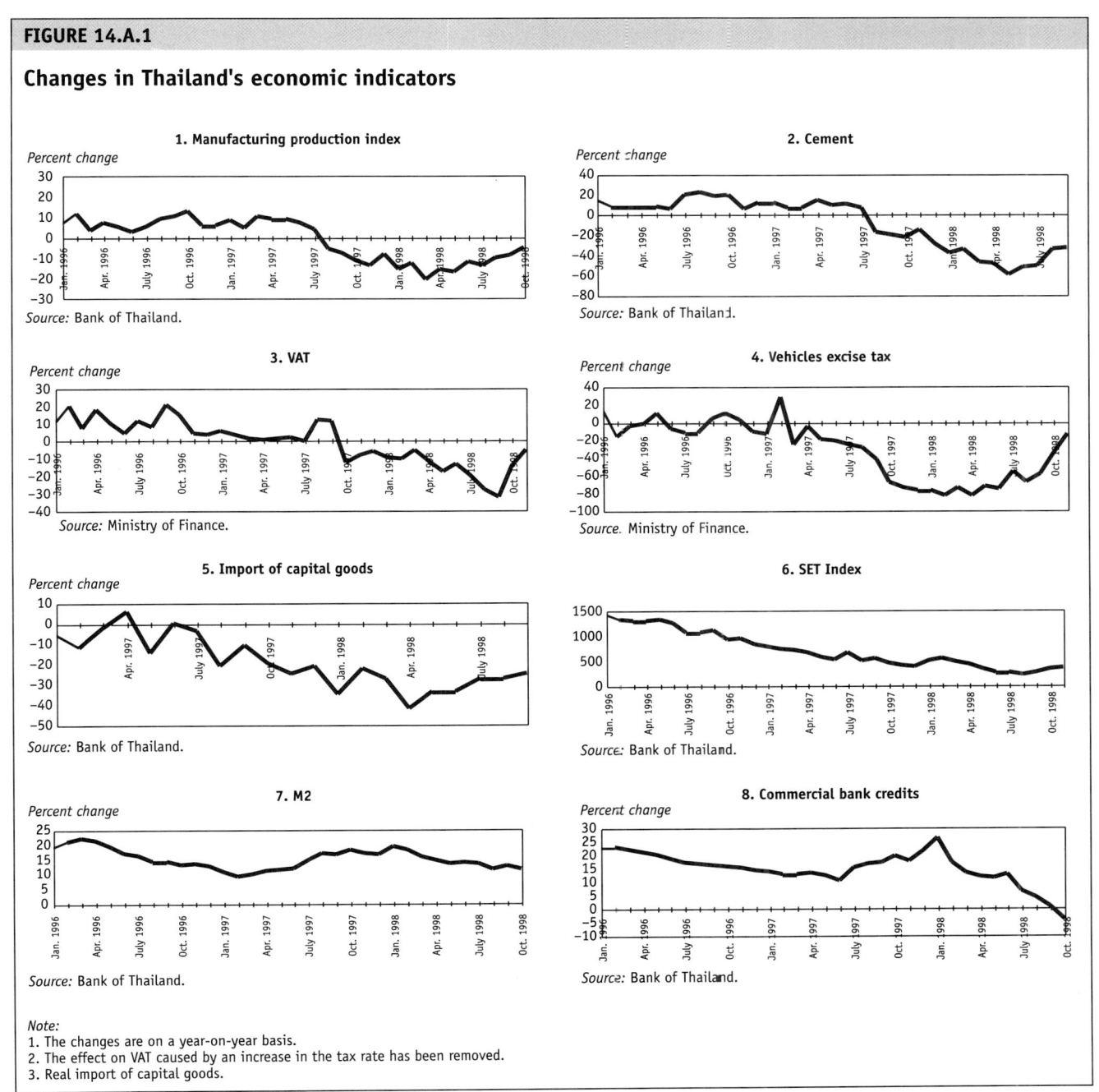

**FIGURE 14.A.1**

Changes in Thailand's economic indicators

Note:
1. The changes are on a year-on-year basis.
2. The effect on VAT caused by an increase in the tax rate has been removed.
3. Real import of capital goods.

## TABLE 14.A.1
### GDP shares of manufacturing commodities

|  | At 1988 prices | | | At current market prices | | |
| --- | --- | --- | --- | --- | --- | --- |
|  | 1994 | 1995 | 1996p | 1994 | 1995 | 1996p |
| Apparel except footwear | 9.21 | 9.79 | 9.78 | 11.52 | 11.44 | 11.70 |
| Other manufacturing industries | 9.13 | 9.68 | 9.29 | 8.93 | 8.87 | 8.18 |
| Electrical machinery and supplies | 9.00 | 8.29 | 7.87 | 8.80 | 8.14 | 7.83 |
| Food | 8.60 | 8.49 | 7.74 | 8.23 | 7.78 | 8.01 |
| Textiles | 8.26 | 7.74 | 7.06 | 7.96 | 7.75 | 6.68 |
| Transport equipment | 8.20 | 7.76 | 7.65 | 7.80 | 8.62 | 8.66 |
| Machinery | 6.86 | 7.36 | 8.83 | 6.55 | 7.28 | 8.37 |
| Petroleum refineries and petroleum products | 6.72 | 7.69 | 8.88 | 6.25 | 6.46 | 7.62 |
| Beverages | 6.61 | 6.87 | 6.81 | 6.24 | 6.45 | 6.36 |
| Nonmetallic mineral products | 6.18 | 6.05 | 6.24 | 5.66 | 5.30 | 5.45 |
| Leather, leather products, and footwear | 3.45 | 3.15 | 2.90 | 4.10 | 3.74 | 3.12 |
| Furniture and fixtures | 3.02 | 3.07 | 2.74 | 3.02 | 2.84 | 2.61 |
| Rubber and plastic products | 2.73 | 2.75 | 3.01 | 2.73 | 3.14 | 2.60 |
| Fabricated metal products | 2.40 | 2.56 | 2.61 | 2.53 | 2.56 | 2.74 |
| Tobacco | 2.22 | 1.89 | 1.97 | 2.39 | 2.10 | 2.13 |
| Chemicals and chemical products | 2.04 | 1.80 | 1.53 | 2.18 | 2.31 | 2.24 |
| Basic metal industries | 1.96 | 1.89 | 1.82 | 1.75 | 1.79 | 1.79 |
| Paper and paper products | 1.58 | 1.57 | 1.70 | 1.39 | 1.54 | 1.77 |
| Wood and wood products | 1.08 | 1.10 | 1.19 | 0.99 | 0.75 | 0.69 |
| Printing, publishing, and allied industries | 0.74 | 0.50 | 0.38 | 0.99 | 1.15 | 1.46 |
| Total | 100.00 | 100.00 | 100.00 | 100.00 | 100.00 | 100.00 |

p. Projected.
*Source:* NESDB, http://www.nesdb.go.th.

## TABLE 14.A.2
### Export shares by commodity group

|  | 1993 | 1994 | 1995 | 1996 | 1997 | 1998 |
| --- | --- | --- | --- | --- | --- | --- |
| Electrical products | 16 | 18 | 19 | 21 | 22 | — |
| Agricultural products | 12 | 11 | 11 | 12 | 10 | — |
| Food | 11 | 10 | 9 | 9 | 8 | — |
| Garments | 10 | 9 | 7 | 6 | 5 | — |
| Textiles | 6 | 6 | 5 | 6 | 5 | — |
| Precious stones and jewelry | 4 | 4 | 4 | 4 | 3 | — |
| Plastic products | 4 | 3 | 4 | 2 | 3 | — |
| Base metal products | 2 | 2 | 2 | 3 | 3 | — |
| Footwear | 3 | 3 | 4 | 2 | 2 | — |
| Vehicle parts and accessories | 1 | 2 | 1 | 1 | 2 | — |
| Furniture and parts | 2 | 2 | 1 | 1 | 1 | — |
| Mineral products | 1 | 1 | 1 | 1 | 1 | — |
| Others | 29 | 29 | 31 | 33 | 35 | — |
| Total | 100 | 100 | 100 | 100 | 100 | 100 |

—: not available
*Source:* Bank of Thailand Monthly Bulletin.

# Annex 14.B

## Methodology

### Missing values

Unfortunately, some firms did not answer all of our questions, and hence the figures shown in the tables sometimes do not add up to the total values.

### Negative equity values

Firms with negative equity values were excluded from any calculations that are related to the firms' equity values such as debt-equity ratio and change in equity financing.

### Outliers in financial data

Before the average calculations, normalization technique using a 95 percent confidence interval was performed to eliminate outliers for the firms' debt-equity ratios, profit margins, interest expenses, and gains or losses from foreign currency. (See statistics or econometric textbooks for more details.)

### Establishment classification

Throughout this paper, we group the surveyed firms using different classifications and compare their results. Definitions for such classifications are shown in table 14.B.1.

**TABLE 14.B.1**
**Establishment classification used in the paper**

| Classification | Definition (percent) |
|---|---|
| *Size* | |
| Small | Employ less than 150 workers |
| Large | Employ at least 150 workers |
| *Export orientation* | |
| Nonexporters | Do not export their outputs directly |
| Exporters | Export at least some of their outputs directly |
| *Volume of exports* | |
| Small | 0 < Export Sales/Total Sales < 0.05 |
| Medium | 0.05 ≤ Export Sales/Total Sales < 0.50 |
| High | 0.50 ≤ Export Sales/Total Sales |
| *Foreign control* | |
| None | 0 ≤ Share of Foreign Equity < 10 |
| Some | 10 ≤ Share of Foreign Equity < 50 |
| Total | 50 ≤ Share of Foreign Equity |
| *FDI firms* | |
| Yes | Share of Foreign Equity ≥ 0 or answered "Foreign-Owned/Controlled Firm" or "Joint Venture with Foreign Firm" |
| No | Otherwise |
| *Borrow in foreign currency* | |
| No foreign debt | Do not have debt denominated in currencies other than baht |
| Have foreign debt | Have debt denominated in currencies other than baht |
| *Heavy debt* | |
| No | Total Debt/Total Equity ≤ 2.0 |
| Yes | Total Debt/Total Equity > 2.0 |
| *Market* | |
| Domestic | Do not export |
| Crisis Countries and Japan | Biggest export markets are Indonesia, Korea, Malaysia, the Philippines, or Japan |
| Noncrisis Countries | Otherwise |
| *Age* | |
| New | Established in and after 1990 |
| Old | Established before 1990 |
| *Location* | |
| Bangkok and Greater Bangkok | Located in Bangkok, Ayutthaya, Nonthaburi, Pathum Thani, Samut Prakan, or Samut Sakhon |
| Non-Bangkok | Otherwise |
| Total | Overall value (all establishments) |

## Notes

This paper was the result of a joint collaboration effort undertaken by Nat Chulkarattana and Dhanoos Sutthiphisal of the Office of Industrial Economics of the Ministry of Industry, and Pongpanu Svetarundra, Chanatip Promphan, and Wanchart Kittisuwan of the Fiscal Policy Office of the Ministry of Finance The authors wish to express their appreciation to Mary Hallward-Driemeier for her invaluable comments and suggestions.

1. These countries are Indonesia, Malaysia, the Philippines, and the Republic of Korea.

2. While the large majority of the firms have decreased their capacity utilization, about one-fifth have been successful in expanding their production since the onset of the crisis. These firms are likely to be food processing or garment plants. They also tend to be large firms that export the majority of their output.

3. As with those firms that increased their capacity utilization, garment and food processing firms are those that were most likely to have increased employment since July 1997—although fewer firms increased employment compared with those that increased capacity utilization. Interestingly, the employment increases were not concentrated among the exporting firms or among the large firms, further indicating the gap between capacity utilization and job creation.

4. The response rate to questions asking for financial and profit information was lower than for the rest of the questionnaire. However, there is no systematic bias in terms of firm characteristics (sector, size, age, export status, ownership, and so on) between those that did and did not answer these questions. As in the section on the description of the survey, it should be noted that the responses are likely to be biased toward favorable results; that the more viable and successful firms are most likely to have provided the requested information.

5. The effects attributable to other factors such as lower gains or losses from foreign exchange might dominate the effects of high interest expenses.

6. One might argue that the increase in debt-equity ratio in 1997 might come from the substantial reduction in equity. However, we found that this was not the case. The average percent change in equity and the average percent change in debt from 1996 to 1997 both had positive signs.

7. The average percent change in equity from 1997 to the first half of 1998 had a positive sign, whereas that of debt had a negative sign.

8. Estimated figure from the Ministry of Labor and Social Welfare as of the end of 1998.

9. For conditions that would be conducive to a credit crunch to have existed, the liquidity of the firms would need to have been so constrained that these firms would not have had the funds necessary to finance the costs of production. However, they would have been able to sell their goods if they had been able to produce them.

10. The extent of product and process innovation and investment in human capital also varied by firm characteristics. With more resources, large firms, exporters (whose majority shares of firms were large firms), and firms with foreign ties invested more on product and process innovation and human capital than small firms.

11. An excerpt from the Ministry of Industry's Industrial Restructuring Master Plan: Executive Summary proposed to the Cabinet, January 1998.

12. Year-on-year percentage changes in macroeconomic indicators from April to November 1998 are as follows: −16.10 percent to 3.40 percent for the manufacturing production index; −12.25 percent to −5.59 percent for VAT; −83.51 percent to 34.08 percent for the excise tax on motor vehicles; and −42.07 percent to −1.55 percent for imported capital goods.

13. The previous spending plans were aimed at budget surpluses and had not been changed to budget deficits until early 1998. This led to a large adjustment in the fiscal budget to stimulate domestic demand between the first and third quarters of 1998. Hence, the government started having large budget deficits in the third quarter of 1998.

14. Comparing the firms' expectations a year ago with their actual performance in 1998, the correlation was weak (0.16). At that time, the firms were overly optimistic about their prospects.

# References

*The word "processed" describes informally reproduced works that may not be commonly available through libraries.*

## Chapter 1

Dasgupta, Dipak, and Kimiko Imai. 1998. "The East Asian Crisis: Understanding the Causes of Export Slowdown, and the Prospects for Recovery." Processed, World Bank, Washington, D.C.

Ito, Takatoshi, and Luiz A. Pereira da Silva. 1998. "The Credit Crunch in Thailand during the 1997–1998 Crisis: Theoretical and Operational Issues Derived from Bank Survey Results." Processed, World Bank, Washington, D.C.

## Chapter 3

Bernanke, B., and M. Gertler. 1995. "Inside the Black Box: The Credit Channel of Monetary Policy Transmission." *Journal of Economic Perspectives* 9(4): 27–48.

Christiano, L., M. Eichenbaum, and C. Evans. 1994. "Identification and the Effects of Monetary Policy Shocks." Working Paper WP-94-7. Federal Reserve Bank of Chicago, Chicago.

Ding, W., I. Domac, and G. Ferri. 1999. "Is There a Credit Crunch in East Asia?" World Bank, Washington, D.C. Processed.

Dollar, D., and M. Hallward-Driemeier. 1998. "Crisis, Adjustment, and Reform in Thai Industry." World Bank, Washington, D.C. Processed.

Fischer, S. 1999. "On the Need for an International Lender of Last Resort." International Monetary Fund, Washington, D.C. Processed.

Goldstein, M. 1998. *The Asian Financial Crisis: Causes, Cures, and Systemic Implications*. Institute of International Economics, Washington, D.C.

IIF (Institute of International Finance). 1998. "Capital Flows to Emerging Market Economies."

JP Morgan. 1999. *Asian Financial Markets, First Quarter 1999*.

Lane, T., A. Ghosh, J. Hamann, S. Phillips, M. Schulze-Ghattas, and T. Tsikata. 1999. "IMF-Supported Programs in Indonesia, Korea and Thailand: A Preliminary Assessment." International Monetary

Fund, Washington, D.C. Processed.

Lee. J., and C. Rhee. 1998. "Social Impacts of the Asian Crisis: Policy Challenges and Lessons." Occasional Paper No. 33, Human Development Report Office, United Nations Development Programme (UNDP), New York.

McKinnon, R. 1998. "The IMF, The East Asian Currency Crisis, and The World Dollar Standard." Paper presented at the 1998 Annual Meeting of the American Economic Association, January 3–5, 1999, Chicago.

Sims. 1992. "Interpreting the Macroeconomic Time Series Facts: The Effects of Monetary Policy." *European Economic Review* 36: 975–1011.

Yusof, Zainal Aznam. 1998. "Economic Reform of Malaysia After the East Asian Crisis." Institute of Strategic and International Studies (ISIS), Malaysia. Processed.

## Chapter 5

Cho, Yoon Je, and Changyong Rhee. 1999. "Macroeconomic Views of the East Asian Crisis." Paper presented to the Conference on Corporate Recovery, Bangkok.

Claessens, Stijn, Simeon Djankov, and Larry Lang. 1999. "East Asian Corporates: Growth, Financing and Risks over the Last Decade." Processed, World Bank, Washington, D.C.

Claessens, Stijn, Simeon Djankov, Joseph Fan, and Larry Lang. 1999. "Ultimate Ownership Structure and Diversification by East Asian Corporations." Processed, World Bank, Washington, D.C.

Demirguc-Kunt, Asli, and Vojislav Maksimovic. 1995. "Stock Market Development and Firm Financing Choices." Policy Research Paper 1461, World Bank, Washington D.C.

Ghosh, Swati R. 1998. "Korea in the Aftermath of the Crisis: Credit Crunch or Lack of Demand." Draft, Processed, World Bank, Washington, D.C. December.

Ito, Takatoshi, and Luis Pereira da Silva. 1999. "The Credit Crunch in Thailand during the 1997–98 Crisis: Theoretical and Operational Issues Derived from Bank Survey Results." Processed, World Bank, Washington, D.C.

Kawai, Masahiro, Hongjoo Hahm, and Giuseppe Iarossi. 1999. "Corporate Foreign Debt in East Asia: Too Much or Too Little?" Paper prepared for the Conference on Asian Corporate Recovery, Bangkok.

Shirazi, Javad K. 1999. "The East Asian Financial Crisis, Financial Sector Restructuring: Progress and Issues." Paper prepared for the Conference on Asian Corporate Recovery, Bangkok.

Stiglitz, Joseph, and Andrew Weiss. 1981. "Credit Rationing in Markets with Imperfect Information." *American Economic Review* 71(3): 393–410.

Waiquamdee, Atchana, Soravis Krairiksh, and Wasana Phongsanarakul. 1999. "Corporates' Views of the Constraints to Recovery." Paper prepared for the Conference on Asian Corporate Recovery, Bangkok.

## Chapter 6

Armstrong, Angus. 1999. *Asia Economics Weekly:* 2.

1999. *Asia Economics Weekly:* 2.

Deutsche Bank Research. 1998. *Global Emerging Markets*. June.

1999. *Far Eastern Economic Review*.

IMF (International Monetary Fund). 1998. *International Capital Markets: Developments, Prospects and Key Policy Issues*. International Monetary Fund, Washington, D.C. September.

Krugman, Paul. 1999. "Balance Sheets, the Transfer Problem, and Financial Crises." January. Processed.

Republic of Korea. 1998. *Progress Report on Korea's Economic Reform*. October.

Shirazi, Javad K. 1998. "The East Asian Crisis: Origins, Policy Challenges, and Prospects." Featured presentation at the Conference organized by the National Bureau of Asian Research and U.S. Army's Strategic Studies Institute, titled "East Asia in Crisis," Seattle, June 9–10.

1999. *Sunday* (Singapore) *Times*, Feb. 28, p.8.

World Bank. 1998. *East Asia: The Road to Recovery*. World Bank, Washington, D.C.

World Bank. 1999. *Thailand Economic Monitor*. World Bank, Bangkok. March.

## Chapter 7

Claessens, Stijn, Simeon Djankov, and Giovanni Ferri. 1998. "Corporate Distress in East Asia: Assessing the Impact of Interest and Exchange Rates Shocks." Forthcoming as an *Emerging Markets Quarterly* paper in December, available on the Web at http://wbln0018.world-bank.org/Research/workpapers.nsf/WPDomesticFinance/?OpenView&count=500000&Topic=Domestic+Finance

Claessens, Stijn, Simeon Djankov, and Larry Lang. 1999. "Who Controls East Asian Corporations?" Research Paper 2054. World Bank, Washington, D.C. This paper is available on the Web at http://wbln0018.worldbank.org/Research/workpapers.nsf/WPPrivateSectorDevelopment/?OpenView&count=500000&Topic=Private+Sector+Development.

Claessens, Stijn, Simeon Djankov, Joseph Fan, and Larry Lang. 1999a. "Diversification and Efficiency of Investment by East Asian Corporations." Research Paper 2033. World Bank, Washington, D.C. This paper is available on the Web at http://wbln0018.worldbank.org/Research/workpapers.nsf/WPDomesticFinance/?OpenView&count=500000&Topic=Domestic+Finance.

Claessens, Stijn, Simeon Djankov, Joseph Fan, and Larry Lang. 1999b.

"Ultimate Ownership Structure and Diversification by East Asian Corporations." World Bank, Washington, D.C. Processed. This paper is available on the Web at http://wbln0018.worldbank.org/research/workpapers.nsf/policyresearch?openform.

Claessens, Stijn, Simeon Djankov, Joseph Fan, and Larry Lang. 1999c. "Expropriation of Minority Shareholders in East Asian Corporations." World Bank, Washington, D.C. Processed. This paper is available on the Web at http://wbln0018.worldbank.org/research/workpapers.nsf/policyresearch?openform.

# Chapter 8

Claessens, Stijn, Simeon Djankov, and Larry H. P. Lang. 1999 "Who Controls East Asia Corporations?" Policy Discussion Paper 2017, World Bank, Washington, D.C.

Dollar, David, Mary Hallward-Driemeier, Giuseppe Iarossi, and M. Chakraborty. 1998. "Short-Term and Long-Term Competitiveness Issues in Thai Industry." In Johanna Witte and Stefan Koeberle, eds., *Competitiveness and Sustainable Economic Recovery in Thailand*. Washington, D.C.: World Bank. Volume II, Background Papers for the Conference "Thailand's Dynamic Economic Recovery and Competitiveness," held in Bangkok in May 1998.

Dun & Bradstreet Credit Services. 1999. *Industry Norms and Key Business Ratios*. Murray Hill, N.J.

Furman, Jason, and Joseph E. Stiglitz. 1998. "Economic Crises: Evidence and Insights from East Asia." *Brooking Papers on Economic Activity* 2: 1–135.

World Bank. 1998. *East Asia: The Road to Recovery*. Washington, D.C.

# Chapter 9

Agarwal, N. 1995. *Indonesia Labor Market Policies and International Competitiveness*. Policy Research Working Paper No. 1515. World Bank, Washington, D.C.

Athukorala, P. C. 1998. *Trade Policy Issues in Asian Development*. New York: Routledge.

Economist Intelligence Unit (EIU). 1998a. *Country Report: Indonesia*. Economist Intelligence Unit, London. Various issues.

———. 1998b. *Country Report: Malaysia and Brunei*. Economist Intelligence Unit, London. Various issues.

———. 1998c. *Country Report: Philippines*. Economist Intelligence Unit, London. Various issues.

———. 1998d. *Country Report: South Korea and North Korea*. Economist Intelligence Unit, London. Various issues.

———. 1998e. *Country Report: Thailand*. Economist Intelligence Unit, London. Various issues.

Garnaut, R. 1998. "The East Asian Crisis." In R. McLeod and R. Garnaut, eds., *East Asia In Crisis*. New York: Routledge.

IMF (International Monetary Fund). 1999. *International Financial Statistics*. International Monetary Fund, Washington, D.C. January.

Lee, E. W. 1998. "Panel Strikes Compromise over Layoff System." *Economic Report:* 17.

Lee, J. H., and D. I. Kim. 1997. "Labor Market Development and Reforms in Korea." KDI Working Paper No. 9703. Korea Development Institute, Seoul.

Kim, S. S., C. H. Rhee, and J. H. Lee. 1992. *A Study of the Institutional Reform in Korean Industrial Relations* (in Korean). Korea Development Institute, Seoul.

Veale, C. 1999. "Unions on the Verge of Boycott." *Australian Financial Review,* 23 February 1999.

# Chapter 13

*Business World*. 1999.

Lamberte, Mario B. 1999. "Currency Crisis: Where do We Go from Here?" Discussion Paper No. 99-10. Philippine Institute for Development Studies, Makati City. April.

Lamberte, Mario B., and Gilberto M. Llanto. 1995. "A Study of Financial Sector Policies: The Philippine Case." In Shahid N. Zahid, ed., *Financial Sector Development in Asia*. Manila: Asian Development Bank.

Lamberte, Mario B., and Josef T. Yap. 1999. "Scenarios for Economic Recovery: The Philippines." Discussion Paper Series No. 99-05. Philippine Institute for Development Studies, Makati City. March.

Virtucio, Felizardo K. 1998. "Social Implications of the Asian Financial Crisis: The Philippine Case." In *EDAP Joint Policy Studies No. 9: Social Implications of the Asian Financial Crisis*. Seoul: Korea Development Institute.

# Chapter 14

Dollar, David, Mary Hallward-Driemeier, Giuseppe Iarossi, and Mita Chakraborty. 1998. "Short-Term and Long-Term Competitiveness Issues in Thai Industry." In Johanna Witte and Stefan Koeberle, eds., *Proceedings of the Thailand's Dynamic Economic Recovery and Competitiveness Conference,* Vol. 2: *Bangkok, May 20–21, 1998*. Bangkok: Office of the National Economic and Social Development Board and the World Bank Thailand Office.

IMF. 1998. *World Economic Outlook*. October.

**DATE DUE**

HIGHSMITH #45230  Printed in USA